Animal
Subjects
2.0

Environmental Humanities Series

Environmental thought pursues with renewed urgency the grand concerns of the humanities: who we think we are, how we relate to others, and how we live in the world. Scholarship in the environmental humanities explores these questions by crossing the lines that separate human from animal, social from material, and objects and bodies from techno-ecological networks. Humanistic accounts of political representation and ethical recognition are re-examined in consideration of other species. Social identities are studied in relation to conceptions of the natural, the animal, the bodily, place, space, landscape, risk, and technology, and in relation to the material distribution and contestation of environmental hazards and pleasures.

The Environmental Humanities Series features research that adopts and adapts the methods of the humanities to clarify the cultural meanings associated with environmental debate. The scope of the series is broad. Film, literature, television, Web-based media, visual art, and physical landscape—all are crucial sites for exploring how ecological relationships and identities are lived and imagined. The Environmental Humanities Series publishes scholarly monographs and essay collections in environmental cultural studies, including popular culture, film, media, and visual cultures; environmental literary criticism; cultural geography; environmental philosophy, ethics, and religious studies; and other cross-disciplinary research that probes what it means to be human, animal, and technological in an ecological world.

Gathering research and writing in environmental philosophy, ethics, cultural studies, and literature under a single umbrella, the series aims to make visible the contributions of humanities research to environmental studies, and to foster discussion that challenges and reconceptualizes the humanities.

Series editor:
Cheryl Lousley, *English and Film Studies, Wilfrid Laurier University*

Editorial committee:
Adrian J. Ivakhiv, *Environmental Studies, University of Vermont*
Catriona Mortimer-Sandilands, *Tier 1 CRC in Sustainability*
and Culture, Environmental Studies, York University
Susie O'Brien, *English and Cultural Studies, McMaster University*
Laurie Ricou, *English, University of British Columbia*
Rob Shields, *Henry Marshall Tory Chair and Professor,*
Department of Sociology, University of Alberta

Animal Subjects 2.0

JODEY CASTRICANO and
LAUREN CORMAN, editors

WLU PRESS

WILFRID LAURIER
UNIVERSITY PRESS

LAURIER
Inspiring Lives.

Wilfrid Laurier University Press acknowledges the support of the
Canada Council for the Arts for our publishing program. We acknowledge the
financial support of the Government of Canada through the Canada Book Fund for
its publishing activities. This work was supported by the Research Support Fund.

Canada

Canada Council   Conseil des arts
for the Arts   du Canada

ONTARIO ARTS COUNCIL
CONSEIL DES ARTS DE L'ONTARIO
an Ontario government agency
un organisme du gouvernement de l'Ontario

Library and Archives Canada Cataloguing in Publication

Animal subjects 2.0 / Jodey Castricano and Lauren Corman, editors.

(Environmental humanities)
Includes bibliographical references and index.
Issued in print and electronic formats.
ISBN 978-1-77112-210-8 (paperback).—ISBN 978-1-77112-211-5 (pdf).—
ISBN 978-1-77112-212-2 (epub)

1. Animal rights. 2. Animal welfare. 3. Animal welfare—Moral and ethical aspects.
4. Human–animal relationships. I. Castricano, Jodey, [date], author, editor
II. Corman, Lauren, [date], author, editor III. Series: Environmental humanities

HV4708.A62 2016   179'.3   C2016-902904-2
                                              C2016-902905-0

Cover design by Blakeley Words+Pictures. Front-cover image by Zokru/iStock.
Text design by Janette Thompson (Jansom).

© 2016 Wilfrid Laurier University Press
Waterloo, Ontario, Canada
www.wlupress.wlu.ca

Chapter 11, "Vegans for Vick," appeared originally, in slightly different form,
in *International Journal of Communication* 7, no. 1 (2013): 780–800.

Contents

For Felix and Harley,
who were with me the first time around

— Jodey Castricano

For Frank (2008–2016), the most loving cat,
whose survival was remarkably entwined with my own

— Lauren Corman

Acknowledgements

This collection had its beginnings in an enthusiastic conversation that I had many years ago in a coffee shop on Commercial Drive in Vancouver, BC, with Lisa Quinn, who was then the acquisitions editor at WLU Press. Based on the success of the previous collection, *Animal Subjects: An Ethical Reader in a Posthuman World* (2008), Lisa agreed that a second collection, focused on new developments in the field of Critical Animal Studies, was a good idea. The next step was to contact my colleague Lauren Corman, of Brock University, and invite her to share in an co-editorial journey that over the years taught us much about collaboration, negotiation, differences, compromises, and agreements as well as about ourselves as colleagues and friends engaged in the work of animal advocacy.

I continue to believe strongly in this work and want to extend my gratitude to those who encouraged it and contributed to the making of the present collection. I wish first to acknowledge the financial support from the Faculty of Creative and Critical Studies at UBC Okanagan in the form of a Book Publication Grant. Thanks also to Lisa Quinn, who, since becoming Director of WLUP, continued to offer leadership in and encouragement for this project while at the same time executing a smooth hand-off of the tiller to Siobhan McMenemy, the incoming acquisitions editor, who kept the work on course even during rough passages. Nearer the end of the journey, Kel Pero earned our immense gratitude for the precision of her editorial eye, to say nothing of her wicked humour. Lastly, thanks go to Rob Kohlmeier, Managing Editor at WLUP, who took over the helm in the final stages of production and steered us into harbour.

Thanks go always to the contributors to this volume, all of whom responded positively to the call for essays and who never missed a beat where revisions and deadlines were concerned. Their contributions are the heart of this collection and I am honoured to have worked on this project with committed scholars, writers, activists, and thinkers whose commitment to animal advocacy serves as a beacon of hope in world where the exploitation of animals routinely and ubiquitously occurs and where we all, at times, feel our interventions are not enough. Still, we keep on and I am grateful for the solidarity within this growing community, especially where it includes those featured in this collection, behind it in production, and beyond it from those whose works and interventions continue to inspire me: Carol Gigliotti, David L. Clark, Rasmus Simonsen, Dana Rilke, Zipporah Weisberg, Harold Brown, Greta Gaard, Carol J. Adams, Julie Andreyev, and so many others.

I also want to acknowledge my students in the upper levels and graduate seminars in Critical Animal Studies, who over the years have taught me a great deal about advocacy and compassion. These students are not only going beyond the classroom to make a difference for animals but continue to inspire me with the courage of their convictions. Special thanks here go to Ellen Campbell, Juawana Grant, Renata Russo, Leah Waffler, Cole Mash, Brittni MacKenzie-Dale, Trystan Carter, Morgan Armstrong, Nishat Tasnim, and Asher J. Klassen. This collection is, in part, dedicated to them.

Last, but not least, I want to acknowledge the canine and feline four-leggeds with whom I share living space: Simon, the little terrier from the SPCA (a.k.a. "Little Bushman"), whose faithful companionship over the years has brought much joy to this house; Max, newer to the household, a chihuahua/corgi cross whose ears put him in the company of Yoda and who came to me last year from a high-kill shelter in Sacramento, where he was rescued at the last moment. He is such a joyful, playful, and sensitive being that I cannot fathom his being put to death. Meanwhile, he been mentored by the cats Eddie, Blue, and Stevie, all of whom can be trusted to give instruction while I'm at the computer and never fail to remind me that cats rule.

Introduction

An Initial Intervention

In 2008, the first volume of *Animal Subjects*—subtitled *An Ethical Reader in a Posthuman World*—came into being to address what Cary Wolfe had earlier identified as a "lag" in critical theory and cultural studies regarding "the question of the animal."[1] To this end, the collection brought together a diverse group of scholars, writers, and activists whose work responded to the social and theoretical lag by calling into question, from a number of positions, the ontological and epistemological borders that historically had marked the divide between the more-than-human world and the claim to universality of the *anthropos*. Indeed, a principal aim of the first volume was to interrogate the disavowal, or withholding, of ethical consideration for nonhumans, given that critical theory and cultural studies had "proved almost impervious to the question of the nonhuman animal owing to an internalized paradox that maintained the very status of the human."[2] This interrogation of such refusal of ethical consideration was predicated upon a critique of *speciesism*, for as Wolfe maintains, "debates in the humanities and social sciences between well-intentioned critics of racism, (hetero) sexism, classism and all other -isms that are the stock in trade of cultural studies almost always remain locked within an unexamined framework of *speciesism* . . . even as we claim for our work an epistemological break with humanism itself."[3] It was the purview of the first collection to stage an intervention in the disavowal of the nonhuman in critical and cultural theory that operates through the normative convention of the human that confers the "exceptionalism" of the Human onto itself.

The current volume, *Animal Subjects 2.0*, picks up where the earlier volume left off but with the aim of giving voice to the diversity, intersectionality, and widespread development in our field. Like the first volume, it is intended to further debates rather than close them down. Indeed, *Animal Subjects* faced resistance from those who argued that the (nonhuman animal) subject did not fall within the purview of cultural studies. Like the first collection, *Animal Studies 2.0* faces another challenge, but this time one that potentially comes from within the field of critical animal studies (CAS) itself.

The first collection posed the question "Cultural studies: what's in a name?" and asked what was meant pedagogically, intellectually, and politically by the term *cultural studies* "for the simple reason that cultural studies is organized around a set of controversies."[4] This collection goes further to draw attention to controversies in the field of CAS that would argue against its inclusion in cultural studies. This is to say that CAS, like cultural studies, has an interdisciplinary history that is equally marked by controversy. It is not the aim of this current collection to exhaustively track the historical, political, and ethical trajectories of the rise of CAS, but it is necessary to situate *Animal Subjects 2.0* in relation to other work being done in the name of CAS. In an interdisciplinary context, the collection is situated in a pluralistic field, one in continuous transition, not only with respect to the formation of knowledge regarding human–nonhuman animal relations but also with regard to its own methods aimed at developing intersectional modes of social justice for and with nonhuman animals. Most significantly, this collection follows the lead of thinkers such as Jacques Derrida, Cary Wolfe, Lori Gruen (whose essay "Navigating Difference (Again): Animal Ethics and Entangled Empathy" appears in this collection) and Matthew Calarco, a continental philosopher who reminds us that "we have ethical and ontological work to do" and that rather than attempting to feverishly seal the borders of CAS, we should accept that "there are several ways into the animal question, via law, literature, art, film, science, and so on."[5] Indeed, Calarco's thoughts on "indistinction" are useful here, for they help us understand what's at stake when "the sharp distinctions that have typically been drawn between humans and animals fall by the wayside" and we are called to see the animal question in relation to social justice and change on other grounds and through different avenues, namely "queer struggles, feminist groups, indigenous peoples, anti-racism and decolonization struggles, alter-globalization activists, radical environmentalists."[6] All of these groups are asking us, says Calarco, "to push back against [the old game of determining human propriety] and eventually end it altogether."[7]

The Pulse of CAS

In pushing back against that determination, this collection acknowledges the challenge posed within the field of CAS regarding the fact that, like gender studies and queer studies, the field cannot be distilled down to the name "critical animal studies" but is intentionally, necessarily interdisciplinary regarding the question of the animal. Indeed, it is the question itself that also obliges us to worry the reduction of "the animal" to a *word* or, as Derrida says, "an appellation that men [*sic*] have instituted, a name they have given themselves the right and the authority to give to the living other."[8]

Now is an important and generative moment in which to question such right and such authority. Indeed, we are still challenging the tendency to exclude the *question* of the animal from fields such as cultural studies. Hence, as editors of this collection, we are explicitly asking about the boundaries of CAS, which since its inception has disavowed what has been called "elitist" theorizing that ostensibly deals only in "metaphysical interpretations" regarding nonhumans and, as such, is unconcerned with the real, embodied exploitation/oppression of nonhumans and the plight of billions of actual animals who, on a global scale, suffer and die yearly in the name of human exceptionalism or human supremacy. Originally, CAS was defined partially through differentiation. Historically, CAS was based on the shared commitments of a collection of people in the early 2000s who were working together through the Centre for Animal Liberation Affairs and who explicitly grounded their efforts in animal liberation. CAS was conceived as being "an interdisciplinary field dedicated to establishing a holistic total liberation movement for humans, nonhuman animals, and the Earth. CAS is engaged in an intersectional, theory-to-action politics, in solidarity with movements to abolish all systems of domination."[9] As Steven Best, co-founder of the field argues, CAS rejects what he calls "mainstream animal studies," based on its apolitical stance, inaccessible jargon, lack of activism, and a paucity of intersectional analyses and critiques of capitalism. The point being made by Best is that academia has largely co-opted and institutionalized the question of the animal, rendering it abstract and devoid of efficacy with regard to achieving social justice and ethical consideration for nonhumans and, specifically included in this, the large-scale exploitation of other animals.

This collection is brought together with the awareness that it may draw criticism, for its aim is to be seen *as a form of activism* if the latter is seen along a continuum. This is to say, this collection aims to establish affinities with the historical iterations of CAS by situating itself along a *continuum* of shared aims with regard to nonhuman beings and social justice. For after all, we think it is safe to say that we are united in the view, to use John Sorenson's words in a newly released book on CAS, "that animals are sentient beings with inherent value that are deserving of justice."[10] But how to seek affinities in a field? As editors, we think all would agree that those of us involved in contemporary CAS share an abiding concern to end the industrialized exploitation of nonhuman animals at national and international levels, notably in the context of the environmental devastation associated with nonhuman animal use.

In this regard, as editors of this collection we agree with others in CAS, that our task is to *analyze* "the social construction and representation of animals, speciesism and the creation of boundaries, intersectionality of various forms of oppression, the structured violence of animal use, and the potential for social change."[11] Indeed, such analysis challenges us in CAS to work as interventionists at all levels with regard to speciesism and its role in sustaining the animal industrial complex, which takes as its rationale the ontological determinations of human exceptionalism and anthropocentrism. Furthermore, many of us in CAS rely on critical theory to critique a variety of hierarchies, which historically have obscured the interconnected workings of power that sustain related oppressions such as sexism, racism, and speciesism in regards to the *question* of the animal *and animals themselves.* This is to say that a posthumanist approach to CAS has many of us highlighting and challenging, like Foucauldian scholar Stephen Thierman, "the political and power-laden dimensions of those interrelations."[12] In this regard, we are concerned with bringing into focus interrelated dominations of both human and nonhuman animals by using methods that, as Derrida might say, do not confirm "a certain *interpretation* of the human subject, which itself will have been the very lever of the worst violence carried out against nonhuman living beings."[13]

Indeed, at the heart of such analysis is a critical concern with the tendency of some animal advocates to rely upon a rights discourse that, as feminist philosopher Kelly Oliver points out, "either uses or repeats identities that historically have been used to oppress or exploit certain groups, or [as is usual in the case of animal rights arguments] it uses values associated with the dominant group as its norm."[14] In this regard, we are partially indebted to poststructuralist thought where it leads into post-anthropocentrism, and by feminist and postcolonial critiques of a normativized understanding of rights and protections. For example, in following feminist thinkers such as Kari Weil, "who have been critical of the way that the very notion of 'women's rights' may reify a fictional identity of women as subordinate and thereby entrench women within their subordination" one question posed in this collection is "how the notion of 'animal rights' might similarly entrench animals under a falsely unifying idea of 'the animal.'"[15] In light of this influence, it also needs be said that some CAS scholars' opposition to poststructuralist thought is based on the criticism that at best, it produces "obscure theories for elite consumption."[16] For example, a recent CAS publication explicitly disavows the "pernicious" influence of thinkers such as Jacques Derrida and Donna Haraway, dismissing them because

> their arcane writing and irrationalism is largely meaningless, as it is dissociated from popular struggles and undermines activism. Deliberately vague and apolitical, postmodern animal studies avoids any direct commitment to animals or to serious criticism of their exploitation. Although typically presented as radical interventions, these works are characterized by obscurantist language accessible only to a tiny number of academics and offer little practical help in terms of efforts to reduce the exploitation of non-human animals and advance the cause of animal rights. This work is not only apolitical, but it also often condones and offers excuses for the continued oppression of non-human animals. (Best, n.d.). In some cases, the ideas promoted by postmodernists working in animal studies are not simply disengaged from any practical relevance to alleviating the oppression of animals, but are in fact deeply inimical to animal advocacy.[17]

As editors of this collection we consider ourselves deeply and ethically implicated in the field of CAS and have sought to present the reader with contributions from scholars, thinkers, writers, and activists who are likewise sincerely concerned and profoundly committed in diverse ways, including drawing on poststructuralism, to end the exploitation of nonhuman animals. While we are not averse to debate within the field of CAS, we are concerned, nevertheless, with schisms within the field created by a partisan stance that has the potential to detract from the arguably *shared* goal of seeking social justice to end the exploitation of nonhuman animals in a unified way. It is the spirit of sharing the goal that has prompted us as editors to include in this collection the works of some scholars who would disagree with us methodologically in our use of poststructuralist thought. And, if this inclusion seems jarring, inconsistent or even contradictory, we stand behind our aim of inclusiveness to provide the reader with a real sense of what occupies those of us in CAS today. In our view, seeking social justice for animals is the common goal and we believe this to be more important than our theoretical differences. Again, we do not mean that constructive criticism is unwelcome; we do mean that in the name of social justice, rather than divisiveness, we seek affinities within CAS where they matter *most* to ending the exploitation of nonhuman animals.

In this context, therefore, we ask the reader of this collection to judge for herself which approaches to the question of the animal are most effective. For example, while only some of us in this collection consider ourselves poststructuralists, we think it safe to say the work of all scholars, thinkers, and activists in *Animal Subjects 2.0* is dedicated to "the task," as John Sorenson eloquently puts it elsewhere, "of creating a global social justice movement that advocates for other animals, as well as for humans" in spite of the claim by some CAS scholars that certain critical approaches are "largely meaningless," "deliberately vague," "apolitical, arcane, and therefore 'safe.'"[18] As editors and scholars, we reject the classical distinction between *praxis* and *theory* and embrace intersectionality as a *thinking* modality rather than an either/or framework of terms. In this sense, we follow the lead of CAS scholars Helena Pedersen and Tobias Linné who, in "'Expanding My Universe: Critical Animal Studies as Theory, Politics, and Practice," assert that "entrenched norms in society (such as meat consumption) [must be] interrogated" via critical theory and, most relevantly for our purposes in this collection, that "work for social change is viewed as *part of* theory rather than *outside* of theory."[19] Therefore, we also understand poststructuralism not to be uncomplicatedly synonymous with postmodernism but see it as a methodology which can effectively "steer a path *between* theory and practice, between modernism and postmodernism," and thus resolve oppositional thinking in relation to ethics *and* aesthetics/theory.[20] In this sense, we seek to explore what Linné and Pedersen refer to as a working "in-between," a space of "both *potential* and *process*."[21]

In this collection, we make space for what may be generally named posthumanist approaches to "the question of the animal" that also, crucially, foreground intersectionality. As Richard Twine aptly notes, "(critical) animal studies is essentially venturing a posthumanist reading of intersectionality, in which the reconceptualization and decentring of the human is inseparable from attempts to resolve both anthropocentric hubris and its exclusionary histories."[22] The current volume resonates with Twine and others in CAS who show the potential of posthumanism, in particularly important ways, to illuminate the unmarked power and manoeuvrings of liberal humanist subjectivity. Such a project, or rather orientation, recognizes continuity with the original articulation of CAS, while noting complementary theoretical tools provided through certain streams of posthumanist thought.

This does not mean, however, that we consider all posthumanist inquiry to be equally worthwhile or useful for addressing the pressing issues of human and nonhuman animal oppression. For example, we note resistance to "academic discourse" (posthumanist or otherwise), whereby scholarship is seen as being woefully incomprehensible and thus inaccessible to a wider range of audiences, including some activist ones. Further, we are also troubled by research (again, posthumanist or otherwise) that finds nonhuman animal issues just the latest trendy topic in a series of faddish academic pursuits, with little to no responsibility shown to those animals who live and die under human-constructed regimes of terror and objectification. In other words, we do not give posthumanism or other theories a blanket pass, but instead maintain that its work should not be dismissed out of hand. Following from this, we acknowledge the vital efforts of cultural studies and other intersectional areas to dismantle—and challenge—the various social axes of difference related to dominating and disavowed forms of race, gender, class, sexuality, and ability, among others that comprise liberal humanist subjectivity, and thus we would also be remiss to neglect the centrality of species in enacting the privileges of the Western humanist subject. Indeed, the persistent assumption that subjectivity is the exclusive domain of humanity must be rigorously and relentlessly interrogated, as various authors working under the banner of posthumanism do.

As editors of this collection we see CAS as a *living* and dynamic field, one that is characterized by *difference* (and, even, to recall Derrida, *différance*). Authors featured in this collection repeatedly move against assimilationist forms of ethics that demand subjects be the same as existing rightsholders. Stressing instead compassion, empathy, relationality, and humility, the version of CAS highlighted here presses for a recognition of shared continuities—*not* similarities—between humans and other animals, wherein we, too, realize that humans are animals, and animals are not the lesser and lacking beings that dominant Western thought has deemed them.

We believe this orientation speaks to a larger turn in this still emergent field toward a more distinct decentring of the liberal human subject. Beginning from the position that appreciation of diversity and difference might be a foundation for ethical relations,[23] rather than homogenization, helps suggest new possibilities for more radically ethical ways of thinking about and being with other animals. In this collection, the authors repeatedly lay claim to the richness of nonhuman animal subjectivities, ones that include but extend beyond the necessary (but nonetheless limited claims) of conventional animal rights discourse that centralizes pain and suffering while too often neglecting nonhuman animals' capacities for pleasure and other sensory experiences.[24]

As such, we build upon Bakhtin's gloss on the "living word," in that the collection and for that matter, CAS, like the "word," is *always already* "entangled, shot through with shared thoughts, points of view, alien words, value judgments and accents," having emerged in "a dialogically agitated and tension-filled environment."[25] In this regard, we can align ourselves with Jacques Derrida's critique of "the industrial, mechanical, chemical, hormonal, and genetic violence to which man [*sic*] has been submitting animal life for the past two centuries."[26] We certainly find nothing in Derrida's assertion in "Violence Against Animals" that would mark it as "arcane" or "apolitical," for as Derrida states,

> this industrial, scientific, technical violence against animals will not be tolerated for very much longer, neither de facto nor de jure. It will find itself more and more discredited. The relations between humans and animals *must* change. They *must*, both in the sense of an "ontological" necessity and of an "ethical" duty. I place these words in quotation marks because this change will have to affect the very sense and value of these concepts (the ontological and the ethical). That is why, although their discourse often seems to be poorly articulated or philosophically inconsistent, I am on principle sympathetic with those who, it seems to me, are in the right and have good reasons to rise up against the way animals are treated: in industrial production, in slaughter, in consumption, in experimentation.[27]

This volume continues the struggle of CAS to name and resist violence, recognizing that violence happens in simultaneous registers, on both material and categorical levels. The non-subject status ascribed to animals and other oppressed groups is not only a physical, social, and emotional degradation but also a fundamental one of figurative erasure, such that the two forms of objectification are indivisibly interlocked and reinforcing.

The Limits of Humanism

As editors of this collection, we offer this thinking about the question of the animal in the spirit of radical pedagogy, including critical and feminist perspectives, wherein "teaching," to draw from bell hooks, "is a performative act" that "offers the space for change, invention, spontaneous shifts" whereby education becomes "the practice of freedom."[28] With regard to theorizing and writing, we take the view that engaging in these modalities is to challenge the assumption that these are irrelevant to staging interventions with regard to the treatment of nonhumans and humans, especially at a time of unprecedented industrial, mechanical, genetic, and chemical violence towards them as Derrida, Calarco, Gruen, and many others have noted. To this end, this collection regards the *question* of the animal as an ethical call *to recognize* "the existence of nonhuman subjects."[29] Thus, *Animal Subjects 2.0* challenges anthropocentrism to stage an encounter with the dominant and limited perception of the subject as *solely human*. In other words, this collection, in the spirit of post-anthropocentrism, urges us "to question the violence and the hierarchical thinking that result from human arrogance and the assumption of transcendental human exceptionalism."[30] In the context of CAS, we see *Animal Subjects 2.0* as offering a fundamental challenge to metaphysical anthropocentrism. Similarly, and perhaps more significantly, we see the works of scholars, activists, and thinkers contained herein as standing in opposition to "the worst kinds of violence, that is, the purely instrumental, industrial, chemico-genetic treatment of living beings."[31] We also see this collection as being an intersectional declaration of solidarity with work done in other areas of CAS as well as in the fields of ecology, animal behaviour, and cognitive ethology, where all of these challenge speciesism and human exceptionalism through a sustained acknowledgement of the capacity of nonhumans to experience a rich range of emotions including empathy and compassion, joy, grief, jealousy, and love. To our way of thinking, this is the ethical domain where posthumanism and ecofeminism(s) are crucial components in the field of CAS.

Notably, however, there are multiple and conflicting definitions of posthumanism; our understanding and use of *critical posthumanism* is guided by Cary Wolfe's view that posthumanism paradoxically "comes both before

and after humanism": before in the sense that it recalls Foucault's historicizing of the appearance of "that . . . specific thing called 'the human'"[32] that
Foucault says was "the effect of a change in the fundamental arrangements
of knowledge";[33] therefore, as Wolfe states, posthumanism comes *after* in
the sense that it "names a historical moment in which the decentering of the
human by its imbrication in technical, medical, informatics, and economic
networks is increasingly impossible to ignore, a historical development that
points toward the necessity of new theoretical paradigms (but also thrusts
them on us), a new mode of thought that comes after the cultural repres-
sions and fantasies, the philosophical protocols and evasions, of humanism as a historically specific phenomenon."[34] Add to this Rosi Braidotti's
thinking on the posthuman as a move beyond anthropocentrism and we
arrive, as Pollack says, at "the set of questions confronting us, and ways of
dealing with these questions, when we can no longer rely on 'the human'
as an autonomous, rational being who provides an Archimedean point for
knowing about the world (in contrast to 'humanism,' which uses such a
figure to ground further claims)."[35] Central to this "set of questions" is the
ubiquitous one of "the animal." But it is not a singular question in that it is
complicated by the fact that "the animal is a word, it is an appellation that
men have instituted, a name they have given themselves the right and the
authority to give to the living other."[36] This reference to the word gives us
to understand what is at stake in editing a collection of essays with respect
to *animal subjects*, and the complication is alluded to by Derrida when he
says "I have never believed in some homogenous continuity between what
calls *itself* man and what *he* calls the animal."[37] Indeed, Derrida's thoughts
on the designation "animal" draws attention to the complexity inherent in
posthumanism in relation to those "living others" of whom we wish we
speak in this collection:

> *animal* is a word that men [*sic*] have given themselves the right to give.
> These humans are found giving it to themselves, this word, but as if they
> had received it as an inheritance. They have given themselves the word
> in order to corral a large number of living beings within a single con-
> cept: "The Animal," they say. And they have given it to themselves, this
> word, at the same time according themselves, reserving for them, for
> humans, the right to the word, the naming noun . . ., the verb, the attrib-
> ute, to a language of words, in short to the very thing that the others in
> question would be deprived of, those that are corralled with the grand
> territory of the beasts: The Animal.[38]

How then to speak of /to/with/as animal subjects?

The first volume approached these questions by exploring the role of empathy and compassion concerning the presence/use/understanding of animals in the ethical domain in which anthropocentrism has been the road-block *and the tautological justification* in philosophy, literary and cultural studies, law, and science with regard to denying nonhumans a place in our ethical communities. Indeed, the first volume concerned itself with bringing animal subjects into the realm of cultural studies. It included a critique of industrialized farming for both animals and workers alike (Haraway); it questioned the tenets of conventional metaphysical humanism in philosophy (Wolfe, Cavalieri), in sociobiological discourse (Preece), and with the capitalistic domination of the natural world (Taylor); it offered a critique of animals in "entertainment" (Sorenson), as well as an ecofeminist meditation on the discourses of vegetarianism in the eighteenth century, and it explored the work of Mary Wollstonecraft with regard to extending sympathy for the suffering of animals (Seeber); it took up the issue of arbitrarily denying the attribution of personhood to nonhumans (Sztybel), and questioned a justice system that posits animals as "property" and "inanimate things" (Bisgould); it included a biologist's critique of biomedical experiments that have been shown to have minimal or no effects in improving human health, but in which many millions of animals suffer and die (Dagg); and, finally, it questioned the denial of the possibility of immortality to nonhuman animals based on distinctions between the rational and the animal soul (Tito). Obviously, a collection such as this could not be all things to all people and many issues that are current to us in the field of posthumanism and CAS—various biological, social, and cultural issues such as gender, race, ability, species, sexual orientation—were not explicitly addressed.

This current volume takes an intersectional approach to animal subjects not only in examining multiple systems of oppression as regards speciesism, racism, ableism, and sexism, but also in exploring the agency of nonhumans in terms of their own interests.

Intrasections

As editors, we decided to structure the collection thematically, although we also recognize that many of the topics are interrelated, which is why we think of the headings as being "intrasections," rather than indicating discrete themes. Accordingly, our intrasections take shape as "Representing

Animals," and we mean this section to demonstrate not only an exploration of *representations of* animals, and not only action to *represent* animals in a legal and social justice sense, but also to signal that representation is not limited solely to the human animal but ought to be considered in the more-than-human sense. In "Intersecting Animals" we explore the various theoretical approaches to human exceptionalism by turning to a discussion at the intersections of disability studies, queer studies, and animal studies; Indigenous perspectives on vegan ethics; the radical potential of ecofeminism and "entangled empathy"; and, of post-anthropocentrism and theory as activism.

Representing Animals

The collection begins with Rod Preece's "Might Makes Right: The Origins of Ethics and the Use of Animals for Human Ends." We chose to begin with this chapter as it advances the aim of the collection regarding extending ethical consideration to the more-than-human. In this work, Preece, the author of more than a dozen books on animals, offers an historical and grounded critique of the origins and development of the idea that humans stand at the apex of the animal realm. Preece argues that those attributes deemed superior human characteristics are no more than those deemed instrumental to the achievement of specifically human aims, usually at great cost to animals. Preece's historical approach shows us that the nonhuman animal has always been central to epistemological and ontological pursuits and that the definition of "human" has relied upon deeming the nonhuman worthy or unworthy of ethical concern. Preece's chapter explores the origins and foundations of ethics in order to see what light they may shed on the justification for the use of animals for human purposes, especially in invasive animal experimentation.

Following Preece, Maneesha Deckha, in "Critical Animals Studies and the Property Debate in Animal Law," engages a leading debate in the field of animal law to examine whether animals' legal status as *property* inhibits meaningful reform for them. An Associate Professor in the Faculty of Law at the University of Victoria, Deckha points out that despite their differences, all positions in the debate operate from liberal premises about animals, law, and justice with regard to property and ownership. This chapter stages an intervention in the "property" debate from the intersectional perspective of CAS to ask whether the law should continue to categorize animals as property. As such, Deckha draws on CAS to unseat the liberalism evidenced in various approaches, offering a remediation and illumination of the unmarked assumptions that undergird the debate.

Shifting from legal to visual representations, J. Keri Cronin's "'Popular Affection': Edwin Landseer and Nineteenth-Century Animal Advocacy Campaigns" considers the recontextualization of Sir Edwin Landseer's (1802–1873) paintings on the pages of pamphlets and publications produced by activists lobbying for better treatment of nonhuman animals in the late nineteenth century. Cronin's chapter argues that reproductions of images like Landseer's well-known painting *The Highland Shepherd's Chief Mourner*, were especially popular selections for these campaigns as this type of image unsettled boundaries between "human" and "animal," and in so doing was part of new ways of thinking about relationships between species that, in turn, supported arguments made by groups such as the Victoria Street Society for the Protection of Animals from Vivisection and the Massachusetts Society for the Prevention of Cruelty to Animals.

Parallel to historical insights made possible through her visual genealogy, Cronin's gaze also casts forward: she argues, "[b]y attending to the politics of representation from previous eras we are better equipped to understand the ways in which images in our contemporary activist culture can work to destabilize dominant understandings of how nonhuman animals should be treated" (p. 82). Indeed, activists today, whether intentionally or not, draw on earlier legacies of representation, including remarkable engagements with visual culture. Cronin's chapter thus underscores the necessity for activists to learn from, and to effectively employ, previous activist strategies so we may better intervene in a "world increasingly characterized by competing visual strategies" (p. 82).

In the realm of storytelling and narrative, the chapter by Rhys Mahannah, "'The Animal,' Systems, and Structures: An Ecofeminist–Posthumanist Enquiry," explores ethical questions surrounding vivisection and the relationship between scientific discourse and speciesism in the context of H.G. Wells' controversial nineteenth-century novel, *The Island of Dr. Moreau*. Mahannah examines the novel's representation of the "Beast People" and, thus, speciesism through the lens of Foucault's notion of biopower, which works to control bodies through a hierarchical social apparatus, thus marking "the animal" as the limit indicating and rationalizing violence perpetrated and perpetuated through the animalization of women and racialized others. To this end, Mahannah takes an ecofeminist–posthumanist approach to Wells' novel, reading it as a scathing critique of anthropocentrism.

Furthering the question of animal representation, particularly animals' own capacities for representation, the chapter by Joshua Russell, "Animal Narrativity: Engaging with Story in a More-Than-Human World," offers not only a critique of humanism's tendency to delineate between what is uniquely human and what is *merely* animal but also a challenge to the widely held assumption that the capacity to tell stories and to *represent* is a marker of the uniquely human. In other words, narrative is seen as that which sets humans apart from nonhuman animals. In this chapter, Russell explores phenomenological descriptions of interspecies encounters to argue on behalf of "animal narrativity," a term that Russell uses to describe a *felt* sense that human and nonhuman animal lives emerge from and are knowable as part of an "ecology of stories." Russell's contemplative chapter engages us in the sense that it draws attention to the paucity of thinking that only human animals can tell their stories.

Beginning with a stirring personal story, Russell deftly bridges theory with lived experience to illuminate a profound interplay between the two. Russell powerfully reminds us of the subjectivity of other animals, including their own vast capacities for intelligence, language, and thought, which are too often denied. The implications regarding interspecies intersubjectivity reveal an undeniable ethical imperative that demands our dialogical relating as much as our reckoning.

Speaking of/to/with/as Animal Subjects: Intersections

Peter Hobbs' "Canine Cartography: On the Curious and Queer Pleasures of Being a Dog" arrives as a kind of theoretical mutt, embodying different voices, histories, and questions as it scratches at our humanism, revealing our own limits. Through science, philosophy, and fiction, Hobbs explores how dogs have been figured as ways of both securing and unsettling truth. If we are willing to pay attention and resist some of our persistent humanist assumptions, we can begin to see dogs as knowing and being in ways that we are unable. Yet, despite the persistent humanist renderings of dogs, their meanings remain unfixed, and both delightfully and frustratingly fluid: They are contestable creatures, evading complete appropriation as they point, snout first, into different ways of knowing and being in the world. They are not us, which is part of what makes them so compelling. Whatever our narratives about them, their totality ultimately eludes us, remaining outside the reductive grasp of humanism.

Reaching across fields of zoology, popular culture, fiction, and non-fiction—and including crucial interlocutors Jacques Derrida and Cesar

Millan, Cary Wolfe, and the Big Bad Wolf—Hobbs' chapter enacts a queer animal studies in pursuit of complicating and impeding the inflated claims of humanism. Such a theoretical approach flips humanism on its tail. Against the inert versioning of dogs, Hobbs shows instead how dogs draw us into their worlds and, because of the limited nature of our own forms of the physical and mental knowledge and bodies, they reveal our *only ever* partial capacity to represent other animals.

Yet, Hobbs' speculative mapping of canine life is as much constructive as it is critical. As he explores various limits of humanism, he also draws together methodologies that demonstrate how we might know and experience dogs differently. As such, we must listen differently, and even uncomfortably, to that which we are unaccustomed to perceiving through humanism's rote filters. Authors such as Donna Haraway, Jakob von Uexküll, Thelma Rowell, Marc Bekoff, and Paul Auster are called upon to engage this task, as Hobbs holds open a crucial space of unknowing. Drawing on earlier work by Agamben, he pursues a kind of knowing that allows dogs to "be outside of being" to dwell in "the zone of non-knowledge."

Similarly invested in different ways of being and relating with animals, Lori Gruen calls for "entangled empathy," what she describes as a form of "moral attention," that values difference and fosters ethical interspecies relationships. Troubled by unjustifiable prejudices and oppressive practices enacted through humanism, Gruen's feminist theory critiques in two directions, both toward the unchecked humanism—most centrally its isolated individualism—that undergirds much of the "humanities" as well as animal advocacy that propagates the "sameness response." "Navigating Difference (Again): Animal Ethics and Entangled Empathy" proposes a posthumanism that refuses to reduce or homogenize while it guides us to inhabit ethical interspecies relationships.

Margaret Robinson also addresses the importance of different kinds of relating, specifically with regard to questions of culture and diet. She examines continuities and compatibilities between veganism and Mi'kmaq culture in her *Animal Voices*' interview with collection co-editor, Lauren Corman. Taking her provocative and lauded article, "Indigenous Veganism: Feminist Natives Do Eat Tofu," as the starting point for their conversation, Robinson offers a postcolonial ecofeminist reading of Mi'kmaq legends as a foundation for a veganism grounded in Indigenous culture. Reflecting on her journey with veganism, Robinson discusses the process of merging vegan ethics with her Mi'kmaq value system. Spanning a broad range of topics throughout the "All My Relations" interview, including gender and human–animal relations in Mi'kmaq legends and culture, impacts of colonialism on food security for Aboriginal communities, and thoughts on the Indigenous fishing industry from a critical Aboriginal perspective, Robinson's nuanced observations draw attention to the specificities of her culture while also challenging the larger stereotype that Indigeneity is necessarily incongruous with veganism.

In "Rampant Compassion: A Tale of Two Anthropomorphisms and the 'Trans-species Episteme' of Knowledge-Making," collection co-editor Jodey Castricano proposes the term "thin(kin)g" to describe a complex ontological and vital materialist interaction between living beings that ceases to be invested in an anthropocentric value hierarchy based on the subject/object distinction of human exceptionalism. Castricano reflects upon "thin(kin)g" as a call to recognize the always already unavoidable relations to all living beings, a relation that raises profound ethical questions with regard to the more-than-human world. This chapter follows the trajectory of Derrida's call to "think the war on compassion," a path made not only urgent in the face of unprecedented violence against animals in bioengineering, in industrial production, in slaughter, in consumption, in experimentation, and in "entertainment," but also an epistemological journey made difficult and paradoxical because, as Derrida argues, "thinking is what we already know *we have not yet begun*." A call to think the war on compassion is, as Castricano, argues, a post-anthropocentric, radically intersectional and, quite possibly, neo-anthropomorphic call to responsibility.

Emerging at the intersection of animal studies and disabilities studies, Kelly Oliver's "The Limits of the 'Human': An Alternative Ethics of Dependence on Animals" gingerly steps into the thicket of Kantian and utilitarian forms of animal ethics. She draws on postmodernist approaches to reconceive of nonhuman animals and our relationships with them, considering service dogs in particular as a generative example to think through society's ambiguous relationship with animals.

Concentrating on the dependence of both nonhuman animals in our homes and people with disabilities, Oliver displaces the humanist fixation on autonomy with an appreciation of vulnerability, a characteristic that might be more usefully acknowledged as constitutive of human and nonhuman animal life. Here she follows Julia Kristeva's work, while she also challenges its dedicated humanism. Critical of ethics predicated upon the assumption that only those who are "like us" ought to be members of the ethical community, she argues along with Cary Wolfe that animal studies *and* disabilities studies are enriched when we challenge forms of ethics tied to the false binary that values so-called rational over non-rational ones.

Garrett M. Broad, in his empathetic and critical chapter, "Vegans for Vick: Dogfighting, Intersectional Politics, and the Limits of Mainstream Discourse," offers a provocative mapping of the Michael Vick dogfighting controversy. He emphasizes the missed opportunity for those in the animal rights movement, who are dedicated to anti-racist and anti-speciesist intersectional analysis, to penetrate the public debate about Vick in a more meaningful way. Broad challenges the mainstream framing of the debate, which was largely dominated by various institutional voices (such as belonging to People for the Ethical Treatment of Animals, the Humane Society of the United States, and the National Association for the Advancement of Coloured People), while those offering a nuanced intersectional analysis were little more than a murmur on its fringes, unable to provide a cohesive counter-narrative.

The small but enduring contingent of the intersectional animal rights movement could have greatly enriched the public dialogue, disrupting its rote positions to engender greater understanding and even potential coalition between multiple anti-oppression causes. Thus Broad turns to this work in his chapter, providing an analysis of the mainstream debate while drawing together those whose opinions fell outside of the mainstream discourse; simultaneously, he pushes for those engaged in both animal rights and racial justice to pursue strategies that will allow intersectional analyses to be amplified in future public discussions.

Interventions

Anthony J. Nocella II merges dis-abilities studies, CAS, and environmental studies to expose ableism within animal advocacy and theory, and like Gruen, to propose productive ways forward that value difference. Specifically, in "Disability, Animals, and Earth Liberation: Eco-ability and Ableism in the Animal Advocacy Movement," Nocella sets out to describe "eco-ability," a new philosophy that stresses intersectionality and the perspective that "nature, nonhuman animals, and people with disabilities promote collaboration, not competition; interdependency, not independence; and respect of difference and diversity, not sameness and normalcy" (p. 329). Beginning with an overview of modernism, Nocella demonstrates various exclusions and disavowals of those subjugated groups who have historically been considered not fully human. He argues that, despite the work of animal advocacy to challenge the human/animal divide, many advocates who attempt to disrupt the hubris of speciesism nonetheless reproduce ableism, as they fail to appreciate that these and other forms of oppressions are mutually reinforcing and predicated on similar constructions of "the human."

Lynda Birke's intimate and contemplative chapter, "On Being a Pragmatist: Reflections on Animals, Feminism, and Personal Politics," examines a series of difficult questions about the direction of both animal advocacy and animal-related scholarship. Here she carries the feminist maxim, "the personal is political," into some of the tenuous debates currently calcifying the boundaries of CAS. In light of these tensions, which in some veins have precipitated a certain rigidity and antagonism toward other forms of (human–)animal studies, Birke reflects on her history with feminist activism and women's studies, providing a kind of cautionary tale about the potential missteps CAS might likewise be making.

Birke's long view suggests that emergent divisions, which can appear as new difficulties in relation to animal advocacy and CAS, were preceded by similar riffs in feminism about reform versus revolution, including the compromises entailed by working within institutions and systems. In a series of self-described "meanderings," Birke lucidly meditates on abolition versus welfare, the question of "keeping pets," and the politics of research that includes animals, to strike a note that rings clearly throughout: dogmatic adherence to particular ideologies should not usurp the practical and pragmatic work of minimizing animals' suffering and—extrapolating from feminist methodological insights—the importance of accountability to others who are currently tangled within relationships and matrices of unequal power relations. Indeed, in some cases, the abolitionist versus welfare approaches may very well exist together, and for the time being, necessarily be simultaneously engaged. For Birke, how we make relationships with animals work *well* is her greatest concern, and that requires diligent attention to animals' subjectivities. It also requires dealing with the messiness of being in the world, and at times the seeming disjuncture between more abstract ideological positions and the real-world accountability that subjects should ethically demand of us.

Also turning toward how we might practically and more effectively engage in animal politics, Carol L. Glasser asks what is at stake when the animal rights movement includes profit-seeking institutions within its campaign strategies. Glasser's "Campaigning with the Enemy: Understanding

Opportunity Fields and the Tactic of Corporate Incorporation" explores this approach, arguing that the tactic can either render the campaign impotent, or worse, undermine it to such a degree that the work becomes counterproductive to the cause.

While sociology has theorized various opportunity structures, including political and cultural opportunities, the field has neglected to recognize an economic framework as well. Thus, Glasser analyzes a theoretical framework—what she calls the *opportunity field*—to both expand existing understandings of social movements and to encourage the animal rights movement to re-evaluate collusion with corporations, or *corporate incorporation*. Consequently, Glasser cautions against the increasing institutionalization of the animal rights movement, a trend reflected in the proliferation of formal animal rights organizations, which occurs when the movement fails to address the economic bias of corporations. Radicalism and controversy are sacrificed to professionalism, while competition in the social movement field is generated.

Re/membering Animals

Jessica Carey's "Nose-to-Tail Eating: A Prematurely Post-Factory-Farm Biopolitics," hones an analysis of new carnivorous eating. Addressing the human supremacy and mastery that constitute the movement, she advances three central observations: the movement's emphasis upon the personal recuperation and transmutation of waste; its articulation of a pastoral power relationship that positions animals as inherently in need of the human care, expressed in husbandry and skilful cooking; and its appeal to a form of totalizing pleasure that encompasses both the humanist mastery over other animals and the immersion in animality.

The chapter sharpens its critique by developing Foucault's biopolitics to reveal the undergirding of a movement committed to a new ethics of interspecies relations. Yet while it masquerades as the avant-garde of eating, it remains deeply unaware of its continuities with the very forms of production and consumption it ostensibly seeks to resist: factory farming and industrialized food. For Carey, the movement may be characterized as "post–factory farm" in the sense of sharing a biopolitical vision with factory farming that, ironically, it is also committed to challenging. Against certain delicate sensibilities, including society's affinity for various pre-packaged and pre-selected cuts of meat, the "nose-to-tail" movement promises a refinement of taste, faux ethical hedonism, and a kind of environmental sustainability that bucks society's otherwise typically aseptic, disembodied, and wasteful forms of consumption.

John Sorenson and Atsuko Matsuoka similarly tackle the rise of the New Carnivore movement, where head-to-toe eating is celebrated as the ethical vanguard and vegetarianism is reduced to hand-wringing puritanism. Throughout "The New Carnivores," Sorenson and Matsuoka map the contemporary landscape of this particular strain of "foodies" who posture as a radical front while often reinforcing tired clichés and conservative notions of animal welfare.

As Sorenson and Matsuoka demonstrate, the emergent carnivorous movement makes the possibility of animals' inherent value unthinkable, hermeneutically sealed within the anthropocentric appeals to personal pleasure while consciences are soothed through consumption of "grass-fed," "organic," "local," and other vaguely defined terms, or through the triumph of the do-it-yourself butchering of animals. Within the new carnivorous movement, the humanist logic of animal welfare resurfaces, draped in different clothes but bearing the same fundamental form of previous ethical positions: What we owe animals is simply a minimization of suffering, and the value of their lives is wholly reduced to a means to humans' ends while we re-establish ourselves at the rightful top of some mythical hierarchy. Frequently imbued with machismo and disdain for vegetarians, the New Carnivores emphasize relationships with animals at the same moment they deny animals' complex subjectivity, reinforce their property status, and impose upon them suffering and premature death without necessity.

Carrying forward themes of animal subjectivity and human malignment of other species, Leesa Fawcett's chapter, "Rats! Being Social Requires Empathy," reminds us that there is not only a supposed cleavage between our species and others, but also among nonhuman animals who are also variously valued and used. What more appropriate animal for the contemplation of the particularity of species, and individuals within that species, than the common brown rat, who so often lands on the bottom rung of Western society's ranking? In contemplating these animals, as Fawcett shows, we inevitably must contemplate—and question—ourselves. As she notes, among myriad places and spaces, rats occupy vivisection laboratories as well as our imaginations; in neither instance do they fare well. Yet, they are not just this but they are *themselves*, even when we fail to acknowledge it. Cognitive ethology, along with her discussion of ecofeminist care ethics, justice, and empathy, suggests different ways of being, feeling, and understanding rats. Fawcett thus helps make the common strange, and opens a space for us to orient otherwise, to raise the possibility of flourishing intersubectivity.

Lauren Corman's chapter, "The Ventriloquist's Burden: Animal Advocacy and the Problem of Speaking for Others," complements Fawcett's arguments regarding animal subjectivity and the need to pay attention to animals themselves, driving the inquiry further into debates about voice appropriation and the politics of voice. Concerned with the hubris potentially implied in advocates' use of the voice metaphor (through phrases such as "the voice of the voiceless"), she argues that insights evidenced within certain pockets of animal activism, cognitive ethology, posthumanism, and—crucially—other social movements and theories can help mitigate the challenges of animals' political representation. These approaches stress richer versions of subjectivity that include, but extend beyond, representations of victimization and suffering.

Grappling with the voice metaphor and the problem of speaking for others, Corman considers how voice in its political register (as opposed to its strictly compositional or literary form) tends to highlight non-unitary subjectivity, notions of resistance, valuation of experiential knowledge, and relationality. These "dynamics of political voice" name subjects' pain and suffering, while they refuse to reduce or flatten Others' subjectivities to pure victimization. Such recognition helps unsettle the humanism involved in advocates' political representation of other animals, as we increasingly shift away from discourses of heroism to ones of (attempted) solidarity.

Conclusion: The Living Animal

How to arrive at a conclusion or solution when the open-ended question of the animal remains before us as never before? As we have seen, this is the very question that humanism is unable to contain and we come to realize that we are left not only with a sense of entanglement with regard to intersectionality but also an immediacy based upon knowledge that, even as this is written, the lives of billions of animals are on the line. In fact, in the twelve seconds it took to write this sentence, as Timothy Pachirat points out, 1 of the 2,500 cattle killed per day at the Great Plains slaughterhouse has gone to her death on the kill floor. As editors we take this collection as the opportunity to put before the reader—to challenge the reader—to consider not only "the industrial, mechanical, chemical, hormonal, and genetic violence to which man [*sic*] has been submitting animal life for the past two centuries,"[39] but also to recognize and acknowledge the shared continuities between nonhuman animals and human animals that can serve as the foundation of more ethical relations. Rather than a "conclusion," the "end" of this collection is an invitation to respond to a question posed in *Animal Rites* by Cary Wolfe: "what would it mean in both intellectual and ethical terms to take seriously the question of the animal—or the *animals*, plural, as Jacques Derrida admonishes us."[40] In Wolfe's view, and arguably in the view of contributors and editors of this collection, taking seriously the question of the animal also has the potential to mean that in the future, "we will look back on our current mechanized and systematized practices of factory farming, product testing, and much else that undeniably involves animal exploitation and suffering—uses that we earlier saw Derrida compare to the gas chambers of Auschwitz—with much the same horror and disbelief with which we now regard slavery or the genocide of the Second World War."[41] Ironically, this call to a future-looking-back comes at a time of "the *unprecedented* proportions of [the] subjection of the animal,"[42] and it's been nearly a decade since the publication of *Animal Subjects: An Ethical Reader in a Posthuman World*. If the first collection called attention to the role of empathy and compassion regarding such horror and the question of the animal, this collection seeks to expand the focus and bring into view the capacity of the nonhuman for cognitive, subjective experiences previously denied them and, in the process, to offer a concrete ethico-political perspective on the question of the more-than-human world. As Matthew Calarco puts it, this amounts to a "thorough reworking of the basic anthropocentric thrust of the Western philosophical tradition."[43]

As editors of this collection, we think it is all too evident, as Derrida says, "that in the course of the last two centuries . . . traditional forms of treatment of the animal have been turned upside down by the joint developments of zoological, ethological, biological, and genetic forms of *knowledge*, which remain inseparable from *techniques* of intervention *into* their object, and from the milieu and world of their object, namely, the living animal."[44] In this collection of essays, we offer our most profound intersectional concerns with the living animal with regard to the ethical community in hope of addressing ethical questions whose social and theoretical relevance can hardly be underestimated.

NOTES

1. Wolfe, quoted in Castricano, *Animal Subjects*, 1.
2. Castricano, "Animal Subjects in a Posthuman World," introduction to *Animal Subjects*, 2.
3. Wolfe, quoted in Castricano, *Animal Subjects*, 2.
4. Castricano, "Animal Subjects in a Posthuman World," introduction to *Animal Subjects*, 4.
5. Calarco, "We Are Made of Meat."
6. Ibid.
7. Ibid.
8. Derrida, *Animal That Therefore I Am*, 23.
9. ICAS, "About."
10. Sorenson, "Thinking the Unthinkable," introduction to *Critical Animal Studies*, xxi.
11. Ibid., xxix.
12. Thierman, "Apparatuses of Animality," 91.
13. Derrida, "Animal That Therefore I Am (More to Follow)," 65 (our emphasis).
14. K. Oliver, *Animal Lessons*, 32.
15. Weil, *Thinking Animals*, 5.
16. Sorenson, "Thinking the Unthinkable," introduction to *Critical Animal Studies*, xxviii.
17. Ibid., xix.
18. Ibid., xxxi.
19. Linné and Pedersen, "'Expanding My Universe,'" 269.
20. B. Oliver, "Modernism."
21. Linné and Pedersen, "'Expanding My Universe,'" 269.
22. Twine, *Animals as Biotechnology*, 12.
23. Bryant, "Similarity or Difference."
24. Balcombe, "Animal Pleasure."
25. Bakhtin, *Dialogic Imagination*, 276.
26. Derrida, *Animal That Therefore I Am*, 26.
27. Derrida and Roudinesco, *For What Tomorrow*, 64.
28. hooks, *Teaching to Transgress*, 11, 13.
29. Wolfe, *Animal Rites*, 123.
30. Braidotti, *Posthuman*, 86.
31. Derrida, "Violence Against Animals," 73.
32. Wolfe, *Animal Rites*, xv.
33. Foucault, *Order of Things*, 387.
34. Wolfe, *Animal Rites*, xv–xvi.

35. Pollock, review of *What Is Posthumanism?*, 235.
36. Derrida, *Animal That Therefore I Am*, 23.
37. Ibid, 30.
38. Ibid., 32.
39. Derrida, "Violence Against Animals, 73.
40. Wolfe, *Animal Rites*, 190.
41. Ibid., 190.
42. Derrida, *Animal That Therefore I Am*, 25.
43. Calarco, *Zoographies*,108.
44. Derrida, *Animal That Therefore I Am*, 25.

BIBLIOGRAPHY

Bakhtin, M.M. *The Dialogic Imagination: Four Essays*. Edited by Michael Holquist. Translated by Caryl Emerson and Michael Holquist. Austin: University of Texas Press, 1981.

Balcombe, Jonathan. "Animal Pleasure and Its Moral Significance." *Applied Animal Behaviour Science* 118, nos. 3–4 (2009): 208–16.

Braidotti, Rosi. *The Posthuman*. Cambridge: Polity Press, 2013.

Bryant, Taimie. "Similarity or Difference as a Basis for Justice: Must Animals Be Like Humans to Be Legally Protected?" *Law and Contemporary Problems* 70 (2007): 207–53.

Calarco, Matthew. "We Are Made of Meat: Interview with Matthew Calarco." *Human–Nonhuman*. Accessed March 15, 2014. http://arzone.ning.com/profiles/blogs/we-are-made-of-meat-the-matthew-calarco-interview.

———. *Zoographies*. New York: Columbia University Press, 2008.

Castricano, Jodey, ed. *Animal Subjects: An Ethical Reader in a Posthuman World*. Waterloo, ON: Wilfrid Laurier University Press, 2008.

———. "Animal Subjects in a Posthuman World." Introduction to *Animal Subjects: An Ethical Reader in a Posthuman World*, edited by Jodey Castricano, 5–11. Waterloo, ON: Wilfrid Laurier University Press, 2008.

Derrida, Jacques. *The Animal That Therefore I Am*. Edited by Marie-Louise Mallet. Translated by David Wills. New York: Fordham University Press, 2008.

———. "The Animal That Therefore I Am (More to Follow)." In *Animal Philosophy*, edited by Peter Atterton and Matthew Calarco, 113–28. London: Continuum Press, 2004.

———. "Violence Against Animals." In *For What Tomorrow . . .: A Dialogue*, by Jacques Derrida and Elisabeth Roudinesco. Translated by Jeff Fort. Redwood City, CA: Stanford University Press, 2004.

Derrida, Jacques, and Elisabeth Roudinesco. *For What Tomorrow. . .: A Dialogue.* Translated by Jeff Fort. Stanford, CA: Stanford University Press, 2004.

Foucault, Michel. *The Order of Things: An Archaeology of the Human Sciences.* New York: Pantheon, 1971.

hooks, bell. *Teaching to Transgress: Education as the Practice of Freedom.* New York: Routledge, 1994.

ICAS (Institute for Critical Animal Studies). "About." Accessed August 24, 2014. http://www.criticalanimalstudies.org/about/ (site since modified).

Linné, Tobias, and Helena Pedersen. "'Expanding My Universe': Critical Animal Studies Education as Theory, Politics, and Practice." In *Critical Animal Studies: Thinking the Unthinkable*, edited by John Sorenson, 268–83. Toronto: Canadian Scholars' Press, 2014.

Oliver, Bert. "Modernism, Postmodernism and Poststructuralism, the Difference." *Thought Leader* (blog), May 24, 2013. Accessed March 2, 2014. http://www.thoughtleader.co.za/bertolivier/2013/05/24/modernism-postmodernism-and-poststructuralism-the-difference/.

Oliver, Kelly. *Animal Lessons: How They Teach Us to Be Human.* New York: Columbia University Press, 2009.

Pollock, Greg. Review of *What Is Posthumanism?*, by Cary Wolfe. *Journal for Critical Animal Studies* 9, nos. 1–2 (2011): 235–41.

Sorenson, John. "Thinking the Unthinkable." Introduction to *Critical Animal Studies: Thinking the Unthinkable*, edited by John Sorenson, xi–xxxvi. Toronto: Canadian Scholars' Press, 2014.

Thierman, Stephen. "Apparatuses of Animality: Foucault Goes to the Slaughterhouse." *Foucault Studies* 9 (2010): 89–110.

Twine, Richard. *Animals as Biotechnology: Ethics, Sustainability and Critical Animal Studies.* London: Earthscan, 2010.

Weil, Kari. *Thinking Animals: Why Animal Studies Now?* New York: Columbia University Press, 2013.

Wolfe, Cary. *Animal Rites: American Culture, the Discourse of Species, and Posthumanist Theory.* Chicago: University of Chicago Press, 2003.

1

Might Makes Right

The Origins of Ethics and the
Use of Animals for Human Ends

Rod Preece

Rather than follow the customary path of investigating current manifestations of ethical principles, the intent here is to look to the origins and foundations of ethics in order to see what light they may shed on the justification for the use of animals for human purposes, especially in invasive animal experimentation. The basic aspects of what an entity is to become are, in many instances, inherent in its origins, just as the oak tree is inherent in the acorn. There is something vital to an entity that will often be obscured when we study the appearances of the developed manifestation alone. Animal ethics are continually informed by the assumptions of their origins.

Like nature, ethics may be seen to have its own evolution, changing in accordance with the underlying modes of consciousness of particular communities. It was such an insight that led the Irish historian William Lecky to declare in 1869 that "there is such a thing as a natural history of morals."[1] The benevolent affections from which our ethics is derived, Lecky opined, have expanded in Western cultural history from being applied to family, to tribe, to class, to nation, to groups of nations, to humanity as a whole, and ultimately to animals, as societies become ever more complex and interdependent. But our earliest ethical sentiments never leave us as new loyalties are added to those we initially have to family and local community.

As we ponder our ethical responsibilities in complex, interdependent societies, we come to perceive that individuals of other nations are similar to ourselves in relevant respects and are accordingly also entitled to our benevolent sentiments, which were previously denied to them. Further, we extend those sentiments across gender, culture, and race borders, and having included all of humanity within our benevolent sentiments, we are prompted to extend those sentiments to animals of other species. However, not only are there different levels of loyalty but most persons have some degree of attachment to each stage of development—on attaining our attachment to nation we do not forgo those we had to family or region. Moreover, our loyalties expand further to include sports teams, political parties, professional groups and ideologies, most of which adherences contain ethical elements. With increasing societal complexity our loyalties become more diffuse and, indeed, fraught with conflict, for the interests of at least some of the groups to which we feel a level of attachment do not always coincide. Each will have a different priority in different circumstances and in many situations the differences between the competing interests will be irreconcilable. Ethical decision-making will thus come to involve a choice of one group's interests over those of another, or an earnest attempt to balance, somehow, the competing interests. It is not, then, that there is merely a natural history of morals, as Lecky observed, but there is also the addition of different dimensions of loyalty to coexist alongside the others, the human–animal relationship being one of the most fraught with conflict.

It is thus that an understanding of the development of benevolent sentiments is conducive to grasping the nettle of the prickly problem of the use of nonhuman species for human ends. Our ethical stance is not simply the product of pristinely impartial intellectual determination but is in greater part a response of our individual social nature to societal developments, as well as intellectual deliberations and personal dispositions. Ethical choices thus tend to appeal to us more according to our dispositions and communal interests than to any intrinsic merit they possess. Contrary to Aristotle's famed pronouncement that man is the political, hence rational, animal, it is perhaps more telling to acknowledge man as above all the rationalizing animal—even if in the guise of pursuing objective inquiry. The justification of animal use for human ends is a telling instance.

The very existence of an ethical sense arises from the benevolent and malevolent emotions, directed toward those we are for and those we are against. They arise from the protection of, and protection by, those to whom we have the most immediate relationship: spouses, parents, offspring, and siblings. They are then extended to tribe, usually about a hundred and twenty strong, which appears to be about the normal size of the primary societal organization beyond the nuclear family. This primary organization is involved in mutual protection and the fulfillment of social needs of its members. Thus arises loyalty to a body toward which our benevolent sentiments and our duties are directed. We come to feel obligated to a body that protects communal interests against those from outside—sometimes other humans from outside the tribe with competing interests for scarce commodities (primarily food and shelter), but also frequently predatory animals, for, as the bone-fossil evidence indicates overwhelmingly, hominids, proto-humans, if you will, were decidedly a prey rather than a predator species, as *Homo sapiens* proper has been, much of the time in rather less dramatic form, since the species' appearance in east Africa slightly less than 200,000 years ago. All those outside the tribe, human and animal alike, are "other," i.e., those to whom the benevolent affections are rarely, if ever, extended. For example, the Makritare of the rain forests of the uppermost Orinoco speak the So'to language. *So'to* means twenty, the number of digits possessed by a human. All non-So'to-speaking people, including their immediate neighbours, the Kariña, are regarded as fearsome animals; that is, they are beneath being truly human. The Kariña are epitomized by the Makritare as their jaguar-shamans who are eighteen-clawed predatory cats. Fear and despisal result in the treatment of non-So'to speakers, animal or human, as beneath entitlement to ethical consideration. But there is also an element of awe that is commonly felt toward the powerful unknown with its potential for destruction. Thus, many animals, especially the most fearsome, can be prayed to, and sacrificed to, in order to escape their wrath, and can even become the very basis of religion without their being esteemed. For example, the Tuamotu of the South Pacific worship the shark. Living at the very edge of shark-infested waters, experience teaches a rational fear and loathing for the creatures that have preyed upon so many of their kin. The purpose of the sacrificial worship is to persuade the sharks to leave their kin unharmed. It is certainly not based on any positive evaluation of the shark or acknowledgement of kinship with it, but is far more redolent of the very reverse.

These anthropological facts are mentioned here in order to cast doubt on the common assumption in the animal rights literature that we have a natural affinity with nonhuman animals based on our kinship with them.

It was a view maintained and furthered by the primary Victorian representative of animal ethics, Henry Salt, and has received widespread approbation. There are, indeed, some indications of a natural affinity when, for example, the orphaned infants of one species will occasionally be nurtured by the adults of another species, even when the natural parents' demise occurred through the predation of the now nurturing caretakers; and there is undoubtedly awe felt by humans toward some of the more formidable animals but awe contains a sense of dread as well as wonder. But these are exceptions. It is not that we are essentially unsympathetic to other species. Rather is it that the relationship is complex, with sympathy for some and abject terror toward others. Rather than acknowledging a primal sympathy through kinship it would appear more appropriate to see the commonality in a recognition of common capacity for pain and suffering and recognize that, at least in Western historical experience, consideration of interests has expanded as the benevolent affections have come to extend ever outward from family and local community toward greater inclusivity, eventually to include the animals, or at least some of the animals, for I doubt that crocodiles, scorpions, and mosquitoes have found an easy entry into the world of benevolent affections. However, those who feel benevolence toward some species will commonly maintain, by logical extension, a respect for those animals toward whom they feel little benevolence. While we have long acknowledged our biological kinship with the animals—at the very least since Presocratic Greece—it was not until the nineteenth century that we came to acclaim that kinship as an appropriate basis for our ethical responsibilities.

If not paradoxically, at least surprisingly, it is precisely when we have gained a measure of control over our predatory foes, as we have in the West, that we can come to accord them benevolent respect, unlike, for example, the inhabitants of the Sundarban region of Bangladesh and northern India who live in daily fear of predator tigers. Sixty-five people were killed by tigers in a four-month period of 1988 alone. In Indian Uttar Pradesh in the summer of 1996, sixty-six children were killed in wolf attacks. The thought of viewing tigers and wolves with some measure of moral equality would be entirely alien to those who are pursued by them. Wolves and tigers are decidedly "other." In Western cultural history Immanuel Kant could write of his own time that wolves were still generally feared and loathed. And Percy Shelley could write of the trepidation felt toward bears in Switzerland. Yet, the dangers were rapidly diminishing and both Kant and Shelley understood the respect and consideration owed to animals in general, including the predators.[2] It is only when we no longer have cause to fear some once formidable animal foe that we can come to accord animals rights as a class.

Two antithetical relationships between human and nonhuman animals began some ten or so thousand years ago. On the one hand, the wolf, or its near relative, from whom all dogs are descended, became a helpmeet in the hunt and thus gradually these fellow hunters became peripheral members of the human tribal community, an attachment that became ever stronger as they became companion animals as well as collaborators in the hunt. On the other hand, those societies that became agricultural rather than remaining solely hunter-gatherer communities began to domesticate and breed relatively compliant species as what Gordon Child called living larders and walking wardrobes, a permanent and renewable source of food and raiment—not as a consequence of human ingenuity but of climate change and increasing scarcity of hunted species. Hunger and want rather than the moral and intellectual superiority of humans drove the inception of agriculture.

As conquered species, the domesticated food animals were treated with disdain by their masters, —just as the Normans treated the Saxons in Britain from the eleventh century on, as did conquerors in a myriad other cases, more as the norm than the exception in human history. These oppressions reflect two relevant and significant facts. First, the control of, and disregard for the interests of, fellow beings was not at all restricted to the human–animal nexus but was a part of human behaviour toward fellow beings everywhere and at all times—slavery was not restricted to the southern United States but was commonplace in Africa, Europe, South America, and Asia as well, and still exists in many instances today. Second, the acceptability, normality, even legitimacy, of what amounted to enslavement of both fellow humans and fellow animals was treated by the conquerors and even the conquered as a part of the natural order of things—simply an essential part of the way of the world. If might did not make right, it was nonetheless accepted as the normal source of practice at a time when there was yet no language of ethics. The stage was set for the justification of dominance, as was most evident in Aristotle's notorious justification of slavery in *The Politics*. The defeated were *ipso facto* the inferiors and the less entitled. The winners not only wrote history but also the ethical rules, which in most instances came to be accepted by the vanquished as well as the victors. The use of animals for human ends was simply assumed as a part of the natural order. The human conquerors determined the ethical rules, even before we had ethical discourse.

Traditionally, the origins of philosophy are said to lie with Thales in Ionia in the eighth century BC (in present-day Turkey but then a Greek colony), though to us it would appear to be an inchoate mixture of philosophical thought, magic, and myth rather than philosophy as such. However, Thales and Anaximander and their fellows were not concerned with ethics but with *physis*, the nature of *things*. Again traditionally, ethical discourse is said to have begun with Socrates in the fourth century BC. As Cicero explained later, Socrates was the first to call "philosophy down from the heavens and set her in the cities of men and bring her into their homes and compel her to ask questions about life and morality and things good and evil."[3] Certainly, one can find veiled hints at ethical discourse before, notably with the Pythagorean Empedocles in the fifth century BC, but it is first with Socrates that we get an explicit recognition of matters ethical. Indeed, Aristotle complained in the *Metaphysics* that Socrates restricted himself to questions of moral philosophy at the expense of metaphysics. It is, in fact, with Socrates that we encounter the first explicit account of relative human–animal status. It was with Socrates that we get the first, albeit implicit, intellectual justification for the use of animals for human ends.

It was Xenophon, contemporary associate of Socrates, who stated Socrates' purported position; for, as is well known, Socrates never put stylus to parchment for posterity. Having made the bald assertion, neither further examined nor explained, that "the beasts are born and bred for man's sake" (*Memorabilia* 4.2)—a proposition somewhat elaborated by Aristotle a short time later, but still mere bald assertion—Xenophon stated what he claimed to be Socrates' view that human uniqueness consists in the possession of hands, speech, erect posture, awareness of the deities, the capacity to anticipate, the enjoyment of learning, and the possession of sexual appetite "unbroken to old age." Socrates via Xenophon was expressing nothing more than the superiority humans had come to feel as a result of their domestication of food animals, other practices such as animal sacrifice, and the success in diminishing predation against themselves. It functioned more as a justification of the then 8,000-year-old practices in the treatment of domesticated food animals, and the eons longer of having hunted and eaten animals, rather than as a description of human uniqueness and the superiority it implied.

The virility "unbroken to old age" category can be dismissed out of hand, since, even if it were true and other animals did not possess the same capacity, it is difficult to imagine why it should confer superior status on humans. Moreover, other species possess many of the attributes had by humans—even if in many instances in different form or lesser degree—and it would be no difficult matter to categorize the attributes of other species that humans do not possess or possess in less exalted degree. What comes immediately to mind are the echolocation of the bats and whales, butterfly migration, the capacity for unaided flight of the birds, the ability of fish to breathe without surfacing, the agility of the mountain goat, or the direction-finding of the honeyguide. Are these not as impressive as human attributes in furthering the goals of these animals, with the needs, wants, and purposes they have?

Certainly, some of the categories Xenophon mentions are impressive. Humans possess hands with opposable thumbs, which permit manual dexterity in a manner alien to other species, but then we must ask of what benefit to other species would the possession of opposable thumbs be in the fulfillment of their needs as the animals they are. Would opposable thumbs be of any greater benefit to whales than, say, hibernation would be to us? Speech is certainly an impressive attribute, though it should be noted that it is a consequence of the *FOXP2* gene rather than of human ingenuity. However impressive the faculty of speech may be, Thomas Hobbes pointed out memorably in the seventeenth century that a prime function of speech is to lie, deceive, and mislead. It is not that other species do not lie. For example, they lead predators away from their young by pretending they are elsewhere. The difference is that we lie more persuasively than other species. Is being persuasive liars the mark of our essential superiority on which we predicate our dominion over the animals and the right to their use? The question is, of course, rhetorical, and it is not suggested that our attributes have only negative aspects, but these do deserve earnest consideration in any scale of nature we may wish to devise. And it is the idea of a scale of nature, with humans at the apex, that lies behind the human species' belief in its right to use other species to its own ends.

Some of Xenophon's categories may be said to be irrelevant—such as upright posture—or spurious half-truths such as enjoyment in learning. One of Xenophon's postulates, however, strikes home, the capacity to anticipate, which, while undoubtedly present in other species, is a hallmark of humanity. More than any other species humans anticipate pain and suffering, which is on occasion itself a form of suffering. It is a capacity entitled to serious consideration in any determination of the use of non-human animals for human ends. Unfortunately, the fact of anticipation is sometimes employed by the proponents of animal use for human ends as a convenient rationalization for the continuation of animal experimentation unabated and unreformed.

A significant moral task, even more relevant today than in Xenophon's time, because of the enormous amount of invasive experimentation, is to seek to determine the relative value of different attributes of different species, so that, principally when the interests of animals and other humans are in conflict, as they so often are, we may be pointed in the direction of appropriate treatment. Nonetheless, serious and honest investigation would appear prima facie to provide no easy answers, indeed, on the face of it, perhaps no answers at all.

Despite reservations we must have about the particulars, what is important about Xenophon's statement of Socrates' views is that in having called ethical philosophy down from the heavens, as Cicero saw it, it gave implicit acknowledgement that the use of animals required a justification. It had indeed been tacitly accepted, if unexamined, for several centuries in Presocratic Greece. When an animal was to be sacrificed to propitiate the gods it was deemed necessary that the victim should acquiesce in the sacrifice. Of course, the acquiescence was obtained fraudulently. The sacrificial victim was anointed with liquid and when the animal moved its head up and down to rid itself of the annoying intrusion, acquiescence was assumed. But the *principle* persisted nonetheless—even if it was merely a lingering and ineffective principle born of the need for self-justification. The practice appears to suggest that at some prior time there had been an unresolved musing whether humans had any rights over the lives of animals. It appears not to have worried the Greeks unduly, however.

It is worthy of note that not all in recorded history have been convinced of human superiority over the animals—and not merely in matters of speed, strength, hearing, sight, and the like. A rare few deemed at least certain animals to be morally and practically superior beings, most notably Plutarch in his parody of Book 10 of Homer's *Odyssey*, with many of the early Greek philosophers, notably Democritus, not being far behind. In addition a number of somewhat obscure French and Italian Renaissance figures expressed the same opinion. To be sure, Plutarch's editor, Ian Kidd, does not think Plutarch is being the least bit serious.[4] Kidd's judgment, however, reflects little more than a common human prejudice that no rational person could think in that manner, rather than being based on internal evidence in the essay or on a comparison with Plutarch's other writings. It must, of course, be conceded that the proclivity to posit non-humans as superior is almost always born of a ploy to prick the bubble of human hubris. That was undoubtedly the primary intent of the satirical Jonathan Swift in "The Beasts' Confession" and *Gulliver's Travels* and of the equally satirical Mark Twain in "Man's Place in the Animal World," but although it is undoubtedly a primary consideration there would appear also to be a degree of seriousness, or at least a raising of serious questions, in Plutarch and some semblance of earnestness about both Swift and Twain. Even the satirical pricking of the human bubble reflects a recognition of humanity's vast overestimation of itself. Nor should it be overlooked that from the eighteenth to the nineteenth centuries major literary figures, and many scientists besides, were adamantly opposed on moral grounds to all animal experimentation. The current more or less ubiquitous acceptance of invasive animal experimentation is born of habit, convenience, and self-interest rather than logic and reason. Like Kidd's judgment of Plutarch, current assumptions about animal experimentation are predicated more on millennia of habit born of human conceit than on evidence. As long as the experiments bore little palpable fruit for humans, and not mere knowledge, they were often abominated. When they redounded to human health benefits they were usually applauded.

By the time of Xenophon, human uniqueness and superiority had, with rare exceptions and a few misgivings, been taken for granted for some millennia. It had not always been so. In earlier times in the struggle for life, the procurement of food and shelter had not favoured the human species. But it now became the norm to accept human superiority and entitlement to greater moral consideration on its account, and to tease out the criteria for that entitlement. The earliest *Homo sapiens* would have found the quest preposterous. Indeed, the human species came very close to extinction some 80,000 years ago, so unsuccessful was it in the struggle for life. Conditions were as unfavourable to it as they later became favourable. In teasing out those criteria of superiority we gradually came to believe we possessed, we have been offered in the course of Western history: reason, speech, a religious sense, anticipation of future goods and ills, opposable thumbs, upright stance, being alone in God's image, the possession of an immortal soul, and having a moral conscience, or all or a number of these at once. It is notable how little different they are from Xenophon's original statement of Socrates' position—a further reflection of the oft-repeated quip that the Greeks said it all before.

A more formalized stage of the representation of humanity's precedence over the animals than that of Xenophon came with Plotinus in the third century AD. Relying on Plato's conception of the irrationality of animals, Plotinus devised what became known as the Great Chain of Being, which became one of the most important presuppositions in the history of Western thought. It remained the predominant conception of relative human–animal status until the end of the nineteenth century, being treated not merely as an evaluation of relative merit but as a scale of indubitable fact. It has remained, at least implicitly, the mode of consciousness prevalent until today, though now denuded of its once important religious significance concerning the reality of evil in a world created by a good God. Nor did Darwinism remove the conception. Indeed, the social Darwinists employed their interpretation of Darwin not only to demonstrate the superiority of humans over animals but of whites over blacks and the supremacy of Western culture over all else—conclusions which were not alien to Darwin himself.

The Chain as devised by Plotinus was popularized by Macrobius in the fifth century, largely by rendering Plotinus's difficult-to-penetrate, abstract Platonic philosophy as it seemed in Greek into something more like popular journalism in Latin. The scale of nature, or scale of creatures as it was sometimes known, posited God at the summit, followed by the angels, humans, the higher, then the lower, animals, plants, and minerals—in descending order. The criterion of relative status was the possession and degree of reason. The model proved so persuasive that as late as 1893, William Minto, Professor of Logic and English at the University of Aberdeen, in his well-received book *Logic: Deductive and Inductive*, could treat the Chain as a product of rigorous and indisputable logic rather than as a convenient yet controversial assumption supportive of human hegemony over the other animals. In fact, as has here been intimated, its origin lay more in human self-indulgence than in science. That reason should be the relevant criterion of merit remained the unquestioned assumption throughout the period of the sovereignty of the Chain, and remains so today in the popular and even the scientific mind. The poet Alexander Pope's was a rare dissenting voice in history—and perhaps his was more a hint than a declaration—when he averred in the eighteenth century that "man has reason enough only to know what is necessary for him to know and dogs have just that too."[5] Greater reason would have been of no benefit to dogs.

Once the Great Chain of Being had become the intellectual norm, "Reason"—always capitalized—was the undisputed ground to confer on humans preferential rights over animals and, indeed, often enough to give the latter little serious consideration at all.

Yet reason is also the source of many human mental ills; sophisticated reason promotes sophisticated crime, especially but not solely in the age of the computer—in the medieval era it consisted most strikingly in the elaborate forgery of church documents conferring land rights. Most importantly, reason is undeniably the source of our desecration of the environment. If exalted reason has provided many human benefits it has also produced the greatest devastation, from weapons of mass destruction to all those ills that have put the very survival of the planet and its inhabitants, human and animal alike, at grave risk. A persuasive case can be made that reason has been the most destructive faculty in the course of our planet's history. Reason certainly has no undisputed claim to allow humans preferential consideration. We may infer that reason was chosen as the reigning criterion of entitlement to preferential consideration for no better reason than that it was the faculty that seemed most important in assisting humans to fulfill their ends, regardless of whether it was a faculty of equal importance in helping other animals achieve their ends.

Protagoras of Abdera observed famously in the fifth century BC that "man is the measure of all things." And, indeed, he is right. But he is only right because man is doing the measuring. Man measures by human standards, not by impartial criteria. Animals are demeaned in the scale of nature because they do not share or do not possess in equal degree the faculties and attributes that are seen as useful for humans to achieve human ends. A great deal of sound research and commentary has been produced in recent years to show that nonhuman animals possess reason, a moral sense, benevolent sentiments, and other worthy passions. But they possess these attributes in lesser degree than humans, and so to measure them is still to accord them a lower place in the relative-status stakes. The groundbreaking research functions, quite unintentionally, as a modern version of the Great Chain of Being with humans still at the apex of the animal world. Certainly, the argument and evidence of these admirable studies demonstrates beyond reasonable doubt that animals are more worthy than they have traditionally been treated, but humans still emerge as the superior creatures. The reality is that other animals have their own attributes, which are not shared or are shared in lesser degree by humans. They are attributes that would appear to be at least no less successful in furthering the fulfillment of the animals' ends—with the needs, wants, and purposes they possess—than human attributes succeed in fulfilling human ends.

What has here been implied is that there are no adequate and certainly no unassailable grounds on which human rights and needs trump those of the animals. But, of course, such a conclusion does not for an instant accord with the reality of our cultural beliefs. Invasive animal experimentation—often conducted, we need remind ourselves, for very worthy ends—is condoned as a necessary evil. That is the context in which, despite the evidence from the origins of ethics, the use of animals for human purposes must be discussed if any advances are to be won. But where do we begin? In accord with Aristotle, there would appear to be no reasonable alternative but to start with how relevant persons do think, and work from there, remembering that many of those who promote human over animal interests have reached their conclusion with earnest and honourable circumspection. It is a far from happy starting point, for it is to *begin* from the context in which human rights and needs are entitled to greater consideration than those of animals. The conclusion is preordained by the premise. Yet we must recognize with Edmund Burke that what may be morally right may be politically wrong: the demand for abolition or wholesale rethinking may hinder piecemeal improvement. To achieve some measure of progress in practical matters, moral compromises may be, almost always will be, necessary. It is not enough to argue that the current practices are blatantly unjust. If we believe they are unjust we are still constrained to accept them for what they are and work within the context of current mores. We must seek what values are shared in common. But we should also note that the current climate favourable to animal experimentation is not a reflection of a perennial norm: all animal experimentation was abominated by the great literary figures, from Shakespeare to Samuel Johnson to Bernard Shaw. But for a quirk of fate, a large proportion of animal experimentation would have been abolished by the British parliament in 1876. The most distinguished figures in the realm, from the Lord Chief Justice to the great reformer, the seventh Earl of Shaftesbury, to Queen Victoria were loud in their condemnation. Only the new-found prestige of science and medicine stood against them. If current mores favour invasive research on animals, they have not always done so and will not necessarily always do so.

Historically, what has been held in common in ethical deliberation, and hence the point of agreement in matters moral, is the paramountcy of sentience. In fact, it would make more sense to talk of the rights of sentience rather than animal rights. The elimination of animal pain and suffering has been pervasively perceived by the commentators on ethics as a primary moral task, at least from the time of the Torah and other early Jewish texts, and repeated frequently thereafter, most notably by Aristotle's successor at the Lyceum, Theophrastus, and by Moses Maimonides in Spain in the twelfth century, and treated as commonly conceived currency by Humphrey Primatt and Richard Dean in the eighteenth century. Even most of those who wrote in opposition to these animal advocates acknowledged that, where it could be avoided, suffering ought not to be inflicted on animals. The presumption of the centrality of sentience received its most celebrated expression by Jeremy Bentham in 1789—the question is not whether they reason, nor whether they talk, but can they suffer? And its most sublime expression came from Rousseau a few years earlier in his educational treatise *Émile*. Many of the most respected philosophers spoke out on behalf of the animals. Of course, there were, on the other side, the Cartesians who denied sentience to animals. But despite their acclaim in other areas, their influence on the animal question was quite negligible, although the Cartesian tenor of mind had something of a renaissance in the age of Pavlov.[6]

But there must be more to the question of ethical value than pain and suffering alone, since, so restricted, incongruences soon appear. A highly regarded animal-welfare scientist remarked to me that he looked after his research cattle well, ensured that they lived a happy and carefree life, and then one day, after their usefulness was over, he had them put to death painlessly and without their suffering. He was convinced he had acted ethically in the matter. I asked him whether he would apply the same criteria to himself. He had, I suggested, lived a satisfying and fulfilling life. Would it then now be appropriate to put the scientist to death painlessly and without suffering? If not, there must be some *essential* difference between human and nonhuman animals if his treatment of the cattle was ethical. If so, I find myself unable to imagine in what the difference might consist. Clearly, our sense of the ethical goes beyond the elimination of pain and suffering to include such considerations as the value of life itself, the quality of life, and the effect of actions on social relationships. And there would appear no good ground for restricting these criteria to human life alone. If there are good grounds we need to be told unequivocally not only what they are but why they should be deemed convincing grounds for distinction. After all, to claim that humans are entitled to preferential consideration because of their superior reason is in principle no more convincing than to claim that dolphins are entitled to preferential consideration because of their superior echolocation.

It has, then, been a common presumption in ethical discourse throughout recorded Western history, but certainly not a well-practised one, that we have a responsibility not to cause, and, if we listen to the Torah, a duty to prevent, pain and suffering to animals. But that, of course, is where the practical problem begins. Supporters and opponents of animal experimentation can claim adherence to that principle, though some, of course, more easily than others. If we have a duty not to harm animals but at the same time have the possibility of alleviating human suffering by harming animals, ethics becomes a precarious juggling act balancing conflicting rights and duties. And while I have argued that humans have no incontrovertible rights over other animals, we have no alternative but to accept for the present that almost all those who legislate, those who conduct invasive experiments, and those who adjudicate on ethics review committees do think we possess those rights, relying, if pressed, on the phylogenetic scale, which, in essence, treats relative rights according to organizational complexity. What prevails in such committees is a view that is called by philosophers *reasonable partiality*, implying that equality and universality are admirable principles that it is appropriate to deviate from on occassion. In the field of invasive research on animals that amounts to the adage that it is wrong in principle to harm animals where no offsetting benefit is achieved, but where we may be reasonably confident in achieving considerable benefits to humans, the experiment is justified. Indeed, that today is the preponderant belief in Western culture.

This general practice reflects, on the surface, the principle enunciated by Russell and Burch over half a century ago when they introduced the 3Rs program of replace, reduce, and refine.[7] A prevailing problem today is that mere lip service is paid to the principle. Less attention is devoted to alternatives than is deserved, especially in epidemiological research—animals, after all, are cheaper than humans and don't have unions and coffee breaks. And, of course, efforts at reduction have been a total failure, in large part for legal protection against being sued rather than because the research

MIGHT MAKES RIGHT **41**

is likely to produce health advantages. Indeed, it is often merely a repetition of research done previously in other jurisdictions, and the results are thus known in advance.

Reasonable partiality is a worthwhile concept to introduce into the debate since it is an omnipresent aspect of human behaviour. For example, we tend to applaud the principle of equality of opportunity in education but know that it is natural for parents to consider the interests of their own children first and foremost—they possess partiality on behalf of their own offspring. We look to government and law to ensure that better-educated, wealthier, and more-concerned parents are not able to provide too great an advantage for their own children while we also uphold, with some degree of tension, the centrality of the family in the social order. The alternative is to adopt Plato's proposal to remove children from their family at birth and deny them all knowledge of their parents. Only thus in Plato's view would the undue partiality of parents be effectively eradicated.

The task of ethics review committees is, or ought to be, analogous with that of government in educational policy, i.e., to represent the potentially disadvantaged. The committees, however, see it as their role to be impartial. Yet in the current cultural milieu, to be impartial is to be partial to the interests of the researchers. In effect the committees represent the interests of the researchers, sharing, by and large, the same belief system and believing in the virtue of so-called reasonable partiality. Only egregious ethical breaches are curtailed. In reality, the committees represent the interests of those already advantaged rather than the disadvantaged.

Unfortunately, formal ethics itself can never provide final answers to ethical questions. It is restricted largely to the consistent and logical ordering of thoughts within a given cultural paradigm. It can have far less to say about the paradigm itself. And the paradigm is at least currently favourable to the human interest, since in practice man *is* the measure of all things. The instrument of measurement is the human yardstick. But if reasonable partiality appears so reasonable to most, important questions still need to be asked. If it is reasonable to favour human over animal interests in some circumstances, and most believe it is, would it not be equally reasonable to discriminate in some circumstances in favour of whites over blacks, heterosexuals over homosexuals, and Christians over Muslims? If there is any case to be made in these instances in favour of reasonable partiality it is usually thought appropriate to favour those who have been traditionally discriminated against, i.e., to level the playing field. The very opposite is true in the case of animals. We discriminate in favour of the advantaged over the disadvantaged.

In animal experimentation reasonable partiality in favour of human interests can only be warranted if we measure human and animal attributes and declare the human attributes, and indeed humankind itself, more worthy. Yet it is a most daunting exercise to seek criteria that would allow the task to be accomplished and invasive research to be justified. The traditional concepts of Western cultural history, such as reason and opposable thumbs, are less than wholly persuasive. We are left with the rights of sentience and the value of life itself as the primary considerations. Unless we can find some means of justifying the valuation of humans more highly than other animals, we must have the most serious moral qualms about what we do in animal experimentation, however beneficial the projected ends. At the very least this implies that animals as the subjects of research are entitled to a great deal more consideration than they currently receive. The animal deserves to be considered no longer "other."

Either the human is an animal in precisely the same way that other animals are animal, and subject to similar considerations, or, if we are to seek a justification for our invasion of animal bodies, we must resort to regarding the human being as a quasi-divine existence, a being of a higher order than our fellow animals. Humanity would have to be designated as a minor deity, a step most would consider absurd, even though in effect that is what has already happened in Western cultural history. Even then it would be a vivid stretch of the imagination to portray humanity as a benevolent deity.

NOTES

1. Lecky, *History of European Morals*, 103.
2. It is not uncommon to read that Kant denied rights to animals on the grounds of lack of self-consciousness. Nonetheless, Kant believed also that it was the moral duty of humankind to treat animals with consideration and respect.
3. Cicero, *Tusculan Disputations*, 435.
4. "Now it need hardly be said that Plutarch himself did not believe a word of this looking-glass world he had conjured up"; in Plutarch, *Essays*, 381.
5. Quoted in Scholtmeijer, *Animal Victims in Modern Fiction*, 17.
6. See Preece, *Brute Souls*, ch. 3.
7. Russell and Burch, *Humane Experimental Technique*.

BIBLIOGRAPHY

Cicero, Marcus Tullius. *Tusculan Disputations*. Rev. ed. Translated by J.E. King. Cambridge, MA: Harvard University Press, 1945.

Lecky, William Edward Hartpole. *The History of European Morals from Augustus to Charlemagne*. New York: D. Appleton & Co., 1869.

Plutarch. *Essays*. Translated by Robert Waterfield. Edited by Ian Kidd. London: Penguin, 1992.

Preece, Rod. *Brute Souls, Happy Beasts, and Evolution: The Historical Status of Animals*. Vancouver: UBC Press, 2005.

Russell, William Moy Stratton, and Rex Leonard Burch. *The Principles of Humane Experimental Technique*. London: Methuen, 1959.

Scholtmeijer, Marian. *Animal Victims in Modern Fiction: From Sanctity to Sacrifice*. Toronto: University of Toronto Press, 1993.

2

Critical Animals Studies and the Property Debate in Animal Law

⋄⊷⫘⊶⫘⊷⋄

Maneesha Deckha

An animal turn is evident in contemporary Canadian and American academia. Investigations of the relationships and interactions humans have with nonhuman animals are on the rise[1] and are generating an emergent field often described as "human–animal studies" or simply "animal studies."[2] Scholarship in this area, though spanning a wide range of disciplines and thus challenging to define, shares a common purpose: to understand the relationships, practices, norms, and/or discourses that organize human encounters with animals.[3] Within this overarching field of human–animal studies, *critical* animal studies (CAS) is emerging as an important strand, emphasizing the undercurrents of power and hegemony that inform our relationships with animals—an emphasis scholars writing in this field note is too absent in mainstream animal studies accounts.[4]

CAS scholars go beyond exploration and analysis of animal experience to take issue with the ideology of human exceptionalism and the species hierarchies it has instituted.[5] It is thus non-anthropocentric in both senses of that word—challenging human benchmarks and experiences as well as the privileging of human interests.[6] As Helena Pedersen argues, it overlaps with posthumanism if the latter is understood to mean a theoretical framework that destabilizes the human–animal divide, values nonhumans as subjects, *and* challenges ways of knowing that reflect human values and experiences to consider the nonhuman as a "knowing subject,"[7] but not reducible to it.[8] CAS more consistently identifies animal exploitation as a problem and freedom from such exploitation as the only acceptable remedy.[9] Inspired by other critical theories coalescing in focus on human-difference-oriented concerns of gender, race, sexuality, etc., CAS centres the problem of species difference and impugns the practices and discourses, both subtle and violent, by which animals are Othered and oppressed.[10] Applied to posthumanist theory in general, it can bring about a more critical version of posthumanism.[11]

At the same time that animal studies acquired more visibility in undergraduate and graduate teaching, and in scholarly research portfolios in the humanities, social sciences, and natural sciences, animals also drew more attention at law schools. In fact, "animal law" is a rapidly developing curriculum area in American law schools;[12] since 1977, when the first animal law course was offered, at least 116 American law schools have offered the course.[13] Much of that growth took place in the last fifteen years.[14] The scope and content of animal law courses varies, but most courses cover the range of common legal issues that involve animals (e.g., "custody" disputes over companion animals when humans separate, estate planning for companion animals upon a human owner's death, claims for damages in tort when the negligent action of a third party harms a companion animal, etc.).[15]

Accompanying the increased curricular attention to legal issues affecting animals is legal scholarship by law professors about the normative dimensions of animals' legal status.[16] The main debates in animal law scholarship have centred on animals' legal status as property under the common law, as leading scholars in the field of animal law have differed over whether property status for animals inhibits meaningful reform. The *Animal Rights Debate: Abolition or Regulation,*[17] a fairly recently published exchange by two prominent scholars, lays out two of the main arguments in this debate. Gary Francione, a groundbreaking American scholar in the animal law field, is well known for his abolitionist position; he claims that the property status of animals must be abolished for any effective social change to occur.[18] In contrast, Robert Garner, an eminent British political scientist, has long asserted that meaningful reforms for animals can develop within the established property regime; he promotes a "broad protectionism" for animals.[19] A third theory stakes a middle ground: David Favre, an influential American legal scholar, has written a number of articles advocating a system of "equitable self-ownership"[20] and "living property"[21] for animals. His work aims to revamp the current conception of property as it applies to animals' legal classification.

Despite the rising prominence in universities of CAS, which employs posthumanist deconstructive methodologies, and the parallel growth of animal law in law schools, CAS has not figured prominently in animal law scholarship. The discourses of difference, Otherness, and marginalization to which CAS centrally attends occupies a relatively minor role within animal law scholarship. Instead, humanist liberal concepts of equality and justice and liberal intellectual traditions of utilitarianism and deontology guide argumentation against speciesism within animal law scholarship (and moral philosophy about animals in general).[22] As we shall see, liberalism also serves as the theoretical framework through which the debate about the potential of animals' propertied status in law to inhibit robust reform proceeds.

Although arguments based in liberalism can illuminate the moral worth of animals and the corresponding need for legal reform, critical theorists operating from feminist, postcolonial, queer, postmodern, and posthumanist vantage points have questioned liberalism's ability to provide justice to marginalized subjects (animal or not).[23] A shared concern among these critical theories is liberalism's reliance on sameness logic; that is, liberalism measures the ethical worth of a marginalized subject through examining that subject's possession of a particular capacity presumed by the dominant group to be important.[24] In the case of animals, liberal arguments have variously concentrated on the capacity animals share with humans to suffer, emote, think, use tools and language, etc.[25] Demonstrating that animals share human qualities and thus should count as humans do is a troubling argumentation route since the human subject remains the benchmark; liberalism's sameness logic thus perpetuates humanism while it critiques anthropocentrism.[26] Liberalism is not, then, posthumanist even in the non-critical sense, let alone the critical posthumanist sense Pedersen calls for, and arguments founded in its concepts and commitments will find it difficult to achieve their desired posthumanist outcomes.[27]

This chapter does not canvass this full critique of liberalism and its ramifications for animal law. Instead, it seeks to intervene in the "property" debate from the perspective of CAS, a theoretical framework that, to recall the above discussion, does not argue for animals based on the "shared capacity" for reasoning. For this reason alone, CAS is posthumanist in a way that liberalism is not. Moreover, in its respect for nonhuman difference, we can understand CAS as a theoretical framework that (1) recognizes species difference as a prime venue of problematic and power-laden social construction and Othering; (2) criticizes human-made ethical boundaries regarding animals as fragile and tenuous hegemonic social constructions; (3) highlights the intersectional nature of our understandings about species difference and animality; and (4) rejects the default ethical position that routinely sacrifices animal interests to human ones.[28] As noted, the "property" debate has operated within liberalism's parameters. As such, discussion about social construction, Otherness, intersectionality, and difference do not figure prominently in this debate. It is thus useful to add another theoretical perspective to the "property" debate to diversify the conversation and investigate the shortcomings in the reasoning behind current positions in the debate. Although the end point—a conclusion about the question of whether the law should continue to categorize animals as property—might be the same through a liberal or CAS framework, considering this question through the latter framework will help fortify/impugn positions arrived at through liberalism and, perhaps more importantly, provide a *critical* posthumanist and difference-centred reading of this debate. The overall "case," then, for the conclusion about whether animals should continue under the legal category of property becomes stronger.

As will be evident, the debate over legal categories overlaps heavily with the long-standing rights/welfare debate found in general animal theory.[29] For the purposes of this chapter, the latter debate is engaged to the extent necessary to elucidate the former. In excavating this recent iteration of the property debate, my intention is to consider which response to the property debate is preferable to the others when examined through a CAS framework. I argue that a posthumanist approach that takes species difference, Otherness, and marginalization seriously, as CAS does, would favour a non-property legal status for animals in the common law. The chapter proceeds in three parts, with the three leading proposals or "sides" to the posthumanist property debate each presented and evaluated from a CAS perspective.

The Desirability of a Non-property Status

Francione's writings on abolitionism for animals within the law are extensive and well known.[30] His contribution to *The Animal Rights Debate* forms his most recent fulsome articulation of his views and it is this text on which

I draw to present his point of view on the abysmal results of animals' propertied legal status.[31] Before delving into Francione's position, it is important to acknowledge that while Francione is deeply committed to ending the exploitation of animals, he has not explicitly aligned his abolitionist theory with posthumanism (or, for that matter, CAS) in his writings. It may be that he would reject both frameworks on principled grounds. The purpose here, however, is not to argue that Francione would himself endorse these theories, but rather that a CAS posthumanist approach to thinking about the welfare-abolition debate clearly favours Francione's abolitionist side.

Francione acknowledges early on that he is "sharply critical of the welfarist position," describing it as a "manifest failure."[32] For Francione, the problems with welfarism are rooted in its acceptance of and resignation to the use of property as a legal category for sentient animals.[33] His aversion to the property category underpins his entire theory; for example, he notes that he uses the term "animal rights" to refer to the abolitionist position he advocates because "[f]or the most part, when I refer to animal rights, I am really referring to *one* right: the right not to be treated as the property of humans."[34]

On Welfarism

Francione's appraisal of the failures inherent in a property status for animals informs his assessment of animal protectionist initiatives. He notes that welfarist measures are only successfully enacted when human economic interests would benefit—i.e., when it becomes cost-effective to improve welfare.[35] He also stresses that the standards of "humane" treatment under anti-cruelty laws are generally defined by animal-use industries, not animal advocates.[36] As a result, he argues, welfarist reforms actually increase animal exploitation by placating the public with the perception that animal exploitation is now more "humane," thus deterring them from demanding more radical change.[37] Further, he argues that most welfarist measures, rather than prompting individuals to question the current legal order, instead bolster the "property paradigm."[38] This is even true, he claims, of the "new welfarist" approach, where animal advocates seek abolition as an end point (and thereby differ from "old welfarists," who only focused on better treatment) but believe that welfarist measures are useful in the meantime since they may eventually lead to abolition.[39] Francione's reasons for holding this view reveal the extent to which property status matters in his analysis. He writes:

> First, welfare reform is . . . always predicated on the notion that we may
> use animals as long as we treat them reasonably well and kill them in a
> relatively painless way. That is, welfarism does not challenge our use per
> se of animals; it challenges only our treatment of them. Second, welfare
> reform is almost always limited by the economic benefits that producers
> or consumers will enjoy if the reform is adopted. That is, welfare reform
> perpetuates the notion that animals are economic commodities without
> inherent or intrinsic value. Animal welfare will never be an incremental
> step toward anything but more animal exploitation and greater accept-
> ance of that exploitation.[40]

Based on his previous work and the examples of various campaigns he gives
in his chapter, Francione here appears to have in mind not the intentions
of new welfarists, but the legislative, political, and economic purposes that
actually motivate legislators or industry executives.[41] His unwavering conviction that welfare measures are useless for engendering a disruption to
the property status of animals is a result of the fact that the welfare measures, by definition, do not contest the property status. Francione's rejection
of welfarist measures also depends on group valuation over individual: it
must be the overall effect of welfare reforms that Francione contends are
useless, since he would recognize the value of a ban on mutilations in factory farming to an individual animal in the industrial farming complex,[42]
even if that measure did nothing to move toward a non-property paradigm
for animals.[43]

The Abolitionist Model

Francione offers up the abolitionist view as the better option for animals,
summarizing the theory as follows: "The rights position as I propose it
maintains that death is a harm for any sentient being and that we cannot
make meaningful distinctions between the quality of sentient experiences
between humans and nonhumans that would justify imposing any pain and
suffering on nonhumans incidental to our use of them as our resources, any
more than we can make such distinctions between or among humans for
the purpose of justifying slavery or otherwise treating humans exclusively
as resources."[44] Francione objects to the welfarist belief that animals do not
suffer the same way humans do when they die prematurely. This theory of
a differential impact of death is grounded in the idea that animals do not
have an autobiographical sense of themselves (deliberately envisioning and
following a life course, planning for the future) as humans do. They are,

instead, seen as "eternally present" beings—in other words, they are living in the present.[45] Beyond this, Francione also questions the welfarist idea of "humane" treatment, asserting that the use of animals as resources is always exploitative. Francione is thus against the current legal order that classifies animals as property.[46] For him, a propertied existence is *always already* to be subjugated.[47]

Francione is unwilling to concede that abolitionism is impractical, instead choosing to present guidance for its future implementation.[48] Garner, of course, presents counter-arguments to this and other aspects of Francione's abolitionist view; some of those are canvassed below in discussing Garner's views on the impact of animals' legal status as property. I wish to keep the focus here, however, on the property debate and Francione's position within it. While we may disagree with Francione as to the practicality of the abolitionist approach or his conclusion that welfare reforms should never be pursued, it is difficult to contest his reasoning that the current property paradigm for animals facilitates their exploitation and is inegalitarian. On this point, the liberal animal law theoretical framework Francione uses matches the conclusions reached by a CAS framework employing posthumanist methodologies. Property entrenches a logic and relationship dynamic of domination that places animals in a legal position of slavery for their owners. This position promotes the Othering of animals by conceptualizing them as commodities and subordinating their interests. It is difficult to reconcile with the tenets of CAS identified earlier that animals are not secondary beings and their relegation to this and even more abysmal places in society is a marginalizing move that can only be justified through anthropocentric and speciesist discourses.[49]

Having outlined the abolitionist view of the property debate and CAS's strong alignment with it, the chapter now turns to the counter-arguments presented by the welfarist approach, to consider whether the CAS framework can support the view that the property status of animals is irrelevant to their suffering.

Discounting Property as a Legal Status: Garner and Broad Protectionism

Garner shares Francione's concern about the exploitation of animals, but prefers to find alternatives to abolitionism in reaching his goals.[50] He calls abolition strategically useful but "find[s] it difficult to reconcile . . . [with] the political art of the possible."[51] He takes care to begin his contribution to *The Animal Rights Debate* by stressing that he "is not criticizing animal rights" in general, but rather rights of the abolitionist variety.[52] Garner assails Francione's conception of animal rights because of its "assertion that the abolition of the use of animals by humans is both ethically desirable and politically possible."[53] Thus, in promoting his theory of broad protectionism, which is ultimately a welfarist approach, Garner is not stipulating a position against rights, although he does take issue with the view that all human use of animals is unethical. He is also skeptical of the viability of the abolitionist viewpoint, especially given the entrenched position that animal exploitation occupies in contemporary society.[54] Garner identifies himself as "welfarist" but adds the adjective "new," thus distinguishing his theory, which he labels "animal protectionism," from "old-style welfarism that has rightly been condemned ethically."[55]

Answering the Abolitionist Critique

What, then, are Garner's main arguments that a non-property legal order is not necessary to generate meaningful change for animals? First, he is unconvinced that welfarism has the prohibitive effect on animal emancipation claimed by Francione (and others). He dismisses the claim that all welfarist measures placate rather than radicalize people as too broad, empirically untested, and speculative.[56] Garner notes, to the contrary, the increasing mainstream societal acceptance of vegetarianism, which he attributes in part to animal welfare advocacy.[57] He also questions the efficacy of abolitionist-based campaigns, noting that they have not been very successful in generating more than "minority support" for their vision.[58] He states that because abolitionist campaigns give the perception that they conflict with human ends and desires, they will very likely continue to have bleak prospects for achieving actual results.[59] The movement, he says, requires "an unprecedented level of altruism"—a level that many humans will not achieve.[60]

The second abolitionist argument to which Garner seeks to respond is the critique that a welfarist approach is ineffective. It is here that he raises the issue of the property status of animals, stating that abolitionists perceive welfarist strategies as ineffective because animals remain the property of human or corporate persons and are thus subject to the exploitation that ownership rights facilitate.[61] In response, drawing from the work of animal ethics theorist Alisdair Cochrane, Garner asks us to consider closely what rights we would like animals to have.[62] He states that if the rights afforded animals are conceptualized as the right not to suffer, rather than the right to life and liberty, ownership does not entail subordination. It is worth quoting his full reasoning:

> it is possible to argue that equality between humans and animals can be consistent with ownership if we adopt the principle that we should treat the interests of animals equally with those of humans. Crucial to the success of this argument . . . is the acceptance of an interest-based conception of rights rather than a choice-based conception. The former sees rights as protecting individual interests whereas the latter sees rights as protecting an individual's autonomy to act.[63]

After explaining that the interest-based model protects the right not to suffer, but not the right to life or liberty, Garner considers what he views as the two most common incidents (features) of ownership—the right to possess and the right to use—and explains why they do not necessarily entail animal exploitation. With respect to possession, his main point is that while "[p]ossession clearly restricts the freedom of animals . . . lack of freedom does not necessarily infringe their interests."[64] It is all contingent "on the species and nature of the restriction."[65] In examining the subordinating potential of the right to use, Garner argues that human use of animals need not contradict the equal consideration of animal interests.[66] Following Cochrane again, Garner states: "equating their property status with inequality follows only if we add the additional claim that animals possess an interest in not being used against their will. If we conceive of animals as not being autonomous (and therefore not having an interest in developing and pursuing their own life plans), then they do not have that interest. Using animals per se, therefore, is not the problem. It is what they are used for that is the key."[67] Garner again stresses that abolitionist concerns about the incident of use evaporate if it is accepted that animals are not autonomous. The trump card, then, for Garner is his premise that animals do not have the capacity for autonomy. Due to this presumed absence, we do not have the duty to abstain from using animals against their will. Garner's support for his belief that animals are not autonomous is the lack, among nonhumans, of "morally significant characteristics,"[68] such as "self-consciousness and a high degree of rationality,"[69] that allow for autonomy.

Protectionism and Property—Compatible Companions?

There are several ideas that one might object to in Garner's claim that continued property status is compatible with equality for animals. First, Garner defines an "interest-based" model as non-autonomous; it does not require the maximization of animal autonomy, just the reduction or cessation of suffering. It is not evident, however, why this should be so. Why should we think that animals do not pursue a life plan or, for that matter, why think that a pursuit of a life plan is the mark of autonomy? The instability and masculinist interpretations of what constitutes autonomy, and which beings exercise it, have been decisively criticized by relational feminists, including ecofeminists,[70] and questioned by posthumanists in general.[71] Yet, Garner's discussion of the right to both possession and use depends on this tenuous characterization.

Even if we accept Garner's premise that animals' autonomy does not have to be respected, we are still left with the question: why can't an interest-based model protect a right to life? The right to life is coupled with the right to liberty; liberty's correspondence with autonomy is clear, but the right to life seems at least as relevant to an interest-based model as to one based on choice. Moreover, his discussion of possession as a critical element of the "bundle of rights" that usually attaches to ownership acknowledges that being a possession can impair an animal's interests. He points to wild animals and animals in factory farms as examples of those whose interests would be, or are, infringed by human ownership.[72] Given that "the use of animals for food is, by far, the most numerically and culturally significant animal use,"[73] and the high (potentially uncountable) number of wild animals on earth,[74] it would seem that the property regime already subordinates a significant number of animals.

When he moves to consider the effect of property status on the introduction and viability of reform measures, Garner's argument is stronger. Here, he states that the intended effect of animal welfare laws is to "limit property rights in order to benefit animals directly."[75] Recall that Francione takes issue with this portrayal of whom it is that animal welfare statutes are intended to benefit. Leaving this dispute aside, we may read Garner here to mean that such laws—whether anti-cruelty or otherwise—have a positive effect on animals, notwithstanding the fact that their purposes are based on a Kantian world view that is essentially humanist. Instituting incremental yet meaningful reforms in factory farming will have a discernible effect on the suffering that a hen must endure and is thus, arguably, effective for that individual hen.

Garner's defence of welfarism as not necessarily counterproductive or ineffective is more convincing than his defence of the possible compatibility of a property status with equality for animals. While a welfare measure that makes a cage larger will likely benefit the hen, she will still suffer as a result of a lack of sunlight, mutilation, poor diet, the inability to nest comfortably, and so on (note that the hen suffers even if one believes she is not an autonomous agent). Even if animal welfare measures could cumulatively address all the suffering a hen could possibly experience while being raised for slaughter (say, in an idyllic family farm setting), it is the property status that subjects her to her eventual fate.[76] This power dynamic inheres in ownership even if one sees property, as Garner does, as "a reflection, and not the cause, of the relatively low worth attached to animals."[77]

Property and Culture

It may be true, as Garner submits, that the real obstacle to elevating animals' moral worth in our society is not their legal status, but their public and industry status.[78] Certainly, as Garner stresses, a change in legal status is not sufficient to bring about an animal utopia.[79] A legal sea change is also unlikely to occur without a wide-scale cultural and political attitudinal shift toward posthumanism. Garner is also right to point out that some animals, such as companion animals, already enjoy good treatment vis-à-vis other animals despite their property status.[80] In this regard, he is keen to emphasize that property as a category does not prohibit good treatment. Although Garner does not explicitly note this point, in making this argument he has recognized the higher cultural status afforded to companion animals. That cultural views shape our laws is clear. But again, to take Garner's example of companion animals, it bears noting that the cultural protections only last as long as the cultural values do. The loving companion of a companion animal may eventually decide, for whatever "legitimate" reasons, to act in a way that maximizes the owner's interests rather than the companion animal's.[81] Moreover, despite the favourable treatment of many companion animals when compared to farm and research animals, the relational work they do for their human owners should not be discounted or romanticized too quickly.[82] It is still the property relationship that allows subservient positionings of companion animals to occur in both cases.

As Francione argues, property is a powerful vehicle for domination and control. To be sure, property owners are regulated, but they also typically have a set of rights that permit instrumentalization, commodification, and exploitation of the thing owned. The nature of property is to permit owners to act to maximize their interests; property is normally envisioned as entitlement to do certain things with the objects owned.[83] Even if the argument often put forth by animal industrialists and researchers—that they care for their animals at a high level in order to produce higher quality food or better research results—is accepted, there is still no legal duty for the owners to act in this way. Animals may be bought, sold, loaned, leased, maimed, and killed in a wide variety of circumstances due to their property status. They are denied a childhood,[84] mating and coupling opportunities, expression of species-typical behaviours, and, finally, the opportunity to live. Welfarist measures, however strong in intention, impose minimal curtailments on these property rights. It is difficult to reconcile these limits with a robust vision of anti-subordination, such as a CAS framework contemplates.[85]

But what if the ownership model of property did not prevail? Or was replaced with a milder, pared-down version? What if the concept of property was revised to actually curtail the ability of owners to act in their own interests, and instead mandated that they act in the interests of their animals? Would this model of property be compatible with equality for animals? This is David Favre's contention and it is examined below.

A More Equitable Property Category?: Favre and "Living Property"

David Favre has offered an alternative to both the abolitionist and new welfarist approaches. He offers the model of "equitable self-ownership" as a hybrid, ostensibly trying to take the best of both approaches and combine them into an innovative solution,[86] and he incorporates it, for domestic animals, into the model of "living property." This section examines both of these related and innovative concepts under a CAS framework.

Equitable Self-Ownership

To understand Favre's model of equitable self-ownership for animals, a brief explanation of equitable interests is required.[87] Ownership interests may be divided into their "law" and "equity" components; thus, the entire bundle of rights that constitutes ownership may be categorized into "legal" and "equitable" interests. Normally, because the same person enjoys both the legal and equitable interests, this distinction goes unnoticed—we rarely, in law or society, speak of "legal owners" or "equitable owners," simply referring to "owners." When the interests are separated between two or more persons, however, we must specify the precise interests involved. The legal concept of the trust provides the most common contemporary example of this bifurcated type of ownership.[88] A trust is an instrument for property transfer where the legal ownership of the trust is vested in person A (the trustee) but the equitable ownership is vested in person B (the beneficiary).[89] The effect of this division is to transfer the beneficial interests (the incidents/rights of use and enjoyment) in ownership to the beneficiary but to keep what may be referred to as the managerial elements of ownership (the incidents/rights of control and possession) with the trustee.[90] This division exerts a critical impact on how the legal owners may manage the property. That is, the legal owner must do so not for her own benefit, but for the benefit of the beneficiary. Thus, in a simple trust, the trustee manages the trust but for the benefit of the trustee.[91]

Returning to Favre's proposal, he wishes the current model of animal ownership, where both legal and equitable interests in an animal are reposed within the same person, to change to a system where the legal and ownership interests are separated. He proposes that the legal person would retain legal ownership of an animal, but the equitable ownership interest would shift to the animal. The animal would then have what Favre calls "self-ownership" in equity.[92] Similar to the trust model outlined above, the legal owner of the animal would have the rights of possession, sale, lease, etc., but would be required to discharge any decisions exerting these rights according to the interests of the equitable owner—the animal.[93] Thus, the entitlement that typically attaches to ownership falls away; in its place is a duty to act in the interests of the animal, with the owner becoming a guardian of the animal.[94] In listing some of the "potential dimensions of the concept," Favre advises that the duty of animal guardians would be shaped by principles from both anti-cruelty laws (providing for basic needs) and the child protection laws that regulate parents' duties toward their human children.[95] The generic and long-standing legal principles of "equity, justice, fair dealing, [and] balancing of interests" also inform the duty.[96] Moreover, the law's attention would be directed at whether, given their available resources, the guardian is able to avoid "substantial interference"[97] in the "life-supporting and species-defining activities" of the self-owned animal.[98]

This bifurcation of animal property rights would therefore require legal consideration of the animal's interests as well as allow the animal to sue and enforce the duties owed to him or her from third parties. Favre points to "custody" disputes over companion animals as an area of the law which would undergo concrete change under his model, with the jurisprudence shifting from an emphasis on standard property law principles to the use of the "best interests" standard currently applied in child custody disputes. Other changes would include the ability of an individual animal to sue her guardian in tort should the duties be violated.[99]

Living Property

Equitable self-ownership is just one component of the new legal status and corresponding rights that Favre outlines for animals. He also proposes a new legal category for animals, called "living property," which he believes would ameliorate their current subordinate state by better respecting their interests.[100] The primary purpose of this status would be to compel legal actors to consider the interests of animals in any decisions taken about them.[101] In the "living property" category, Favre includes all living beings, subject to some exceptions (the exclusion of plants and invertebrates, for example) that he inserts into his model for practical reasons.[102] Due to his desire to effect a change in animals' legal status while working within the present property system, he also limits the category to animals that are already propertized.[103] Having established which animals' interests will be counted, Favre then lists the interests that matter under his scheme. As a "starting point," he lists the following:

- fighting for continued life,
- finding and consuming food daily,
- socializing with others (usually of the same species),
- mating,
- caring for their young,
- sleeping,
- accessing sunlight (or not),
- exercising their inherent mental capacities, and
- moving about in their physical environment.[104]

Deciding whether these interests might trigger a positive legal change depends, Favre writes, on asking the following questions: "Do we understand the interests in question (science information)? Is the interest in conflict with the interests of humans or the government? Can the legal system provide a useful remedy with the resources available? Do other public policies trump the animal's interests?"[105]

The "judgment call" required in posing the above questions will involve a balancing act.[106] Favre does not provide precise direction as to how one might balance these interests, but he does give examples throughout the article that offer a sense of how the new legal status might impact particular issues. For example, Favre concludes that the sterilization of cats and dogs is acceptable because of the larger public interest at stake (animal interests in mating may be trumped by the human interest in controlling the cat and dog population), while the lifelong constraint of chimpanzees in research laboratories is not compatible with a "living property" status, because of the level of interest impairment involved for the chimpanzees.[107] He also suggests that greyhound racing should be prohibited, given the treatment of the dogs in the industry and the corresponding lack of important human interests involved; he notes that a human desire for gambling may be satisfied through other venues.[108]

Favre is quite clear that he finds the continued property categorization of animals "ethically acceptable" and that he rejects the abolitionist view that would prohibit all animal use and ownership.[109] He believes that "positive human communities can include animals that are owned and used by humans."[110] As such, he does not find anything problematic in the term "ownership" when used to describe the relationship between humans and animals. Instead, Favre points out that "the concept of ownership as applied to an animal can be either beneficial, as when the relationship is respectful, or detrimental, when the relationship is oppressive."[111] In his 2000 article discussing the "equitable self-ownership" concept, Favre stated that abolishing animals' property status was "neither advisable nor feasible at this time," specifically pointing to the fact that contemporary ownership principles at least assign responsibilities to animal owners and provide a clear system of human responsibility for any given animal.[112] For Favre, uncommodifying animals would create a situation of abandoned yet dependent animals, who are unable to care for themselves and are now forced to deal with hostile environments on their own.[113] In 2010, when discussing "living property," Favre does not change his position on this point.[114]

Moreover, Favre believes that animals' current property status does not preclude their interests from being counted in law. He gives various examples, mostly from anti-cruelty statutes, but he also points to the American system of pet trusts that allows owners to provide for animals in their estates, as well as the recent United States Supreme Court decision about the impact of Sonar training on nearby marine mammals, in attempting to illustrate that the law presently concerns itself with animal interests.[115] For Favre, a judicial balancing that puts less weight on harm to an animal than on a human interest in harming the animal for food, medical research, or national defence does not take away from the fact that the animal's interests still matter under the law.[116] He concedes that the resulting rights are "modest" but views them as rights all the same.[117] At a minimum, under this approach, animals can be rights-holders and the remedy for any harm will be conceptualized or understood in the eyes of the law as flowing directly to them.[118]

Animal Interests and Rights to Be Recognized

An advantage Favre sees in this approach is its ability to alter the status quo for at least some animals while still remaining pragmatic. Indeed, he is responsive to the "piecemeal" and "incremental" nature of legal reform and has outlined a relatively comprehensive way to move forward with respect to the domestic animals who are incorporated into the current property regime.[119] In addition, the "living property" model is able to register a wide variety of animal interests. At a conceptual level, Favre is willing to include all living beings in his proposal, even if he does value vertebrates as more worthy due to their capacity for pain, and practically excludes invertebrates and plants.[120] The animal interests he would recognize are robust compared with those the law currently responds to. Most importantly, Favre is clear that legal recognition of these interests would establish rights for animals that restricted the interests and rights of humans.[121] The "living property" status would establish the following rights for animals:

1. Not to be held for or put to prohibited uses.
2. Not to be harmed.
3. To be cared for.
4. To have living space.
5. To be properly owned.
6. To own property.
7. To enter into contracts.
8. To file tort claims.[122]

Favre gives brief descriptions of what each right would mean. For the first—the right not to be held for or put to prohibited uses—Favre explains that this right would not compel society to prohibit any particular use of animals, but simply provide that animals have the right not to be held or put to any use that the law chooses to ban. Favre asserts that "the list of prohibited uses can be developed by using the general principle that a use should not constitute a significant interference with the well-being of the animals involved."[123] The second right—the right not to be harmed—is meant to build upon existing welfare legislation by enacting a higher level of regulation for industries that are minimally or insufficiently regulated today. Favre intends that this right would remove the exemptions granted to the agricultural and research industries under current welfare statutes.[124]

The right to be cared for has a similar purpose. It is meant to place a duty on owners to consider animal needs beyond the basics of food, shelter, and physical injury, which are currently addressed by anti-cruelty legislation.[125] Here, Favre highlights the ability of the "living property" status to attend to the "social needs" animals have, such as having a companion of their own species or bonding time with their mother, as well as their need to exercise the other capabilities and behaviours that are necessary for their species, as he puts it, to "experience the fullness of life, as provided by their genetic heritage."[126] He states that "[i]t is unethical for humans to use animals unless the method of use allows the animal to experience the critical components of life for that animal, and the law should reflect this duty."[127] The fourth right, the right to have living space, builds upon this attempt to direct attention toward social needs.[128] Favre's fifth right, which provides animals with the right to be properly owned, operates like a remedy. It secures the ability of an animal to have his title transferred to another person when his owner does not respect the first four rights.[129] Again, as Favre notes, some anti-cruelty legislation already provides for this remedy against a defendant who is convicted.[130] Favre's articulation of the right is meant to extend this remedy to other situations. Also, the right is meant to require that the "best interest" standard govern animal custody disputes, rather than the traditional family law rules of property division, so that the human who most cares for the animal will own the animal upon family dissolution.[131] The remaining rights—the rights to own property, enter into contracts, and sue in torts—give animals elements of legal personality that they currently do not have.[132]

Critical Assessment

Favre's proposal is intended to promote better regulation, create new owner duties, and perhaps even prompt judicial conversation and subsequent enhancement of animal treatment prohibitions. Indeed, the "living property" proposal would direct the law's attention to animal interests in ways

that could have a meaningful impact for them. For example, a "best interests" standard in family law disputes would likely generate positive effects
for animals. Yet, this sort of tangible change to a legal rule that does not lead
to animal instrumentalization is rare in the living property model. From
the examples that Favre gives, it is clearly the domestic and companion animals that would benefit from conversion into living property. In his article
devoted to explaining equitable self-ownership, Favre's examples again primarily stem from the companion animal sphere.[133] How the guardianship
model would work for factory-farmed animals is never explained. Without
this guidance, it is not clear how a for-profit use of animals would be
compatible with an equitable self-ownership model where human guardians are meant to care for animals as human parents for their children.[134]

Further, if guardianship of human children is the best legal guide for
the development of guardianship for animals, it is not clear why Favre
prefers a non-property approach for human children but not for animals.
Recall that Favre's main reasons for believing that the removal of domestic
animals from their property status "is not feasible or desirable at this time"
are (1) domestic animals' dependent status and their poor prospects if left
on their own in a free state; and (2) the power of ownership to impose
responsibilities on owners to take care of their charges.[135] These two points
could easily apply to human children, who are also unable to care for themselves very well; yet this does not lead Favre to advocate the necessity of
legally classifying human children as property.

This is not to say that the living property model with equitable
self-ownership is without benefit to animals. According animals some elements of legal personality, as the living property model does, is a major
advance in the law. Although Favre's model would grant animals direct
standing to sue for harm and allow them to transact economically, the right
to sue in tort does not entail suing against the instrumental use of the animal by the owner, and the right to receive property or be compensated for
any prizes the animal receives does not include the right not to have one's
labour appropriated in the first place. The rights are limited to breaches of
the first four rights that Favre lists, which are themselves primarily welfarist
in design. The living property approach tolerates the property category and
thus the instrumentalized uses it enables. The rights it would create do not
change this. To give another example, the right to be cared for may, as Favre
wishes, generate a new law that animals may not be removed from their
mothers for a period of time; but neither this nor any of the other rights will

prevent that animal from being used and killed. Certainly, we can imagine that the bonding time would improve the early period of an animal's life, in terms of both mental and physical well-being, but the end point for the animal is still the same—to live and die a life planned by humans and not the animal herself. And while the fourth right—to have living space—could also generate an immeasurably better quality of life for zoo animals, the living property model does not prevent captivity. Favre is very clear that this right is to be a "substitute for the human right of personal liberty."[136]

In accepting the instrumental use and possession of animals for human purposes, Favre's model presents concerns under a CAS framework in line with a posthumanist philosophy. There are no clear guidelines, other than the mandate to consider the interests of animals, to limit their use and possession.[137] There is nothing in the model to reconceptualize humans' relationship with animals or compel a judge to otherwise move beyond mainstream contemporary social values. For the largest group of industrially exploited domestic animals—those used for food—there is little respite from their end fate.[138] Favre suggests that the balancing act of interests that his model entails should lead to a situation where the interests of animals in concentrated animal feeding operations are given "considerably more weight."[139] He also recognizes, however, that the interests of corporate owners, the human public, and animals who wish to avoid slaughter may not be reconciled or be amenable to being "balanced out."[140] Favre's proposal seems most capable of protecting animals where human interests that enjoy widespread social support are absent. Thus, his examples of a living property model leading to a ban on the sale of cats (as opposed to transfer by gift or inheritance) seems more possible in a "balancing act" guided by contemporary social values because cats have social value and public opinion strongly supports controlling the cat population and acquiring animals from shelters rather than from breeders.[141]

There is, of course, nothing wrong with a model that asks judges to consider animals' interests directly. This is a vast symbolic improvement on the current regime. Yet, the proverbial and perhaps literal elephant in the room is the limit that will be applied to human interests in assessing those of animals. Favre's approach gives animals direct consideration, but no use permitted today is prohibited (despite the fatal end they often involve for the animals), since animal interests may be sacrificed for human ones. Favre is correct to acknowledge that no human rights are absolute: they also undergo a balancing act.[142] But our attitude toward humans is different.

Despite any dominant social values, certain basic limits that the rule of law among other legal norms is supposed to respect vis-à-vis humans do not extend to animals. Most humans do not hold animal interests in high regard; most of us consider them to be "lesser" interests that are more easily trumped. Human interests are not sacrificed in favour of those of animals to the same extent or degree, especially when human physical injury or life is at stake.

Despite the balancing act Favre claims to desire, no element of the "living property" model changes this. Perhaps it could, by prompting legal actors to question outdated norms in the animal agriculture and laboratory industries and influencing change in the outcomes of anti-cruelty cases, thereby elevating animal interests to a higher level.[143] But there is nothing in the model that guarantees this, equalizes interests between animals and humans, or even provides that an animal's interest in her life should always outweigh a corporate interest in profit. The model is comfortable with the incremental change that comes from waiting until judges or legislatures are ready to move in more animal-friendly directions.[144] Apart from the discursive use of "rights" language, it is difficult to distinguish the living property model from the broad protectionist/new welfarist model Garner espouses. The rights provided do not act as "trumps" against instrumental use as they do for humans.[145]

The same may be said of the potential for recognition of new duties for owners under the living property model. As an example, Favre writes about the need for owners to attend to animals' mental well-being, an area in which he notes that current American law is overwhelmingly silent.[146] He is hopeful that the model, in granting the right to be cared for, will encourage judges to consider the mental health of animals in addition to the physical needs that have traditionally constituted the focus of anti-cruelty stat-utes.[147] Favre notes that animals confined in cages in zoos and laboratories would certainly benefit from this principle given what is known of the mental anguish these animals suffer.[148] But again, there is little in his approach that delineates the extent of this duty. Favre leaves the scope of the duty in specific situations up to the "balancing act." He states that the purpose of his model is "to establish that there is a duty, and that this duty is owed to the animal."[149] This is a positive and substantive change compared to the existing property regime. Yet, the concrete effects of the change are in no way guaranteed by a model that lays down no limits on how, when, or why human interests should trump animal ones.

Interestingly, Favre adopts a different approach to wild animals. In a companion piece to those discussed here, Favre addresses how the law needs to change to properly respect wildlife.[150] Notably, he argues that the law should regard wild animals as legal persons, not property.[151] Favre is insistent about this: "At this pivotal point in time, the future of wildlife within our legal system turns upon the issue of legal personality. As individuals, species, and occupiers of ecosystems, wildlife should be recognized as possessing their own legal personalities, rather than a resource to be managed."[152]

It is not clear whether Favre views personhood as a necessary legal status for wild animals (but not for domestic ones) because human action will eventually devastate wildlife to the point of extinction, whereas domestic animals will continue, generation after generation, because they bring humans profit. Shortly after the above passage, Favre analogizes wild animals to humans, pointing to factors about the former's ethical and legal worth (desire to "live out their lives" and "biological parallels") that also apply to domestic animals.[153] Yet, later still, Favre draws a distinction between the two legal categories for animals that seems to privilege dependence on humans as the salient determinant of their legal status. He writes:

> The interests of self-owned wildlife, unlike those of domestic animals, do not exist in the same context of human possession, which focuses the law upon the obligations of the human owners as guardians to meet the needs of animals to the extent those animals are unable to take care of themselves. Wildlife have the capacity to meet their needs without human interference. While living property is defined as animals removed from their natural environment and possessed by humans, wildlife's living interest exists in the context of the natural environment. To satisfy the needs of wildlife, their rights should be legally distinct from the rights of domestic animals.[154]

The basis for the difference in legal status, then, seems to rest on the independence of wildlife and the fact that they mostly live apart from humans.[155] With his discussion of this latter factor, Favre seems to intimate that wildlife need the status of personhood to fend off further human-caused ecological destruction; mere property status will not be enough. This implies, however, that property status *does* limit the extent of the interests that can be protected for "living property"; the "balancing act" can only go so far.

Favre's jurisprudential model for wildlife also incorporates a balancing act. From his discussion, one can see that granting personhood to wild animals does not immunize them from state killing as it does human persons (except for those on death row).[156] Nonetheless, the partial personhood Favre grants wild animals has an effect. With wild animals Favre is careful to articulate that "[a] critical question in drafting and implementing the law is how to determine the weight that should be given to wildlife interests when in conflict with human interests."[157] Favre does not specify a global standard, but later suggests that simple profit motives should not lead to destruction of habitats or the animals themselves.[158] For living property, on the other hand, Favre accepts a pure profit motive for their use and death.[159] Clearly, the difference in property status between wild and domestic animals that Favre posits creates a better starting point for animals who are viewed as wild when their interests are weighed against humans than those viewed as domestic. This difference is ostensibly justified by wild animals' independence from humans. Privileging independence as a reason for a higher legal status follows classic, liberal, masculinist, and ableist theory that stigmatizes "dependent" actors.[160] It also raises the issue of the human role both in the initial domestication of animals and in causing their dependence. It is not a position that disrupts animals' Othered status or one that is in line with a critical posthumanist perspective.

Finally, it is worth noting that the communicative value of property also subsists despite the change in priority of interests. We do not easily see something that is owned as equal to the status of the owner; the model is not reciprocal. Objections may also arise because the model is paternalistic. It is not clear that the pragmatism obtained by revising rather than subverting the property model compensates for a paradigm where animals cannot be persons and persons are still in control, however benevolently they are now required to act.

Conclusion

The efforts of both Garner and Favre to chart new legal methods for improving the lives of animals are commendable. Both approaches show a willingness to work within the current private property regime for animals, and the resulting change in standards of care and the extent of owners' duties could be far-reaching. This result is not to be discounted in terms of the better lives that individual animals may lead. Nevertheless, both approaches are premised on the subordination of animal interests to human ones. In their models, animals are important, but they are not as important as humans. The abolitionist approach, here represented by the writings of Francione, is the only position in the property debate that does not establish a hierarchy that places human interests over those of animals. For this reason, it is the most compatible with a CAS framework and with a critically oriented posthumanism more broadly. Although it may be that ownership relationships can be benign—as they are for many companion animals[161]—the status of being owned usually leads to instrumental use for the vast majority of animals who reside in this legal category. Moreover, the state of ownership enacts violence against concepts of equality and dignity, unless, perhaps, one has freely contracted into this state.[162] This, of course, is not the case for animals. As Favre notes, most animals come under private ownership by one of two methods: they were wild, but then were caught or killed; or, they were born to an owned mother.[163] Removing animals from their propertied status is thus necessary for a legal framework to reflect CAS's theoretical approach and achieve meaningful posthumanist results in altering the conditions of animals' lives.[164]

NOTES

1. Shapiro and DeMello, "State of Human–Animal Studies," 307; Datson and Mitman, "How and Why of Thinking with Animals," 2; and Rohman, "Animal among Others," 1.
2. Pedersen, "Critical Animal Studies," 2; and Pick, "Creaturely Bodies," introduction to *Creaturely Poetics*, 2.
3. Pedersen, "Critical Animal Studies," 2; Calarco, "Question of the Animal," introduction to *Zoographies*, 2.
4. Pedersen, "Release the Moths," 65, 67.
5. Pedersen, "Critical Animal Studies," 2; Wolfe, "Subject to Sacrifice," 100–107; Fudge, *Animal*, 113–58.
6. Boddice, "End of Anthropocentrism," introduction to *Anthropocentrism*, 1.
7. Wolfe, "Human, All Too Human," 571–72. This is not to suggest that scholars who accept the CAS label for their work would also accept the posthumanist one. See, for example, Pedersen, "Release the Moths," 67–68. For an example of a prominent "animal studies" author who is critical of the posthumanist

term see Haraway, *When Species Meet*, 17. For a compilation of the multiple
definitions of posthumanism see Pedersen, "Release the Moths," 74.

8. Pedersen, "Release the Moths," 65–67.

9. Pedersen, "Critical Animal Studies," 2; Oliver, *Animal Lessons*. Oliver discusses
   the place of animals in the works of various humanist and anti-humanist
   thinkers, encouraging contemplation on the meaning of such philosophical
   terms and supplementing a posthumanist perspective and the role of CAS
   therein.

10. Pedersen, "Critical Animal Studies," 4–10; Castricano ("Animal Subjects in
    a Posthuman World," introduction to *Animal Subjects*, 5–11) articulates the
    place of animal studies within critical studies more generally. Luke ("Taming
    Ourselves or Going Feral?") explores the challenges of crafting a CAS
    framework that resists patriarchy, thus linking the subject of animal oppression
    to other subjects of marginalization.

11. Pedersen, "Release the Moths," 75.

12. Deckha, "Teaching Posthumanist Ethics in Law School," 287n3; Wagman,
    "Growing Up with Animal Law," 206–7.

13. Senatori and Frasch, "Future of Animal Law," 211.

14. Miller ("Rise of Animal Law," 28–31) attributes the very rapid rise of
    animal law at American law schools to the snowball effect of the $1 million
    endowment donations that celebrity Bob Barker made to seven highly regarded
    law schools in different regions of the United States. The funds came with the
    condition that the schools offer a course in animal law at least every other
    year and host an animal law conference or similar event in alternative years.
    Once top-tier schools started to offer animal law courses, many other schools
    followed suit. For a critique of how the loose drafting of the gift agreements has
    thwarted the potential of these Barker endowments in ensuring that schools
    apply the funds to animal law purposes, see Bryant "Bob Barker Gifts," 237.

15. Sankoff, "Charting the Growth"; Wagman, "Growing Up with Animal Law."

16. Contribution to legal scholarship is not limited to law professors. For example,
    John Sorenson—a professor of CAS, globalization and anti-racism at Brock
    University—has criticized Canada's approach to anti-cruelty legislation in his
    article "'Some Strange Things,'" and more recently his book *About Canada*.

17. Francione and Garner, *Animal Rights Debate*.

18. For examples of Francione's work, see *Animals, Property, and the Law*;
    Rain Without Thunder; *Animals as Persons*; "Animal Welfare"; "Animals in
    Biomedical Research"; and "Reflections."

19. For examples of Garner's work, see *Animal Ethics*; *Animals, Politics, and
    Morality*; "Political Ideology"; "Animals, Ethics, and Public Policy"; and
    "Politics of Animal Protection."

20. Favre, "Equitable Self-Ownership," 473.

21. Favre, "Living Property," 1022.
22. Wolfe, *Animal Rites*, 33.
23. Kapur, "Human Rights in the 21st Century."
24. Bryant, "Similarity or Difference," 207.
25. Corbey, *Metaphysics of Apes*.
26. Oliver, introduction to *Animal Lessons*, 21.
27. Pick, *Creaturely Poetics*, 2.
28. See Pedersen, "Critical Animal Studies," 1–4; Richard Twine provides an exploration of such a CAS framework in his discussion of livestock genetic corporations, and describes this perspective as one which contests the "persistent norms of the 'human' and the ethical and spatial invisibility of the 'animal'" (Twine, "Revealing the 'Animal–Industrial Complex,'" 9). Steven Best contrasts *mainstream* to *critical* animal studies, describing the latter as opposing "all forms of discrimination, hierarchy, and oppression as a complex of problems to be extirpated from the root, not sliced off at the branch" ("Rise of Critical Animal Studies," 12). Animal law scholarship does consider other sites of difference such as gender and race, but most often as parallels or comparators to, rather than in interaction with, species difference. See, for example, Kathy Hessler, where, in a more pragmatically oriented discussion, Hessler defends the creation of an Animal Law Clinic as a means of teaching engagement with critical social justice initiatives generally, by signalling the parallels between human and animal oppression ("Role of the Animal Law Clinic," 282–83).
29. See Francione, *Rain Without Thunder*.
30. See generally the sources at note 18.
31. Francione and Garner, *Animal Rights Debate*, 1–102. Francione's section of the book is entitled "Abolition of Animal Exploitation."
32. Francione and Garner, *Animal Rights Debate*, 3. Francione is careful to note that he is "not making any moral judgments about welfarists as individuals" and that he has "affection and respect for many of them as individuals" (ibid.).
33. Ibid., 27, 42.
34. Ibid., 1 (emphasis in original).
35. Ibid., 27–29.
36. Ibid., 29.
37. Ibid., 26.
38. Ibid., 29–30, 51, 58. Francione points to several animal advocacy campaigns as examples of the way in which the welfarist further entrenches a status quo approach to animals (ibid., 30–40).
39. Ibid., 48.
40. Ibid., 58.
41. See Francione, *Animals as Persons*. For his discussion of the reasons for the

success of legal reform and other campaigns targeted at specific corporations, see Francione and Garner, *Animal Rights Debate*, 30–58.

42. Francione devotes six pages to descriptions of the various slaughter methods that are being debated among welfarists, employing vivid imagery to describe the suffering of the chickens (Francione and Garner, *Animal Rights Debate*, 30–36): "I have been very careful in all of my writing to make clear that less suffering is always better than more suffering but that the fundamental moral question is whether we have the right to use animals at all" (ibid., 231).

43. "[S]uch reforms are not only problematic as a matter of theory; they are also useless at best because they rarely go beyond what is necessary to make exploitation economically efficient and . . . mean that legislation or even voluntary industry changes will provide little, if any, welfare benefits to animals" (ibid., 84).

44. Ibid., 24–25.

45. Ibid., 15–16. Ironically, a growing number of humans are attempting to tame anxiety about the future by "living in the present"; for examples of self-help books which promote this goal, see Kuypers, *What's Important Now*; Tolle, *Power of Now*; and Beazley, *No Regrets*. For a sampling of the academic literature emphasizing the clinical uses of this mindset, see Williams, "Mindfulness, Depression," along with other discussions of mindfulness found in the same issue; Borkovec, "Life in the Future"; and Orsillo and Roemer, *Acceptance and Mindfulness-Based Approaches to Anxiety*.

46. Francione and Garner, *Animal Rights Debate*, 1, 85.

47. Ibid.

48. Ibid., 25.

49. Recall the four tenets of CAS outlined in the introduction to this chapter: (1) the recognition of species difference as a venue for Othering; (2) a criticism of human-made ethical boundaries regarding animals; (3) an acknowledgement of the intersectional nature of our understanding about animality; and (4) a rejection of the default ethical position that sacrifices animal interests to human ones.

50. Francione and Garner, *Animal Rights Debate*, 103–74. Garner's section is called "A Defense of a Broad Animal Protectionism."

51. Francione and Garner, *Animal Rights Debate*, 104.

52. Ibid., 103.

53. Ibid.

54. Ibid., 144.

55. Ibid., 104.

56. Ibid., 122–24.

57. Ibid., 123.

58. Ibid.

59. Ibid., 125–26.

60. Ibid., 126.

61. Ibid., 127. Garner points to Francione, *Animals*; *Rain Without Thunder*; Wise, *Rattling the Cage*; and Kelch, "Toward a Non-property Status"—as works presenting the view that the property status of animals makes welfarism ineffective.

62. Citing Cochrane, "Ownership and Justice," 424.

63. Francione and Garner, *Animal Rights Debate*, 128. It is curious that Garner makes a claim about the equality of humans and animals since his protectionist approach is based on the premise that the moral worth of humans exceeds that of animals (ibid., xi).

64. Ibid., 129.

65. Ibid.

66. Ibid.

67. Ibid.

68. Ibid., 192.

69. Ibid., 191.

70. See, for example, Lori Gruen, "Dilemmas of Captivity," drawing upon Mackenzie and Stoljar's influential volume, *Relational Autonomy*.

71. For a critique where the authors use the language of agency over autonomy see Donaldson and Kymlicka, *Zoopolis*.

72. Francione and Garner, *Animal Rights Debate*, 129.

73. Ibid., 2.

74. Matheny and Chan, "Human Diets and Animal Welfare."

75. Francione and Garner, *Animal Rights Debate*, 130.

76. Further, absent from the discourse is the appreciation of animal pleasure, see Balcombe, "Animal Pleasure." Balcombe calls for an expansion of the scholarly discussion of animal sentience: "If we view animals' interests solely in terms of avoiding pain and suffering, then the case for their moral protection appears sound. When we include their capacity for pleasure, the case is made stronger," 215. I am grateful to Lauren Corman for recommending this article.

77. Francione and Garner, *Animal Rights Debate*, 131.

78. Ibid., 131–32.

79. Ibid., 130.

80. Ibid., 131–32.

81. Reasons for de-emphasizing the companion animal's interests may include a change in family structure (the addition of an animal-adverse human, for example), the loss of financial stability (undermining the support of the companion animal), or a switch in home locations.

82. For a CAS critique of companion animal relationships, see Kim, "Petting Asian America."

83. Singer, *Entitlement*.

84. Bryant, "Denying Animals Childhood."
85. Indeed, Garner seems to acknowledge that exploitation may continue even after welfare reforms have revamped a particular industry when he writes: "I do not accept the premise that we should not accept reforms that fall short of banning the use of animals completely, even if that means animals remain exploited" (Francione and Garner, *Animal Rights Debate*, 137).
86. Favre, "Equitable Self-Ownership," 476.
87. Favre himself provides a basic overview of the history and workings of equity and equitable ownership in his article (ibid., 484–90). For further information, see Gillese and Milczynski, *The Law of Trusts.*
88. Gillese and Milczynski, *Law of Trusts*, 5.
89. Ibid., 5–6.
90. Ibid.
91. Ibid.
92. Favre, "Equitable Self-Ownership," 476, 479–80.
93. Ibid., 497.
94. Ibid., 496. Favre prefers "guardian" instead of "trustee" as the appropriate term for the owner to avoid the latter's traditional connotation of financial matters. He writes that an owner has "being" accountability and not "financial accountability" to the animal, which the term "guardian," commonly associated with parent's obligations to human children, more accurately conveys (ibid.).
95. Ibid., 497.
96. Ibid.
97. Ibid., 499.
98. Ibid., 498.
99. Ibid., 499.
100. Favre, "Living Property."
101. Ibid., 1023.
102. Ibid., 1043–47.
103. Ibid., 1047.
104. Ibid.
105. Ibid., 1052.
106. Ibid., 1052–53.
107. Ibid., 1053.
108. Ibid., 1063.
109. Ibid., 1023.
110. Ibid., 1024.
111. Ibid., 1043.
112. Favre, "Equitable Self-Ownership," 495.
113. Ibid.
114. Favre, "Living Property," 1023.

115. Ibid., 1034–40.
116. Ibid., 1042.
117. Ibid., 1043.
118. Ibid., 1060.
119. Ibid., 1030, 1049, 1051, 1057.
120. Ibid., 1043–46. Of his exclusion of invertebrates Favre writes: "This is not to suggest that invertebrate animals are not worthy of ethical concern, as they do have individual interests, even if they might sit more lightly on the scale of our moral concerns" (ibid., 1046).
121. Ibid., 1024.
122. Ibid., 1062.
123. Ibid., 1062–63.
124. Ibid., 1064.
125. Ibid., 1065.
126. Ibid., 1065–66. Although Favre uses the term "capabilities," he does not reference Martha Nussbaum's work in extending capabilities theory to animals and thus does not state whether the list she has developed there is wholly incorporated into his model. A larger issue suggested by the use of capabilities language, which Favre also does not mention, is the critique capabilities theory offers of rights theory, the latter of which Favre implicitly supports with his "living property" model. See Nussbaum, *Frontiers of Justice*.
127. Favre, "Living Property," 1066.
128. Ibid.
129. Ibid., 1067–68.
130. Ibid., 1067.
131. Ibid., 1068. This approach has been used in a few American cases, but is still the exception more than the norm. See, for example, *Raymond v. Lachmann*, 695 N.Y.S. 2d 308 (Sup. Ct. App. Div. 1999); *Whitmore v. Whitmore*, 2011 Va. App. LEXIS 57 (Va. Ct. App. 2011); and *Juelfs v. Gough*, 41 P.3d 593 (Alaska Sup. Ct. 2002). For further discussion and examples, see Stroh, "Puppy Love"; Newell, "Animal Custody Disputes"; and Huss, "Separation, Custody."
132. Favre, "Living Property," 1067.
133. Favre, "Equitable Self-Ownership," 489–90, 498–99, 501–2.
134. Favre writes: "The closest parallel to the nature of equitable self-ownership and the relationship between legal and equitable ownership is that of minor children with their lawful guardians" (ibid., 500).
135. Ibid., 495.
136. Favre, "Living Property," 1066.
137. Favre writes that "the primary public policy consideration for living property is that the interests of the animal should be taken into account" (ibid., 1056).
138. This is a point that Francione makes; he chooses to focus on food animals in

his discussion because they constitute the majority of animals subsumed into human use (Francione and Garner, *Animal Rights Debate*, 2).

139. Favre, "Living Property," 1058.
140. Ibid., 1056.
141. Ibid., 1055.
142. Ibid., 1053.
143. Ibid., 1057–58.
144. Ibid., 1057.
145. Ronald Dworkin first popularized the image of rights as trumps. See Dworkin, "Rights as Trumps."
146. Favre, "Living Property," 1059.
147. Ibid., 1058.
148. Ibid.
149. Ibid.
150. Favre, "Wildlife Jurisprudence."
151. Ibid., 462.
152. Ibid., 476.
153. Ibid.
154. Ibid., 478.
155. The distinction may be insufficient to neatly and easily categorize all animals. For discussion of animals that may seem to straddle these categories, see Palmer, *Animal Ethics*, 7–8.
156. Favre writes: "Eventually, the goal is the adoption of laws acknowledging that wildlife's living interest should be considered and balanced against human economic interests before humans can exploit and kill them" (Favre, "Wildlife Jurisprudence," 477, 479–81). In particular, Favre's second principle in his theory of wildlife jurisprudence is that if they must be killed then the killing should "not inflict unnecessary pain and suffering" (ibid., 481).
157. Ibid., 478.
158. Ibid., 500–508.
159. Favre, "Living Property," 1056.
160. Feminist and disability studies scholars have highlighted the exclusionary premises of the idealized human actor in law and political life—the autonomous and rational individual. They have noted how liberal understandings of autonomy typically equate this highly prized value of subjectivity with independence and thus view those who are dependent on others or necessarily thrive in relation to others as leading compromised, non-ideal lives. Relational feminist theory has underscored the unrealistic nature of this understanding of autonomy given that all humans exist in a web of relationships during their lives; they claim that an association of autonomy with independence rather than relationships reflects an androcentric (and generally impoverished) viewpoint

that downplays the role of women in giving birth to, nurturing, and sustaining purportedly independent male actors and distorts the relational aspects of the lives we all lead. Disability studies scholars have added to this critique by demonstrating the value in dependency and the multiple ways that those who lead intensely dependent lives (due to their disabilities and/or the ableist norms of society that do not accommodate them) can reciprocate and otherwise exercise agency in their relationships; in this critique, dependency is not a bar to agency or autonomy, but a precondition of it. For further discussions of these points, see Ruddick, *Maternal Thinking*; Smart, *Feminism and the Power of Law*; Nedelsky, *Law's Relations*; and Arneil, "Disability, Self-Image." For an animal-centric critique of the stigmatization of dependence, see Donaldson and Kymlicka, *Zoopolis*, 82–85, 102–8, citing Arneil, "Disability, Self-Image."

161. Even here, however, animals perform relational work for their owners, serving as companions, substitute mates, children, etc. This dynamic has its troubling dimensions. For further discussions, see Kim, "Petting Asian America"; Gaard, "Ecofeminism on the Wing"; Tuan, *Dominance and Affection*; and Shell, "Family Pet."

162. For a discussion of the need to respect contracts where people have sold themselves into servitude, see Satz, "Voluntary Slavery."

163. Favre, "Living Property," 1054.

164. With the desirability of the non-property status established, the question remains as to which legal status should replace property. Should it be personhood, as Francione and other abolitionists suggest, or another status rooted more in vulnerability and embodiment? While an important question, addressing it here exceeds the scope of this chapter.

BIBLIOGRAPHY

Arneil, Barbara. "Disability, Self-Image, and Modern Political Theory." *Political Theory* 37, no. 2 (2009): 218–42.

Balcombe, Jonathan. "Animal Pleasure and Its Moral Significance." *Applied Animal Behaviour Science* 118, no. 3 (2009): 208–16.

Beazley, Hamilton. *No Regrets: A Ten-Step Program for Living in the Present and Leaving the Past Behind.* Hoboken, NJ: Wiley & Sons, 2004.

Best, Steven. "The Rise of Critical Animal Studies: Putting Theory into Action and Animal Liberation into Higher Education." *Journal for Critical Animal Studies* 7, no. 1 (2009): 9–52.

Boddice, Rob. "The End of Anthropocentrism." Introduction to *Anthropocentrism: Humans, Animals, Environments*, edited by Rob Boddice, 1–20. Lieden: Brill, 2011.

Borkovec, T.D. "Life in the Future versus Life in the Present." *Clinical Psychology: Science and Practice* 9 (2002): 76–80.

Bryant, Taimie L. "The Bob Barker Gifts to Support Animal Law." *Journal of Legal Education* 60, no. 2 (2010): 237–62.

———. "Denying Animals Childhood and Its Implications for Animal-Protective Law Reform." *Law, Culture and the Humanities* 6, no. 1 (2010): 56–74.

———. "Similarity or Difference as a Basis for Justice: Must Animals Be Like Humans to Be Legally Protected from Humans?" *Law and Contemporary Problems* 70 (2007): 207–54.

Calarco, Matthew. "The Question of the Animal." Introduction to *Zoographies: The Question of the Animal from Heidegger to Derrida*, 1–14. New York: Columbia University Press, 2008.

Castricano, Jodey. "Animal Subjects in a Posthuman World." Introduction to *Animal Subjects: An Ethical Reader in a Posthuman World*, edited by Jodey Castricano, 5–11. Waterloo: Wilfrid Laurier University Press, 2008.

Cochrane, Alasdair. "Ownership and Justice for Animals." *Utilitas* 21, no. 4 (2009): 424–42.

Corbey, Raymond. *The Metaphysics of Apes: Negotiating the Animal–Human Boundary*. Cambridge: Cambridge University Press, 2005.

Datson, Lorraine, and Greg Mitman. "The How and Why of Thinking with Animals." Introduction to *Thinking with Animals: New Perspectives on Anthropomorphism*, edited by Lorraine Datson and Greg Mitman, 1–14. New York: Columbia University Press, 2010.

Deckha, Maneesha. "Teaching Posthumanist Ethics in Law School: The Race, Culture and Gender Dimensions of Student Resistance." *Animal Law* 16 (2008): 287–315.

Donaldson, Sue, and Will Kymlicka. *Zoopolis: A Political Theory of Animal Rights*. London: Oxford University Press, 2011.

Dworkin, Ronald. "Rights as Trumps." In *Theories of Rights*, edited by Jeremy Waldron, 153–67. Oxford: Oxford University Press, 1984.

Favre, David. "Equitable Self-Ownership." *Duke Law Journal* 50, no. 2 (2000): 473–502.

———. "Living Property: A New Status for Animals within the Legal System." *Marquette Law Review* 93, no. 3 (2010): 1022–71.

———. "Wildlife Jurisprudence." *Journal of Environmental Law and Litigation* 25 (2010): 459–510.

Francione, Gary L. "Animal Welfare and the Moral Value of Nonhuman Animals." *Law, Culture and the Humanities* 6, no. 1 (2010): 24–36.

———. *Animals as Persons: Essays on the Abolition of Animal Exploitation*. New York: Columbia University Press, 2008.

———. *Animals, Property, and the Law*. Philadelphia: Temple University Press, 1995.

———. *Rain Without Thunder: The Ideology of the Animal Rights Movement*. Philadelphia: Temple University Press, 1996.

———. "Reflections on *Animals, Property, and the Law* and *Rain Without Thunder.*" *Law and Contemporary Problems* 70, no. 1 (2007): 9–58.

———. "The Use of Nonhuman Animals in Biomedical Research: Necessity and Justification." *Journal of Law, Medicine & Ethics* 35, no. 2 (2007): 241–48.

Francione, Gary L., and Robert Garner, eds. *The Animal Rights Debate: Abolition or Regulation?* New York: Columbia University Press, 2011.

Fudge, Erica. *Animal.* London: Reaktion, 2002.

Gaard, Greta. "Ecofeminism on the Wing: Perspectives on Human–Animal Relations." *Women & Environments International Magazine* 52–53 (2001): 19–22.

Garner, Robert. *Animal Ethics.* Cambridge: Polity, 2005.

———. "Animals, Ethics, and Public Policy." *Political Quarterly* 81, no. 1 (2010): 123–30.

———. *Animals, Politics, and Morality.* New York: Manchester University Press, 2004.

———. "Political Ideology and the Legal Status of Animals." *Animal Law* 8 (2002): 77–91.

———. 1995. "The Politics of Animal Protection: A Research Agenda." *Society & Animals* 3, no. 1 (1995): 43–60.

Gillese, Eileen E., and Martha Milczynski. *The Law of Trusts.* 2nd ed. Toronto: Irwin Law, 2005.

Gruen, Lori. "Dilemmas of Captivity." In *Ethics and Animals: An Introduction,* 149–51. Cambridge: Cambridge University Press, 2011.

Haraway, Donna. *When Species Meet.* Minneapolis: University of Minnesota Press, 2008.

Hessler, Kathy. "The Role of the Animal Law Clinic." *Journal of Legal Education* 60, no. 2 (2010): 263–84.

Huss, Rebecca J. "Separation, Custody and Estate Planning Issues Relating to Companion Animals." *University of Colorado Law Review* 74, no. 1 (2003): 181–240.

Kapur, Ratna. "Human Rights in the 21st Century: Take a Walk on the Dark Side." *Sydney Law Review* 28 (2006): 665–87.

Kelch, Thomas. "Toward a Non-property Status for Animals." *New York University Environmental Law Journal* 6, no. 3 (1998): 531–85.

Kim, James. "Petting Asian America." *MELUS* 36, no. 1 (2011): 135–55.

Kuypers, John. *What's Important Now: Shedding the Past So You Can Live in the Present.* Burlington, ON: Present Living & Learning, 2002.

Luke, Brian. "Taming Ourselves or Going Feral? Toward a Nonpatriarchal Metaethic of Animal Liberation." In *Animals and Women: Feminist Theoretical Explorations,* edited by Carol J. Adams and Josephine Donovan, 290–319. Durham, NC: Duke University Press, 1995.

Mackenzie, Catriona, and Natalie Stoljar, eds. *Relational Autonomy: Feminist Perspectives on Autonomy, Agency, and the Social Self.* New York: Oxford University Press, 2000.

Matheny, Gaverick, and Kai M.A. Chan. "Human Diets and Animal Welfare: The

Illogic of the Larder." *Journal of Agricultural and Environmental Ethics* 18 (2005): 579–94.

Miller, Greg. "The Rise of Animal Law." *Science* 332 (2011): 28–31.

Nedelsky, Jennifer. *Law's Relations: A Relational Theory of Self, Autonomy, and Law.* Oxford: Oxford University Press, 2011.

Newell, Barbara. "Animal Custody Disputes: A Growing Crack in the Legal Thinghood of Non-human Animals." *Animal Law* 6 (2000): 179–84.

Nussbaum, Martha. *Frontiers of Justice: Disability, Nationality, Species Membership.* Cambridge, MA: Harvard University Press, 2006.

Oliver, Kelly. *Animal Lessons: How They Teach Us to Be Human.* New York: Columbia University Press, 2009.

Orsillo, Susan M., and Lizabeth Roemer, eds. *Acceptance and Mindfulness-Based Approaches to Anxiety: Conceptualization and Treatment.* New York: Springer, 2005.

Palmer, Clare. *Animal Ethics in Context.* New York: Columbia University Press, 2010.

Pedersen, Helena. "Critical Animal Studies and Education Research: A Background." In *Animals in Schools: Processes and Strategies in Human–Animal Education,* 1–16. West Lafayette, IN: Purdue University Press, 2010.

———. "Release the Moths: Critical Animal Studies and the Posthumanist Impulse." *Culture, Theory and Critique* 52, no. 1 (2011): 65–81.

Pick, Anat. *Creaturely Poetics: Animality and Vulnerability in Literature and Film.* New York: Columbia University Press, 2011.

Rohman, Carrie. "The Animal among Others." In *Stalking the Subject: Modernism and the Animal,* 1–28. New York: Columbia University Press, 2009.

Ruddick, Sara. *Maternal Thinking: Towards a Politics of Peace.* Boston: Beacon, 1989.

Sankoff, Peter. "Charting the Growth of Animal Law in Education." *Journal of Animal Law* 4 (2008): 105–48.

Satz, Debra. "Voluntary Slavery and the Limits of the Market." *Law & Ethics of Human Rights* 3, no. 1 (2009): 87–109.

Senatori, Megan A., and Pamela D. Frasch. "The Future of Animal Law: Moving Beyond Preaching to the Choir." *Journal of Legal Education* 60, no. 2 (2010): 209–36.

Shapiro, Kenneth, and Margo DeMello. "The State of Human–Animal Studies." *Animals & Society* 18 (2010): 307.

Shell, Marc. "The Family Pet." *Representations* 15 (1986): 121–53.

Singer, Joseph William. *Entitlement: The Paradoxes of Property.* New Haven: Yale University Press, 2000.

Smart, Carol. *Feminism and the Power of Law.* New York: Routledge, 1991.

Sorenson, John. *About Canada: Animal Rights.* Black Point, NS: Fernwood, 2010.

———. "'Some Strange Things Happening to Our Country': Opposing Proposed Changes in Anti-cruelty Laws in Canada." *Social & Legal Studies* 12, no. 3 (2003): 377–402.

Stroh, Heidi. "Puppy Love: Providing for the Legal Protection of Animals When Their Owners Get Divorced." *Journal of Animal Law and Ethics* 2 (2007): 231–53.

Tolle, Eckhart. *The Power of Now: A Guide to Spiritual Enlightenment.* Vancouver: Namaste, 2004.

Tuan, Yi-Fu. *Dominance and Affection: The Making of Pets.* New Haven: Yale University Press, 1984.

Twine, Richard. "Revealing the 'Animal–Industrial Complex'—A Concept and Method for Critical Animal Studies?" *Journal for Critical Animal Studies* 10, no. 1 (2012): 12–39.

Wagman, Bruce. "Growing Up with Animal Law: From Courtrooms to Casebooks." *Journal of Legal Education* 60, no. 2 (2010): 193–208.

Williams, J. Mark G. "Mindfulness, Depression and Modes of Mind." *Cognitive Therapy and Research* 32, no. 6 (2008): 721–33.

Wise, Steven M. *Rattling the Cage: Towards Legal Rights for Animals.* Cambridge, MA: Perseus, 2000.

Wolfe, Cary. *Animal Rites: American Culture, the Discourse of Species, and Posthumanist Theory.* Chicago: University of Chicago Press, 2003.

———. "Human, All Too Human: 'Animal Studies' and the Humanities." *PMLA* 124, no. 2 (2009): 564–75.

———. "Subject to Sacrifice: Ideology, Psychoanalysis, and the Discourse of Species in Jonathan Demme's *The Silence of the Lambs* (with Jonathan Elmer)." In *Animal Rites: American Culture, the Discourse of Species, and Posthumanist Theory,* 97–121. Chicago: University of Chicago Press, 2003.

"Popular Affection"

Edwin Landseer and Nineteenth-Century Animal Advocacy Campaigns

⊰⊱⊷⊶

J. Keri Cronin

At the end of the nineteenth century there was increased attention paid to the treatment of nonhuman animals in both Britain and North America. By this time organizations such as the Royal Society for the Prevention of Cruelty to Animals (RSPCA; formed in 1824), the Massachusetts Society for the Prevention of Cruelty to Animals (MSPCA; formed in 1868), and the Canadian Society for the Prevention of Cruelty to Animals (CSPCA; formed in 1869) had been in operation for a number of years, each spearheading a wide range of campaigns in an attempt to improve the lives of nonhuman animals. Some of the reform efforts undertaken by these groups included improving conditions for workhorses, the establishment of humane education programs, and the targeting of "fashionable" practices such as the "check rein" or the addition of animal body parts to hats and dresses. The headquarters of these organizations were in cities like London, Boston, and Montreal, and the proximity of certain animals in these urban spaces often dictated the direction of these campaign efforts. It was frequently the animals who were most intertwined with city life—workhorses or stray dogs, for example—who received the most sustained attention from these organizations.

These campaigns aimed at improving the lives of nonhuman animals often had a strong visual component, and the politics of sight—what is rendered (in)visible in a given context—played an important role in these advocacy efforts in a number of different ways. First, illustrations and graphic images could be used in a didactic manner as was the case with published diagrams depicting the change in a horse's posture when restrained by a check rein versus her posture when not restrained by this device. Second, imagery was also used as part of the process of "bearing witness" to acts of cruelty. In some cases this took the form of documenting an event or activity, in other instances imagery was used to make visible that which had remained out of sight, either through deliberate concealment or through the fact that some of the behaviours now being deemed "cruel" were so normalized as to not be noticed by passers-by.

Visual culture has played—and certainly continues to play—an important role in the realm of animal advocacy. As W.J.T. Mitchell reminds us, "Images are active players in the game of establishing and changing values."[1] By attending to the politics of representation from previous eras we are better equipped to understand the ways in which images in our contemporary activist culture can work to destabilize dominant understandings of how nonhuman animals should be treated. As is the case today, activists working on bettering the world for nonhuman animals in the late nineteenth century found themselves embroiled in a battle of representations. How the issues were characterized, normalized, and troubled depended largely on representational strategies. Paying attention to the strategies used in previous reform efforts is especially critical in a world increasingly characterized by competing visual strategies. After all, many of the actions that contemporary animal rights activists are attempting to stop are, themselves, the product of a long history of representation. As Virginia DeJohn Anderson notes in her history of domesticated animals, "since England's experience with livestock husbandry was so widespread and stretched so far back in time, inhabitants could not help but see it as normative."[2]

A case investigated by the Canadian Society, the CSPCA, during the late nineteenth century illustrates how complex the visual culture of animal advocacy can be. In June 1898 a photographer was brought in as part of the CSPCA's investigation into allegations of cruelty towards the horses who hauled barges along the Chambly and Beauharnois canals in Quebec. The horses in this case had been made to work long hours in harsh weather, and had severe sores where the harnesses had rubbed against their bodies, an indication of just how difficult these conditions were for these animals at these particular worksites. The photographer documented the wounds with his camera, but as he went to leave he was roughed up by some of the workers at the canal and a number of the photographic plates he had just obtained were deliberately destroyed. The surviving images were published in the newspapers, with one reporter remarking, "It is inconceivable that no one has noticed the condition of the animals before this. They have been passing up and down the canal for weeks, even months perhaps, and must have been noticed by many people."[3] This tale points to the complexity of "bearing witness" via visual imagery; the power to both reveal and conceal the acts of cruelty towards the horses, the public outcry when the pictures were published, and the reporter's pointed remarks about the camera making visible what had already been in plain sight underscore that the visual history of animal advocacy is anything but straightforward.

From illustrated lectures to graphic images depicting institutionalized cruelty in the context of antivivisectionist campaigns, these reform movements relied heavily on visual culture in both a pedagogical and a performative sense. In turn, visual culture played an important role in these campaign efforts; as art historian Diana Donald notes, "[v]isual representations . . . exert a power that is denied to verbal communication. . . . At the simplest level, they have a materiality that brings 'real' animals before our eyes."[4] The following discussion focuses on one specific visual phenomenon that occurred within these campaigns: the images of well-known artworks on the pages of publications circulated by those doing animal advocacy work at the end of the nineteenth century.[5] In particular, I focus on the ways the paintings of Sir Edwin Landseer functioned within this context, because of the frequency with which these images appear in these campaign materials produced in both Britain and North American during this era.[6]

Sir Edwin Landseer (1802–1873) was a British artist who achieved considerable fame during his lifetime.[7] He was a member of the Royal Academy and first had his work included in an Academy exhibition in 1815 when he was just thirteen years old. He became famous for his animal-themed paintings, many of which were reproduced as prints. Landseer is best remembered for two distinct types of animal pictures: paintings of wildlife and paintings of dogs.

Landseer's 1851 painting entitled *Monarch of the Glen* is typical of his wildlife paintings in that it focuses on an isolated, majestic animal situated in a rugged landscape (in this case, the Scottish Highlands). The stag depicted in *Monarch of the Glen* is represented as existing outside the realm of human society, although the fact that this painting was intended to hang in the House of Lords belies this reading; this specific species in this specific landscape stands as a symbol of aristocratic pursuits in the Scottish Highlands, including hunting expeditions.[8]

In contrast, Landseer's dog paintings make overt references to relationships between human and nonhuman animals, and it is these images from Landseer's *oeuvre* that were most frequently reproduced in early animal advocacy campaigns.[9] Many art historians have read these works primarily as explorations of human activities, systems, and values. For example, Richard Ormond has noted that "[t]hrough the character of the dogs and the settings in which they are placed, we are led to speculate about their absent owners, whose status and occupations they reflect; on the nature of the relationship between man and dog; and, by extension, on the human values that the animals represent."[10] But what happens when we consider the dogs in these paintings *as dogs*? When we think about the politics of representing canine subjects in their own right, rather than see them as symbols of human values as Ormond suggests, how does the meaning of these paintings shift? The fact that many undertaking animal advocacy in the late nineteenth century selected from this body of work when they were choosing images to include in periodicals and campaign literature indicates that they did not read these paintings in the way Ormond suggests they should be read. For these activists the dogs represented in Landseer's paintings were significant *because they were dogs*.

In his provocatively titled book *What Do Pictures Want? The Lives and Loves of Images*, W.J.T. Mitchell discusses the importance of understanding pictures as "complex individuals occupying multiple subject positions and identities."[11] In other words, the meaning of an image is never fixed or static and changes according to the context in which it is viewed. Further, the oil-on-canvas version of a Landseer painting hanging in a Royal Academy exhibition takes on a very different set of meanings than a reproduction of the very same painting circulated on a pamphlet produced by an antivivisection group. Given the frequency with which Landseer paintings were reproduced and circulated during this era, it is important to consider the multiplicity of meanings that would have been attached to these pictures, including those arising from their circulation in animal advocacy discourses.

Late-nineteenth-century animal advocacy groups often went to considerable expense to include illustrated material in these campaigns, a testament to the relative importance they placed on the ability of visual material to convince people to change the ways in which they thought about and treated nonhuman animals. For example, in the preface to an 1888 publication produced by the Toronto Humane Society (THS), J. George Hodgins, then vice-president of the THS, made a point of stating that the organization had hoped to distribute it for free, however, the cost of including images made it impossible to do so.[12] That the THS opted to include images despite the additional cost is significant.

In the context of late-nineteenth-century animal advocacy, the reprints of such well-known Landseer paintings as *A Distinguished Member of the Humane Society*, *Saved!*, and *The Highland Shepherd's Chief Mourner* stood as important visual reminders that the certainty with which distinctions between humans and other animals could be made was up for debate. In each of these paintings—which I discuss in more detail below—the non-human animal (the dog) is the dominant actor, where the human with whom he relates is either absent, dead, or saved from drowning by the dog. Further, in each of these pictures the dog is represented as having qualities more frequently assigned to humans: loyalty, bravery, and the ability to mourn. These images were repeated over and over again on the pages of animal advocacy publications produced during this era. Landseer's paintings became a critical part of animal advocacy because of the ways in which the images were adapted into thinking about what it meant to be "human" and what it meant to be "animal." For example, Landseer pictures showing dogs acting in heroic and "brave" ways—rescuing humans from drowning, for example—were frequently used in antivivisection literature. By placing these specific images in this specific context, reformers were using visual language to ask viewers to consider who really was the "beast"—the selfless dog working to help others, or the human who ignores the feelings of others in pursuit of his or her own gain. Further, when reproduced in these campaigns these images underscored the fact that certain patterns of behaviour were common to both human and nonhuman animals. Simply put, these images forced viewers to confront the reality that an activity like rescuing someone from drowning was not something exclusive to humans. In this context the continued reproduction and circulation of well-known Landseer imagery became part of a larger dialogue about the commonalities between species, a dialogue that became intensified in the wake of Charles Darwin's published writings.

In his recent thought-provoking essay entitled "Thoughts Out of Season on the History of Animal Ethics," Rod Preece notes that Darwin's work has perhaps been given too much credit in animal advocacy discourses.[13] Preece notes that many of the core ideas found in texts like the *Descent of Man* had previously been articulated by others and, as such, do not represent the groundbreaking status usually afforded to Darwin's writings. Further, Preece points out that in his writing Darwin does not unequivocally lobby to erase hierarchies between and within species. Preece's point is well taken: the writings of Charles Darwin contain many complex nuances that are often not addressed by those linking his texts to discussions around animal rights. However, another angle needs to be considered in this dynamic, namely that popular understandings of Darwin's writings during the nineteenth century—however simplified or incorrect these understandings may or may not have been—were generated through a wide range of cultural objects, including visual imagery. Janet Browne notes, for instance, how in the years following the publication of Darwin's books one could encounter "Darwinism" in such items as songs, advertisements, Wedgwood ware, statues, and cartoons.[14] In many cases these examples dealt with ideas that were distorted or even absent from Darwin's original writings. However, the mass production and circulation of this kind of material certainly went a long way towards generating common understandings of the implications of Darwin's writings, namely that human and nonhuman animals had much in common. In other words, what I am arguing is that while neither Darwin nor Landseer were themselves part of organized animal advocacy in the nineteenth century, the popular understandings of their work had much in common with animal advocacy. It is the broader implications of the work of these men in this context, coupled with the perceived relationships between their creative and intellectual output, that is the focus of this chapter.

Art historian Diana Donald has written about the connections that many would have made in this period between the writings of Darwin and the paintings of Landseer. As Donald notes, "Landseer's later animal paintings were hailed as expressions of Darwinian concepts."[15] I would extend this notion to some of Landseer's earlier work as well—namely, the pieces discussed in this essay—given the ways in which facsimiles of these paintings were appropriated and circulated. The perceived connections between Darwin and Landseer were also expressed in the popular press during this era; as one reporter opined, "Mr. Darwin and his opponents appeal to the judgment of all classes, because Landseer had taught the humblest ignoramus that ever gazed into the window of a print-shop to look with new eyesight at his familiar cur."[16]

In his discussion of the Schönbrunn Menagerie in nineteenth-century Vienna, Oliver Hochadel talks about how the zoo acted as a "powerful medium of Darwinism."[17] He notes that the zoo "not only amplified Darwinism but also reshaped and adapted it."[18] In much the same way, I consider the multitude of reproductions of Landseer paintings in the context of late-nineteenth-century animal advocacy as being a "medium of Darwinism" in that they extended the dialogue about commonalities between species. I want to be very clear: I am not arguing that those working in the context of organized animal advocacy in the late nineteenth century were necessarily direct proponents of Darwin's theories; in fact, very little was said about Darwin on the pages of their publications. Rather, I am interested in exploring how the specific visual strategies used by anti-cruelty advocates were part of the broader discourses about nonhuman animals in Britain and North America at this time. Why did they select these specific paintings at this specific historical moment, several decades after they were first painted and exhibited? The sheer number of Landseer prints that were circulating at this time makes it necessary to consider alternative readings of these images.

In his introduction to the third edition of Darwin's *The Expression of the Emotions in Man and Animals*, Paul Ekman reminds readers that the central purpose of the work was "to show, through the study of expression, that humans are not a separate divinely created species."[19] Landseer, similarly, has been credited with being able to alter dominant ideas about nonhuman species through his artwork. As an 1873 article from *Bell's Life* noted, "nowadays, we cannot take up a book, a review, a newspaper, without feeling that the whole attitude of man towards brutes is completely changed.... If there is one man who, by the force of his native genius, is the cause of this extraordinary change, it is Sir Edwin Landseer."[20] As Donald's research demonstrates, the direct connections and specific spheres of influence that may have existed between Darwin and Landseer during their lifetime are uncertain and, for the most part, "must remain a matter of conjecture."[21] However, the point that Donald argues, and one that is central to my discussion in this chapter, is that in the minds of the public, links were frequently made between the works of these two men. This sense of connection was undoubtedly heightened in the 1870s as both the death of Landseer and the publication of Darwin's *Expression of the Emotions* were widely discussed in various venues at this time. Building on Donald's arguments, the remainder of this essay looks at how popular perceptions of the similarities between Darwin and Landseer's work could have contributed to the frequency with which Landseer's images appeared in animal advocacy campaigns. In this context, images that Landseer had painted earlier in the century were revisited and invested with a renewed sense of cultural currency. While these images may not have been overtly and directly linked to the writings of Darwin, they function here in a much more subtle way in terms of the broader cultural dialogue about similarities between species unfolding at this time.

Much has been made of Landseer's status as one of the favourite artists of Queen Victoria and Prince Albert. In addition to painting portraits of the royal family and their dogs (see, for instance, *Windsor Castle in Modern Times*, 1841–54), Landseer offered private art lessons to the queen.[22] Landseer's status as a favourite of the nineteenth-century animal advocacy movement, on the other hand, has all but been ignored by both art historians and by scholars studying early animal protection movements. While it certainly is to be expected that images of animals would adorn the leaflets, newsletters, and flyers of organizations dedicated to animal advocacy, the selection of specific images for use is significant and worth a closer look. The images explored in the following discussion are neither scientific illustrations nor derived from photographs—two forms of visual culture used by those working in organized animal advocacy to extend the process of witnessing cruelty through the perception of objectivity associated with these forms of picturing, both in the nineteenth century and today.[23] In this context, however, many of the images reproduced in these publications had been recognized and well-loved animal paintings recontextualized in a new arena. This process of recontextualization opens up new meanings for these images; as Steve Baker reminds us, representations of animals are "constantly open to negotiation."[24]

The concluding chapter of Baker's groundbreaking study, *Picturing the Beast*, focuses on forms of visual culture that he sees as being especially useful for contemporary animal rights movements. As part of this discussion, Baker encourages a process of "unsettling" what he describes as "cute" animal imagery.[25] The case study that Baker focuses on is Disney-related imagery, specifically the familiar symbol of Mickey Mouse. In his analysis Baker points to an example of activists donning souvenir Mickey Mouse "ears" while protesting a cosmetic company's tests on laboratory mice.[26] The blurring of boundaries between "human" and "animal" in Baker's case study unsettles assumptions about both. While I do not wish to suggest that twentieth-century Disney imagery and reproductions of nineteenth-century Landseer paintings are somehow interchangeable—there certainly are many important differences!—I do believe that Baker's insights about "cute" or popular animal imagery can be useful when we are thinking about how reformers in previous eras working for better treatment of nonhuman animals chose to use visual culture. Baker asks "how the animal rights movement might choose to respond to Disney's animals, and how it might understand its own responses."[27] Likewise, I am interested in thinking about how previous generations of activists responded to, utilized, and made sense of some of the most popular animal images of the day. In this context, Landseer's imagery brought to the forefront many important philosophical questions about relationships between human and nonhuman animals at the end of the Victorian era.

By the end of the nineteenth-century Landseer's animal paintings were widely reproduced and easily recognized. His art was highly celebrated; he was touted as the "*Raffaelle des Chiens*"[28] and the "Shakspeare [*sic*] of Dogs."[29] His brother, engraver Thomas Landseer, produced many of the reproductions of his work, and it was through these images that many people became familiar with Edwin Landseer's art. As one writer in the period noted about Landseer's art, "the thousands who go to exhibitions, public galleries, and private collections, are few compared with those who day by day study the learned prints for which we are indebted to the skilful hand of Mr. Thomas Landseer."[30] And it was not only Thomas Landseer who was responsible for producing the replicas of Landseer images so popular with nineteenth-century audiences. Over the course of Edwin Landseer's career more than a hundred engravers were commissioned to create reproductions of his paintings, resulting in what one biographer has termed a "thriving industry."[31] An 1873 article in *The Times*, announcing the artist's death, pointedly remarked that "his paintings are well known in the household of every educated man through the length and breadth of the land."[32] The same article also reminds readers about the significance of printmaking technologies in the popularization of Landseer's art, stating that his paintings of dogs "are well known to the world by the engravings of them."[33] In other words, when nineteenth-century animal advocacy groups selected Landseer imagery to use in their publications they could most certainly count on readers recognizing them due to the sheer volume of prints produced of his work. As Donald has noted, Landseer's animal paintings "were almost universally familiar to the artist's contemporaries, and . . . they have never quite lost that familiarity to the public at large."[34]

It was frequently argued in the nineteenth-century periodical press that, in addition to simply being recognizable, Landseer's art had the ability to shape the way the public perceived nonhuman animals and their place in modern society. He "had the gift of controlling, directing, and even forming the popular thought, the popular imagination, and the popular affection," an 1873 article in *Bell's Life* noted.[35] Likewise, a review in *The Ladies' Treasury* notes that while other artists had painted canine subjects throughout the history of art, "none ever painted such dogs as Landseer's. He bestows upon them not only new graces of form and colour, but occasionally imparts an intelligence calculated to involve the question of instinct and reason in still further perplexity than ever."[36] These kinds of reviews acknowledge Landseer's skills in the formal and compositional aspects of painting, but also seriously consider how these images functioned within the popular discussions and debates about the status of nonhuman animals taking place at this historical moment.

The phenomenon of works of art being reproduced on the pages of animal advocacy campaign materials was in many ways similar to the use of visual culture in other social reform movements. For instance, the movements for temperance and for the abolition of slavery both adopted visual culture as part of campaign and educational materials because of the immediacy of imagery. In both instances artists produced prints addressing themes of the campaigns—Hogarth's *Gin Lane* (1751) and William Blake's *A Negro Hung Alive by the Ribs to a Gallows* (1796) come to mind here.[37] However, one big difference exists between the use of visual culture in these movements and in animal advocacy at the end of the nineteenth century, namely that the visual culture I focus on here was comprised almost entirely of images repurposed for these campaigns. They were not originally created for animal advocacy purposes. These were images painted several decades prior to becoming icons of late-nineteenth-century animal advocacy. The act of appropriating and recirculating these images in these campaigns, then, becomes central to their use by such groups as the Victoria Street Society. While Landseer certainly seemed to care about the welfare of certain species of animals—for instance, he was "strongly against" the practice of cropping dogs' ears,[38] and he agreed to serve as vice-president of the RSPCA (the Royal Society for the Prevention of Cruelty to Animals) in 1869[39]—he was not directly associated with the majority of the advocacy groups who would later repurpose his images for the pages of their campaign materials, as many of them were formed after the artist's death.

The idea that art could both reflect and shape the dominant understandings of relationships between humans and nonhuman animals was discussed in an 1887 issue of *The Animal World*, the official publication of the RSPCA: "And has not art promoted our work also? The pencils of old masters, and those of a hundred modern animal painters, among whom Landseer will ever be prominent, have taught us to love animals, and when we cannot love, to be in sympathy with them as fellow creatures. The walls of the Academy year after year keep up this theme, and delineate particularly man's companionship with animals."[40] The prints of Landseer's paintings on the pages of animal advocacy campaign literature necessarily added another layer of meaning to these familiar pictures. Despite his lack of direct involvement in many of the late-nineteenth-century animal advocacy movements, the popular discourses surrounding Landseer credited him with achieving one of the primary objectives hoped for by those movements, namely asking viewers to recognize that nonhuman animals are as deserving of care and compassion as human beings.

These images, in other words, could create a sense of sympathy for and empathy with other species. For example, an article published in *Bell's Life* shortly after the artist's death argued that "whatever dogs do, their hope, their fear, their rage, their pleasure, their delights, their discourse, was the *farrago* of Landseer's painting. . . . We were acquainted with it all before, but had really never *seen* it till we saw it in Landseer's pictures."[41] This popular understanding of the ability of Landseer's paintings to present the emotional qualities of nonhuman animals very much aligned him with the Darwinian discourses that were so hotly debated at this time. Domesticated animals—particularly the dog and the cat—also figured prominently in Darwin's *Expression of the Emotions*, published just one year before Landseer's death. It is, as Donald notes, the "strong sense of dogs' inner life, and its connection with the evolving sensibilities of mankind" that we find in the work of both of these men.[42]

An important aspect of late-nineteenth-century animal advocacy campaigns was asking people to imagine what a specific animal might be feeling in certain situations. Creative tactics such as poems or books narrated from the point of view of a horse, bird, or dog, or images in which roles were reversed and humans were represented in places that nonhuman animals typically appeared (e.g., pulling a cart) asked people to think about what it would feel like to encounter both kindness and cruelty. These reflective exercises were seen as an important way to change behaviour. As Frank B. Fay, secretary of the MSPCA (Massachusetts Society for the Prevention of Cruelty to Animals), noted in the April 1871 issue of the MSPCA's magazine, *Our Dumb Animals*, "If we had a better appreciation of their message and pleading looks directed to us, we should be more thoughtful and more merciful."[43] It is significant to note that on the page opposite to Fay's comments is a replica of Landseer's well-known 1829 painting, *High Life*.

High Life was the companion piece to *Low Life*, each canvas focusing on an individual dog—in the former, a sleek deerhound living in an aristocratic household, while the latter depicts a gruff terrier in a stark butcher's shop.[44] These two paintings were meant to be viewed together, and the common reading of these images is of a study in human class differences. For example, the website of the Tate Gallery, the institution that now owns these paintings, states that Landseer's "intention was to juxtapose two dogs from different worlds and different social classes as representations of their absent owners."[45] However, the commentary that accompanied these images in the 1871 issues of *Our Dumb Animals* (*High Life* appeared in April, and *Low Life* in the following month's issue) spoke more of the commonalities between species. In the April issue, the following words accompanied the reproduction of *High Life*: "There seems to be the same difference in the culture and taste of dogs as of men and women; and like men and women they are very likely to be influenced by the habits of those about them."[46] In the following month's issue, the dog in the reproduction of *Low Life*—here referred to as *The Butcher's Dog*—was described as "not necessarily an ugly dog or without good manners." George T. Angell, the editor of *Our Dumb Animals* at this time, further notes that "[t]his dog does not exhibit the polish nor are his surroundings as elegant as those of the High Life Dog in our last. And yet the fidelity of the butcher's dog may be fully equal, and his bravery superior. We must not judge men or dogs by their exterior altogether. And we may be sure that kindness will not be lost on either."[47] As these examples show, Landseer's imagery often served as a launching point for discussions around the social, cultural, emotional, and intellectual qualities of *both* human and nonhuman animals. The sense of immediacy associated with imagery and the direct appeal of visual culture in nineteenth-century periodicals made Landseer's paintings a particularly savvy selection for campaigns run by groups like the Victoria Street Society for the Protection of Animals from Vivisection, and the Massachusetts Society, the MSPCA.

A chance encounter between Landseer and a Newfoundland dog named Paul Pry resulted in one of the paintings that would later be adopted by animal advocacy groups. As the story goes, the artist was out for a walk and came across a striking-looking Newfoundland dog carrying a basket of flowers in his mouth. Landseer received permission from the dog's human companion to have the dog pose for him in the studio, and the resulting image was *A Distinguished Member of the Humane Society* (Figure 3.1).[48] This picture was exhibited at the Royal Academy in 1838 and proved to be so popular that in 1839 the artist's brother, Thomas Landseer, was commissioned to make an engraving of it so that copies could be sold.[49]

The Newfoundland breed of dog has a reputation for being especially skilled at water rescue, and it is this ability that Landseer celebrates with *A Distinguished Member of the Humane Society*. In this painting, a large black and white dog rests on the water's edge, his paws dangling casually over the

FIGURE 3.1   Edwin Landseer, *A Distinguished Member of the Humane Society* (exhibited in 1838). Public domain.

edge of the cement dock, while sea birds hover in the background. Whether this dog is catching his breath after a recent rescue or waiting attentively to be called into service is not clear, however, what is emphasized in this image is the legendary life-saving abilities attributed to this breed of dog. The Humane Society referred to in Landseer's title is the Royal Humane Society of Britain, which was formed in 1774 and originally called the Society for the Recovery of Persons Apparently Drowned. Landseer's playful reference to this dog as a member of this organization both acknowledges the extraordinary rescue efforts performed by Newfoundland dogs as well as the "selfless" qualities attributed to all who perform marine rescues, human or canine. This relationship between image and text, in other words, focuses our attention on both the qualities that make this breed of dog unique and on those that make this breed of dog seem decidedly *like us*. This did not escape the notice of those writing about this picture during the nineteenth century—for example, one review of this painting draws the reader's attention to the "semi-human pathos of the dog's eyes."[50]

This tension between "animality" and qualities thought to exemplify the very best of human behaviour resurfaces again several decades later when the Victoria Street Society adopted the by-then familiar face of Paul Pry as its logo (Figure 3.2). The well-known reformer Frances Power Cobbe founded the Victoria Street Society in 1875 as a means to lobby against the

FIGURE 3.2 Logo of the Victoria Street Society for the Protection of Animals from Vivisection (ca. 1883).

practice of experimentation on live animal bodies.[51] This was an organization that was especially prolific in terms of publishing campaign materials—as Harriet Ritvo notes, "by 1892 the Victoria Street Society alone had published 320 books, pamphlets, and leaflets, of which over 270,000 copies had been distributed."[52] That the specific dog who served as Landseer's inspiration was undoubtedly long dead did not matter to Cobbe and the other members of the Victoria Street Society; it was what this dog had come to stand for that was of interest to these antivivisection activists.

In 1856 Landseer once again painted an image celebrating the legendary marine rescues performed by Newfoundland dogs (Figure 3.3). *Saved!* features the dramatic action that *A Distinguished Member of the Humane Society* lacks. In this painting Landseer chose to depict a scene just moments after the canine rescuer has brought a young child safely back to land. The child lies unconscious on the rocky shoreline while the dog, clearly exhausted from the rescue effort, looks upwards, perhaps towards the anxious family of the young girl.

As was the case with *A Distinguished Member of the Humane Society*, this picture was adopted by those working in organized animal advocacy later in the nineteenth century. For example, it was included in a publication by the THS (Toronto Humane Society), an organization formed in the late 1880s by newspaper reporter and reformer, J.J. Kelso.[53] In 1888 the THS

FIGURE 3.3   Edwin Landseer, *Saved!* (1856). Public domain.

published *Aims and Objects of the Toronto Humane Society*, which contained 112 illustrations, images that had also been used by other animal advocacy groups.[54] Landseer's *Saved!* is reproduced in black and white on page 171 of this publication (Figure 3.4), alongside a story entitled "Newfoundland Dogs as Savers of Life."[55] The juxtaposition of this specific visual representation with tales of dogs rescuing humans from drowning powerfully underscores the fact that these kinds of images—no matter how far removed from the actual, living, breathing animal that inspired them—could not be easily separated from the complex relationships that exist between human and nonhuman animals, a point to which I return below.

FIGURE 3.4   From THS's *Aims and Objects*, featuring a reproduction of *Saved!* (published in 1888).

This same image also appears on the cover of *Vivisection in America*, published by Frances Power Cobbe and Benjamin Bryan at the end of the century (Figure 3.5). Here again an organization aimed at abolishing vivisection adopts an image that apparently has nothing to do with medical research or laboratory experimentation. Instead of showing animal bodies being restrained or cut open (as Cobbe would do in other publications), the visual strategy in these examples is to focus the viewer's attention on the exemplary qualities, achievements, and abilities of nonhuman animals. This coupled with the antivivisection sentiment of the publication serves as a plea to support efforts to keep these animals safe from harm—if they are

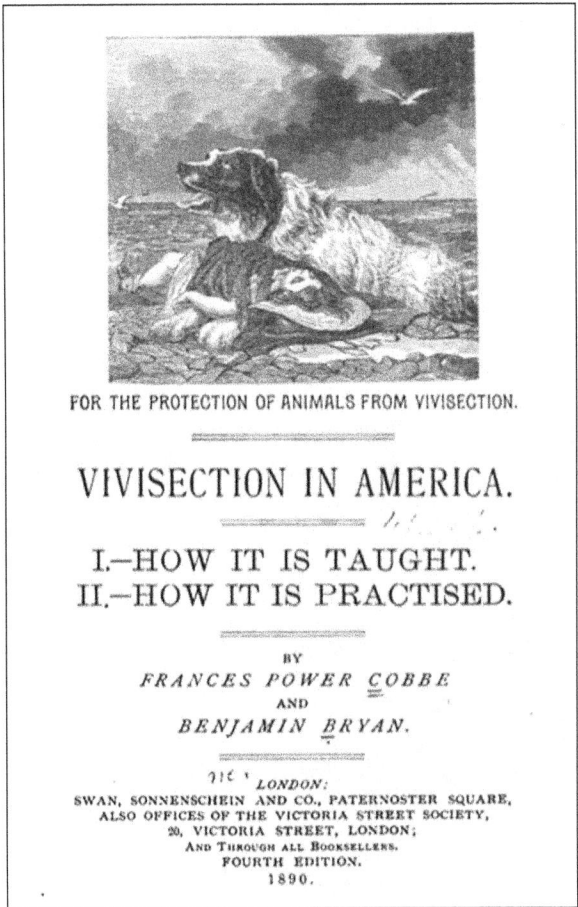

FIGURE 3.5 Cover of *Vivisection in America*, 4th edition (1890).

willing to help us, the campaigners demand, why, then, is it such a struggle for us to repay the courtesy?

The Highland Shepherd's Chief Mourner is probably Landseer's most well-known painting (Figure 3.6).[56] This picture was painted in 1837 and exhibited at the Royal Academy that same year. This sentimental scene of a faithful dog refusing to leave his human companion's side even in death is considered by many to be the definitive Landseer image. In *Modern Painters* John Ruskin had high praise for this image, calling it "one of the most perfect . . . pictures." Ruskin goes on to emphasize the

> exquisite execution of the glossy and crisp hair of the dog, the bright sharp touching of the green bough beside it, the clear painting of the wood of the coffin and the folds of the blanket, are language—language clear and expressive in the highest degree. But the close pressure of the dog's breast against the wood, the convulsive clinging of the paws, which has dragged the blanket off the trestle, the total powerlessness of the head laid, close and motionless, upon its folds, the fixed and tearful fall of the eye in its utter hopelessness, the rigidity of repose which marks that there has been no motion nor change in the trance of agony

FIGURE 3.6   Edwin Landseer, *The Highland Shepherd's Chief Mourner* (1837). Copyright © Victoria and Albert Museum, London.

since the last blow was struck on the coffin-lid, the quietness and gloom of the chamber, the spectacles marking the place where the Bible was last closed, indicating how lonely has been the life—how unwatched the departure of him who is now laid solitary in his sleep;—these are all thoughts—thoughts by which the picture is separated at once from hundreds of equal merit, as far as mere painting goes, by which it ranks as work of high art, and stamps its author, not as a neat imitator of the texture of a skin, or the fold of a drapery, but as the Man of Mind.[57]

Ruskin was one of the most highly respected art critics of the era and his complimentary remarks about this image certainly went a long way towards ensuring the popularity of this picture for nineteenth-century audiences.[58] It is, however, in another contemporary commentary on this painting that we find a perhaps even more poignant understanding of its influence on this period's thought. In a newspaper article published on the occasion of Landseer's death in 1873, *The Highland Shepherd's Chief Mourner* was celebrated for its ability to shift a viewer's understanding of the relationship between human and nonhuman animals: "by the 'Shepherd's Chief Mourner' we have all been cheated out of the pride of our humanity. And, losing this pride, we find that it has hidden from us a whole world of knowledge."[59] This painting, in other words, has revealed for the writer—and presumably at least for some of the readers who would have read this article in the days following the famous painter's death—the extent to which a painting like this can reduce the "pride of humanity" and, in so doing, open the door to the recognition that human and nonhuman animals have much in common.

The MSPCA reprinted *The Highland Shepherd's Chief Mourner* in an 1881 issue of its monthly newspaper, *Our Dumb Animals*, and declared it to be "eminently appropriate" for this publication (Figure 3.7).[60] As was the case with *Saved!* and *A Distinguished Member of the Humane Society*, the reproduction of this image emphasizes exemplary qualities and behaviours of nonhuman animals, and its use in this context once again asks readers how human society could perpetuate cruelty and unkind acts towards creatures who are apparently so kind and loyal to our species.

While Edwin Landseer remains one of the best-known artists to have work adopted by organizations like the MSPCA, THS, and Victoria Street Society, he was not the only artist who had work reproduced in nineteenth-century animal advocacy literature. For example, Landseer's

FIGURE 3.7 *The Highland Shepherd's Chief Mourner*, Landseer's painting of the same title as published in *Our Dumb Animals* (in March 1881). Image reproduced with permission of the Massachusetts Society for the Prevention of Cruelty to Animals.

FIGURE 3.8 Thomas Landseer, *Three Members of the Temperance Society*, after J.F. Herring's painting of the same title, as published in *Our Dumb Animals* (in February 1878). Image reproduced with permission of the Massachusetts Society for the Prevention of Cruelty to Animals.

brother, Thomas, produced an engraving after J.F. Herring's *Three Members of the Temperance Society* that appeared on the pages of *Our Dumb Animals* in February 1878 (Figure 3.8). Here Herring's painting of three horses drinking from a water trough is reproduced for supporters of the MSPCA who are also invited to the Society's offices to view Thomas Landseer's original engraving.[61]

The article accompanying this image in *Our Dumb Animals* argued that "no one can fail to observe the intelligence, almost human, in the faces of these faithful members of the temperance society, and the indisputable proofs each gives of a long descent from noble blood. Are we to stand neutral and see such animals starved, or overloaded, or abused in any way? Do they not unconsciously plead for justice in return for their priceless services to man? And plead for all their race?"[62] While both the species depicted and the formal qualities of Herring's image differ from Landseer's well-known and often-reproduced images discussed above, there are similar representational strategies at work in this example. The inclusion of the title of the image, *Three Members of the Temperance Society*, of course, points to another related social reform movement taking place at the time. The image–text relationship in this example suggests that these animals are engaging in behaviour that is highly desirable (from a British and/or American middle-class perspective)—in fact, much more desirable than that which many humans engage in. Further, it is emphasized that these animals are "almost human" while the implication is that those who are not supporters of temperance behave like "beasts." Just like Baker's twentieth-century example of animal rights activists donning Mickey Mouse ears, in these instances the boundaries of "human" and "animal" become blurred.

These kinds of images functioned in a very different way than those provided as "evidence" of cruelty (e.g., the CSPCA example with which I opened this discussion). While, for example, Landseer's *A Distinguished Member of the Humane Society* may have been inspired by an actual, living, breathing dog, this image's currency came from a much broader sense of canine identity. There is a tension between the actual flesh-and-blood dog and the representation he inspired. Undoubtedly the representational techniques informing the continued replication of this image generated meanings beyond the individual identity of a single dog; in this picture we are no longer dealing with an actual dog. Rather, this is a representation, once removed, and continually recirculated through the multiple prints and publications in which it appeared. In this dynamic, I recognize that there are, indeed, symbolic qualities at play, however, unlike Ormand, I do not see this painted version of a Newfoundland dog as representing "human values" above all else. Further, I think it is necessary to imagine this picture's influence on actual animal bodies, bringing the cycle of representation back around to "real" dogs once again. While it is impossible to know just how many people were influenced by animal advocacy campaigns featuring images like this, we can confidently speculate that at least some who viewed these images in the context of this reform movement were moved to modify behaviours and/or attitudes towards nonhuman animals. As Anderson notes, "how people think about animals influences how they interact with them,"[63] and it is precisely this point that makes these kinds of representations so influential in the context of animal advocacy. In this context, pictures have a profound ability to shape, confirm, or disrupt dominant patterns of thought. As Mitchell so eloquently argues, "We need to ponder that we don't just evaluate images; images introduce new forms of value into the world, contesting our criteria, forcing us to change our minds. . . . Images are not just passive entities that coexist with their human hosts, any more than the microorganisms that dwell in our intestines. They change the way we think and see and dream."[64] Nineteenth-century reformers hoped that by reproducing pictures like the ones discussed in this chapter they would reach the hearts and minds of a broad public, convincing them to change the way they perceived and ultimately treated the nonhuman animals with whom they shared the planet.

Conclusion

A number of reasons can be given for why reproductions of paintings such as *A Distinguished Member of the Humane Society*, *Saved!*, and *The Highland Shepherd's Chief Mourner* appeared on the pages of the periodicals and campaign materials produced by animal advocacy organizations in the late nineteenth century. Undoubtedly the visual appeal of the images reproduced on the pages of campaign materials made them popular choices; in an age where illustrated periodicals competed with one another for readership this cannot be forgotten. However, the selection of *which* artworks to reproduce on these pages points to a much more sophisticated pattern of representation than simply inserting interesting-looking animal pictures. As discussed above, many of the paintings selected for publications like *Our Dumb Animals* were often those in which nonhuman animals were depicted as having traits exemplary of the most "civilized" human behaviours, what Marc Bekoff refers to as "secondary emotions"— loyalty, compassion, bravery, or self-restraint, to name just a few.[65] In this context, these images become part of a broader dialogue focusing on the emotions, morality, and sentience of nonhuman animals. In other words, the reproduction of these images placed them right in the midst of Darwinian-inspired debates about the similarities between species during this era. For groups attempting to convince the public that nonhuman animals needed to be treated kindly, images that visually addressed these concepts were valuable resources.

The recontextualizaton of these types of images on the pages of animal advocacy campaign literature was a complex process. On the one hand, these animals are presented as having much in common with humans—in fact, in some cases, demonstrating better behaviour than exemplified by a large number of humans. And yet, at the same time, these representations are much more than just four-legged symbols of humans and their behaviours. The context in which these images appear—in advocacy and educational publications—ensures, by definition, a recognition of the nonhuman status of these creatures.

Landseer's paintings worked especially well in the context of nineteenth-century animal advocacy because these images resist easy categorization of what it means to be "human" and to be "animal." That so many advocacy organizations chose to reproduce these images over and over again stands as a testament to this effect. The blurring of boundaries found within the frames of these images was fundamental to the campaign efforts of such groups as the Victoria Street Society, the THS, and MSPCA. The recognition that animals could, in many ways, be "like us" underscored an uncomfortable awareness of the ability of other species to feel pain and experience emotions. And yet these images also point out that these animals are not quite "like us" in that they were unable to protect themselves from human cruelty and exploitation and, as such, legitimize the existence of these organizations at this time.[66]

NOTES

1. Mitchell, *What Do Pictures Want?*, 105.
2. Anderson, *Creatures of Empire*, 8.
3. Johnston, *For Those Who Cannot Speak*, 18.
4. Donald, *Picturing Animals in Britain*, iii.

5. For the sake of clarity I use the phrase "animal advocacy" to encompass a broad range of approaches and actions aimed at making the world a kinder place for nonhuman animals during the historical period under consideration. It is important to note that late-nineteenth-century reform movements aimed at bettering the treatment of nonhuman animals were not homogenous; some were focused more on what we may now understand to be "welfare" issues (improving the conditions of animals used in agriculture or industry), while other reformers considered themselves to be "abolitionists," although this concept was typically applied to a single issue. The reformers associated with the British Union for the Abolition of Vivisection, for example, were focused on ridding the country of experimentation on live animal bodies, but were relatively silent on other issues such as the treatment of animals in agriculture.
6. I have chosen to focus on these two geographic areas because of the ways in which advocacy groups from Britain and North American shared and exchanged material. During the late nineteenth century there was much reciprocity between British, Canadian, and American animal advocacy groups.
7. Edwin Landseer was knighted in 1850.
8. On a similar note, Queen Victoria and Prince Albert decorated Balmoral Castle in Scotland with Landseer prints.
9. Landseer's wildlife paintings did appear in early animal advocacy work, in particular in the context of humane education. See, for example, Krause, *Manual of Moral and Humane Education*. It was, however, Landseer's dog paintings that were by far the more common choice for 19th-century animal advocacy groups.
10. Ormond, *Sir Edwin Landseer*, 94.
11. Mitchell, *What Do Pictures Want?*, 47.
12. Hodgins, *Aims and Objects*, v.
13. Preece, "Thoughts Out of Season," 365–78.
14. Browne, "Darwin in Caricature," 496–509.
15. Donald, Introduction to *Endless Forms*, 23.
16. *Bell's Life*, "Influence of Landseer," 6.
17. Hochadel, "Darwin in the Monkey Cage," 82.
18. Ibid.
19. In Darwin, *Expression of the Emotions*, xxv.
20. *Bell's Life*, "Influence of Landseer," 6.
21. Donald, "'Mind and Conscience,'" 209.
22. Lennie, *Landseer*, 122.
23. For example, Frances Power Cobbe, the Victorian antivivisection activist, frequently reproduced pictures of animal bodies being experimented on directly from scientific texts. She deliberately chose this method of picturing to avoid accusations of embellishing the situation or of being overly sentimental.

Cobbe relied on the perceived objectivity of science—and, by extension, scientific imagery—to lend credibility to these visual campaigns.

24. Baker, *Picturing the Beast*, 226.
25. Ibid.
26. Ibid., 228.
27. Ibid., 227.
28. *Ladies' Treasury* (London), "Pets," 97.
29. Bucke, "Cyno-psychoses," 470.
30. Stephens, *Sir Edwin Landseer*, 13.
31. Lennie, *Landseer*, 162.
32. *Times* (London), "Sir Edwin Landseer," 10.
33. Ibid.
34. Donald, *Picturing Animals in Britain*, 127.
35. *Bell's Life*, "Influence of Landseer," 6.
36. *Ladies' Treasury* (London), "Pets," 97.
37. Lansbury, *Old Brown Dog*; Blocker, Fahey, and Tyrrell, *Alcohol and Temperance*; Lewis-Jones, "Minds in Chains."
38. *Royal Cornwall Gazette*, "Queen and Sir Edwin Landseer on Cropping Terriers' Ears," 3. See also, Lennie, *Landseer*, 85.
39. *Morning Post* (London), "Royal Society for the Prevention of Cruelty to Animals," 5.
40. RSPCA, "Day at the Royal Academy," 147.
41. *Bell's Life*, "Influence of Landseer," 6.
42. Donald, "'Mind and Conscience,'" 210.
43. Fay, Annual Report of the Secretary, 87.
44. *High Life* and *Low Life* were painted in 1829 and exhibited in 1831.
45. Tate Gallery, "Summary: Sir Edwin Henry Landseer, *Low Life*, 1829," Tate Gallery website, http://www.tate.org.uk/art/artworks/landseer-low-life-a00702.
46. Angell, Children's Department, 88. The reproductions in these issues were flipped from left to right.
47. Ibid., 98.
48. This story is recounted in Lennie, *Landseer*, 93.
49. Ormand, *Sir Edwin Landseer*, 11.
50. Stephens, *Sir Edwin Landseer*, 79.
51. Williamson, *Power and Protest*, 126. The Victoria Street Society was originally known as the Society for the Protection of Animals Liable to Vivisection. In 1898 the group became known as the National Anti-Vivisection Society, the name it still goes by today.
52. Ritvo, *Animal Estate*, 162.
53. Jones and Rutman, *In the Children's Aid*.
54. Hodgins, *Aims and Objects*, vi.

55. Ibid., 171.
56. This painting is also known as *The Old Shepherd's Chief Mourner* and is in the collection of the V&A in London. For more on this image see Donald, *Picturing Animals in Britain*, 155–58.
57. Ruskin, *Modern Painters*, 9.
58. In the context of this chapter it is worth noting that Ruskin resigned from Oxford in 1855 after the University voted to include vivisection in its curriculum.
59. *Bell's Life*, "Influence of Landseer," 6.
60. MSPCA, "Our March Paper," 76.
61. MSPCA, "Three Members of the Temperance Society," 72.
62. Ibid.
63. Anderson, *Creatures of Empire*, 7.
64. Mitchell, *What Do Pictures Want?*, 92.
65. Bekoff, *Emotional Lives of Animals*, 8.
66. I would like to thank Martin Danahay and Hilda Kean for earlier discussions that sparked ideas in this chapter. I would also like to thank Jodey Castricano and Lauren Corman for their feedback on earlier drafts of this manuscript.

BIBLIOGRAPHY

Anderson, Virginia DeJohn. *Creatures of Empire: How Domestic Animals Transformed Early America*. Oxford: Oxford University Press, 2004.

Angell, George T. Children's Department. *Our Dumb Animals* 3, no. 11 (April 1871): 88; and no. 12 (May 1871): 98.

Baker, Steve. *Picturing the Beast: Animals, Identity and Representation*. Manchester: Manchester University Press, 1993.

Bekoff, Marc. *The Emotional Lives of Animals*. Novato, CA: New World Library, 2007.

Bell's Life in London and Sporting Chronicle. "The Influence of Landseer." London, October 18, 1873.

Blocker, Jack S., David M. Fahey, and Ian R. Tyrrell. *Alcohol and Temperance in Modern History*. ABC-CLIO, 2003.

Browne, Janet. "Darwin in Caricature: A Study in the Popularisation and Dissemination of Evolution." *Proceedings of the American Philosophical Society* 145, no. 4 (2001): 496–509.

Bucke, W. Fowler. "Cyno-psychoses: Children's Thoughts, Reactions, and Feelings toward Pet Dogs." *Pedagogical Seminary* 10 (1903): 459–513.

Darwin, Charles. *The Expression of the Emotions in Man and Animals*. Oxford: Oxford University Press, 1998.

Donald, Diana. "'A Mind and Conscience Akin to Our Own': Darwin's Theory of Expression and the Depiction of Animals in Nineteenth-Century Britain." In

Endless Forms: Charles Darwin, Natural Science and the Visual Arts, edited by Diana Donald and Jane Munro, 195–214. New Haven: Yale University Press, 2009.

———. Introduction to *Endless Forms: Charles Darwin, Natural Science and the Visual Arts*, 1–27. New Haven: Yale University Press, 2009.

———. *Picturing Animals in Britain, 1750–1850*. New Haven: Yale University Press, 2007.

Fay, Frank B. Annual Report of the Secretary. *Our Dumb Animals* 3, no. 11 (April 1871): 86–87.

Hochadel, Oliver. "Darwin in the Monkey Cage: The Zoological Garden as a Medium of Evolutionary Theory." In *Beastly Natures: Animals, Humans and the Study of History*, edited by Dorothee Brantz, 81–107. Charlottesville, VA: University of Virginia Press, 2010.

Hodgins, J. George. *Aims and Objects of the Toronto Humane Society*. Toronto: Toronto Humane Society, 1888.

Johnston, Beatrice. *For Those Who Cannot Speak: A History of the Canadian Society for the Prevention of Cruelty to Animals, 1869–1969*. Laval, QC: Dev-Sco, 1970.

Jones, Andrew, and Leonard Rutman. *In the Children's Aid: J.J. Kelso and Child Welfare in Ontario*. Toronto: University of Toronto Press, 1981.

Krause, Flora Helm. *Manual of Moral and Humane Education*. Boston: Atkinson, Mentzer & Co., 1910.

Ladies' Treasury (London). "The Pets." June 1, 1857.

Lansbury, Coral. *The Old Brown Dog: Women, Workers, and Vivisection in Edwardian England*. Madison, WI: University of Wisconsin Press, 1985.

Lennie, Campbell. *Landseer: The Victorian Paragon*. London: Hamish Hamilton, 1976.

Lewis-Jones, Huw. "Minds in Chains." *Apollo* 166, no. 547 (2007): 112–14.

Mitchell, W.J. Thomas. *What Do Pictures Want?: The Lives and Loves of Images*. Chicago: University of Chicago Press, 2005.

Morning Post (London). "Royal Society for the Prevention of Cruelty to Animals." July 1869.

MSPCA (Massachusetts Society for the Prevention of Cruelty to Animals). "Our March Paper." *Our Dumb Animals* 13, no. 10 (March 1881): 76.

———. "Three Members of the Temperance Society." *Our Dumb Animals* 10, no. 9 (February 1878): 72.

Ormond, Richard. *Sir Edwin Landseer*. Philadelphia: Philadelphia Museum of Art, 1981.

Preece, Rod. "Thoughts Out of Season on the History of Animal Ethics." *Society & Animals* 15 (2007): 365–78.

Ritvo, Harriet. *The Animal Estate: The English and Other Creatures in the Victorian Age*. Cambridge, MA: Harvard University Press, 1987.

Royal Cornwall Gazette, Falmouth Packet, and General Advertiser. "The Queen and Sir Edwin Landseer on Cropping Terriers' Ears." Truro, June 3, 1869.

RSPCA (Royal Society for the Prevention of Cruelty to Animals). "A Day at the Royal Academy." *Animal World* 18, no. 217 (October 1, 1887): 147–49.

Ruskin, John. *Modern Painters.* New York: John Wiley & Sons, 1888.

Stephens, Frederick G. *Sir Edwin Landseer.* 3rd ed. London: Sampson Low, Marston, Searle & Rivington, 1880.

Times (London). "Sir Edwin Landseer." October 2, 1873.

Williamson, Lori. *Power and Protest: Frances Power Cobbe and Victorian Society.* London: Rivers Oram Press, 2005.

4

"The Animal," Systems, and Structures

An Ecofeminist-Posthumanist Enquiry

Rhys Mahannah

Suddenly, as I watched their grotesque and unaccountable gestures, I perceived clearly for the first time what it was that had offended me, what had given me the two consisting and conflicting impressions of utter strangeness and yet of the strangest familiarity. The three creatures engaged in this mysterious rite were human in shape, and yet human beings with the strangest air about them of some familiar animal. Each of these creatures, despite its human form, its rag of clothing, and the rough humanity of its bodily form, had woven into it—into its movements, into the expression of its countenance, into its whole presence— . . . the unmistakable mark of the beast.[1]

Edward Prendick, in *The Island of Dr. Moreau*

The Animal Within

H.G. Wells' fantastically grim novel *The Island of Dr. Moreau* (1896) is more than a commentary dealing with moral questions surrounding vivisection and scientific discourse in general. Indeed, some critics have examined the allegorical meaning of the novel with regard to the "mythical" quality of implicit racial hierarchies: working within this framework, the "performativity" of "race"—and therefore its illusory, unreal nature—becomes explicit. The drive to eliminate the "animality" of the Beast Men through scientific alteration, as well as the forced internalization of the Law, is Moreau's way of containing and controlling the "excess" of the foundational event that is the performativity of "difference."[2] From a critical animal studies perspective, as Sherryl Vint's analysis cogently shows, the novel reveals the inherently speciesist attitudes that allow for the subjugation and exploitation of animals by the scientific community.[3] It is the reinforcement of this speciesism, ineluctable within the tradition of human exceptionalism, that creates "the animal" as a scientific "problem," an object of contemplation and a site of transfiguration for the "mad scientist"—a being whose goal is to "tame" or "control" nature and its constituent elements. And it is precisely the unexamined nature of scientific discourse—including its methods, purposes, and goals—that becomes problematic, for it normalizes the constructed nature of an anthropocentric hierarchy which privileges "man" over "nature."[4]

However, the focus on science as an ideological apparatus that problematizes the moral and ethical concerns of "the animal" is only one crucial aspect in examining and exposing the violence directed towards "animality" or "the animal" (at the conceptual level) and animals themselves (at the level of praxis and practicality) within rationalist anthropocentric discourse(s).[5] Indeed, by reading *The Island of Dr. Moreau* through a more discursive lens, one begins to understand that these speciesist attitudes can be extrapolated to a more comprehensive, more totalizing framework: firstly, at the level of "internal" belief, the thoughts and feelings of the individual(s); and secondly and more broadly, society's collective (un)conscious. This "internal" belief is manifested in "external" systems, institutions, and material practices—the physical acts informed by those beliefs. That is, violent "implicit" beliefs are inextricably intertwined with—indeed, lead to the manifestations of—the violent "explicit" actions they provoke.

Examining the effects of this implicit/explicit violence, then, one may see similar attitudes enacted and directed towards "the animal"—the Beast Men, more specifically—in *The Island of Dr. Moreau*. The novel begins in *media res*, with the protagonist, Edward Prendick, adrift in the ocean following a shipwreck. Picked up by a vessel transporting animals, Prendick is nursed back to health by Montgomery, whose companion, "a misshapen man, short, broad, and clumsy, with a crooked back, a hairy neck, and a head sunk between his shoulders," both fascinates and repulses Prendick.[6] The ship reaches a mysterious island, where the caged animals, Montgomery, the strange companion (later discovered to be named M'ling), and Prendick are left with a Dr. Moreau. While on the island, Prendick discovers more strange creatures with uncanny semblance to both humans and animals. He comes to learn that Dr. Moreau, a once famous physiologist banished from England for performing horrific experiments on animals, is engaging once again in animal vivisection—"A humanizing process," Moreau calls it, in which he hopes to "create" men from animals.[7] Problems arise when the Law, a human-based social system used by Moreau to "control" the Beast Men eventually begins to degrade, and rapidly so after the death of Moreau while tracking one of his creations gone rogue—that is, "control" in the sense of ideological interpellation, where the Beast Men, as "recognized" (quasi-)subjects, self-regulate. Soon thereafter, Montgomery dies in an accident and, having previously burned a life raft in which Prendick planned to escape, leaves Prendick stranded on the island. Subsequently, Prendick comes to live in relative safety with the Beast Men for ten months. He later discovers a derelict vessel and sets sail from the island, and is rescued by a ship heading to San Francisco. Back in London, the horrific events of the island cause Prendick to retire from the city, haunted by the idea that, potentially, the "degradation of the Islanders will be played over again on a larger scale."[8]

Significant within the novel is Prendick's interactions with the strange Beast Folk. Walking through the vegetation of Moreau's island shortly after arriving, Prendick comes across a group of strange creatures—beings that are uncannily[9] human-like, but, within an anthropocentrism that abides by the creation and strict categorization of identities, impossibly so, for they reveal "that transitory gleam of [their] true animalism"[10] in their movements and actions, material markers of, for Prendick and the humanist tradition in general, identity delineation. After noting, for example, that the Beast Men "began leaping in the air, first one and then the other, whooping and grunting," and, shortly thereafter, how "one slipped, and for a moment was on all fours,"[11] Prendick's cavalier observation/recognition of, first and foremost, the "inhuman" physical movements of the creatures *always already* sets the stage for destabilizing conflict: what is human *cannot* be animal, for they are "inherently different." The Beast Men are thus immured to the inferior realm of "nonhumanness." But this schism, this "definitive" separation, is challenged when Prendick, while contemplating one of these beings, asks himself, as well as the reader, perhaps the ultimate humanist question: "What on earth was he—man or beast?"[12] Indeed, the implications of this enquiry are greater than a merely superficial recognition of a "particular," "knowable," "concrete" ontological definition. It asks, "Are you human?" If so—if, indeed, the question is answered in a human tongue— then the individual asked is automatically/immediately and conventionally attributed the "privilege" of reason and rationality (in most cases, anyway). It says, "You can speak, you talk in my (human) language. You are thus relevant, important, worthy of social, moral, and ethical consideration. You are superior!"[13] Perniciously, it also asks the antipode (the question, already predetermined, is illogical): "Are you a beast? Are you nonhuman?" An affirmative "answer," that significant marker of the nonhuman that is either silence or the cries unheard, the language(s) of assent, immediately rejects the being, pushing it out of the realm of "humanness" and into the abyss of the "object," the "thing," the "unwanted."[14] What the affirmative answer says, it says in, perhaps, a mocking manner, simply to satiate the human and human condition, for of course the animal cannot, is not supposed to, understand this eternal verdict: "You lack rationality, reason, and therefore moral consideration. You lack Self. You are abject, you are Other, and thus you are subjected to what I, all-powerful human (man), see fit."

Prendick's question, then, reveals an internalized belief of "normality" (human) versus "abnormality" (animal), and their separation into distinct, concretized categories. His anxiety and psychological stress surrounding this "distinction," or lack thereof, is most explicit at the end of the novel, where Prendick, at home in England, begins to see the "beast" in all humans, the uncanny spectre, or trace, of "the animal" residing in the very heart of all human society: "I feel as though the animal was surging up through [these people]; that presently the degradation of the Islanders will be played over again on a larger scale. I know this is an illusion; that these seeming men and women about me are indeed men and women, men and women forever, perfectly reasonable creatures, full of human desires and tender solicitude, emancipated from instinct and the slaves of no fantastic Law—beings altogether different from the Beast Folk."[15] For Prendick, the division between what constitutes "animality" and "humanity" falls into a realm of obscurity; a slippage begins to occur—aporias of and within these identities begin to surface—and the illusory, arbitrary categories of "man" and "beast" begin, unabated, to reveal themselves as such. The ability of the Beast Folk to communicate through (human) language—and, it would seem, by use of reason, no matter how primordial—further blurs that already precarious contour of the human/animal divide. And in a move that further distorts or deconstructs this line, Prendick himself seems to re(in)state the "Humanist Law": men and women are "reasonable" creatures, they have "human desires" and "tender solicitude," they are emancipated from "instinct," and they are no slaves of a "fantastic Law" (does the Humanist Law become a parody of the Beast Folk's Law, or is it the other way around? Which law becomes an illusory perception of truth?). He desperately wants to believe that these people, his people, are—they *must* be—different from the Beast Folk; and in a twist of perhaps poignant irony, it appears that he is indeed desperately clinging to a "Human Law," a construction that is as painfully (un)real as the "Beast Law," itself a parodic mirror that reveals the very arbitrariness of all such "Laws."[16] As Friedrich Nietzsche contends in his essay "Truth and Lying in an Extra-moral Sense" (1873), "[man] will always obtain illusion instead of truth";[17] Prendick's belief and intense desire of an inseparable, distinctive line of the human/animal binary thus reveals itself as an illusion, one which he desperately wants to retain as "truth," for such a decisive summation upholds his position as "man" at the summit of an ontological hierarchy.

As a result, Prendick becomes another (anxious) figure of the human exceptionalist tradition in the novel (Moreau is the primary figure of this nature, through both his implicitly violent beliefs and the explicitly violent actions which follow—namely and most obviously, vivisection). The obscurity of "animalness" and "humanness," and Prendick's anxiety surrounding the ambivalence about what truly constitutes each of these identities, reveals a potential breakdown of the ideological "apparatus," as Michel Foucault calls it, which, through ideological institutions (or "ideological state apparatuses," to use the terminology of Louis Althusser), systematically upholds a "necessity" of binary definition and identification (man/woman, reason/sentiment, Self/Other, Man/Animal, etc.) in order to reaffirm the human's "inherently" superior position; this also simultaneously removes "the animal" from a position of privilege, of moral and ethical consideration. With its whole concept of "truth" built upon the illusion of "real" differences, however, this ideological apparatus reveals its fragility when confronted with the definitional limit that is "the animal," that marker of Otherness.[18] Indeed, what "the animal" is, what it does, and its importance to the human exceptionalist tradition becomes, importantly, what Jacques Derrida calls the "the question of animality": that which "represents the limits upon which all the great questions are formed and determined, as well as all the concepts that attempt to delimit what is 'proper to man,' the essence of the future of humanity, ethics, politics, law, 'human rights,' 'crimes against humanity,' 'genocide,' etc."[19] Thus, in an ideology that "creates" identities, privileges particular identities over others, and develops a hierarchy of being through a system of binary definitional differences, "the animal" represents that outermost boundary of definitional possibility in this apparatus—including and even making possible what it means to be "human," as a privileged entity.

"The Animal"

If Prendick's anxiety—indeed, the anxiety of an entire humanist tradition—surrounding the categories "human" and "animal" is the result of a realization that neither is "true-in-itself," that both are merely arbitrary constructions that, upon further examination, inevitably blur and collapse into one another, then perhaps we may take a different approach to Prendick's profoundly anthropocentric question. If, through a dialectic of negative definition, "the human" requires "the animal" to exist (since what is human but that which is not animal?) and "the animal" requires "the human" to exist (what is animal but that which is not human?), then perhaps there comes to be another possible answer to Prendick's question: the Beast Man is simultaneously *both* human *and* animal. Perhaps he/it always already was. If this is true—if we are to accept what may at first appear to be a radical *conjunctive* possibility—the implications could be extraordinary: if one has never been either man *or* beast, but has always already been both man *and* beast, then "human" and "animal" have never existed as distinct, essential possibilities. Within the context of posthumanism, which challenges the epistemological boundaries of identity itself, we may understand this notion of identity, of ontological possibility, as that which is not essential and static, but is always already rewritten, remade, re-understood. If this is the case, then perhaps we can re-imagine, not only what identity is, but also what the ethical implications of such a shift entail.

In this chapter, I explore how the Otherness of "the animal," as implicated in a patriarchal ideology, is intimately and inveterately connected with the Otherness that is women and racialized beings (among other Others). More specifically, I will critically examine how the systematic violence employed by the Western patriarchal apparatus works to marginalize these groups

through *fundamentally similar ideological methods*: these figures are inextricably linked in and through a network of illusory inferiority that nonetheless
has real and deplorable effects in the varying degrees of violence against individuals—from derogatory comments to the documented horrors of factory
farms to the rationalization of genocide, all of which, in one way or another,
reinforce each other as methods of (rationalized) violence. At the same time,
however, "the animal" inhabits a unique Othered position, ostensibly apart
from both women and racialized Others, and yet is still inextricable from
these oppressions. In this regard, one may show that, in fact, it is "the animal" that exposes the arbitrariness of the apparatus. Beginning with Louis
Althusser's theory of ideology and ideological state apparatuses, I examine
ideological frameworks as "'world outlooks' [that] are largely imaginary"[20]—
that is, they don't correspond to reality—but which nonetheless have real and
material effects: the construction of Otherness is a reality of hierarchy, where
those "below" the human are conceptualized, "created" (just as "the human"
is "created"), and treated as inferior, both implicitly (by internalization of
particular beliefs) and, consequently, explicitly (the material practices that
uphold those beliefs). Next, I examine Foucault's notion of "biopower," as a
particular ideological apparatus, which produces the (human–animal) body
as a dense transfer point of knowledge: subjects are regulated and controlled
through numerous techniques for achieving the subjugation of bodies. Thus,
the creation of "norms" necessarily leads to, and is entirely reliant upon, the
development and dissemination of "perversions." And while these (sexual)
perversions have traditionally been attributed to human "subjects"—for
Foucault, the diagnosis of the Other is manifested in and by the homosexual,
the hysterical woman, and the masturbating child—the animal body *also*
becomes a site that is subjected to knowledge discourses. These discourses
support a particular economic ideology, where bodies and systems revolve
around the motive of productivity and, more broadly, capital and profit.[21]
However, the position of "the animal" reveals itself as a definition that
works at the very conceptual limit of the Western patriarchal apparatus that
constructs and upholds identities (and, simultaneously, helps to construct
the "animalized" identities of women and racialized Others). This occurs
through, as I will focus on in this essay, the employment of what Carol J.
Adams deems the "absent referent," a semantic violence that uses metaphor
to describe one being's experience using the language of another, seemingly
unrelated being; the inferior groups within the apparatus, as a result—
women, racialized Others, and animals—reinforce the marginalization that

each identity experiences at both the conceptual and material level. However, the ideological interpellation—the "hailing" of a subject into an ideology, defined as such by Althusser—of "the animal" becomes problematic. Can an animal become a subject-of-a-life in this patriarchal apparatus? What are the implications in exploring this? In thinking about these questions, I want to examine how taking an ecofeminist perspective of "the animal" affects the Western patriarchal apparatus. Indeed, the role and implications of the apparatus and what it does can, at the very least, be questioned through the deconstruction of interrelated oppressive systems, combined with a particular "ethics of care," an ethical outlook purported by Carol Gilligan and, more recently, Diane Antonio, that recognizes the necessity of emotion *and* reasons in deconstructing the subject/object divide. Thus, though it may potentially face problems with identity essentialism, ecofeminism nonetheless offers a critical perspective in dealing with "the animal" in a posthumanist context, posthumanism being a movement that (re)imagines "the human" as that which is not yet, is yet to become, is always in the process of becoming, and thus never "fully" becomes "human." Indeed, posthumanism can be thought of as a "[humanism that] forever rewrites itself as posthumanism."[22] (Post)humanism is thus a "movement [that] is always happening," one which "cannot escape its 'post-.'"[23] Posthumanism, then, ostensibly looks "beyond" the definitions of "the human," as well as "the animal," in order to explicitly promote the atemporal arbitrariness of such ontological constructions, which have traditionally been upheld in social constructionism(s)—those ideological social conventions that morally and ethically approve of the domination and "progression" of the human condition.

The Ideological Subject

To begin this examination of "the animal," as well as its (inter)connectedness with the position of women and racialized Others, an outline of what ideology is and what it does becomes crucial. According to Louis Althusser, in his seminal essay "Ideology and Ideological State Apparatuses" (1970), ideology is the result of "the existence of a small number of cynical men who base their domination and exploitation of the 'people' on a falsified representation of the world which they have imagined in order to enslave other minds by dominating their imaginations."[24] One would be mistaken, however, to assume that these "small number of cynical men" ("men" being a key term here, within a patriarchal enterprise) devised such an ideology, then implemented it, such as would be the case with, say, the architectural plans of a building; to conceptualize ideology in this way presupposes an "outside," one that imagines a power of application controlled by a "user" that remains detached from the "system" applied.[25] That is, everyone becomes both a *subject of* an ideological system (in the sense subjects are indispensable to the system's very existence, and contribute to the ideology's identity through their "beliefs" and material actions) *and subject to* it (in the sense that all subjects "work" within the confines of the system and its dominant "ideas" and "notions"). (Of course, who or what counts as an *everyone*, as opposed to an *everything*, and what this means in terms of interpellation— that "hailing," or "recognition," of the subject's "concrete" position within ideology—comes to be a salient question. As I will later address, uncertainty as to whether it is even possible to imagine "the animal," a being without language in the human exceptionalist tradition, as capable of being interpellated reveals its stubborn resistance to the human/animal divide.)

Important is the idea that an ideology is imaginary (an *illusion*)—that is, it does not correspond to "reality," in the sense that it is indubitably tied up with the essence of what reality is. At the same time, however, ideology becomes an *allusion* to "reality," in the sense that ideology relates to something that is seen to really exist "out there."[26] Thus, ideology is the process of "[m]en representing their real conditions of existence to themselves in imaginary form"[27]—that is, the ways of understanding or "constructing" the world are developed arbitrarily as ways of dealing with, for instance, from a Marxist point of view, the alienation and reification of capitalist means of production and the way such relationships between the labourer and the product are disseminated into the rest of the labourer's existence. Over time, this representation comes to be internalized and naturalized.

Fundamental to the implementation, reinforcement, and continuation of certain ideological beliefs are *material* practices. "'Ideas' or 'representations' . . . which seem to make up ideology do not have an ideal . . . or spiritual existence, but a material existence."[28] This "material existence" is reinforced in and through a variety of ideological apparatuses—schools, religious or scientific establishments, government facilities, and so on. In a cyclical relationship of ideological interpellation, subjects are endowed with a certain perceived "free consciousness" that allows them to "freely choose" what they "believe" in. Thus, "the individual in question behaves in such and such a way, adopts such and such a practical attitude, and, what is more, participates in certain regular practices which are those of the ideological apparatus on which 'depend' the ideas which he has in all consciousness freely chosen as a subject."[29] Ideas and beliefs, then, exist only insofar as they are (materially) practised by a subject: the physical act of praying in a church, the physical act of allowing one rights while revoking the same rights from others, and so on. This process of reciting, as it were, the material practices based on an individual's "beliefs" that are informed by ideology and its apparatus(es) relies on the notion of *interpellation*.

Interpellation, metaphorically speaking (for this is the only way that we, as ideological subjects, can conceptualize this phenomenon), is the "calling" or "hailing" of subjects into a particular ideology. First and foremost, the recognition that ideology understands us to be concrete, individual knowable subjects is "obvious": "it is clear that you and I are free subjects.... Like all obviousness, including those that make a word 'name a thing' or 'have a meaning' (therefore including the obviousness of the 'transparency' of language) the 'obviousness' that you and I are subjects—and that that does not cause any problems—is an ideological effect, the elementary ideological effect."[30] We as subjects cannot *fail to recognize* that we are indeed interpolated into a particular system of naming, identification, and organization, which, as a result of our "awareness" of it as a particular system as such, presents no problems. And furthermore, because this system of "hailing" is always already happening (it is an atemporal mechanism), it follows that we are constantly (re)interpellated as subjects by all of our "practices"—and again, these come in many subtle and overt forms, from a certain conscientiousness of how we walk to the act of (religious?) praying.[31] That is, everything that we "believe" or act upon is/always was working in an ideological mode; and because these "beliefs" and actions stem from this ideological basis, are part and parcel to an ideology, they serve only to reinforce it and ourselves as subjects within it. With this in mind, the next step to understanding the subjects within ideological discourse(s) becomes important in order for one to understand its implications. Are all subjects the same? Are animals in some sense "subjects?" Do all subjects—including, perhaps, animals—react in the same way, become interpellated in a similar manner, reinforce ideology "as they should"?

The Bodies Speak

To engage these questions further, an examination of Michel Foucault's ideological mechanism of "biopower," as seen in his highly influential book *The History of Sexuality* (1976), is revealing, specifically with regard to the treatment of the body as a centre of knowledge discourses. Around the eighteenth century, according to Foucault, concepts of the body, power, and power distribution began to change. Unlike the top-down approach of older hegemonic systems, power came from everywhere: specifically, it was the "multiplication of discourses" of the individual (meticulous self-regulations), between individual subjects (regulation of others through observation), and within particular institutions (scientific and religious apparatuses, such as psychiatrists and religious confessionals).[32] Thus, as an ideological system, the *material* practice of "creating" certain (mythical, illusory) discourses surrounding the body worked within a particular economic apparatus. Foucault's definition of the apparatus, quoted by Stephen Thierman, is as follows:

> [A] thoroughly heterogeneous ensemble consisting of discourses, institutions, architectural forms, regulatory decisions, laws, administrative measures, scientific statements, philosophical, moral and philanthropic propositions—in short, the said as much as the unsaid. Such are elements of the apparatus. The apparatus itself is a system of relations that can be established between these elements.[33]

The body, as a result, became a dense transfer point of "knowledge" discourses. Through the "professional" practices in this apparatus—physicians being the most prominent figure here—biopower was used to regulate and control subjects of ideology through an explosion of numerous and diverse techniques for achieving the subjugation of bodies. Sex, as a result, "became an issue, and a public issue no less; a whole web of discourses, special knowledge, analyses, and injunctions settled upon it," and so a particular ideal of sexuality and health arose, creating a certain bodily "norm."[34] Consequently, the development, or "discovery," of perversions surrounding the body surfaced as well.

But upon further examination, these "multiple implantations of 'perversions'"[35] can be understood to extend beyond both sexuality and the human body. Indeed, while perversions "allowed for the diagnosis of 'otherness'" in terms of sexuality—most notably the homosexual, the hysterical woman, and the masturbating child, as Foucault recognizes them[36]— the "knowledge" of the "perverse," Othered body, which Marjorie Spiegel explores in her book *The Dreaded Comparison: Human and Animal Slavery* (1997), also becomes apparent with regard to "the animal." As Jean Baudrillard puts forth in his essay "The Animals: Territory and Metamorphoses" (1994), the ideological apparatus of scientific discourse became a way of "making animals speak, as one has made the insane, children, sex (Foucault) speak"; that is, "every day [they] would deliver their 'objective' . . . messages in laboratories."[37] Thus, for instance, the attribution of the psychic life allowed for new ways of controlling "the animal": "With ingenuity, one thus discovers, like a new and unexplored scientific field, the psychic life of the animal as soon as he is revealed to be maladapted to the death one is preparing for him. In the same way one rediscovers psychology, sociology, the sexuality of prisoners as soon as it becomes impossible to purely and simply incarcerate them."[38] What Baudrillard alludes to here is that this "objective" message is the result of a patriarchal ideology and its apparatuses finding exactly what is required in order to reinforce the dominant (masculine) human position: the "discovery" and the "knowledge" of "the animal" that, in some way or another, reveals it to inhabit a lower ontological position in juxtaposition with the human. Through a constant proliferation of discourses surrounding the (animal) body, then—"perverse" discourses which "find" and further rationalize "the animal" as an inferior, Othered entity—animals are removed and stringently held from a position of moral and ethical consideration, the realm of the uniquely human, and instead become and remain targets of domination and exploitation.

Similarly, by situating Friedrich Nietzsche's provocations of the power of language to develop particular "truths," specifically with regard to "the animal," within patriarchal discourse, one may find a perspective particularly salient to this notion of (man-made) "objectivity":

> If somebody hides a thing behind a bush, seeks it again and finds it in the self-same place, then there is not much to boast of, respecting his seeking and finding; thus, however, matters stand with the seeking and finding of "truth" within the realm of reasons. If I make the definition of the mammal and then declare after inspecting a camel, "Behold a mammal," then no doubt a truth is brought to light thereby, but it is of very limited value, I mean it is anthropomorphic through and through, and does not contain one single point which is "true-in-itself," real and universally valid, apart from man.[39]

"The animal," that conceptual identity which is conferred upon all non-human beings (and, importantly, even some human beings) within the apparatus of scientific discourse is "created" and defined as inferior through language and discourse; the human as the superior entity is only through an ostensible coincidence reinforced by this "truth" (as opposed to the "truth-in-itself," possible only in the realm of *objective* science, which, as Althusser contends, lies outside the ideological subject). Nietzsche, in a Foucauldian fashion, discovers that discourse empowered by the language of the human has allowed for—has, indeed, led to—the development of illusory discourses about the body, human and animal alike: "Speaking is a beautiful folly: with that man dances over all things. How lovely is all talking, and all the deception of sounds!"[40] Humans have, according to Nietzsche, observed the animal, learned from the animal, have become wise from the animal, are indeed moral, at least in part, because of the animal. But stories, myths, conceptions of our (human) selves have led to a breaking of the human from the animal—to creating a storyline in which the all-mighty human is distinct from, and superior to, the lowly beast. And so the human forgets its humble beginnings, and instead remembers itself as transcending that bestial state, evolving beyond the animal, forgetting that the animal, too, also evolves; the pride of the human overcomes, suppresses, forgets its memories and its past that has perversely resulted in "all these voices [of ideology and of human language] which have spoken so long in our civilization—repeating the formidable injunction to tell what one is and what one does, what one recollects and what one has forgotten, what one is thinking and what one thinks he [*sic*] is not thinking":[41] "The beginnings of justice, as of prudence, moderation, bravery—in short, of all we designate as the *Socratic virtues*, are *animal*: a consequence of that drive which teaches us to seek food and elude enemies. Now if we consider that even the highest human being has only become more elevated and subtle in the nature of his [*sic*] good and in his [*sic*] conception of what is inimical to him [*sic*], it is not improper to describe the entire phenomenon of morality as animal."[42] Instead of a celebration of the intimate, moral connection and knowledge-sharing between "the animal" and "the human," however, the animal body serves only to reinforce what the capitalist wants. The "discovery" of the "truths" of the body occurs in the "professional" scientific setting, where the animal "only furnish[es] the response one asks for."[43] Indeed, as Nietzsche further posits, just "as the astrologer contemplated the stars in the service of man and in connection with their happiness and unhappiness, such a seeker contemplates the whole world as related to man."[44] Thus, "the animal" constantly "reaffirms" its complacency and acceptance of the binary system of identification—a system where they inhabit the position of inferior "object," and where "man" automatically inhabits the position of superiority; these "facts," naturally, come to be/are "transparent."

Oppressed: Brothers and Sisters

"The animal," then, within Foucault's concept of the apparatus, and which resonates within Nietzsche's contemplation of humans, animals, language, and society, comes to inhabit the lowest position of the (humanist) onto-logical hierarchy.[45] But the abject position of "the animal" in this hierarchy also serves to reflect and reinforce that of women and racialized Others. Indeed, these oppressions are *fundamentally similar* in their systematic ideological marginalization. It becomes important, Spiegel warns, not to focus on this violent subordination of Othered groups as *separate* acts, but instead to realize and confront the fact that "[these systems of oppression] share the *same basic essence*, [that] they are built around the *same basic relationship*—that between oppressor and oppressed."[46] This requires us "to link oppressions in our minds, to look for the common shared aspects, and work against them as one."[47] Similarly, in her book *The Sexual Politics of Meat* (1989), Carol J. Adams argues that, upon closer examination, one can see that there is an intimate "relationship between violence against humans and violence against animals, including the direct relationship between child and animal abuse, and woman-battering and animal abuse";[48] thus, Adams's book focuses on "demonstrat[ing] the ways in which animals' oppression and women's oppression are linked together."[49]

Adams makes this connection of oppressions, most notably, through her concept of the "absent referent." With regard to the similar ontological position as Other that animals and women share, there exists "[a] struc-ture of overlapping but absent referents [that] links violence against women and animals"; this reveals, consequently, the fact that "patriarchal values [are] institutionalized."[50] Patriarchal ideological apparatuses, which work as an identification system of binary terms (man vs. animal, man vs. beast), simultaneously creates "man" as the ideal being (and also the ideal human), versus women and animals; this directly affects the attribution of "rights" to certain individuals—man existing, of course, as the entity that is privileged over all. All other groups are dialectically opposed to man in varying degrees of Otherness (but Otherness nonetheless). For instance, when evaluating the marginalized position of animals within the binary, "the experience of women ... becomes a vehicle for describing [these] oppressions. Women, upon whose bodies rape is most often committed, become the absent referent when the language of sexual violence is used metaphorically";[51] the linguistic violence of this metaphorical process, as a result, means that "women's experiences [are recalled] but not women."[52] When one describes the stripping of resources from a habitat, for example, one may talk about how a process of economic "necessity" has led to the "raping of the land." Here, the experience of a psychologically traumatic moment—and, importantly, a signifier of the violence directed towards women (and, of course, men, boys, and girls)—recalls, implicitly, the systematic patriarchal violence directed towards those deemed "objects."

This process of recalling an experience of one marginalized Other to describe the violence done to another Other is a circular process. Indeed, just as when violence directed toward or upon female bodies is used to describe the violence done toward nature and animals (the image of the "mad scientists," previously mentioned as a figure who looks to "tame" nature), "when women are the victims of violence, the treatment of animals is recalled."[53] Women, when treated as a sexualized object, for instance, may refer to themselves as being treated "like a piece of meat." This recalls, implicitly, the violence of a patriarchal ideology of economy that butchers animals for the consumer public. Of course, this violence that is done to "the animal" (body) is what is recalled, not the animals themselves (and, furthermore, the *individuality* of the animals is neglected, as they do not own that "privileged" position of being interpellated as singular "concrete" subjects located within an ideology, although, as previously explored, they are violently implicated within it).[54]

The patriarchal (linguistic) violence done to both animals and women through the structure of the absent referent can also be equally extended to another position of Otherness: the racialized Other; or, as Spiegel alludes, the slave. Indeed, Spiegel thoroughly explores the connection of the animal/ slavery metaphor in her book *The Dreaded Comparison*, where she states, in a mode very similar to Althusser, that a certain "obvious" ideological system has allowed "[m]asters [to] have built into society a long succession of supposed defenses and justifications for systems of oppression and slavery, designed to confound the public into complacency."[55] As a result, in recalling the violence done toward the racialized Other/slaves, as well as using the violence done toward these groups as metaphor for explaining other types of violence (women and animals), "a dialectic of absence and presence of oppressed groups occurs."[56] Similar to the recollection of animals and women, what is absent "has theoretical implications for class and race as well,"[57] and so there comes to exist a triad of oppressive identities (of which, importantly, "the animal" inhabits the lowest realm). Philip Armstrong also examines "the animal" and its connection to the postcolonial Other in his essay "The Postcolonial Animal" (2002), stating that "the definition of 'the animal' is inextricably bound up with the formation of other notions fundamental to the work of colonialism,"[58] where one can see the metaphor of a marginalized position at work. So, when one makes a comment that women's working conditions are similar to those of "slave labour," the systematic violence of the Western patriarchal apparatus with regard to *actual* slavery is brought to the forefront; the slaves as beings, however (or, more accurately, as "objects" within the apparatus), are forgotten.

Similarly, in her article "'The Beast Within': Race, Humanity, and Animality" (2000), Kay Anderson explores how Western conceptions of "animality" have, from the realm of nature, transgressed into social relations and, more specifically to her analysis, into the constructions of racialized Others as being "animal-like." She explores "the discursive production of social groups identified by their base drives, proximity to 'nature,' infantility, eroticism, and absence of civilized manners."[59] Such traits are, she explains, applicable to the "identity politics" of "various savage peoples, the mentally disordered, some women, and the so-called 'dangerous classes' who in different ways have been deemed either beyond, or potentially improved by, the cultivation of self-government."[60] Anderson, in a similar vein to Spiegel, Adams, and Armstrong, thus recognizes the dialectical employment of the (subordinate) identity of animals to describe the position of an "inferior" category of humans. Indeed, "animality has been a state of being to which whole categories of humans have been *referred back.*"[61] "The animal," devoid of a moral or ethical identity that rationalizes its subordinate position, has allowed for the "justifying [of] particular racist regimes."[62] Anderson then takes her framework of discursive practices working in and among political identities of "human" and "animal" to show how Central Australian aborigines, moving to Sydney to pursue new opportunities, were quickly conceived of as problematic in perniciously racist and animalistic terms, both of which served to reinforce each identity's existence as "inferior." She refers to the specific allusions of "indolence, promiscuity, drunkenness, and degeneracy"[63] that the aborigines embodied, resembling "early man";[64] not coincidentally, the aborigines were also referred to as "vermin"[65] and as constituting a "human zoo."[66] These identity labels are, as Anderson points out, dialectically oppositional to Western white peoples, individuals who are not a "savage peoples" (for they are civil and domesticated) or slave to animalistic instinct, and thus are not animals (for they have "control" of those "bestial desires"). In making this statement—a statement cannily similar to Prendick implicitly upholding a Humanist Law, a definition of human that *is not* animal—either implicitly or explicitly, the idea of a "superior" Western identity at once recognizes and absolves traits of the savage man with those of the animal; they are, in essence, for the Western white individual, traits of overlapping and common occurrence.

The Capital Subject

It becomes important to recognize that these particular discourses surrounding the marginalization of the (human and animal) body, which help to regulate and control it, ultimately exist within the (Western patriarchal) ideology of *capitalism*, or the mode of economy. The absent referent often refers to the *economic* object, as well as the economically and ontologically intersect position that women, the racial Other/slaves, and animals inhabit. Indeed, Foucault states that "[o]ne of the great innovations in the techniques of power . . . was the emergence of 'population' as an economic and political problem."[67] Spiegel, too, recognizes that "profitability" was the main motive for these discourses of power: "[t]he heightened *institutionalization* of oppression of blacks (in the form of legalized slavery), and animals (in factory farming and vivisection), can be attributed to the profit motive."[68] This was resituated within the ideas of "'humanism,' 'normality,' [and] 'quality of life'" that "were nothing but the vicissitudes of profitability."[69] It is apparent that the subjects—the sexualized human (especially women), the racialized Other, and animals—are different individual victims; they are, however, suppressed by *similar ideological systems of oppression* built around the motive of economy and, as a result, privilege.

Ultimately, this power of oppression works through the ideological institutions (or apparatuses) of a patriarchal ideology, which thus lead those "recognized" subjects (who always already "recognize" themselves as subjects) to internalize their position within a binary system. Indeed, the "ambitious" woman, the discontent slave, and "the animal" soon "learn[ed] that [they would] win approval . . . by suppressing [their] own desires and conforming to those of the omnipotent human [the white male] who legally owns [them]."[70] Those who didn't suppress their desires became "deviant" (see Foucault's notion of the "perverse implantation") and, therefore, problematic. However, the promise of "normality" through suppression of desire and subscription to a patriarchal system only serves to reinforce the permanent inferior placement of the Other (the complicit slave, the docile mastiff, and the passive, silent woman).

The Interpellated (?) Animal

The examination of "the animal" as Other, however, which shares this marginalized position with women and racialized Others, becomes problematic. Stephen Thierman examines the possibility of using the concept of Foucault's apparatus "to investigate another important facet of human life, namely, our interactions with other 'nonhuman' animals."[71] As previously examined, women and racial Others always are interpellated into their subordinate position within the Western patriarchal apparatus; they materially "practise" their placement, and thus internalize a certain "norm" of binary definitions, where they are opposed to the ideal subject that is man (man vs. women, man vs. racial Other, man vs. animal—essentially, man vs. not man).

But does it make sense to implicate animals within this ideological apparatus? Can animals inhabit the position of a subject-of-a-life—a "subject," rather than an "object," position? Thierman analyzes this precise question: "can we think of . . . animals as 'subjects' . . . as beings whose very existence is shaped and constituted by power in some significant way?"[72] Indeed, "the animal" within patriarchal ideology is constructed as being incapable of actively taking part in this process of ideological (self-)regulation. Yet, at the same time, "the animal" inhabits a position within the apparatus as a body subjected to a certain system that "creates" or "discovers" a "normal" or "perverse" being. For Foucault, the concept of biopower required, in the beginning, *confession*: that is, the constant discourse about one's desires, one's feelings, and so on. (Those who were incapable of confession, or who refused to confess, were, perhaps, the first problematic subjects—the first to "reveal" their own "perversity.") Telling someone about one's internal desires allowed for institutionalized regulation, as well as self-regulation; if a professional knows one to be "unhealthy," then certain regulations of power and control can be exercised on that individual—either through incarceration or a "cure," however that may be defined. This reveals a fundamental problem regarding "the animal": indeed, where is "the animal"

located, if it cannot negotiate within the framework of biopower, interpellation, and ideology in a "normativized" human-centred fashion?

In confronting this question, it is worth examining what Baudrillard
has to say about the "language of silence" of "the animal": "In a world bent
on doing nothing but making one speak, in a world assembled under the
hegemony of signs and discourse, their silence weighs more and more heavily on our organization of meaning."[73] That is, the inability of animals to
materially—through *human speech*—acknowledge their own "deviance"
problematizes our subordination of them; they neither "truly" reaffirm nor
reject our consensus of their Othered position. This animal "silence," then,
becomes deafening. Science as an apparatus looks to "destroy" the "animality" of "the animal" (see: Dr. Moreau): "Animals must be made to say
that they are not animals,"[74] and this is done in the "professional" context
of the lab, where "every day they deliver their 'objective' messages."[75] But
this fails. The animal silence seems to reflect the humanist values that we
ascribe to them, the values that present "the animal" as a body, an object of
scientific, economic knowledge discourse(s). As a result, the fragility of the
apparatus becomes apparent; the limit of the apparatus, "the animal" itself,
and its inability to be (ostensibly) absolutely recognized reveals a system
of meaning built on illusion (if it were not—if animals truly inhabited a
realm of inferiority in comparison to humans—would not the "true-to-it-
self" meaning, as Nietzsche calls it, become knowable for us?). Thus, "the
animal" rejects a possible subject position within, though animals continue to be subject to, the patriarchal apparatus, existing within a space that
the apparatus wants to deny. And though the problematic "silence" of the
animal exposes the ultimately illusory, unreal nature of the apparatus, the
real and material effects of this apparatus as an ideology become violently
apparent—indeed, animals become "useful" because they are a source of
"raw" (economic) materials.

Stephen Thierman, however, believes that the animal as an "object"
within this apparatus is more complicated. He states that animals "are
certainly subjected to our objective capacities, that is, they are modified,
used, consumed, and destroyed in a variety of ways";[76] but even with
that acknowledged, it remains difficult to "[characterize] them simply as
'things.'"[77] Rather, he contends that the existence of animals is "shaped and
constituted by power in some significant way."[78] But can—or should—we
accept this proposal? Though admittedly animals are "not inert objects
without the ability to react or respond,"[79] they are still trapped within a

fundamentally *anthropocentric* discourse of meaning, where they inevitably—indeed, necessarily—become a peripheral figure, one that appears to exist outside the human realm of moral consideration (among other things). Thus, the position of "the animal" within this patriarchal economic ideological apparatus sustains no "knowable," "solvable" position. It is not enough to imagine an animal implicated within a system in which it becomes an object of economic motive. But this does not mean there is not more to be done when examining this position. Indeed, in addressing Derrida's "the animal question," the discourses surrounding ecofeminism may offer invaluable insights.

New Ethic(s): An Ecofeminist Perspective

Though a relatively new social and political movement (the term was coined by French feminist Françoise d'Eaubonne in 1974),[80] ecofeminism has opened up new ways of thinking about feminist theory. Ecofeminism connects feminist thinking with ecology. It posits, as previously explored through the role of the absent referent, that patriarchal ideology and its apparatuses, which serve to oppress women and minority groups (including racialized minorities), are interconnected with the thinking that leads to the (material) exploitation of nature and the natural environment. As a result, woman, nature, and the racial Other become assigned to the category of Other in opposition to the superior position of man.

Ecofeminism thus recognizes the connection of oppression between minority groups. As previously examined, there is a clear (inter)connection between the subordinate status of women, the racial Other, and animals.[81] Indeed, ecofeminism importantly posits that the systems of oppression employed against both women and nature are *fundamentally similar*. And rather than conceptualizing and confronting the suppression of nature and women (as well as the racial Other) as separate, disconnected issues, ecofeminism stresses the importance—indeed, the necessity—of recognizing them as being inextricably intertwined. Birke brings attention to this very idea, highlighting Vandana Shiva's notion that "women engaged in survival struggles . . . are, simultaneously, [engaged in the] struggles for the protection of nature," which, as a result, reveals that "women and nature are intimately related, and their domination and liberations similarly linked."[82] To effectively tackle this inherently problematic relation (which, again, though a construction, has real and material effects), one must realize, as

Birke says, quoting Andrée Collard, that "feminist values and principles directed towards the ending of oppression of women are fundamentally linked to ecological values and principles directed towards ending the oppression of nature."[83] As a result, recognition of this construction, historically speaking, of woman *as* nature, nature as women, as well as the implication of the racial Other as being intertwined with this oppression, is required in order to expose and facilitate meaningful discourse.

Once the fundamentally similar systems of the oppression of women, the racialized Other, and animals are recognized and approached as such, then discourse surrounding a new kind of ethics—an "ethic(s) of care"—becomes possible. Such an ethic(s) was first conceptualized by Carol Gilligan, whose notion of an "ethic of care" identifies, as explained in Donovan and Adams' *The Feminist Care Tradition in Animal Ethics*, "a women's 'conception of morality' that is 'concerned with the activity of care . . . responsibility and relationships,'" as opposed to a men's 'conception of morality as fairness,' which is more concerned with 'rights and rules.'"[84] Such an approach to a world of unique, autonomous beings—both human *and* animal—emphasizes flexibility and responsibility, not merely abstract systems: indeed, such an ethics becomes "concerned with 'sustaining connection . . . keeping the web of relations intact."[85] That is, rather than a masculine ethics based on concerns "with rights, rules, and an abstract ideal of justice," this feminist approach "offers a more flexible, situational, and particularized ethic."[86] Diane Antonio, in her essay "Of Wolves and Women" (1995), explores an "ethics of care" firmly entrenched in Gilligan's philosophy. She succinctly describes what she believes such an ethics would look like: "Developing an ethic of care and respect toward nonhuman animals is a challenge to the feminist moral imagination. It will necessitate an examination of our relationship not only of the similarities underlying all animal life, but also the development of many new ways of relating to differences. Such an examination touches on the sources of racism and classism, for ecofeminism generally contends that moral failures of perception and imagination between human and nonhuman realms of nature are symptomatic of similar failures between men and women, races, and social classes."[87] This "ethics of care," then, challenges the patriarchal apparatus based upon a system of binary identification. No longer does identification—the very nature of our (recognized) being—rely on negative definition. Instead, differences between beings are celebrated, accepted, and become a focal point of positivity and new imagination.

It is important to note, however, the potential problems associated with developing a monolithic political identity for the explicit purpose of critiquing patriarchal suppression and, in response to it, re-envisioning a particular ethics associated with women, nature, and animals. In her important work, *The Good-Natured Feminist*, Catriona Sandilands clarifies and highlights the dangers of assuming an essentialist notion of identity in feminist liberal politics. Sandilands defines identity politics as the "attempt to create a politically coherent bridge across the empirical fact of a group's existence and its political representation as a group with a particular set of knowledges and experiences."[88] From a pragmatic standpoint, in a patriarchal system that reinforces the object position of particular entities through institutionalized ideological measures (i.e., the absent referent, slaughterhouses, slavery), the desire to bring together these similar experiences of exploitation to create an identity for resistance may appear attractive in its political potential. The danger in this practice, though, may lie in the very *desire* for resistance—a resistance that, due to the real and material effects of violent ontological differentiation, calls for immediate liberal action—based on ostensibly fundamental similarities. This desire relies upon a certain idealization of identity. Thus, identity in a political context ultimately "involves the construction of a story about the 'cause' of identity in which that identity must be seen as pre-political and specifically *not* constructed or chosen."[89] For women, racialized others, nature, animals, and so on, the similarity in the experiences of subjugation in an oppressive regime becomes that fundamental point of agreement from which to build essentialized connections.

However, this very process of monolithic identity production—and this is the key point—only reinforces precisely what these politics purport to challenge: the privileging of certain identities over others. Sandilands purports, importantly, that "no identity can ever fully capture the multiplicity of potential forms of meaning, nowhere more so than in the context of the broadening and deepening of points of political conflict."[90] The category "woman," for example, is a power-laden discursive site that constructs, and thus limits, ideas of what "actually" constitutes women. That is, because there exist many unique women's identities—lesbians, women of colour, working-class women, and so on—to conceive of identity as a fixed concept relies upon differentiations and exclusions, not only of certain identities, but also of their associated vested political interests. This process becomes even more problematic when one considers that nature and animals, which do not have a "voice" in the traditional sense (i.e., the human voice), are *spoken for* in a liberal initiative (or any initiative, for that matter). Indeed, animals, or "the animal," may have an identity constructed as a means to an end for a particular feminist political goal; the political and moral interests of the animals, or "the animal," may thus be forgotten or, worse, ignored. It is therefore important to understand that identities are a particular construction used to further the ends of particular political initiatives; this understanding, furthermore, highlights identity as a certain "doing" or "practice" that falls under the same exclusionary practices that patriarchal ideology relies upon.

However, even with the problems associated with essentialized identities, there is at least a movement towards rethinking the very ethical paradigms which have, so far, developed an arbitrary hierarchy that privileges certain ontologies. Understanding an ethics of care that focuses on the individual, the question is thus no longer, as Prendick in Well's *The Island of Dr. Moreau* puts it, "man or beast," but "man *and* beast"; it is no longer "one or the other" but "one *and* the other." Again, such a notion cannot rely on a *system* , an ultimately illusory and depersonalizing process, but a personal one. Indeed, as Antonio highlights further, we must "agree that our emotional attachments to individual animals and species are moral realities that need to be illuminated."[91] Personal relationships, then—which rely on this emotional connection that recognizes and respects both similarities *and* differences—have "to be forged out of the stuff of our own experience with an individual animal or out of a concrete situation in nature, such as imminent species extinction."[92] Of course, such a philosophy, set aside in favour of dominating masculine systems, takes time to understand and implement, but at the very least it is a step in the right direction for an ethical or moral system that looks to be more inclusive, that does not ignore the individual, but does away with the dialect of "massification" that allows for the suppression of feelings of guilt to rationalize and perpetrate horrors onto others. Rather, such a notion emphasizes the individual, the relationship individuals have with other individuals, and how care, trust, and mutual respect come to be at the forefront of such relationships. When one takes seriously these ideas, concepts, and realities, and puts them into practice, then a step into rethinking both "the animal" and "the human" in a posthumanist way will be possible.

Posthumanism: A Question of Continuum

Posthumanism can be understood, in one of its definitions, as a movement that attempts "to . . . critique . . . humanism, emphasizing a change
in our understanding of the self and its relations to the natural world,
society, and human artifacts"; at the same time, it also advocates for the
"develop[ment]—in ways that are safe and ethical—[of] technological
means that will enable the exploration of the posthuman realm of possible modes of being."[93] That is, posthumanism looks to break out of this
categorical means of identification, and looks to explore being as a continuum, one that transcends our preconceived, constructed, and arbitrary categories of identification, which have had very real and violent
(material) effects.[94] As Cary Wolfe asks, can we "respond to the redefin-
ition of humanity's place in the world by both the technological and the
biological or 'green' continuum in which the 'human' is but one life form
among many?"[95] Indeed, this question becomes one of necessity when
confronting and re-examining both "the animal question" as well as "the
human question" (including their traditional interdependence) from a
perspective of both ecofeminism and posthumanism, movements that are
connected in their goals of change and liberation from the institutionalized violence that occurs within the apparatus.

In trying to renegotiate the position of "the animal," however, there
is a danger in naïvely assuming we can work in a context separate from
the patriarchal/anthropocentric ideological frameworks that we as subjects
currently reside within—that of a posthumanist perspective, where we may
attempt to imagine the unimaginable. We may, for instance, try to conceptualize "[the subject of the animal that] relies on the fantasy of a subject
who escapes the constitutive blindness[96] (that is, the contingency and selec-
tivity) that in fact makes knowledge possible."[97] That is, the posthumanist
may want to (re)imagine the (newly identified) animal as being *outside* the
realm of (ideological) science and "truth," creating the "ideal" animal figure
as something removed from this anthropocentric discourse. Ideologically
speaking, however, this becomes impossible, for, as Althusser contends,
"[i]deology *has no outside* (for itself), but at the same time . . . *it is nothing
but outside* (for science and reality)."[98] Cary Wolfe also acknowledges this
impossibility when he says that "[t]he 'post-' of posthumanism does not
(and, moreover, cannot) mark or make an absolute break from the legacy
of humanism."[99] To do so, or to make this the goal of posthumanism, is to

bring our ideas and conceptions right back into a humanist mode of thinking—it falls back into that "either/or" system of "distinctive" categories. That
is, our models of knowledge and truth rely on already identifiable systems
of knowledge, and so we are forced to work with the conceptual apparatus
within these systems. So does the question of "the animal" become possible
in the current (humanist) ideological framework? While there is no answer
to this, it does reveal certain fragilities—certain possibilities—in the system
(including, perhaps, the significance of the "the" in "the animal"). Through
a posthumanist and ecofeminist lens, which aids in exposing the ultimately
arbitrary systems and institutions of the patriarchal apparatus, we can begin
to work within the aporias that these systems fundamentally rely upon for
points of resistance.

Conclusion

Because the question of "the animal"—a definition inextricably bound up
with "the human"—is implicated in a patriarchal ideological apparatus that
relies on systems and institutions of binary meaning and ontological hierarchy, a closer examination of these features of ideology becomes instruct-
ive. As "human" subjects, we are interpellated into a particular (economic)
ideology, which "calls" us, through a variety of interconnected systems
within an ideological (economic) apparatus, into being as "recognizable,"
"concrete," "individualized," and "naturalized" entities. This relies on a certain binary system of meaning, based on negative definition—man is *not* an
animal/woman/racialized Other. With regard to "the animal," however, this
process of interpellation becomes incredibly complex for two reasons. First,
"the animal" represents the limit of definitional possibility in this apparatus,
as revealed through the use of the absent referent. Indeed, "the animal" and
"the animal experience" inhabit the lowest position, or the periphery, of the
ontological hierarchy, and thus "the animal experience" becomes a metaphor for the oppressed experience of both women and racialized minorities
(and vice versa), as well as other Others; there is, importantly, no experience "beyond" "the animal." Second, "the animal" seems to inhabit two
positions simultaneously within the apparatus: that of "object," and that of
the "quasi-subject." The animal becomes an "object" of economy—literally
"a body", as Foucault describes, through the apparatus of biopower—and
so serves the consuming public. At the same time, however, for this process to "create" and maintain that body as an economic object, "the animal"

is "endowed" with a psychic life, so as to create a "perverse" body (was it not already perverse to the human?) and a "normal" body that can both be regulated. Thus, "the animal" was and is "discovered" to have suicidal traits, which could be regulated and controlled (much like the "deviant" characters of sexuality; see Chapter 1, page 34, on the animal's perceived willingness to be sacrificed).[100] This liminal, impossible positioning of "the animal," then, reveals the fragile (arbitrary and illusory) foundation upon which the patriarchal apparatus is built.

As a result, "the animal" opens up the aporias of this patriarchal (economic) apparatus—it renders the ideological system to critical exposure. Ecofeminism, as a particular social and political movement, recognizes that this arbitrary system does have real and material effects: such an analysis identifies this through the fundamental similarities of the patriarchal ideological systems that are used to subordinate groups of Otherness. While ecofeminist political initiatives, like some other feminist liberal groups, may problematically engage with identity essentialism, ecofeminism nonetheless recognizes, importantly, that to tackle the issue of subordination is to tackle *all* subordination, and so the movement of liberation requires cooperation between all groups—including that of "dominant man." Indeed, while some have critiqued the focus on the morality surrounding animals and animal issues—they ask, don't humans around the world face enough injustices that have yet to be resolved?—the salient notion here is that these injustices, all part of an underlying rationality, can and must be tackled, conceptually and materially, at once. Part of this process is to recognize the importance of an "ethic(s) of care": the acknowledgement of emotion *and* rationality (as opposed to the traditional, masculine realm of reason alone) as modes of feeling–thinking in order to work towards this goal. This requires a personalizing process—as opposed to *systems* and *institutions*—where personal, emotional relationships are made and where differences as well as similarities are celebrated and respected. Thus, it becomes human *and* animal (as opposed to *or*). If this occurs, then, from a posthumanist perspective, it will allow for a radical reconceptualization and transformation of both "the human" and "the animal." Consequently, this movement also asks us to redefine our ideologies (and what "us" includes) into ways that allow for a more sustainable future for all.

NOTES

1. Wells, *Doctor Moreau*, 100.
2. Christensen, "'Bestial Mark' of Race."
3. Vint, "Animals and Animality."
4. Kelly Oliver discusses some of the ways in which this (pre)ordained superiority over the natural and animal Other has been rationalized by the human: "In the history of philosophy, the necessity of human existence has been justified with appeals to an eternal realm of forms or reason, divine providence or design, nature or natural laws, and perhaps the most influential alternative to the hand of God: the hand of Nature through the law of natural selection. What these religious or secular accounts of the origin of man share is their insistence on necessity over chance, providence over accident. Man's existence is preordained by God or Nature; it is *not* an accident." *Animal Lessons*, 2 (emphasis in original).
5. Matthew Calarco—whose brief analysis of Heidegger's metaphysics regarding animals' negative definitional relationality to humans can be found in Peter Atterton and Matthew Calarco's *Animal Philosophy*—defines "anthropocentrism" as I conceive of it in this essay: "By anthropocentrism I mean simply the dominant tendency within the Western metaphysical tradition to determine the essence of animal life by the measure of, and in opposition to, the human." *Animal Philosophy*, 29.
6. Wells, *Doctor Moreau*, 78.
7. Ibid., 120.
8. Ibid., 78. The spectre of "degeneration on a larger scale" that haunts Prendick—and, perhaps, the entire humanist tradition—is twofold. Prendick fears a "regression" of his fellow humans back to a "bestial state," a transfiguration of the "recognizably" human to something other, some Other. This anxiety, however, is also enveloped with the "desecration" of the very ideology that Prendick clings to for his very identity—the same "desecration" whose occurrence he witnessed happen with the Beast People, where the explicit imposition of Montgomery's Law degrades into the realm of arbitrary obscurity from which it was first summoned. This degradation becomes a mirror, then, of the potential disruption to all such ideological laws.
9. Prendick's trouble understanding what he is confronted with in the Beast Men is indeed uncanny, in the sense in which Andrew Bennett and Nicholas Royle define it: "'the uncanny' has to do with a *troubling* of definitions, with a fundamental disturbance of what we think and feel. The uncanny has to do with a sense of strangeness, mystery or eeriness. More particularly it concerns a sense of unfamiliarity which appears at the very heart of the familiar, or

else a sense of familiarity which appears at the very heart of the unfamiliar."
Introduction to Literature, 34; original emphasis. Throughout the novel, an
intermingling of the human and animal continuously arises, distorting and
defying Prendick's ability to understand, define, or comprehend these creatures
in a rationalist fashion.

10. Wells, *Doctor Moreau*, 101.

11. Ibid., 100–101.

12. Ibid., 101. Advertisement posters of William Henry Johnson, better known
as "Zip the Pinhead," a famous freak performer in P.T. Barnum's circus
shows, asked a similar question: "What Is It?" This question, then, materially
embodied as a spectacle—Johnson as the "freak"—is a literal performance of
the anthropocentric desire for the either/or distinction.

13. Of course, as critical feminist discourse puts forth, the "human" is an ever-
present complex, dynamic binary in and of itself (man/woman, black/white,
etc.). In each binary, the "superior" entity within these dualisms—those
usually on the left side of the slash—invokes power over the "inferior" Other.
Val Plumwood (*Environmental Culture*, 4) describes this general relationship
in terms, specifically in her analysis, of culture and nature: "Rationalism and
human/nature dualism have helped create ideals of culture and human identity
that promote human distance from, control of and ruthlessness towards the
sphere of nature as the Other, while minimizing non-human claims to the
earth and to elements of mind, reason and ethical consideration."

14. Hearing the cries of the Puma Man in the adjacent room, Prendick
contemplates language as a marker of "humanness," and thus as a marker of
ethical and moral significance: "The crying [of the Puma] sounded louder
out of doors. It was if all the pain in the world *had found a voice*. Yet had I
known such pain was in the next room, and had it been dumb, I believe—I
have thought since—I could have stood it well enough. *It is when suffering
finds a voice and sets our nerves quivering that this pity becomes troubling to us*"
(*Doctor Moreau*, 97; emphasis added). Later on, Prendick comes face to face
with another creature, but his response to it is quite different from the other
Beast Men—precisely due to the creature's capacity for language: "I did not
feel the same repugnance towards this creature which I had experienced in my
encounters with the other Beast Men. 'You,' he [the creature] said, 'in the boat.'
He was a man, then—at least as much as a man as Montgomery's attendant—
for he could talk" (110; emphasis added).

15. Ibid., 173.

16. Oliver's fascinating analysis of how philosophers Jean-Jacques Rousseau and
Johann Gottfried Herder define the human by the human relationship *to*
animals is particular enlightening here: "In . . . passages in which they delineate
what distinguishes man from animals, both Rousseau and Herder turn to

animals to illuminate their arguments. Their animals do not merely serve as examples against which they define man. Rather, these animals belie the very distinction between man and animal that their invocation seeks to establish. . . . [T]he examples and metaphors of animals that inhabit these texts ape or mock assertions of any uniquely human characteristics (*Animal Lessons*, 2). Prendick, in his attempt to uphold a particular definition of the human, relies on a cannily similar method of (unconscious or blind) reasoning: that is, he attempts to uphold the definition and value of the (constructed) human through precisely its (constructed) opposite in the animal Other, though this apparently indelible requirement eludes his rationalization.

17. Nietzsche, "Truth and Lying," 262.
18. Oliver: "By uncovering the latent humanism in antihumanist texts, we continue to witness the ambivalence toward animality and animals that has *defined* Western philosophy and culture. This ambivalence is all the more striking in these philosophies of ambivalence. The very psychoanalytic notion of ambivalence itself is linked to the history of using and disavowing animals. Engaging with animal figures in these texts, however, reveals the *dependence of man, human, humanity, and subjectivity on animal, animals, and animality.* Looking to animals in these texts can help us acknowledge our *dependence on animals on all levels of our existence, physical, imaginary, and symbolic*" (*Animal Lessons*, 5; emphasis added). As Oliver's analysis of Rousseau, Herder, and Heidegger (among others) points to, as well as Prendick's attempt to differentiate the Beast Men from "actual humans," "the animal" is indispensable to the human in terms of (human) identity and the humanist systems and hierarchies employed in world epistemologies.
19. Derrida, in Derrida and Roudinesco, *For What Tomorrow*, 62.
20. Althusser, "Ideology," 693.
21. Plumwood effectively outlines the notion of an "economic rationalism," inextricably linked to the patriarchal tradition, that this essay addresses as the primary ideology: "Some have termed the application of the rationalist agenda in the economic sphere 'economic rationalism,' but it has also been called 'economism,' 'neo-liberalism,' 'laissez-faire economics,' 'economic fundamentalism,' and more recently 'extreme' or 'turbo-capitalism'. . . . Economic rationalism has replaced the classical warrior of earlier rationalism by the corporate warrior of the global economy. It establishes their privilege through the subordination of all other aspects of social life to the form of economic organization controlled by corporations and loaded in their favor, the rationalist 'free-market.' The market is portrayed as a detached, disengaged, supremely rational mechanism, free from 'irrational' interference, as the supreme social end and the measure of worth ('efficiency') of other social ends. But it can only appear in this neutral and dispassionate guise as 'rational

machinery' *because the historical social relations that have selected its rules and established its cast of players in far from neutral ways have disappeared from view.* Once this abstraction from historical reality has been achieved the culture of market rationalism can proclaim the supremacy of the market as the ultimately fair and rational way of ordering life" (*Environmental Culture*, 22; emphasis added). In this present ideology, subjects come to trust the "rational" of the market system—it becomes the dominant mode of thoughts, beliefs, and actions—and so the ways in which we as subjects interact with and within life, from the micro to macro, all contribute in some way or another to the system of capital and profit.

22. Badmington, *Posthumanism*, 9.
23. Ibid.
24. Althusser, "Ideology," 694.
25. Stephen Thierman, quoting Foucault, explains this idea clearly: "power [can]not be conceived of abstractly, or as a possession that exists apart from individuals that they can decide to retain or alienate" ("Apparatuses of Animality," 97). It is essential to note that those perpetrating this violence are themselves victims in an ideology of difference that inevitably leads to ontological hierarchies with real (non)privileges.
26. Althusser, "Ideology," 693–94. To understand this relationship of ideology being an illusion of/allusion to reality, one must first carefully distinguish the differences between Althusser's concepts of "objective science" and the "ideology of science": "objective science" posits that there exists a certain objective reality that works outside the confines of ideology and the subject; this "objective science," however, is absolutely unknowable to us as subjects, and is hence referred to by Althusser as a "subject-less discourse" (698). The "ideology of science," on the other hand, can be referred to as a "subjective" science: it is what we as subjects perform in the way of experiments, observations, recordings, and other such measures that are within a certain (ideological) scientific discourse.
27. Ibid., 694.
28. Ibid., 695.
29. Ibid., 696.
30. Ibid., 698.
31. Questions of interpellation, subjectivity, and the notion of "obviousness" come to be a, if not *the*, major critical intervention with regard to the position of "the animal" within this patriarchal discourse. Stephen Thierman analyzes this precise question: "can we think of . . . animals as 'subjects' . . . as beings whose very existence is shaped and constituted by power in some significant way?" ("Apparatuses of Animality," 97). As Althusser importantly recognizes,

the transparency of *language* comes to play the elementary role in how we conceive of "the animal" within this apparatus, for it is the ability to have/use language, or at least what is recognized *as language* by humans, that excludes "the animal" from human consideration.

32. Foucault, *History of Sexuality*, 18.
33. Thierman, "Apparatuses of Animality," 90.
34. Foucault, *History of Sexuality*, 26.
35. Ibid., 37.
36. Ibid., 38.
37. Baudrillard, "Animals," 136–37.
38. Ibid., 132.
39. Nietzsche, "Truth and Lying," 264.
40. Nietzsche, *Thus Spoke Zarathustra* (Walter Kaufmann trans.), in Atterton and Calarco, *Animal Philosophy*, 3.
41. Foucault, *History of Sexuality*, 60.
42. Nietzsche, *Daybreak* (R.J. Hollingdale, trans.), in Atterton and Calarco, *Animal Philosophy*, 4.
43. Baudrillard, "Animals," 138.
44. Nietzsche, "Truth and Lying," 264.
45. Here, I consider "the animal" as an entity of "nature" more broadly. "Nature," of course, has many ontological forms; from a patriarchal perspective, these various forms may be organized into particular hierarchies, though I do not explore this idea here.
46. Spiegel, *Dreaded Comparison*, 28 (emphasis added).
47. Ibid., 30.
48. Adams, *Sexual Politics*, 20.
49. Ibid., 25. It is worth mentioning that, specifically within second-wave feminist thought, some feminists wished to mitigate the connection of subordination between women and animals in the political pursuit of achieving equal rights for women (versus, and in line with, men). But as Adams, among others, explains, the explicit acceptance of such a connection is imperative in order for any and all forms of such conceptual and material violence to be effectively deconstructed. Such a recognition and acceptance is, I believe, a maturing of the feminist position into a more significant and effective movement.
50. Ibid., 67.
51. Ibid., 68.
52. Ibid.
53. Ibid.
54. Josephine Donovan and Carol J. Adams explore the significance of the "massification" of individuals—of individual animals, of individual racialized

Others, and so on—as a process that allows for the transformation of uniquely singular beings into a dialectical (and thus, in the way it is conceived, a materially real) object; this, in turn, frees the oppressors from feelings of guilt: "Their [animals,' but also any other Others'] 'massification' allows our [the oppressor's] release from empathy. We cannot imagine ourselves in a situation where our 'I-ness' counts for nothing. We cannot imagine the 'not-I' of life as a mass term" (Adams, "War on Compassion," 24, in Donovan and Adam's *Feminist Care Tradition*). Donovan and Adams extend this idea, appropriately, to the genocide in Rwanda: "To kill a large number of people efficiently, the killers succeed when they have made the people they are targeting into a mass term. Philip Gourevitch . . . : 'What distinguishes genocide from murder, and even from acts of political murder that claim as many victims, is the intent. The crime is wanting to make a people extinct. The idea is the crime. No wonder it's so difficult to picture. To do so you must accept the principle of the exterminator, and see not people, but *a people*'" (ibid.; emphasis added).

55. Spiegel, *Dreaded Comparison*, 103.
56. Adams, *Sexual Politics*, 69.
57. Ibid.
58. Armstrong, "Postcolonial Animal," 414.
59. Anderson, "'Beast Within,'" 302.
60. Ibid.
61. Ibid., 310 (emphasis in original).
62. Ibid.
63. Ibid., 314.
64. Ibid.
65. Ibid., 315.
66. Ibid., 316.
67. Foucault, *History of Sexuality*, 25.
68. Spiegel, *Dreaded Comparison*, 83.
69. Ibid., 131.
70. Ibid., 41.
71. Thierman, "Apparatuses of Animality," 91.
72. Ibid., 97.
73. Baudrillard, "Animals," 137.
74. Ibid., 129.
75. Ibid., 137.
76. Thierman, "Apparatuses of Animality," 99.
77. Ibid., 99.
78. Ibid., 77.

79. Ibid., 98.

80. Sandilands, *Good-Natured Feminist*, 6.

81. Importantly, some feminists believe that focusing on the rights of animals may direct attention away from the ultimate goal of female liberation from a patriarchal system. Adams responds: "I have met and corresponded with animal advocates around the world who are immersed in forwarding both issues (of female and animal oppression) since *they recognize how intertwined they are*" (*Sexual Politics*, 21; emphasis added).

82. Birke, *Feminism, Animals*, 24.

83. Ibid., 23.

84. Donovan and Adams, *Feminist Care Tradition*, 2.

85. Ibid.

86. Ibid.

87. Antonio, "Wolves and Women," 213.

88. Sandilands, *Good-Natured Feminist*, 29.

89. Ibid., 40–41.

90. Ibid., 46.

91. Antonio, "Wolves and Women," 217.

92. Ibid., 214.

93. Bostrom, *Posthumanism*.

94. It should be noted that posthumanism is a mode of understanding, not a means to the end of violence and oppression. Rather, a *subsiding* of violence over time, such as that which has been explored in this article, would be a possible result of a posthumanist understanding.

95. Wolfe, "What Is Posthumanism?"

96. The concept of "blindness" to which Wolfe refers is derived from Paul de Man's *Blindness and Insight*, originally published in 1971. De Man's metaphorical use of "blindness," in his examination of Maurice Blanchot, Georges Poulet, and others, is outlined succinctly in de Man's forward to his seminal text: "In all of them [literary critics] a paradoxical discrepancy appears between the general statements they make about the nature of literature (statements on which they base their critical methods) and the actual results of their interpretations. Their findings about the structure of texts contradict the general conception that they use as their model. Not only do they remain unaware of this discrepancy, but they seem to thrive on it and owe their best insights to the assumptions these insights disprove" (*Blindness and Insight*, ix).

97. Wolfe, "'Animal Studies,'" 117.

98. Althusser, "Ideology," 700.

99. Quoting Neil Badmington, Wolfe, "'Animal Studies,'" 121.

100. See Baudrillard's "Animals."

BIBLIOGRAPHY

Adams, Carol J. *The Sexual Politics of Meat: A Feminist-Vegetarian Critical Theory.* Twentieth Anniversary Edition. New York: Continuum Publishing, 2010.

——. "The War on Compassion." In *The Feminist Care Tradition in Animal Ethics: A Reader,* edited by Josephine Donovan and Carol J. Adams, 21–36. New York: Columbia University Press, 2007.

——. "Woman-Battering and Harm to Animals." In *Animals and Women: Feminist Theoretical Explorations,* edited by Carol J. Adams and Josephine Donovan, 55–84. Durham, NC: Duke University Press, 1995.

Althusser, Louis. "Ideology and Ideological State Apparatuses." In *Literary Theory: An Anthology,* 693–702. Edited by Julie Rivkin and Michael Ryan. Cambridge: Blackwell, 2004.

Anderson, Kay. "'The Beast Within': Race, Humanity, and Animality." *Environment and Planning D: Society and Space* 18 (2000): 301–20. Accessed July 4, 2012. doi:10.1068/d229.

Antonio, Diane. "Of Wolves and Women." In *Animals and Women: Feminist Theoretical Explorations,* edited by Carol J. Adams and Josephine Donovan, 213–30. Durham, NC: Duke University Press, 1995.

Armstrong, Philip. "The Postcolonial Animal." *Society & Animals* 10, no. 4 (2002): 413–17.

Atterton, Peter, and Matthew Calarco. *Animal Philosophy: Ethics and Identity.* New York: Bloomsbury Academic, 2004.

Badmington, Neil, ed. *Posthumanism.* New York: Palgrave, 2000.

Baudrillard, Jean. "The Animals: Territory and Metamorphoses." In *Simulacra and Simulation,* 129–41. Translated by Sheila Faria Glaser. Ann Arbour: University of Michigan, 1994.

Bennett, Andrew and Nicholas Royle. *Introduction to Literature, Criticism and Theory.* 3rd ed. Harlow, Essex: Longman, 2004.

Birke, Lynda. "Exploring the Boundaries: Feminism, Animals, and Science." In *Animals and Women: Feminist Theoretical Explorations,* edited by Carol J. Adams and Josephine Donovan, 32–54. Durham, NC: Duke University Press, 1995.

——. *Feminism, Animals and Science: The Naming of the Schrew.* Buckingham: Open University Press, 1994.

——. "Intimate Familiarities? Feminism and Human–Animal Studies." In *Society & Animals* 10, no. 4 (2002): 429–36.

Bostrom, Nick. *Posthumanism.* Accessed April 1, 2011. http://www.posthumanism .com/.

Christensen, Timothy. "The 'Bestial Mark' of Race in *The Island of Dr. Moreau.*" *Criticism* 46, no. 4 (2004): 575–95.

de Man, Paul. *Blindness and Insight: Essays in the Rhetoric of Contemporary Criticism,* 102–41. Minneapolis: University of Minnesota Press, 1971.

Derrida, Jacques, and Elisabeth Roudinesco. *For What Tomorrow . . .: A Dialogue.* Translated by Jeff Fort. Stanford: Stanford University Press, 2004.

Donovan, Josephine. "Animal Rights and Feminist Theory." *Signs* 15, no. 2 (1990): 350–75.

Donovan, Josephine, and Carol J. Adams. *The Feminist Care Tradition in Animal Ethics: A Reader.* New York: Columbia University Press, 2007.

Foucault, Michel. *The History of Sexuality.* New York: Vintage Books, 1988.

Haraway, Donna. "A Manifesto for Cyborgs: Science, Technology, and Socialist Feminism in the 1980s." In *The Haraway Reader,* 7–46. New York: Routledge, 2004.

Mies, Maria, and Vandana Shiva. *Ecofeminism.* Halifax, NS: Fernwood, 1993.

Nietzsche, Freidrich. "On Truth and Lying in an Extra-moral Sense." In *Literary Theory: An Anthology,* edited by Julie Rivkin and Michael Ryan, 262–65. Cambridge: Blackwell, 2004.

Oliver, Kelly. *Animal Lessons: How They Teach Us to Be Human.* New York: Columbia University Press, 2009.

Plumwood, Val. *Environmental Culture: The Ecological Crisis of Reason.* New York: Routledge, 2002.

Sandilands, Catriona. *The Good-Natured Feminist: Ecofeminism and the Quest for Democracy.* Minneapolis: University of Minnesota Press, 1999.

——. "Mother Earth, the Cyborg, and the Queer: Ecofeminism and (More) Questions of Identity." *NWSA Journal* 9, no. 3 (1997): 18–40.

Spiegel, Marjorie. *The Dreaded Comparison: Human and Animal Slavery.* New York: Mirror Books, 1996.

Thierman, Stephen. "Apparatuses of Animality: Foucault Goes to a Slaughterhouse." *Foucault Studies* 9 (2010): 89–110.

Vint, Sherryl. "Animals and Animality from the Island of Moreau to the Uplift Universe." *Yearbook of English Studies* 9, no. 3 (1997): 85–102.

Wells, H.G. *The Island of Doctor Moreau.* 1896. Edited by Mason Harris. Toronto: Broadview, 2009.

Wolfe, Cary. "'Animal Studies,' Disciplinarity, and the (Post)Humanities." In *What Is Posthumanism?*, 99–126. Minneapolis: University of Minnesota Press, 2010.

——. "What Is Posthumanism?," University of Minnesota Press website. Accessed May 28, 2016. https://www.upress.umn.edu/book-division/books/what-is-posthumanism.

5

Animal Narrativity

Engaging with Story in a
More-Than-Human World

-◆-▷-━◐ ◑━-◁-◆-

Joshua Russell

Canadian poet and scholar Robert Bringhurst writes:

> Each of us tells stories, and each of us is a story. Not just each of us
> humans, but each of us creatures—spruce trees and toads and timber
> wolves and dog salmon. We all tell stories to ourselves and to each
> other—within the tribe, within the species, and way beyond its bounds.
> Roses do this when they flower, finches when they sing, and humans
> when they speak, walk, sing, dance, swim, play a flute, build a fire, or
> pull a trigger.[1]

What does this passage suggest about the presence of stories within a
more-than-human world? At first glance, it suggests that stories abound
in the natural world within the voices, movements, and embodiments of
myriad living beings. Looking deeper, however, the quote plays with the
hubris of thinking *Homo sapiens* to be a being apart from the rest of nature.
Human exceptionalism is often based on strict notions of language, cognition, and future-thinking, all aspects of narrative as it is traditionally
understood in humanist terms. I want to propose a wider notion of narrative thinking, one that takes our encounters with other beings and their
storied existences seriously. Bringhurst's quote above suggests that stories—not simply linguistic objects but unfolding, living, and communicative

happenings—exist within a vast ecology of sights, sounds, and movements. All creatures live within "a net of stories and interconnections from which, even in death, there is no escape."[2] The bodies, minds, and relations of living beings as well as the non-living processes on which they depend provide multiple kinds of dwelling places within which stories are cultivated, thrive, evolve, and presumably pass away. Still, on the supposedly "enlightened" side of the chasm between human and animal, *Homo sapiens* remains the sole proprietor of narrative, the only being capable of perceiving stories and of spinning a tale.

This chapter challenges the assumption that narrative is a capacity that distances humans from all other animals and from the natural world. In order to broaden the scope of narrative thinking, I will investigate a phenomenon I am calling "animal narrativity." Animal narrativity describes the qualitative, felt sense that stories are present in animal bodies, gestures, and relationships. It also situates narrative within the more-than-human world, rather than categorizing it as a uniquely human characteristic. In what follows, I explore what it means to think of narrativity as part of our own animality, a process through which we participate in multi-species relationships and communities. Animal narrativity attends to a heterogeneous spectrum of animality, acknowledging that stories abound in a wide web of otherness, among individuals, communities, and between species. I argue that stories emerge from the bodies and minds of creatures in relation with each other: that beginnings, endings, and complex causal chains or plots abound in the world. How such stories are perceived and what meanings they convey are matters of epistemic and ethical importance, and the narratives created by storytelling creatures—of which humans may be just one—impact the lives of beings in relational space profoundly. I also argue that narrative imagination, as a response to animal stories, provides a potent way of engaging with other kinds of being, paving the way for ethical actions toward the creatures with which we share our world. In the same way, it is through failings of narrative imagination that we perpetrate and are complicit in the continued suffering and deaths of other beings.[3]

Throughout this chapter, I focus in particular on the narrativity of animal deaths. Some of the stories below are personal, while others arise in various forms of visual media and literature, and some stories are actually shared by other animals. This focus on animal death is intentional, as death is a challenging theme in Western thinking, not only about animals but about language and narrative as well. On the one hand, the experience of death has been repeatedly denied to other animals on the shaky premise that they are incapable of contemplating their own mortality. Exploring the murky relation between animality, language, and death has the profound effect of bringing us "face to face with the inadequacies of our language, or at least with the rational and logical thinking it enables."[4] As such, I find stories of animal death to be particularly generative for an investigation of animal narrativity, for the sense that certain experiences, beings, and even entire lifetimes are recognized as having a "greater degree of 'narrativeness' than" others. Whose actions, lives, and deaths are recognized as possessing narrativity, and whose stories are overlooked, forgotten, or silenced drives this investigation. In addition, inspired by the narrative work of Richard Kearney, I also wonder: How are we to respond to other beings we encounter in this world full of stories?

To begin, I would like to share a story of my own.

Beginning with an Ending: A Dog Dies

A typical post-Christmas drive back home to Toronto is generally nothing special. With our dog, Penny, in the back seat next to piles of new books and clothes, my partner and I drive through the wintry landscape of southern Ontario. The scenery is quite pleasant, as the Queen Elizabeth Way cuts through vineyards, along the Niagara Escarpment, and parallel to the shores of Lake Ontario. We try to avoid large crowds, but the traffic always picks up about forty-five minutes outside of Toronto, where you'll find plenty of white-knuckle stretches of highway driving before even glimpsing the big city skyline with its iconic CN tower.

Any time I am outdoors, I have a propensity to look out for wildlife. Ever since I was a child, I have always been highly attuned to the possibility of seeing other creatures, and riding or driving in cars leads to many good sightings. Wintertime is particularly good for spotting red-tailed hawks, as the leafless trees cannot always mask their feathery masses sitting stoically on branches right above the roadside. I also typically keep a rather haphazard tally of roadkill: raccoons, squirrels, birds, skunks, deer, and on rare occasions snakes or porcupines. Those who ride with me would tell you I often frown at these sights and sometimes I lament the unfathomable numbers of wild animals that must be killed on roads around the world each year.[5] Sometimes, I try to imagine what that particular animal's life was like, or how it may have experienced its last few moments.

On a particular drive home, we were witness to a tragic event. The landscape, typically a blend of whites, blues, and grays in winter, was painted from a palette of yellows and browns on account of the uncharacteristic lack of snowfall. A stopped police car about a kilometre ahead of us drew our attention before it turned off its flashing lights and drove away. We noticed cars pulling into the right hand lane and as we approached the scene I saw a yellow flash dart across the road. The truck ahead of us pulled onto the shoulder and so did I. When I was close enough I noticed that the flash was, in fact, a dog—a yellow lab—covered in mud, running along the grassy median. She was hard to make out from afar, as her golden fur blended in seamlessly against the background of dead reeds and grasses. The men in the truck ahead of us, dressed in coveralls and flannel coats, jumped out and began calling to her. I slowed down to stop behind them, rolled my window down, and began calling and whistling. The dog glanced at each of us before she began to pick up her pace and head in the opposite direction. She looked frantically over both shoulders, clearly frightened. My partner jumped out of the car and began whistling toward the dog, but it was too late; she panicked and ran across the road. We lost sight of her amid a group of oncoming cars. I looked away in shock with my shoulders scrunched up to my ears and my hands tightly gripping the steering wheel. I sat in silence with my eyes closed for a few moments, before I noticed the driver of the truck in front of me shouting loudly and cursing. "How could they hit that poor dog??" He was outraged that the oncoming drivers did not stop or avoid the dog, but the events happened so quickly and the moment had now passed.

When I turned back to look, I saw that the dog was not yet dead. Pulling herself forward with her front legs, she was struggling to drag her clearly paralyzed back legs off of the road and to safety. The dog did not make it far before she lay down completely and stopped moving. A woman, presumably one of the drivers who struck the dog, pulled off the road about 500 metres past and began running back, while the police car that had been stopped earlier returned to the scene. Together, they waited for a break in the traffic and pulled the dog's body off the road. We were unsure if the dog would survive, but we knew she was—at the very least—suffering, and probably in shock. We assume that the dog died, as the woman who pulled her off the road was visibly weeping over her body, now motionless on the pavement. Weeping ourselves, we got back into the car and continued our drive home.

For the rest of our ride back to Toronto we were haunted by the events. Each subsequent glimpse of an animal lying dead on the road, each movement of our own dog in the back seat, and each resurfacing of the scene in our own minds broke the silence, causing us to speak to each other about what we witnessed. I tried to imagine where the dog was coming from, whom she lived with and where. Was her home a comfortable place that she was returning to, or somewhere abusive that she was running from? Did she have human companions, children who loved her, adults that cared for her? It was impossible to know, and the frustration of not knowing and not being able to do anything for her or those who possibly cared for her was upsetting.

Narrative Animality

Upon reflection, what struck me most about witnessing the dog's death was my automatic assumption that her tragic end was the conclusion of a story, *her* story. Prior to narrating the event of her death to others, my lines of thinking looked back into the unknowable aspects of the dog's own past in order to formulate a story, one that would help me understand her better. I think that such thinking entails a profound attempt to know another being, and I also argue that such acts of narrative imagining are not only common, but epistemically and ethically significant.

While most strands of narratology focus on the unique linguistic capacities of human animals, the experience of animal narrativity presents a subversive, counter-hegemonic, and more inclusive approach, recognizing that humans are not the sole subjects, agents, authors, or proprietors of stories. Yet, language is typically the realm in which narrative is situated rather than in the complex bodies and minds of storying beings in relation to each other. Since language is still widely considered to be a uniquely human capacity, animal narrativity requires a wilder, more inclusive understanding of language and mind, one that is inherently ecological, relational, and embodied. This will take us into various phenomenological, ethological, and literary forays that I believe support both the personal, consciously felt quality of animal narrativity as well as the integral ecological, historical, and social processes that function in more-than-human communicative practices.

Disciplinary approaches to animal narratives privilege the human being's singular capacity for narrative construction, often denying true agency or subjectivity to nonhuman beings within the narrative form.[6] Within posthumanist literary analyses, such questions of agency and subjectivity are tackled. Susan McHugh argues thoughtfully that literary animals are key figures in the ever-shifting biopolitical terrain of human–animal relations, ultimately calling for a form of "narrative ethology" which "emphasizes embodied relations of agency and form" tying knowledge about species and narrative to a common "ethics premised on feelings honored as concrete, intense, and shared."[7] Yet, there remains a hesitation within such work to allow for a serious turn of imagination, for as McHugh notes, "no one to date seriously argues that squirrels write poetry," and perhaps rightfully so.[8] Given the epistemic grounds on which so much species knowledge stands, such a claim might lead to investigations that only serve to solidify the uniqueness of human aesthetic forms. Perhaps those of us interested in "the question of the animal," seeking to critique the ongoing fantasies of a human/animal divide that, not only intellectually but materially, comes at the price of so many other creaturely existences, ought to challenge such hesitations.

Narrative is a highly popular methodological, theoretical, and practical approach to research and scholarly writing, but its assumptions about where stories come from, who is speaking or can speak, and who deserves to be heard or seen need to be laid bare. The narrative form, with all its aesthetic elements, is a widely exercised cultural phenomenon. It is commonly considered a universal aspect of human cultures, stretching back to our earliest beginnings as a hominid species. As such, I would like to turn the focus initially to the role of narrative within the lives of *human* animals, and to acknowledge the ways in which other animals participate in similar narrative enactments.

Homo narratus

Folk psychologist Jerome Bruner refers to narrative as a culturally enacted knowledge domain:[9] "a domain . . . is a set of principles and procedures, rather like a prosthetic device, that permits intelligence to be used in certain ways, but not in others. . . . [T]hese domains, looked at in another way, constitute something like a culture's treasury of tool kits . . . the attraction of this view is, of course, that it links man [*sic*] and his knowledge-gaining and knowledge-using capabilities to the culture of which he and his ancestors were active members."[10] Understood as "prosthetic devices," narratives provide a communicative forum for symbolic systems of beliefs, desires, habits, and morals to be instilled, exchanged, and altered over time by the individuals within a given culture or community. Narratives come to shape and give meaning to our experiences as we reflect on them personally and as we share them with others. This cultural enactment is on display in personal stories, autobiographies, cultural histories, national histories, and across a wide variety of media. Narratives are shared orally, in writing, and pictorially using a range of performative methods for diverse audiences.

Narratives are considered to be a universal feature of human cultures, discursive objects that organize and communicate both real and imagined events: our personal and communal histories as well as our fictions and fantasies. Yet narratives are largely considered a strictly human domain. Political theorist Hannah Arendt suggests that the primary distinction between human and nonhuman life comes from the unique ability of human beings to constitute their lives biographically. Humans, she argues, possess a unique capacity to represent birth and death—and the living in between—through the act of narration.[11] This distinction between "mere" biological living (*zoe*) and uniquely human living (*bios*) can be traced back in Western philosophical history to the works of Aristotle, particularly his discourse in *Poetics*, and it remains today. Alisdair MacIntyre claims that life itself evokes a narrative form.[12] More recently, in his book *On Stories*, Richard Kearney writes that "every human existence is a life in search of a narrative," and following Aristotle, that "human existence is a life of 'action' . . . conducted *in view of some end*—even if that end is itself."[13]

Narrative is clearly a potent feature of *human* culture, but I argue it is so because its form emerges from our temporal and spatial experiences. Kearney's phenomenology of narrative provides insight into the appeal of the narrative form, but it also shines a light on the possibility of an implicit, pre-narrative experience within each of our lifeworlds, a term that describes "the world of our immediately lived experience, as we live it, prior to all our thoughts about it."[14] Drawing upon anthropocentric notions of being, including Heidegger's famous notion of *Dasein* as "Being-towards-death," Kearney and the others mentioned above and below make no reference to the possible narrative lives of nonhuman animals. In fact, the silences that remain surrounding animal stories dismiss animal experiences of temporality, identity, language, or of their possible experiences of living or dying, relegating them to a "mere" biological existence.[15] Ricoeur makes a familiar appeal to the unique human relation to action, through our singular competence in language: "In this respect, human life differs widely from animal life, and, with all the more reason, from mineral existence. We understand what action and passion are through our competence to use in a meaningful way the entire network of expressions and concepts that are offered to us by natural languages in order to distinguish between *action* and mere physical *movement* and psychophysiological *behaviour*. . . . In this network we find all the components of the synthesis of the heterogeneous."[16] Ricoeur's "synthesis of the heterogeneous" as well as his joined notions of concordance and discordance expose the active, intentional nature of narrative formation; but why deny such capacities to other beings, who clearly exist on a whole plane of heterogeneity, who encounter and engage with each other through drastically discordant forms of embodiment, language, and communication? The answer lies partly in the prioritization of narratives as artifacts over the more sensuous experience of story emerging from the joining and parting of disparate lifeworlds.

Perhaps it is the constitution of narratives—the textual representation of experience or image in a narrative form—that empowers the distinction between human beings and animals for thinkers such as Arendt and Kearney. After all, human beings seem to be the only creatures, on our planet anyway, that write stories down or express them orally with the intention of sharing them with others. Our narratives are expressed in oral or written forms. According to Gregory Currie, narratives are "intentional-communicative artefacts: artefacts that have as their function the communication of a story, which function they have by virtue of their makers' intentions."[17] What this suggests is that the capacity for narrative itself requires knowledge of a *storyteller*, a being that intends to communicate a story through narrative construction. This standard is easily assumed to be applicable only to the human species, partly because of a lack of evidence and, I argue, because of a lack of perception and imagination in our epistemic endeavours.

Currie offers a slight shift in thinking, however, one that is generative for investigating a wider, more-than-human storyworld. He suggests that it is not narrative as a categorical concept that is interesting so much as the sense that certain events and subjects possess varying degrees of narrativity. While narratives provide representations of things—people, actions, events, objects, and animals—narrativity describes "connotatively a felt quality, something that may not be entirely definable or may be subject to gradations."[18] Narrativity denotes something beyond a linguistic object with a given structure, focalization, or particular voice; it alludes to the quality that is sensed or experienced in the momentousness of events, communicative encounters, and even within music, imagery, or bodies that seek to negotiate and articulate meaning. While this shift in narrativity allows us to imagine a more complex storyworld surrounding us, Currie falls back in line with the exceptionalist trap by suggesting that only human beings have the linguistic capacities whereby narrative could evolve as both a culturally and biologically mediated mechanism of communicating.[19] Other animals, capable only of rudimentary signalling, are limited to a sort of economics of cheap and possibly deceptive communications about territory, predators, mates, and food. Nature, in this view, is not only red in tooth and claw, but in word and deed as well.

Humans' Animal Stories

Despite these prevailing ideas about humans' singular mastery over language and narrative as a communicative endeavour, our actual storytelling practices belie an underlying unease with such distinctions. In fact, our narratives have long since been tied to the more-than-human world as setting and to animals as vital characters in our lives and communities. This is evidenced in the presence of animals in much Indigenous narrative cultures rooted in oral, rather than written, exchange. Indigenous author Thomas King suggests that the assumed sophistication of written over oral stories is closely tied not only to the ways in which oral traditions utilize language, but to what they say. In comparing Christian and Native creation stories, for example, he notes that the strategies of his Native storytelling involve a conversational voice, highlighting "the exuberance of the story," but diminishing "its authority, while the sober voice in the Christian story makes for a formal recitation but creates a sense of veracity."[20] David Abram similarly reminds us that culture is deeply embedded within storytelling practices, but as oral cultures die out and as written cultures embrace universal languages and alphabets, we lose not only the tie between language and the more-than-human world but also the possibilities of other ways of knowing and living, ways that avoid less violence. But as King reminds us, for our current capitalist, Judeo-Christian world, "the talking animals are a problem."[21]

The story I told at the beginning of this chapter takes stock of a series of events and provides those events with an order, temporal extension, and significance in the mindful, hopeful, and stylized process of storytelling recognizable by a particularly Western audience. There are thousands of animal stories shared like it every day, though hopefully not as tragic. Listen to those who have companion animals share stories of their dogs, cats, or birds: stories full of anthropomorphism and revealing a deep belief in animal subjectivity, personality, and intelligence. There are cultural forces at play in these communicative dances and storytelling moments. Alongside these interpersonal, oral narratives is the rapidly growing technological story-telling apparatus that exists in cyberspace. Blogs, online videos, and social media allow individuals who experience both the mundane and unexpected encounters of interspecies life to capture, fashion, edit, and store them online in myriad forms. Spend an afternoon searching the Internet for ani-mal stories and you will come across spectacular videos of dogs rescuing each other from danger, fantastical human encounters with wild animals, politically driven accounts of domesticated animals set to mood-enhancing music, or great migrations filmed in slow motion or high definition. You will also encounter millions of hours of footage featuring "adorable" cats, singing dogs, or moments woven into compelling viral videos. Each of these technologically mediated accounts connects thousands—perhaps millions—of strangers to unknown characters and events that seem to war-rant special recognition. Viewers are invited to comment, like, or dislike the videos on YouTube, establishing new technocultural modes of mediating knowledge or exchanging ideas about what is right. But what does this say about our perception of the story *behind* the production?

Interest in animal narratives is also voiced in fictional, historical, and academic literatures: *The Island of the Blue Dolphins, My Friend Flicka, Where the Red Fern Grows*. Levinas writes about a dog, Bobby, who greeted the workers in a Nazi concentration camp. Freud wrote several accounts of his dogs' participation in his analytic sessions. These fictional and non-fictional accounts of animals in the lives of various literary characters, scholars, and authors, in addition to the growing library of Internet videos and the sharing of everyday encounters between those in our interpersonal communities, indicates a wide breadth of meaning attributed to or derived from human–animal encounters. Some of these tales, like the tragic story I told above, draw upon the significance of singular events, while others fold the entirety of shared lives and deaths into narrative arcs with longer plots, more developed characters, and perhaps some sense of narrative closure in the form of a moral, a resolution, or a punchline.

When we stop to examine these stories further, analyzing their struc-tural, thematic, and performative elements, we cannot help but notice how these moments of living and dying together blur our experiences of self and other and trouble the waters of our deeply interconnected lives with other creatures. These stories allow us to explore the intersubjective and interspecies communities in which we live, to assess the bonds that are truly important in our lifeworlds. Donna Haraway's stories of "companion species" acknowledge the historical and material intertwining of organisms, troubling categories of being such as "human," "animal," and even "companion animal" that maintain the fictions of biological and philosophical species boundaries.[22] In thinking through the implications of companion species ontologically, epistemically, and ethically, Haraway makes reference to "a looping story of figuration, of ontics, of bodies in the making, of play in which all the messmates are not human."[23] The very suggestion that her analysis plays out as a "story" points us again to the felt sense of narrative presence within a wider range of bodies, beings, and processes in the world. New plots become possible that reject the requirements of univocality or singular points of view and allow for multi-species, hybrid voices to share in relationally significant forms of biological, historical, and mythical narratives.

We are storying beings, and our co-evolution with members of other species has a long past that draws upon narrative engagements. Haraway draws our attention to the very basic self–other couplings that blur species boundaries, even at the level of our DNA. Thinking through animal narrativity does not require us to delve so deeply, although I think it is aligned with such thinking. Individuals do not precede their relations, and stories of individuals are situated within long histories of species evolving together. Here, the imaginative anthropologies of thinkers like Paul Shepard acknowledge that human minds and cognitive capacities are a product of evolution in natural places and in relation to other beings: "The human mind is the result of a long series of interactions with other animals. The mind is inseparable from the brain, which evolved among our primate ancestors as part of an ecological heritage. That heritage . . . arboreal and terrestrial, is not unique to our descent but is widespread among monkeys and apes, so that to understand our kind of consciousness—higher-level thinking, artistic expression, and abstraction—requires some further explanation and is linked to our perception of animals."[24] Perceiving animal narrativity follows from this evolutionary heritage, taking our encounters with other beings and their storied existences seriously as part of our own development. Clearly, other species' own histories follow similar trajectories of co-operation, co-ordination, and co-evolution leading to a wide range of capacities, some far beyond our own comprehension.

I want to suggest that this co-evolution with other animals in complex communities of co-operation and competition is part of the popular appeal of what McHugh and Bekoff refer to as "narrative ethology."[25] We appeal to narrative forms in our epistemic endeavours as evidenced in many popular approaches to natural history, anthropology, literature, and ethology. Curious as to "what kinds of knowledge we as humans ever can have about other species," McHugh suggests a need for further articulations of animal knowledge in new, imaginative narrative forms. Such work, she notes, has profound potential for shifting "patterns of engagement between species."[26] Heeding this call, might it be a vital step to attributing narrative imagination and our knowledge of a rich, multi-species world to our species' perceptual heritage? Can we trace animal narrativity through our natural and historical pasts?

Nonhuman Animal Narrators

One can trace Western thinking about animals through various scientific and philosophical discourses about their capabilities and qualities, typically in comparison with human beings. Upon this tenuous and anthropocentric foundation, we place our pillars of epistemology and ethics. "Qualities such as mind, communication, consciousness and sensitivity to others" set the epistemic boundaries by which we determine various moral standards: a creature either possesses these qualities—becoming worthy of moral regard—or they are left outside the circle of considerable beings.[27]

If we were to follow such reasoning, then Bringhurst's suggestion that other species tell stories becomes difficult in light of the questions above. However, there are theories hypothesizing that other animals may actually possess narrative intelligence—that perhaps *Homo narratus* does not stand alone in its use of stories and its experiences of storyworlds. A particular thread of evolutionary and cognitive research puts forth the *narrative intelligence hypothesis* (NIH), suggesting an "intertwined relationship between the evolution of narrative and the evolution of social complexity in primate societies."[28] NIH postulates that there is an evolutionary advantage for narrative capacity within highly social animals—notably primates—that maintain individualized societies, in particular the ability to keep track of relationships and to communicate with others about third-party members.[29] This theory draws upon comparisons between narrative development in human infants and children and the potential for non-verbal, transactional narrative forms in, at the very least, great apes. Great apes are, after all, possessors of mirror neurons, the neuropsychological foundation for scientific theories of empathy and intersubjectivity. NIH has interesting implications for both animal studies *and* robotics, including for the development of socially intelligent agents and artificial intelligence.[30]

The epistemic manoeuvres involved with inquiring about other animals' narrative intelligences are essentially the same as those that Plumwood and others critique as built on hegemonic and anthropocentric narratives of mastery: a human quality or capacity, considered to be unique to our species, is being sought out scientifically in other closely related beings.[31] It has been argued in many places that these empirical, positivist endeavours serve no other purpose than to maintain our species' centrality within our tenuous cosmologies, thus preserving our own egoistic self-interests. Drawing this speciesism in parallel with other endeavours of mastery allows us to recognize that self-interests and the recognition that we owe our existence to relational ontologies within a vast, more-than-human realm are not mutually exclusive.[32] The continued appeal to traditional extensionist modes of ethics is drawn out elsewhere as a great paradox of animal ethics. When it is a requirement for ethics that other beings have the same capacities as those in the "centre" (be they human, male, white, or European), large groups of beings are excluded. It requires imagination to think beyond those traditional paradigms, or at the very least to reconfigure them.[33] A fear of imagination and anthropomorphism within traditional ethical models, as well as the repeated appeals for empirical evidence, maintains a positivism and anthropocentrism that an acknowledgement of animal narrativity seeks to subvert. Animal narrativity is an epistemic and an ethical phenomenon grounded in humans' shared evolutionary and cultural histories with other-than-human animals, and in that sense NIH presents significant parallels. However, in addition to NIH's maintenance of a 'burden-of-proof' epistemology, it maintains a closedness regarding interspecies knowledge, evolutions, and communications.

What do gorillas say to each other in the wild? How do other species communicate about the events and lives that maintain a similar sense of meaningfulness? I do not think it is fruitful to require other species to prove that they have the capacity for narrative; in fact, NIH maintains a hegemonic epistemic of proof. I do think, however, that we can begin to recognize animal lives and actions as possessing degrees of narrativity both for them and for "us." It is perhaps the best we can do to avoid closing the door on the possibilities narrative allows. In J.M. Coetzee's novel *The Lives of*

Animals, the main character, Elizabeth Costello appeals to the possibility of "sympathetic imagination" in addressing a similar concern. She argues that imagination is the key to understanding the existence of other beings, but as others point out, the often drastic differences between human perception and knowledge and the diverse forms of animal life on the planet call such an ability into question.[34] Still, if what we share with other creatures is, at the very least, a life in pursuit of various relationships and meanings and a life temporally bounded by birth and death, then narrativity is clearly an emergent property of animal life, one that allows us to work around our perceptual differences.

Narrativity and Animal Lifeworlds

One can never be sure whether squirrels, apes, or any other nonhuman species write poetry or tell stories. They certainly do not make art for us, and if they did we would likely fail to notice it.[35] However, life forms can be recognized as possessing various aesthetic qualities, artistic lines of movement, musical sounds, lives full of narrativity, and not just *for* human beings. In addition, narratives are complex forms that engage with meaning, and meanings are abundant within the natural world whether they are articulated verbally or not. The hesitancy to attribute poetic or narrative capacities to other creatures belies an underlying unease with their capacity for complex thought and language, a cornerstone of Cartesian doubts about the animal world. However, mind and language can be thought of as emergent properties of intersubjective and interaffective living, the result of shared intentions and feelings. In order to better understand how narrative emerges in a similar way, we must imaginatively consider the kinds of language, gesture, and signs that allow storying beings to negotiate meaning in their varied encounters with otherness.

Animal Lifeworlds

Jakob von Uexküll, the Estonian biologist, made several contributions to the fields of ethology and is considered by some to be the forefather of biosemiotics. Uexküll's frustration with the objectification of animal life led him to explore animals' perceptual worlds in his work. Perhaps his most famous and intriguing contribution to the study of animal behaviour and biology is the notion of Umwelten: the perceptual worlds that surround animal subjects, represented metaphorically by a soap bubble surrounding each individual animal's body.[36] The Umwelt provides a crucial component for understanding animal perception and subjectivity, as the essential process that is its body-in-environment contributes not only to the animal's own experience of reality and self but to its interpretations of signs in complex environments. Uexküll argues that there are as many Umwelten as there are organisms, and as such, no one being is capable of a complete view of reality. It is the relations that arise between Umwelten that generate meanings in nature.

Uexküll's concepts have been taken up by a number of philosophical and environmental theorists because of their contributions to ontology and metaphysics, notably Heidegger, Merleau-Ponty, and Deleuze.[37] Uexküll's theory of animality bonds organisms and lifeworlds together in the interpretation of and response to signs. These are the very conditions wherein I argue that narrativity is experienced, particularly for those creatures whose response is subsequently to communicate these signs and the conditions under which they are encountered within a story form. In A *Theory of Meaning*, Uexküll tells a brief story about an experience he had while hearing a Mahler symphony performed in Amsterdam. A nearby patron explained that by following the musical score, he was able to follow not only the individual tones and voices of the orchestra and performers, but also to understand the piece as a whole. Uexküll uses this anecdote to introduce a favoured metaphor for the workings of the natural world: the musical score. In fact, he questions "whether it is the task of biology to write the score of Nature."[38] This metaphor of nature as symphony provides an inroad for our task of recognizing animal narrativity as emerging from a wider, more-than-human world of stories.[39]

In addition to the example above, large sections of Uexküll's work rely on musical and symphonic metaphors to establish the relational quality of life, "a theme that is interwoven in a thousand variations into the orchestration of the living world."[40] If we imagine, following Uexküll's suggestion, that the task of biology is to "write the score of Nature," then we must consider that this singular task suggests—at a deeper level—a felt sense that subjects interpret meanings within the natural world through charting the voices, bodies, movements, and processes of other beings. Sharing meaning is how organisms, in their very different Umwelten, negotiate livelihoods. While Uexküll preferred to think of musical tones and harmonies, this is not altogether different from considering that individual organisms are stories unfolding in relation to one another. Further, this suggests that attentiveness to the movements, bodies, and language of others—other humans, animals, or beings—brings forth an opportunity both for empathic engagement and for gaining knowledge. Animals may tell stories through echolocation, through scent or other chemical markers, or through dramatic visual displays; our inability to see or hear beyond our own human range does not negate the possibility (see Chapter 6 on 'pheromones' in dogs).

Still, I want to remain cautious. Uexküll's theories suggest that meaning is always partial, given our perceptual capacities and limits, our soap bubbles. Life is meaningful insofar as other bodies and beings enter what Neil Evernden calls our "fields of care,"[41] and so knowledge becomes a matter of intersubjectivity. While this makes knowledge of the world always partial and subject to the availability and interaction of self with other, for Evernden it also requires attentiveness to the lifeworlds of other organisms. In this sense, a creature that we encounter, whether human or more-than-human, "does not have a world-view; it *is* a world-view."[42]

Animal Languages and Minds

Recognizing others as having or even being a world view opens us up to the necessities of interpretation. In *Becoming Animal*, David Abram likewise suggests that there is a language in the flesh of the world that one can become attuned to:

> All things have the capacity for speech—all beings have the ability to communicate something of themselves to other beings. Indeed, what is *perception* if not the experience of this gregarious, communicative power of things. . . . Not just animals and plants, then, but tumbling waterfalls and dry riverbeds gusts of wind, compost piles and cumulus clouds, freshly painted houses . . . are all expressive, sometimes eloquent, and hence participant in the mystery of language. Our own chatter erupts in response to the abundant articulations of the world: human speech is simply our part of a much broader conversation.[43]

Abram makes this suggestion following the lead of phenomenologist Maurice Merleau-Ponty. Merleau-Ponty's notion of the flesh of the world is generative for the notion of narrativity that I am seeking to set forth. First, Merleau-Ponty articulates an animal world that is more complex than Heidegger and others allowed in previous ontological articulations, an animal world that displays culture, intelligence, and embodied rationality as evidenced by a wide range of ethological observations. Second, "Flesh" is Merleau-Ponty's articulation of the intersubjective fabric of sensation and affect. Organisms or beings in contact are capable not only of perceiving each other but equally as being perceived, something Merleau-Ponty extended not only to humans but to other beings as well.[44] Finally, the notion of "Flesh" in Merleau-Ponty's work also works to decentre language from individual human minds or knowledge-makers and establishes meaning in a wider range of movements, gestures, and processes: not just those of the animal world, but in a larger realm of being, indicating that meaning already exists before it is given specific human codes or forms. This hopefully decentres narrativity as well, for while a narrative may indeed be formulated according to human cultural norms, the meanings and the stories are already there before a form or genre is chosen and a narrative created.

One particularly potent way to develop a more accurate knowledge of and a balanced, mutual livelihood within the world—if indeed that is our task—is to engage in ethical communication with other beings and to see their bodies and gestures, indeed the processes we witness in the world, as being historical and indicative of meaningful lives. This requires not just speaking to other creatures, or recognizing their *capacity* for language, but in being attentive to otherness when and how it presents itself to us. At base, I believe this is what we already do in both the most mundane interactions we share with other creatures and in those we deem momentous and seek to explore and retell in depth. This is at the heart of recognizing the narrativity in animal lives.

Barbara Smuts draws critical connections between embodiment, language, and minds while recounting her time spent with baboons as well as in her stories about living with her canine companions. Speaking about her experience with baboons, she notes that while her intention entering the field with them was to gather particular kinds of behavioural data, she found herself instead negotiating meaning with radically different forms of sociality and selfhood. They were not only highly individual, but also remained selves within a tightly knit community. These experiences and others with her companion dogs shifted her consciousness:

> Before . . . if I were walking in the woods and came across a squirrel, I would enjoy its presence, but I would experience it as a member of a class, "squirrel." Now, I experience every squirrel I encounter as a small, fuzzy-tailed, person-like creature . . . this squirrel [could] reveal itself as an utterly unique being, different in termperament and behavior from every other squirrel in the world. In addition, I am aware that if this squirrel had a chance to get to know me, he or she might relate to me differently than to any other person in the world.[45]

It is precisely this shift that animal narrativity espouses: first the recognition that animals, both as species and as individuals, are unique, that their lives are indeed a story apart from others; and then, the understanding that only in relation to others are they knowable, and that if we choose to engage with that relationship, our experiences will reveal that our story is, indeed, entwined with their own. While this may be more available in lifelong relationships, such as those we share with companion species or other human beings, they are possible elsewhere given enough attentiveness and imaginative engagement. Perhaps this is why I so readily imagined the yellow dog's life story, for I am quite familiar with dogs in my own experience. As I will explore below, this may be more difficult in animals that lie outside our realms of intimate knowledge: so-called wild animals, domestic animals whose lives are hidden from our view, microscopic organisms, or animals whose bodies and Umwelten are drastically different from our own. Yet, as Smuts suggests in her work with dogs, baboons, and other animals, by exploring our relational coexistences with other beings, we arrive at a sense of mutuality, recognizing others as selves with histories and stories of their own.[46]

An Ethics of Animal Narrativity

The promise of recognizing animal narrativity for new commitments to epistemic explorations and for living ethically with other creatures returns our attentions to some of the questions raised above concerning the connection between stories and the perceived human/animal divide. In a sense, thinking through narrativity brings us back, full circle, to actual narratives and their epistemic and ethical features. Yet, there are many possibilities for rethinking a narrative ethics that takes seriously the intersubjective and interspecies processes of creaturely encounters. The first requirement, flowing from the above discussions, obviously entails the perception of animal stories. This echoes much of what is said by Cheney and Weston when they argue that we must move away from using knowledge-based criteria for moral consideration and toward a complex, ethical approach to both similarities *and* differences.[47] The result, which they call "environmental etiquette," recognizes the potential intentionality of the other, and an openness to discover it through dialogue built upon attention to embodiment. Working with these ideas, Traci Warkentin posits the idea of an "interspecies etiquette," consisting of attentiveness, invitations, and "a keen awareness of embodiment, our own and the bodiments of other animals, to grasp continuities and negotiate key differences."[48] This entails something like a particular kind of attunement, an opening up of one's self to possibilities built on awareness and humility, but equally recognizing the possibility of never hearing a response. I suggest this fits well within the expanded, inclusive, and multi-species approaches to meaning, language, and mind presented above.

From such attentiveness, we are left with the question of how to respond to animal narrativity, to the stories we feel compelled to retell. Linda Vance traces several narratives concerning animals through historical discourses within ethics, particularly environmental ethics. Her analysis suggests that through these ethical narratives, animals are constructed as essentially silent, without voice or agency. Outlining ideological narratives within animal liberation, the land ethic, and deep ecology, Vance concludes that there is a middle path to approaching narrativity—seeking neither master narratives nor innocence in storytelling—which illuminates the locational specificity of stories and hopefully encourages us to "restore some balance between humans and animals."[49] She suggests four criteria for such narratives: "(1) they should be ecologically appropriate to a given time and place; (2) they should be ethically appropriate in that time and place; (3) they should give voice to those whose stories are being told; and (4) they should make us care."[50]

I find Vance's criteria very promising for the creation of narratives in social discourses and in theory, but engaging with animal stories requires a step back from the formation of narratives and their emplotment to include an acknowledgement of meaning and narrativity within creaturely encounters that is prior to textual configuration. The resulting narratives, following Vance, ought then to become inclusive of the multiple voices present in such encounters, thus subverting traditional human/animal boundaries. In addition, Vance's criteria return us to Newton's framework for narrative ethics as a process involving serious responsibilities. Working from the core relationalities of these two approaches, we can begin to imagine how other-than-human beings are indeed agents within experiences of animal narrativity. In attending to animal narrativity, the dualism of human beings as the storying animal, *Homo narratus*, and all *other* animals as non-storying beings is rejected. So how do we reimagine narrative and ethics as part of an intersubjective, interspecies process?[51]

Beyond merely thinking of narratives as ethical objects, Adam Newton suggests that it is the *process* of narrating that lends itself to ethical consideration. Newton's foundational claim is that "listening is an ethical act."[52] Just as importantly, the telling of a story—the very speech act—is a moment of outreach. In "saying," we are asking others to hear and, possibly, respond. There is at one point an anxiety in rendering self into narrative or when we "affect others narratively," just as there is an answerability that arises in the listener to recognize the other's singular uniqueness in time and space—a singularity that "enjoins responsibilities both aesthetic and ethical."[53] The ethical relation arises in an incomplete telling, listening, and responding between selves and others. Newton presents a "triadic structure" of narrative ethics, the first part of which is the dialogical exchange between tellers, listeners, and witnesses. Perhaps the best example of what an interspecies dialogical exchange might look like comes from Val Plumwood. Plumwood notes that we cannot simply extend moral considerability to other species in light of some mechanism they share with human beings. Using the example of intentionality, a cornerstone of continental philosophy, an extensionist paradigm would focus on which species are capable of intentional thought—and thus subjectivity so confined—and subsequently deem them morally considerable. Instead, she suggests that instead of abandoning the notion of intentionality altogether, we might expand the concept so that it "is more inclusive and different," a vital step forward requiring openness or attentiveness: "our openness to the non-human other's potential for intentionality, including their potential for communicative exchange and agency . . . is important ethically not as evidence of 'qualifications' for moral status but primarily because it is part of providing a counter-hegemonic alternative to the hegemonic stance of reductionism and closure."[54] Plumwood is recognizing both continuity and discontinuity between humans and other-than-human animals. She notes that even if we argue that other-than-human species' intentionality is of a lesser order, it does not necessarily follow that there are any ethical implications. Rather, we need a recognition of and respect for difference that will lead us toward higher orders of ethical *complexity* rather than hierarchy.

Of representation in narrative ethics, the second structure in the triad, Newton says: "the concept of 'life-turned-into-story' implies . . . the small but still momentous distance . . . taken up when selves represent or are represented by others."[55] This distance for Newton is in representing persons as characters in a story, which certainly applies to animal narrativity but must also be taken up in terms of the distance between experience and the form it is given. Representation is a problematic concept that is exposed in many postmodern and feminist critiques of language for its tendency to essentialize the subjectivity of individuals and groups and in its closure around the "real" versus the "unreal," a distinction that postmodernism problematizes. While I agree that we cannot make definitive claims as to the subjective experiences of others or the reality of events in our communal pasts, being within an ecology of stories requires us to reflect upon our narrative representations and to imagine alternatives based on new information, experiences, or stories that we encounter. Kearney suggests that one way we can address this problem of representation is by combining narrative's empathic functions in literature, history, and other disciplines with the scientific community's objective methods in a complementary way, an appeal that directly corresponds with the possibilities inherent in new narrative ethologies.[56] This attends to suggestions made above by McHugh, Bekoff, and Smuts.

The last concept within our triadic structure is that of hermeneutic responsibility. It is here that we can return to Kearney's hermeneutic approach, noting that "it is the task of narrative . . . to provide us with specific ways of imagining how the moral aspects of human behavior may be linked with happiness or unhappiness."[57] Coming from a distinctly humanist tradition, the focus here on "human behavior" does not require us to completely disregard the possibilities of narrative in ecological or other-than-human relationships. Animal narrativity requires a critical hermeneutic responsibility for experiences that cannot be expressed adequately in words. This does not preclude us from employing imagination in a storying of our relationships with others in the world. This builds partly from Kearney's notion of "a hermeneutic model of narrative, resolved in spite of all to say something about the unsayable, to imagine images of the unimaginable, to tell tales of the untellable."[58]

Newton similarly recognizes that the reading or hearing of another's story calls us into responsibility; if we contend that the creation of narratives happens as a matter of the impulse to communicate the narrativity of our experiences with otherness, then the reading of or listening to another's story puts us in a position of "answerability . . . what readers answer for . . . is their separateness before another's helplessness."[59]

Ecofeminist scholars remind us that we are not only responsible or response-able within human–human encounters: "Responsibility—the ability to respond to the other—cannot be restricted to human–human encounters when the very boundaries and constitution of the 'human' are continually being reconfigured and 'our' role in these and other reconfigur-ings is precisely what 'we' have to face. A humanist ethics won't suffice when the 'face' of the other that is 'looking' back at me is all eyes, or has no eyes, or is otherwise unrecognizable in human terms."[60] How do we engage with animal narrativity? We must try to imagine, know, and encounter other beings on their own terms, so as to avoid engaging "in narcissistic projec-tions and miss what is important and valuable to them from their point of view."[61] Reimagining narrativity in terms of what is valuable to and experi-enced by other animals we encounter, we will undoubtedly recognize that our differences are vast. Still, we share with other beings a vulnerability which is at the crux of assessing our moral obligations, requiring us to take seriously the tasks of listening, making meaning, and becoming responsible for our interpretations of stories, be they personal, historical, or fictional. This will undoubtedly be difficult, as the various cultures of which we are a part maintain strong, deeply embedded, hegemonic narratives of div-ision, allowing humans mastery over companion, domesticated, and wild animals; but imagining a being's life as a story, no matter how uncertainly, holds many possibilities for shifting individual and cultural practices.

Ending with an Ending: A Hawk Dies

A group of friends and I were driving across New York state from Buffalo to New York City for a wedding last summer. I sat in the front seat keep-ing the driver, Tara, company, while the other two passengers remained relatively quiet in the back, reading, listening to music, or sleeping. I was not sure. At some point, Tara asked me about the topic of my dissertation. Cringing ensued. I began what was a well-rehearsed response: "I'm inter-ested in children's experiences of animal death. Coming from a background in environmental education, I recognize that much of our teaching and learning revolves around tragedy, loss of biodiversity, loss of habitat, and endangerment/extinction. I'm curious about how children make sense of animal death and loss in their own lives, how they tell their own stories about their experiences."

Tara was intrigued, she asked me about my own experiences with the topic as a child. I recounted how I was unsure of experiencing animal death per se, though I had many experiences with loss after my parents got rid of various pets I had growing up: birds, a cat, a dog. These were formative for me, as was the loss of the thick woods behind our house to construction and Dutch elm disease. I talked about my own personal mixture of awe in nature as well as what can only be described as melancholy over the loss of animal species and habitats, a combination of feelings I have experienced since childhood.

I was about to ask her about her own experiences, when suddenly a red-tailed hawk took off from the shoulder and flew directly in front of the car. Tara shouted through the windshield, "What are you doing?" But it was too late; the front of the car hit the hawk, which drifted up over the windshield in an invisible current of air. I looked back quickly to see his body land on the road behind us. He was motionless for as long as I could see him, and we presumed he was dead.

Tara was visibly and audibly upset; she cried and asked for reassurance that it was not her fault. Clearly, there was nothing she could have done differently as neither of us noticed the hawk until it was flying directly into the path of the car. We were both shaken by the experience. We assured each other that the safest thing to do was keep driving; anecdotally we remembered learning that people who swerve to avoid animals while driving cause more accidents and injuries. Unable to pull over anywhere, Tara kept driving, managing somehow to keep her emotions in check, when one of the passengers in the back seat spoke up: "Who knew hawks were so stupid?" I do not want to read too much into my friends' comment about hawk intelligence, especially since I consider him to be a genuinely good person. Still, I found his comment deeply insensitive and unsettling. I was angry he said it. Did he not recognize the tragedy of the situation? Could he not see what Tara or I saw, that is, the violent ending of an individual's life, the end of its story? Perhaps what is most illustrative about his comment was that it quickly breached the gap between an individual being and the entirety of a species; not only was *that* hawk stupid, but by extension, *all* hawks were stupid. It is a clear avoidance of epistemic and moral responsibility, drawn from a failure of imagination: my friend was unable to imagine that the hawk we hit with our car was an individual, with a story uniquely his own. The hawk was part of a species, yes, but he was also undoubtedly an individual being with physical, emotional, and cognitive differences from others of his kind, whether we knew him or not. I could not help but think that the failure was in recognizing that hawk's own life, his own *story*; and I worry that such perceptual and imaginative failures engender an ongoing silence about the often violent and perhaps preventable deaths of hundreds, thousands, or millions of individuals every day.[62]

NOTES

1. Bringhurst, "Tree of Meaning," 14.
2. Ibid.
3. Kearney, *On Stories*.
4. Weil, "Killing Them Softly," 87–96.
5. While precise numbers are often unattainable, a cursory statistical review is quite sobering. There are typically between 14,000 and 15,000 *reported* wildlife/vehicle collisions (WVCs) in Ontario alone each year. However, reported WVCs are typically those involving large mammals such as white-tailed deer and moose, and reports of bird, reptile, and amphibian strikes could effectively be measured in the millions per annum, as reported in *A Guide to Road Ecology in Ontario* (Ontario Road Ecology Group). Companion animals suffer similar fates, although the only estimate I found was a report from 1998, which estimated that over 5.4 million cats and 1.6 million dogs were killed on roadways in 1997 in the US alone, as per Braunstein, "Roadkill."
6. See Wolfe, *What Is Posthumanism?*; and McHugh, *Animal Stories*.
7. McHugh, *Animal Stories*, 218.
8. Ibid., 10.
9. The phrase, *Homo narratus*, is from Dautenhahn, "Origins of Narrative."
10. Bruner, "Narrative Construction," 2–3.
11. Kristeva, *Hannah Arendt*, 8.
12. MacIntyre, *After Virtue*.
13. Kearney, *On Stories*, 129.
14. Abram, *Spell of the Sensuous*, 40.
15. Buchanan, "Being with Animals," 278.
16. Ricoeur, "Life in Quest of Narrative," 28.
17. Currie, *Narratives and Narrators*, 6.
18. Abbott, *Introduction to Narrative*, 24.
19. Ironically, Currie also suggests that the human capacity and "taste for significantly narrativized accounts" coincided with a decrease in the ability to use language deceptively (*Narratives and Narrators*, 47). As we learned to tell more complex stories, he argues, we also made it more difficult to lie through our narratives. This leads to interesting questions, worth exploring, about the development of justice in our species, something other narrative thinkers like Paul Ricoeur, connect to our narrative preferences.
20. King, *The Truth about Stories*, 22–23.
21. Ibid., 23.
22. See Haraway, *Companion Species Manifesto*, and *When Species Meet*.
23. Haraway, *When Species Meet*, 165.
24. Shepard, *Others*, 15.

25. See McHugh, *Animal Stories,* 217–18; and Bekoff and Pierce, *Wild Justice.*
26. McHugh, *Animal Stories,* 23.
27. Plumwood, *Environmental Culture,* 144.
28. Dautenhahn, "Origins of Narrative," 98.
29. There is certainly anecdotal evidence that great apes do possess such narrative intelligence. When asked about his mother, Michael, a lowland gorilla taken from Cameroon and raised by the Gorilla Foundation in California, responded with the following sequence of signs: "Squash-meat-gorilla. Mouth-tooth. Cry-sharp noise-loud. Bad-think trouble-look face. Cut neck-lip (girl)-hole." For the video, see Cohn, "Michael's Story." It was largely interpreted to be a recounting of his mother's violent death as part of the bush-meat trade that remains an ongoing problem for species conservation efforts all over the world. Michael recounted this story about his mother, through a similar pattern of signs, regularly throughout his life. Michael was telling a story not only of his own life, but also of the life of his mother. Michael, together with his more famous companion, Koko, developed unique signs of their own, apart from the American Sign Language researchers had taught them. Doing so, they became the focus of much scientific and philosophical discussion about animal intelligences and language. See Patterson and Gordon, "Personhood of Gorillas."
30. Dautenhahn, "Origins of Narrative," 118–19.
31. Code, *Ecological Thinking.*
32. Plumwood, *Mastery of Nature.*
33. Calarco, *Zoographies.*
34. Sellbach, "Lives of Animals."
35. The ongoing popularity of creating and selling art made by captive animals like elephants and apes challenges my assumption here, although I would argue that such artistic creation is structured by the experience of confinement, boredom, and human mastery within zoos and aquaria. Elephants are handed paint brushes and canvases in order to prevent them from being bored, and arguably, they are instructed how to paint by human beings who take those paintings away to be sold.
36. Buchanan, *Onto-ethologies.*
37. Ibid., 3.
38. von Uexküll, *A Foray,* 186.
39. This emphasis on musicality and orchestration also reveals an uneasy aspect of Uexküll's work: a teleological bent. The postmodern unease with teleology— especially in discussions of a "naturalized" plan or trajectory of life—roots itself in the historical, relative, and contingent basis for constructing concepts like "nature" and "culture" in the first place. This mistrust of teleology, translated as "end purpose," flows also throughout the biological sciences, often misaligned

with Darwinian determinism. However, Uexküll's teleology is only loosely defined throughout his work and is largely a product of his alignment with the work of the biological theories of Karl Ernst von Baer. The distinction between Uexküll's notion of a plan and the so-called naturalist teleology of Aristotle rests on Uexküll's rejection of the very anthropomorphic treatment of teleology given by philosophy at that time: that only ends capable of being articulated or seen by humans count in the formulation of "grand plans." For Uexküll, the notion of an Umwelt arises from the very complex and yet ordered and musically harmonious workings of nature's interwoven web of relations. The plan, however, is likely beyond any singular being's comprehension. Still, the parallels here raise the question as to whether narrativity points toward a kind of plan inherent in nature or the mere sense that storying beings are part of a larger narrative. See Buchanan, *Onto-ethologies*, 8–12; see also Weber and Varela, "Life after Kant."

40. von Uexküll, "Concept of Umwelt," 118.
41. Evernden, *Natural Alien*.
42. Ibid., 80.
43. Abram, *Becoming Animal*, 172.
44. Dillard-Wright, *Ark of the Possible*.
45. Smuts, "Encounters," 301.
46. Ibid., 308.
47. Cheney and Weston, "Environmental Ethics."
48. Warkentin, "Interspecies Etiquette," 118.
49. Vance, "Beyond Just-So Stories," 176.
50. Ibid., 176–77.
51. Importantly, we must do so while acknowledging that narratives are not necessarily morally just. In fact, stories can be created and misused to appropriate the lives of others, to politically interfere with their own living, or to create distorted boundaries between morally considerable subjects and beings unworthy of consideration (Kearney, "Narrative and Ethics"). There are complex and intricately woven narratives behind some of the greatest failings of human morality; no doubt the crises claimed by environmentalists and animal rights proponents fit within those terms. In addition, ecofeminist authors point out that there are hundreds, perhaps thousands, of narratives claiming the status of *the* Grand Narrative. For now, I think we can leave those homogenizing meta-narratives aside and first consider what might be required of human beings that will encourage a genuine recognition of our ethical relationships with other-than-human beings at individual and communal levels in acknowledgement of animal narrativity.
52. Newton, *Narrative Ethics*, 17–21.
53. Ibid., 31–46.

54. Plumwood, *Environmental Culture*, 181.
55. Newton, *Narrative Ethics*, 18.
56. See Kearney, "Narrative and Ethics"; also, McHugh, *Animal Stories.*
57. Kearney, "Narrative and Ethics," 31.
58. Kearney, *On Stories,* 10.
59. Newton, *Narrative Ethics*, 21.
60. Barad, *Meeting the Universe*, 392.
61. Gruen, "Attending to Nature," 34.
62. This chapter was written with the support of a generous research fellowship granted by the Animals and Society Institute at Wesleyan University.

BIBLIOGRAPHY

Abbott, H. Porter. *The Cambridge Introduction to Narrative*. 2nd ed. New York: Cambridge University Press, 2008.

Abram, David. *Becoming Animal: An Earthly Cosmology*. New York: Pantheon Books, 2010.

——. *Spell of the Sensuous: Perception and Language in a More-Than-Human World*. Toronto: Vintage Books, 1997.

Barad, Karen. *Meeting the Universe Halfway: Quantum Physics and the Entanglement of Meaning*. Durham, NC: Duke University Press, 2007.

Bekoff, Marc, and Jessica Pierce. *Wild Justice: The Moral Lives of Animals*. Chicago: University of Chicago Press, 2009.

Braunstein, Mark Matthew. "Roadkill: Driving Animals to Their Graves." *Animal Issues* 29, no. 3 (1998): 1–11.

Bringhurst, Robert. "The Tree of Meaning and the Work of Ecological Linguistics." *Canadian Journal of Environmental Education* 7, no. 2 (2002): 9–22.

Bruner, Jerome. "The Narrative Construction of Reality." *Critical Inquiry* 18, no. 1 (1991): 1–21.

Buchanan, Brett. "Being with Animals: Reconsidering Heidegger's Animal Ontology." In *Animals and the Human Imagination: A Companion to Animal Studies*, edited by Aaron Gross and Anne Valleley, 265–88. New York: Columbia University Press, 2012.

——. *Onto-ethologies: The Animal Environments of Uexküll, Heidegger, Merleau-Ponty, and Deleuze*. Albany, NY: SUNY Press, 2008.

Calarco, Matthew. *Zoographies: The Question of the Animal from Heidegger to Derrida*. New York: Columbia University Press, 2008.

Cheney, Jim, and Anthony Weston. "Environmental Ethics as Environmental Etiquette: Toward an Ethics-Based Epistemology in Environmental Philosophy." *Environmental Ethics* 21, no. 2 (1999): 115–34.

Code, Lorraine. *Ecological Thinking: The Politics of Epistemic Location*. New York: Oxford University Press, 2006.

Cohn, Ronald. "Michael's Story." Gorilla Foundation video, 0:52. February 26, 2010. http://www.koko.org/michaels-story.

Currie, Gregory. *Narratives and Narrators: A Philosophy of Stories*. Toronto: Oxford University Press, 2010.

Dautenhahn, Kerstin. "The Origins of Narrative: In Search of the Transactional Format of Narratives in Humans and Other Social Animals." *International Journal of Cognition and Technology* 1, no. 1 (2002): 97–123.

Dillard-Wright, David. *Ark of the Possible: The Animal World in Merleau-Ponty*. Toronto: Lexington Books, 2007.

Evernden, Neil. *The Natural Alien: Humankind and Environment*. 2nd ed. Toronto: University of Toronto Press, 1993.

Gruen, Lori. "Attending to Nature: Empathetic Engagement with the More Than Human World." *Ethics & the Environment* 14, no. 2 (2009): 23–38.

Haraway, Donna. *The Companion Species Manifesto: Dogs, People and Significant Otherness*. Chicago: Prickly Paradigm Press, 2003.

———. *When Species Meet*. Minneapolis: University of Minnesota Press, 2008.

Kearney, Richard. "Narrative and Ethics." *Proceedings of the Aristotelian Society, Supplementary Volumes* 70 (1996): 29–45.

———. *On Stories*. New York: Routledge, 2002.

King, Thomas. *The Truth about Stories*. Toronto: House of Anansi Press, 2003.

Kristeva, Julia. *Hannah Arendt: Life Is a Narrative*. Toronto: University of Toronto Press, 2001.

MacIntyre, Alasdair. *After Virtue*. 3rd ed. South Bend, IN: University of Notre Dame Press, 2007.

McHugh, Susan. *Animal Stories: Narrating across Species Lines*. Minneapolis: University of Minnesota Press, 2010.

Newton, Adam. *Narrative Ethics*. Cambridge, MA: Harvard University Press, 1995.

Ontario Road Ecology Group. *A Guide to Road Ecology in Ontario*. Scarborough, ON: Ontario Road Ecology Group, 2010.

Patterson, Francine, and Wendy Gordon. "The Case for Personhood of Gorillas." In *The Great Ape Project: Equality Beyond Humanity*, edited by Paola Cavalieri and Peter Singer, 58–79. London: Fourth Estate, 1993.

Plumwood, Val. *Environmental Culture: The Ecological Crisis of Reason*. New York: Routledge, 2002.

———. *Feminism and the Mastery of Nature*. New York: Routledge, 1993.

Ricoeur, Paul. "Life in Quest of Narrative." In *On Paul Ricoeur: Narrative and Interpretation*, edited by David Wood, 20–33. New York: Routledge, 1991.

Sellbach, Undine. "The Lives of Animals: Wittgenstein, Coetzee, and the Extent of the Sympathetic Imagination." In *Animals and the Human Imagination:*

A Companion to Animal Studies, edited by Aaron Gross and Anne Vallely, 307–30. New York: Columbia University Press, 2012.

Shepard, Paul. *The Others: How Animals Made Us Human*. Washington, DC: Island Press, 1997.

Smuts, Barbara. "Encounters with Animal Minds." *Journal of Consciousness Studies* 8, nos. 5–7 (2001): 293–309.

Vance, Linda. "Beyond Just-So Stories: Narrative, Animals, and Ethics." In *Animals and Women: Feminist Theoretical Explorations*, edited by Carol J. Adams and Josephine Donovan, 163–91. Durham, NC: Duke University Press, 1995.

von Uexküll, Jakob. *A Foray into the Worlds of Animals and Humans*. Translated by Joseph D. O'Neil. Minneapolis: University of Minnesota Press, 2010.

———. "The New Concept of Umwelt: A Link Between Science and the Humanities." *Semiotica* 134, no. 1 (2001): 111–23.

Warkentin, Traci. "Interspecies Etiquette: An Ethics of Paying Attention to Animals." *Ethics & the Environment* 15, no. 1 (2010): 101–21.

Weber, Andreas, and Francisco J. Varela. "Life after Kant: Natural Purposes and the Autopoietic Foundations of Biological Individuality." *Phenomenology and the Cognitive Sciences* 1, no. 2 (2002): 97–125.

Weil, Kari. "Killing Them Softly: Animal Death, Linguistic Disability, and the Struggle for Ethics." *Configurations* 14 (2006): 87–96.

Wolfe, Cary. *What Is Posthumanism?* Minneapolis: University of Minnesota Press, 2009.

6

Canine Cartography
On the Curious and Queer Pleasures of Being a Dog

Peter Hobbs

A trip to the dog park is a trip to Sodom, with dogs of all different shapes and sizes forming daisy chains of dog on dog on dog. Both purebred and mutt shamelessly engage in sexual acts that are hard to ignore, and bring home the difference between sex and reproduction and between sex and gender. Even the spayed or neutered police dog runs the risk of being outed as a sexual outlaw. Canine sexuality (doggie style) will not be denied.

On the other hand, dogs are long-standing spokespersons of capital and civility, the very embodiment of a pervasive disciplinary apparatus. On television and out on the streets they perform as both the tail-wagging yes-men and the snarling watchdogs of a canine industrial complex.[1] Stay! Beg! Fetch! Roll over! Cover me with kisses! Through these eager brown-nosers, discipline in all its abrupt and subtle forms becomes second nature.

These two opposing generalizations help jump-start a speculative mapping of canine life, as they call attention to how dogs come to embody moral values and how such values are in turn pressed on society as a whole. It is important to remember that in this canine inscription the twin refrains of "Good dog" and "Bad dog," along with "Good girl" and "Bad boy," are never fixed and today's "Good dog" will often prove herself to be tomorrow's "Bad dog." It is this fluidity of embodiment—its inherent contestability—that I want to pursue as an unresolved adventure. Rather than come out in favour of one side of a great divide that attempts to mark dogs as either bad or good, social or asocial, compliant or perverse, I am much more interested in mapping canine life as an uncertain and lively terrain. In the combined biting spirit of Michel Foucault and Donna Haraway, this chapter asserts a biopolitics of dogs in which sex, citizenship, and animality are inextricably woven. Haraway's dog book, *When Species Meet* (2008), serves as a primary guide, as she presents the world of dogs as a muddy biopolitics of competing interests.[2] Like Haraway, I want to rehearse some of the discourse surrounding dogs to show how they are both objects and subjects (products and producers) of meaning. My aim is to delineate a queer animal studies in which dogs teach us both philosophical and concrete lessons about the limitations and possibilities of being human.

Along with Haraway and Foucault, I need to acknowledge my dog, who, as a representative of a unique assortment of divergent beings, acts as an emissary or ambassador, providing me with glimpses of a furry ontology, albeit forever partial, ever emergent. This canine world, in turn, complicates discipline and innateness so that we are forced to concede that, like humans, dogs are neither solely social constructs nor biological phenomena, neither solely docile bodies nor feral spirits. My plan is to invoke a canine world view or cartography in the form of three overlapping maps, each pursuing a different type of ontological inquiry: philosophy, ethology, and fiction.

In this proposed canine cartography my dog functions as an actor/informant whose map-making takes place both in plain sight and hidden from human comprehension. As something of a first principle, my dog obstinately refuses the lead that would have me following her about documenting her daily routines and passing my notes off as a definitive log of her behaviour and psyche. She turns her nose up at such a straightforward ethnography. She demands that we take an ever-winding route, reminding me that if I aspire to a canine cartography or psycho-geography, I need to adopt a dog frame of mind. But as she and Jacques Derrida's cat point out, such an attempt is complicated by the fact that animals remain naked and aloof (I will return to the lessons of Derrida's cat below).

By referencing "my dog" I am not trying to hide behind her and pretend that she is making all the decisions in writing this essay. For the most part she is invoked here to stress nonhuman intelligence and to reference dog-training books. Anyone familiar with these books will know that this trope, "my dog," is used as a marker of authority that usually extends to the standard author's photograph on the cover or back of the book. The conventional images of authors kneeling beside their dogs are supposed to lend credence to their words, as if they co-wrote or ghostwrote their texts with their canine muses/companions. My invocation of "my dog" is not meant to carry the same weight, as I am not claiming to speak for her or for dogs in general. But I am also not interested in presenting canine life as an unfathomable abyss. Instead of barking up this old oak, I want to stress the ecological interdependency of life and how dogs, like all living things, promise an open-ended adventure, the adventure of existence itself. In this spirit, my dog draws me into an embodied way of knowing (an affective and tacit ecology) in which she gnaws on my flesh and bones, softening their rigidity, helping me realize that my flesh and bones are never solely human. Her evident curiosity and pleasure, her lust for life, is contagious and solicits similar feelings. On a daily basis she reminds me that, like her, I am aging animal flesh and eventually I too will be consumed as fodder. In this respect, she is an unyielding materialist.

I want to begin my canine cartography by referencing Bruce Bagemihl's *Biological Exuberance: Animal Homosexuality and Natural Diversity* (1999) and Joan Roughgarden's *Evolution's Rainbow: Diversity, Gender, and Sexuality in Nature* (2004). Both texts challenge heteronormativity by documenting the animal kingdom as a thoroughly queer bestiary in which animals of all types engage in various homosexual acts. In this way, Foucault's insistence that the homosexual is a modern invention that emerges from the institutional discourses of the nineteenth century is given new traction, new legs, as these texts reveal how the discourses of zoology have struggled with same-sex desire.[3] Of course Bagemihl and Roughgarden also complicate Foucault's all-too-human configuration of homosexuality, as they render the homosexual as having claws, scales, fur, wings, and gills. By being no longer contained within the discursive frame of the all-too-human, the homosexual desire exhibited by animals contradicts heterosexist claims that such acts are sins against nature. But the will of heteronomativity is not easily thwarted and can play both sides of the same coin. When nature is shown to be undeniably queer, the exact opposite position is voiced so that homosexual desire is damned as all-too-animal. As Stacy Alaimo reminds us, "if conservatives are hell-bent on damning homosexuals, they will, no doubt, simply see all this queer animal sex as shocking depravity and consign those of us who are already outside the Family of Man to the howling wilderness of bestial perversions."[4]

In my desire to map canine life, I turn to Alaimo's exemplary essay, "Eluding Capture: The Science, Culture and Pleasure of 'Queer' Animals," in which she argues that while we should embrace the idea of queer animals, we should also be wary of our enrolling animals in ways that would curtail their sense of alterity. Echoing Haraway, Alaimo insists that animals exist, just like their human counterparts, as fleshy complex beings full of inconsistencies and contradictions that frustrate efforts to forge/capture universal truths by bracketing them within limited categories. In this way, Haraway and Alaimo extend the feminist and queer critique that bodies matter to include animal bodies. Just as faceless figures of women and homosexuals (and women as homosexuals) have been pressed into service in the binary logic of patriarchy, the divergent lives of animals have similarly been enrolled to perpetuate a world view that demarcates and assigns positive and negative value to the proper and the improper, the normal and the abnormal, male and female, dominance and passivity, the human and the animal. This entrenched, reductive, and hierarchical world view in turn lends weight to the heteronormative axiom that animals are willed by a biological imperative to reproduce and continue the species line.

Alaimo takes aim at this imperative to reproduce and how it is perceived as an instinctual force that structures all life. She asserts that pleasure, as an end to itself, is regularly purged from popular and scientific accounts of animal sex. To substantiate this claim, Alaimo references the sexology of Susan Block, who presents herself as a subversive champion of bacchanalian pleasure. Block gained celebratory status as a television sex-show host and animal advocate by promoting what she calls an "ethical hedonism" and "the Bonobo Way." But even Block's celebration of female bonobos engaged in "a sisterhood of pleasure" is made subservient to the "greater good of bonobo society."[5] To this end, Alaimo states: "Block's philosophy of the ethical hedonism of the bonobo is indicative of a general understanding, in wider culture, that the 'reason' bonobos have so much sex, including same-sex sex, is to reduce social conflicts. Such explanations may well make all that mounting seem just another chore."[6] In this way, Block's unconventional wisdom, her advocating "peace through pleasure," does little to dispel the convention that animals are hard-wired to reproduce and keep the peace. She ultimately denies the bonobos any sense of pleasure that would conflict with the social and biological reproductive will to power.

Alaimo goes on to delineate the rhetorical contortions and slippages that scientists have deployed so that animals continually appear to be unquestionable agents of sociobiological reproduction. In their insistence in producing what Alaimo refers to as a "landscape of Byzantine heterono-mativity,"[7] these accounts perpetuate this underlying will in which the sexual pleasures of animals, regardless of how much they might deviate from the norm, are read as *always already* heterosocial (although the full significance of social life is ultimately denied animals, so they are contradictorily configured as natural social agents without true agency and sociability). In such a landscape, the apparent queer pleasures of animals are enrolled so that any sense of either queerness or pleasure is all but erased.

Alaimo's essay serves as a helpful template, as she insists on the complications and contradictions inherent in the diversity of life. First she argues the constructionist position that sex and pleasure manifest as forever implicated in the inscription of power. But she also insists that animals (humans and bonobos alike) engage in pleasures beyond narratives of biological and social reproduction. In this way, Alaimo voices the posthumanist idea that life exists beyond the human, beyond the constrictive reach of ideology, beyond the ethical and physical limits that are embodied in our being all-too-human. It is important to keep in mind that such a position is far from advocating a version of nature as a separate and untainted domain, or a return to neutral objectivity.

Like Alaimo, I too want to insist on the twists and turns inherent in life as a way of pursuing a queer animal studies. To offset my own conscription of dogs, I will foreground assorted curiosities and pleasures on the part of dogs and their human interlocutors. My intention is to mix a variety of voices—zoology and popular culture, fiction and non-fiction, Jacques Derrida and Cesar Millan, Cary Wolfe and the Big Bad Wolf—as a means to develop a queer animal studies that has elements of camp, Bakhtin's carnivalesque, and the posthuman, such that things and concepts are flipped on their heads and the lowly (in the form of the bodily and the animal) impede and complicate the high claims of humanism. More specifically, I hope, by putting these voices together to invoke the queer potential or character of dogs, to show how they constitute a world view or ontology that is necessarily queer/queering from our perspective. Dogs cannot help themselves in this respect. Like other animals, dogs pull us into worlds that underscore the physical and mental limits of human knowledge and the human body and our subsequent limited ability to speak for and represent other animals. Dogs never tire of teaching us this posthumanist lesson despite our unwillingness to listen.

Before beginning my canine cartography I should reference Derrida's encounter with his cat as a model of posthuman inquiry. In his legendary ten-hour lecture on the question of animals (as part of a conference dedicated to his work in 1997 at Cerisy-la-Salle) Derrida introduces the idea of *animalséance* in the form of an anecdote. His story has him stepping out of the shower to find himself standing naked before his cat. He proceeds to present this everyday occurrence as a primal scene of shattering consequences. In his cat's gaze, the naked philosopher reads both curiosity and indifference, which causes him an accumulating sense of shame:

> It is as if I were ashamed, therefore, naked in front of this cat, but also ashamed for being ashamed. A reflected shame, the mirror of a shame, ashamed of itself, a shame that is at the same time specular, unjustifiable, and unavowable. At the center of this reflection would appear this thing—and in my eyes the focus of this incomparable experience—that is called nudity. And about which it is believed that it is proper to man, that is to say, foreign to animals, naked as they are, or so it is thought, without the slightest consciousness of being so.[8]

Thus Derrida attempts to give voice not so much to his cat but to the ontological distance separating them. Both he and his cat are revealed to occupy a series of contradictory positions, which in turn makes him feel strange within the familiar confines of his bathroom.[9]

There is the very real sense that what unsettles Derrida is the revelation that there is another being in the room, as if he were just recognizing the full significance of his cat, as another somebody in the bathroom, for the first time. What Derrida recognizes is that this cat is not just anybody. She/he is not a stranger but an intimate, a constant companion, but one who remains furred, naked, and aloof. Despite this ontological gap, there is an exchange of looks and an indication of shared curiosity, as Derrida's cat gazes back, looking at the naked philosopher "from head to toe, as it were just to *see*, not hesitating to concentrate its vision—in order to see, with a view to seeing— in the direction of my sex. *To see*, without going to see, without touching yet, and without biting, although that threat remains on its lips or the tip of its tongue."[10] There is a tacit understanding that the cat knows that Derrida is vulnerable in his nakedness, a vulnerability of which the cat should be blissfully ignorant because "it is naked, without *existing* in nakedness."[11] The cat also appears to focus her/his attention on Derrida's penis, perhaps recognizing it as the source of the philosopher's vulnerability and shame. The uncertainty of the exchange is a definite part of its charm, its allure.

Just as Derrida's nameless cat pulls him into an ontological breach, my dog knowingly gazes at me and in the process hails/interpellates me as all-too-human. Again I want to stress that this gap between Derrida and his cat, and between me and my dog, should not be used to support claims of exclusion and exceptionalism. The following three theoretical maps attempt to push beyond such definitive claims of us and them, human and non-human, and to get on with the messy business of mapping these breaches.

Map 1: Little Dogs and Big Bad Theorists

Anyone who likes cats or dogs is a fool.

> Gilles Deleuze and Félix Guattari,
> *A Thousand Plateaus: Capitalism and Schizophrenia*

The first nodal point or coordinate I want to pause/paws on in mapping a canine cartography is Deleuze and Guattari's (D&G's) infamous assessment of cats and dogs. It is not surprising that my dog has no time for D&G and looks on with a puzzled expression, as if to question why I would choose to chew over such old bones. I am drawn to D&G because of their talk of political and methodological sorcery, as well as their talk of lines of flight, deterritorialization, and diagramming. But as I slog through *A Thousand Plateaus* I become more frustrated than inspired. Determined to write off all pets as agents of capitalism and Oedipal desire, D&G present the dog as a traitorous embodiment of the wolf. While the wolf pack refuses the domesticated heat of the primal campfire, the dog is a whimpering counter-revolutionary and collaborator. "These animals," D&G assert, "invite us to regress, draw us into a narcissistic contemplation, and they are the only kind of animal psychoanalysis understands, the better to discover a daddy, a mommy, a little brother behind them . . . *anyone who likes cats or dogs is a fool.*"[12] Ensconced in the drawing room, on a rug in front of the familial hearth, as well as finding a place on the analyst's couch, D&G's dog is the smiling face of bourgeois comfort and contempt.

Along with wolves, D&G champion other pack animals including rats, whales, and tortoises, or rather the vengeful rats from *Willard*, the great white from *Moby Dick*, and the snapping and stubborn tortoises that appear in the poems of D.H. Lawrence. For D&G, the common ground shared by these fictive creatures is their ability to displace or deterritorialize the docile subject position that they attribute to cats, dogs, and elderly women: "Ahab's Moby-Dick is not like the little cat or dog owned by an elderly woman who honors and cherishes it. Lawrence's becoming-tortoise has nothing to do with a sentimental or domestic relation. . . . But the objection is raised against Lawrence: 'Your tortoises aren't real!' And he answers: Possibly, but my becoming is, my becoming is real, even and especially if you have no way of judging it, because you're just little house dogs."[13] To question the validity or force of D&G's collection of animals is to be met with a strong rebuke: how would you begin to question the epic texts of Melville and Lawrence when you and your kind are no more than little house dogs?

As Haraway points out, the ultimate aim in D&G's attack on dogs is to produce a scapegoat, to give a face to Oedipal desire and bourgeois consumption. "Little house dogs and the people who love them," she states, "are the ultimate figure of abjection for D&G, especially if those people are elderly women, the very type of the sentimental."[14] In this way D&G create a great divide with little house dogs and elderly women on the one side and wolves and anti-Oedipal/anti-capitalist theorists on the other. Despite all their grandstanding, D&G's portrayal is disappointingly mundane. We have heard it all before. In their positing of nature and culture as primary categories that frame and organize life, they repeat much of the plot of Nietzsche's *Thus Spake Zarathustra* (1885) and Freud's *Civilization and Its Discontents* (1930). We know this story and its outcome: civilization came at a price and we subsequently live with the unbearable burden/guilt of being all too human. Fashioned as the quintessential outsider, wolves also suffer in this schism, occupying the dangerous position of being both envied and hated, both lauded and hunted. Their nature is presented as an unaffected or feral will to power that humans foolishly traded or bartered away at the gates of the city. Rather than troubling these sublime but worn tropes, D&G invoke them as axiomatic, as self-evident principles or open secrets, so that dogs and women are *fixed* as *always already* castrated and castrating, as thoughtless flag bearers of social passivity, who cannot help but triangulate Oedipal desire and capitalism. As stated above, D&G invoke this Medusa-like fusion of dogs and women as a scapegoat, as the very thing that must be expelled in their becoming animal. But how often have we heard frustrated males similarly condemn "the little bitch" that has made their lives miserable? How is D&G's condemnation any different? How is it a line of flight that breaks new ground? And how does D&G's joint inscription and rejection of female power, as a passive but all-consuming will that saps life of its feral spirit, constitute a radical rejection of psychoanalysis and its ideology of lack? To my foolish, dog-loving ears and nose it sounds and smells like crap.

D&G promise "a politics of sorcery" that they contend is capable of unleashing havoc and causing "a rupture with the central institutions" of thought and governance.[15] To conjure this political sorcery they invoke the definitively male prose of Henry Miller and F. Scott Fitzgerald. They state:

> We have seen sorcerers serve as leaders, rally to the cause of despotism, create the countersorcery of exorcism, pass over to the side of the family and descent. But this spells the death of the sorcerer, and also the death of becoming. We have seen becoming spawn nothing more than a big domestic dog, as in Henry Miller's damnation ("it would be better to feign, to pretend to be an animal, a dog for example, and catch the bone thrown to me from time to time") or Fitzgerald's ("I will try to be a correct animal though, and if you throw me a bone with enough meat on it I may even lick your hand"). Invert Faust's formula: So that is what it was, the form of the traveling scholar? A mere poodle?[16]

This offhand allusion to Goethe's "mere poodle" appears to present the ultimate object of D&G's scorn. It is the poodle in *Faust* who follows the distraught protagonist home and then transforms into the devil-trickster Mephistopheles. But why do D&G reject Mephistopheles, the Devil himself, from their select covenant of true sorcerers? Because they do not clarify this allusion we are left to wonder if it is Mephistopheles' dandy-like character that they so revile. Their scorn does not seem to be limited to dogs and the elderly women who love them, but also appears to be concentrated in the figure of the dandy and his poodle companion. Dandies, along with female prostitutes, have long served as scorned figures of bourgeois decadence. Again, by simply playing off these conventions rather than examining them, D&G miss another opportunity to expand their critique and their notion of political sorcery.

The ease with which D&G write off people and animals who do not fit in their schema of becoming animal irks me. What makes them so certain that the little old lady walking her poodle is worthy of their scorn? Why do they see her as an unquestionably passive agent? Could she and poodle not be going to a protest rally? Could her bags not be filled with shoplifted booty or a firebomb? Why is she automatically disqualified as a possible political sorcerer? Is it simply her class, her age, her gender, and her poodle that disqualify her in D&G's eyes? And what about the poodle? Could she/ he not be a political sorcerer in sheep's clothing? "My, what big teeth you have, Professors Deleuze and Guattari!"

My frustration with D&G reiterates Haraway's chiding comments in *When Species Meet*. She too becomes angry for what she sees not only as a missed opportunity on the part of D&G, but also as a glaring case of misogyny. She underscores how D&G add insult to injury by following their vilification of women and dogs with a similarly charged line of flight, which they identify as "becoming-woman." "Despite the keen competition," she declares, "I am not sure I can find in philosophy a clearer display of misogyny, fear of aging, incuriosity about animals, and horror at the ordinariness of flesh, here covered by the alibi of an anti-Oedipal and anticapitalist project."[17] In sharp contrast to D&G's deployment of clichés that tell us next to nothing about the rich significance of dogs, wolves, or women, Haraway presents detailed accounts of specific dogs, wolves, and women who pull us in directions that frustrate our attempts to reduce life to a world with obedient house dogs and housemaids on one side, and wolves and radical theorists on the other.

By detailing various dog stories in *When Species Meet* that involve women zoologists, anthropologists, biologists, dog breeders, and dog lovers, Haraway also invokes an alliance between dogs and women. In other words, like D&G, she too invokes the hybrid figure of a dogwoman. But unlike D&G's dogwoman or Freud's Wolfman, Haraway does not invoke this figure to make sweeping claims that are meant to hold true for all women or all dogs. Haraway's dogwoman is much more of a shifter, in both the linguistic and the shamanistic senses of the word. She/they/it is/are meant to come away at the seams/cuts. Haraway's dog is several dogs but not all dogs, just as her embodied dogwoman is strung together from several women but makes no claims to be about all women. Haraway has long argued for the specificity and richness that matter and thick description lend to our assessments of life. Her insistence that matter matters, that the materiality of the world complicates and augments our attempts to inscribe order, is a key principle fuelling her work, evident in her detailed accounts of female primatologists, biologists, and ethologists working against the grain of traditional science, in her thorough analysis of the inscription of women and female bodies in the discourses of science and popular culture, and in her catalogue of scientific oddities and queer misfits that she champions throughout her work, including the female/man cyborg, the Harvard oncomouse, feminist vampires, and the microscopic symbionts living in our intestines.

One of my favourite portraits in *When Species Meet* is that of Thelma Rowell, the ethologist cum sheep farmer who sets "out a twenty-third bowl in her farmyard in Lancashire when she has only twenty-two sheep to feed."[18] As Haraway explains, this extra bowl is representative of Rowell's efforts to attend to the possible lessons that her ovine companions can teach her as they settle down for their evening meal. "That homely twenty-third bowl," states Haraway, "is the open, the space of what is not yet and may not ever be; it is a making available to events; it is asking the sheep and the scientists to be smart in their exchanges by making it possible for something unexpected to happen."[19] With this talisman in the form of an extra bowl, Rowell engages in the sort of mindful/methodological sorcery that is promised in *A Thousand Plateaus* but is forfeited by D&G's pressing desire to separate the true sorcerers and the true animal spirits from all the charlatans, the old crones, the mindless herds of sheep, and the mere poodles.

I want to end this first canine map on this image of the twenty-third bowl, as emblematic of Rowell's curiosity and her brand of *animalséance*. But perhaps I am being too philosophical and, by invoking Haraway as a good-philosopher dog and Deleuze and Guattari as bad, I have left the physical world of dogs far behind me. To compensate, in the next map I shift to a much more corporeal understanding of dogs. Specifically, I want to focus on dogs urinating and scent-marking as a form of canine cartography. This next map examines how the routine behaviour of scent-marking has been configured as a form of canine communication or dogspeak. The aim here is twofold: (1) to find further examples of ethology like Rowell's that adopt a methodological sorcery; and (2) to further argue that dogs occupy a world that is necessarily queering/deterritorializing and rebukes our attempts to claim mastery over it/them.

Map 2: On a Canine Public Sphere

We begin such a stroll on a sunny day before a flowering meadow in which insects buzz and butterflies flutter, and we make a bubble around each of the animals living in the meadow.... A new world arises in each bubble.

Jacob von Uexküll, *A Foray into the World of Animals and Humans*

A dog can never tell you what she knows from the smells of the world, but you know, watching her, that you know almost nothing.

Mary Oliver, "Her Grave"[20]

Jakob von Uexküll's *A Foray into the Worlds of Animals and Humans* (1934) is a thoughtful, unpresuming text that, for the most part, does not jump to conclusions or make grand claims. Instead, it offers a methodically slow-moving phenomenology of animal behaviour. In this text we are presented with an example of canine cartography in which the author follows his dogs about so as to determine something of their perceived world. In this respect, von Uexküll beat me to the chase by several decades. Von Uexküll traversed this ground as a way to develop the concept of the "Umwelt," the idea that animals, through their unique sense of perception, occupy worlds that are concretely alien from the ways in which humans perceive the world. It is from von Uexküll (and Mary Oliver) that I borrow the idea of a canine world view that manifests both in front of our eyes and hidden from our comprehension.

Von Uexküll's text includes a map that is meant to illustrate the spots where the ethologist's two dogs urinated and scent-marked in a combined effort to relieve themselves and mark territory (Figure 6.1). However, this map, like many of the illustrations in the text, is more confusing than clarifying. The map shows a god's-eye view of the footpaths of the Hamburg Zoo. Sprinkled on the paths are numerous small black dots that are perhaps meant to represent the puddles produced by von Uexküll's two canine subjects. Cutting across the left side of the map is an unexplained railroad-like path that breaks off in two directions and ends with two arrows. In addition to the black dots there is also a liberal sprinkling of clear dots, which perhaps indicate the zoo animals and/or their markings, as these further dots appear off the indicated footpaths. There is no legend to clarify this confusion. Neither does the author spend much time explaining his map. He simply states: "Figure 34 represents a map of the Hamburg Zoo, with the paths on which two male dogs who were walked daily urinated on these daily walks. The places where they left their odor marks were the same as those that were easily recognizable to the human eye. Whenever both dogs were walked at the same time, a urinating contest regularly occurred."[21] Von Uexküll is exceedingly rational in his assessment of what his two dogs appear to be doing. But his map does not support his claim that what is going on here is "easily recognizable to the human eye." As I have just explained, the map in fact makes it extremely difficult, if not impossible, to determine exactly where the dogs are leaving their urine and scent marks. Despite all this urine and von Uexküll's earnest charting, the map provides no clue to why these dogs are so liberal or generous in spreading their mark/scent.

Von Uexküll is keen to present scent-marking as an eager contest of canine supremacy, but the confusion of this map suggests that there is much more to it than that. In other words, von Uexküll's map is necessarily confusing as it attempts to document a canine Umwelt that makes little sense when we deploy traditional methods of inquiry, such as the all-seeing, god's-eye view of conventional map-making. Here the all-seeing god sees next to nothing.

Konrad Lorenz, von Uexküll's peer in German ethology, similarly presents scent-marking as a simple matter of competition and supremacy in which dogs use their urine as a clear and indelible marker to claim territory. Lorenz presents this scenario in his classic 1949 text, *Man Meets Dog*: "the visit of a strange member of his own species releases in the average male dog a response which is not welcome to every house-wife. The leg-lifting of a dog has a very definite meaning which is, paradoxically, exactly the same as that of a nightingale's song: it means the marking of the territory, warning off all intruders by telling them as clearly as their sense can perceive it that they are trespassing on the ground owned by somebody else."[22] Lorenz's offhand remark about housewives who are forever frustrated trying to free their homes of the urine and the scent produced by leg-lifting

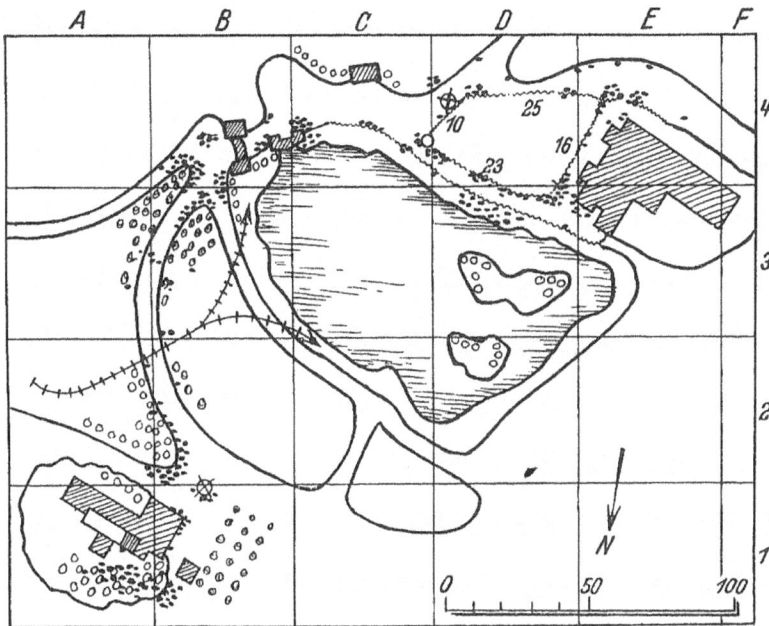

FIGURE 6.1   Von Uexküll's map of the Hamburg Zoo, from *A Foray into the Worlds of Humans and Animals* (1934).

male dogs echoes the same sort of misogyny and incuriosity voiced by D&G. Throughout his book, Lorenz expresses (both directly and indirectly) a taxonomic order in which things and bodies are clearly marked as belonging to specific domains, such that individuals across gender and species lines are presented as knowing and not questioning their place.

In my edition of Lorenz's book, an illustration inserted into the body of the text shows a terrier lifting his leg to mark the kitchen table (Figure 6.2). The fact that this illustration physically interrupts the flow of Lorenz's texts lends itself to the humorous notion that this imagined terrier is lifting his leg to pee on Lorenz's resolve in seeing this behaviour as a simple matter of dogs exercising property rights. By interrupting the text to pee on the table leg, the terrier is reminding Lorenz and his readers, in a not-so-subtle fashion, that dogs generally have a difficult time with the notion of ownership. Despite this defiant/deviant terrier and the countless dogs like him, who, on a daily basis, will wear away at their owner's property (as a consequence of being trapped inside), the notion that canines mark territory as means to establish property rights is persistent in the ethological and popular literature on dogs. My point here is not to dispel the idea that dogs are territorial (I have been chased by vigilant guard dogs and even my dog will growl and snap if I try to separate her from her bone). The point is to question the ease in which we attribute to dogs a natural sense of ownership,

keep dogs. That is simple consideration for others, not only because a dog fight gets on most people's nerves—it does not worry me personally because my dogs usually win—but because the visit of a strange member of his own species releases in the average male dog a response which is not welcome to every house-wife. The leg-lifting of a dog has a very definite meaning which is, paradoxically, exactly the same as that of a nightingale's song: it means the marking of the territory, warning off all intruders by telling them as clearly as their senses can perceive it that they are trespassing on the ground owned by somebody else. Nearly all mammals mark their territory by means of scent, as being one of their strongest sense faculties. A

FIGURE 6.2 Lorenz's naughty terrier, from *Man Meets Dog* (1949).

property rights, or competition, obvious capitalist values. The point is to resist the temptation to configure dogs as simple guardians or totems of the status quo. As this fictive terrier would suggest, most dogs have more bite than that.

In her 2009 best-seller, *Inside of a Dog: What Dogs See, Smell, and Know*, zoologist Alexandra Horwitz contradicts Lorenz by pointing out that dogs do not generally urinate in their own homes if they can help it. She argues that the dog's penchant for wanting to go out for a pee cannot be written off as a matter of good housebreaking. For dogs, peeing is a public event that takes place beyond the confines and concerns of territory. To this end, she states: "The 'territory' notion is also belied by the simple fact that few dogs urinate around the interior corners of the house or apartment where they live. Instead, marking seems to leave information about who the urinator is, how often he walks by this spot in the neighborhood, his recent victories, and his interests in mating. In this way, the invisible pile of scents on the hydrant becomes a community center bulletin board, with old deteriorating announcements and requests peeking out from underneath more recent posts of activities and successes."[23] Instead of using their urine solely to declare territory, Horwitz's dogs engage in a collective or pack enterprise that produces a convoluted and layered public script. While I am encouraged that Horwitz's notion of scent-marking is much more complex than Lorenz's, I am disturbed by her consistent use of the male pronoun in speaking about dogs (she only adopts the female pronoun "she" when she is speaking about Pump, her long-time canine companion), as this consistency perpetuates the myth that only male dogs engage in scent-marking and in the construction of this canine public script.

As a corrective to Lorenz's limited version of scent-marking, this idea of dogs contributing to a collective communal text or discourse with their urine has found a place in both popular and zoological accounts of canine life. The notion of a canine community bulletin board or doggy newspaper is of course also clearly ideological and anthropomorphic, conjuring up kitschy images of dogs dressed as beat reporters sniffing out juicy stories about the lives of their fellow canines. But this interpretation of scent-marking accounts for dogs' acute sense of smell and for their ability to exchange an elaborate range of messages through their pheromones. In this way, dogs are attributed with a much greater sense of agency, as they are seen as engaging in a form of non-human intelligence that is nuanced and subject to interpretation (and misinterpretation). Rather than engaging in

a simple act of colonial flag-planting, dogs are portrayed as active participants, collectively contributing to a canine public sphere of pheromones.[24]

But simply representing scent-marking as a collective canine text does
not guarantee a generous understanding of dogs. For example, Stanley
Coren's *How to Speak Dog: Mastering the Art of Dog–Human Communication*
(2000) champions the idea of a canine communal text, but one in which
dogs appear to merely reinforce conventional human behaviours. On
the back cover of Coren's book we learn that the author is a professor of
psychology at the University of British Columbia, the host of a television
program called *Good Dog*, and the author of several popular dog books.
Like Horwitz, Coren stresses that the physiognomy of a dog's nose makes
the canine world much richer with regard to things they can smell and the
information they can glean from the experience. "The average person," he
explains, "has around 5 million scent receptors in his or her nose, which
puts us in the lower third of mammals in our smell sensitivity. The average
dog has around 220 million receptors in its nose, which potentially makes
its sense of smell forty-four times more sensitive than ours."[25] He further
explains that the variety of messages that dogs are now known to derive
from pheromones displaces earlier notions of scent-marking:

> The original belief was that these smells simply told male animals when
> females were in season, and then served as a means to excite them to
> track the females and mate with them. Today, we know that these per-
> sonal chemicals carry a lot more information than sexual readiness.
> Different hormones are secreted when an animal is angry, fearful, or
> confident. Some chemical signatures identify the sex of the individual,
> and others tell us how old the dog is. There is a lot of sexual information
> as well, such as where the female is in the estrus cycle, if she is pregnant
> or having a false pregnancy, and even if she has given birth recently.[26]

In this excerpt we get a sense of Coren's respectful curiosity about
scent-marking (so far, so good). And to further explain scent-marking,
Coren too invokes a canine free press. "If reading scents," he continues,
"is for dogs the equivalent of reading a written message, then the canine
equivalent of ink is urine."[27] Reading these lines, I was initially excited to
find a description that fit with my goal of mapping a canine cartography
in which dogs are configured as nonhuman agents collectively engaged in
the construction a canine public sphere. And with Coren's emphasis on the
signature and the trace, I thought I might be able to put him in conversation

with Derrida. But my enthusiasm quickly turned sour as Coren uses this opportunity to present an exceedingly sappy representation of canine communications, one in which scent-marking serves as a literal mirror image of the personal columns, and a rather sanitized version of the personal columns to boot. He states:

> When my dogs are busily sniffing at their favorite spot or tree on a city street frequented by other dogs, I sometimes fantasize that I hear them reading the news aloud. Perhaps this morning's edition goes: "Gigi, a young female miniature poodle, has just arrived in this neighborhood and is looking for companionship—neutered males need not apply," or, "Rosco, a strong middle-aged German shepherd, is announcing that he is top dog now, and is marking this whole city as his territory. He says that anybody who wishes to challenge this claim had better make sure their medical insurance is current and paid up."[28]

According to Coren's coy fantasy, the notion of male dogs claiming territory is restored and canine pheromones are reduced to a series of clear-cut signals that transmit clichés of femininity, masculinity, and heterosexual romance. In this way, we get a taste of Coren's brand of psychology and what his idea of a "good dog" consists of. This reductive interpretation is also in keeping with his assertion that we can all master dogspeak if we just follow his lead. Ultimately, Coren's version of Doctor Doolittle and his art of dog–human communication leaves little to the imagination.

Rather than dwell on the heterosexual matrix that buttresses Coren's art of dog–human communication, I want to press on to a further example of ethology that deals with canine scent-marking. In his 2006 collection of essays and field notes, entitled *Animal Passions and Beastly Virtues: Reflections on Redecorating Nature*, Marc Bekoff argues for a mindful or "deep ethology" that shares much in common with the methodological sorcery evident in Rowell's strategy of leaving out a twenty-third bowl for her sheep. "As a deep ethologist," explains Bekoff, "I, as the see-er, try to become the seen. I become coyote. I become penguin. I try to step into animals' sensory and locomotor worlds to discover what it might be like to be a given individual, how they sense their surroundings, and how they behave and move about in certain situations."[29]

In keeping with this mindfulness for his animal subjects, Bekoff designed an experiment in which he patiently followed his dog, Jethro ("a 35 kg neutered male mix"), over the course of several winters in Boulder,

Colorado, gathering up the yellow snow produced by the dog to determine recurring patterns of scent-marking. Bekoff's aim, in other words, was to get Jethro to tell us something of the messages communicated through dog urine. He provides the details of his yellow-snow experiment in the form of field notes. He states:

> Immediately after Jethro or other dogs (known males and females) urinated on the snow, I scooped up the clump of yellow snow (about 4 cm × 4 cm) in gloved hands while Jethro was elsewhere and did not see me pick it up or move it. Before picking up urine the gloves were cleaned thoroughly using clean snow to minimize odor cues. I kept track of which other dogs were present and did not use the urine of the same dogs for at least a week, and Jethro had not previously sniffed the other dogs' urine during a given session. After being moved, yellow snow was matted by hand into other snow to minimize visual cues.[30]

These detailed notes give a sense of the extreme care Bekoff put into his experiment, his meticulous efforts not to run roughshod over the data that could emerge.

The objective of this experiment was to place the yellow snow at three different distances along the path so as to record and measure Jethro's reactions to each of the piles. In one version of the experiment "Jethro's urine was moved 57 times, that of other males 38 times, and that of females 49 times."[31] Bekoff also goes to the extent of applying a mathematical formula and laying out his collected data with an elaborate chart. Despite Bekoff's care, or rather because of the excessive detail, it becomes confusing for the reader to follow along. In this way, Jethro and the reader are placed in a similar predicament, trying to determine whose urine is whose. The reader experiences the same sort of confusion resulting from von Uexküll's map of the Hamburg Zoo, but the two ethologists come to very different conclusions.

Bekoff found that overall "Jethro paid less attention to his own displaced urine than he did to displaced urine from other males or females . . . [and that he] showed about the same amount of interest in displaced urine from other males and displaced urine from females."[32] If Jethro was simply marking territory as his property, we would not see the fluctuating patterns in behaviour that he continued to display, which suggest that dogs engage in a cognitive process that demands subtle degrees of discretion, interpretation, and interaction. Jethro, in other words, appeared to be both picking out who he wanted to be in communication with, as well as selecting the types of messages he wanted to send to his fellow canines.

Bekoff's experiment is admirable for its mixture of elaborate detail and rather simple mechanics, as he practises a methodological sorcery that any dog enthusiast or budding ethologist can adopt as long as they live in a cold climate and have access to fresh snowfall and compliant dogs. There are no Pavlovian bells and whistles to poke and prod dogs to exhibit behaviour. Bekoff's intentions are much more gracious and respectful of animals. But Bekoff's humility has broad implications, as he is also aware that by asking us to acknowledge the complexity of canine life, he is targeting the very foundations of our being all-too-human. He is aware, in other words, that our stubborn refusal of nonhuman intelligence is essential to our claims of being human and not animal. For Bekoff, this arrogance is clearly not conducive to the ecology of the planet and his goal as a deep ethologist is to unearth empirical evidence that proves that, like humans, animals lead lives that are mentally, emotionally, and physically rich. Our second map ends on this wonderful image of Bekoff carefully moving piles of yellow snow as an effective means to chart canine cognition and communication, while gnawing away at our claims of human exceptionalism.

Map 3: Gnawing and Desiring Against the Grain

> Whatever Mr. Bones knew of the world, whatever he discovered in the way of insights or passions or ideas, he had been led to by his sense of smell.
>
> Paul Auster, *Timbuktu*

To begin this final map, I want to return to my dog one final time and clarify how she speaks to me. On my desk sits a worn copy of the March 2008 edition of *National Geographic* with a photographic portrait of Betsy on the cover (Figure 6.3). This dog has been following me around for four years, from one apartment to the next, and even from one country to the next. She seems to have taken up a permanent place on my desk and has become "my dog."

Betsy is the celebrated Border collie living in Germany who is reported to have mastered "a vocabulary of more than 300 words."[33] By learning the names of different stuffed toys and fetching them on command, Betsy has surpassed the cognitive skills of Rico, a fellow Border collie living in Germany, who "learned the names of some 200 toys."[34] Beyond *National*

Geographic, the cognitive skills of these two dogs have drawn the attention of such prestigious institutions as *Science* (considered to be the leading scientific journal), and the Max Planck Institute for Evolutionary Anthropology in Leipzig. Above the cover image of Betsy is a bright red banner that reads "Inside Animal Minds." The banner, and Betsy's slightly tilted head and pensive expression, combine to form an imperative statement or demand that in effect stares down our attempts to ignore the evidence of non-human intelligence and continue to maintain that cognition somehow belongs exclusively to the domain of humans. In this way, Betsy's mug, her doglike mugging, gives face to non-human intelligence and to our stubbornness to acknowledge this intelligence. She stares at me as if she were saying, "Come on, Peter. Get real. Wake up and smell the coffee."

I invoke Betsy as "my dog," as my ghost dog, to enact Derrida's *animalséance* and to make a point about affect. While I agree with Haraway that animals are good to live with, I do not believe that these animal companions need to be living in one's home or even need to be living to experience their material existence. I am not trying to be ghoulish, but dead dogs never truly sleep and we carry on living with and learning from companion animals long after their demise. A photographic image on a tattered magazine may seem like a poor substitute for the real thing, but I am not in the financial position to live with a dog, and Betsy offers me a sense of communion with the two dogs I grew up with and who significantly informed who I am.

FIGURE 6.3 The author's desk, featuring Betsy's mugging face on the cover of *National Geographic*. Photo by Peter Hobbs. The *National Geographic* photo was taken by Vincent J. Musi.

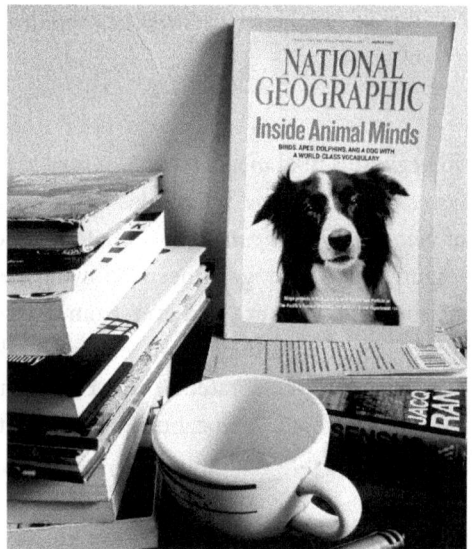

My two childhood dogs were considered black sheep of the family and when they died (Nicky was run over chasing a truck and Tootles mysteriously disappeared) I remember being truly horrified that I seemed to be the only family member who saw these deaths as tragedies that could have been easily avoided if the dogs received more care and respect. For a queer kid growing out in the outskirts of Toronto, both dogs, Nicky and Tootles, acted as something of queer siblings, as they both seemed to prefer the company of their own sex and would shamelessly engage in polymorphous sexual acts. I didn't know I was gay as a kid, but I did know that I didn't want the bickering, depression, drinking, and infidelities that heterosexual marriage appeared to offer. My two dogs confirmed that other pleasures and curiosities lay elsewhere.

Fiction similarly served as a vehicle for imaging a life beyond the familiar. I want to turn to the speculative and world-making function of fiction and address the role animals play in imagining life otherwise. The manner in which animals are enrolled to tell stories and envision life is the subject of much debate that crosses academic disciplines and is contested under the monikers of posthumanism, critical animal studies, and eco-criticism. Susan McHugh's 2011 publication, *Animal Stories: Narrating across Species Lines*, is extremely helpful in wading through these debates. What excites me about McHugh's book is her adoption of what she refers to as a "narrative ethology" and how she uses this method to recoup animal stories that have been vilified as "too sentimental," "too childish," "too populist," and "too anthropomorphic."[35]

McHugh situates her discussion of narrative ethology by referencing the popularity of turn-of-century animal fictions such as Anna Sewell's *Black Beauty* (1877), (Margaret) Marshall Saunders' *Beautiful Joe* (1894), and Ernest Thompson Seton's *Wild Animals I Have Known* (1898), and how Theodore Roosevelt (and other iconic masculine figures) criticized these authors as "nature fakers." This public debate was mostly focused on the reading habits of children and what animal tales would be considered "proper and improper," "fit or unfit." As McHugh explains, social Darwinism played a defining role: "Premier American naturalist John Burroughs thought these texts so dangerous to education about wildlife, especially regarding legislation of the land, that in 1903 he publicly denounced their authors for promoting distorted views of animal happiness, the supposed outcome of natural benevolence, at the expense of the harsh realities of survival, or the inevitable misery involved in the contests that supposedly prove Darwinian fitness."³⁶ In conjunction with social Darwinism and the promotion of "realistic" portrayals of the violence of animal life, Burroughs was also advocating for wilderness conservation, which underscores how nature is conscripted so that competition and aggression are envisioned as products of nature, as the very nature of nature. In other words, the wilderness or nature that Burroughs was arguing to conserve was also a way of conserving the dog-eat-dog tenets of social Darwinism. It is this discursive doubling of nature, so that the nature of nature is *always already* cultural, that Haraway references in her use of the neologism "natureculture."³⁷

As a way of recouping these discredited texts and other such animal stories, McHugh proposes narrative ethology, which she in part accredits to D&G and their emphasis on affect as means of "deterritorialization" (a term/idea I have been using throughout my essay without properly attributing it to D&G). In her introduction, McHugh briefly sketches the purview of narrative ethology: "Challenging the assumption that literature is merely a reflection of ideology, the following chapters highlight some of the ways in which animal narratives also pointedly appeal to the power of affect and defy the regimes that benefit from separation, isolation, and fragmentation of our lives and theirs.... Put plainly, my purpose in sketching these very specific animal narrative histories is to insist that story forms serve as spawning grounds for forms of species and social agency."³⁸ By foregrounding affect, McHugh, like Alaimo and Haraway, also makes a bid for animal life beyond the limits of the all-too-human. Echoing Isabelle Stengers, McHugh refers to this shift to affect as a shift from biopolitics to that of "cosmopolitics," a critique that attempts to move beyond the conventions of discourse analysis to account for the interrelations of species across scales and temporal constraints.³⁹

Inspired by McHugh, I want to use the space remaining to pursue a narrative ethology (or canine cosmopolitics) that isolates some of the ways novelists use sentiment and affect to produce dog stories that run counter to ideology. Because of space constraint, I have chosen to focus on one text: Paul Auster's 1999 novel, *Timbuktu*. Auster tells this comic-tragic tale about the love and companionship shared between a poet drifter (Willy G. Christmas) and his dog (Mr. Bones) from the dog's point of view. At the outset of the story, Mr. Bones can sense that years of living on the road, as well alcohol and drug abuse, have taken their toll and that Willy's death is imminent. Mr. Bones can also tell from his companion's anxiety that Willy too is aware that he does not have long to live. Part of Willy's anxiety is that he does not want to leave Mr. Bones homeless, and with this in mind the two set off to Baltimore in search of Bea Swanson, Willy's high-school teacher. For Willy, Mrs. Swanson (or "swan song") is the only person who can be trusted to take care of both his dog and his notebooks filled with his poetry. We soon learn that Willy, formerly William Gurevitch, took his vow of poverty and his Saint Nick persona (complete with a tattoo of Santa Claus on his arm), in part to rebel against his Jewish mother. We also learn that Willy has not seen his former teacher for seventeen years. The fact that Mrs. Swanson could be long dead adds to the sheer desperation of their quest.

Timbuktu addresses some of the same issues covered in this essay, as much of the story revolves around the ontological gap between the worlds of humans and dogs. The novel also stresses the idea that the canine world is an olfactory one that is necessarily alien to the ways in which humans experience life. In a scene that is very reminiscent of Marc Bekoff's yellow snow experiments with Jethro, Willy builds a makeshift maze or labyrinth in the sub-basement of his mother's apartment building to chart/map what he refers to as a "symphony of smells."[40] To determine if Mr. Bones can distinguish the difference between lust and sentiment, Willy scatters rags through the maze soaked in the urine of female dogs in heat alongside an assortment of his own dirty clothes. The fact that Mr. Bones does not show any clear preference does not deter Willy's enthusiasm (or suggest to Willy that Mr. Bones might desire him). Mr. Bones, on the other hand, sees the experiment as inherently flawed, as he disagrees with Willy's working premise that sentiment and lust can be parsed out as separate things, smells, feelings or sensations: "For once, Mr. Bones was glad that he had not been endowed with the power of speech. If he had, he would be forced to tell Willy the truth, and that would cause him much pain. For a dog, he would have said, for a dog, dear master, the fact is that the whole world is a symphony of smells. Every hour, every minute, every second of his waking life is at once a physical and a spiritual experience. There is no difference between the inner and the outer, nothing to separate the high from the low."[41] Mr. Bones' pragmatic thinking, along with his concern not to offend Willy's feelings, is consistent with his overall persona, as he is repeatedly shown to be far more caring/humane than Willy and the various other humans he encounters.

Following Willy's death, Mr. Bones is faced with a harsh, indifferent world, finding a brief respite in the companionship of Henry Chow, a young Chinese boy and fellow misfit who is forced to hide Mr. Bones in a crate behind his family's take-out restaurant. Eventually, Mr. Bones finds himself in the suburbs and is adopted by a white suburban family (the Joneses), who can provide him with what he initially thinks is an ideal home. After being transformed into a "proper dog" fit for the suburbs, he realizes that this existence is no life for any "self-respecting dog." This transformation sees him being neutered, groomed, leashed to a "running wire" in the backyard, forced to live in a doghouse, and renamed Sparky. Disillusioned, Mr. Bones is comforted by the bond he shares with Polly Jones, who also feels trapped in her role as a suburban housewife. Once Mr. Jones (Dick—there is no subtlety in Auster's choice of names) leaves for work, Polly defies her husband by sneaking Mr. Bones/Sparky into the house to lounge and shed hairs on the matrimonial bed and to eat scrambled eggs at the kitchen table.[42] Polly and Mr. Bones also commiserate their shared fate by taking long drives together in the family minivan. Despite this bond, Mr. Bones cannot accept his new life as Sparky and is haunted by his memories of Willy, who in one frightful dream appears as a demon and vehemently chastises Mr. Bones for selling his canine soul. Mr. Bones' inner turmoil will not rest and he decides to end his own life, like Nicky, by playing the losing game of dodging traffic on a busy highway.

By telling this epic journey from Mr. Bones' point of view, Auster invokes a canine world view or Umwelt that addresses the limits of human and animal bodies and experiences, while showing how these limits are never clear-cut. Instead, lives and world views are easily contaminated, as they intermingle, distort, and inform one another so that it becomes impossible to mark off clearly where one world stops and another begins. Life, as such, is inherently alien, exuberant, and uncontainable. The novel underscores this ontological theme in its numerous graphic scenes detailing the deterioration of both Willy and Mr. Bones, as they excrete sweat, vomit, drool, snot, blood, and shit. But with all this emphasis on bodily fluids, it is significant that sex is all but absent. While Auster underscores the heterosexuality of both Mr. Bones and Willy (for example, both briefly refer to past sexual encounters), neither expresses any inkling of sexual desire. I suspect that Auster holds back on sex to quash the spectres of homosexuality and bestiality in this already complicated buddy narrative. In other words, to explicitly express sexual desire in such an otherwise carnal and carnivalesque text would be going too far for Auster, as it would risk the innocence of Willy and Mr. Bones' cross-species relationship.

There is significantly more to say about *Timbuktu* and if I had more space I would expand on its portrayal of homelessness, as well as its queer pastiche of Jack Kerouac, and its use of racial and ethnic stereotypes as a way to map American culture. As a final word, it is important to emphasize that *Timbuktu* is by no means a journey of redemption in which all the loose ends are tied up and order is restored. Instead, the reader is left to ponder the messiness of life as an open-ended adventure.

I want to close my canine cartography in a similar open-ended and messy fashion by reiterating Derrida's promise of more to follow. There are many noteworthy dogs and dog people that demand to be heard (Barbara Smuts' canine ethology, with her emphasis on embodied knowledge, is a glaring omission, as are J.R. Ackerley's wonderfully queer canine narratives). Having initiated this *animalséance* or canine cartography, I find myself obliged to pursue a litany of divergent voices and affects. This sense of obligation is the result of the constitutive relationship we share with animals as our interlocutors/fellow creatures. It is also important to echo both Derrida's and Haraway's warnings that critiques of humanism, especially those that use the language of "post" or "beyond" (as I have), should never lose sight of or attempt to surpass either the animal or the human by succumbing to a teleology in which humans have evolved/mutated to shed their all-too-animal fur or their all-too-human frock coats to emerge on the other side of an ontological divide. Betsy, Nicky, Tootles, Jethro, and Mr. Bones won't be given the slip by such a dry and deluded morsel. They need a story they can sink their teeth into, a tale that doesn't make them or their human companions (foolish or otherwise) obsolete.

NOTES

1. On the animal industrial complex see Noske, *Beyond Boundaries*.
2. Haraway, *When Species Meet*. This text is a much-extended version of the arguments that Haraway raises in her earlier publication, *Companion Species Manifesto*.
3. On the inscription of the homosexual see Foucault, *History of Sexuality*, 43.
4. Alaimo, "Eluding Capture," 55.
5. Susan Block's essay, "The Bonobo Way."
6. Alaimo, "Eluding Capture," 62.
7. Ibid., 63.
8. Derrida, *Animal That Therefore I Am*, 4.
9. In *When Species Meet*, Haraway praises Derrida for the significance he allots to his cat as an agent who shatters the ontological space of his daily routines, but she also criticizes him for not delving into the specific material character

of his cat. She argues that Derrida misses a valuable opportunity by invoking his cat as a generic marker of alterity, rather than pursuing something of his cat's phenomenological life and behaviour and how this cat-ness of the cat constitutes "a possible invitation, a possible introduction to other-worlding" (20).

10. Derrida. *Animal That Therefore I Am*, 4.
11. Ibid., 5.
12. Deleuze and Guattari, *A Thousand Plateaus*, 240.
13. Ibid., 244.
14. Haraway, *When Species Meet*, 30.
15. Deleuze and Guattari, *A Thousand Plateaus*, 247.
16. Ibid., 248.
17. Haraway, *When Species Meet*, 30.
18. Ibid., 33.
19. Ibid., 34.
20. This poem is part of a 2013 collection by Oliver entitled *Dog Songs*, which includes similar eulogies for departed and lost dogs, expressing how they constitute thoughtful emissaries of a canine world and worlding.
21. von Uexküll, *A Foray*, 106.
22. Lorenz, *Man Meets Dog*, 93–94.
23. Horwitz, *Inside of a Dog*, 84.
24. On the canine public sphere see Uddin, "Canine Citizenship."
25. Coren, *How to Speak Dog*, 183.
26. Ibid., 185–86.
27. Ibid., 186.
28. Ibid.
29. Bekoff, *Animal Passions*, 7.
30. Ibid., 116–17.
31. Ibid., 117.
32. Ibid., 119.
33. Morell, "Animal Minds," 49.
34. Ibid., 48.
35. McHugh, *Animal Stories*. See especially her concluding chapter, "Towards a Narrative Ethology."
36. McHugh, *Animal Stories*, 213.
37. For an elaboration of naturecultures see the first section of Haraway's *Companion Species Manifesto*, "Emergent Naturecultures."
38. McHugh, *Animal Stories*, 19.
39. Stengers, "Cosmopolitical Proposal."
40. Auster, *Timbuktu*, 42–43.
41. Ibid. By pointing the metaphysical leaps and binaries that are used to construct

the ontological boundaries or limits that are, in turn, perceived as universal laws, like the separation of the human from the animal, men from women, homosexuality from the heterosexuality, cultural from nature, the mental from the physical, Mr. Bones echoes the French critique of Western metaphysics associated with Derrida, Foucault, Deleuze and Guattari, Luce Irigaray, and Bruno Latour.

42. Auster's choice of "Polly" could be read as a reference to Homer's *Odyssey*, in which another Polly or Penelope is similarly left to care for the dog, Argos, when her husband, Odysseus, goes to work.

BIBLIOGRAPHY

Alaimo, Stacy. "Eluding Capture: The Science, Culture and Pleasure of 'Queer' Animals." In *Queer Ecologies: Sex, Nature, Politics, Desire*, edited by Catriona Mortimer-Sandilands and Bruce Erickson, 51–72. Bloomington: Indiana University Press, 2010.

Auster, Paul. *Timbuktu*. New York: Picador, 1999.

Bagemihl, Bruce. *Biological Exuberance: Animal Homosexuality and Natural Diversity*. New York: St. Martin's Press, 1999.

Bekoff, Mark. *Animal Passions and Beastly Virtues: Reflections on Redecorating Nature*. Philadelphia: Temple University Press, 2006.

Block, Susan. "The Bonobo Way: Peace through Pleasure," *The Bonobo Way* (author's website). www.blockbonobofoundation.org.

Coren, Stanley. *How to Speak Dog: Mastering the Art of Dog–Human Communication*. New York: Free Press, 2000.

Deleuze, Gilles, and Félix Guattari. *A Thousand Plateaus*. Minneapolis: University of Minnesota Press, 1987. First published 1980.

Derrida, Jacques. *The Animal That Therefore I Am*. New York: Fordham University Press, 2008.

Foucault, Michel. *The History of Sexuality*. Vol. 1. New York: Vintage Books, 1978. First published 1976.

Haraway, Donna. *The Companion Species Manifesto: Dogs, People, and Significant Otherness*. Chicago: Prickly Paradigm Press, 2003.

——. *When Species Meet*. Minneapolis: University of Minnesota Press, 2008.

Horwitz, Alexandra. *Inside of a Dog: What Dogs See, Smell, and Know*. New York: Scribner, 2009.

Lorenz, Konrad. *Man Meets Dog*. 1949. London: Routledge, 2005.

McHugh, Susan. *Animal Stories: Narrating across Species Lines*. Minneapolis: University of Minnesota Press, 2011.

——. *Dog*. London: Reaktion, 2004.

Morell, Virginia. "Animal Minds." *National Geographic* 213, no. 3 (March 2008): 49.

Noske, Barbara. *Beyond Boundaries: Humans and Animals*. Montreal: Black Rose Press, 1997.

Oliver, Mary. *Dog Songs*. New York: Penguin Press, 2013.

Roughgarden, Joan. *Evolution's Rainbow: Diversity, Gender, and Sexuality in Nature*. Berkeley: University of California Press, 2004.

Shukin, Nicole. *Animal Capital: Rendering Life in Biopolitical Times*. Minneapolis: University of Minnesota Press, 2009.

Stengers, Isabelle. "The Cosmopolitical Proposal." In *Making Things Public*, edited by Bruno Latour and Peter Weibel, 994–1003. Cambridge, MA: MIT Press, 2005.

Terry, Jennifer. "Unnatural Acts: Scientific Fascination with Queer Animals." *GLQ: A Journal of Lesbian and Gay Studies* 6, no. 2 (2000): 151–93.

Uddin, Lisa. "Canine Citizenship and the Intimate Public Sphere." *Invisible Culture: An Electronic Journal for Visual Culture* 6, 2003.

von Uexküll, Jakob. *A Foray into the Worlds of Animals and Humans*. Minneapolis: University of Minnesota Press, 2010. First published 1934.

Wolfe, Cary. *Animal Rites: American Culture, the Discourse of Species, and Posthumanist Theory*. Chicago: University of Chicago Press, 2003.

7

Navigating Difference (Again)

Animal Ethics and Entangled Empathy

Lori Gruen

"Speciesism," "humanormativity," "human exceptionalism"—these are terms that have been used to identify a perceived ethical problem with human attitudes toward, and treatment of, other animals. Speciesism, akin to sexism and racism, is the view that our species is superior to others in virtue of a morally irrelevant characteristic—species membership; humanormativity, akin to heteronormativity (and later homonormativity), is the view that humans are the gauge or normative measure against which other species are judged deficient, deviant, lacking;[1] human exceptionalism harkens back to nationalist theories that set one nation or one people apart from and above others. The attitudes evoked by these terms and the practices that emerge from and support them are increasingly viewed to be unjustifiably prejudicial and oppressive, but they are also at the very core of scholarship in virtually every field in the "humanities."

Humanism rests on a deeply entrenched value hierarchy—we define the human, human action, human mindedness, human morality, human creativity, human knowledge against the animal and just below the divine. We construct animals as others, and ourselves in the image of God—presumably to elevate our value, but in the process we lower theirs and fundamentally, and often perilously, deny our own animality.[2] The limitations of humanism have led some to advocate a "posthumanistic turn" and I think that is a good idea, but some posthumanisms are more appealing than others. In what follows I first briefly elaborate my understanding of humanism and its limitations. I then discuss the most prominent response to these limitations that comes from animal advocates, what I call the "sameness response," and discuss some worries with it. I then turn to feminist rejections of the sameness response that are critical of the isolated individualism central to both humanism and the sameness response to it. I end by advocating my preferred alternative, what I have been calling "entangled empathy," which might be considered a type of posthumanism that helps us navigate difference and build meaningful, ethical interspecies relationships.

"We Are Not Them" Humanism

A commitment to human uniqueness has deep roots, going back to ancient texts in both Eastern and Western traditions. Theorists often go to great lengths to establish humans as different from and better than animals. Consider this from Augustine:

> Though in fact we observe that infants are weaker than the most vulnerable of the young of other animals in the control of their limbs, and in their instincts of appetition and defense, this seems designed to enhance man's superiority over other living things, on the analogy of an arrow whose impetus increases in proportion to the backward extension of the bow.[3]

These days, there are less contorted but perhaps more complicated attempts to distinguish us from them:

> An animal might be aware of her experiences and of herself as the subject of those experiences, and yet her attitudes might still be invisible to her, because they are a lens *through* which she sees the world, rather than being parts of the world that she sees.... The experiences that she was aware of having would still be experiences of things as "to-be-eaten" "to-be-fled" "to-be-cared-for" and so on; and her responses to those things would still be governed by the teleological content of her experiences.
>
> But as rational beings we are aware of our attitudes. We know of ourselves that we want certain things, fear certain things, love certain things, believe certain things, and so on. And we are also aware of the potential influence of our attitudes on what we will decide to do. We are

aware of the *potential grounds* of our actions—of the ways in which our attitudes incline us to respond. And once you are aware of the influence of a potential ground of action, you are in a position to decide whether to allow yourself to be influenced in that way or not. . . . you now have a certain reflective distance from the impulse that is influencing you, and you are in a position to ask yourself, "but *should* I be influenced in that way?" You are now in a position to raise a *normative* question, a question about whether the action you find yourself inclined to perform is *justified*.[4]

Of course there are differences between humans and other animals. Indeed, all animals are different one from the other, as members of biological groups and as individuals. Chimpanzees are closer to humans genetically and evolutionarily than either is to another great ape, the gorilla. All great apes are markedly different from ungulates, carnivores quite distinct from herbivores, monotremes very unlike cats. Given the tremendous variety of animal shapes, sizes, social structures, behaviours, and habitats, separating humans from all other animals is a peculiar way to categorize organisms. But these constructs have purposes and in this case differentiating the human from the animal establishes animals as "others" of lesser worth, others that can be readily used for human ends.

Sameness Response

The standard response to the "we are not them" construct is to turn both to empirical work to show that such a view defies reality and to ethical argumentation that demands that like cases be treated alike. If ethological and cognitive research shows that other animals share many of the qualities that we admire in ourselves and to which we attach moral significance, then we ought to admire and value those qualities in whatever bodies they arise. As I've discussed elsewhere, many species of nonhumans have rich social relationships—orangutan mothers stay with their young for ten years and even though they eventually part company, they continue to maintain their relationships over time. Less solitary animals, such as chimpanzees, baboons, wolves, and elephants maintain extended family units built upon complex individual relationships, for long periods of time, in some cases up to fifty years. Meerkats in the Kalahari desert are known to sacrifice their own safety by staying with sick or injured family members so that the fatally ill will not die alone. Like humans, many nonhuman animals negotiate their social environments by being particularly attentive to the emotional states of others around them. When a conspecific is angry, it is a good idea to get out of his way. Animals that develop lifelong bonds are known to suffer terribly from the death of their partners. Some are said to die of sorrow.[5] Recent studies in cognitive ethology have suggested that some nonhumans engage in manipulative and deceptive activity, can construct "cognitive maps" for navigation, act altruistically, and some nonhumans appear to understand symbolic representation, and are able to use language. It appears that many, if not most, of the capacities that are thought to distinguish humans have been observed, often in less elaborate form, in the nonhuman world.

Some of the work that has been done to explore attributes that we may share with other animals has led to new avenues of inquiry that help us rethink how we have conceptualized certain ideas and practices. Consider the idea of norms and norm governance. The general social scientific understanding is that norms are standards of social behaviour that are expected by a group. When a norm is transgressed there is generally a group recognition of the transgression and typically there is a response. The responses to norm violations vary with context. If a new member of the group is being taught a norm, the reaction to its violation will tend to be different than when a so-called "troublemaker" violates the norm, particularly if it is a repeated violation. Most of the literature on social norms treat them as unique to humans. For example, Sripada and Stich write, "Humans are unique in the animal world in the extent to which their day-to-day behavior is governed by a complex set of rules and principles commonly called *norms.*" And Fehr and Fischbacher suggest that "[t]he human capacity to establish and enforce social norms is perhaps the decisive reason for the uniqueness of human cooperation in the animal world. The evidence indicates that other animals largely lack the cognitive and emotional capacities that are necessary for social norms." Sripada and Stich even suggest that the ability to recognize and respond to norms is part of innate psychological mechanisms that are "universal, [human] species-typical emotional structures," structures that serve in both the norm acquisition function and the norm implementation function.

The sameness response to such claims of human uniqueness allows us to refocus inquiry by challenging the human-centred assumptions being made. Are these emotional structures unique to humans? It seems that these very structures developed to serve a social purpose and it is unlikely, although possible, that closely related species facing similar social pressures would develop very different psychological mechanisms to address those pressures. It is at least plausible that the capacity to recognize and respond to norms may exist in other social animals in addition to the human animal.

There is a large and growing body of literature that supports the view that co-operation and sanction do occur among relatively large groups of animals who are not direct kin. Chimpanzees provide excellent examples. In natural settings where populations are not threatened, chimpanzees live in fission–fusion societies in which their smaller, tighter-knit groups of 4–10 come together with the larger community of approximately 100 individuals on a fairly regular, although not day-to-day, basis. The ability to share resources, exchange information, and to manage social interactions in such a large group would best be facilitated through adherence to some sort of norms. In addition, the complex behaviours exhibited in these regular meetings would also be best explained by the existence of norms. Chimpanzees have long-term memory, they are socially tolerant and intelligent, they have quite flexible social repertoires, they have complex communicative abilities (some can even can use basic human symbolic language systems), they understand and respond to the emotions of others, they understand the consequences of their and others' actions, and there is at least some evidence that they are able to inhibit their behaviours. They also engage in complex behaviours that researchers have variously described as "fairness," "other-regarding behaviour," "inequity tolerance," "punishment or sanction," "co-operation," and "retaliation." It is possible that this is the wrong way to describe the behaviours, but at least in some cases, norm-based descriptions do seem apt. Here are some of those cases:

In Bossou, chimpanzees are occasionally observed crossing roads that intersect with their territories. One of the roads is busy with traffic, the other is mostly a pedestrian route, both are dangerous to the chimpanzees. On video recording of chimpanzee behaviour at the crossings, adult males were found to take up forward and rear positions, with adult females and young occupying the more protected middle positions. The positioning of dominant and bolder individuals, in particular the alpha male, was found to change depending on both the degree of risk and number of adult males present. Researchers suggested that co-operative action in the higher-risk situation was probably aimed at maximizing group protection. This sort of risk-taking for the sake of others is also often observed in male patrols of territorial boundaries in other parts of Africa. In these instances, a bold male, who may or may not be the alpha of the group, together with others with whom he has an alliance, begins a patrol with the goal of potential food rewards as well as protecting the group from neighbouring threats.⁶

De Waal and Brosnan developed a series of tests to try to analyze co-operative behaviour (foodsharing) among chimpanzees in captivity. They found that adults were more likely to share food with individuals who had groomed them earlier in the day. They suggested that the results could be explained in two ways: the "good-mood hypothesis," in which individuals who have received grooming are in a benevolent mood and respond by sharing with all individuals, or the "exchange hypothesis," in which the individual who has been groomed responds by sharing food only with the groomer. The data indicated that the sharing was specific to the previous groomer. The chimpanzees remembered who had performed a service (grooming) and responded to that individual by sharing food. De Waal and Brosnan also observed that grooming between individuals who rarely did so was found to have a greater effect on sharing between partners who commonly groomed. Among partnerships in which little grooming was usually exchanged, there was a more pronounced effect of previous grooming on subsequent food sharing. They suggest that being groomed by an individual who doesn't usually groom might be more noticeable and thus warrant greater response in the form of food sharing, or what they call "calculated reciprocity." They write, "Not only do the chimpanzees regulate their food sharing based on previous grooming, but they recognize unusual effort and reward accordingly."⁷

In a different set of studies, de Waal and his collaborators have described reconciliation behaviours in which a high-ranking female will work to help two male chimpanzees "make up" after an altercation. This kind of behaviour, in which the female first attends to the "winner," then reassures the "loser" and encourages him to follow her to a grooming session with the winner, has no obvious or immediate benefit for the female but does impact social harmony. Once the males begin grooming each other, she will usually leave them alone.⁸

One of the clearest indications that there are norms in place is activity that corresponds to reactions to violations of norms. De Waal describes one such incident at the Yerkes Field Station:

> Jimoh detected a secret mating between Socko, an adolescent male, and one of Jimoh's favorite females. Normally the old male would merely chase off the culprit, but for some reason—perhaps because the female

had repeatedly refused to mate with Jimoh himself that day—he this time went full speed after Socko and did not give up. He chased him all around the enclosure—Socko screaming and defecating in fear. Before Jimoh could accomplish his aim, several females close to the scene began to "woaow" bark. This indignant sound is used in protest of aggressors and intruders. At first the callers looked around to see how the rest of the group was reacting, but when others joined in, particularly the top-ranking female, the intensity of their calls quickly increased until literally everyone's voice was part of a deafening chorus. The scattered beginning almost gave the impression that the group was taking a vote. Jimoh broke off his attack with a nervous grin on his face, he got the message.[9]

Consider also some of the behaviours I witness when I visit a group of chimpanzees with whom I periodically interact: When I arrive, there is usually a lot of excitement; I imagine this is both because it is something different from the daily routine and also because I bring lots of treats. During one visit, Keeli, an adolescent male, started displaying in ways that are inappropriate for a chimpanzee in his position in the social hierarchy. At one point, Darrell, then the alpha male, decided it was time to put Keeli in his place and began displaying and chasing Keeli around the enclosure, smacking him when he got close enough. While this was going on the other chimpanzees in the group tried to get out of their way, which is quite typical, but on this occasion Sarah, the older female, began "woaow" distress vocalizations. Upon hearing the vocalizations, Darrell continued chasing Keeli around the enclosure but also began reassuring all the other chimpanzees as he did so. The reassurance not only calmed the other chimps down but also slightly distracted Darrell from the intensity of his pursuit. When he eventually caught Keeli, he smacked him, but not as hard as he might have had he been in full pursuit. The next day Keeli sat apart from the group, pouting.

On another occasion I observed a surprising set of behaviours. Sarah likes to look at books, so when I visit I occasionally bring her children's books that can withstand chimpanzee handling for at least a few minutes. I gave Sarah her book and before she could really start "reading" it, Harper, a young male chimpanzee, came over and took it away. Sarah didn't struggle with Harper when he took it. Then moments later, Sheba a very smart female chimpanzee (the daughter of Nim Chimpsky), who didn't appear to me to have noticed Harper's behaviour—because she was happily eating her dried mangos—went over to Harper and took the book from him. This in itself wouldn't be surprising as taking things that others have is typical among members of a group that aren't clearly dominant. What was surprising was that rather than keeping it herself, she promptly gave it back to Sarah. There were no vocalizations that I was aware of that might indicate Sarah was distressed by Harper's thievery, nor that Sheba was trying to appease any distress. It just looked to me as though Sheba was setting things right.

How might we explain the risky behaviour the males engage in to protect the group? Or the strategic exchange of food and grooming? Or reconciliation behaviours? Or the sanctioning/reassuring behaviour and the rectification behaviour? One plausible explanation would be that the chimpanzees are trying to promote social harmony or well-being (in addition to furthering their own) and that they achieve this, in part, by recognizing and acting on certain norms. In the case of the male protection of the group there is coordinated activity that the strong engage in for the sake of the others. In the case of food exchange for grooming, individuals remember the behaviour of others and reward it, particularly when longer term positive social engagement is desired. The behaviours I observe among my chimpanzee friends may best be explained by positing that the chimpanzees understand social norms, those that distinguish right or apt or appropriate behaviour from wrong or inappropriate behaviour, and act to enforce the norms. I'm quite certain that these chimpanzees don't ask themselves whether they should be acting the way they are acting or whether their actions are justified, but I do think they are acting under normative forces.

If we can see that the force of norms might be felt in social groups that aren't made up of humans, then we can ask ourselves different conceptual questions about the nature of norms and normativity. Yet, while sameness views can provide openings for thinking about ourselves, our practices, and our concepts in new ways, it is also deeply problematic when those holding these views unwittingly project human capacities or extend our conceptions of motivation onto other animals.

To illustrate this worry about unwitting projection, consider a controversy that has been going on for decades in research into what is called "theory of mind." When Sarah (mentioned above) was tested originally in the 1970s, she was given tasks that were based on our own conception of mentation and what it means to have and understand mental states such as "intentions," "knowledge," "belief," "thinking," "guessing," "pretending," and "liking." Sarah was shown a set of four videotaped recordings of a human facing a problem and the tape was stopped just before the human was to solve the problem. She was then presented with photographs, one of which depicted the solution to the problem. She was asked to pick the photograph that solved the problem for the human in the video and she passed the test well above chance levels, which indicated to David Premack and Guy Woodruff that Sarah could "impute mental states to herself and to others" and thus had a "theory of mind."[10]

Yet when other chimpanzees at other laboratories were tested, they all failed miserably.[11] It appeared that no other chimpanzees could pass what are called "non-verbal false belief tests," often used with human children before they can speak. A test was designed to determine whether chimpanzees understood that seeing meant knowing. Two humans would stand outside an enclosure with a desirable food item. One of the humans would not be able to see the chimpanzee. (Her eyes might be covered, she would have a bucket over her head, or she would be looking away.) The other human would be looking right at the chimpanzee. If the chimpanzee went to the human that could see him and asked for food, rather than going to the human who could not see him to ask for food, researchers could conclude that the chimpanzees understood that seeing was an important part of the way individuals formed mental states. But the chimpanzees approached the humans randomly in this set of experiments.[12] None of this work supported the original conclusion that chimpanzees could attribute wants, intentions, beliefs, or purposes to themselves or others. Indeed, quite the opposite was being claimed. Cecilia Heyes even suggested that since "there is still no convincing evidence of theory of mind in primates. . . . We should stop asking Premack and Woodruff's question."[13]

But when chimpanzees were not viewed as hairier, stronger versions of human children and researchers started to pay attention to chimpanzee differences, the theory-of-mind tests could be reformulated. Brian Hare and his colleagues noticed that chimpanzees did seem to understand something about the visual perception of other chimpanzees.[14] Hare created an experiment in which a subordinate chimpanzee and a dominant chimpanzee were put in competition over food, and showed that the subordinate would systematically approach the food the dominant could not see and avoid the food the dominant could see.[15] In a variation on this theme, a subordinate watched food being hidden that the dominant could only sometimes see, depending on whether or not the dominant chimpanzee's door was open or closed during the time of hiding. When the dominant was released, the subordinate would only approach the food that the dominant had not seen being hidden, even though the dominant could see it now. After a series of experiments, the researchers claimed, "[w]e therefore believe that these studies show what they seem to show, namely that chimpanzees actually know something about the content of what others see and, at least in some situations, how this governs their behavior."[16] They concluded, "[a]t issue is no less than the nature of human cognitive uniqueness. We now believe that our own and others' previous hypotheses to the effect that chimpanzees do not understand any psychological states at all were simply too sweeping."[17] The researchers attribute the chimpanzee's success in demonstrating an understanding of another's psychological state to the ecological relevancy of the experiment. Observing differences, in this case that competing for food is a more typical behaviour for chimpanzees than begging for it from a human, led to a recognition of complex social cognitive abilities.

That the sameness view leads to empirical problems is troubling, but it also leads to theoretical problems. When what we are looking for are similarities—how we might share the same general type of intelligence or cognitive skills, the same sensitivities and vulnerabilities, the same emotional responses—we tend to obscure or overlook distinctively valuable aspects of the lives of others. We assimilate them into our human-oriented framework, we grant them consideration in virtue of what we believe they share with us, we allow them to be seen, perhaps for the first time, through our distinctively human gaze. And in our magnanimous embrace of the other, we end up reconfiguring a dualism that will inevitably find some "other" to exclude.

Feminist theorists have long been critical of this standard humanist problem. As Naomi Schor put it, "If othering involves attributing to the objectified other a difference that serves to legitimate her oppression, saming denies the objectified other the right to her difference, submitting the other to the laws of phallic specularity. If othering assumes that the other is knowable, saming precludes any knowledge of the other in her otherness."[18]

Varieties of Difference

There are (at least) three types of feminist responses to the sameness view. Each rejects the abstract individualism of liberal humanism and its sameness shadow in favour of contextualizing relationships and recognizing both the ontological and ethical implications that spring from them. The first feminist response focuses on the particularities of relationships, rather than intrinsic capacities generalized over, to try to determine what is ethically salient in our attitudes and actions toward other animals. As I will show, however, this view reverts to a different sort of humanism. The second type of response emerges from the new turn towards material feminism. Material feminism is undoubtedly posthumanist; in this view there are no individual humans to elevate above all else. But I worry here that this view may go too far in valuing every kind of material relation. The third response is what I am calling engaged or entangled empathy that draws on the previous two views, as well as some important insights from the sameness response to humanism, but differs significantly from each.

Particular Familial Relations

Feminist theorists have long been critical of faulty universalism that has been a cornerstone of so much theorizing in ethics, political philosophy, epistemology, and theories of personal identity. Drawing on these criticisms, feminist philosophers Elizabeth Anderson and Eva Kittay have recently taken on the sameness response to thinking about other animals and those who promote such responses. In particular, they are responding to sameness arguments that equate the moral considerability of nonhuman animals with that of significantly cognitively impaired humans (a thorny debate that brings animal studies, feminism, disability studies, and practical ethics into dialogue). Their rejection of sameness views, most pointedly those of Jeff McMahan and Peter Singer, are based on the view that species-specific social relations make a difference from an ethical perspective.

According to Anderson, a human person's normative commitments do not emerge solely from her intrinsic psychological capacities (those very capacities that sameness proponents have been trying to discover or illuminate); rather such commitments are constructed and made meaningful in social relations with other humans. To illustrate what she is thinking in terms of relations to others who are not moral agents (or "persons" as they are called in the mainstream ethics literature), such as most nonhuman animals and human moral patients, she has us consider an individual with a profound case of Alzheimer's. This individual is unable to recognize herself or others, to reason, or to care for herself. Anderson argues that this individual's dignity would be violated if she was:

> not properly toileted and decently dressed in clean clothes, her hair combed, her face and nose wiped, and so forth. These demands have

only partially to do with matters of health and hygiene. They are, more fundamentally, matters of making the body fit for human society for presentation to others. Human beings need to live with other humans, but cannot do so if those others cannot relate to them as human. And this specifically human relationship requires that the human body be dignified, protected from the realm of disgust, and placed in a cultural space of decency.

If the relatives of an Alzheimer's patient were to visit her in a nursing home and find her naked, eating from a dinner bowl like a dog, they might well describe what shocks them by saying, "They are treating her like an animal!" The shock is a response to her degraded condition, conceived in terms of a symbolic demotion to subhuman animal status. This shows that the . . . dignity of humans is essentially tied to their human species membership, conceived hierarchically in relation to nonhuman animals and independently of the capacities of the individual whose dignity is at stake.[19]

Yet there is no obvious reason to invoke a hierarchy of moral status here. Species-based relationships don't seem to obviously answer the value question. One can imagine that if one treated a dog like a horse, or a chimpanzee like a child, or a bear like a ballerina, some might object in a similar vein without invoking a value hierarchy.

Of course, specific social relations will determine how moral agents come to understand their attitudes to moral patients. Indeed, a family who has their mother with Alzheimer's in a top-of-the-line facility might find the state-run care "undignified"; they might even think that the state-run facility "treats people like animals." But this judgment could be the result of snobbery or speciesism, and we should not draw moral conclusions from such judgments. These judgments in themselves don't show that human non-persons, by virtue of their social relations with other, sometimes judgmental, human persons are due more consideration or attention than nonhuman non-persons.

Eva Kittay has made similar arguments. As the mother of a severely cognitively impaired daughter, Sesha, Kittay is vividly attuned to the role of social relations in understanding our moral commitments to others. When we think of moral patients she urges us to think of them as "someone's child. . . . That social relationship [entails] a series of appropriate emotional and moral responses. . . . It is morally (and emotionally) appropriate to care for one's child for the child's own sake. It is the practices that define parenthood, and not simply the intrinsic properties of the product of the pregnancy."[20] She too wants to focus on species-specific social relations, particularly those that model the family. She writes:

> Family membership is conditional on birth lines, marriage, and (under particular conditions) adoption, not on having certain intrinsic properties. . . . Families (or adequate substitutes) are critical when we are dependent, as in early childhood, during acute or chronic illness, with serious chronic conditions including disability, and in frail old age. At these times, we are generally best served by close personal ties. Families are called on in times of moral crisis for the support of family love and loyalty. Similarly, I propose that membership in a group of moral peers based solely on species membership has as its appropriate moral analogue family membership, not racism. . . . As humans we are indeed a family.[21]

Here, Kittay is suggesting that partiality to one's own family needn't be thought of as necessarily prejudicial. She is urging us to think of speciesism—favouring one's own species over members of other species—as on par with favouring one's own family. Insofar as we think it is ethically permissible to grant greater weight to the interests and desires of members of our own family, so is it permissible to grant greater weight to the interests and desires of members of our own species.

There are a number of worries about this view even if we accept the premise, as I do, that species-specific social relations do matter from a moral point of view. It might simply be suggested that ultimately we aren't morally justified in caring more about our own children and family members than the children and family members of our neighbours and colleagues; it is just a function of the way we have arranged our social relations and institutions that we are psychologically oriented towards favouring our own family members and, practically, it works out well if every family takes care of its own. There are, in fact, different cultural practices and alternative family arrangements in which caring for one's own family members more than for other people is not thought to be justifiable. Favouring one's own family and how we understand who counts as a family member are arguably artifacts of our particular social and cultural practices. And cultural practices are often the very sorts of practices that should be held up to ethical interrogation, because they tend to make certain kinds of prejudices seem natural. Even within our own culture, there are limits beyond which favouring one's own family members becomes questionable. We cannot go to any lengths to further the interests of our own children over the interests of other people's children. In addition to being limited, partiality to one's own family members is not thought to be ethically required. We don't think that the parent who sends her children to public school and sends the money she would have spent sending them to private school to support education in the developing world is doing something unethical; indeed, many would find that admirable. So, partiality to family looks more like a contingent feature of our social relations and not obviously a principle for organizing those relations and the ethical obligations that might spring from them.[22]

Even if an argument could be made in favour of partiality to one's family, it is important to recognize that families come in many forms and I'd argue that families and intimate social units can include more than just humans. My immediate family (I prefer to call it a pack) for quite some time has not included any other humans but does include other animals. Just as Kittay finds it offensive when Sesha is compared to animals, I find it problematic that my intimate social unit is considered less valuable, less genuine, less meaningful than one that is made up exclusively of humans or humans and their "pet."

Consider Dawn Prince-Hughes, an autistic writer and anthropologist, who found the most comfort in the company of animals; it was through her observations of, and work with, gorillas that she was eventually able to enter into a human family. Prince-Hughes, by spending time watching captive gorillas who were "so sensitive and so trapped," began to understand herself, the world, and other humans. Through them she learned that "persons are more than chaotic knots of random actions" and "that as people we are reflected in one another. Because the gorillas were so like me in so many ways, I was able to see myself in them, and in turn, I saw them—and eventually myself—in other human people."[23] Bonds of kinship extend beyond the species border, in our own culture and in others. If other animals can be part of families, then the family does not serve as a model for identifying morally relevant distinctions between species.

Before I turn to the material feminist view, I want to say one more thing about Kittay's criticism of the sameness model, and add a small wrinkle. Kittay is concerned (even disgusted) when Sesha is compared with an animal, but those who work with and study animals are also troubled when perfectly healthy, cognitively functioning nonhumans are compared to cognitively impaired humans. The sameness construct distorts both and leaves little room for nonhuman animals who themselves have cognitive disabilities. I know a chimpanzee named Knuckles who has cognitive and motor-control deficits believed to be due to cerebral palsy. Knuckles has lived at the Center for Great Apes, a sanctuary in Florida, since he was two years old. He receives around-the-clock care from human caregivers, while also being allowed supervised visits with other chimpanzees. He is quite distinct in his abilities from other non-cognitively-impaired chimpanzees, who are also quite distinct from humans with cognitive impairments. If we want to get an accurate picture of the range of beings who deserve our moral attention, attending to the variety of differences is essential.

Kittay and others who have personal stakes in the lives of humans with cognitive impairments have made the importance and value of their lives, experiences, and interests more vivid. They have reminded us of the centrality of relationships and the importance of epistemic humility. But there is no reason to extend that humility to only human relationships, then stop when relationships cross the species border. Those studying and caring for nonhuman animals have also enlivened our understanding of the value of the lives, experiences, and interests of other animals, and the relationships these individuals form with one another are meaningful and enlivening.

Material Matters

Material feminists, though by no means univocal, push epistemic boundaries and encourage a reassessment of our illusory understandings of nature as something distinct from and opposed to culture, a binary that is central in maintaining the "we are not them" construct. Material feminists are particularly dismayed by feminists who have eschewed nature and the study of science for fear of being labelled essentialists or positivists as well as postmodernists who reduce the other-than-human world to discourse.[24] They see such views as reproducing a kind of anthropocentric dualism that is reminiscent of the sameness response discussed earlier.

Donna Haraway has long tried to correct this and find ways to talk about nature, animals, and the material world in other than dualist terms. Her recent focus on companion species has us recognize that animals and organisms are not passive others, but, as Stacey Alaimo and Susan Hekman suggest "agentic forces that interact [or intra-act] with and changes the other elements in the mix, including the human."[25]

One of the central insights of material feminism is that we are already in relations with all sorts of life forms and, for the most part, we have not been recognizing this. That we are already in relations should ground the demand for more conscientious ethical reflection and engagement. Since we necessarily exist in relation with other animals, and our perceptions, attitudes, and actions are entangled with them in ways that make their experiences better or worse, which in turn affects our own experiences to varying degrees, then this is a social/natural fact that should be attended to. The ontological recognition that we are in unavoidable relations to all sorts of other beings and organisms raises profound ethical questions. As Karen Barad puts it, "the ethical questions that we will want to consider are not only about how nonhuman animals are being appropriated for human desires but also how our desires and our beings are co-constitutively reconfigured as well."[26] And the path to answers to such questions is not clear.

Attending to all life forms, finding agency and intra-agency in other animals as well as whole ecosystems and even the dirt, may go so far that the ethical questions become overwhelming.[27] Our relations to other organisms are varied and the meaning and significance of particular relations also varies. Some of these relations are more tangible: animals that are in the relation as the eaten, animals made homeless by increased human consumption and habitat destruction and the effects of climate change, animals slaughtered for fun or profit. Some relations are less tangible: our relations to the bacteria that are part of our guts and the viruses and other animals' DNA that are now a part of the human genome. While a recognition of these relations has important epistemic implications, it is also clear that not all relations are ethically equivalent. If we are all parts of bioassemblages, companion species, coexisting and co-evolving and co-constituting, then an ethic of respect and right perception provides an epistemic anchor but it can't help navigate the ship through complex terrain. We live in a world of conflicts and need guidance about how to resolve at least some of that conflict, some of the time.

The other day I was driving to my university to meet a colleague who is a stem cell biologist and I was reminded again of the importance of difference and making distinctions. I came across some Canadian geese lined up along the side of a street, staring into the road where one of their kin lay dead, presumably recently hit by a car. I was quite moved by this sight. Perhaps these geese were mourning, standing together in grief at the death of a member of their community, their gaggle. Perhaps they were merely responding to change—but even so, their response to change is qualitatively different from a stem cell's response to change. The death of the goose is, to my mind, profoundly different than the destruction of an *in vitro* embryo to create stem cell lines or the death of those cells when the medium in the dish becomes contaminated. The material feminist recognition of life and its various entangled processes and their commitment to deconstructing sameness/difference, masculine/feminine, organic/machine, and culture/nature binaries may leave us unable to ethically respond to differences between kinds of fellow creatures.

The ethical implications of this expansive ontology suggest that the life that sustains us in our communities matters, and it certainly does. As Judith Butler has recently suggested:

> we are reciprocally exposed and invariably dependent, not only on others, but on a sustained and sustainable environment. Humanity seems to be a kind of defining ontological attribute. . . . But what if our ontology has to be thought otherwise? If humans actually share a condition of precariousness, not only just with one another, but also with animals, and with the environment, then this constitutive feature of who we "are" undoes the very conceit of anthropocentrism. In this sense, I want to propose 'precarious life' as a non-anthropocentric framework for considering what makes life valuable.[28]

But this appears to be a new form of vitalism that does not seem any better prepared to address the practical problems that attended earlier versions promoted by some environmental ethicists. Perhaps, in the same way that philosopher William Goodpaster encouraged us to think beyond the human and the animal and to consider valuing life itself over thirty years ago, the focus on the significance of complex intra-actions among living things is meant to focus our "sensitivity and awareness" rather than to guide our actions.[29]

What is most troubling about the ethical shift that some material feminists seem to be calling for is that it appears to miss, or divert attention away from, the deep ways in which our emotional, cognitive, and embodied connections are oriented towards particular others with whom we share or can share a particular quality of connection. I take this to be an important insight of both the sameness response proposed by many animal advocates and the family focus that Anderson and Kittay recommend. I can't connect with embryonic stem cells or microbes (even those that are part of me) and my connection to bugs is thin. I am not moved to act for their sakes if there are other conflicting values in play. While I do feel a deep sense of grief when humans fell old trees or pave meadows or dump toxics in wetlands, that grief is driven by concern for the creatures that made their lives and their homes in these places, by my one-sided projection of connection, and perhaps by my feeling of "species shame." Clearly there is value to be attended to in all the places of the earth that sustain life, but that value is abstract; I am not connected to the meadow or the wetland or the insects that inhabit them in the way that I can be to the animals, fish, and birds who make their homes there. My sense is that the reason I can't connect is because it isn't possible to be in direct *ethical* relation to ecosystems or organisms that exist in ways that I can't imagine, beyond metaphor or projection, what it is like to be like.[30]

Entangled Empathy

Being in ethical relation involves, in part, being able to understand and respond to another's needs, interests, desires, vulnerabilities, hopes, perspectives, etc., not by positing, from one's own point of view, what they might or should be. To recognize another's distinct orientation does not mean that we are not also, as the material feminists note, shaping and co-constructing each other's needs, interests, desires, even identities. While everyone is entangled with particular others and to some extent with various forms and forces of life, not recognizing that there is a particular embodied being who organizes her perceptions and attitudes can be problematic. We need only reflect on the various ways that those in positions of power have obscured or disavowed the subjectivity of those they seek to dominate and the struggles for recognition that follow to realize the importance of holding on to the self, however porous or shifting her boundaries may be. Empathy is a way of connecting to specific others in their particular circumstances and thus is a central skill for being in ethical relations.

As I understand it, entangled empathy is a process whereby individuals who are empathizing with others first respond to the other's condition (most likely, but not exclusively, by way of a precognitive empathetic reaction).[31] There are a myriad of ways such reactions can go wrong, but they are also often right, especially in guiding needed attention in the right directions and there are often important details to be gleaned from these initial reactive attitudes. From these reactions, we move to reflectively imagine ourselves in the position of the other, and then make a judgment about how the conditions that she finds herself in may contribute to her perceptions or state of mind and impact her interests. These perceptions will involve assessing the salient features of the situation and require that the empathizer seek to determine what is pertinent to effectively empathize with in the being in question. Entangled empathy requires that there be room to correct empathetic responses.

So, entangled empathy involves both affect and cognition. The empathizer is also attentive to both similarities and differences between herself and her situation and that of the fellow creature with whom she is empathizing. She must move between her own and the other's point of view. As Diana Meyers has recently written: "Given that people aren't transparent to one another, accurate empathy seems to require gradually building up propositional and intuitive knowledge of the other that is then fed into an imagined scenario, which may in turn be corrected and reimagined after further observation and thought, and so on. In other words, alternating between the first-person perspective of the individual you are empathizing with and your own third-person perspective on her is part and parcel of empathy."[32] This alternation between the first- and third-person points of view will minimize narcissistic projections, a worry associated with some forms of empathetic engagement.

Many standard accounts of empathy suggest that what one does when one empathizes is put oneself into another's shoes. This does not require that the empathizer accurately characterize the person or being with whom she is empathizing, as the empathizer can maintain her own perspectives, values, beliefs, and attitudes but from someone else's embodied position, as it were. This way of understanding anthropomorphizing with animals is problematic and can lead to profound mistakes both in judgment and in practice (though not all anthropomorphizing is problematic).[33] But in moving between the first- and the third-person perspective, as Meyers suggests, one must genuinely attempt to understand how the one being empathized with experiences the world and this requires gaining as much knowledge of the ways she lives as is possible. In the case of other animals, to empathize well, one must understand the individual's species-typical behaviours as well as her individual personality, and that is not easy to do without observation, over a period of time. Many current discussions of the claims animals make on us fail to attend to the particularity of individual animal lives. The overgeneralizations that Kittay, Anderson, and others criticize in sameness accounts can be avoided if one is engaged in entangled empathetic interactions.

Some have argued that empathy with others needn't bring about good results for the individuals who are being empathized with, as it doesn't have any motivational pull. Some have even suggested that "good" torturers are good empathizers and that allows them to more fully access the tortured individual's weak spots. Yet, in the psychological literature, empathy is often coupled with a motivational state that leads to "helping action."[34] If the development and exercise of empathy involve both affective empathy (emotional contagion, imitation, etc.) and cognitive empathy (reflective engagement with the feelings of the other, perspective taking, etc.), then it is likely that empathy is motivational. But the motivations can take different forms. Some people moved to help a distressed individual with whom they are empathizing may be motivated to end the distress because it causes them discomfort; others may be moved because they are unable to imagine themselves in a situation in need in which others do not come to their aid; others may be motivated because their sense of themselves as an empathetic person requires it. Indeed, some combination of motivations may be operating much of the time. Unlike sympathizing with someone in distress in which the sympathizer feels bad or sorry for the person, entangled empathy involves the empathizer directly and thus is motivating.[35]

Entangled empathy as I am construing it involves both affect and cognition and will necessitate action. The empathizer is attentive to both similarities and differences between herself and her situation and that of the fellow creature with whom she is empathizing. How might this process of empathetic engagement help to overcome the problems with the sameness approach and the dualism and anthropocentrism that it threatens? Because entangled empathy involves paying critical attention to the broader conditions that undermine the well-being or flourishing of those with whom one is empathizing, this requires those of us empathizing to attend to things we might not have otherwise (much as the material feminists would have us do) and figure out how to better navigate difference. Entangled empathy requires gaining wisdom and perspective and, importantly, motivates the empathizer to act ethically. I suggest that entangled empathy with other animals is a form of moral attention that focuses our perception on the claims they make on us, and it helps us to reorient our ethical sensibilities and overcome the limitations that standard humanist responses to them pose. It is also an ethical skill that can assist us in navigating various forms of human difference, a skill that in our violent world still needs to be taken up and thoughtfully honed.[36]

NOTES

1. See Warner, *Fear of a Queer Planet*; and Duggan, *Twilight of Equality?*
2. There are other ways of understanding "humanism" and my interest is not in staking out any particular territory for understanding and refuting "humanism" or "posthumanism" per se, I am primarily interested in the set of prejudicial ideas that have become associated with humanism.
3. Thanks to Mary-Jane Rubenstein for bringing this remarkable quote to my attention. It is from *Concerning the City of God Against the Pagans*, trans. Henry Scowcroft Bettenson (London: Penguin Books, 1972).
4. Korsgaard, "Evolution of Morality."
5. Gruen, "Moral Status of Animals."
6. Hockings, Anderson, and Matsuzawa, "Road-Crossing in Chimpanzees."
7. Brosnan and de Waal, "Variations on Tit-for-Tat," 141.
8. de Waal, "Primates."
9. de Waal, *Good Natured*, 91–92.
10. Premack and Woodruff, "Does a Chimpanzee Have a Theory of Mind?," 515. Sarah is an "enculturated" chimpanzee; she has spent most of her life in regular interactions with humans.
11. Povinelli et al., "What Young Chimpanzees Know."
12. Ibid.
13. Heyes, "Theory of Mind," 102. For an interesting discussion of how rearing history might influence results see Bulloch, Boysen, and Furlong, "Visual Attention."
14. Hare, Call, Agnetta, et al., "Chimpanzees Know What Conspecifics Do and Do Not See."
15. Hare, Call, and Tomasello, "Do Chimpanzees Know What Conspecifics Know?"
16. Tomasello, Call, and Hare, "Chimpanzees Understand Psychological States," 155.
17. Ibid., 156.
18. Schor, "This Essentialism." See also Gruen and Weil, "Teaching Difference."
19. Anderson, "Animal Rights," 282.
20. Kittay, "Margins of Moral Personhood," 111.
21. Ibid., 124.
22. There is a lot of interesting work about familial partiality. See, for example, Kolodny, "Which Relationships Justify Partiality?"
23. Prince-Hughes, *Songs of the Gorilla Nation*, 3.
24. The claim that feminists are "biophobic" has been challenged, most notably by Sara Ahmed; see "Open Forum Imaginary Prohibitions." However, judging from the backlash against ecofeminism and the repeated, yet mistaken, claims

that ecofeminism is essentialist (see Gaard, "'Ecofeminism' Revisited"), there is force to the material feminist view that some feminists eschew "nature."

25. See Alaimo, "Transcorporeal Feminisms," 251. See also Kari Weil's discussion in "Shameless Freedom."

26. Barad, "Queer Causation," 335.

27. Alaimo quoting McWhorten on dirt, in "Transcorporeal Feminisms," 247.

28. In Stanescu, "Species Trouble," 576.

29. As Goodpaster wrote, "It seems to me that there clearly are limits to the operational character of respect for living things. We must eat, and usually this involves killing (though not always). We must have knowledge, and sometimes this involves experimentation with living things and killing (though not always). We must protect ourselves from predation and disease, and sometimes this involves killing (though not always). The regulative character of the moral consideration due to all living things asks, as far as I can see, for sensitivity and awareness, not for suicide (psychic or otherwise)" ("Morally Considerable," 324).

30. When I say I am not connected to these abstract places I don't mean to suggest that others who have formed particular, meaningful connection to such places aren't really connected. But their situated knowledge may ground their connections in ways that it can't ground mine. Of course, whether the connection is reciprocated or metaphorical will need to be considered.

31. This discussion builds on my earlier work on what I was calling "engaged empathy." See for example, Gruen, "Empathy and Vegetarian Commitments," and "Attending to Nature" (*Ethics and the Environment*).

32. Meyers, *Victim's Stories*, 154.

33. See, for example, Keeley, "Anthropomorphism."

34. See, for example, Bateson's research in the *Altruism Question*, and Hoffman on internalization and guilt in *Empathy and Moral Development*.

35. Because of the variability around the understanding of the terms "empathy" and "sympathy," not everyone would agree here. For example, Stephen Darwall claims that "empathy can be consistent with the indifference of pure observation" whereas sympathy involves concern for the person sympathized with and this concern is motivational (in "Empathy, Sympathy, and Care"). It should be clear from my discussion that empathetic distress is not something one can remain indifferent to and this is the case whether or not the empathizer has concern for the individual with whom she is empathizing.

36. This chapter was originally published in Gregory R. Smulewicz-Zucker, ed., *Strangers to Nature: Animal Lives and Human Ethics* (Lanham, MD: Lexington Books, 2012). Parts of this discussion are drawn from my book *Ethics and Animals: An Introduction* (Cambridge: Cambridge University Press, 2011). Since the original publication, I published *Entangled Empathy: An Alternative Ethic for Our Relationships with Animals* (New York: Lantern Press, 2015).

BIBLIOGRAPHY

Ahmed, Sara. "Open Forum Imaginary Prohibitions: Some Preliminary Remarks on the Founding Gestures of the "New Materialism."" *European Journal of Women's Studies* 15, no. 1 (2008): 23–39.

Alaimo, Stacy. "Transcorporeal Feminisms and the Ethical Space of Nature." In *Material Feminisms*, edited by Stacy Alaimo and Susan Hekman, 237–64. Bloomington: Indiana University Press, 2008.

Anderson, Elizabeth "Animal Rights and the Values of Nonhuman Life." In *Animal Rights: Current Debates and New Directions*, edited by Cass R. Sunstein and Martha Nussbaum, 277–98. Oxford: Oxford University Press, 2004.

Antonello, Pierpaolo and Roberto Farneti. "Antigone's Claim: A Conversation with Judith Butler." *Theory & Event* 12, no. 1 (2009). https://muse.jhu.edu/journals/ theory_and_event/summary/v012/12.1.antonello.html.

Barad, Karen. "Queer Causation and the Ethics of Mattering." In *Queering the Non/ Human*, edited by Noreen Giffney and Myra Hird, 311–38. Hampshire: Ashgate Publishing, 2008.

Bateson, C. Daniel. *The Altruism Question: Toward a Social Psychological Answer.* Hillsdale, NJ: Lawrence Erlbaum, 1991.

Brosnan, Sarah, and Frans de Waal. "Variations on Tit-for-Tat: Proximate Mechanisms of Cooperation and Reciprocity." *Human Nature* 13, no. 1 (2002): 129–52.

Bulloch, Megan, Sally Boysen, and Ellen Furlong. "Visual Attention and Its Relation to Knowledge States in Chimpanzees, *Pan troglodytes*." *Animal Behaviour* 76, no. 4 (2008): 1147–55.

Darwall, Stephen. "Empathy, Sympathy, and Care." *Philosophical Studies* 89, nos. 2–3 (1998): 261–82.

de Waal, Frans. *Good Natured.* Cambridge, MA: Harvard University Press, 1996.

———. "Primates: A Natural Heritage of Conflict Resolution." *Science* 289, no. 5479 (2000): 586–90.

Duggan, Lisa. *The Twilight of Equality?* Boston: Beacon Press, 2003.

Fehr, Ernst, and Urs Fishbacher. "Social Norms and Human Cooperation." *Trends in Cognitive Science* 8, no. 4: 185–90.

Gaard, Greta. "'Ecofeminism' Revisited: Rejecting Essentialism and Re-placing Species in a Material Feminist Environmentalism." *Feminist Formations* 23, no. 2 (2011): 26–53.

Goodpaster, Kenneth. "On Being Morally Considerable." *Journal of Philosophy* 75, no. 6 (June 1978): 308–25.

Gruen, Lori. "Attending to Nature." *Ethics and the Environment* 14, no. 2 (2009): 23–38.

———. "Empathy and Vegetarian Commitments." In *Food for Thought: The Debate over Eating Meat*, edited by Steve Sapontzis, 284–294. New York: Prometheus

Press, 2004. Reprinted in Carol Adams and Josephine Donovan, eds., *The Feminist Care Tradition in Animal Ethics* (New York: Columbia University Press, 2007), 333–44.

———. *Entangled Empathy: An Alternative Ethic for our Relationships with Animals.* New York: Lantern Press, 2015.

———. *Ethics and Animals: An Introduction.* Cambridge: Cambridge University Press, 2011.

———. "The Moral Status of Animals." In The *Stanford Encyclopedia of Philosophy* (Fall 2014 edition), edited by Edward N. Zalta. Palo Alto: Center for the Study of Language and Information, Stanford University. Article published July 1, 2003; substantively revised September 13, 2010. http://plato.stanford.edu/entries/moral-animal/.

Gruen, Lori, and Kari Weil. "Teaching Difference: Sex, Gender, Species." In *Teaching the Animal*, edited by Margo DeMello, 127–44. New York: Lantern Books, 2010.

Hare, Brian, Josep Call, Bryan Agnetta, and Michael Tomasello. "Chimpanzees Know What Conspecifics Do and Do Not See." *Animal Behaviour* 59, no. 4 (2000): 771–86.

Hare, Brian, Josep Call, and Michael Tomasello. "Do Chimpanzees Know What Conspecifics Know?" *Animal Behaviour* 61, no. 1 (2001): 139–51.

Heyes, Cecilia. "Theory of Mind in Nonhuman Primates." *Behavioral and Brain Sciences* 21, no. 1 (1998): 101–14.

Hockings, Kimberly, James Anderson, and Tetsuro Matsuzawa. "Road-Crossing in Chimpanzees: A Risky Business." *Current Biology* 16, no. 17 (2006): 668–70.

Hoffman, Martin. *Empathy and Moral Development.* Cambridge: Cambridge University Press, 2000.

Keeley, Brian L. "Anthropomorphism, Primatomorphism, Mammalomorphism: Understanding Cross-Species Comparisons." *Biology & Philosophy* 19, no. 4 (2004): 521–40.

Kittay, Eva. "At the Margins of Moral Personhood." *Ethics* 116, no. 1 (2005): 100–131.

Kolodny, Niko. "Which Relationships Justify Partiality? The Case of Parents and Children." *Philosophy & Public Affairs* 38, no. 1 (2010): 37–75.

Korsgaard, Christine. "Reflections on the Evolution of Morality." *Amherst Lecture in Philosophy* 5 (2010): 1–29. http://www.amherstlecture.org/korsgaard2010/.

Meyers, Diana Tietjens. *Victims' Stories and the Advancement of Human Rights.* New York: Oxford University Press, 2016.

Povinelli, Daniel J., Timothy J. Eddy, R. Peter Hobson, and Michael Tomasello. "What Young Chimpanzees Know about Seeing." *Monographs of the Society for Research in Child Development* 61, no. 3 (1996): i, iii, v–vi, 1–189.

Premack, David, and Guy Woodruff. "Does a Chimpanzee Have a Theory of Mind?" *Behavioral and Brain Sciences* 1, no. 4 (1978): 515–26.

Prince-Hughes, Dawn. *Songs of the Gorilla Nation: My Journey Through Autism.* New York: Harmony Books, 2004.

Schor, Naomi. "This Essentialism Which Is Not One." *Differences* 1, no. 2 (1988): 38–58.

Sripada, Chandra, and Stephen Stich. "A Framework for the Psychology of Norms." In *The Innate Mind.* Vol. 2, *Culture and Cognition,* edited by Peter Carruthers, Stephen Laurence, and Stephen Stich, 280, 294. New York: Oxford University Press, 2006.

Stanescu, James. "Species Trouble: Judith Butler, Mourning, and the Precarious Lives of Animals." *Hypatia* 27, no. 3 (2012): 567–82.

Tomasello, Michael, Josep Call, and Brian Hare. "Chimpanzees Understand Psychological States—The Question Is Which Ones and to What Extent." *Trends in Cognitive Sciences* 7, no. 4 (2003): 153–56.

Warner, Michael. *Fear of a Queer Planet.* Minneapolis: University of Minnesota Press, 1993.

Weil, Kari. "Shameless Freedom." *JAC* 30, nos. 3–4 (2010): 713–26.

Zamir, Tzachi. *Ethics and the Beast.* Princeton: Princeton University Press, 2007.

8

All My Relations
Interview with Margaret Robinson

-◦≻══◑ ◐══≺◦-

Interviewed by Lauren Corman

Dr. Margaret Robinson is a Mi'kmaq woman, feminist scholar, and bisexual activist who, at the time of this interview, lived in Toronto, Ontario. The following *Animal Voices* interview with Robinson explores Mi'kmaq values, veganism, and social justice. The interview was originally broadcast on April 23, 2013, in Toronto, on CIUT 89.5 FM.

LAUREN CORMAN (Host): Hello, and welcome to *Animal Voices*. You're listening to CIUT 89.5 FM, as well as CFBU in the beautiful city of St. Catharines. Today we have a very special guest, somebody I've been looking forward to speaking with for a couple of years now, because I've been teaching a very provocative, interesting article of hers called "Indigenous Veganism: Feminist Natives Do Eat Tofu." We are joined today by Margaret Robinson. She is a status Mi'kmaq woman. She has a PhD in theology, and she currently works for the Centre for Addiction and Mental Health as a researcher in Toronto. It's my pleasure to welcome Margaret to the show. Hi, Margaret.

MARGARET ROBINSON (Writer, "Indigenous Veganism: Feminist Natives Do Eat Tofu"): Hi, thanks for having me.

LC: It's wonderful to have you here today. There's a lot to say about this article and your research, so we'll jump right into it. Can you give us a quick synopsis of "Indigenous Veganism: Feminist Natives Do Eat Tofu"?

MR: Sure. The article proposes a postcolonial ecofeminist reading of Mi'kmaq legends as a basis for a veganism rooted in Aboriginal culture. In the Mi'kmaq legends I examined, animals are portrayed as siblings to humanity. I argue that these legends offer an alternative to the Christian colonial stewardship and domination model of human–animal relations. I suggest that veganism is in keeping with the cultural values expressed in our legends, although it wasn't part of our traditional practices. The development of an Aboriginal veganism is complicated by gender roles in Mi'kmaq culture, in which manhood is associated with hunting, for example, and I examine that as well. There is a tendency for people to locate cultural authenticity in the replication of what our ancestors did. In the article, I argue that coming up with new ways to express the values our ancestors held could also be authentically Native. So an ecofeminist exegesis of Mi'kmaq legends can provide us with an Indigenous grounding for vegan practice.

LC: Right. So there's continuity, even if the practice is different.

MR: Exactly.

LC: So what about your own journey to veganism?

MR: I started for superficial reasons. I wanted to drop some weight, and I thought, "What a great and easy way to cut my fat consumption! I won't have to count calories or think about any of those details." Of course I was wrong. I lost no weight at all. But over time, it started to mean something to me. The activity of not eating meat sensitized me to what I had been doing psychologically in order to eat meat. I had ignored the aspects of meat that reminded me it was someone's body—the veins and tendons, for example. I'd been brought up on supermarket meat, which comes dissected in white styrofoam packages. It's difficult, seeing a piece of chicken breast, to imagine it was part of anything living. The packaging is designed to help us forget what meat really is. Then I moved to the Chinatown and Kensington Market area of Toronto. And here, they sell the animals as they are. There's a pig head or an entire gutted goat hanging in the butcher shop. The chickens have heads and feet. I bought a fish, and instead of a clean white fillet in a package it was an entire fish, with eyes, and teeth and everything. And as I was trying to butcher it with my blunt kitchen tools I suddenly realized, "This isn't meant to come apart." I realized the fish's body was designed for its own life—not for my chowder. In philosophical terms, I realized that the ontology of the fish—its essence as a being—was different than I had previously thought. It wasn't *for me*, it was for *itself*.[1]

Living in Chinatown and Kensington, the reality of meat-eating is extremely visible, and it made me realize I had separated myself from other animals, and created walls in my psyche to enable me to see animals as objects that could be exploited. In her book, *The Sexual Politics of Meat*, Carol Adams talks about the detachment process where the concept of meat replaces the concept of the animal, and the meat gets renamed in ways that further erase the animal. She calls this "the absent referent."[2] But in my neighbourhood there's no way to separate meat as a concept from the carcass of the dead animal, because it's right there, clearly identifiable. Once that illusion was gone, I had to ask myself if I was willing to pay the emotional and moral price it was going to take in order to continue to consume animals. And I wasn't. Lots of people see the same things I do and make a different choice. Farmers eat meat. Hunters eat meat. Butchers eat meat. But for me, once I saw the reality of the system, it wasn't something I could support.

LC: So it opened up a space for you to ask some ethical questions?

MR: Very much so. My partner and I went vegan together, and we realized that it's changing how we see the world, and it's changing what kind of people we want to be. We'd adopted four cats, and our daily interaction with them reminded us how animals have personalities and moods. And that helped us make the connection between the internal mental life of every living creature, and our dietary choices.

LC: Did it seem immediately evident to you that this would square with your Mi'kmaq culture?

MR: Yes and no. It squared with the values I had grown up with, but it didn't at all square with the traditions I had grown up with.

LC: So how did you navigate that?

MR: It was tricky, because my family was culturally assimilated in a lot of ways. My grandmother lost her status when she married a man who was not Native, which was a method the federal government used to reduce the number of people eligible for treaty rights, and she didn't receive her status back until 1985. But that status didn't extend to the rest of us, so we grew up as non-status Natives, which meant we couldn't live on reserve, or access treaty rights, and that separated us from a lot of cultural activities. I grew up knowing we were Native, but people didn't talk about it very often, partly as a strategy to avoid racism. So I grew up with traditions that I didn't think of as Native until, in retrospect, I began seeing how our family had things in common with other Native families, and there were things about my upbringing that were very different than, say, your average White girl. But veganism certainly wasn't part of that tradition.

LC: Then you began transitioning into a vegan diet, and you have that past that you're bringing to it [. . .] and so where did you go from there in terms of starting to see connections?

MR: I had to hammer out the connections for myself, because there wasn't a body of literature that talked about modern approaches for neo-Indigenous living. As a person who grew up without status, I didn't have easy access to traditional teachings. What's been accessible for me has been written works, and they're often written by White people examining Mi'kmaq culture through a historical-anthropology lens. Knowing how people lived and what they did two or three hundred years ago is interesting, but I don't want to recreate how my ancestors lived. I want to find authentic ways to live today, in downtown Toronto.

Much of what I found by other Aboriginal people was written from a traditionalist perspective, and focused on countering the erasure of tradition. And I had a hard time with what I saw as a suspicion of newness, and a suspicion of feminism, in traditionalist writing. So the more I read, the more alienated I felt. I was trying to find a space where I could be a contemporary person and also feel connected with my culture. And eventually I realized that I was going to have to start talking about the space I find myself in now, and see if there are other people that that will resonate with.

LC: Was there a concern that you would be viewed by other Mi'kmaq people as maybe being co-opted by a Western imperialist point of view, or an animal rights agenda? You mentioned feminism, that somehow you had been assimilated that way?

MR: I was very concerned that I was going to come across as assimilated. I've been to Aboriginal events where they had traditional meat-based dishes. And of course, I don't eat those. So I'd eat a lot of bannock, or I'd fill up on wild rice and blueberries. When you interact with people who aren't vegan, you end up asking a lot of questions about the ingredients, so you don't get unpleasantly surprised. But having dietary boundaries singles you out as separate, and when you're trying to fit into a community, being singled out can be very painful. So I was hesitant to ask questions. I didn't want people to think I was being difficult, or condescending.

LC: Has it gotten easier?

MR: It's gotten much easier, in part because event organizers make sure they have vegetarian options now. It's become standard to ask, "Do you have any dietary issues?" Native people are also becoming more aware of food justice issues such as access to, and the cost of, fresh produce. We're more conscious about issues such as diabetes, and we're looking critically at the kind of food that we eat, and what shapes our food choices.

LC: Yeah, your article "Indigenous Veganism: Feminist Natives Do Eat Tofu" really resonated with what I've read and learned about the environmental justice movement, in particular people talking about things like food deserts, and how particularly communities of colour, poorer communities don't have access to nutrient-dense, healthy foods. And that's something that you raised at the beginning.

MR: Exactly. Food deserts are an increasing problem for racialized people living in urban areas. In some areas you can walk for blocks and not find a grocery store, but there could be a McDonald's every block and a half.

LC: You tie this in the beginning of the article into a critique of colonialism and a discussion about food and poverty in reservations. Can you say more about that?

MR: Sure. Reserves in Canada were located in isolated places that nobody else wanted, and laws enabled the colonial government to move reserves if they got too close to White settlements. In Nova Scotia, where I'm from, reserve land was usually rocky with a thin layer of topsoil. Yet Native people were encouraged to farm. And of course, it failed miserably. People became reliant on purchasing food, and food in a reserve store can be enormously expensive. Professor of human ecology Kim Travers found that Mi'kmaq people living on reserve were eating highly processed protein such as peanut butter, wieners, or bologna.[3] That's a poverty issue, and a class issue, in addition to being a cultural issue.

LC: You make the argument that what we come to see in terms of dominant Canadian culture as Native food is actually food of poverty.

MR: Absolutely. When we eat inexpensive foods often enough they become seen as traditional, when in reality, they're an expression of our economic oppression. So an Aboriginal restaurant such as Tea-N-Bannock, has bologna, wieners, and Klik canned meat wrapped in fry bread on their menu. What we're doing is traditionalizing our own poverty.

LC: So what do you think now of a kind of counter-claim that veganism can presume access to certain foods (such as organic produce) while ignoring that these foods are higher priced? In other words, some people continue to see veganism as potentially classist, elitist, certainly White food; what do you think about those sorts of arguments or claims?

MR: I encounter that view a lot, and it seems like an ethnocentric argument. There are enormous numbers of people who are vegetarian or vegan on the planet. India alone has 600 million vegetarians.[4] And it's not because they have money to burn. There's nothing particularly elitist or expensive about vegan basics. The "veganism is expensive" argument overlooks the fact that in some places, meat and dairy industries are subsidized by the government. In Canada, for example, beef production is subsidized. If vegetables were equally subsidized and as equally promoted, I don't think you would see that kind of argument going on.

LC: So you don't feel like you're eating a very expensive, elitist diet when you're eating vegan in Toronto, for example?

MR: Not at all. I made minimum wage most of my life, and I tend to be pretty frugal.

LC: I wanted to come back to the connections that we were touching on at the very beginning of the interview, this notion that there was continuity between the values you saw represented within animal liberation, animal rights, and what you were talking about in terms of traditional Mi'kmaq values, that although the manifestation of the practice was different, the value itself was there. There was a connection there. Can you speak more about that?

MR: Well, I think the idea that Native authenticity and veganism are separate is rooted in stereotypes about Aboriginal people, particularly the double-sided coin of noble savage and ignoble savage. The ignoble savage stereotype portrays us as too savage to have any ethics, or as having some sort of primal nature that is too backward to live on anything but meat. There's a certain aggressive masculinity in that stereotype, that sees anything other than a hunter lifestyle as effeminate and weak. The noble savage paints us as inherently closer to nature, and assumes this gives us a special right to eat animals. I found myself questioning both of these stereotypes, whether I encountered them in White or in Aboriginal communities. The Mi'kmaq have a philosophy tradition. Reflecting on how best to live has been something we've done for a long time. I wanted to bring all my intellect to bear on the question of how to live as a Mi'kmaq woman in the twenty-first century. So I went to our legends looking to find something that would resonate with the kind of person that I am, and the kind of politics I was developing.

I grew up in a family where people respected animals and understood them as having their own selfhood. Although my family ate meat, it was seen as a regrettable thing that had to be done. As I grew older, I realized that it *is* a regrettable thing, but it actually *doesn't have* to be done. I began rethinking what that could mean. I found myself questioning why particular practices were traditions, what values those traditions embodied, and started asking myself whether those were *my* values or not.

The Mi'kmaq legends answered some of my questions. Mi'kmaq legends portray human beings as intimately connected with the world around us. In Mi'kmaq legends, Glooscap is kind of the archetype of the Mi'kmaq person. He's formed from the red clay of the PEI soil. In the creation story he doesn't hunt, he just hangs out with the other animals. In the story of Nukumi and Fire, Glooscap meets his grandmother, Nukumi, who cannot live on plants and berries alone. So Glooscap asks Marten to give his life so Nukumi can live, and Marten agrees because of his friendship with Glooscap. In return, Glooscap makes Marten his brother. This story represents the basic relation of the Mi'kmaq people with the creatures around us. The animals are willing to provide food and clothing, shelter and tools, but always they must be treated with the respect given a brother and friend.

Well, that deal between Glooscap and the animal world is based on the need to eat meat in order to survive. Given the fact that this is no longer the case, I concluded that dying for food is something that we no longer have to ask our animal siblings to do for us. And given how we've treated animals through overfishing and overhunting and the wholesale slaughter and destruction of their homes, I think the animals would like to get out of the bargain as well.

LC: Well, that makes sense. Can you tell us more about Glooscap and some of the other stories? You really stress animal agency, so the ability for animals to make conscious choices in the world. That was something that came through really strongly in the article.

MR: Well, Glooscap is kind of neat. He's very much an all-purpose hero figure. And in his interactions with animals, he's usually an arbiter of disagreements, and he's first and foremost their friend. Aboriginal people have a phrase called "all my relations," and by relations we mean not only the people and the ancestors to whom we're related, but also the other animals to whom we're related. And those are the kinds of things that you see in Mi'kmaq legends. There isn't a sharp human/animal divide. Humans turn into animals or vice versa. Animals are anthropomorphized in that they're seen as types of people. There's a story about Muin, a boy raised by bears, and his experience of bonding with the bears changes the way that his human community interacts with bears. Of course other people have similar stories. Romulus and Remus, for example, are suckled by a wolf after they're exposed to die. For me the issue isn't whether a real bear would nurture a human child, but rather the idea of a basic kinship between humans and other animals.

LC: Do you have a favourite animal story?

MR: Some of them are pretty weird. There's one where a man falls in love with a beautiful woman, who it turns out is a whale in human form, and after they have a child together, he notices that she's becoming despondent, particularly when the whale pod comes by and calls. She goes off to join the pod, taking her child with her, and he's left alone. But he knows that she and the child are happy, because they're with their whale people. I find that it's a very strange story. It's an interesting combination of a were-creature story and a tragic romance.

LC: I wanted to go back to just a point that you had raised before about masculinity and hunting and how those get paired together, and if you're not participating or supporting hunting that you're somehow weaker, or effeminate. And in your telling of the connections between Mi'kmaq culture and its resonance with veganism, there is a profound feminist perspective that you bring, and I was hoping you could tell us more about that.

MR: I really noticed the ecofeminism connection when I was doing my PhD in theology. We studied the idea that the suppression of women and the suppression of nature were linked, particularly in Christian theology, and looked at ways that women were equated with nature. In *Gaia and God*, for example, Rosemary Radford Ruether examines how patriarchal culture has associated women with nature and the emotions, while associating men with transcendence and rational thought. Ruether argues that the image of a monotheistic male God has been used to justify the domination of "men over women, masters over slaves, and (male ruling-class) humans over animals and over the earth."[5] And I carried that insight with me, and noticed the places where Mi'kmaq women were equated with vegetables and vegetarianism, and men were associated with hunting. The feast celebrating the birth of Glooscap's mother, for example, is described as consisting of plants, roots, berries, nuts, and fruit.[6] And some of this gendering is purely descriptive, since traditionally, Mi'kmaq men were hunters. But of course it's not always clear-cut. Women traditionally gutted and butchered the animal, and prepared the meat for consumption. But this activity wasn't central to their femininity in the way that hunting was connected with masculinity and its maintenance.

And so when I read Carol Adams' book, *The Sexual Politics of Meat*, and saw the connections she made between food and the expressions of hierarchical values, that helped me place my values and my practices in a feminist political framework. Adams outlines a cycle of objectification, fragmentation, and consumption, which she applies to both animals and women. "Objectification," she writes, "permits an oppressor to view another being as an object. The oppressor then violates this being by object-like treatment: e.g., the rape of women that denies women the freedom to say no, or the butchering of animals that converts animals from living breathing beings into dead objects."[7] So both women and other animals are treated as objects to be dissected for our desirable parts, reduced, for example, to breasts and thighs, and dehumanized as objects for consumption. That kind of cycle isn't in keeping with Mi'kmaq values of respect and kinship. And for a queer activist for over twenty years, that kind of aggressive, heterosexist masculinity is problematic, especially when it's paired with dismissing things as effeminate because they're not matching up to a heteronormative masculine standard. As a feminist and a bisexual woman, those kind of gender associations are a real red flag.

LC: Right, this kind of larger sense of femininity being degraded: its lower status. So in terms of masculinity being linked with hunting and meat and killing of animals, is that something coming out of Mi'kmaq culture, or is dominant Canadian culture projecting that onto you?

MR: It's difficult to tell, because Aboriginal and mainstream cultures aren't entirely separate. Mik'maq culture and Nova Scotian culture, for example, overlap in a lot of ways. Mi'kmaq culture is one of the foundations, next to English, Scottish, and French culture, upon which Nova Scotian culture is built. Hunting culture in general tends to have inherent assumptions about masculinity, even if it's women who are doing the hunting. There's often a type of manliness associated with it. And some of that is present in Mi'kmaq culture too. For example some Mi'kmaq believed that if a menstruating woman came in contact with your musket it would fail you in hunting or in battle, and maybe lead to impotence in other areas.[8] So there's a parallel between the rifle and the penis, which leads me to think that heteronormative masculinity of hunting is cross-cultural.

LC: So, I'm curious about whether or not in your discussions now with people about veganism, perhaps just your role in the community, or maybe after you published the article "Indigenous Veganism: Feminist Natives do Eat Tofu," what the responses were, and in particular, if people were threatened by the kinds of claims you were making.

MR: Actually, the response has been positive, although it's mostly other vegans who have even seen the work, so that's not really a random sample. I hoped I would hear from other Aboriginal people, but most of the people who responded are excited White people. I originally presented the article at an academic conference on religion, and the response there was positive. But Aboriginal people are disproportionately excluded from the academy, and I'm usually the only Native in the room. I later posted a draft of my presentation on my website, where it was picked up by *The Scavenger*, and it's possible that *The Scavenger* and my website have a predominantly White audience. *The Canadian Journal of Native Studies* is publishing a revised and expanded version, so I may have more Native responses in the future. Anytime you publish something that takes a strong point of view, you're going to encounter people who disagree with it. That hasn't happened for me yet, but I'm not particularly nervous about it. I have a lot of opinions that people find strange, so I'm used to that.

LC: So you were anticipating maybe a bit of resistance, but so far haven't encountered anything too strong?

MR: Yeah. I was expecting that I might encounter people who disagreed, maybe even people who were really upset. Because I said some pretty strong things about my opinions on the Aboriginal fishery, for instance, which touches on our treaty rights.

LC: Such as?

MR: I argued that the commercial fishery is further removed from our Mi'kmaq values, as presented in our legends, than vegan practices are. The commercial fishery treats fish as objects to be collected for money, while veganism is rooted in a relationship of respect. The commercial fishery is presented as a solution to the economic disenfranchisement that the Mi'kmaq have experienced—which, given the serious decline of the fishing industry in the Maritimes, is a bit of a joke. People who want to promote a Mi'kmaq fishery try to make a link between our traditional fishing practices, which were for survival, and our participation in the fishing industry. I think that parallel is a false one. We have fishing as a treaty right—I strongly affirm that—but I don't think that how sea fishing is practised now reflects our traditional values. The fishing industry reflects the White settler attitude that nature is there to be exploited for gain. And wholesale slaughter in exchange for economic power is not commensurate with the Mi'kmaq values that I inherited. That's something that was imported here by the French and the English and reinforced through the fur trade.

LC: So there's the publishing of the article, but then there's how you move through the world as a Mi'kmaq person. How have people in general been responding to your point of view within your community? I was really curious about people's responses in your own family.

MR: They've joked about it. Like, "Oh, are you still doing that?" as if veganism was a phase I would grow out of. My parents were initially very concerned about where I was going to get my protein, and all of those things that omnivores ask. But there was never any question about the ethical basis for it, because I think my parents got that part right away, which was nice. We didn't have any kind of intellectual debate about it. Plus, the Mi'kmaq have a value of non-interference in one another's lives, so even if people disagree with what you're doing, they're usually not confrontational about it. There's a tradition of letting people be as strange and as weird as they want, as long as it's not interfering with other people. And if animals are our siblings, as the legends claim, I think there's an argument to be made to extend this philosophy of non-interference to their lives as well.

LC: So you said that you had a lot of excited White people, and of course, Dan [Daniel Angrignon, producer and fellow host of *Animal Voices*] and I are both sitting here, "excited White people." We're excited about the ideas presented in your article, but your target audience, you said, wasn't us! So I'm curious if you can say a little bit more about, you know, you've talked about the *Canadian Journal of Native Studies* picking up the article, and that's excellent. But were you trying to initiate a conversation or a dialogue about these issues within Aboriginal communities in Canada?

MR: Well, I wrote it when I was thinking about issues of postcolonialism, which is important to me personally because I'm a Mi'kmaq woman, and was important academically because I'm on the board of Postcolonial Networks, a community that brings scholars, activists, and other movement leaders together to foster decolonized relationships, scholarship, and social transformation.[9] So I was working through my own cultural values in relation to issues of assimilation and colonialism. And these issues are rarely black and white. Agriculture, for example, particularly the growing of corn and root vegetables, was encouraged by the British as a solution to Mi'kmaq migration. They wanted to pin the Mi'kmaq down to one location. So it's legitimate to argue that vegetarianism or veganism is historically aligned with colonial forces. At the same time many Mi'kmaq did farm and were pushed off their fertile land by British settlers with the consent and support of the government. Mi'kmaq farmers were labelled as squatters, and their barns and homes were burned. So it's also legitimate to see vegetable cultivation as an activity that was thwarted by colonialism too.

In terms of my target audience, I imagined that my readership consisted of other people interested in colonialism and assimilation, and I assumed that those would be people like myself. I underestimated how interested settler colonial people are in colonialism as a concept. I hope it's not just a case of exotification. People sometimes tell me, "Oh, Indian things are so 'in' right now!" As if my interest in my own culture is a trend I should exploit. So I hope it's not that. But I think, especially given the Idle No More movement,[10] that Canadians are becoming increasingly aware that Native culture isn't frozen in time. Native people use cellphones, we're online, and half of us live in cities. I think there's an increasing awareness that issues of food justice matter, and that issues of assimilation matter. Aboriginal people are acting out our values in modern ways all the time. Idle No More raises issues related to environmental exploitation such as mining and pollution. For example, the federal government is passing laws enabling them to pollute and exploit rivers in ways that seriously affect the animals that live in them and the people and animals that rely on those rivers. It's classic colonialism. So I think my expectation that my audience would be primarily other Aboriginal people underestimated the degree to which the settler colonial population is starting to get their head around these issues as well.

LC: One of the things that we've tried to address on the program for a while has been around issues of White supremacy and racism within the animal rights movement as practised in North America, and you know, it's seen as predominantly a White movement, and there has been certain racist discourses and actions that have taken place in the name of animal rights and liberation. With an article like this, I'm sure that some people would see you as being aligned with the animal rights and liberation movements—which of course, I don't see as being strictly racist and White supremacist; I am a member of them!—but I'm wondering about what you think about some of those claims, such that, you know, sometimes people talk about animal rights as being "animal Whites."

MR: I think the accusation can be both true and false. The distinction between conservationists and Aboriginal people is artificial. For example, when settler fishermen in Nova Scotia objected to Mi'kmaq fishermen exercising their treaty rights, it was framed as "White fishermen are conservationists preserving this limited supply of fish from these Mi'kmaqs who are going to fish them to extinction." Well, that portrayal ignores the fact that it is White fishermen who have fished those animals to the point of extinction. The Mi'kmaq have these treaty rights, but we're unable to exercise them in part because of White overfishing. So I would prefer that, rather than setting it up as this dichotomy where Natives are on one side and emotionally compromised or embarrassed White activists are on the other side, I think there's a lot of common values that people could seek to explore. Common values on both sides.

Many Aboriginal people are standing up for the environment and its inhabitants against powerful and destructive economic forces, such as the oil industry, or the mining industry. But their work usually isn't labelled as animal rights activism. I'd like to see them get more credit for the work that is being done. I'd also like to see animal rights activists be more aware of the way that their tactics, and the battles they choose to fight, reinforce colonialism. For example, I think the seal hunt is a terrible idea! I think seals should be left alone. However, having a bunch of White people come and protest the seal hunt when they could be protesting things that have a greater environmental impact—things that White people are doing, for example—is a little hard to swallow. The majority of people involved in the seal hunt are White, yet the issue is often framed as one of White animal rights activists versus Aboriginal hunters. And that just isn't the reality of what's going on.

LAUREN CORMAN: Well, this issue came up around the Short Hills protest. I don't know if you watched the unfolding of that. But there were members of the Haudenosaunee Council that wanted to and then engaged in an Aboriginal hunt of deer in Short Hills Park, and this really divided the animal rights community here in St. Catharines and beyond, and I assume what you just said about the seal hunt would also apply, then, perhaps to this. I mean, people saw it potentially as [. . .] some people in the animal rights movement felt that it was important to be in support of this hunt continuing, because the people that wanted to engage in it were enacting their treaty rights.

MR: Well, we have a variety of treaty rights, and some of them are really vague, and some of them are bizarrely specific. If you start reading the treaties, which most White Canadians have never done, you realize that the treaties are often specific to particular areas. The 1752 treaty between the British and the Mi'kmaq, for example, indicates that the Mi'kmaq have the right to hunt and fish, and to sell skins, feathers, fowl, fish, or other animal products. Treaties signed in 1760 and 1761 detail that we're only allowed to sell these products in truckhouses—specific markets designed for trade and administered by the British government. Almost immediately after the treaties were drafted, truckhouses were replaced by a licenced trader system, which was itself phased out in the 1780s. But the right to hunt and fish and to sell the products of that labour remained. And there's a concern that if we don't exercise our treaty rights then they won't be acknowledged by the Canadian government—which, let's face it, has a history of breaking the treaties whenever it suited them to do so.

But these treaties were based in a time when our lifestyles—both Mi'kmaq and settler—were very different than they are now. And while I think it's acceptable to revisit them, that has to be done on both sides. Simply curtailing treaty rights on the Aboriginal side is unjust. I have environmentalist friends who think we should just prevent Aboriginal people from hunting, period. And I've asked them, "What are you willing to surrender in exchange? Are you willing to move to a different area of town? Are you willing to surrender large swathes of crown land?" They haven't thought through the fact that the treaty gives *them* something. They just see it as some sort of welfare system for Native people.

LC: So they're missing a larger analysis of colonialism.

MR: Absolutely. They're missing the big picture of what a treaty actually is. And there needs to be more awareness of how colonialism has helped shape the practices that they're opposing, such as commercial hunting, trapping, or fishing. Exploitative relations with nature have been economically rewarded for hundreds of years, so it's not going to be surprising that you have Aboriginal people who see themselves as traditional, but whose relationship to the animals has been shaped by colonial-initiated and supported practices such as commercial trapping. Opposing the practice is fine, but people need to be more aware of the origins of the practices.

LC: We're just down to probably the last ten minutes or so. We've covered a lot of ground on the show so far, but I wanted to turn it over to you, if there're particular things that you wanted to speak about.

MR: I guess one thing I wanted to say was about the tendency to think of Aboriginal people as hunters rather than gatherers or even farmers. It's a reflection of the homogenization of Native cultures—the idea that all Native people fit one mould. In reality, there's a number of different Aboriginal cultures, and a number of different Aboriginal nations throughout Canada, the US, Mexico, and down into South America. There's an enormous variety of Native cultures. In some, vegetables are the predominant diet. So the tendency to stereotype Natives as hunters, and to attach authenticity to meat-eating as quintessentially Aboriginal ignores our cultural variety. Even within any given First Nation, there's a variety of food traditions. And so you can't say that only one way of being, or way of eating, is authentically Native.

LC: One of the things that comes through really strongly when you speak is that there's a diversity of opinion within groups of people; groups of Mi'kmaq people are having these discussions. These debates sound alive and well, and it's not like even within a particular group, everybody's thinking one way, or has come to one decision about issues.

MR: Absolutely. I think the fact that we can communicate online has made the variety of opinions within any group more accessible. It's easier to communicate. It's easier to organize political movements. One of the things that has enabled movements like Idle No More to happen is the power of people communicating through social media. And that's exciting to me, because the image of what the Native person is in Canadian culture is still frozen in that antiquated model, and people ignore modern expressions of Aboriginal values. Whether it's hip hop or graffiti art or veganism, these cultural expressions are often dismissed as "not Native enough." My ancestors didn't fight 400 years of colonialism so I could be told what makes me a real Mi'kmaq and what doesn't. I feel like we've gotten to a point where we can be visible as modern Aboriginal people. And *we* get to decide what that looks like. That's a place that we've never been before in terms of being able to shape the media and the way that people see us. That's never been within our reach prior to the existence of the Internet.

LC: I wanted to ask a question about space. It was one of the things that you raised right at the beginning of the interview, about creating a space or speaking from the space that you are. Where are you finding your kind of lifeblood at this point, and what are the spaces that are inspiring you, either online, if there're communities that people can check out, or particular groups in Toronto? You mentioned that, you know, you're part of a board that looks at postcolonial issues, but I was just curious about where you're feeling connected lately.

MR: Intellectually, postcolonialism has been really stimulating, and I've enjoyed connecting with people across vast distances around the ways that colonialism has affected us. And for that I recommend the Postcolonial Networks website. Being in Toronto has been strange for me. I'm surrounded by a Native culture that isn't my own. So I have to ask myself, as a settler in this province, how do I relate to the people for whom this is their traditional territory? Because this is not my traditional territory. I've been anxious about coming into Native spaces here, as a woman with White-skin privilege who doesn't eat animal products and doesn't know the local traditions. But I've adapted. I know more Ojibwa than I know Mi'kmaq. I've found it slightly easier to connect with two-spirited people since I moved here, because even if we're from different nations, we have shared experiences of homophobic colonialism and we can bond over that.

One of the challenges I face is finding spaces in Toronto where I can feel connected with the land, because in a city it's easy to see human beings as the be-all and end-all. When you grow up in a rural environment you're constantly aware of the fragility of the human being in relation to our environment. Canada is a country where it's really easy to die if you're outside too long. It's easy to forget our vulnerability when you live in a place where your needs are catered to. Being reminded of our vulnerability is a humbling experience.

LC: I like that point, too. I think it brings us back to something I always try to ask my interviewees about, which is, you know, real animals, and you had mentioned at the beginning of the show too that you've had connections with real animals throughout your life that continue to inspire you, and it sounds like being in natural spaces is grounding in a similar kind of way. They remind you about the lack of centrality of human beings, or that kind of delusion that we have sometimes, that is false.

MR: Yes. When you interact with wild creatures in their environment, you realize that the human being is not at the top of the great food chain, but is part of a web of interdependence. We're not great at running, we're not great at swimming. It's kind of a minor miracle that we've made it this far, in part because we're able to think and build tools. So when you interact with other animals, especially wild animals, the fragility of human life can be really alarming. And when you're constantly alarmed it can be hard to see other animals as friends, or as siblings. I grew up in the woods by a lake, and most of my interactions with animals, apart from pets, were with animals that depended on the lake in some way—deer, porcupine, bears, loons, fish, and frogs.

One day, after a big rainstorm, my dad came in the house, and said, "Hey kids, I need your help. A frog laid a bunch of eggs in this puddle out back, and it's drying up now, and they're all going to die if we don't get them into the pond." So for the next two hours we moved frog eggs and tadpoles from this shrinking puddle into the pond. And that was such a fundamental experience with my dad, of caring for creatures without any gain involved. I mean, frogs don't do anything for us, other than eat mosquitos. We weren't going to harvest them or anything. But it made me realize that to him, the fragility of these animals mattered in the same way that our fragility mattered. So for me, that was a very concrete experience of what "all my relations" actually means.

NOTES

1. I use the gender neutral pronoun "it" here because at the time of this incident the fish in question was dead, and given the state of my moral reflection at the time, the animal wasn't yet a *someone* to me.
2. Adams, *Sexual Politics*, 51.
3. Travers, "Using Qualitative Research."
4. Hughes et al., *World Food India*.
5. Ruether, *Gaia and God*, 3.
6. Augustine, "Mi'kmaq Transcript."

7. Adams, *Sexual Politics*, 58.
8. Romero, *Making War*, 28.
9. Postcolonial Networks website, http://postcolonialnetworks.com.
10. Idle No More website, http://www.idlenomore.ca.

BIBLIOGRAPHY

Adams, Carol J. *The Sexual Politics of Meat*. Tenth Anniversary Edition. New York: Continuum, 2000.
Augustine, Stephen. "Mi'kmaq Transcript." *Four Directions Teaching*. Accessed January 2013. http://www.fourdirectionsteachings.com/transcripts/mikmaq.html.
Ellingson, Ter. *The Myth of The Noble Savage*. Berkeley: University of California Press, 2001.
Hughes, Martin, Sheema Mookherjee, and Richard Delacy. *World Food India*. Oakland, CA: Lonely Planet, 2001.
Romero, R. Todd. *Making War and Minting Christians: Masculinity, Religion, and Colonialism in Early New England*. Amherst: University of Massachusetts Press, 2011.
Ruether, Rosemary. *Gaia and God: An Ecofeminist Theology of Earth Healing*. San Francisco: Harper Collins, 1992.
Travers, Kim. D. "Using Qualitative Research to Understand the Socio-cultural Origins of Diabetes among Cape Breton Mi'kmaq." *Chronic Diseases in Canada* 16, no. 4 (1995): 140–43.

9

Rampant Compassion

A Tale of Two Anthropomorphisms and the "Trans-species Episteme" of Knowledge-Making

Jodey Castricano

In 1978, at the Modern Language Association Convention, critical theorist Monique Wittig's announcement that "I am a lesbian, not a woman" created disquiet in her audience.[1] Later, in "One Is Not Born a Woman," Wittig's materialist feminist analysis of de Beauvoir's view of the "myth of woman"[2] leads to her critique of "the idea that women are a 'natural group,'"[3] and to her radical and provocative assertion in "The Straight Mind" that "Lesbians are not women."[4] As has been pointed out by feminist scholars such as Judith Butler, Wittig's aim was to critique the heteronormative category of "sex" as well as the system of compulsory heterosexuality to which it is tethered. At the time, Wittig concluded that "that the category 'woman' as well as the category 'man' are political and economic categories not eternal ones."[5] In effect, Wittig challenged "the idea of 'woman' as an essentialist concept"[6] by *historicizing* and thereby undoing the perception that women are a *natural* group. Wittig went on to say that "'Woman' is there . . . to hide the reality 'women,'"[7] thereby drawing attention to "a biologizing interpretation of history" that has served in the oppression of women.[8] More recently, scientist and feminist Donna Haraway follows in Wittig's footsteps to advocate for "a feminism that does not embrace Woman but is for women."[9]

Beyond Wittig, though, in an interview with Haraway regarding recent debates about the human/posthuman, Nicholas Gane took things even further when he remarked that the classical conception of "a bounded human subject . . . has become difficult to sustain in light of recent challenges to *what counts as being 'human.'*"[10] Indeed, these recent challenges take us to the water's edge regarding the human subject, as can be heard in the provocative question posed in the title of the interview with Haraway: "When we have *never been human,* what is to be done?"[11] In fact, contemporary debates about what counts as being human challenge us even further to radically rethink the concept of the *social,* for, as Haraway declares, "social relationships include *nonhumans* as well as humans."[12] In other words, nonhuman beings called *animals* pose philosophical and ethical questions that go to the root not just of what we can think, but also of who we (think we) are. In this regard, Haraway's questions resonate not only within feminism but also within "posthumanism" and post-anthropocentrism, an intersectional field of theories and critical practices out of which come further questions aimed at interrogating the borders of "human exceptionalism," as well as critiquing the role played by "speciesism" in maintaining what critical theorist Cary Wolfe calls "that fantasy figure called 'the human.'"[13] This chapter aims to go beyond a critique of speciesism and to offer an ontological paradigm shift from the *anthropos* to that more-than-human world of "living beings" with regard to the singularity and embodiment of animals known not only on the basis of suffering but also through the capacity of nonhumans for joy, pleasure, grief, family relations, etc.

In line with these seismic interrogations, Bruce Mazlish, in *The Fourth Discontinuity,* identifies four ruptures in the history of modernity that, in the names of Copernicus, Darwin, Nietzsche, and Freud, have forced a rethinking of what it means to be human (or not) by substantively troubling the notion of human exceptionalism to the extent that the polarization of the human and nonhuman can no longer hold. In this chapter I engage with Derrida, Cary Wolfe, Matthew Calarco, Rosi Braidotti, and Gay Bradshaw in considering the significance of posthumanism and, beyond that, post-anthropocentrism to critical animal studies (CAS), in which proposing a post-species episteme signals the emergence of a *fifth rupture,* one that, as Cary Wolfe argues, troubles "the concept of 'the human' that the human falsely 'gives to itself'" and, in the process, as Cary Wolfe suggests, is what "binds us to nonhuman being in general, and within that to nonhuman animals, as the *very condition of possibility* for what we know and for sharing it with one another."[14] The condition for this possibility is what I am calling "post-species episteme," a term that follows from eco-psychologist Gay Bradshaw's "trans-species psychology," in which she takes the view that "there is no scientific basis for maintaining separate fields and models for animal and human psychology."[15] In this regard, a post-species episteme takes us to the limits of identity politics through which the extending of rights, personhood, moral consideration, or compassion towards the more-than-human has unfolded.

The point I will be making is at least twofold: one fold takes the form of a question and necessarily leads directly into posthumanist/post-anthropocentric territory: How can we apply the rights of persons to animals if the very distinction between animals and persons is inherent in the notion of rights?[16] Kelly Oliver argues, for example, that there are problems with using terms of identity to liberate when those same terms have been used to subordinate. In other words, she asks, what happens when rights discourse "either uses or repeats identities that historically have been used to oppress or exploit certain groups or [uses] the values associated with the dominant group as its norm"?[17] In other words, what we have is a Catch-22 situation, as indicated by Oliver's question, "How can we apply the rights of persons to animals if the very distinction between animals and persons is inherent in the notion of rights."[18] This very question was asked, word for word, earlier in this paragraph.

The second fold involves ameliorating the rights dilemma by adopting an ethos predicated upon what Kelly Oliver has called, following Merleau-Ponty, "strange kinship," which can be seen as a non-hierarchical ethical turn based, as Oliver says, "not on blood or on generation but on *a shared embodiment and the gestures of love and friendship* among living creatures made possible by bodies coexisting in a world on which we all depend."[19] Environmentally and ethically, this means realizing that the human/animal divide is also ethico-political and the divide sets up the very possibility of politics. Thus this notion of *kinship*, however "strange," leads us to consider the interrelatedness of all forms of oppression based on the logic of domination and biopower that functions socially, culturally, and politically through what Foucault calls the "apparatus," by which he means

> a thoroughly heterogeneous ensemble consisting of discourses, institutions, architectural forms, regulatory decisions, laws, administrative measures, scientific statements, philosophical, moral and philanthropic

propositions—in short, the said as much as the unsaid. Such are the elements of the apparatus. The apparatus itself is the system of relations that can be established between these elements.[20]

In Giorgio Agamben's terms, the apparatus is

anything that has in some way the capacity to capture, orient, determine, intercept, model, control, or secure the gestures, behaviours, opinions, or discourses of living beings.[21]

Agamben's take on the apparatus amounts, as Stephen Thierman points out, to a "shift from [the] 'human' to 'living beings' [and, thus,] helps us to begin to acknowledge that the experiences (and subjectivities) of other creatures may also be deeply shaped by the apparatuses within which they are situated."[22] The shift from the "human" to *"living beings"*[23] also has the advantage of radicalizing ontology by the inclusion of love and friendship to the extent that "such recasting . . . [as Thierman observes,] allows us to expand imaginatively beyond the exclusively human realms of concerns" and therefore "to throw into radical question the schema of the human" upon which the issue of rights has traditionally and often paradoxically rebounded.[24] But what's wrong with rights?

In an interview with Elisabeth Roudinesco, Jacques Derrida expresses concern with the notion of extending rights to animals, for, as he points out, the concept of right and rights is part of a tradition whose conceptual system trades on excluding, exploiting, and disavowing animals or anyone seen to be "like animals." As Derrida puts it, "rights discourse" has a way of reconfiguring hierarchies and subtly confirming a certain interpretation of the human subject that has been instrumental in maintaining the oppositional and exclusionary limit between "man" and "the animal," especially where the latter is a class without individuals. These reconfigurations are one reason why Derrida has grave concerns about extending rights to some animals and not others. He mentions, for example, the Great Ape Project: "to want absolutely to grant, not to animals but to a certain category of animals, rights equivalent to human rights would be a disastrous contradiction. It would reproduce the philosophical and juridical machine thanks to which the exploitation of animal material for food, work, experimentation, etc., has been practiced (and tyrannically so, that is, through an abuse of power)."[25] As Kelly Oliver points out, what Derrida is worried about is "that giving rights to some animals but not all would repeat the exclusionary logic of the Cartesian subject and the juridical conception of individuality and freedom resulting from it,"[26] and it is this logic that has justified and sustained the practice of exploitation of animals all along. According to Oliver, the contradiction regarding "rights" comes in when we realize not only that the history of rights is based on the ideals of autonomy, rationality, individuality, and sovereignty—which, in part, one might argue, *can* be extended to animals—but also, and more significantly, that such ideals are always already built on opposing them to "animality" and "animal nature." This is to say, as Derrida does, that "[t]o confer or to recognize rights for 'animals' is a surreptitious or implicit way of confirming a certain interpretation of the human subject, which itself will have been the very lever of the worst violence carried out against nonhuman living beings."[27]

In this regard, any question of "thinking about animals" becomes moot unless we first come to terms with the epistemological structures that *organize* how we know, how our knowledge gets transmitted and accepted, and why and how it is received. Furthermore, it becomes apparent that in the exclusionary logic of the Newtonian/Cartesian epistemological paradigm, the subjective *as well as the affective* are not only suspect but also strongly repudiated as "unscientific" or "irrational," for, as Brian Luke rightly observes, "the terms 'rational' and 'irrational' distinguish between positions worthy and unworthy of being heard."[28]

In this context, it is telling that similar epistemological aporias regarding the reason/emotion divide appear within the discourse of animal rights and resonate with what Derrida has called "the war on pity."[29] Consider Tom Regan's oft-cited assertion that it is "reason—not sentiment, not emotion" that is key in making the case for animal rights,[30] since only by "making a sustained commitment to rational inquiry" instead of "indulg[ing] our emotions or parad[ing] our sentiments" can any progress be made.[31] As Brian Luke points out, the "reason/emotion dualism . . . and the privileging of principles" are "structural elements" of an animal rights theory based on a metaethics that, Luke argues, has "developed within a framework of patriarchal norms, which includes the subordination of emotion to reason [and] the privileging of abstract principles of conduct."[32] The point of such critiques, however, is not merely a matter of reversals; it is not, as Luke contends, "to instead place emotion over reason—but rather to suggest that in ethics reason and emotion *work together*, so that attempts to expunge emotion from theoretical ethics are artificial and self-defeating."[33]

One might also argue that it is a critique of traditional metaethics that Cary Wolfe has in mind when he expresses concern over the reiteration of a certain anthropocentrism in CAS, saying, "Just because we direct our attention to the study of nonhuman animals, and even if we do so with the aim of exposing how they have been misunderstood and exploited, that does not mean that we are not continuing to be humanist—and, therefore, by definition, anthropocentric."[34] This is to say, of course, that there are gaps, fissures, and slippages with regard to the place of anthropocentrism in CAS and in Wolfe's critique; anthropocentrism relies, in part, methodologically upon the denial or suppression of affective knowledge to sustain the rationalist framework of humanist thought, and this amounts to, as Brian Luke observes, "a dualism of reason over emotion" that "makes so little sense theoretically."[35]

Thus, it remains to posthumanism and a post-species episteme to draw attention to the necessity of conceptual shifts in the *questions* that must be asked, not only of theoretical approaches to CAS, but also of what sustains the humanist world at the symbolic level with regard to the singularity and embodiment of animals, with respect to their suffering as well as their capacity for joy, pleasure, fear, family relations, etc. Furthermore, in the realm of necessities, it is the "question of the animal" itself that has brought us to this moment, even though, as Matthew Calarco points out, "the *question* of the animal is already a *response* to some thing or some event that has preceded it" and, thus, what gives rise to ethical debates over animals has less to do with their "ability" or "capacity" for suffering than with "an encounter with an animal's *inability* or *in*capacity to avoid pain, its fleshly vulnerability and exposure to wounding."[36] This encounter is what Derrida has in mind when he observes that "mortality [is] the most radical means of thinking the finitude that we share with animals, the mortality that belongs to the very finitude of life, to the experience of compassion, to the possibility of sharing the possibility of this nonpower, the possibility of this impossibility, the anguish of this vulnerability and the vulnerability of this anguish."[37] Responding to the possibility of non-power means an encounter, as Calarco puts it, at "the site where one's egoism is called into question and where compassion is called for."[38]

In other words, the question of the animal turns upon how anthropocentrism reiterates a figure familiar to us with regard to Cartesian ontology and epistemology: the figure of the "thinker," the sovereign subject of human exceptionalism, the *cogito ergo sum* animating what Cary Wolfe calls "the . . . figure of the human who, imbued with individual consciousness, reiterates the anthropocentric subject–object divide in relation to the object of study: the animal."[39] Indeed, this anthropocentric divide is a tricky one to negotiate because it can self-identify as posthumanism while sustaining humanism by virtue of the fact that while acknowledging compassion, the human can remain at "a safe *ontological* distance" and, as Wolfe argues, be able to apprehend the nonhuman other "in a gesture of self-flattering 'benevolence' wholly characteristic of liberal humanism."[40]

In this regard, the interventions of Derrida, Wolfe, Oliver, and others carry the force of an epistemological shock wave delivered along the already unstable fault lines of anthropocentrism. Thus, if anything could be said to embody a post-species episteme, it is an accounting of "the [ongoing] 'question of animality,'" which, as Derrida asserts, "is difficult and enigmatic in itself [because] it . . . represents the limit upon which all the great questions are formed and determined."[41] If such an accounting *is* to be possible, how can a post-species episteme bring us not to the familiar threshold of "benevolence" that can be seen implicated in the subject/object divide, but to the opportunity to undermine that architecture in more radical ways?

To consider this opportunity, and in the name of the posthuman, I shall now reflect briefly upon that condition of possibility that, to recall Wolfe earlier, "binds us to nonhuman being in general, and within that to nonhuman animals."[42] As Wolfe remarks, it is "a less visible . . . bond between human and nonhuman animals as beings who not only live and die as embodied beings, but also communicate with each other in and through a second form of finitude that encompasses the human/animal difference, forming a bond that is all the more powerful because it is 'unthinking' and in a fundamental sense *unthinkable*."[43] Herein, of course, emerges the epistemic paradox of an *unthinkable* epistemology that does not give to itself the human of humanism but rather recalls, at every turn, the implications of a trans- and post-species perspective that relies on *bidirectional inferences* that charge us, as Gay Bradshaw contends, "with a re-creation of ethics and reasons and ways of knowledge-making that reflects our understanding that animals are fully sentient beings."[44] Such knowledge-making is based on "the force of evidence from neuroscience, ethology and psychology [which, as Bradshaw argues,] has made it *impossible* to retain the idea that only humans have emotions, culture, and all the other attributes that are used to *justify* human privilege over other species."[45] Furthermore, what is significant about such knowledge-making is that it "provides a collective language that links scientific objectivity with subjective knowledge and experience to create [what Bradshaw calls] a science of the heart."[46]

With respect to knowledge-making, a science of the heart contests the view that claims of animal consciousness lack firm empirical evidence and are specious because heavily freighted with emotional baggage. This is the stance taken by Oxford professor of animal behaviour Marian Stamp Dawkins, who claims that threats to "the very basis of ethology" take the form of what she calls "rampant anthropomorphism,"[47] a term used by Dawkins to discredit the view taken by cognitive ethologists, such as Marc Bekoff, that animals have rich emotional lives and experience joy, empathy, grief, embarrassment, anger, and love. But rather than setting up a duality by resisting Dawkins, Bekoff meets her remarks head-on with the assertion that an effective cognitive ethology actually means "[c]areful anthropomorphism *is alive and well, as it should be,*" but also with the rebuttal that "claims that anthropomorphism has no place in science, or that anthropomorphic predictions and explanations are less accurate than more mechanistic or reductionist explanations are *not* supported by any data."[48] Indeed, it can be seen that charges of anthropomorphism are grounded in anthropocentrism, and Bekoff's view sidesteps this anachronistic charge by demonstrating that an ethics of care would be radically *transformative*; it would change how *science is done* to the extent that, as Bekoff asserts, "the burden of proof would . . . shift to the side of the skeptics, who would have to 'prove' *their* claims that animals don't experience emotions."[49] In this regard, a move towards "careful anthropomorphism" acknowledges the significance of empathy and compassion, love and friendship as being key to living a trans- and post-species episteme. Indeed, to shift the burden of proof turns the tables on Dawkins and suggests that what is so threatening about such "rampant" anthropomorphism is its *potential* for a paradigm shift in that it just might, as Bekoff argues, "actually reflect a very accurate way of knowing."[50] In other words, Bekoff's careful anthropomorphism is disquieting to some because it draws attention to what lies at the heart of the "strange kinship," advocated by Kelly Oliver, that I mentioned earlier—a kinship that Oliver says is "based on gestures of love and friendship" as well as compassion. It is this moment of recognition that Derrida has in mind when he states that "one of the leading questions of our age" revolves around "the question of violence and compassion toward animals."[51] According to Derrida, the question appears at a time of "the worst kinds of violence" involved in "the [unprecedented] purely instrumental, industrial, chemico-genetic treatment of living beings."[52]

RAMPANT COMPASSION **257**

Further to Derrida's observation is the question of whether an appeal to compassion sustains an onto-theological humanism that remains firmly anthropocentric. That is, does an appeal to compassion inadvertently reconstitute the human subject? Perhaps, especially when, as Matthew Calarco points out, the question of "how to think otherwise about animal life and its place in ethics and politics" means "seeking to rethink differences between human beings and animals in a nonhierarchical and nonbinary way."[53] This means not *just* a decentring of human subjectivity, "but rather a thought of the Same–Other relation where the Same is not simply a *human* self and where the Other is not simply a *human* other."[54] This thought is well beyond the human/animal divide and is concerned with "*life as responsivity*, where life is understood not exclusively but broadly and inclusively from human to animal and beyond."[55]

As I understand it, this "thought" of life-as-responsivity is what Rosi Braidotti has in mind regarding *life beyond species*, which is a "postanthropocentric shift away from the hierarchical relations that had privileged 'Man'"; this shift "requires a form of estrangement and a radical repositioning on the part of the subject."[56] This repositioning not only stresses "the more compassionate aspect of subjectivity," but also, and perhaps just as radically, involves "a non-human definition of Life as *zoe*, or a dynamic and generative force."[57] According to Braidotti, the best method by which to accomplish this involvement is "the strategy of defamiliarization . . . from the dominant vision of the subject," a "dis-identification" that would disrupt "familiar habits of thought and representation in order to pave the way for creative alternatives."[58] While a post-species episteme might involve such a creative alternative, it is only the first step towards understanding life as responsivity, because although it makes an appeal to compassion, it may also surreptitiously retain the onto-theological human of humanism and its anthropocentric underpinnings predicated upon nostalgia for the human subject. How, then, to think otherwise? Here we encounter, once again, an epistemic paradox of an *unthinkable* epistemology, which does not give to itself the human of humanism.

If we consider Thomas Laqueur's claim that "systems of knowledge determine what can be thought within them,"[59] we appear to arrive at an impasse, for in an onto-theological tradition the *anthropos* and *bios* are seen as "categorically distinct from the life of animals and non-humans, or *zoe*,"[60] and thus serve to give sense to the term "human" by virtue of exclusions. Indeed, it is the centrality of *anthropos* that posthumanism or postanthropocentrism challenges, and in the process such thinking-through is not only radically intersectional, it requires, as Calarco asserts, "abandoning, or at least inhabiting in a hypercritical manner, the hierarchical humanist metaphysics that we have inherited from the ontotheological tradition, for it is this tradition that blocks the possibility of thinking about animals in a non- or other-than-anthropocentric manner."[61] It is *this* possibility for thinking about animals that points to the war between violence and compassion that (as a generation of ecofeminists pointed out prior to Derrida) is grounded in Kant's rejection of sentiment or sympathy and his universalizing but discriminatory concept of ethics. Significantly, ecofeminists have also critiqued an "inherent bias in contemporary animal rights theory [Singer/Regan] toward rationalism,"[62] even while focused on suffering, and have brought attention to the interconnectedness of oppressions with regard to racism, sexism, and speciesism where all of these function to support the biopower of anthropocentrism. Here the point is that while ecofeminists have for decades been addressing the "war on compassion,"[63] the initial approach has been limited to a recognition of the capacity of animals for suffering and, in the process, the "war" appears, at times, to be waged on the premise that humanism can be decisively left behind. But the problem with this aim, as Braidotti argues, is that it "subscribes to a basic humanist assumption with regard to volition and agency, as if the 'end' of Humanism might be subjected to human control, as if we bear the capacity to erase the traces of Humanism from either the present or an imagined future."[64] The point of this situation is the "difficulty of erasing the trace of epistemic violence by which a non-humanist position might be carved out of the institutions of Humanism"[65] and which remains inextricable from anthropocentrism. And what, then, of rationality with regard to moral reasoning? Of compassion? What *of* suffering? What of a CAS that appears methodologically and ideologically to turn in a feedback loop reiterating humanism? Thus, as Cary Wolfe points out, "we continue to think of the question [of the animal] in terms of persons and 'a subject centered semantics,' that is, precisely, in terms of humanism."[66]

At the same time that we apprehend an unprecedented violence against animals, we also witness "the counterforce of animal protection" that is "engaged in a protracted struggle over the extent of pity and compassion toward animals."[67] As Derrida contends, we are now hearing the voices of those who seek "to awaken us to our responsibilities and our obligations with respect to the living in general" and, in this regard, the war on compassion or pity is a timely call in that, as Derrida says, we are "passing through a critical phase. We are passing through that phase and it passes through us. To think the war we find ourselves waging is not only a duty, a responsibility, an obligation, it is also a necessity, a constraint that, like it or not, directly or indirectly, everyone is held to. Henceforth and more than ever. And I say 'to think' this war because it concerns what we call 'thinking.' The animal looks at us, and we are naked before it. Thinking perhaps begins there."[68] Matthew Calarco points out just how significant the reference to "thinking" by Derrida actually is, as it indicates that "this question [of violence and compassion] is situated at the limits of philosophy and the metaphysical tradition and that the resources to think through this question are not likely to be found wholly within that tradition,"[69] given its onto-theological and anthropocentric determinations. The question of violence and compassion and how "to think the war" leads, necessarily, into the "end" of humanism and thus the "end" of Man. What would such "thinking" with regard to a call to responsibility look like?

In *Specters of Marx*, Derrida—who uses the figure of the "scholar" to demonstrate that *thinking* is *not* logic and *not* metaphysics—recalls Heidegger's insistence that a system emerges only when a certain view of thinking comes to an end. As Heidegger sees it, "thinking" itself is "poetic" and since we do not take the poetic "seriously," we have, paradoxically, *yet* to "dwell" in it. Instead, says Heidegger, we "dwell unpoetically" in a "curious measure of frantic measuring and calculating."[70] Derrida also makes the point that philosophy has deprived itself of poetic thinking and settled for "philosophical knowledge."[71] Out of a world view built upon "frantic measuring," "calculating" and "philosophical knowledge" appears a binary logic of identity built upon a subject who, as Rosi Braidotti explains, "is equated with consciousness, universal rationality, and self-regulating ethical behaviour" and stands in opposition to Otherness, which is "defined as its negative," as well as to difference, which "spells inferiority."[72] What does it mean, then, "to think the war" when an earlier Derrida asserts that "[t]hinking is what we already know *we have not yet begun.*"[73]

Perhaps we have not yet begun the "thinking" as alluded to by Derrida because in the humanist tradition the thinker is an anthropocentric subject who confronts the world as a separate, inanimate object, whereas post-anthropocentric subjectivity is no longer "the exclusive prerogative of *anthropos*" but understands itself as belonging to "*an assemblage that includes non-human agents.*"[74] Perhaps the significance of such an "assemblage" in being able "to think the war" can be understood in Heidegger's thinking of *gathering* in the Old High German sense of the word "*thing*," which according to Heidegger means, specifically, "a gathering to deliberate on a matter under discussion, a contested matter"; here "the thing" refers to an *active, deliberative assembly* rather than merely denoting "whatever is or may be an *object of thought*"[75] or an inanimate object. In other words, Heidegger's sense of deliberation and assemblage is relational and implies a vital kinship, rather than a separation between "thinking" and "things" or subject and object.

This turn away from the subject/object distinction and from the subject of humanism is what I'd like to term a *thin(kin)g* in that such turns imply, even necessitate, a cognitive and relational entanglement, a kinship, with "things," so much so that, as Braidotti might say, we must have not only "a new concept of 'matter' [that] is both affective and auto-poetic [recalling Heidegger on living poetically] or self-organizing,"[76] but we must also recognize new subjectivities. In this entanglement, *thin(kin)g* describes a complex ontological and vital materialist interaction between living beings that ceases to be invested in a value hierarchy defined by "*human* action, *human* mindedness, *human* morality, *human* creativity, or *human* knowledge against the animal and just below the divine."[77] Moreover, such *thin(kin)g* is associative, entangled, yet indeterminate, in that it calls upon us to recognize, as Lori Gruen points out, that "we are *already in relations with all sorts of life* forms and, for the most part, we have *not* been recognizing this."[78] Similarly, *thin(kin)g* as such could be said to involve "the ontological recognition that we are in *unavoidable relations* to all sorts of other beings and organisms," which "raises profound ethical questions."[79]

The recognition that we are always already in "unavoidable relations" enables us to understand the epistemological and ontological complications of what Derrida has in mind when he enjoins us "to think the war" *because*, he says, "it concerns what we *call* 'thinking.'" Instead of engagement, what has been called "thinking" has been given over to the philosophical, social, and political naming and classification of *things*, thereby naturalizing an ontology and epistemology based on sustaining what Derrida refers to as "the sharp distinction between the real and the unreal, the actual and the inactual, the living and the non-living, being and non-being . . . in the opposition between what is present and what is not."[80] In other words, instead of engagement, entanglement, we have classification, which, as Susanne Kappeler asserts, is "an expression of the subjectivity of power" and, being thus, is "neither neutral, being put to political use 'thereafter,' nor is it objective: it is itself an act of social and political discrimination."[81] What this means is that philosophical knowledge is implicated in the politics of classification, and is, therefore, unable "to think the war," if only because classification and philosophy have served to institutionalize, justify, and naturalize the worst kinds of violence against living beings.

At this point, it might seem as if the question of the animal(s)[82]—the/a *real* animal—has taken a back seat to what has been called "elitist" theorizing, dealing only in "metaphysical interpretations" of such questions and being unconcerned with the real, embodied exploitation/oppression of nonhumans, of the plight of millions or more actual animals who, on a global scale, suffer and die yearly in the name of human exceptionalism. But this is *not* the case, for behind the *question* is an urgent call to think the war in the face of the unprecedented violence against animals in bioengineering, in industrial production, in slaughter, in consumption, in experimentation, and in "entertainment." The urgency of this call and the question of the animal are one and the same and are based, as Derrida says, on "what everybody knows": "the industrial, mechanical, chemical, hormonal, and genetic violence to which man has been submitting animal life for the past two centuries. Everybody knows what the production, breeding, transport, and slaughter of these animals has become."[83] Indeed, it is true that "everybody knows" and the tendency has been to foreground these terrifying *images* or to bring them to mind because they "open the immense question of pathos and the pathological, precisely, that is, of suffering, pity, and compassion."[84] And this is certainly effective, to a point. To speak of the *question* of the animal is not to *forego* activism, however: it is in itself a viable and necessary form of praxis that leads to being able "to think the war"; such thinking means to arrive at "the place that *has* to be accorded to the *interpretation* of this compassion, to the *sharing* of this suffering among the living, to the law, ethics, and politics that must be brought to bear upon this experience of compassion. What has been happening for two centuries now involves *a new experience of this compassion.*"[85]

The import of such arrivals heralds a sea change regarding different levels of intervention in relation to activism in the face of the violence wreaked upon animals. In this context, the interpretation of compassion stands in relation to direct action and takes as one of its aims the dismantling of "the *discourse* that supports [the violence] and attempts to *legitimate* it."[86] That such dismantling is critical, strategic, and compassionate can be heard in Derrida's appeal to address specifically modern forms of violence, and thus to increase the purview of the realms of advocacy, all of which can agree that

> [t]his industrial, scientific, technical violence will not be tolerated for very much longer, neither de facto nor de jure. It will find itself more and more discredited. The relations between humans and animals *must* change. They *must*, both in the sense of an "ontological" necessity and of an "ethical" duty. I place these words in quotation marks because this change will have to affect the very sense and value of these concepts (the ontological and the ethical). That is why, although their discourse [that of "rights" or of direct action] seems to me poorly articulated or philo-sophically inconsistent, I am on principle sympathetic with those who, it seems to me, are in the right and have good reasons to rise up against the way animals are treated: in industrial production, in slaughter, in consumption, in experimentation.[87]

I include this long quotation because it reflects upon the work that is neces-sary to law, ethics, and politics in addition to more familiar forms of activism in that it seeks to establish a kinship between CAS scholars and grassroots activists, all of whom understand "the right and good reasons to rise up." In this regard, such work is inextricable from the "new experience of com-passion" I mentioned above and, as such, calls for and provokes thinking as *poiesis*. In other words, it involves, as Derrida says, a "thinking concerning the animal, [and] if there is such a thing [it]derives from *poetry*."[88]

The reader will recall Derrida's insistence on "think(ing) the war," and it is this war, he says, that is "waged over the matter of pity."[89] In the pas-sage I quoted earlier, the reader might recall Derrida's assertion that "to think the war" is a duty, a responsibility, and an obligation, and that the possibility of such thinking can "perhaps begin" where "the animal looks at us and we are naked before it."[90] What Derrida is referring to in this instance is not only an awareness that animals have agency, but also that the animal's look is a disruption of the anthropocentric sense that *only humans do the looking* (at animals). Instead, Derrida refers to the fact that the animal who, in its "unsubstitutable singularity"[91] "looks at us" is a liv-ing, agential being and that to be *aware of being seen* by an animal is to be aware of the embodied entanglement always already existing "between human and nonhuman animals as beings who . . . live and die as embodied beings" and who "communicate with each other in and through a second form of finitude that encompasses the human/animal difference,"[92] but that has been ignored or disavowed via anthropocentrism. Those whose gaze has never intersected with an animal's directed at them, or who took no account, "neither wanted nor had the capacity to draw any systematic consequence from the act that an animal could, facing them, look at them, . . . and in a word, without a word, *address them*. They have taken no account of the fact that what they call 'animal' could *look* at them, and *address* them from down there, from a whole other origin."[93] The entanglement is grounded in a certain thin(kin)g that makes possible the "bond" between living beings, one that, as Cary Wolfe has said, "is all the more powerful because it is 'unthinking' and in a fundamental sense unthinkable."[94] Such a thin(kin)g is political, compassionate, and ethical, and, in a post-anthropocentric, post-species world is predicated upon what Lori Gruen calls "entangled empathy."

To live a post-species episteme of knowledge-making and decision-making, therefore, has the potential, as Foucault might say, "to shake up habitual ways of working and thinking, to dissipate conventional familiarities, to re-evaluate rules and institutions starting from this re-problematization, to participate in the formation of a political *will*."[95] In the case of a post-species episteme, such a political will is based upon an ecological, eco-critical, and post-anthropocentric ethic of care that not only involves a new experience of compassion but also does not reiterate and revitalize humanism. There is great potential in this moment, but many challenges as well. As John Sanbonmatsu puts it in an interview with Direct Action Everywhere, "The challenge we all face, emotionally and even 'existentially,' is how to keep advocating radical social change in the face of a pervasive and deep-seated global culture of terrible violence."[96] Recognizing this challenge means putting an end to "the war on compassion"[97] because to do so enables us to respond to the urgency of the ontological and ethical turn involved in Derrida's call "to think the war." Indeed, this call is a moment in human history that provides us with the opportunity to challenge the human species' right and to recognize the lives of animals as being worthy of respect and protection.

NOTES

1. *GLTB Literature*, "Monique Wittig."
2. de Beauvoir quoted in Wittig, "One Is Not Born a Woman," 11.
3. Ibid., 9.
4. Wittig, "Straight Mind," 32.
5. Wittig, "One Is Not Born a Woman," 14.

6. Ibid.

7. Ibid., 16.

8. Ibid., 10.

9. Haraway, *Haraway Reader*, 329.

10. Gane, "When We Have Never Been Human," 142 (emphasis mine).

11. Haraway, *Haraway Reader*, 329.

12. Ibid.

13. Wolfe, *Animal Rites*, 6.

14. Wolfe, "'Animal Studies,'" in *What Is Posthumanism?*, 118 (emphasis mine).

15. Bradshaw, "What We Do."

16. See Donovan, in "Animal Rights and Feminist Theory," who writes that "in the articulation of Locke and the framers of the US Declaration of Independence and Constitution not all humans were in fact considered sufficiently rational . . . to be considered 'persons' entitled to rights: only white, male property owners were deemed adequately endowed to be included in the category of personhood. Indeed, much of the nineteenth-century women's rights movement was devoted to urging that women be considered persons under the Constitution. Here, as elsewhere in Western political theory, women and animals are cast together" (353–54). In Canada, one need only recall the in/famous Person's Case (*Edwards v. A.G. of Canada*) in which women were finally in 1929 given the status of persons through an appeal to the Judicial Committee of the Privy Council of London, which had reversed an earlier verdict of the Supreme Court of Canada stipulating that the word "person" did not apply to women.

17. Oliver, *Animal Lessons*, 32.

18. Ibid., 29.

19. Ibid., 228 (my emphasis).

20. Quoted in Thierman, "Apparatuses of Animality," 90.

21. Quoted in ibid., 91.

22. Ibid., 92.

23. Ibid.

24. Ibid., 99.

25. Derrida, "Violence Against Animals," in Derrida and Roudinesco, *For What Tomorrow*, 65.

26. Oliver, *Animal Lessons*, 35.

27. Derrida, "Violence Against Animals," in Derrida and Roudinesco, *For What Tomorrow*, 65.

28. Luke, "Taming Ourselves," 299.

29. Quoted in Adams, "War on Compassion," 32.

30. Regan, *Case for Animal Rights*, 24.

31. Regan, *Case for Animal Rights*, xii.

32. Luke, "Taming Ourselves," 292.

33. Ibid.

34. Wolfe, *What Is Posthumanism?*, 99.

35. Luke, "Taming Ourselves," 292.

36. Calarco, *Zoographies*, 118.

37. Derrida, in Calarco, *Zoographies*, 118–19. See Derrida, *Animal That Therefore I Am*, 396.

38. Calarco, *Zoographies*, 118.

39. Wolfe, *What Is Posthumanism?*, 236.

40. Ibid.

41. Derrida, "Violence Against Animals," in Derrida and Roudinesco, *For What Tomorrow*, 62–63.

42. Wolfe, "'Animal Studies,'" in *What Is Posthumanism?*, 118.

43. Wolfe, *What Is Posthumanism?*, 123.

44. *Animal Visions*, "Trans-species Living."

45. Ibid.

46. Bradshaw, "Overview."

47. Quoted in Bekoff, "Dawkins' Dangerous Idea."

48. Bekoff, *Emotional Lives of Animals*, 126.

49. Ibid., 123–27.

50. Ibid., 131.

51. Quoted in Calarco, *Zoographies*, 113.

52. Derrida, "Violence Against Animals," in Derrida and Roudinesco, *For What Tomorrow*, 73.

53. Calarco, *Zoographies*, 105.

54. Ibid., 106.

55. Ibid.

56. Braidotti, *Posthuman*, 88.

57. Ibid., 86.

58. Ibid., 88–89.

59. Laqueur, *Making Sex*, 13.

60. Braidotti, *Posthuman*, 65.

61. Calarco, *Zoographies*, 112.

62. Donovan, "Animal Rights and Feminist Theory," 351.

63. Adams, "War on Compassion," 34.

64. Braidotti, *Posthuman*, 30.

65. Ibid.

66. Wolfe, *Animal Rites*, 119.

67. Calarco, *Zoographies*, 113.

68. Derrida, in Calarco, *Zoographies*, 113. See Derrida, *Animal That Therefore I Am*, 29.

69. Calarco, *Zoographies*, 113.

70. Heidegger, "Poetically Man Dwells," in *Poetry, Language, Thought*, 228.

71. Derrida, *Animal That Therefore I Am*, 7.

72. Braidotti, *Posthuman*, 15.

73. Derrida, "Of Grammatology," in *Derrida Reader*, 53 (emphasis mine).

74. Braidotti, *Posthuman*, 82 (emphasis mine).

75. Heidegger, "Thing," in *Poetry, Language, Thought*, 174.

76. Braidotti, *Posthuman*, 158.

77. Gruen, "Navigating Difference," 213 (emphasis mine). See Chapter 7, p. 203.

78. Ibid., 225 (emphasis mine). See Chapter 7, p. 218.

79. Ibid., 226. See Chapter 7, p. 218.

80. Derrida, *Specters of Marx*, 11.

81. Kappeler, "Speciesism, Racism, Nationalism," 338.

82. I use the plural here to address the issue raised by Derrida in *The Animal That Therefore I Am*, regarding "the discourses of common sense, which at bottom are the same . . . tend to confuse all animal species under the grand category of 'the animal' versus 'man (without taking into account differences between sexed and non-sexed animals, mammals and nonmammals, without taking into account the infinite diversity of animals . . . (59). Likewise, Derrida asserts that "there is an immense multiplicity of other living things that cannot in any way be homogenized, except by means of violence and willful ignorance, within the category of what is called the animal or animality in general. . . . The confusion of all nonhuman living creatures within the general and common category of the animal is not simply a sin against rigorous thinking, vigilance, lucidity, or empirical authority, it is also a crime. Not a crime against animality, precisely, but a crime of the first order against the animals, against animals" (48).

83. Ibid., 26.

84. Ibid.

85. Ibid. (emphasis mine).

86. Derrida, "Violence Against Animals," in Derrida and Roudinesco, *For What Tomorrow*, 64 (emphasis mine).

87. Ibid.

88. Derrida, *Animal That Therefore I Am*, 7 (emphasis mine).

89. Ibid., 29.

90. Ibid.

91. Ibid., 9.

92. Wolfe, *What Is Posthumanism?*, 123.

93. Derrida, *Animal That Therefore I Am*, 13.

94. Wolfe, *What Is Posthumanism?*, 123.

95. Foucault, quoted in Graham, *Representations*, 44 (emphasis mine).

96. Sanbonmatsu, "Interview."

97. Adams, "War on Compassion," 33.

BIBLIOGRAPHY

Adams, Carol J. "The War on Compassion." In *The Feminist Care Tradition in Animal Ethics*, edited by Josephine Donovan and Carol J. Adams, 21–38. New York: Columbia University Press, 2007.

Animal Visions. "Trans-species Living: An Interview with Gay Bradshaw." Blog, 17 September, 2010. Accessed August 25, 2013. https://animalvisions.wordpress.com/2010/09/17/trans-species-living-an-interview-with-gay-bradshaw/.

Bekoff, Marc. "Dawkins' Dangerous Idea: We Really Don't Know If Animals Are Conscious." *Huffington Post* blog, July 15, 2012. http://www.huffingtonpost.com/marc-bekoff/animal-consciousness_b_1519000.html.

———. *The Emotional Lives of Animals*. Novato, CA: New World Library, 2007.

Bradshaw, Gay. "Overview," *Kerulos Center*. http://www.kerulos.org/what_we_do/overview.html (site since modified).

———. "What We Do." *Kerulos Center*. http://www.kerulos.org/what_we_do/tspsych.html (site since modified).

Braidotti, Rosi. *The Posthuman*. Cambridge: Polity Press, 2013.

Calarco, Matthew. *Zoographies*. New York: Columbia University Press, 2008.

Derrida, Jacques. *The Animal That Therefore I Am*. Edited by Marie-Louise Mallet. Translated by David Wills. New York: Fordham University Press, 2008.

———. *A Derrida Reader: Between the Blinds*. Edited by Peggy Kamuf. New York: Columbia University Press, 1991.

———. *Specters of Marx*. New York: Routledge, 1994.

Derrida, Jacques, and Elisabeth Roudinseco. *For What Tomorrow . . .: A Dialogue*. Translated by Jeff Fort. Stanford, CA: Stanford University Press, 2004.

Donovan, Josephine. "Animal Rights and Feminist Theory." *Signs* 15, no. 2 (Winter 1990): 350–75.

Gane, Nicholas. "When We Have Never Been Human, What Is to Be Done?: Interview with Donna Haraway." *Theory, Culture & Society* 23, nos. 7–8 (December 2006): 135–58.

GLTB Literature. "Monique Wittig." Accessed October 26, 2013. http://www.glbtq.com/literature/wittig_m.html, accessed October 26, 2013 (site discontinued).

Graham, Elaine L. *Representations of the Post/Human: Monsters, Aliens and Others in Popular Culture*. New Brunswick, NJ: Rutgers University Press, 2002.

Gruen, Lori. "Navigating Difference (Again): Animal Ethics and Entangled Empathy." In *Strangers to Nature: Animal Lives and Human Ethics*, edited by Gregory R. Smulewicz-Zucker, 213–34. New York: Lexington Books, 2012.

Haraway, Donna. *The Haraway Reader*. London: Routledge, 2004.

Heidegger, Martin. *Poetry, Language, Thought*. Translated by Albert Hofstadter. New York: Harper Colophon Books, 1971.

Kappeler, Susanne. "Speciesism, Racism, Nationalism . . . or the Power of Scientific Subjectivity." In *Animals and Women: Feminist Theoretical Explorations*, edited by Carol J. Adams and Josephine Donovan, 320–52. Durham, NC: Duke University Press, 1995.

Laqueur, Thomas Walter. *Making Sex: Body and Gender from the Greeks to Freud.* Cambridge, MA: Harvard University Press, 1990.

Luke, Brian. "Taming Ourselves or Going Feral?: Toward a Nonpatriarchal Metaethics of Animal Liberation." In *Animals and Women: Feminist Theoretical Explorations*, edited by Carol J. Adams and Josephine Donovan, 290–319. Durham, NC: Duke University Press, 1995.

Mazlish, Bruce. *The Fourth Discontinuity: The Co-evolution of Humans and Machines.* New Haven: Yale University Press, 1993.

Oliver, Kelly. *Animal Lessons: How They Teach Us to Be Human.* New York: Columbia University Press, 2009.

Regan, Tom. *The Case for Animal Rights.* Berkeley and Los Angeles: University of California Press, 1983.

———. "The Case for Animal Rights." In *In Defense of Animals*, 13–26. Edited by Peter Singer. New York: Basil Blackwell, 1985.

Sanbonmatsu, John. "Interview with John Sanbonmatsu, Associate Professor of Philosophy at Worcester Polytechnic Institute," by Saryta Rodriguez. *Direct Action Everywhere* blog. Accessed July 12, 2015. http://directactioneverywhere .com/theliberationist/2014/12/1/interview-with-john-sanbonmatsu-associate -professor-of-philosophy-at-worcester-polytechnic-institute.

Thierman, Stephen. "Apparatuses of Animality: Foucault Goes to a Slaughterhouse." *Foucault Studies* 9 (September 2010): 89–110.

Wittig, Monique. "One Is Not Born a Woman." In *The Straight Mind and Other Essays*, 9–20. Boston: Beacon Press, 1992.

———. "The Straight Mind." In *The Straight Mind and Other Essays*, 21–32. Boston: Beacon Press, 1992.

Wolfe, Cary. *Animal Rites: American Culture, the Discourse of Species, and Post-humanist Theory.* Chicago: University of Chicago Press, 2003.

———. *What Is Posthumanism?* Minneapolis: University of Minnesota Press, 2010.

10

The Limits of the "Human"

An Alternative Ethics of Dependence on Animals

Kelly Oliver

In this chapter, I explore mainstream culture's ambivalent relationship to our dependence on animals, particularly the animals in our homes, by turning to discussions at the intersection of disability studies and animal studies. Critically revisiting the debate between some from disability studies (Eva Kittay and Licia Carlson) and some from animal studies (Peter Singer and Jeff McMahan), over the comparative moral status of animals with higher IQs and some severely mentally disabled people, points to problems with the very framework of the debate. Furthermore, comparisons between supposedly non-rational human beings and non-rational animals—so called "marginal cases"—continue to vex both utilitarian (Singer and McMahan) and Kantian (Cheshire Calhoun and Christine Korsgaard) approaches to animal ethics, as well as disability studies. Here, spelling out some of the problems with both of these mainstream approaches to questions of animal ethics, I propose the need for an alternative approach to questions of both animals and disabled persons. Drawing on postmodernist resources, including Jacques Derrida's writings on the human/animal opposition, Cary Wolfe's Derridean-inspired analysis of posthumanism, a critical engagement with Julia Kristeva's work on disability, and my own past work on animal ethics, I suggest some ways forward through the thickets of moral status when it comes to living beings considered "non-rational," particularly those with whom we share intimate domestic space. I begin with the nonhuman animals literally at the intersection of disability and animal studies: service dogs.

The Ambiguous Status of Service Animals

Last spring, actress Ashley Judd took heat in the blogosphere for "coming out" as having "psychological support" dogs to help her cope with depression. Some people responded calling her "crazy," a "beyotch," and a "service dog snob."[1] Registered as service animals, Judd's dogs go everywhere with her, especially her favourite, "Shug," whom she calls her "four-legged companion." Yet the status of emotional support dogs is ambiguous. Technically, only service animals, and more recently only trained dogs, including physical and psychiatric but not psychological, therapy, or emotional support dogs, are legally considered service animals.[2] According to the ADA (Americans with Disabilities Act) regulations, service animals are for use by people who suffer from physical or mental disability. Rather than pets, companions, or even helpers, the law describes them as akin to tools that enable disabled people to navigate the world.[3] Several reports describing the difference between pets that serve as therapy or emotional support animals and service dogs make comparisons between service animals and equipment like "assistive aids such as wheelchairs."[4] The Justice Department requires that all service dogs (or other animals) must be specifically trained to perform certain "tasks." The calming or therapeutic effect of their company is not enough. They must perform a service such as picking up dropped keys, counterbalancing dizziness, or turning on lights. The Justice Department draws a distinction between "psychiatric service dogs" and "emotional support" or "therapy dogs." The former are legally recognized under the ADA, while the latter are not, even as relatively new subcategories of "service" animals have been designated to provide us with not only physical assistance (as guide dogs do) but also with emotional and therapeutic support.

Doctors are prescribing dogs instead of pills for everything from post-traumatic stress to depression. In addition, "comfort dogs" are now being used in courtrooms to provide emotional support to children called to testify in difficult cases.[5] Both Yale Law School and Harvard Medical School have instituted programs whereby students can "check out" a dog from the library and play with it for thirty minutes to help alleviate stress.[6] It is noteworthy that an article in the *Yale Daily News* reporting the success of the program, ends: "the library also checks out umbrellas, soccer balls, goal posts and bicycles."[7] And an article in the *Harvard Gazette* says, "Cooper [therapy dog] can be checked out by Harvard ID holders, just like a library book."[8] There are programs like this popping up all over as evidence mounts that companion animals reduce stress and disease, and promote learning, coping, and social adjustment for all ages.[9]

In spite of growing recognition of the important role that companion animals play in our lives, legally animals enter our households and intimate family units either as pets or as service animals; in either case, their legal status is like that of property, even if expensive or prized property.[10] Pets still have the legal status of quasi-property, like things. And although there are anti-cruelty laws in all states, as Gary Francione powerfully demonstrates in his book *Animals, Property, and the Law*, animals can still be disposed of at will by their "owners" or city officials and these laws do little to stop abuse of animals.[11] While new types of service animals are legally sanctioned not only for physical support but also for psychological and emotional support, the laws are clear that these animals are tools used for very specific tasks.[12] These laws, however, cannot prevent people from becoming emotionally attached to their service animals; they do not prevent the animals from providing companionship as well as performing specific functions. Service animals, even strictly defined, do much more for their human counterparts than turn on lights or pick up keys. Yet, in spite of growing evidence of the mental and physical health benefits of animals in the home, our psychological and emotional relationships to animals continue to be circumscribed by laws that relegate animals to forms of property.

These laws suggest that public policy does not take seriously dependence on animals, particularly our emotional dependence, without turning them into assistance devices like wheelchairs, machines performing tasks, or medication to be prescribed by doctors. These seemingly mainstream cultural and legal attitudes suggest that people who are dependent on their animals for anything other than amusement or entertainment are abnormal or unhealthy. Valuing animals as companions or loving them as friends and family, and more especially depending on them for emotional comfort, is seen as a sign of weakness or quirkiness at best, and at worst a sign of "craziness" or mental illness.

The Questionable Status of Military Service Dogs

This ambivalent attitude towards service animals is manifest in the military, where dogs have served alongside US service men and women for decades.[13] While the history of dogs in the military demonstrates changing attitudes towards service animals, at the same time it highlights continuing ambiguity in our relationship to companion animals. New programs offer dogs as service animals or as pets to military personal suffering from post-traumatic stress or emotional problems resulting from war and active military duty. Organizations outside the military such as Pets for Patriots, Puppies Behind Bars, and Paws and Stripes provide trained service dogs for veterans as part of a test program partially funded by the military to study the effects of emotional support dogs on veterans suffering from post-traumatic stress disorder (PTSD) and other emotional problems as a result of active service in a war zone.

Following federal policy, however, the military is clear that emotional support animals are not service animals, and that service animals are still the only animals legally protected under the ADA. Delineating differences between pets and service animals, Military.com puts it this way: "The term "service animal" includes a wide range of animals highly trained for specific types of needs, such as signal dogs (for the deaf) or seeing eye dogs (for the blind). In a key distinction from other types of animals, *federal law does not consider these or other service animals pets*; they are viewed as *equipment* [my emphasis] necessary for disabled people to manage the basic tasks of daily living."[14] Following federal policy, the military continues to draw sharp distinctions between companion animals and service animals. Legally, the former are considered pets, while the latter are "viewed as equipment."

Yet, the goal of the new study is to determine whether companion dogs can provide a form of treatment to vets suffering from PTSD. Early results suggest that the answer is yes.[15] So while the emotional connection between humans and companion animals (in this case, dogs) is being studied and proving significant to the scientific community, and while "pet owners" testify to the importance of their companion animals to their everyday well-being, the status of these animals is still ambiguous in terms of public policy. Their importance as tools or equipment is acknowledged, while the importance of their emotional support is either suspect or must be quantified in terms of functionality on the part of the dogs and the people they serve.[16] In other words, these animals are valued in terms of what tasks they perform and how those jobs enhance the performance of human beings. Furthermore, all of these studies and discussions about them revolve around the benefits for humans rather than whether or not there are benefits for the animals themselves.

Although it is only recently that dogs are being used by the military for emotional support to help soldiers deal with PTSD, since at least World

War II the United States military has used dogs in active duty as messenger dogs, sentry dogs, attack dogs, tactical dogs, scout dogs, casualty dogs who helped find wounded soldiers, pack dogs, and bomb sniffers to find land mines.[17] One military history of working dogs begins: "The call of modern warfare as the Gulf war demonstrated in 1991, exemplified our use of the most sophisticated, technologically advanced equipment that the US could procure to bring swift and decisive victory for a just cause. . . . But although the face of war changed, some fundamental *tools and weapons* used have not. As a matter of fact, the US followed certain paths laid out by the ancient peoples of Persia and Assyria with their use of *four-legged technology* in warfare."[18] Echoing what has been standard military protocol since World War II, Staff Sargent Tracy English, the author of this military report, refers to military service dogs as "tools," "weapons," and "technology." Since the 1949 Federal Property and Administrative Services Act, military dogs have been classified as equipment. And as such, until 2000 with the passage of H.R. 5314 by Congress, which allowed handlers and others to adopt retired dogs, military dogs were treated as any other worn out equipment and "disposed of after they were no longer useful."[19]

Despite the fact that bonds between military dogs and their handlers are often very close, military dogs are still currently classified as equipment. The 2005 *Military Working Dog (MWD) Field Manual* describes working dogs as living equipment: "MWDs [military working dogs] are a unique item; they are the only living item in the Army supply system. Like other highly specialized equipment, MWDs complement and enhance the capabilities of the military police. MWD teams enable the military police to perform its mission more effectively and with significant savings of manpower, time, and money."[20] It is noteworthy, however, that a congressional committee is currently considering introducing a bill that would make military working dogs akin to soldiers rather than equipment. In an about-face in military policy, this 2012 bill acknowledges that "[m]ilitary working dogs perform critical and varied roles that go far beyond their current designation as 'equipment'"; it calls for a change in classification of working dogs from equipment to "canine members of the armed forces"; and like other service members, they will be eligible for a "variety of other forms of decoration consistent with the reclassification of military dogs as canine members of the military."[21] If this bill passes, it will radically change the way military service dogs are classified and presumably, therefore, the ways in which they are treated. Rather than mere things or equipment, they will become canine members of the military. Thus, their status as service dogs will be more akin to that of service members than to serviceable equipment.

Kantian Obligations to Service Dogs

That the United States military and federal ADA regulations describe animals as more like things than persons follows the long history of regarding animals as property. Although some animal welfare and animal rights advocates argue that (at least some) animals should have the legal and moral status of persons, we might ask, why must animals be either things or persons? Is there no way to extend our moral community without making animals persons? In other words, can they enter the moral community as animals? This is a question that vexes some Kantians, such as Christine Korsgaard and Cheshire Calhoun, who are trying to recuperate Kant's position on animals and our duties toward them. Before returning to the question of our obligations to military service dogs, which is the centrepiece of Cheshire Calhoun's attempt to articulate a Kantian animal ethics, I briefly sketch the main conclusions of Calhoun's and Korsgaard's arguments for duties to nonhuman animals. My aim is to show how both theorists rely on "like us" arguments even while they agree with Kant that animals are not rational, and therefore neither of them explicitly takes issue with Kant's designation of animals as *things*, which proves problematic. Ultimately, my goal is not a sustained engagement with Kantian arguments for including animals in the moral community, but rather to highlight the types of arguments they use to make the claim that "Kantian ethical thought is more promising than is utilitarianism" on "the animal question," and to show how in important ways, these Kantians are making some of the same conceptual moves and assumptions as some utilitarians, specifically Singer and McMahan.[22]

Both Korsgaard and Calhoun quote Kant referring to animals as *things* that we can dispose of as we see fit: a person is "a being altogether different in rank and dignity from *things*, such as irrational animals, with which one may feel and dispose at one's discretion."[23] "Beings . . . without reason, have only a relative worth, as means, and are therefore called *things*, whereas rational beings are called *persons* because their nature . . . marks them out as an end in itself."[24] And while neither remarks on the designation of animals as *things*, both argue for duties to animals. While Calhoun argues that our duties to animals come from analogous duties to humans, Korsgaard goes further to suggest that animals may be members of the moral community in their own right as "fellow creatures" with their own natural goods and bads and on that basis moral patients if not moral agents to whom we are directly obligated.[25] Both find the source of our duties to animals in our duties to ourselves as animals.

Engaging Korsgaard, Calhoun argues, "[i]n her view, we cannot consistently place value on our own animal nature while refusing similarly to value nonhuman animals' animal nature. But of course, when we value our animal nature, we do so within a wider set of evaluative commitments, including most fundamentally, valuing our own rational nature—a nature animals do not share. It would thus seem that we still need a positive account of why the morally significant differences between animals and humans do not warrant discounting (perhaps severely discounting) animal interests."[26] Calhoun identifies the central problem for a Kantian animal ethics, namely that the kingdom of ends and thus the moral community is populated by self-legislating rational beings, so how can non-self-legislating, non-rational beings enter either one? Through several books and articles, Korsgaard has tried to show how Kantian principles can be—must be—applied to animals even though they are neither self-legislating nor rational. Calhoun follows suit yet seems to reject Korsgaard's solution, which is to divide human beings into two parts, the rational and the animal. Korsgaard goes on to argue that the rational part legislates on behalf of the animal part in humans, and therefore we humans have an obligation to legislate on behalf of the animal part in animals (which is to say the whole of animal nature). Or in Korsgaard's words: "we are the beings who create the order of moral values, the beings who choose to ratify and endorse the natural concern that all animals have for themselves. But what we ratify and endorse is a condition shared by the other animals. So we are not the only beings who matter. We are the only beings who on behalf of all animals can shake our fists at the uncaring universe, and declare that in spite of everything we matter."[27] Calhoun, on the other hand, argues for a spirit of gratitude and generosity towards animals that comes from not only our duty to ourselves as animals but also analogies to human experiences. In the end, like Kant, she suggests that gratitude and generosity towards nonhuman animals may make us better people. When push comes to shove, however, Calhoun cannot find rational grounds upon which to argue for direct duties to animals. She does argue, however, that persons with properly moral characters should behave in ethical, considerate ways towards animals. Thus, following fellow Kantian Tom Hill, she asks, what sort of person would want to behave in ways that are ungrateful to the animals, particularly the animals who serve them?[28] She concludes, "[a]nimals present us with reasonable analogues of positive moral behavior and thereby occasions for practicing gratitude, respect for property, and fairness. Perhaps this will improve our moral performance towards fellow humans, as Kant thought it would. But even if it does not, such practice is a way of generously honoring the spirit of morality."[29]

Calhoun's main example is that of military service dogs. With this example, she attempts to show how a Kantian approach is better than a utilitarian one: "But regardless of how well valuable animal equipment is treated, taking an entirely instrumentalist valuing attitude towards beings who are in fact more like us than like assault rifles may strike us as ethically deficient. From a Utilitarian viewpoint, attitudes are ethically worrisome only insofar as they tend to result in ethically condemnable action. Kantian ethical thought takes our attitudes themselves, apart from the consequences of holding those attitudes, to be assessable."[30] And this leads Calhoun to what she sees as the ethical heart of the matter, which is the failure to reward the long, faithful service of military working dogs.[31] She argues that an ethics of gratitude for services rendered cannot be captured when only considering animal interests or welfare as utilitarians do. Because a military working dog is "a co-worker who faithfully served his handler, and in so doing, the US," Calhoun argues that they are analogous to human co-workers and therefore deserve gratitude and rewards.

Indeed, throughout her essay "But What about the Animals?" Calhoun argues that animals and animal behaviour are analogous to humans and human behaviour, not because animals are rational or intelligent, but rather because animals and humans *function* in similar ways. For example, the function of instinct in animals is analogous to the function of rational willing in humans. So, although the basis of the analogy is not that animals are the same as humans, animals' actions and emotions can be—perhaps should be—interpreted by us as analogous in terms of value. In other words, although animals may be different and have different motivations, their being and actions have equal value to our own; they are equally important by reason of analogy. While Calhoun's analysis may apply to service animals, and these are her central examples, it is more difficult to see how it applies to all animals. Even in the case of service animals, it is their service to their handlers and their faithful work that deserves reward, which is not to say that they have intrinsic value in the way that human beings do for Kant. The emphasis is on their service to us. More generally,

Calhoun's appeal to gratitude for loyal service of co-workers seems complicit with an economy that values productive and able-bodied workers over non-productive or disabled bodies that cannot be integrated into a workforce. I return to this point later in my discussion of Julia Kristeva's call for interaction with, rather than integration of, what she calls "people in the condition of handicap."

For now, I appeal to another proponent of rights for disabled persons, Eva Kittay, who in response to Singer's and McMahan's analogies between disabled people and animals argues that analogies always privilege one term over the other. Kittay explains: "When we assert that A is like B, we take B as the template—its features are salient—and the features of A not found in B lose their salience. That is, if B is characterized by the features x, y, and z, then we come to see A only in terms of its similarity with respect to x, y, and z even if in other contexts A's features, a, b, and c, are the salient ones. The pernicious reductive comparisons between humans and nonhuman animals take such an asymmetrical form."[32] Although Kittay is challenging the comparison of disabled humans with animals that may have higher mental capacities, her analysis also applies to Calhoun's use of analogies between animals and humans. In both cases, it is the intellectual abilities or reason that are salient features and not the ways in which animal bodies (in the case of Calhoun) or disabled bodies (in Kittay's challenge) do not fit into the template set up by the comparison. I will return to this point later.

Neither Korsgaard nor Calhoun can put animals *directly* into the kingdom of ends or the moral community without much, and sometimes complex, argumentation and strong interpretations of Kant. Following, yet diverging from, Kant, conceptually at least, they do so indirectly, and always by comparison to human beings. For Korsgaard this means that our obligations to animals come from our obligations to our own animal natures, while for Calhoun it means that our obligations to animals—if we have any, which remains an open question for her—come from analogical reasoning that renders animals analogous to humans; moreover for Calhoun, our treatment of animals becomes a testament to our own moral character. We could say that for both Korsgaard and Calhoun, man is still the measure of all things. And while things may have value because humans will them to, they cannot give themselves value (unless perhaps we will that they will themselves value), since it seems that we also will that we are the only beings who have rationally self-constituting wills. Korsgaard describes what we might call this "bootstrapping" of value whereby we give ourselves morality: "The *decision* to regard ourselves as the source of legitimate normative claims is the *original act* that brings the world of normative reasons and values into existence."[33] But, we might ask, of what kind is the originary decision for us to be the kind of beings who make decisions? And, what kind of being were we before we made the decision to become rational, self-legislating beings that give ourselves values? These questions take us back to at least the beginning of secular philosophical thinking about the origins of humanity and dilemmas about whether we were once like other animals that one day became human.[34] Korsgaard circumvents any such questions by positing an original decision that made us rational self-legislating beings and thus human. This postulation seems especially problematic given Korsgaard's assumption that there is a human nature that is given as a natural fact that exists before we add value to it; does this human nature exist before the original decision or only after? And if it exists before, then how can rational will be part of human nature? If it exists only after, then what are we before that fateful day of our first rational decision? Animals or humans? Perhaps Korsgaard isn't bothered by such questions because her extension of Kant's ethics to animals is based on a split between our rational selves and our animal selves, as if the two can be so easily separated. And if they can, doesn't this bold re-inscription of the abyss between the two, with the rational one properly legislating the animal other, perpetuate the hierarchy of reason over non-reason that has excluded animals from the moral community? Doesn't it make Korsgaard's animal ethics a form of benevolent dictatorship of our rational selves over not only our own animal selves but also over all animals?

Our Obligations Towards "Marginal Cases"

One of the main problems for Kantians in including animals in the moral community is the requirement for reciprocity of the will. Kant maintains that we are all bound by moral rules because we are all rational rule-givers. How, then, do non-rational beings enter the moral community, those who are not self-governing or self-legislating, the so-called "marginal cases"? We have already seen how Calhoun and Korsgaard deal with this problem. Korsgaard makes an interesting argument about "marginal cases" that takes me to the next phase of my analysis in this essay, namely the intersection of animal studies and disability studies. She maintains that each species has its own *functional unity* or *natural way of functioning*. A human being's natural way of functioning involves reason while an animal's does not. Human beings who are not fully functional in terms of their reason, infants or mentally disabled, are what Korsgaard calls "undeveloped" (infants) or "defective" (mentally disabled).[35] She argues, "[t]he sense in which such people 'lack reason' is entirely different from the sense in which a nonhuman animal 'lacks reason' for the nonhuman animal functions perfectly well in his own way without it.... there is a difference, morally as well as metaphysically, between being a defective being of a certain kind and being a different kind."[36] Her argument that animals are different kinds of beings, however, further complicates the split in human beings that she describes as animal selves and rational selves; furthermore, it makes the question of what kind of beings we were before the original decision more striking since the difference between humans and nonhuman animals is not one of degree but rather one of kind. Korsgaard's suggestion that animals and disabled humans lack reason in different ways resonates with Eva Kittay's insistence that whatever disabled people do, however imperfectly they do it, they do it as humans and not as animals.[37] In her ethics of care, Kittay also maintains a difference in kind between human beings and other animals, a difference that for her, as for Korsgaard, is morally significant. This is a fundamental difference between Kantian animal ethics and utilitarian animal ethics, which usually takes the differences between humans and other animals as a matter of degree rather than kind, at least when it comes to intellectual abilities.

While I agree with Korsgaard that non-rational animals and non-rational human beings lack reason in different ways (if we can speak this way about having or not having rationality, which I think is questionable and to which I will return), her functional definition of species being is problematic on several fronts. First, the characterization of mentally disabled persons as "defective" human beings seems uncharitable at best and dangerous at worst. The notion of "defect" suggests a thing that is broken and should be fixed or discarded. Second, it proposes ideals for species membership that easily lead to subpar designations and metaphysical and moral hierarchies of the very type she is trying to avoid. Even if species membership is guaranteed by something other than rationality, we risk dividing human beings into defective and normal or inferior and superior in ways that, as we know, can become politically dangerous when they become justifications for discrimination, oppression, and even genocide.

Another of Korsgaard's arguments against utilitarianism is that "we cannot generally weigh the interests of other animals against the interests of human beings. We need another way of thinking about how we should treat them."[38] I completely agree that we cannot weigh the interests of other animals against those of human beings, but I have serious reservations about her alternative way of thinking about them. She maintains that while utilitarians are concerned only with the consequences of an action and therefore with sums of pain and pleasure in the world, Kantians are concerned with relationships between people, and on her analysis, also between people and other animals. Kantians, she claims, want morally proper relationships and all actions must be evaluated in terms of whether or not they promote such relationships.

While I am sympathetic to many of Korsgaard's criticisms of utilitarianism, her arguments seem to share problems that result from taking human rationality as the standard or ideal. For example, she claims that utilitarianism allows killing animals when the benefits of killing them outweigh the harms of doing so.[39] This points to a broader problem with utilitarian analysis insofar as it is based on a comparison of both quantity and quality of pains and pleasures, harms and benefits, which, at the extreme, makes it seem like philosophers such as Peter Singer and Jeff McMahan suggest that in some cases it might be better to kill (or let die) disabled people than able-bodied animals. I agree with Korsgaard that we cannot weigh animal interests against those of humans. Indeed, I would go further and argue that the kind of comparative analysis upon which utilitarian reasoning relies seems inherently problematic in that it requires some outside criteria by which to adjudicate the claims of one individual or group against another. Moreover, for the sake of objectivity, even if we could come up with those criteria (using purely utilitarian reasoning), they would have to be applied to each particular situation by an impartial external judge. When adjudicating between species it becomes clear that no such judge exists. Korsgaard makes a different, yet related, argument when she says, "it may be that the goods of different subjects can't be added at all: what's good for me plus what's good for you isn't *better*, because there is no one *for whom* it is better."[40]

Yet, Korsgaard "solves" this problem by claiming that humans are the only beings who make value. Other animals may have "goods and bads" according to their natures—that is to say, things that are good and bad for them—but only human beings create normative values or moral goods. And, we may do so not just for ourselves but also for all animals. Of course, this is a problem for animal ethics generally. But it does sound a

bit strange, after her complicated extension of Kant's philosophy of reciprocal self-legislation and a subject split between her rational self and her animal self, that Korsgaard concludes:

> We may interact with the other animals as long as we do so in ways to
> which we think it is plausible to think they would consent if they could—
> that is, in ways that are mutually beneficial and fair, and allow them to
> live something reasonably like their own sort of life. If we provide them
> with proper living conditions, I believe, their use as companion animals,
> aides to the handicapped and to the police, search and rescue workers,
> guards, and perhaps even as providers of wool, dairy products, or eggs,
> might possibly be made consistent with this standard.[41]

She argues that we cannot imagine that any animal would consent to its
own death. But given *what she can imagine* that animals would consent to,
listed above, it is difficult to say how we would judge what a fair bargain
would be in terms of animal life. Moreover, this sort of bargaining with
their happiness and their consent starts to sound a lot like utilitarian cost–
benefit analysis.

Korsgaard also argues against Peter Singer's claim that human beings
have "more to lose" by death than other animals because humans have a
sense of the future and make plans, taking issue with his position in *The Lives
of Animals* where, in a fictitious conversation with his daughter over her dog
Max, he suggests that an individual dog's happiness may be lost absolutely
if that dog dies, but as long as there are other dogs, there could be as much
dog happiness in the world. In other words, animals—or at least dogs—are
interchangeable, perhaps in ways that humans are not. At the extreme, it
seems that this utilitarian argument cannot account for the singularity of
each individual life. But the same seems true of the Kantian position. Insofar
as Korsgaard and others assume that there is a human nature and that it is
rational and self-legislating, any individuals who do not measure up to this
ideal become problematic or "marginal cases." Indeed, insofar as at times
when each one of us does not live up to the ideal of rational self-legislating
human nature (when we are sick, asleep, under the influence of drugs or
alcohol, etc.), we risk falling outside the moral community. Given that Kant
sets the bar pretty high in terms of what counts as a moral act, we could say
that no one ever measures up to the Kantian ideal of rational self-legislating
good will. Korsgaard claims that this would not be the case for Kant or
Kantians, because we are all embraced by the category "human." Yet, what

makes us human and distinguishes us from other animals in Kant's view is precisely the rational self-legislating will. Following Derrida we might ask, how can we be so sure that animals don't have it and that we do?[42]

Within the framework of Kantian ethics, it seems problematic to claim that species membership is based on what Korsgaard calls a *natural fact*: "As animals, we are beings for whom things can be good or bad: that is just a natural fact. When we demand to be treated as ends in ourselves, we confer normative significance on that fact."[43] Yet, until we confer normative significance, what is the status of any fact? Korsgaard skirts this question by asserting that (animal) facts come first and then (human) values are imposed on them. In addition, she too easily slips from an idea of natural goods to the notion of moral good, or at least moral obligations to those who have natural goods, which might include plants and machines.[44] Again we encounter the "bootstrapping" circularity of Korsgaard's argument. Korsgaard's appeal to *natural facts* and *human nature* is problematic for other reasons; as history has shown us, definitions of human nature and human biology can and have changed, and can and have been used for political ends.

What's So Special about Human Beings?

In the end, both Korsgaard and Calhoun defend versions of human exceptionalism, or what Singer would call speciesism. Korsgaard and Calhoun, following Kant, see animals as different kinds of beings from humans, while Singer, McMahan, and other utilitarians see a continuum between humans and animals. Yet, both Kantians and utilitarians look for what we share with the animals, whether it is our rationality in the case of higher primates according to Singer, or our animal natures according to Korsgaard. Animals are granted moral consideration, on these accounts, by virtue of what they share with us, either directly or indirectly through analogy. Normal adult human intelligence is taken as the standard in both accounts, the template that sets the framework for what is considered salient, to use Kittay's formulation in her challenge to comparisons between humans and nonhuman animals. For Korsgaard and Calhoun, all animals do not have reason and intelligence and all humans are part of a species that has them; for Singer and McMahan, some animals do have them and some humans do not, and species is irrelevant.

Peter Singer challenges two related views, which he sees as speciesist: "that species membership is crucial to moral status, and that all human life is of equal value."[45] Singer proposes a graduated view of moral standing that applies to both humans and animals based on cognitive abilities, since some animals have higher IQs than some humans. Against Kantians who claim that only human beings are properly members of the moral community because only we are autonomous and self-legislating, Singer argues: "because of the overlap in cognitive ability between some humans and some nonhuman animals, attempts to draw a moral line on the basis of cognitive ability, as Kant and the contractarians try to do, will require either that we exclude some humans—for example, those who are profoundly mentally retarded—or that we include some nonhuman animals—those whose level of cognitive ability are equal or superior to the lowest level found in human beings."[46] I completely agree with Singer that Kantians cannot maintain a consistent position with regard to non-rational human beings and non-rational animals, not only because some animals may be capable of reasoning, but also because they take human reason as the ideal against which the moral community is measured. Singer, however, also takes human reason and intellectual abilities to be the criterion for membership in the moral community. Given that he has committed his philosophical career to arguing for animal welfare, it seems strange that he accepts the traditional values of autonomy and rationality even as he argues that some animals possess them. This valuation is part and parcel of the ideology that has, and continues, to denigrate animals and our own animality. Indeed, neither Kantians Calhoun and Korsgaard nor utilitarians Singer and McMahan challenge the commitment to autonomy and rationality as the criteria for membership in the moral community. Even while Singer (in his work with the Great Ape Project) quotes Bentham asking whether or not animals also suffer, he does not appeal to the suffering of all creatures but rather to the intellectual abilities of some.[47] And subsequently, with his example of the dog Max, he even discounts animal suffering when he claims that human beings suffer more.[48]

Here I agree with Korsgaard that, in absolute terms at least, we cannot compare the suffering of one against another as qualitatively more and therefore more important. While in our everyday lives we may have to weigh considerations of relative suffering, this does not mean that we can assign moral worth to them as natural facts. Or at least, if and when we are called upon to do so, we can do so only and always provisionally, which is to say not from or towards universal moral rules that bind us to assign moral worth in all such situations. Comparative analysis such as

Singer's and McMahan's leads to various problems and dangers set out by Eva Kittay and Licia Carlson in their responses to the comparison between nonhuman animals and disabled human beings, including not viewing disabled human beings as persons or viewing them as subpar, and therefore justifying discriminating against them or possibly even letting them die.[49] In other words, treating them "like animals."

Herein lies one major problem with Kittay's and Carlson's responses. Kittay in particular expresses her outrage using words like "revulsion," "hideous," and "horrific" to describe the comparison between disabled people and nonhuman animals. Specifically, Kittay expresses her disgust at the comparison as a mother because it includes her mentally disabled daughter, Sesha:

> For a mother of a severely cognitively impaired child, the impact of such an argument [McMahan's argument that our treatment of animals is governed by stronger restraints than traditionally supposed while our treatment of the cognitively impaired is governed by weaker restraints than traditionally supposed] is devastating. How can I begin to tell you what it feels like to read tests in which one's child is compared, in all seriousness and with philosophical authority, to a dog, pig, rat and most flatteringly a chimp; how corrosive these comparisons are, how they mock those relationships that affirm who we are and why we care?[50]

While I am sympathetic to Kittay's emotional response at hearing her child compared to an animal, it seems to me that the comparison is only unflattering because of our current views of animals. If we respected animals, even revered them, and treated them well, would Kittay find the comparison so insulting? The fact that Kittay herself suggests a hierarchy between animals wherein it is less insulting to compare her daughter to a chimp than a dog or a rat is evidence not just of our negative attitudes towards animals, but also our differential negative attitudes towards some animals. In other words, not all animals are alike. This is obvious in terms of their appearance, biology, habitat, behaviour, etc. But it is also apparent in our attitudes towards them. We prefer chimps to rats. Human beings love some animals as pets, exterminate some as vermin, and eat others.

Against Singer and McMahan who group the severely cognitively impaired or disabled into one category or group, Kittay and Carlson argue that each disabled person is unique with singular abilities and disabilities and therefore cannot be referred to en masse. But, as Jacques Derrida's *The*

Animal That Therefore I Am makes so powerfully clear, we should not group animals into one category and refer to them en masse. To do so is to overlook significant differences between species and between individuals within each species. I have argued elsewhere that the human/animal opposition not only leads to overlooking differences between animals and grouping them all together, but it also leads to overlooking differences between humans; there I suggest that by opening up one side of the binary to multiplicity of differences, we may begin to open the other.[51]

Even Licia Carlson, who argues for a more cooperative approach between disability studies and animal studies, and who acknowledges that historically the oppression of some people at the hands of others has been justified by comparing the former group to animals, insists that we should not compare disabled people to animals.[52] Yet, the animalization of people only works because to be an animal, or to be called an animal, is derogatory and disrespectful; to be an animal or to be treated like one is to be without rights or recourse when faced with abuse, torture, or killing. Since historically it has been morally blameless to farm, slaughter, and eat animals, to use them for laboratory testing, to wear their pelts and skins as clothing, it is risky to call humans animals. The risk is that humans may be treated in these ways. But, imagining humans treated in these ways makes clear the horrific (to use one of Kittay's words) breach of morality inherent in such treatment.

Engaging in the kind of comparison that she and Kittay challenge in Singer and McMahan, Carlson argues that the difference between disabled children and animals is evidenced by the fact that we are outraged by keeping "retarded children" locked in rooms without toilets, naked, and deprived of human touch, but we aren't outraged when animals are given the same treatment.[53] This type of argument is suspicious on multiple fronts. First, it is absurd to compare humans without clothes to animals without clothes. Second, who are these people who would not be outraged if an animal was kept in a room alone, without contact with another animal and without human touch? The thought of no toilet for a well-trained companion animal seems inconsiderate at best and abusive at worst. Obviously children and animals are different in important ways that should not be discounted. This raises various questions, including: Who can be admitted into the moral community as either moral patients or moral agents in light of, even because of, their differences? Do they have to meet some criteria established on the basis of adult human normalcy?

While the Kantians draw comparisons by analogy between humans and animals because in their view humans and animals are different kinds of beings, the utilitarians draw comparisons arguing for degrees of intelligence and rationality, suggesting that whether or not we are different kinds of beings, we share certain salient characteristics. This leads to "line drawing" in order to determine where to cut off lower levels of intelligence, or pain and suffering, and thereby membership in the moral community. This becomes a difficult, if not impossible, exercise that, as Kittay points out, can have risky if not dangerous political consequences for those who do not make the cut. Kittay, however, is concerned with human beings who may not make the cut and not with animals. Even while she challenges such comparisons and line drawing, Kittay herself engages in a similar type of moral calculation when she insists that she feels more deeply her connection to her daughter than even the most ardent dog lover could feel for their canine companion: "There is no comparison between the feelings for a beloved child of normal capacities and those for a beloved canine. And I can tell you that there is also no comparison when that child has intellectual disabilities."[54] Here, as a dog lover herself, Kittay is perhaps speaking as J.S. Mill's connoisseur who has loved both and therefore can tell others which love is more intense. Certainly, when Kittay says, "there is no comparison" she is speaking rhetorically and really means that love for the child is stronger than love for the dog. Later, she makes a less personal and seemingly more objective claim when she says that a parent has a "morally and objectively more significant relationship" with his or her child than "a pet owner does with his beloved pet."[55] By making these kinds of comparisons, Kittay also engages in normalizing judgments about which relationship has more moral import than another. And, while these kinds of judgments are necessary to make in our everyday decision-making, as universal principles or objective facts they seem problematic at best.

How can Kittay judge what other people *feel* towards their companion animals? Are the people who "admit" that they love their companion animals like children, or as much as or even more than their own children morally suspect, possibly immoral? I appreciate Kittay's emphasis on caring relationships as the basis of ethics, which resonates with Korsgaard's extensions of Kantianism as a concern for relationships. But, while I agree that our relationships with others are the basis of our ethical obligations to them, I think it is dangerous to set out objective and morally decisive measurements of what relationships count morally. This is especially vexing considering Kittay's insistence throughout her work that dependence and not independence is not only definitive of human beings but also of ethics, and that, rather than deny our dependence on others, we should embrace it. Only by embracing dependence rather than independence or autonomy as the starting point of ethics can we hope for an ethics of care, or moreover, an ethics of difference or otherness, or, indeed, what I have called elsewhere an ethics of responsiveness.[56]

Ethics of Dependence

Throughout her work on ethics, Kittay has proposed an ethics based on our dependence on one another rather than autonomy or independence. Recently, she restates her position: "According to the most important theories of justice, personal dignity is closely related to independence, and the care that people with disabilities receive is seen as a way for them to achieve the greatest possible autonomy. However, human beings are naturally subject to periods of dependency, and people without disabilities are only 'temporarily abled.' Instead of seeing assistance as a limitation, we consider it to be a resource at the basis of a vision of society that is able to account for inevitable dependency relationships between 'unequals' ensuring a fulfilling life both for the carer and the cared for."[57] In her earlier work, which I have quoted often, Kittay maintains that a subject who "refuses to support this bond [of dependency] absolves itself from its most fundamental obligation—its obligation to its founding possibility."[58] Yet for all intents and purposes, we are indirectly and directly as dependent upon animals as we are on other human beings. We depend on animals as sources of food, clothing, other goods and services, entertainment, experimentation, and companionship. We are utterly dependent on animals in virtually every facet of life. Indeed, it is hard to imagine that we could or would exist without them. Without other animals, we would be a very lonely species. In the words of John Berger: "With their parallel lives, animals offer man a companionship which is different from any offered by human exchange. Different because it is a companionship offered to the loneliness of man as a species."[59] If our dependence on other beings for our very being obligates us to them, then we are also morally obligated to nonhuman animals. Indeed, I have often used Kittay's claim that our dependence on others, including other animals, is our founding possibility and this is the ground of our ethical obligations to others.[60]

Although Carlson appeals to the significance of the *human face* of disabled persons, she follows Alisdair MacIntyre's insistence that in addition to the virtues of independence, we need to value the virtues of dependence, particularly since only by acknowledging these can we hope to develop a notion of "human flourishing."[61] Carlson argues, "we might more fully realize an ethical relationship toward individuals with intellectual disabilities and broaden our conception of human flourishing. Thus it is in our dependence and vulnerability that we recognize that we are *human* animals, and insofar as all human beings experience these conditions (to a greater and lesser extent), there is an important way in which the line between able-bodied and disabled begins to disappear."[62] Again following MacIntyre, Carlson argues that we are not animals plus something else, which, recall, is the Kantian position. Rather, our animality is central to what and who we are as human beings. This leads Carlson to embrace an inclusive rather than exclusive approach in the relation between nonhuman animals and disabled humans. She concludes, "far from the margins, the individual with severe disabilities represents what is most centrally human: dependence, and our animal nature."[63] If this is the case, then many nonhuman animals may also represent what is most centrally human, or at least, as I have argued elsewhere, teach us what it means to be human.[64] In *Animal Lessons* I argue that recognizing ourselves as human, what Carlson might call seeing our "human face" and its significance, is the result of our relationships with animals.

Sharing the Earth, Even If We Don't Share a World

Recently, several philosophers including Judith Butler, Julia Kristeva, and Ann Murphy have embraced the notion that it is our vulnerability and not our autonomy that defines us as human, and therefore it is our vulnerability that should be the basis of any ethical theory. Yet, what some of these theorists overlook is that we also share vulnerability with other animals.[65] This is why Derrida, following Bentham, takes up the question of what it means to suffer. If all creatures have the capacity for suffering, Derrida asks, if all living beings are vulnerable to suffering, then what kind of capacity is this?[66] Certainly it is not a capacity of our active willing or rational autonomous agency, and moreover, it is one that we share with all animals and perhaps with all living beings.

Julia Kristeva proposes making vulnerability a fourth term of Enlightenment humanism, along with liberty, equality, and fraternity: "Inscribing vulnerability at the center of the political pact (understood as taking care of others) seems to me the best antidote to barbarity."[67] She suggests that a new form of humanism is emerging that acknowledges differences rather than finding its basis in similarities. In particular, she claims that considering disability transforms our notions of the human and of democracy and calls forth this new humanism.[68] This new humanism is based on our shared vulnerability, in the face of the fact that each suffers his or her vulnerability in a way that is unique and therefore unsharable. Specifically, Kristeva argues that disabled people are vulnerable in a way that is different from the vulnerabilities of other groups. Their physical vulnerability is not something that can be repaired or overcome only through politics or by applying traditional notions of "human rights." It is not something that can be shared. She calls it the "irreparable."[69] And yet, she insists that there is something irreparable in each of us, which is not to say that we are all disabled. Rather, the new humanism must recognize the singularity of the irreparable of each person.

Resonant with Kittay and Carlson, Kristeva argues that each disabled person is disabled in his or her own way; each disability is singular, as is their exclusion. But, rather than calling for *integration* of disabled persons into the public sphere, Kristeva argues for *interaction* based on sharing and caring.[70] Again resonant with Kittay, Kristeva suggests a politics informed by an ethics of caring for others in their vulnerabilities. Thus, she argues against trying to turn everybody into a productive worker through integration programs that define the value of humanity in terms of the ability to work or tasks they perform.[71] It is noteworthy that as we have seen, current public policy values service animals only in terms of the tasks they perform and not in terms of the emotional support they provide. Indeed, Kristeva claims that our culture's "maniacal surge of productivity" is an attempt to deny our fundamental vulnerability, which is also manifest in traditional philosophies based on rational autonomy of the will.[72]

Although she talks of disabled persons as "emerging subjects," Kristeva also insists on the phrase "people in a situation of handicap" in order to indicate that disability is not just a physical or mental condition but also a social response, "in other words, a 'situation' created for the disabled person by society's reception of them."[73] Considering disabled people when thinking about political rights and moral responsibilities challenges traditional notions of rights and equality based in rational autonomy. Kristeva suggests that it forces us to rethink democracy not in terms of contracts but in terms of proximity. Although Kristeva excludes animals even as she argues against the exclusion of disabled people on the basis of their vulnerability, and even as she argues for a democracy of proximity, she does not consider that our proximity with animals (dead and alive) necessarily challenges traditional notions of contractarian democracy.

Adding vulnerability to the notion of humanism forces us "toward a concern for sharing."[74] Once we come to terms with our own vulnerability, which cannot be equated with that of the disabled, we confront our own limits in ways that give us the ability to share in the incommensurable vulnerability of disabled others. Kristeva describes this sharing as neither fusion nor osmosis, nor identification, but rather as participating together through recognition of what cannot be shared.[75] This sharing, then, is recognition of what is beyond sharing and is grounded in our dependence on one another because of our differences. It is not an integration of those others into the rights discourse of traditional versions of humanism, but based on the "irremediable," which is to say what cannot be redeemed within traditional conceptions of the social or political order.[76]

Given Kristeva's analysis of the singular exclusion of disabled persons and the need for a new approach that takes us beyond traditional humanism with its emphasis on human rights and autonomy, and given her insistence on recognizing the unique vulnerability of each through caring and sharing as the starting points of such a venture, we might think that her analysis could be useful in describing how a concern for animals might affect notions of humanism and democracy. And indeed, it might be. For her part, however, Kristeva is clear that in spite of its limitations, she embraces humanism and furthermore, that the vulnerability she diagnoses is uniquely human insofar as it is the wound or fracture that results from what she calls our "untenable" position between *zoe* and *bios*, biology and language. Risking a problematic comparison between animals and disabled persons, yet not wanting to endorse it in the ways drawn by either Kantians or utilitarians, it seems that animals, while not like disabled persons, are also singularly excluded from traditional notions of humanism. They, too, challenge our notions of the human and of democracy in their vulnerability, particularly in their vulnerability to us and our destruction of their habitats, and our control over every aspect of the lives of those we breed to eat, etc.

Indeed, might an equally radical challenge to liberal notions of humanism and democracy come from animal studies, or animal studies in solidarity with disability studies?

As Cary Wolfe argues in *What Is Posthumanism?*, both animal studies and disability studies challenge liberal notions of rationality, autonomy, and agency as the standard or norm for membership in the moral community.[77] Wolfe reminds us that all living creatures share finitude and vulnerability, and all animals, including human animals, have vulnerable bodies that suffer and die. Along with recent philosophers such as Butler, Kittay, Carlson, and Kristeva who propose a politics and ethics based on human vulnerability rather than autonomy, Wolfe argues for an ethics of dependency that now acknowledges our dependence on animals and not just on other human beings. The ethical imperative to care for each other based on what Kittay might call our "founding possibly," Wolfe says extends "across species lines and bind us, in our shared vulnerability, to other living beings who think and feel, live and die, have needs and desires, and require care just as we do."[78] "Such a project," he concludes, "points us toward the necessity of an ethics based not on ability, activity, agency, and empowerment but on *compassion* that is rooted in our vulnerability and passivity."[79]

Ethical compassion, I would add, is rooted in a fundamental obligation to acknowledge our dependency on other animal bodies that sustain our own. With compassion towards other bodies in need, and obligations to those bodies that sustain us, we have an ethical obligation to share the planet even with those with whom we do not share a world. Here, we are back to a certain Kantian ethics that comes from an obligation to hospitality born out of the finite surface of the Earth and the need to share the planet with others, both human and nonhuman animals.[80] And not because we share common features, but rather because of what we cannot share, our irreparable wounds and vulnerabilities that shape our worlds. Even though we may not share a world, we do share the Earth.

Beginning to articulate what this sharing would look like, Wolfe proposes a new way of seeing, what Kristeva might call "emerging subjectivities," as "shared trans-species being-in-the world."[81] His prime example is a magazine cover representing a blind woman accompanied by a German shepherd service dog. Wolfe argues that the service dog is not just a prop or tool (or piece of equipment) that allows the disabled person to be mainstreamed or integrated into liberal society. Rather, he suggests, the interaction between the woman and the dog becomes "an irreducibly different and unique form of subjectivity—neither *Homo sapiens* nor *Canis familiaris*, neither 'disabled' nor 'normal,' but something else altogether . . . constituted by complex relations of trust, respect, dependence and communication."[82] While Wolfe's suggestion is provocative, still, it is important to consider the dog as a living being with its own needs and desires apart from its servicing interactions.

The seeing-eye dog shows us that there are many ways of seeing, and all of them implicate each of us in a network of relationships and perspectives. Wolfe's proposal of a trans-species being-in-the-world gives us a more positive way of looking at both service animals and people with disabilities. Rather than see service animals as mere equipment to be used, and rather than see disabled people as deficient or defective when measured against an ideal norm, both have a positive valuation, particularly manifest in their relationships to each other. Wolfe concludes his discussion of the intersections of disability and animal studies by invoking Derrida on blindness, which Derrida insists is not the opposite of sight, but perhaps even the truth of vision.[83] He quotes Derrida: "The eye would be destined not to see but to weep. . . . The blindness that opens the eye is not the one that darkens vision. The revelatory or apocalyptic blindness, the blindness that reveals the very truth of the eyes, would be the gaze veiled by tears."[84] It is only if we "see" vision as the proper—and perhaps only—function of the eye, that we see blindness as a defect. What if, instead, we take the function of the eye to be crying, crying for those in need or in pain? These would be tears of compassion for all other living beings in need of care. These would be tears of recognition of our ethical obligations to them based on our dependence on them, whatever species they may be.

NOTES

1. See comments posted in response to *ABC News* web-report, "Ashley Judd Keeps a 'Psychological Support' Dog."
2. Federal law allows business owners to ask only two questions of people using service animals; otherwise they risk charges of discrimination or harassment. According to the US Justice Department ADA (Americans with Disabilities Act) 2010 revised requirements, "When it is not obvious what service an animal provides, only limited inquiries are allowed. Staff may ask two questions: 1. Is the dog a service animal required because of a disability? and 2. What work or task has the dog been trained to do? Staff cannot ask about the person's disability, require medical documentation, require a special

identification card or training documentation for the dog, or ask that the dog demonstrate its ability to perform the work or task." Quoted from US Department of Justice website ("Revised ADA Requirements: Service Animals," US Department of Justice (Civil Rights Division, Disability Rights Section), 2010, www.ada.gov). Some people are taking advantage of the fact that the law does not require that a disabled person provide documentation, and growing awareness and concern for the needs of people with disabilities, and are passing off what the law considers pets as service animals. In fact, it is easy to buy special vests for dogs that say "service animal," and that alone seems to answer the first of the two questions allowed by law (if falsely). "For $249, customers visiting the site for Service Dogs America, for example, can buy a special doggie vest and ID cards that label the dog as a service animal. The company claims the package, along with a self-administered test, helps owners 'clearly identify your dog as a service dog and avoid awkward confrontations when entering public places with your dog.'" See Hobbs, "Fake Service Dogs."

3. See, for example, Bazelon Center, "Right to Emotional Support Animals." See also the Pets for Patriots' statement on emotional support versus service dogs, "What Is a Service Animal?" The Americans with Disabilities Act defines service animals thusly: "Service animals are defined as dogs that are individually trained to do work or perform tasks for people with disabilities. Examples of such work or tasks include guiding people who are blind, alerting people who are deaf, pulling a wheelchair, alerting and protecting a person who is having a seizure, reminding a person with mental illness to take prescribed medications, calming a person with Post Traumatic Stress Disorder (PTSD) during an anxiety attack, or performing other duties. Service animals are working animals, not pets. The work or task a dog has been trained to provide must be directly related to the person's disability. Dogs whose sole function is to provide comfort or emotional support do not qualify as service animals under the ADA." US Department of Justice, 2010 revised definition, "How 'Service Animal' Is Defined," under "Service Animals," *ADA Requirements*, at the Department's website, http://www.ada.gov/service_animals_2010.htm.

4. Bazelon Center, "Right to Emotional Support Animals," 1.

5. For legal overview of practice see Dellinger, "Using Dogs for Emotional Support." For one news story on the use of "comfort dogs" in court, see Glaberson, "By Helping a Girl Testify." See also Sandoval, "Court Facility Dogs."

6. See Lalwani, "YLS Dog Rentals": "A pilot program last month that allowed law students to rent Monty—a brown, hypoallergenic 21-pound border terrier mix — was so well received that the library will allow students to borrow the dog in May before final exams." Harvard Medical School has instituted a similar program (see Koch, "Doggone That Stress").

7. Lalwani, "YLS Dog Rentals."

8. Koch, "Doggone That Stress."

9. See Braun et al., "Animal-Assisted Therapy." See also Jones, "In the Company of Animals"; Allen, "Are Pets a Healthy Pleasure?"; and Jenkins, "Physiological Effects." Support Dogs, Inc. has started the PAWS for Reading program that places dogs in classrooms in St. Louis as an incentive for children to read. And in Rochester, Teacher's Pet pairs hard-to-adopt dogs with at-risk kids in a program to train the dogs while helping the kids learn to interact in positive ways.

10. For a discussion of laws governing pet ownership, see Jasper's *Pet Law*.

11. Francione, *Animals, Property, and the Law*.

12. See "Proposed Rules, pages 34465–34508," in *Federal Register Online via GPO Access*, June 17, 2008 (vol. 73, no. 117), wais.access.gpo.gov. The Department is proposing new regulatory text in s. 35.104 to formalize its position on emotional support or comfort animals, which is that "[a]nimals whose sole function is to provide emotional support, comfort, therapy, companionship, therapeutic benefits, or promote emotional well-being are not service animals." The Department wishes to underscore that the exclusion of emotional support animals from ADA coverage does not mean that persons with psychiatric, cognitive, or mental disabilities cannot use service animals. The Department proposes specific regulatory text in s. 35.104 to make this clear: "The term service animal includes individually trained animals that do work or perform tasks for the benefit of individuals with disabilities, including psychiatric, cognitive, and mental disabilities. This language simply clarifies the Department's longstanding position" (33473).

13. War dogs have been used for centuries, since at least the time of the Roman Empire when armoured dogs with spiked collars were used (see English, *Quiet Americans*).

14. Pets for Patriots, "What Is a Service Animal?" It is perhaps noteworthy that the revised ADA policy is that only trained dogs can be service animals.

15. Lorber "For the Battle-Scarred"; see also Rick Nauert, "Canine Therapy for Military PTSD."

16. Some media and public suspicion of emotional support dogs or therapy animals is evidenced by reactions to Ashley Judd's announcement that she has therapy dogs (see note 1). Compare this to some reactions to Jill Abramson's (the first woman editor in the history of the *New York Times*) "The Puppy Diaries," which elicited an article in the online magazine *The Gawker*, entitled "Your Fascination with Your Dog Is an Embarrassment (To You)"; the author suggested that it was silly and undignified for the editor of an important newspaper to write about her attachment to her puppy. Although these are just two examples, they are representative of at least one strand of popular opinions about companion animals that does not take them seriously as companions or family members.

17. English, *Quiet Americans*.

18. Ibid., 3 (emphasis mine).
19. Senator Bob Smith (NH), "Disturbing DOD Policy," 146 Cong. Rec. S10787 (October 19, 2000)—proposes bill that will prevent the disposing of wartime service dogs. "The 1949 Federal Property and Administrative Services Act, enacted after World War II, reclassified military working dogs as equipment. According to the military mentality, any piece of equipment no longer operable becomes a hardship to the unit and must be disposed of. In 1997, the Federal Property and Administrative Services Act was amended. The law was altered to permit federal dog handlers, such as those in the Drug Enforcement Administration, to adopt their aging K-9 partners after their service in law enforcement was completed. The DOD's K-9 partners were the only federal canine group not included in the modification. . . . The bill that I am speaking in support of today, H.R. 5315, will amend the law to allow a handler to adopt a retired military working dog. I believe that legislation was constructed with the best interest for all parties involved" (10787–88).
20. *Military Working Dog (MWD) Field Manual*, Department of the Army, July 2005, FM 3-19.17, Department of the Army Headquarters, Washington, DC.
21. See Canine Members of the Armed Forces Act, H.R. 4103, 112th Cong., 2d Sess., especially at 2–3 (February 28, 2012).
22. See Calhoun, "But What about the Animals?," 2–3.
23. Immanuel Kant, *Anthropology from a Pragmatic Point of View* (Robert B. Louden trans.), quoted in Calhoun, "But What about the Animals?," 196.
24. Immanuel Kant, *Metaphysics of Morals* (Mary Gregor trans.), quoted in Korsgaard, "Interacting with Animals," 99.
25. See Calhoun, "But What about the Animals?"; and Korsgaard, "Fellow Creatures."
26. Calhoun, "But What about the Animals?," 16.
27. Korsgaard, "Fellow Creatures," 108–9.
28. Calhoun, "But What about the Animals?"
29. Ibid., 30.
30. Ibid., 7.
31. Ibid., 7–8.
32. Kittay, "Personal Is Philosophical," 612–13.
33. Korsgaard, "Fellow Creatures," 101 (emphasis mine); see also her "Interacting with Animals," 106.
34. Cf. Oliver, *Animal Lessons*.
35. Korsgaard, "Interacting with Animals," 116.
36. Ibid.
37. Kittay, "Personal Is Philosophical," 617.
38. Korsgaard, "Interacting with Animals," 96.
39. Ibid., 95.
40. Ibid., 95–96.

41. Ibid., 110.

42. See Derrida, *Animal That Therefore I Am*.

43. Korsgaard, "Interacting with Animals," 109.

44. See Korsgaard, "Fellow Creatures," 106n69.

45. Singer, "Speciesism and Moral Status," 581.

46. Ibid., 574.

47. Singer, "Speciesism and Moral Status," 575.

48. Singer, "Reflections," 87–88.

49. Kittay, "Personal Is Philosophical."

50. Ibid., 610.

51. See Oliver, *Animal Lessons*.

52. Carlson, *Intellectual Disability*, 145.

53. Ibid., 152.

54. Kittay, "Personal Is Philosophical," 610.

55. Ibid., 623.

56. See Oliver, *Witnessing*; *Animal Lessons*.

57. Kittay, "Ethics of Care," 49.

58. Kittay, "Welfare, Dependency," 131. See also Kittay, *Love's Labor*.

59. Berger, "Why Look at Animals?," 6.

60. See Oliver, *Witnessing*; *Animal Lessons*.

61. Carlson, *Intellectual Disability*, 158.

62. Ibid.

63. Ibid.

64. See Oliver, *Animal Lessons*.

65. Cf. Oliver, *Witnessing*; *Animal Lessons*; Wolfe, *What Is Posthumanism?*, 140.

66. Derrida, *Animal That Therefore I Am*.

67. Kristeva, *Hatred and Forgiveness*, 34.

68. Ibid.

69. Kristeva, "Limits of Living," 224.

70. Ibid., 223; *Hatred and Forgiveness*.

71. Kristeva, "Limits of Living," 221–22.

72. Ibid., 222.

73. Kristeva, *Hatred and Forgiveness*, 37.

74. Ibid., 42.

75. Ibid., 43.

76. See Ibid.

77. Wolfe, *What Is Posthumanism?*, 127.

78. Ibid., 140.

79. Ibid., 141.

80. In "Perpetual Peace," Kant argues for a principle of hospitality, the third article of perpetual peace, grounded in the finite surface of the planet we inhabit

together: "They have it by virtue of their common possession of the surface of the earth, where, as a globe, they cannot infinitely disperse and hence must finally tolerate the presence of each other" (1795).
81. Wolfe, *What Is Posthumanism?*, 141.
82. Ibid.
83. Ibid., 132–33.
84. In ibid., 142; Derrida, *Memoirs of the Blind*, 126–27.

BIBLIOGRAPHY

ABC News, "Ashley Judd Keeps a 'Psychological Support' Dog." March 19, 2012. http://abcnews.go.com/blogs/entertainment/2012/03/ashley-judd-keeps-a -psychological-support-dog-to-help-deal-with-her-depression/.

Allen, Karen. "Are Pets a Healthy Pleasure?" *Current Directions in Psychological Science* 12, no. 6 (2003): 236–39.

Bazelon Center for Mental Health Law. "Right to Emotional Support Animals in 'No Pet' Housing." Fair Housing Information Sheet 6. Accessed July 15, 2012. http://www.bazelon.org/LinkClick.aspx?fileticket=mHq8GV0FI4c%3D&tabid=245.

Berger, John. "Why Look at Animals?" In *About Looking*, 3–29. New York: Vintage, 1992.

Braun, Carie, Teresa Stangler, Jennifer Narveson, and Sandra Pettingell. "Animal-Assisted Therapy as Pain Relief Intervention for Children." *Complementary Therapies in Clinical Practice* 15, no. 2 (2009): 105–9.

Calhoun, Cheshire. "But What about the Animals?" In *Reason, Value, and Respect: Kantian Themes from the Philosophy of Thomas E. Hill, Jr.*, edited by Mark Timmons and Robert N. Johnson, 194–214. New York: Oxford University Press, 2015.

Carlson, Licia. *The Faces of Intellectual Disability*. Bloomington: Indiana University Press, 2010.

Dellinger, Marianne. "Using Dogs for Emotional Support of Testifying Victims of Crime." *Animal Law* 15, no. 2 (2009): 171–92.

Derrida, Jacques. *The Animal That Therefore I Am*. Translated by David Wills. New York: Fordham University Press, 2008.

———. *Memoirs of the Blind: The Self-Portrait and Other Ruins*. Chicago: University of Chicago Press, 1993.

English, Tracy L. *The Quiet Americans: A History of Military Working Dogs*. San Antonio, TX: Office of History, Lackland Air Force Base, 2003.

Francione, Gary L. *Animals, Property, and the Law*. Philadelphia: Temple University Press, 1995.

Glaberson, William. "By Helping a Girl Testify at a Rape Trial, a Dog Ignites a Legal Debate." *New York Times*, August 9, 2011.

Hobbs, Andy. "Fake Service Dogs: Pet Owners Exploit ADA Loopholes." *Federal Way Mirror*. Last modified April 12, 2012. http://federalwaymirror.com/news/147080865.html.

Jaspers, Margaret. *Pet Law*. New York: Oxford University Press, 2006.

Jenkins, Judy. "Physiological Effects of Petting a Companion Animal." *Psychological Reports* 58, no. 1 (1986): 21–22.

Jones, Karen. "In the Company of Animals, Healing for Humans." *New York Times*, November 1, 2011.

Kant, Immanuel. "Perpetual Peace: A Philosophical Sketch." In *Kant's Political Writings*, 93–130. Edited by Han Reiss. Translated by H.B. Nisbet. Cambridge: Cambridge University Press, 1970. First published 1795.

Kittay, Eva. "The Ethics of Care, Dependence, and Disability." *Ratio Juris* 24, no. 1 (2011): 49–58.

———. *Love's Labor: Women, Equality and Dependency*. New York: Routledge, 1998.

———. "The Personal Is Philosophical Is Political: A Philosopher and Mother of a Cognitively Disabled Person Sends Notes from the Battlefield." *Metaphilosophy* 40, nos. 3–4 (2009): 606–27.

———. "Welfare, Dependency, and a Public Ethic of Care." *Social Justice* 25, no. 1 (Spring 1998): 123–45.

Koch, Katie. "Doggone That Stress: Around Harvard, Relief Comes in Unlikely—and Fluffy—Forms." *Harvard Gazette Online*. Last updated September 22, 2011. http://news.harvard.edu/gazette/story/2011/09/doggone-that-stress/.

Korsgaard, Christine. "Fellow Creatures: Kantian Ethics and Our Duties to Animals." In *The Tanner Lectures on Human Values*, vol. 25/26, edited by Grethe B. Peterson, 77–110. Salt Lake City: Utah University Press, 2005.

———. "Interacting with Animals: A Kantian Account." In *The Oxford Handbook of Animal Ethics*, edited by Tom Beauchamp and R.G. Frey, 91–118. New York: Oxford University Press, 2011.

Kristeva, Julia. "At the Limits of Living." Translated by Claire Potter. *Journal of Visual Culture* 5, no. 2 (2006): 219–25.

———. *Hatred and Forgiveness*. Translated by Janine Herman. New York: Columbia University Press, 2010.

Lalwani, Nikita. "YLS Dog Rentals to Continue." *Yale Daily News Online*. Last updated April 21, 2011. http://yaledailynews.com/blog/2011/04/21/yls-dog-rentals-to-continue/.

Lorber, Jan. "For the Battle-Scarred, Comfort at Leash's End." *New York Times*, April 13, 2010.

McMahan, Jeff. "Cognitive Disability and Cognitive Enhancement." *Metaphilosophy* 40, nos. 3–4 (2009): 582–605.

Nauert, Rick. "Canine Therapy for Military PTSD." *Psych Central* (online magazine), July 9, 2010. http://psychcentral.com/news/2010/07/09/canine-therapy-for-military-ptsd/15444.html.

Oliver, Kelly. *Animal Lessons: How They Teach Us to Be Human*. New York: Columbia University Press, 2009.

———. *Witnessing: Beyond Recognition*. Minneapolis: University of Minnesota Press, 2001.

Pets for Patriots, "What Is a Service Animal and Do I Really Need One?" *Military.com*, December 26, 2011. http://web.archive.org/web/20120304201939/ http://www.military.com/entertainment/pet-corner/what-is-service-animal-and -do-i-really-need-one.

Sandoval, Gabriela N. "Court Facility Dogs—Easing the Apprehensive Witness." *Colorado Lawyer* 39 no. 4 (2010): 17–22.

Singer, Peter. "Reflections." In *The Lives of Animals*, edited Amy Gutman, 85–92. Princeton: Princeton University Press, 1999.

———. "Speciesism and Moral Status." *Metaphilosophy* 40, nos. 3–4 (2009): 567–81.

Wolfe, Cary. *What Is Posthumanism?* Minneapolis: University of Minnesota Press, 2009.

Vegans for Vick

Dogfighting, Intersectional Politics, and the Limits of Mainstream Discourse

Garrett M. Broad

Once one of the most popular players in the NFL, Michael Vick was convicted of a federal felony in 2007 for his involvement in an illegal dogfighting ring. After serving 19 months in prison, Vick returned to the NFL as a starting quarterback and has since become a leading campaigner for anti-dogfighting efforts. This chapter explores some of the key issues that emerge when the case of Michael Vick—NFL star and convicted proprietor of an interstate dogfighting ring—is approached from intersectional anti-speciesist and anti-racist perspectives. In this work, I make no attempt to excuse the cruel actions that were undertaken by Vick during his days as part of the Bad Newz Kennels dogfighting operation. I do, however, suggest that the philosophical foundations of ethical veganism, when enacted in conjunction with an anti-racist praxis, point toward a set of interpretations that differs from those that dominated public discourse on the case.[1] Further, I seek explanations as to why this intersectional counterpublic ideology barely surfaced in the mass-mediated discussions that helped to shape the Vick controversy for the broader public.

Not surprisingly, the Michael Vick dogfighting case sparked outrage on the part of major animal rights organizations, as groups such as People for the Ethical Treatment of Animals (PETA) characterized Vick as a sociopathic monster unfit for civil society.² At the same time, the controversy spurred significant public discourse about the racist implications of his public and legal prosecution. Key figures from organizations such as the National Association for the Advancement of Colored People (NAACP), for instance, argued that Vick's treatment was illustrative of the systemic racism present in US culture and its institutions.³ Less visible in the mediated public sphere, however, were the ideas of those who took an intersectional anti-speciesist/anti-racist approach. By anti-speciesist, I refer to the philosophical position that rejects human superiority to nonhuman animals and calls for an end to their exploitation. By intersectional, I refer to those perspectives that recognize that multiple axes of identity shape experiences of injustice.⁴ Those who take an intersectional anti-speciesist/anti-racist approach link the historical realities of human *and* animal oppression as a way to better understand social phenomena and to build long-term strategies for change—solutions that aim to simultaneously reduce human and nonhuman animal suffering alike. In this work, I contend that the absence of this intersectional perspective during the Vick controversy resulted in large part from a lack of organizational leadership on these issues. Ultimately, it represented a missed opportunity for advocates of an intersectional politics to influence the public debate that ensued.

When Michael Vick signed with the Philadelphia Eagles after his release from prison, I was forced to confront an uneasy tension. I wondered—as a lifelong Eagles fan as well as a committed activist on animal rights *and* social justice issues—what was the appropriate stance for me to take? After a critical interrogation of the issues, I came to the conclusion that the case could be a powerful entry point into several much-needed public dialogues—about human–animal relations, about structural racism, and about the potential for coalition-building among activists in the animal rights and civil rights communities. This work is one product of that exploration.

In this chapter, I first draw from a number of animal rights theorists and social justice practitioners to articulate the foundations of a joint ethical vegan/anti-racist stance. I assert that, while far from a majority opinion, this intersectional perspective has been consistently present *within* the counterpublic that is the animal rights community.⁵ From there, I explore the reasons why an intersectional ethical argument in support of Michael Vick has not gained greater traction, with a focus on three key organizations that emerged as influential media voices throughout the case. By highlighting the practices of the Humane Society of the United States

(HSUS), PETA, and the NAACP, I illustrate the shortcomings of mainstream organizational discourse on intersectional animal rights and social justice issues. Finally, I conclude with thoughts on how those interested in the intersections between media, animal rights, and structural racism might intervene as a way to further progressive change in these arenas. It is my hope that future controversies similar to Vick's might be parlayed into more constructive dialogue as well as into collective action that could bind together activists from both the animal rights and civil rights communities.

The interpretive analysis of this chapter draws from a review of dozens of journalistic accounts of the Vick controversy; from an analysis of the websites of three advocacy organizations that played a key role in shaping public understandings of the Vick case—that is, HSUS, PETA, and the NAACP; and an analysis of posts and comments from the official blog of PETA, known as the *PETA Files.* Several online search engines were used to amass a complement of articles that could provide insight into the ongoing arguments surrounding the Vick case. Search terms included variations and combinations of the phrases "Michael Vick," "dogfighting," "animal rights," and "racism." Key search engines used in this process included LexisNexis Academic, Google, and Philly.com as well as the internal search engines of the organizational websites described above. These accounts were analyzed for prominent themes through an iterative constant comparative method.[6]

Social Controversy and the Public Sphere

Inspired by Jürgen Habermas's discussion of the public sphere, a number of scholars have investigated the role of social controversy for advancing and/ or constraining deliberative discourse.[7] Locating social controversies across various potential sites—including participation in governance processes, in the distribution of resources, and in the administration of social justice— Kathryn M. Olson and G. Thomas Goodnight defined the concept as "an extended rhetorical engagement that critiques, resituates, and develops communication practices bridging the public and personal spheres," adding, "Social controversy occupies the pluralistic boundaries of a democracy and flourishes at those sites of struggle where arguers criticize and invent alternatives to established social conventions and sanctioned norms of communication."[8]

Rhetorical scholar Kendall R. Phillips outlined the two dominant treatments of social controversy that characterized most of the literature on the topic to that point.[9] Many traditional scholars saw controversy as fundamentally blocking the consensus that underlies social action in the public sphere. Others took a more optimistic tack and suggested that the publicity of oppositional arguments that comes through social controversy actually opens a space for reflection, such that it draws more communicative practices into the traditional arena of public deliberation.

Phillips leaned more toward the latter perspective, but differed in that he sought to disconnect theories of social controversy from a conception of a single grand public sphere. He was influenced, in part, by theorists like Nancy Fraser, who articulated the concept of *subaltern counterpublics,* what she defined as "parallel discursive arenas where members of subordinated social groups invent and circulate counter-discourses, which in turn permit them to formulate oppositional interpretations of their identities, interests, and needs."[10] With this in mind, Phillips suggested that the process of controversy leads neither to the "grand conclusion of a public sphere nor to the chaos of postmodern aporia; rather, controversies provide momentary opportunities to resist, change, and reform the local practices of those involved."[11]

It is based on a similar understanding of social controversy that this analysis unfolds. First and foremost, this work is concerned with the ideological positioning of a specific subaltern counterpublic—that of the ethical vegan/animal rights community—and the set of responses that emerged from within this counterpublic in response to the Michael Vick controversy. It is also interested in the extent to which any of these arguments effectively resisted, changed, and reformed the practices of those involved in the case, including the public at large. As will be outlined in full below, while present within this counterpublic discursive domain, an intersectional anti-speciesist/anti-racist perspective was noticeably absent from mainstream public discourse during the Vick controversy.

Michael Vick: Newport News, Bad Newz, and NFL Newsmaker

Michael Vick was born in June 1980 in Newport News, Virginia, a port city at the southeastern end of the Virginia peninsula. He was the second child of four, born to Brenda Vick and Michael Boddie, who were sixteen and seventeen, respectively, at the time Michael was conceived. Life was challenging growing up in the Ridley Circle housing project in the primarily

African-American East End section of Newport News. The economically depressed part of town in which the family lived was nicknamed "Bad Newz" on account of its poverty and drug and gang activity. Vick's competitiveness and athletic ability were his way out, and his talents were clear from an early age.

As a child, he played basketball and baseball at a local boys' club and was steered by a coach toward football when he was about nine or ten years old.[12] He started to flash signs of his superior ability as a three-year starting quarterback with the Warwick High School Raiders in the mid-1990s.[13] He was considered a top national recruit and eventually accepted a scholarship from the Virginia Polytechnic Institute and State University (Virginia Tech), where he would spend the first year redshirting before taking the reins as the starting quarterback. As the redshirt freshman quarterback of Virginia Tech, Vick put on a remarkable performance, leading his team to an undefeated regular season and finishing third in the Heisman Trophy voting. A year later, with the top pick in the 2001 NFL draft, the Atlanta Falcons selected Vick to be their quarterback and the foundation of their franchise moving forward.

After seeing limited action in his rookie year, in his second season, Vick started fifteen of sixteen games in 2002 and was named to his first Pro Bowl team. A broken leg the following season kept him off the field for much of the year, but Vick returned with another Pro Bowl effort in 2004 and led the Falcons deep into the playoffs. In late 2004, the Falcons inked Vick to a ten-year, $130 million contract extension—the richest ever in league history.[14] Vick was hardly a perfect football player, often taking criticism for not working hard enough and for inconsistent passing accuracy.[15] Still, with his rare combination of speed, arm strength, and on-field awareness, the twenty-four-year-old Vick was generally regarded as the most electrifying man in the game, with potential to be one of the greatest quarterbacks of all time.

When he was not showcasing his football talents, however, Vick's personal associations and some poor decision-making contributed to his persona as a controversial public figure. In 2004, police charged two men in Newport News with drug trafficking after marijuana was found in their car. Both men had criminal records and were old friends of Vick's, and the car was registered in Vick's name. In 2005, Vick settled a lawsuit with a former girlfriend who claimed he knowingly gave her a sexually transmitted disease. Vick was also fined by the NFL in 2006 after he gave the middle finger to his own Atlanta Falcons fans following a losing performance. Around the same time, Vick was subject to police questioning when a water bottle with a secret compartment, alleged to contain a marijuana-like substance, was confiscated by airport officials.[16] As journalist Alan Judd described: "The incidents surrounding Vick have followed a consistent arc: Public embarrassment; followed by private talks with team officials, often described as 'stern'; and concluding with Vick's pledge to do better."[17] That successful formula, however, would be impossible to follow once allegations of Vick's involvement in an illegal dogfighting ring began to surface.

On July 17, 2007, Vick, along with Quanis Phillips, Tony Taylor, and Purnell Peace—three old friends from the Newport News area—were indicted by a federal grand jury and charged with "conspiracy to travel in interstate commerce in aid of unlawful activities and to sponsor a dog in an animal fighting venture." A fifth defendant, Oscar Allen, was charged in October. An investigation uncovered that, from late 2002 to late April 2007, the defendants purchased and developed a Virginia property as a staging area for housing and training pit bull dogs and conducting dogfights.[18] Their group—Bad Newz Kennels—engaged in interstate commerce through the dogfighting operation, as gambling purses of tens of thousands of dollars were placed on fights in several states.[19] Vick initially denied any involvement in the day-to-day operations of the dogfighting ring, but a failed polygraph test was used as leverage to obtain a confession. Ultimately, Vick was identified as the primary financier of Bad Newz Kennels, and he also admitted to being a personal witness to the killing of a number of dogs in training that were deemed unsuitable for dogfighting.

A *Sports Illustrated* profile from 2008 gave some insight into the conditions that investigators discovered when the grounds of Bad Newz Kennels were searched:

> The water in the bowls was speckled with algae. Females were strapped into a "rape stand" so the dogs could breed without injuring each other. Some of the sheds held syringes and other medical supplies, and training equipment such as treadmills and spring bars (from which dogs hung, teeth clamped on rubber rings, to strengthen their jaws). The biggest shed had a fighting pit, once covered by a bloodstained carpet that was found in the woods. According to court documents, from time to time Vick and his cohorts "rolled" the dogs: put them in the pit for short battles to see which ones had the right stuff. Those that fought got affection, food, vitamins and training sessions. The ones that showed no taste for

blood were killed—by gunshot, electrocution, drowning, hanging or, in at least one case, being repeatedly slammed against the ground.[20]

In August 2007, Vick pleaded guilty to the criminal dogfighting charges and was sentenced to twenty-three months in federal prison, to be followed by three years of supervised release. At this time, he was suspended indefinitely from the NFL. Vick also settled civil charges through his plea deal, in which he agreed to pay for the costs associated with the long-term care and/or humane euthanasia of fifty-three pit bulls rescued from the site.[21] A wide array of other financial sanctions were handed down from the NFL, from his endorsement partners, and through other business ventures. In all, Vick's financial loss was estimated to be in the hundreds of millions of dollars.[22] After serving eighteen months at a federal penitentiary in Leavenworth, Kansas, Vick was released on July 20, 2009, to a three-year probationary period.

Shortly after his release, Vick was offered a conditional reinstatement by the commissioner of the NFL, and in August 2009 he signed a deal with the Philadelphia Eagles. After playing a limited role as a backup for a season, an injury to Eagles quarterback Kevin Kolb meant that Vick was thrust back into the role of starting quarterback in 2010. Vick excelled in his reclaimed spot, was named to his fourth career Pro Bowl team, and was given the NFL's Comeback Player of the Year award. Before the start of the 2011 season, Vick signed a six-year, $100 million deal with the Eagles, with $35.5 million guaranteed. Vick still owed some $18 million to creditors at the time of the signing and had been living on a court-restricted bankruptcy budget. However, the new contract and several new endorsement deals meant that Vick could finally dig himself out of his financial hole, with plenty to spare.[23]

Race, Animal Rights, and the Michael Vick Backlash

Vick's road back to NFL stardom was hardly universally lauded. From the time the initial reports of his involvement in the dogfighting operation surfaced, Vick became one of the most intensely vilified public figures in the United States. From the start, his court hearings were beset by protestors, many affiliated with animal rights groups like PETA. Back in 2007, a Gallup poll found that 58 percent of Americans surveyed believed Vick should never be allowed to play again in the NFL, with nearly 90 percent believing he should serve some jail time.[24]

To further intensify the case, Vick's public prosecution was undoubtedly racially charged from the start. An analysis of the same Gallup poll from 2007 confirmed what to many was conventional wisdom about the influence of race on perceptions of Vick. Whites who were surveyed expressed significantly harsher attitudes than did African-Americans with respect to both Vick's criminal punishment and the prospects of his NFL reinstatement.[25] Some prominent black leaders aimed to explicitly point out the racial elements of the case, including the outspoken Rev. R.L. White, president of the Atlanta chapter of the NAACP. White urged the NFL and Vick's commercial sponsors to continue to support Vick through the ordeal: "In some instances, I believe Michael Vick has received more negative press than if he would've killed a human being," White was quoted as saying.[26]

The prosecution of Vick took place in the media well before his case made its way through the judicial system. He received a fairly brutal and unforgiving treatment in the press, as journalists individualized his behaviour as personal acts of moral monstrosity. Many (mostly white) commentators consistently insisted that race had no place in the discussion of the case, as they suggested that Vick's cruelty toward animals would be condemned in the same ways regardless of his racial background. Despite these protestations, journalistic tendencies to dehumanize Vick and to emphasize his actions as barbaric acts of cruelty did serve to reinforce long-standing negative portrayals of black athletes. The common depiction of Vick as a *beast*—the true animal among the dogs in his ring—undeniably played off of a history of the dehumanization of black men in US culture.[27]

Not all black leaders felt that Vick should be excused for his actions on account of these racial implications, and there were differences of opinion even within the ranks of the NAACP. Then interim president of the national office of the NAACP, Dennis Courtland Hayes, urged against a common media assertion that dogfighting was an acceptable part of African-American life and rejected the idea that Vick was a victim. Hayes, did, however, situate the reaction of some segments of the African-American community in a broader context. He argued: "We have to understand that what we're hearing expressed by some African-Americans is their anger and their hurt, distrust, in a criminal justice system that they feel treats them like animals."[28]

Vick's reinstatement to the NFL after his release was met with continued controversy. PETA argued on its blog that, even though the legal system said he would be allowed to walk free, "that doesn't mean it is acceptable to put him in the position in which children will look up to him as a role model and wear any new jersey that bears his number."[29] Much of the mainstream animal rights narrative continued to target Vick as not just a criminal but an out-of-control monster. In January 2009, for instance, PETA sent a letter to the league asking that Vick be subjected to a psychological test and an MRI brain scan to look for evidence of clinical psychopathy or antisocial personality disorder. PETA argued that "these tests can help determine if Vick can ever truly understand that dog fighting is a sick, cruel business. Or, they could suggest that he's doomed to repeat mean, violent behavior in the future—whether with dogs or other human beings."[30]

Taking a strikingly different tack, the Philadelphia chapter of the NAACP organized a march to show its support for Vick as he prepared to play his first game back in the NFL. Standing alongside the Black Clergy of Philadelphia and other local civil rights groups, J. Whyat Mondesire, president of the Philadelphia NAACP chapter, explained the organization's position in direct opposition to groups like PETA. He stated: "We believe Michael Vick has served his time, paid his debt to society and deserves a second chance and the animal rights groups want to hold him hostage for the rest of his life."[31]

This sentiment was echoed in part by the HSUS, the nation's leading animal welfare organization (an approach distinct from animal rights, as will be detailed below). Through a partnership with HSUS, Vick became active upon his release in various anti-dogfighting efforts. Subject to its own criticism from Vick's many opponents—devoted dog lovers included—HSUS described its reasons for partnering with Vick: "He served his time in prison, he admitted his wrongdoing, and his regret, and he determined to make amends. His work in reaching out to important audiences now buttresses that of the leading antidogfighting group in the nation in its broad efforts to attack the problem."[32] Vick was in the public eye as he testified before Congress, side by side with the HSUS president, to call for stricter anti-dogfighting laws. That said, most of Vick's advocacy involved speaking to relatively small groups of students at inner-city schools across the country about the dangers of getting involved in activities such as dogfighting. Vick was quoted as saying, "I know that there are people who will never forgive me, and I understand that. What I did was inhumane. I can't change people's minds, I can't change that—if I could, I would. All I can do is what I am doing, to try to help more animals than I hurt, to try to be part of the solution instead of part of the problem."[33]

Vegans? For Vick?

A few years removed from his prison release, Vick had achieved a good deal of success repairing his football career and, to some extent, his personal image. Still, Vick was right to believe that there would remain a significant segment of the public whose opposition would never cease. In 2012, three years after his release from prison, a poll featured by *Forbes* magazine placed Vick as the single most disliked athlete in all of sports, with a 60 percent dislike rating. The story read: "Hardcore NFL fans love him, but Vick still struggles with the casual fans that still know him mainly for his dog fighting legal troubles."[34]

The rationale offered by *Forbes* is a common narrative. Football fans are apt to forgive a convicted criminal like Vick, the argument goes, so long as his performance on the field makes him worthy of praise. Meanwhile, those uninterested in the NFL, along with animal lovers and far-left animal rights activists, think that Vick has gotten off too easy, if anything, and certainly does not deserve to be back to making millions of dollars. Indeed, the maimed dogs from Bad Newz Kennels were hardly afforded that type of opportunity. The thrust of this narrative was supported, for instance, in August 2011, when sixty or so protesters showed up on a steamy summer day in New Jersey to make their presence felt at a Michael Vick autograph signing. Holding signs emblazoned with the PETA logo and photos of abused dogs, the protesters called Vick a monster and compared him to Hitler and Jeffrey Dahmer. On the other side of the street, more than 300 fans were excited to get a chance to meet the starting quarterback of their favourite team.[35]

Still, there is evidence to suggest that this commonly accepted narrative is not altogether reflective of the spectrum of opinions that the Michael Vick controversy engendered, especially given the great divergence in philosophy between those who identify with the causes of animal rights and everyday animal lovers, the latter of whom are unlikely to embody the ideals of ethical veganism. Indeed, I take particular issue with the characterization of animal rights advocates as exclusively portraying Vick as a monster and for insisting that he does not deserve any level of forgiveness due to his undoubtedly heinous acts. While this may be the opinion that is made most visible in media depictions of animal rights activists, my work suggests that there is another important perspective within the animal rights community—a minority perspective, no doubt, but one that has been ignored at the expense of a more grounded understanding of the case.

The ethical vegan case in support of Michael Vick is really quite simple. It begins with the foundations of an ethic of animal liberation, as articulated by scholars such as Peter Singer, among others. Singer was one of the first to discuss the concept of speciesism, defined as a prejudice or attitude of bias in favour of the interest of members of one's own species and against those of members of other species. As he argued, "speciesists allow the interests of their own species to override the greater interests of members of other species."[36] Singer asserted that the interest of a species is not based on her possession of reason or of language but rather her capacity for suffering and enjoyment, which is a prerequisite for having any interests at all. No matter what the nature of the being, he wrote, if it "suffers there can be no moral justification for refusing to take that suffering into consideration."[37] Importantly for the case of Michael Vick, an animal liberation ethic does not favour "cute" or "people-friendly" animals above others. Rather, it sees contemporary US society's general commitment to the prevention of cruelty against nonhuman companion animals like dogs and cats—while other nonhuman animals like chickens, cows, and monkeys are slaughtered and abused in food production and medical research (among other domains)—as a socially constructed phenomenon without a strong basis in moral philosophy. In this sense, an ethical vegan stance rejects the dualism created by humans *within* the nonhuman animal community as strongly as it rejects the dualism *between* humans and nonhuman animals on the whole.

This chapter is not the first effort by an animal rights activist to call attention to the hypocrisy of Michael Vick's vilification. Indeed, several academics, ethicists, philosophers, and others have taken similar public stances. They have argued that, while Vick's actions are undoubtedly cruel and deserving of punishment, they must also be understood within a broader social context in which untold cruelty toward nonhuman animals is consistently ignored, even celebrated. Peter Singer himself weighed in on Vick's case in an interview with the *Philadelphia Inquirer* in which he suggested that "the people who are very quick to jump on Michael Vick maybe could spend some time thinking about how they participate in the cruelty to animals just by walking into the supermarket, spend some time thinking about what happened to that animal before it was turned into meat."[38] Similarly, Francione argued that the case was demonstrative of America's "moral schizophrenia" around animal issues: "How removed from the screaming crowd around the dog pit is the laughing group around the summer steak barbecue?"[39]

On a connected path, several other writers have attempted to use the Vick case to link our understandings of animal rights with issues of structural inequality and historical racial oppression. These arguments build upon a rich history of intersectional analysis and activism that has brought together anti-racist and anti-speciesist perspectives. Prominently in that history, Marjorie Spiegel's *The Dreaded Comparison* drew parallels between the institutions of slavery and animal domination. In that work, the author wrote, "When both blacks and animals are viewed as being 'oppressible', the cruelties perpetrated upon them take similar forms."[40] It is not surprising, then, that many of the historical leaders who have looked to advance animal liberation have also been involved in struggles to deconstruct institutions of human oppression. As Singer suggested, "[i]ndeed, the overlap between leaders of movements against the oppression of blacks and women, and leaders of movements against cruelty to animals, is extensive; so extensive as to provide an unexpected form of confirmation of the parallel between racism, sexism, and speciesism."[41]

Working from this foundation, social justice activist Dany Sigwalt articulated the feeling that, in holding both anti-racist and anti-speciesist ideologies, she often found herself at odds with almost everyone in terms of the Michael Vick debate. These intersectional anti-oppression ideologies forced her to, "realize that dog fighting circles are frequently located in low income communities and communities of color where the practice has provided a resource for financial survival."[42] Similarly, the ethicist Kathy Rudy called attention to what she saw as unjust treatment for animal-related crimes that were more likely to implicate African-Americans: "We need to face the fact that dog fighting is not the only 'sport' that abuses animals. Cruelty also occurs in rodeos, horse and dog racing (all of which mistreat animals and often kill them when no longer useful). . . . But I see one important difference between these more socially acceptable mistreatments and the anger focused on Vick: Vick is black, and most of the folks in charge of the other activities are white."[43]

Indeed, one need not look further than the Philadelphia Eagles roster to see this racialized double standard in action. Kevin Kolb, the West Texas–born white quarterback whose injury paved the way for Vick to take over the Eagles' starting job, grew up honing his skills not just as a football player but also as an "avid outdoorsman"—that meant hunting, fishing, and rodeo. In a 2007 profile of the recently drafted quarterback, Kolb outlined his hunting tactics: "The dogs corral 'em pretty good. When you know it's your turn, when you get a slot, you go in and you grab (the hog) by the back legs first. Depending on how big it is, you flip it over, jump on it, and stab it in the heart."[44]

Kolb, of course, broke no laws in his hunting excursions, but legality alone hardly explains why there was little to no public outcry based on his treatment of animals, either from the mainstream animal rights movement or from everyday animal lovers. Instead, it is affirmation that a nuanced understanding of Vick's case necessarily requires an intersectional perspective, one that is cognizant of the multiple dualisms at play with respect to human–nonhuman animal relations, socio-economic status, and race. It is also, in many ways, an indictment of an animal rights movement (and a civil rights movement, for that matter) that has heretofore failed to articulate such a perspective to the public at large.

Importantly, my analysis also suggests that this perspective is not limited to professional ethicists and social justice activists, but also *is* present within the rank and file of the animal rights community itself. As an example, in December 2010, Vick made more off-the-field headlines when he gave an interview with a website called *The Grio*. In that discussion, he remarked that he would love to be able to get a dog for himself and his children, after the court-mandated moratorium that prohibited him from doing so expired. This story was excerpted with commentary on the official blog of PETA. Following the tenor of PETA's long-standing rhetoric in the Vick case, the blog post took a strong stance against his desires: "The guy whose name has become synonymous with hanging, electrocuting, drowning, and shooting dogs and forcing them to rip each other to pieces in dogfighting rings is now bemoaning the fact that he can't have a canine companion."[45]

An additional 164 comments were written in response to this posting.[46] Most participants took a stance similar to the PETA staffer and argued that Vick was unfit and undeserving to have any companion animal in his presence. Yet a small but stalwart group of defenders made their voices heard on the *PETA Files* message board. Indeed, out of the 164 posts, about 20 were in direct support of Vick. These commenters implored others to show some compassion and to offer Vick a second chance in life. One explicitly suggested that Vick would not be treated with such animosity if he were a white man, others drew attention to the negative influence of Vick's social environment, and a number argued that Vick could serve as an influential role model to help dissuade young people from getting involved in dogfighting. In the view of these participants, Vick's cruelty toward animals was no more heinous than the cruelty that animals in the food system, for instance, face every day and on a vastly larger scale. Participants like Jon saw constructive forgiveness as the logical move: "Michael Vick is doing and saying all the right things. He has truly changed and is doing everything that he can to be part of the solution, including speaking out against dog fighting on a weekly basis. . . . The fact of the matter is that people can change. This is evident of course, by the example of the millions of vegetarians who have converted from a non-vegetarian diet. By your logic, PETA, all vegetarians should spend the rest of their life being punished for once eating meat."[47]

Taken as a whole, this analysis challenges the commonly held understanding of animal rights activists and their response to Michael Vick. In no way does it demonstrate that a majority of this counterpublic community held an intersectional, anti-oppression ideology that compelled them toward support for Michael Vick's reclamation project. However, it is clear that a small but strident portion of the community has made efforts to use the case of Vick as a way to call attention to the constructed nature of society's concern for specific companion animals. These advocates have also pointed out that the case of Michael Vick should be understood within a social context in which dogfighting was largely normalized through his world view. The racial implications of Vick's treatment have also been called into question, as several activists and scholars have suggested that Vick's identity as an African-American male has played a role in his vilification throughout the media and in the public eye. Finally, a number of these "Vegans for Vick" have looked forward to the potential good that Vick could do to spread an anti-animal-cruelty message, particularly to youth in predominantly urban and ethnic minority communities. The question remains, then, as to why this intersectional message has been largely absent from the broader public discourse surrounding the Michael Vick case. Why has it been isolated in a few academic op-eds and as a minor thread of online commentary?

Intersectional Politics and the Limits of Mainstream Organizations

A critical reflection on the ideology of two of the leading anti-animal-cruelty organizations in the United States as well as of the nation's oldest and largest civil rights organization provides some insight into this topic. Ultimately, it demonstrates that, when analyzing the influence of counterpublic perspectives on the discourses of social controversies, it is important to keep in mind the influence of organizations that are able to gain access to mainstream media and therefore can shape the discursive environment in the mediated public sphere.

Focusing first on the animal organizations, both HSUS and PETA have played vocal but mostly opposing roles throughout the Michael Vick case. HSUS has made Vick the centrepiece of its anti-dogfighting efforts, and they have partnered on the production of public service announcement videos, testified together in front of Congress, and appeared at dozens of schools across the nation as a way to connect with at-risk youth. Yet HSUS is a self-described animal protection organization, not an organization that advocates for animal rights or liberation. Its topics of interest range from stopping puppy mills to ending animal fighting to finding retirement homes for chimpanzees once used in laboratory testing. Its guide to "Humane Eating" suggests "embracing the Three Rs—reducing the consumption of meat and other animal-based foods; refining the diet by avoiding products from the worst production systems (e.g., switching to cage-free eggs); and replacing meat and other animal-based foods in the diet with plant-based foods."[48]

This is not to say that HSUS does not do important work in the domain of animal protection or that its moderate approach is not a useful one in connecting to a US population that has become accustomed to being ignorant toward widespread animal suffering. Yet it is clear that HSUS does not ask society to fundamentally question its relationship to animals. Terms such as *speciesism* are nowhere to be found in HSUS literature—even the words *vegetarian* and *vegan* are noticeably absent from the website's guide to "Humane Eating." It is therefore difficult to expect that an organization like HSUS would parlay the Michael Vick case into a broader conversation about society's relationship to animals, one that goes beyond a focus simply on the wrongs of dogfighting. In short, its approach in no way compels everyday animal lovers to take stock of the moral schizophrenia exhibited by much of the US public in its relationship to nonhuman animals.

Contrast this to PETA, which describes itself as the largest animal *rights* organization in the world. It is an organization that consciously takes anti-speciesism as its foundation and cites authors like Peter Singer as influential in guiding its operations. The PETA website asserts that "Animal rights is not just a philosophy—it is a social movement that challenges society's traditional view that all nonhuman animals exist solely for human use.... If you wouldn't eat a dog, why eat a pig? Dogs and pigs have the same capacity to feel pain, but it is prejudice based on species that allows us to think of one animal as a companion and the other as dinner."[49] With this in mind, the campaigns of PETA take a much harder line than does the work of HSUS. The organization explicitly calls for people to switch to a vegan diet, to abstain from wearing any clothes in which animals were used in the production process, and calls for an end to animal use in research laboratories and in the entertainment industry.

Much of what has put PETA on the map has been its use of various controversial tactics, including the use of nude celebrities in their "I'd rather go naked than wear fur" campaign, gallery exhibits that juxtapose pictures of factory farming alongside photos of enslaved Africans and Holocaust victims, and the types of protest actions that were seen during the Michael Vick saga. PETA argues that such colourful and controversial tactics are the best way for the organization to attain media coverage and spread the message of kindness to animals around the world. Yet PETA has come under significant criticism over the years for what is seen as a lack of sensitivity in terms of both sexism and racism.

For instance, in describing PETA's exhibit comparing the slavery of Africans with factory farming, "The Animal Liberation Project," Breeze Harper argued that "PETA's campaign strategies often fail to give a historical context for why they use certain images that are connected to a painful history of racially motivated violence against particular nonwhite, racialized humans."[50] PETA's efforts were also opposed by Marjorie Spiegel, author of *The Dreaded Comparison: Human and Animal Slavery*, who (unsuccessfully) sued PETA for copyright infringement. In response to criticism over an exhibition that compared the Holocaust to the treatment of nonhuman animals, a PETA staffer argued that the organization's ultimate goal was "apolitical" and that it seeks the "elevation of our concept of animals as beings who merely live to beings who share with humans the 'form or manner of living peculiar to a single individual or a group.'"[51] This avoidance of identity politics exemplifies the lack of intersectional, anti-oppression interests of PETA, which in many ways illustrates a broader trend of white domination in the animal rights movement in which other struggles for social justice are not taken into account.[52] The Michael Vick case lays bare the reality that, for many in the mainstream (white) vegan community, issues of social justice are entirely off their radar.

What makes the Vick case particularly compelling is that attention to *only* its racial and social justice implications is also incomplete. That is why it is necessary, as well, to interrogate the role of an organization like the NAACP, as it, too, maintains a distinct dualism between animal rights and racial justice. It is clearly beyond the interests of the organization to take on concerns related to animal rights as part of its mission, and that is understandable to a certain extent, given the scope of civil rights goals toward which its resources are focused. However, the Michael Vick case is not the only instance in which spokespersons from the NAACP have directly *opposed* animal rights activists broadly and PETA in particular, and this opposition has come at the expense of finding common ground in a struggle against oppression at large. Members of the NAACP have opposed PETA's exhibits that contrast human and animal slavery; in 2005, Scot Esdaile, then president of the Connecticut and Greater New Haven chapters of the NAACP, demanded a display be taken down, adding, "We were used like animals to build this country for free; the comparison of black rights with animal rights is not a good one."[53] When NAACP leaders have attempted to stand up for animal issues—as did president and chief executive Kweisi Mfume when he signed on to a 2003 PETA campaign urging KFC (and its parent company, Yum! Brands) to employ more humane slaughtering methods—a harsh rebuke can be expected from the broader organization. In the instance of the KFC issue, under pressure from NAACP members for diverting their focus, a spokesperson for the organization quickly declared that, after speaking with the company, Mfume's single letter would mark the end of his involvement in the campaign.[54]

Time and again, the NAACP has shown that it lacks an interest in drawing connections between human and nonhuman animal suffering. Rather than serving as a force to educate the mainstream animal rights movement about the value of an intersectional approach to deconstructing oppressive structures, it has instead helped to perpetuate a dualistic distinction. Writing on the Vick case, Claire Jean Kim asserted that this myopic focus consistently "subsumes, deflects and ultimately denies the other moral question being raised, the animal question."[55] Indeed, NAACP president Hayes argued that African-Americans' anger with respect to the treatment of Vick emerged from a "criminal justice system that they feel treats them like animals," a tacit approbation of the systemic exploitation of nonhuman life that goes a long way in describing why an intersectional politics has not sprung forth from mainstream organizing for civil rights and racial justice.

Taken together, these examples demonstrate the key influence that the connection between major advocacy organizations and mainstream media outlets plays in shaping public discourse during social controversies. In the case of Michael Vick, the voices of traditionally subaltern counter-publics—including activists from civil rights, animal welfare, and animal rights—*were* featured in major media stories. Yet these discussions did not encompass the full breadth of opinions from within these subaltern communities. Instead, those that espoused an intersectional, anti-speciesist/anti-racist perspective were not sufficiently represented in organizational nor in mediated domains. As scholars like Manuel Castells have articulated, social movement power in our contemporary network society is *communication power*, as discourses are "generated, diffused, fought over, internalized, and ultimately embodied" through communicative action from within local–global networks of individual, mediated, and organizational actors.[56] Absent this access to communication power, the intersectional perspective was unable to significantly "resist, change, and reform" the practices of those involved in the Vick controversy.[57]

Conclusion

How, then, might we advance a different narrative—one that puts at the forefront an intersectional concern over the systematic oppression of people *and* nonhuman animals? How might we bring greater attention to the mainstream animal rights community's inattention to overlapping issues of systemic racism at the same time as we encourage those interested in social and racial justice to consider the animal question? And what might we do to push those animal lovers who vilify Vick as a sociopathic monster to recognize the arbitrary and constructed nature of a speciesist society's differential treatment of different kinds of nonhuman animals? Voices of both scholars and everyday activists have attempted to draw these connections, but, clearly, none of the major organizations that have emerged as important parts of the Vick debate—from the NAACP to PETA to HSUS—have sufficiently attempted to bridge these important gaps.

A fundamental starting point, it seems, is the foundation from which most movements begin—that is, these disparate voices must find a way to coalesce into some sort of coherent and holistic form. There are minor rumblings at the grassroots level to this effect, but to make a broader impact, a more concerted, national, and media-oriented structure might be required.[58] HSUS, PETA, and the NAACP are all characterized by national structures with local chapters, and individually each helps shape the course of its respective movement—animal welfare, animal rights, and civil rights. At this time, however, none of these organizations, and none of the movements in which they are situated, gives voice to those who are committed to deconstructing oppression at the intersection of animal rights *and* racial justice. This lack of institutional voice was brought into relief during the Michael Vick controversy and was exemplified most clearly in the near media blackout of advocates who could speak to these issues from an intersectional perspective.

But what of the next social controversy that begs for an analysis of the intersections between animal rights and racial justice? A push toward organizing like-minded individuals represents the only way to ensure that intersectional politics will have a voice in the discussion and, ultimately, the opportunity to reduce the suffering of nonhuman animals while also deconstructing racism in its modern institutional forms. Again working from Castells, the importance of *communication power* in such instances cannot be overstated.[59] To intervene in future social controversies, the intersectional perspective must be seen and heard in the relevant organizational and media platforms that help to shape discursive reality.

Given the prominence of organizations such as the NAACP and PETA, along with their access to influential media systems, the best strategy might be to attempt to work from within these institutions and bring new intersectional insights into their everyday practices. Advocates could push for an intersectional ethic by urging leaders to open up inter-organizational dialogues and could participate as rank-and-file members by bringing up such issues in meetings, through online platforms, and in organizational literature. It would take time for significant returns to be realized, but the potential for future impact would make the efforts worth the long-term struggle. If such institutions proved to be consistently unwilling to shift from their well-established ideologies, it might be time for the "Vegans for Vick" to strike out on their own; perhaps the external pressure would force the established organizations to reconsider their own relationships to intersectional politics moving forward.

NOTES

This chapter originally appeared, under the same title, as an article in the *International Journal of Communication* 7 (2013): 780–800. It has since been revised slightly by the author.

1. As Gary Francione explains, "Although veganism may represent a matter of diet or lifestyle for some, ethical veganism is a profound moral and political commitment. . . . Ethical veganism is the personal rejection of the commodity status of nonhuman animals, of the notion that animals have only external value, and of the notion that animals have less moral value than do humans" ("Abolition of Animal Exploitation," 62).
2. Shannon, "Is Michael Vick a Clinically Diagnosable Psychopath?"
3. Kim, "Slaying the Beast."
4. Deckha, "Intersectionality."
5. The term *ethical vegan* is used somewhat interchangeably with the terms *animal rights* and *anti-speciesist* in this work and elsewhere.
6. Charmaz, "Grounded Theory."
7. Habermas, *Communicative Action.*
8. Olson and Goodnight, "Entanglements of Consumption," 249.
9. Phillips, "Rhetoric of Controversy."
10. Fraser, "Rethinking the Public Sphere," 67.
11. Phillips, "Rhetoric of Controversy," 495.
12. Maske, "Playing to Wrong Crowd."
13. Stewart and Kennedy, "Michael Vick Biography."
14. *Jet,* "Falcons Quarterback."
15. Such criticisms have often been levelled against so-called running quarterbacks, many of whom are African-American. Indeed, there is an ongoing discussion about the role of race (and racism) in the evaluation of both white and black quarterbacks. See, for example, Billings, "Depicting the Quarterback."
16. Glazer, "Obscene Gesture."
17. Judd, "Game of Life," par. 51.
18. Haaser, "Bad Newz Kennels."
19. Piquero et al., "Race, Punishment."
20. Gorant, "What Happened to Michael Vick's Dogs."
21. Haaser, "Bad Newz Kennels."
22. Piquero et al., "Race, Punishment."
23. Tamari, "Creditors."
24. Jones, "Most NFL Fans."
25. Piquero et al., "Race, Punishment."
26. *CNN,* "NAACP Official."
27. Kim, "Slaying the Beast"; Laucella, "Analysis of Press Coverage."
28. Johnson, "Vick Case Divides African-American Leaders."
29. Flavell, "Michael Vick Is Back."
30. Shannon, "Is Michael Vick a Clinically Diagnosable Psychopath?," par. 3.
31. Paolantonio, "Eagles Hope to Avoid 'Ugly Scene,'" par. 5.
32. HSUS, "Michael Vick and the HSUS's Work," par. 4.

33. Bowen and Domowitch, "Vick on Dogfighting," par. 11.
34. Van Riper, "America's Most Disliked Athletes," par. 2.
35. Fleming, "The Dog in the Room."
36. Singer, *Animal Liberation*, 9.
37. Ibid., 8.
38. Rubin, "An Animal-Rights Activist Stands Up for Vick," par. 9.
39. Francione, "We're All Michael Vick."
40. Spiegel, *Dreaded Comparison*, 27.
41. Singer, *Animal Liberation*, 221.
42. Sigwalt, "Vegan's Perspective," par. 4
43. Rudy, "Michael Vick, Dogfighting and Race," par. 4.
44. Bowen, "Kevin Kolb," par. 8.
45. Pollard-Post, "Michael Vick Wants a Dog," p. 1.
46. Earlier versions of this article included an in-depth thematic analysis of these user comments.
47. Pollard-Post, "Michael Vick Wants a Dog," p. 15.
48. HSUS, "Humane Eating," par. 3.
49. PETA, "Why Animal Rights?"
50. Harper, *Sistah Vegan*, xiv.
51. Guillermo, "Response."
52. Nocella, "Challenging Whiteness."
53. Brune, "Blacks Cry Out for More Ethical Treatment," par. 11.
54. Cohn, "Mfume Endorses PETA Campaign."
55. Kim, "Slaying the Beast," 22.
56. Castells, *Communication Power*, 53.
57. Phillips, "Rhetoric of Controversy."
58. In the time since the original publication of this work, a number of intersectional anti-racist/ethical vegan activists have indeed begun to come together, largely through online discussion. With that said, the organizing power of these groups remains nascent.
59. Castells, *Communication Power*.

BIBLIOGRAPHY

Billings, Andrew C. "Depicting the Quarterback in Black and White: A Content Analysis of College and Professional Football Broadcast Commentary." *Howard Journal of Communications* 15, no. 4 (2004): 201–10.

Bowen, Les. "Kevin Kolb: A Texas Outdoorsman." *Daily News Online—Eagletarian Blog*, September 4, 2010. http://www.philly.com/philly/sports/eagles/102215629 .html.

Bowen, Les, and Paul Domowitch. "Vick on Dogfighting: 'What I Did Was Inhumane.'" *Daily News Online—Eagletarian Blog*, November 23, 2010. http://www.philly.com/philly/blogs/dneagles/Vick_on_dogfighting_What_I_Did_was_inhumane.html.

Brune, Adrian. "Blacks Cry Out for More Ethical Treatment." *Hartford Courant*, September 20, 2005. http://articles.courant.com/2005-09-20/features/0509200182_1_animal-rights-ethical-treatment-peta.

Castells, Manuel. *Communication Power*. Oxford: Oxford University Press, 2009.

Charmaz, Kathy. "Grounded Theory in the 21st Century: Applications for Advancing Social Justice Studies." In *Handbook of Qualitative Research*, edited by Norman K. Denzin and Yvonne S. Lincoln, 509–37. 2nd ed. Thousand Oaks, CA: Sage, 2000.

CNN. "NAACP Official: Vick Shouldn't Be Banned from NFL." Last updated August 23, 2007. http://www.cnn.com/2007/US/law/08/22/vick/index.html?_s=pm:us.

Cohn, Meredith. "Mfume Endorses PETA Campaign." *Baltimore Sun*. Last updated September 12, 2003. http://articles.baltimoresun.com/2003-09-12/business/0309120172_1_mfume-peta-kentucky-fried-chicken.

Deckha, Maneesha. "Intersectionality and Posthumanist Visions of Equality." *Wisconsin Journal of Law, Gender & Society* 23, no. 2 (2008): 249–67.

Flavell, Shawna. "Michael Vick Is Back in the NFL." *PETA Files*. Last updated July 27, 2009. http://www.peta.org/b/thepetafiles/archive/2009/07/27/michael-vick-is-back-in-the-nfl.aspx.

Fleming, David. "The Dog in the Room." *ESPN*. Last updated August 25, 2011. http://espn.go.com/espn/commentary/story/_/id/6889579/espn-magazine-examining-michael-vick-where-dogfighting-falls-continuum-cruelty.

Francione, Gary L. "The Abolition of Animal Exploitation." In *The Animal Rights Debate: Abolition or Regulation?*, edited by Gary L. Francione and Robert Garner, 1–103. New York: Columbia University Press, 2010.

———. "We're All Michael Vick." *Philadelphia Daily News*. Last updated August 14, 2009. http://articles.philly.com/2009-08-14/news/24986151_1_atlanta-falcons-quarterback-vick-illegal-dog-dog-fights.

Fraser, Nancy. "Rethinking the Public Sphere: A Contribution to the Critique of Actually Existing Democracy." *Social Text*, nos. 25–26 (1990): 56–80.

Glazer, Jay. "Obscene Gesture Will Cost Vick $20k." *Fox Sports*. Posted January 27, 2005. http://web.archive.org/web/20070127210848/http://msn.foxsports.com/nfl/story/6217588.

Gorant, Jim. "What Happened to Michael Vick's Dogs." *Sports Illustrated*, December 29, 2008. http://nationalcanineresearchcouncil.com/uploaded_files/tinymce/SI%20Gorant%20Article.pdf.

Guillermo, K. "Response to Nathan Snaza's (Im)Possible Witness: Viewing PETA's

'Holocaust on Your Plate.'" *Animal Liberation Philosophy and Policy Journal* 2, no. 1 (2004): 1–20.

Haaser, Brian L. "Bad Newz Kennels, Smithfield, Virginia—Animal Fighting." Report of Investigation. United States Department of Agriculture, Office of Inspector General. August 28, 2008. http://www.usda.gov/oig/webdocs/ BadNewzKennels.pdf.

Habermas, Jürgen. *The Theory of Communicative Action: Lifeword and System: A Critique of Functionalist Reason.* Vol. 2. Boston: Beacon Press, 1985.

Harper, A. Breeze. *Sistah Vegan: Black Female Vegans Speak on Food, Identity, Health and Society.* New York: Lantern Books, 2010.

HSUS (Humane Society of the United States). "Humane Eating." Accessed January 3, 2013. http://www.humanesociety.org/issues/eating.

———. "Michael Vick and the HSUS's Work to End Dogfighting." Last updated March 30, 2012. http://www.humanesociety.org/issues/dogfighting/qa/vick_ faq.html.

Jet. "Falcons Quarterback Michael Vick Signs Richest NFL Deal in History." January 17, 2005. http://findarticles.com/p/articles/mi_m1355/is_3_107/ai_ n9771537 (site discontinued).

Johnson, M.A. "Vick Case Divides African-American Leaders." *NBC Sports,* August 23, 2007. http://nbcsports.msnbc.com/id/20411561/site/21683474 (site since modified).

Jones, Jeffrey M. "Most NFL Fans Say Vick Shouldn't Be Allowed to Play Again." Gallup. Last updated August 29, 2007. http://www.gallup.com/poll/28540/ majority-nfl-fans-say-vick-should-allowed-play-again.aspx.

Judd, Alan. "In Game of Life, Vick Blitzed by Trouble." *Gadsden Times,* July 22, 2007. http://www.ajc.com/sports/content/sports/falcons/stories/2007/07/21/0722vickbio .html (site since modified).

Kim, Claire Jean. "Slaying the Beast: Reflections on Race, Culture, and Species." *Kalfou* 1, no. 1 (2009): 1–34.

Laucella, Pamela C. "Michael Vick: An Analysis of Press Coverage on Federal Dogfighting Charges." *Journal of Sports Media* 5, no. 2 (2010): 35–76.

Maske, Mark. "Playing to Wrong Crowd." *Washington Post,* August 21, 2007. http://wapo.st/119kF82.

Nocella, Anthony, II. "Challenging Whiteness in the Animal Advocacy Movement." *Journal for Critical Animal Studies* 10, no. 1 (2012): 142–54.

Olson, Kathryn M., and G. Thomas Goodnight. "Entanglements of Consumption, Cruelty, Privacy, and Fashion: The Social Controversy over Fur." *Quarterly Journal of Speech* 80, no. 3 (1994): 249–76.

Paolantonio, Sal. "Eagles Hope to Avoid 'Ugly Scene.'" *ESPN.* Last updated August 26, 2009. http://sports.espn.go.com/nfl/trainingcamp09/news/story?id=4423883.

PETA (People for the Ethical Treatment of Animals). "Why Animal Rights?" Accessed January 3, 2013. http://www.peta.org/about/why-peta/why-animal -rights.aspx.

Phillips, Kendall R. "A Rhetoric of Controversy." *Western Journal of Communication* 63, no. 4 (1999): 488–510.

Piquero, Alex R., Nicole L. Piquero, Marc Gertz, Thomas Baker, Jason Batton, and J.C. Barnes. "Race, Punishment, and the Michael Vick Experience." *Social Science Quarterly* 92, no. 2 (2011): 535–51.

Pollard-Post, Lindsay. "Michael Vick Wants a Dog." *PETA Files.* Last updated December 15, 2010. http://www.peta.org/b/thepetafiles/archive/2010/12/15/ michael-vick-wants-a-dog.aspx.

Rubin, Daniel. "An Animal-rights Activist Stands Up for Vick." *Philadelphia Inquirer.* Last updated August 17, 2009. http://articles.philly.com/2009-08-17/ news/24986154_1_michael-vick-animals-dogs-fight.

Rudy, K. "Michael Vick, Dogfighting and Race." *Duke Today.* Last updated August 29, 2007. http://today.duke.edu/2007/08/vick_oped.html.

Shannon, Dan. "Is Michael Vick a Clinically Diagnosable Psychopath or a Reformed Dogfighter?" *PETA Files.* Last updated January 21, 2009. http:// www.peta.org/b/thepetafiles/archive/2009/01/21/is-michael-vick-a-clinically -diagnosable-psychopath-or-a-reformed-dogfighter.aspx.

Sigwalt, Dany. "A Vegan's Perspective on Dogfighting and Michael Vick." *Racialicious.* Last updated August 3, 2009. http://www.racialicious.com/2009/08/03/a-vegans -perspective-on-dogfighting-and-michael-vick.

Singer, Peter. *Animal Liberation.* 1975. New York: Ecco Press, 2002.

Spiegel, Marjorie. *The Dreaded Comparison: Race and Animal Slavery.* Philadelphia: New Society Publishers, 1988.

Stewart, M., and Kennedy, M. "Michael Vick Biography." Accessed January 3, 2013. http://www.jockbio.com/Bios/Vick/Vick_bio.html.

Tamari, Jonathan. "Creditors Encouraged by Vick's Deal." *Philadelphia Inquirer.* Last updated August 31, 2011. http://articles.philly.com/2011-08-31/sports/ 29949583_1_michael-vick-ross-reeves-bankruptcy-case.

Van Riper, T. "America's Most Disliked Athletes." *Forbes,* February 7, 2012. http:// www.forbes.com/pictures/eddf45fkhi/americas-most-disliked-athletes.

12

Disability, Animals, and Earth Liberation

Eco-ability and Ableism in the Animal Advocacy Movement

Anthony J. Nocella II

Disability rights activists, animal advocates, and environmentalists form social movements that fight for traditionally oppressed groups. These groups—nonhuman animals and people with disabilities—have much in common, and they have arguably been marginalized more than any other segment of the ecological world, which is itself dominated, as shown by contemporary ecological crises. One way the connection between these three subjugated groups (and in the case of the ecological world, we could say a subjugated "mass") manifests is through insult. To wit, in the colonized and civilized world, it is an affront to human dignity to be referred to as "animal" (nonhuman), "wild" (uncultivated, as in nature), or a "freak" (disabled).[1] As was the case with women and people of colour in the Western world less than fifty years ago, and still is today, if one is not recognized as fully human, there is cause to marginalize—and in some cases exploit—that individual. Of course, the species *Homo sapiens* is a general categorization within which all human beings fit, but not neatly, for within the human species are socially constructed ideas of who and what is "normal" and "abnormal." In kind, this chapter analyses the webbed oppression of nonhuman animals, those with disabilities, and the environment. This foundation serves as an introduction to the emergent intersectional, activist theory, *eco-ability*. This theory is so new, in fact, that the first book on the concept, entitled *Earth, Animal, and Disability Liberation: The Rise of the Eco-ability Movement*, was just published in October 2012, of which I was a contributing editor.[2]

As Castricano notes in the introduction to *Animal Subjects* (2008), that collection was "long overdue in cultural studies where critiques of racism, sexism(s) and classism have radically changed the face of the humanities and social sciences but which have also historically withheld the question of ethical treatment from nonhuman animals."[3] This raison d'être of *Animal Subjects* was noble, timely, and theoretically significant. That said, as a scholar of disability studies, I cannot help but comment upon Lesli Bisgould's chapter in that first volume: "Power and Irony: One Tortured Cat and Many Twisted Angles to Our Moral Schizophrenia about Animals." To be clear, Bisgould's chapter is an importantly disturbing, powerful, and effective critique of the paradoxical nature of animal law in Canada. However, her use of the term "moral schizophrenia," popularized by law professor Gary Francione, whom she cites, goes unnoticed as an ableist expression that I will critique later in this chapter. This, if effective, is what I hope to bring to the theoretical table as *Animal Subjects 2.0* makes its debut: exposure of the long invisible ableism inherent in the environmental and animal liberation movements.

In keeping with the original and continued goals of *Animal Subjects*, I want to include treatment of nonhuman animals within the social and political critiques that are the lifeblood of humanities and social sciences scholarship and street-level activism, but I also want to head in a new direction through consideration of how those with disabilities factor into the historical picture of oppression and constructions of "normalcy." And in deference to the classic feminist rallying cry of the "personal is political," within that analysis I will start with my own story to frame the ideas explored in this chapter.

The Emergence of Eco-ability

Before first grade, I was diagnosed as having severe mental disabilities. With this diagnosis, I was enrolled in special education classes from first to fourth grade. Those years were a nightmare for me. I shook all the time, and I had difficulty focusing my energy both in and outside the classroom. At times, I and other students would be held down or removed from class. One of my classmates died because of a medical condition that wasn't properly treated. Aside from family interactions, the only fulfilling and meaningful relationship I had during those years was with my cat, Sparkle; this feline was my best friend and someone with whom I was able to communicate expressively. (While I was still a child, Sparkle was killed by three dogs. My emotional response to hir[4] death inspired me to eventually become involved in the animal rights movement.) During my time with Sparkle, I was also introduced to forests, lakes, and rivers through the Cub Scouts, which allowed me to develop a number of important human friendships and love for the natural world. From fifth to twelfth grade I went to a separate school for students with mental and learning disabilities. These bifurcated institutions—schools for the "normal" and schools for the "different"—alerted me to the social institutions that stigmatize those who do not learn or interact with other humans in standard ways.[5]

My early education and relationship with Sparkle and the Cub Scouts allowed me to connect the social construction of ableism, speciesism, and nature. Ableism, a term created by activists with disabilities, is the discrimination of people with disabilities; it promotes normalcy via structural barriers, personal actions, and theories.[6] Speciesism is discrimination against nonhuman animal species; this ideology proposes that humans are superior animals whose needs and desires trump those of other animal species.[7] Both speciesism and ableism are social constructions interwoven so securely into Western culture that they have been rendered imperceptible until recently. Even those who experienced or witnessed these types of oppressions did not have a name for them, so they too were forced to endure—though not necessarily like—what passed for the "normal" ordering of things.

Eco-ability attempts to make those constructions evident by exposing the power lines that promote normalcy and Western, rationalist intellectualism. In effect, it questions the "project of modernity." An extended history of modernity is outside the purview of this chapter, so I will briefly contextualize. Current Western conceptions of modernity arose out of the European and American Enlightenment period of the seventeenth and eighteenth centuries. Rosenau (1992) poses modernity as "a progressive force promising to liberate humankind from ignorance and irrationality."[8] Similarly, the goal of prominent, rationalist continental philosophers of the Enlightenment, such as René Descartes and Immanuel Kant, was to create theoretical conceptions of reality that divide themselves—meaning white, moneyed, Christian males—from everything that was considered savage, abnormal, and deviant, such as nature, nonhuman animals, women, people of colour, and people with disabilities. Snyder and Mitchell explain how the narrative of modernity was key to constructing disability as deviant and undesirable:

> Modernity gives birth to the culture of technology that promises more data from less input. This unique historical terrain is characterized by Bauman as "the morally elevating story of humanity emerging from pre-social barbarity" (2001b, 12). This progressive narrative is key to the development of disability as a concept of deviant variation. In a culture that endlessly assures itself that it is on the verge of conquering Nature once and for all, along with its own "primitive" instincts and the persistent domain of the have-nots, disability is referenced with respect to these idealized visions. As a vector of human variability, disabled bodies both represent a throwback to human prehistory and serve as the barometer of a future without "deviancy." . . . In other words, for modernity, the eradication of disability represented a scourge and a promise: its presence signaled a debauched present of cultural degeneration that was tending to regress toward a prior state of primitivism, while at the same time it seemed to promise that its absence would mark the completion of modernity as a cultural project.[9]

In sum, the "deviant" and the "disabled" are those that need to be conquered if human beings are to continue an effective evolution from the "pre-social barbarity" that will complete the modernist project. Most humans in the Western world have already successfully distanced themselves from nonhumans through collective, unquestioning acceptance of the human/animal binary. And although it cannot be labelled as a group in the traditional sense of the term (as in a marginalized group of persons), the environment has also been a casualty of modernity.

When colonizers first came to what we now refer to as the Americas, the wilderness was treated as an adversary that needed to be defeated as much as did the "uncivilized" Native peoples inhabiting the land.[10] Establishing a link between the environment as a monolithic entity with individualized groups—i.e., animals and people with disabilities—is a key component of eco-ability. Adams and Socha contend that "because *supposed* nonsentient life does not react with sound or movement that humans can [or want to] perceive, the correlations between sentient and nonsentient existence are often ignored."[11] In response to the historic project of modernity, eco-ability is the theory that nature, nonhuman animals, and people with disabilities promote collaboration, not competition; interdependency, not independence; and respect of difference and diversity, not sameness and normalcy. Eco-ability liberation is the intersectional activist philosophy linking animal liberation, disability liberation, and Earth liberation. Eco-ability studies is about the intersectional academic philosophy linking critical animal, disability, and environmental studies.

Eco-ability is a philosophy that respects differences in abilities with an absence of domination (i.e., ecological management or stewardship). Eco-ability is in its infancy as a concept, and I encourage further dialogue and discussion of its implications. Further, eco-ability is *needed* because, unfortunately, even within a culturally marginalized cause such as the global animal advocacy movement, one that attempts to dissolve the human/animal socially constructed binary, oppressive rhetoric and actions still exist, especially against people with disabilities. The global animal advocacy movement, also referred to as animal liberation and animal rights, arose in response to, and attempts to destroy, the view that nature and nonhuman animals are inferior to humans and the cultures they have created. Native American, Indigenous, and First Nations, on the other hand, while they did

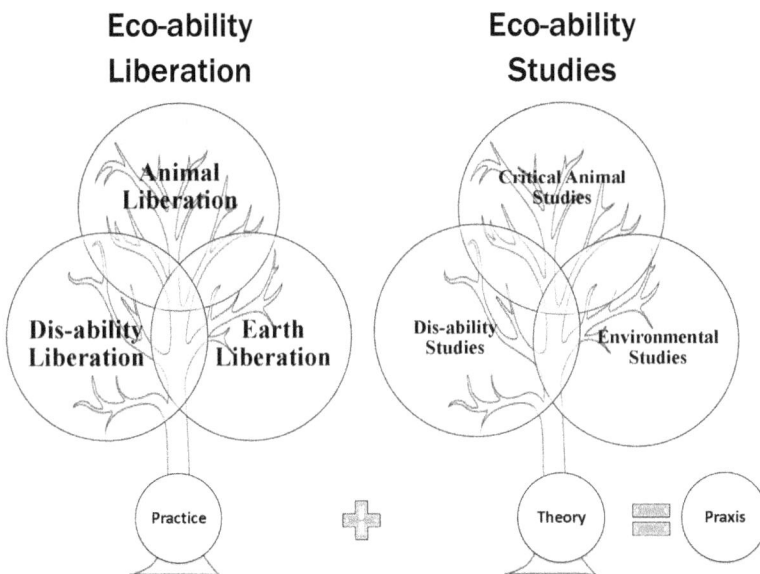

FIGURE 12.1 Eco-ability Liberation plus Eco-ability Studies

utilize natural and nonhuman animal resources (which some see as oppressive), never fully distanced themselves from the circle of life, nor did they stigmatize nature as a violent place to be dominated and overcome.

Ableist Rhetoric in the Animal Advocacy Movement

Western culture is replete with comments meant to demean humans through their comparison to nonhuman animals: "you are such a pig," "you are acting like an animal," "stop acting like a bitch," "he's a dog," "you are as fat as a whale," etc. Similarly, people with disabilities are stigmatized and marginalized with popular comments such as: "you are retarded," suggesting a person is not cool; "you are a freak," suggesting a person has uncommon sexual behaviours or simply acts outside the norm; "why are you acting so lame?," suggesting that a person is boring; and "you are acting crazy," suggesting that a person is not in control of their actions.[12] Many ableist conversations also occur in the animal advocacy movement. Meat eaters are referred to as "crazy," "stupid," "dumb," "idiotic," or "retarded." I have personally overheard such conversations, and when I question the speaker's word choice, the individual will more often than not be defensive rather than reflective.

Often even within social movements whose mission is to end oppressions of all kinds, homophobic, racist, classist, and sexist language is employed. For example, a connection between ableism and speciesism has recently manifested in the animal advocacy movement with the concept of being a "vegan freak." First coined by Bob and Jenna Torres, authors of *Vegan Freak: Being Vegan in a Non-vegan World* and dedicated animal advocates and vegans, the term and the book title were developed ironically to spotlight the social deviance of those who chose veganism, as those who eschew animal products may be marginalized for their "abnormal" behaviour.[13] Torres and Torres write, "So, regardless of how 'normal' you are, in a world where consuming animal products is the norm, you're always going to be seen as the freak if you obviously and clearly refuse to take part in an act of consumption that is central to our everyday lives, our cultures, and even our very own personal identities."[14]

Torres and Torres are social justice scholar-activists who, like most animal advocates who challenge the assumption that veganism is an "oddity," do not critically address the use of the term "freak" or other ableist language. Only once in the book do the authors possibly make a disability reference. Torres and Torres write, "If you're like Bob, planning ahead is something for organized people without ADHD, so it may strike you as incredibly dull."[15] This sentence, which was not critically deconstructed in the book, suggests that people like Bob Torres who perhaps have ADHD are disorganized and that being disorganized is somehow exciting. Further, because this sentence is not critiqued, it is not clear if Bob has ADHD or if the authors are simply making a common ableist "joke." (My assumption is that the latter is taking place.)

Freak is a term historically applied to those with disabilities. As defined by Robert Bogdan in *Freak Show*, a freak has historically been referred to as either those that are not colonial and European, such as Native Americans, First Nations, and Indigenous groups or, "the second major category of exhibit [in the freak show] consisted of 'monsters,' the medical term for people born with a demonstrable difference. *Lusus naturae*, or 'freaks of nature,' were of interest to physicians for whom the field of teratology, the study of these so-called monsters, had become a fad."[16] Bogdan provides a critical summary of certain responses toward people with physical disabilities (i.e., freaks) as an historical social construction. He writes, "Our reaction to freaks is not a function of some deep-seated fear or some 'energy' that they give off; it is, rather, the result of our socialization, and of the way our social institutions managed these people's identities. Freak shows are not about isolated individuals, either on platforms or in an audience. They are about organizations and patterned relationships between them and us. 'Freak' is not a quality that belongs to the person on display. It is something that we created: a perspective, a set of practices—a social construction."[17] Those who view vegans from an ableist and speciesist perspective overtly reinforce two myths about why people become vegan: (1) veganism is a behaviour that people with disabilities adopt or (2) people manifest a mental disability when they adopt a vegan diet. Ableist and speciesist perspectives devalue veganism. They are underpinned by the assumption that anyone who deviates from the traditional meat-based diet must have a disorder because they refuse to take part in their culture's traditions. Torres and Torres might be able to get away with reclaiming the term freak if they took the time to explain the history of the term and/or also showed consciousness of doing so. Most importantly, to reclaim a term for empowerment and liberation, they themselves would have to be identified as freaks through social and medical means.

Being a "vegan freak," however, is not the only ableist term in the animal advocacy movement, for we also have *moral schizophrenia* to consider, which has gained enough cultural meaning to become part of a title in the first volume of this book, as noted in my introduction. Introduced by Gary Francione, a law professor at Rutgers University, in his book *Introduction to Animal Rights: Your Child or the Dog?*, moral schizophrenia refers to how people care for nonhuman animals such as dogs and cats while they exploit other species for food, product testing, clothes, and entertainment.[18] In short, moral schizophrenia is hypocrisy: saying one thing, that animals matter, but doing the opposite, treating animals as if they don't matter. Francione uses the term schizophrenia not in a medical manner, as he is not an MD or a psychiatrist, but to stigmatize those who do not support animal liberation. After a number of Internet critiques arguing that Francione's use of the term schizophrenia is ableist, he published a defence on his blog:

> Some people accuse me of confusing moral schizophrenia with multiple/split personality. . . . When I talk about moral schizophrenia, I am seeking to describe the delusional and confused way that we think about animals as a social/moral matter. That confusion can, of course, include conflicting or inconsistent ways of looking at animals (some are family members; others are dinner) but that does not mean that I am describing a classic split or multiple personality. Our moral schizophrenia, which involves our deluding ourselves about animal sentience and the similarities between humans and other animals, and an enormous amount of confusion about the moral status of nonhumans, is a phenomenon that is quite complicated and has many different aspects.[19]

Francione begins his argument by differentiating schizophrenia from multiple or split personality disorder. However, he has not addressed the remaining problem that *both* schizophrenia and multiple/split personality are medically determined disorders, regardless of the fact that the average person often confuses the two diagnoses. Neither term should be use to casually insult or categorize a person or a group, much the same way that "freak" and "lame" are unacceptable terms from a disability studies perspective. Schizophrenia often conjures up images of violent behaviour, so that rhetoric only serves to reinforce the stereotype, as "moral schizophrenia" is conceptually applied to those who regularly engage in the violent acts of eating meat, wearing animal skins, etc.

Francione did apologize to people who were offended by his use of medical terminology in a stigmatizing manner, while continuing to defend his rationale: "Some people think that by using the term, I am stigmatizing those who have clinical schizophrenia because it implies that they are immoral people. I am sincerely sorry—and I mean that—if anyone has interpreted the term in that way and that is certainly not what I intended. Schizophrenia is a recognized condition that is characterized by confused and delusional thinking."[20] Now, he identifies schizophrenia as a "condition," which quickly snowballs into describing it as a "disorder" that is not culturally "desirable," as stated in the following passage from that same post:

> To say that we are delusional and confused when it comes to moral issues is not to say that those who suffer from clinical schizophrenia are immoral. It is only to say that many of us think about important moral matters in a completely confused, delusional, and incoherent way. I am certainly not saying that those who suffer from clinical schizophrenia are immoral! ... To say that moral schizophrenia stigmatizes clinical schizophrenics is like saying that to talk about "drug use spreading like cancer" stigmatizes cancer victims. Moreover, cancer does not spread quickly, rather it often takes many years for it to grow into something deadly and also is not contagious. I hope this clarifies what I mean when I talk about our moral schizophrenia when it comes to animal ethics. I also hope that it is clear that I am not using that term in a way that does or is intended to convey that clinical schizophrenics are immoral. ... Some critics argue that it is sufficient to say that our moral views about nonhuman animals are contradictory or confused. No, it's not sufficient. When it comes to nonhuman animals, our views are profoundly delusional and I am using that term literally as indicative of what might be called a social form of schizophrenia. Some critics claim that it is sufficient to use "delusional." But delusion is what characterizes the clinical form of schizophrenia and anyone who objected to the use of schizophrenia as ableist would have the same, and in my view groundless, objection to "delusional." Some critics claim that schizophrenia is different from cancer because no one would think that having cancer is a good thing. I confess that this objection is puzzling. I am unfamiliar with anyone who argues as a general matter that cancer or clinical schizophrenia are desirable conditions to have. Yes, there are people who claim that their schizophrenia has led them to great insight; but the same is true of cancer victims. In any event, if "moral schizophrenia" is ableist, then so is the expression "drugs are a cancer on society" or "our polices in the Middle East are shortsighted" or "we are blind to the consequences of our actions" or "when it comes to poverty, our proposed solutions suffer from a poverty of ambition."[21]

The problem here, of course, is that those with cancer are stigmatized as victims in contemporary American culture, and not as inferior or a threat, which is the case for most individuals with physical and mental disabilities (and those who use drugs, for that matter). Quite the opposite is true for those with cancer, as they are often given sympathy and kindness. Thus, Francione has offered a faulty analogy to prove his point, making his apology mere professional apologia. Also, his inability to critique his own ableism is proven by his suggesting that the phrases with which he ends the blog post above are not offensive (i.e., "blind" and "short-sighted"). On the contrary, those who use those phrases, analogies, and comments *are* ableist; whenever someone is describing an individual or group in a negative or insulting manner by using labels that have been historically or are currently meant to describe people with physical or mental disabilities, they are by definition stigmatizing and, more specifically, they are being ableist.

Francione strives to make the parallel between cancer and schizophrenia, yet one is a disease while the other is a personal characteristic that makes up who that person is. In our ableist society, both of them are considered disabilities. Therefore, moral schizophrenia demeans those who have schizophrenia and reinforces the idea that people should not be schizophrenic (as if there is a choice). Francione is certainly not the only ableist in the animal advocacy movement. There are many who use phrases such as "we must cripple the animal agriculture industry," "society is blind to the exploitation of animals," and "vivisectors are idiots." Even many presenters at a recent Thinking about Animals/10th Anniversary North American ICAS (Institute for Critical Animal Studies) conference at Brock University in St. Catharines, Ontario, used Francione's term "moral schizophrenia," which I publicly critiqued to hold people accountable for their ableism. I do not want to dismiss what Francione offers the animal liberation movement, such as his scholarship in the realm of veganism, animal abolition, and critiques of animals as property. I do not use Francione as an example because he is the only one using ableist rhetoric, but because he is such a prominent figure within the animal rights movement that he can aid in ending ableism.

Most of the leaders within the animal advocacy movement, from queer/trans scholar-activists to anarcho-ALF supporters, use language and strategies that are ableist. On blogs and Facebook, fellow activists are calling animal abusers—and each other—"idiots," "blind to the truth," "psychotic," etc. However, using these medical terms without any sense of self-reflection suggests that those individuals are being reactionary and, albeit unintentionally, oppressive. They likely do not have any expertise in medicine, psychology, or psychiatry, but they borrow terminology from those industries that have aided in the construction of normalcy in a futile attempt to fight oppression. In other words, they are attempting to fight oppression with a form of oppression that they cannot or will not acknowledge.

Academics, Facebookers, and bloggers are not the only one's using ableist language. At a fur protest recently I heard two classic chants: "When animals are abused, what do you do? Stand up! Fight back!" and "Stop the murder! Stop the pain! [the company name here] is insane!" The first chant is ableist because of its lack of inclusion of those that are not able to physically stand. The second chant is ableist because of the use of the term "insane," which stigmatizes those with mental disabilities as being violent.

These critiques of ableism parallel similar critiques against sexism and patriarchy within the animal advocacy movement. I can say first-hand that I learned a great deal about challenging my own sexism and patriarchy and how the organizations and campaigns I was involved with promoted it. I believe that the disability and eco-ability community can learn from and dialogue with feminists and eco-feminists within the animal advocacy movement on successful inclusive educational approaches and activist tactics. Some actions employed were conference walkouts, conference takeovers, blogs dedicated to the issue, boycotting campaigns, mediations, and accountability dialogues. I have begun to confront groups and individuals, but there are so few individuals that are socio-politically conscious about disability within the animal advocacy movement that, at this time, only a few activists exist to critically inform others of their ableism, one of whom is A.J. Withers.

In *Earth, Animal, and Disability Liberation*, Withers adds an important critique of People for the Ethical Treatment of Animals (PETA) by stating that PETA "warned that eating fish 'can cause mental retardation and physical disability in children' (PETA, n.d., para. 7). PETA also ran a billboard campaign called 'Got Autism?' that depicted a bowl of milk with Cheerios arranged in a sad face that (falsely) linked dairy consumption to autism (PETA, n.d.)."[22] On June 16, 2008, on the *PETA Files*, the official blog of PETA, a post was published titled, "Top Five Reasons Only Stupid Girls Brag about Eating Meat." This post reinforced ableism and sexism by suggesting that any intelligent female wants to be thin because it is the social norm of attractiveness in Western culture. Such rhetoric creates a stigma by what I term "thin supremacists" against those who do not meet a weight ideal crafted by corporations, advertisers, and other forms of media. I am opposed to using the term "fat-phobic" or any form of phobia in relation to discrimination of others because it puts the blame on the marginalized and makes those that are phobic, such as homophobic or Islamophobia, apparent victims of a disability. However, these "phobic" individuals do not have a disability; they are simply prejudiced against those that they fear and find to be a threat to normalcy, which promotes speciesism, racism, anti-LGBTQIA attitudes, ageism, sexism, and other forms of oppression and domination. Withers further critiques two more animal advocacy organizations, the National Anti-vivisection Society and In Defense of Animals, which focus mostly on antivivisection and animal testing. Withers writes that these two organizations "depict disability as solely negative, and something that resources should be used to avoid. Both organizations argue that 'birth defects' should be prevented, and call on human genetic research to achieve this."[23]

This critique of the animal advocacy movement would not be complete without mention of Peter Singer, author of *Animal Liberation*, the book that launched the modern animal advocacy movement. I argue that because Peter Singer is the founding philosopher of modern animal advocacy, the movement is, by nature, ableist. Singer reinforces the stigmatization of people with disabilities and suggests that being a nonhuman animal is more valuable than an individual with disabilities. For example, as Ida Hammer of the *Vegan Ideal* blog notes, Singer writes in *Rethinking Life and Death*, "To have a child with Down syndrome is to have a very different experience from having a normal child. It can still be a warm and loving experience, but we must have lowered expectations of our child's abilities. We cannot expect a child with Down syndrome to play the guitar, to develop an appreciation of science fiction, to learn a foreign language, to chat with us about the latest Woody Allen movie, or to be a respectable athlete, basketballer or tennis player."[24] With these words, Singer reinforces the value of normalcy by stressing that children with disabilities are deficient and that parents raising such children will not have a complete parenting experience because of all the activities they will miss out on (i.e., talking about Woody Allen). However, children with Down syndrome can excel in music, sports, education, language, art, and, as even Singer admits, they are capable of love and warmth. Withers' chapter also notes Singer's following statement: "When the death of a disabled infant will lead to the birth of another infant with better prospects of a happy life, the total amount of happiness will be greater if the disabled infant is killed. The loss of happy life for the first infant it outweighed by the gain of a happier life for the second."[25]

Singer writes in *Practical Ethics* (1993), "Killing a disabled infant is not morally equivalent to killing a person" (191). It is not surprising then that the disability liberation community has protested Singer. Paula Routly writes in her article, "To Die For," "Singer has plenty of detractors. According to *The New Yorker* magazine, he's perhaps the 'most controversial philosopher alive. He's certainly among the most influential.' When Princeton University hired him on as a professor of bioethics in 1999, a group called Not Dead Yet circulated a petition in opposition, characterizing his views as a 'blatant violation of Princeton University's policy of respect for people with disabilities."[26] Routly goes on to cite Eli Clare, author of *Exile and Pride: Disability, Queerness, and Liberation*, a writer and activist who protested Singer at the University of Vermont because, as he states, "I wouldn't have made Peter Singer's criteria" as one to be spared death.[27] Further, Clare is fearful that if Singer's philosophy was put into policy, infants would become viable research subjects.

The Eco-ability Movement

Similar to the global animal advocacy movement, the environmental movement has emerged out of the Western-colonial, Euro-American paradigm, and it was founded and dominated by white, heterosexual, able-bodied, wealthy, Christian males who ate nonhuman meat and exploited others. The environmental movement has been challenged by many for its contradictory romanticization and destruction of nature. For example, Indigenous and First Peoples argue against a Christian global conquest advocated by the Western environmental movement;[28] ecofeminists challenge patriarchal domination, exploitation, and domestication of nature, nonhuman animals, and women;[29] green anarchists shed light on the commodification of nature and nonhuman animals by capitalism and authoritarianism;[30] and environmental justice activists address the intersectional connection of the destruction of the planet to the destruction of communities of colour, both being polluted and exploited for labour and resources.[31] If the global animal advocacy and environmental movements want to grow, they must challenge, resist, and critically examine their white, heterosexual, able-bodied, wealthy, formally educated male-dominated leadership along with their concomitant theories and histories.

Currently, these two movements are advocating that if you look professional and physically attractive, you are more able to persuade people to support your cause. Indeed, this may be true, but this is a reality that must be challenged, not enforced, by social justice movements. Some of the leading organizations are telling their employees to read *The 7 Habits of Highly Effective People* by Stephen R. Covey instead of books about animal and environmental ethics. These two movements, rather than moving toward a grassroots volunteer-based paradigm, are adopting a corporate model, which in turn sees underground and civil disobedience actions as a liability and antithetical to their goals. Rather than growing more radical and critical, the animal and environmental movements are becoming sanitized and "green-washed."

Eco-ability is the only theory and movement to make an intersectional connection between nonhuman animals, the ecological world, and those with dis-abilities. Those involved in this movement hope that eco-ability will grow and be taken as seriously as those critical perspectives noted above. Eco-ability challenges and resists speciesism, ableism, and unrestrained cultural "civilization," while also dismantling the socially constructed binaries of human vs. animal, normal vs. abnormal, and domestic vs. wild.

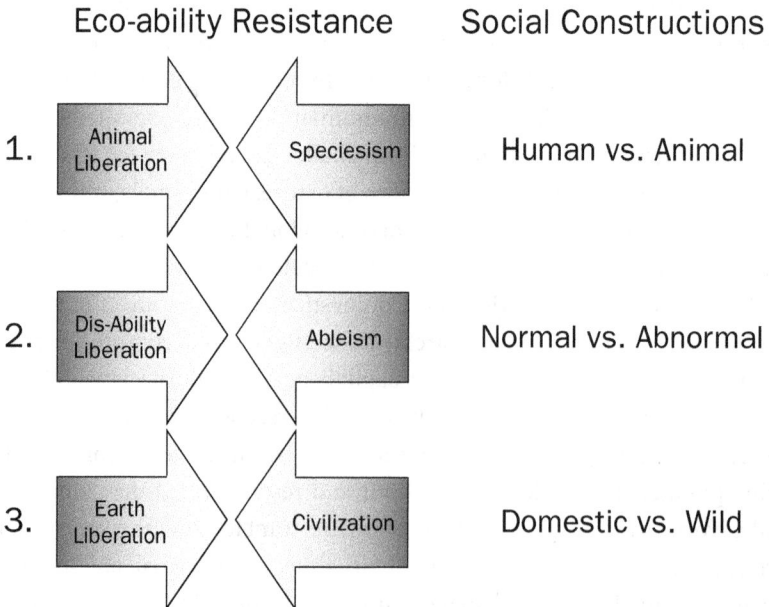

FIGURE 12.2   Eco-ability Resistance and Social Constructions

Eco-ability is not welfarist, reformist, or conservative. Eco-ability opposes the views and work of Temple Grandin, a professor and doctor of animal science with autism who has become famous for her design of so-called humane slaughterhouses and livestock farms. Eco-ability acknowledges the inherent contradiction within the idea and practice of humane slaughter. Grandin argues that her experience as a woman with autism allows her to relate to and understand nonhuman animals; this perspective simplifies and generalizes all nonhuman and autistic human experiences.[32] Just as eco-ability is opposed to welfarism, it is also opposed to apolitical, detached, theoretical analysis of the relationship between non-human and human animals, such as in the fields of animal studies, human–animal studies, and posthumanism. It is a philosophy that aligns itself under the field and movement of critical animal studies that is also against all domination and notions of normalcy while championing an interwoven, interdependent, collaborative relationship with all and a respect of differ-ence. Eco-ability, therefore, is not about paving pathways through the forest for those with wheelchairs, nor is it about establishing paths for walkers to enjoy nature or to exploit dolphins, horses, dogs, or any other nonhuman animal in the name of service, rehabilitation, testing, entertainment, pro-tection, or food. Eco-ability praises the different abilities one has—flying, crawling, swimming, rolling, or walking—and promotes a locally grown, non-packaged, non-processed, organic, vegan-based diet. This movement is for the liberation of all animals, the planet, and those with disabilities; it is for defending their voices in a world that often refuses to acknowledge that nonhumans, humans with disabilities, and the ecological world do, in fact, have voices. Because the relationship between disability and animals is fairly new, it is important that that relationship is maintained by animal liberationists and those with disabilities. Those without disabilities should be strong allies who can cite the work of, provide space for, and move to the side to support the voices of those with disabilities. Those with dis-ability and animals are not mere subjects or concepts to be studied, but an oppressed group wanting liberation.

Eco-ability views disability not as a medical condition, but rather as a social construction that targets those who are oppressed and excluded. For example, women and people of colour are disabled because society is patri-archal and racist. Moreover, nonhuman animals in a speciesist society are also disabled. There are, of course, certain human and nonhuman animals deemed more disabled mentally and physically than others, such as those in wheelchairs and those that have depression. Consideration of disabilities has recently extended to nonhuman animals; there are wheelchairs for dogs, prosthetics for elephants and turtles, and therapy and medication for nonhuman animals with mental disabilities. In the past, such nonhuman animals would have been euthanized, and many still are. Yet this forward momentum, however slight, challenges normalcy and promotes the value of differences.

Eco-ability is against normalcy and standardization, the needed theoretical concepts of capitalism, which are commonly promoted in the packaging and processing of standard products within in a factory. Eco-ability is against any medical or digital technology modifications for economic profit or socio-political control. I have developed eight values of eco-ability: (1) difference and diversity, (2) holistic transformation through dialogue

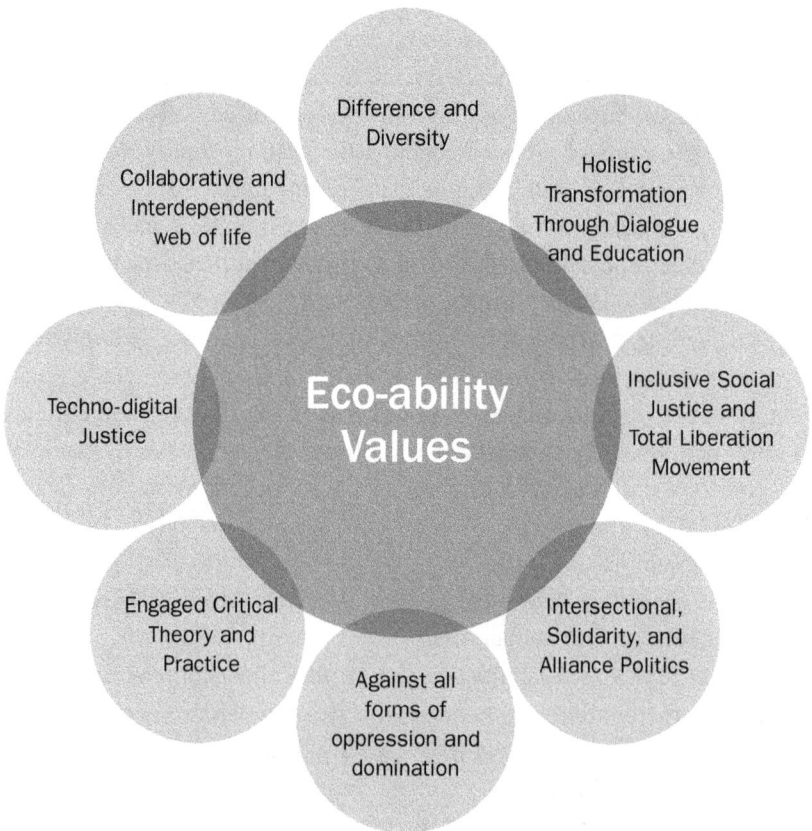

FIGURE 12.3 Eco-ability Values

and education, (3) inclusive social justice and a total liberation movement (dedicated to liberating all and to ending all forms of domination), (4) intersectionality, solidarity, and alliance politics, (5) opposition to all forms of oppression and domination, (6) engaged critical theory and practice, (7) techno-digital justice, and (8) a collaborative and interdependent web of life. These values are noted in the diagram below.

Eco-ability acknowledges the mass environmental destruction and animal exploitation produced in developing digital technology. For that reason, eco-ability argues that if one is to use technology, it must be to help others and the planet. Digital technology should not be used merely as fun, convenient, entertaining gadgets around our offices, homes, or on vacations as we partake in capitalist indulgences. Technology is not apolitical or natural; therefore, whoever uses digital technology should use it to promote social justice and peace. Digital technology should not be used as entertainment or for the use of economic profit from the lands that are destroyed to mine for it and the nonhuman animals on which it is tested.

Similar to the environmental justice movement, eco-ability also calls for a new path to protect and live in the world, arguing that the environmental movement and environmental studies are rooted in domination, purification, and the so-called normalcy of the ecological world. Through their images and narratives, Western environmentalists have traditionally constructed the idea of nature as peaceful/majestic/perfect/ideal.[33] Their stories construct the perfect/ideal snake, perfect/ideal shark, perfect ladybug, perfect hummingbird, perfect lion, perfect tree, etc. Muir writes in *Our National Parks*, "It took more than three thousand years to make some of the trees in these Western woods—trees that are still standing in perfect strength and beauty, waving and singing in the mighty forests of the Sierra."[34] Muir goes on to write in *John of the Mountains: The Unpublished Journals of John Muir*, "No synonym for God is so perfect as Beauty. Whether as seen carving the lines of the mountains with glaciers, or gathering matter into stars, or planning the movements of water, or gardening—still all is Beauty!"[35] The constructed images of perfection are perpetuated in art, tattoos, logos, mascots, books, magazines, cartoons, and movies, and these same narratives "freakify" those that deviate from socially constructed images of what is natural and, consequently, normal. Eco-ability is a powerful challenge to these narratives and images.

To conclude, this chapter is dedicated to opening the discussion of disability liberation, which was missing from *Animal Subjects* (2008).

Eco-ability opposes any theory for animal advocacy that is solely focused on the primacy of intelligence, mind, or sentience of a living being because it reinforces the concepts of normalcy and respectability. To be successful, global animal advocacy cannot be about the status of the Other, but about one's own morals, ethics, and actions grounded in respect of all, void of exploitation, control, or oppression of any element, plant, or animal.[36]

NOTES

1. Snyder and Mitchell, *Cultural Locations*.
2. Nocella et al., *Earth, Animal, and Disability Liberation*.
3. Castricano, *Animal Subjects*, 2.
4. *Hir* is a gender nonconformist pronoun to replace the socially constructed gender binary of *his* or *her*.
5. Corrigan, *Stigma of Mental Illness*.
6. Davis, *Bending Over Backwards*.
7. Dunayer, *Speciesism*.
8. Rosenau, *Post-Modernism and the Social Sciences*, 5.
9. Snyder and Mitchell, *Cultural Locations*, 31.
10. Spiegel, *Dreaded Comparison*, 16.
11. Adams and Socha, "Shocking into Submission," 169 (emphasis mine).
12. Snyder and Mitchell, *Cultural Locations*.
13. Torres and Torres, *Vegan Freak*.
14. Ibid., 8.
15. Ibid., 33.
16. Bogdan, *Freak Show*, 6.
17. Ibid., x–xi.
18. Francione, *Introduction to Animal Rights*.
19. Francione, "Moral Schizophrenia."
20. Ibid.
21. Ibid.
22. Withers, "Disableism," 112.
23. Ibid.
24. Singer, *Rethinking Life and Death*, 213, quoted in Hammer, "Ableism and the Eugenics of Peter Singer."
25. Ibid., 163.
26. Routly, "To Die For."
27. Ibid.
28. Churchill, *Struggle for the Land*.
29. Mies and Shiva, *Ecofeminism*.

30. Zerzan, *Against Civilization*.
31. Pellow, *Garbage Wars*.
32. Adams and Socha, "Shocking into Submission."
33. See, for example, Muir, *My First Summer*.
34. Muir, *Our National Parks*, 364.
35. Muir, *John of the Mountains*, 208.
36. I would like to thank Kim Socha for working with me and helping me edit and clarify many points in this chapter.

BIBLIOGRAPHY

Adams, Deanna, and Kimberly Socha. "Shocking into Submission: Suppressive Practices and Use of Behavior Modification on Nonhuman Animals, People with Disabilities, and the Environment." In *Earth, Animal, and Disability Liberation: The Rise of the Eco-ability Movement*, edited by Anthony J. Nocella II, Judy K.C. Bentley, and Janet Duncan, 159–73. New York: Peter Lang, 2012.

Amster, Randall, Abraham DeLeon, Luis Fernandez, Anthony J. Nocella II, and Deric Shannon, eds. *Contemporary Anarchist Studies: Anthology of Anarchy in the Academy*. New York: Routledge, 2009.

Binet, Alfred. *The Mind and the Brain: Being the Authorised Translation of l'Âme et le Corps*. London, 1907. Repr., Charleston, SC: BiblioBazaar, 2007.

Best, Steven and Anthony J. Nocella II. *Igniting a Revolution: Voices in Defense of the Earth*. Oakland, CA: AK Press, 2006.

Bodley, John H. *Cultural Anthropology: Tribes, States, and the Global System*. New York: McGraw Hill, 2005.

Bogdan, Robert. *Freak Show: Presenting Human Oddities for Amusement and Profit*. Chicago: University of Chicago Press, 1998.

Castricano, Jodey. *Animal Subjects: An Ethical Reader in a Posthuman World*. Waterloo, ON: Wilfrid Laurier University Press, 2008.

Churchill, Ward. *Struggle for the Land: Native North American Resistance to Genocide, Ecocide, and Colonization*. San Francisco: City Lights, 2002.

Corrigan, Patrick W. *On the Stigma of Mental Illness: Practical Strategies for Research and Social Change*. Washington, DC: American Psychological Association, 2006.

Davis, Lennard. *Bending Over Backwards: Disability, Dismodernism and Other Difficult Positions*. New York: New York University Press, 2002.

———. *The Disability Studies Reader*. New York: Routledge, 1997.

DeSilva, Jr., D. "Mental Disorders of the Criminally Insane." *Insider's Health* (online magazine). Accessed April 5, 2012. http://www.insidershealth.com/article/mental_disorders_of_the_criminally_insane/4649.

Dunayer, Joan. *Speciesism*. New York: Lantern Books, 2004.

Effron, Lauren, and Russell Goldman. "Environmental Militant Killed by Police at Discovery Channel Headquarters." *ABC News*, September 1, 2010. http://abcnews.go.com/US/gunman-enters-discovery-channel-headquarters -employees-evacuated/story?id=11535128.

Francione, Gary L. *Introduction to Animal Rights: Your Child or the Dog?* Philadelphia: Temple University Press, 2000.

———. "A Note on Moral Schizophrenia." *Animal Rights: The Abolitionist Approach* (blog), August 12, 2009. http://www.abolitionistapproach.com/a-note-on-moral -schizophrenia/.

Hammer, Ida. "Ableism and the Eugenics of Peter Singer." *Vegan Ideal* (blog). Mayfirst.org, May 12, 2008. http://veganideal.mayfirst.org/content/ableism-and -eugenics-peter-singer.

Harding, Sandra, ed. *The Feminist Standpoint Theory Reader: Intellectual and Political Controversies.* New York: Routledge, 2003.

Lynch, Michael J., and Raymond Michalowski. *Primer in Radical Criminology: Critical Perspectives on Crime, Power, and Identity.* Monsey, NY: Criminal Justice Press, 2006.

Mies, Maria, and Vandana Shiva. *Ecofeminism.* London: Zed Books, 1993.

Muir, John. *John of the Mountains: The Unpublished Journals of John Muir.* Madison, WI: University of Wisconsin Press, 1938.

———. *My First Summer in the Sierra.* New York: Riverside Press Cambridge, 1911.

———. *Our National Parks.* Madison, WI: University of Wisconsin Press, 1981. E-book.

Nocella, Anthony J., II. "Emergence of Disability Pedagogy." *Journal for Critical Education Policy Studies* 6, no. 2 (2008). http://www.jceps.com/wp-content/ uploads/PDFs/6-2-05.pdf.

Nocella, Anthony J., II, Judy K.C. Bentley, and Janet M. Duncan, eds. *Earth, Animal, and Disability Liberation: The Emergence of the Eco-ability Movement.* New York: Peter Lang, 2012.

Pellow, David Naguib. *Garbage Wars: The Struggle for Environmental Justice in Chicago.* Cambridge, MA: MIT Press, 2002.

PETA (People for the Ethical Treatment of Animals). "Top Five Reasons Only Stupid Girls Brag about Eating Meat." Blog. PETA website, June 16, 2008. http://www .peta.org/blog/top-five-reasons-stupid-girls-brag-eating-meat/.

Pfohl, Stephen. *Images of Deviance and Social Control: A Sociological History.* 2nd ed. Long Grove, IL: Waveland Press, 2009.

Rosenau, Pauline M. *Post-Modernism and the Social Sciences: Insights, Inroads, and Intrusions.* Princeton: Princeton University Press, 1992.

Routly, Paula. "To Die For." *Seven Days* (blog), October 6, 2004. http://www .sevendaysvt.com/vermont/to-die-for/Content?oid=2129027.

Schou, Nick. *Killing the Messenger: How the CIA's Crack-Cocaine Controversy Destroyed Journalist Gary Webb.* New York: Nation Books, 2006.

Scott, Peter Dale, and Jonathan Marshall. *Cocaine Politics: Drugs, Armies, and the CIA in Central America.* Updated ed. Berkeley: University of California Press, 1998.

Singer, Peter. *Practical Ethics.* 2nd ed. Cambridge, UK: Cambridge University Press, 1993.

———. *Rethinking Life and Death: The Collapse of Our Traditional Ethics.* New York: St. Martin's, 1994.

Snyder, Sharon L., and David T. Mitchell. *Cultural Locations of Disability.* Chicago: University of Chicago Press, 2006.

Spiegel, Marjorie. *The Dreaded Comparison: Human and Animal Slavery.* New York: Mirror Books, 1996.

Swan, Jim. "Disabilities, Bodies, Voices." In *Disability Studies: Enabling the Humanities,* edited by Sharon L. Snyder, Brenda Jo Brueggemann, and Rosemarie Garland-Thomson, 283–95. New York: Modern Language Association of America, 2002.

Torres, Bob, and Jenna Torres. *Vegan Freak: Being Vegan in a Non-vegan World.* Colton, NY: Tofu Hound Press, 2010.

van der Pijl, Kees. *Nomads, Empires, States: Modes of Foreign Relations and Political Economy.* Vol. 1. London: Pluto Press, 2007.

Webb, Gary. *Dark Alliance: The CIA, the Contras, and the Crack Cocaine Explosion.* New York: Seven Stories Press, 1999.

Withers, A.J. "Disableism within Animal Advocacy and Environmentalism." In *Earth, Animal, and Disability Liberation: The Rise of the Eco-ability Movement,* edited by Anthony J. Nocella II, Judy K.C. Bentley, and Janet Duncan, 111–25. New York: Peter Lang, 2012.

Zerzan, John. *Against Civilization: Readings and Reflections.* Port Townsend, WA: Feral House, 2005.

13

On Being a Pragmatist

Reflections on Animals, Feminism, and Personal Politics

⊰⊱

Lynda Birke

I came of age through and with feminist politics. I was involved in both women's and environmental activism in the UK during the 1970s, and in both activism and associated scholarly inquiry. They were heady days. But all too soon, the alliances we had built seemed to crumble as internecine strife developed; squabbles ensued over who had the moral high ground, over who was the most oppressed, over who did the most to change the world. And, as women's studies gained its ground within the ivory towers of academia, so it seemed to me to separate from much of the activism that had borne it.[1]

So it is with some trepidation that I watch what seems to me to be a tension between critical animal studies (CAS) and what Best refers to as "mainstream" animal studies.[2] One of the pleasures of working in human–animal studies over the past years has been that, for me, some of it is still directly associated with the radical politics of animal activism (another pleasure is that it has provided me with a scholarly excuse for doing what I have most loved over my life: being with, and thinking about, nonhuman animals). My experiences of feminist politics make me worry about divisions and their impact on what we are trying to do in CAS. Those anxieties were brought home to me at a recent international conference, while observing participants in discussion separating themselves off—CAS from the rest of human–animal studies, CAS from animal science.

My starting point for this chapter, then, is a concern to find ways to retain dialogue and discussion without schisms. But I also want to draw on other lessons from feminism to explore several themes in thinking about animals. While my perception of the changes wrought in feminism—what I see as its over-academicization, for example—might bring a salutary lesson, there are also several ideas in feminist theory that can positively contribute to human–animal studies, too.[3] Feminist debates about embodiment and about how to make research accountable are particularly relevant here.

As this is, in part, personal reflection, perhaps I should begin with biographical background. Trained originally as a biologist, doing research in animal behaviour, I was also working in the newly emerging field of women's studies. Research interests shifted, and I came to focus more on how biological ideas impacted other areas of inquiry—in feminism, and in human–animal studies.[4]

Studying biology in the first place inevitably brought problems to someone who was passionate about animals and who read antivivisectionist pamphlets in primary school. It was a love of nature that drew me to biology, yet this same field of study also used methods that dismembered nature. Specializing in animal behaviour—where I could study whole animals— was a response to that dilemma. So, too, was my continuing interest in the animal experimentation controversy—the topic of a later research project.[5] Biological practices use methods that are often invasive and cause animal suffering; yet it is also the discipline of biology that yields much knowledge *about* other animals—especially through work in cognitive ethology.[6]

Still, I have lived all my life with various companion animals (mostly dogs and horses)—which in turn has contributed to the interdisciplinary connections that have dominated my research. It is that linkage that I want to use here, in particular connections between human–animal studies and feminist ideas and politics.[7] What can feminism contribute to our thinking about human relationships to nonhuman animals? This chapter is a personal reflection on some issues that continue to bother me in thinking about animals. It is very much a personal statement rather than an argument for a particular position—a soliloquy on some issues that I see as worrying both for my research and for my own day-to-day engagement with animal others. And it is a plea for us to work to avoid potential divisions and to seek ways in which both theory and activism can coexist and nourish each other.

Splitting (Animal) Hairs

As already noted, my golden memories of feminist activism are tempered by recollections of divisions within the movement. I remember well my dismay as, over time, the connection with direct action began to erode: women's "studies" was born and seemed to bring with it new recruits interested in "gender" as a theoretical construct, but often having little experience in the collective practices of feminism. Splits emerged between activists and theorists, between feminists with different political perspectives. Are we in danger of similar divisions within animal advocacy?

To be sure, there may be grounds for concern that some studies of humans and animals seem rather arcane, divorced from any understanding of how humans *oppress* other animals. But there is space for combining activism and theory, especially in CAS; indeed, that is its strength, as made evident by contributors to this volume who seek to bring certain ethical and political commitments to the fore in their writing. Doesn't such breadth of understanding help to build stronger politics? Theory is vitally important, but theory without practice will not change the world. For all my feelings that feminist activism and scholarly inquiry often diverge, there is also recognition that we need both. Maggie Humm put it succinctly: "The feminist fight is not on the page but in the home, at work and on the streets. But the struggle comes from ideas. Feminist theory is a river fed by different feminisms and different feminists."[8] So, too, we can say that CAS needs many tributaries.

The possibility of splits within the broad field of human–animal studies also concerns me deeply. Particularly worrying is the risk that CAS, with its emphasis on understanding (and challenging) speciesist oppression, becomes distanced from the rest of human–animal studies. Now, perhaps some will say that much of the latter is already depoliticized and too focused on theoretical abstractions, too concerned with dwelling within the house of respectable academic conventions. At times, studies in human–animal studies can seem merely to shore up the processes of power that keep animals oppressed, rather than providing means to question them. Yet it is doubtful that splitting apart helps anyone much. I was very troubled by a recent suggestion, for example, that CAS "challenges human–animal studies as reinforcing single-issue politics and the false binary of human–animals and is opposed to animal studies as being an oppressive field of study that exploits and murders nonhuman animals."[9] Such claims are, I believe, damaging; they produce schisms that potentially restrict our ability to work together for change and can help to depoliticize human–animal studies more broadly.

One major reason why splits are problematic is because they can decrease possibilities for change. There are myriad ways in which change might be effected: we can work toward cultural shifts in attitudes to animals, to achieve better status for them all; we can work within (or against) political systems, either through direct action, through consumer choices, or through the ballot box. No doubt we will disagree over appropriate strategies for bringing about a new world—and those disagreements are important, not least because they generate discussion and development of new ideas. But ongoing schisms and naked accusations within our ranks are liable to reduce our discursive power, decreasing our collective ability to win over hearts and minds. Whether one believes in gradual change through existing institutions, or more radical challenges to speciesist capitalism, it matters that we find ways to reduce strife. It matters not only for long-term survival of animal advocacy but also, more importantly, for animals themselves: if infighting reduces effectiveness, then change won't happen.

In what follows, I pick up on three, somewhat disparate themes that have concerned me in my work and day-to-day encounters with animals. These are practical pragmatism, "pets," and politics in research. In each case, my thinking has been informed by experiences in engaging with feminist politics, which, I will argue, can bring some important ideas to thinking about nonhuman animals. To the irritation of many, I tend to meander around a middle ground on each of these. But it is precisely middle ground that I hope we can all find, as some way to meet across the divides. At the end, drawing again on feminist debates, I argue for a greater emphasis on making research and writing more accountable to other animals.

On Pragmatism

As the title implies, I consider myself a pragmatist, in the sense that I am willing to work on several levels, *even if*, ideologically, these are contradictory. No doubt some who read this will disagree profoundly, believing that any argument for practical pragmatism lets the side down. I have met many who believe, for example, that doing something to improve the lot of laboratory animals is morally wrong because it merely shores up the practices of animal exploitation. Much though I might desire radical change, however, it is not on the imminent horizon and we must do the best we can, however imperfect. It is simply not possible to live completely free from contradictions. I well remember, in my early years as a radical feminist, learning about the women who set up women-only communes. "Living outside the patriarchy," they called it. That seemed fine to me, until I learned that most of them were claiming benefits from the (patriarchal) state. However much we might have wanted to end patriarchy, and however much we sought to live our lives consistent with feminist politics, we still had to deal with everyday life. There are always going to be contradictions.

While I abhor the myriad cruelties and abuses humans inflict on non-humans and am sympathetic to ideas of animal liberation, I am unhappy with the notion that we should *only* work to abolish exploitative practices, rather than intervening to make animals' lives a little easier here and now. This is one way in which being pragmatic, working on several levels at once, makes more sense for me. For instance, although I loathe many practices that go on in laboratory science, my responses are deeply ambivalent. Of course I hate the suffering that goes on, and I am glad that there are people brave enough to go undercover and discover what is happening in labs, or to take direct action. But I am also happy that there are people doing research to find out ways of improving the lot of animals who currently have to live in labs, to make their lives more comfortable, and I want to see emphasis on providing for these animals' behavioural needs alongside broader political challenges to the very existence of animal experiments. So, I support efforts to understand laboratory animal welfare and to find better ways to enrich the lives of those animals. Similarly, I have many reservations about the existence of zoos; but *while they exist* I want to see efforts to ameliorate the living conditions of the animals held captive there.

Having been in several labs and seen the animals there, I would rather go away knowing that something had been done to make better the lives of *those* animals. I might prefer that they weren't there at all, but can I really go away having gazed into their eyes and ignore those individual lives? That specific suffering? I remember one animal technician telling me that they had to keep the animals in their lab in opaque cages, because the scientists didn't like it "when the animals were watching." Gazing back makes it personal. These animals are no longer so easily relegated to numbers—and most laboratory animals are depersonalized in precisely this way[10]—rather, they become individuals. And it is the individuals whose lives can be improved by schemes to provide enrichment and promote welfare, *despite* the ethical case for abolition.

Another reason for my ambivalence is that I know all too well that much of what I have learned in biology about animals—their behaviour, their physiology—has come historically from the selfsame scientific practices. This is certainly not to condone them, nor to suggest that the studies necessarily have validity across species (they don't—extrapolation often does not work),[11] but simply to recognize that animal pain and suffering has indeed historically produced much of what we call scientific knowledge. Looking at physiology textbooks I studied as a student, I see diagrams (literally) embodying a history of animal bodies, used to provide the knowledge represented by the diagram.

Furthermore, it is highly unlikely that these practices will go away in the near future, however much we might challenge them; they are too deeply rooted in global economic interests. Objections to vivisection have been around for a very long time (and organized political protest for over a century;[12] see Chapter 3, on the movement's use of art in the nineteenth century). While governments may pay some heed to these protests, and to wider public opinion, they also heed demands from scientists and from commercial interests whose ethical frameworks usually prioritize human medical progress over what happens to animals. Resulting legislation is thus inevitably a compromise: the UK's Animals (Scientific Procedures) Act of 1986, for example, has been described as simultaneously the tightest system of regulation in the world by researchers, and a whitewash to protect scientists by antivivisectionist organizations.[13] The practices so abhorred by opponents are, moreover, embedded within a wider culture—requirements to test substances for safety, for example, imply animal testing at some point in development, and national legislation is always framed by legal requirements or their lack elsewhere in our globalized world.

There is undoubtedly continuing opposition to laboratory animal use, which has made some gains: direct testing of potential cosmetics on animals is no longer carried out in the UK, for instance (though it could be transferred to other countries). But the practices of animal experimentation are profoundly entrenched within the economies of most countries in the world. If, then, animals are still being used—in large numbers[14]—then I believe we should both be protesting such use and at the same time working hard to ensure that they suffer as little as possible and that their welfare needs are met. The crucial phrase here is "at the same time": trying to understand how to ameliorate lab animals' living conditions and to provide for their welfare does not mean we can't simultaneously work for alternatives to using them at all.

There are, however, undoubtedly ethical problems with prioritizing welfare for such animals, as Francione argued some while ago (1996), in that it can be interpreted as undermining possibilities for radical change.[15] Later, Francione drew a comparison between animal welfare and postmodern feminism, suggesting that both reinforced exploitation of, respectively, animals and women (2007);[16] in both cases, he suggests, there is an emphasis on producing "happy" commodification—the "happy" but exploited production-line pig, the woman working "by choice" in the sex industry.[17] I should point out that he goes on to suggest that: "Both postmodern feminists and welfarists make frequent calls for 'movement unity,' which is code for the position that those who disagree should stop disagreeing and support the postmodern feminist or welfarist position."[18]

My personal advocacy of both/and (political challenge and simultaneously working to ameliorate living conditions) rather than either/or is undoubtedly a form of new welfarism, in Francione's words. And undoubtedly it might be seen as code never to disagree. No doubt there will be many arguments over how to achieve goals, about what is or is not ethical. Debate—and even disagreement—is vital. But in the meantime, many animals endure terrible suffering; if we can't (yet) abolish the practices involved, then trying to find ways to *improve* these animals' lives is, I believe, important.

On "Pets"

Perhaps one of the more significant sources of ambivalence for some in the animal movement is our relationship with "pets," or companion animals. Many people do live with such companions and gain greatly from the association (and perhaps occasionally the animals do, too); indeed, sharing our lives with these animals is a considerable driving force for the very scholarship and politics of animal advocacy. I admit that much of my motivation to think about human relationships with nonhuman others stems from daily gazing into animal eyes, and my amazement at their ability to read me and to get me to do things. Yet living with companion animals is also problematic, grounded as it is in a culture in which humans dominate, and "own" companion animals.

Our relationships with nonhuman others are always deeply and profoundly intersected with power and exploitation. There are no human–animal relationships that can stand outside, including those with "pets."[19] There are parallels and differences here with feminism: similarity in that we can say that no woman can stand outside patriarchal structures of power, but dissimilarity in that some are more privileged than others, through structures of (for example) race and class. In that sense, those women (myself included) have degrees of access to institutional power in ways that few, if any, nonhumans have. And such layers of exploitation intersect with other forms of domination—even if the category of species too often gets omitted from scholarly discussions of intersectionality.[20]

Exploitation among humans both structures and feeds into (and feeds off) human exploitation of other living things.[21] Our relationships with animals are shot through with dominance and power, and many of the practices in which we encounter other animals are deeply detestable and abusive (some animal experiments, intensive agriculture, for example). Most people would probably agree on these particularly exploitative examples. But, like Erika Cudworth in her analysis of our shared social worlds, I consider that some less abusive relations are possible—even shared love.[22] I am troubled by "pet-keeping" even though we live with "pets," and I anguish over veterinary decisions to euthanize a much-loved animal member of our family; I acknowledge Tuan's argument that "pets" represent a kind of dominion over nonhumans, and I am very well aware that the majority of "pets" have a pretty rough time at human hands.[23] Yet dogs seem to have chosen to join us as much as we have domesticated them,[24] so presumably they found advantage in doing so—and perhaps some dogs do have a relatively comfortable life shared with their humans (though clearly a great many do not). I would like to think that the dogs and horses who live with me have some positive experiences of the relationship, and I try to make sure that is so (while recognizing that that depends on my anthropocentric perception of their experiences). Perhaps they sometimes, as Cudworth ponders, experience the relationship as love—even at times without the food bowl.

Living with animals in such ways is undoubtedly one source of both unease and pragmatism. What I have learned about these particular animals and their sentience has come in part from living with them, from my passionate attachments to them, which in turn has fuelled all the work I've done in human–animal studies as well as my training in animal behaviour.

I remain uneasy, yet love the nonhumans in my household; they are, as they are to so many others, kin.[25] This is not to deny that, ultimately, we have power over their lives. It is we who will make decisions at that awful veterinary visit, even if we console ourselves with a belief that the animal herself had made choices by lying down and refusing food, with the belief that now she is no longer suffering. Do we have the moral right to take her life? Do we have a moral right to "keep" her in the first place?

Since I do "keep" animals, then it is clear that I accept (with reservations) the existence of "pets," alongside these difficult ethical dilemmas. This involves, undoubtedly, a duty of care, but it can also permit close bonds—even love, as Cudworth emphasizes. There is an imbalance, in that I make most of the decisions, some of which do indeed constrain their actions. However, it seems to me that it has some parallels with the way we raise children. We do not usually expect human kids to be allowed to follow their every whim; on the contrary, they must be socialized, they are required to do things they may dislike (like going to school). In a similar vein, we socialize our pets, and we do sometimes expect them to behave in ways that fit in with the way we organize our social lives and institutions. That is, we expect that children and animals will be controlled and will learn to control themselves; we call this socialization—although, unlike kids, our pets cannot readily make use of this socialization to become independent and they have no legal status except as possessions. Like children, those nonhuman individuals who cannot or do not learn to behave will probably be punished in some way—but unlike children, that punishment for the nonhuman is liable to be that we take away their lives.[26]

Amongst the nonhuman animals I live with are horses, some of whom I ride. This activity provokes mixed reactions from others in animal advocacy. Some recognize the magic of living with horses, while others are concerned that the act of riding is inevitably one of domination. To some extent, I must concede this point, at least insofar as they may no more choose to be ridden than most children choose to go to school. I have no doubt that they would prefer going straight outside to munch grass to going trotting off with me on board. But "domination" seems a tricky word to use, especially with regard to a very large animal and a rather small woman. It conjures up a sense of force that would be impossible for me to produce.

I understand the domination criticism, and it continues to bother me. Whatever actions the horse and I perform together, it is at my behest. There are times when I ask the horse to do things he or she does not like, such as keeping one of them indoors in July because he was developing laminitis (a serious disease of the feet, causing lameness) caused by the rich grass encouraged by our English rain. In that sense, my closing the gate is an act of domination, incarcerating him inside, even if I do so for reasons of his ultimate welfare. More generally, horse–human relationships (like those with other animals) are always embedded in a society in which animals have little or no power. Our relationships with horses are thus structured by those inequalities.

Yet I also want to understand how the relationship of horse and human *works*. At its best, it seems to me that it is a choreography, a well-orchestrated dance that requires mutual respect and attention. And at its worst, it can become a battle in which humans can get hurt, and ultimately, in which the horse will probably lose his or her life. As long as "keeping" horses remains part of our civilization, then it seems to me that it is important to try to understand what that mutual relating involves, and how it can work for or against the interests of either participant. I want to ask, what do we need to do to ensure that relationships between individual people and animals work well, to the benefit of both? I have watched and worked with horses all of my life and I do believe that, at times, they too get something out of the working together. Most experienced horse people will relate anecdotes about horses who would "do anything" for their person. Should we simply assume that this is wishful thinking, a form of anthropomorphism, or are these people giving voice to an experience of mutual relating?

Many of us live with a range of companion species—animals who continue to inspire us and our engagement in human–animal studies. I want to understand these animals better, I want to know what they may (or may not) gain from that engagement. I want to know more about what makes interspecies relationships work, or not. I want to know, too, how humans understand these interrelatings. It is to these ends that some of my research and writing centres on the horse–human relationship, particularly how it is produced by both participants.[27]

Such interrelatings are profoundly corporeal, especially through riding—which brings me back to feminist thinking. Ann Game suggested that riding comes to be a *process*, in which both horse and human bodies express and anticipate the other.[28] Horses and human riders, Game suggests, carry the memory of shared movements in their muscles, nerves, and sinews. The horse is, in her discussion, a subject with a mind of her or his own, someone who can resist, or become part of a social contract.[29] Indeed, as Thompson points out, there is a deep intercorporeality in riding, in which the rider must become part horse, and the horse part human.[30]

Thinking about such intercorporeality draws on feminist theorizing about the body, and it is important to thinking about relationships with other animals. In interacting through/with the body of an other, whoever they are, embodiment *becomes* relational.[31] In short, who I am is always in the process of being produced in mutuality with others, many of whom have four legs, or are furred or feathered. Such "relatings" impact our lives and how we experience embodiment in ways that need more detailed analysis,[32] I would suggest, as does the impact of such embodiment on the lives of animal companions.

Relationality produces a kind of emergent order; exploring the implications of what this might mean is, to me, where a synergy between feminist inquiry and human–animal studies could be most fruitful, precisely because it is in engagement with those most unlike us that our ways of thinking will be most troubled. How relationalities are constituted, and how such relationalities become (inter)corporeal are questions that matter to feminism—and they are questions much enriched when we acknowledge differences of species. But these questions, however fascinating they may be and however much they may illuminate our relationships with other animals, raise an underlying issue about the ethics of doing research at all with animal subjects—questions that are, ultimately, about politics.

On Politics (and Research)

While some research in human–animal studies does not intervene in animal lives (focusing on, say, animal representations), many studies do directly use animals—including some of my own current work with horses. Is this ethical? Should we do research if doing so involves putting animals into a position of use? Do they thereby become commodities in the research process, means to an end? For some people I have met, the answer is clearly no. They would argue that the research process itself serves to reinforce the subservient status of the animal that, politically, they would eschew. Using animals in any way does not fit with this politics. Now, inevitably I have some problems with this; I am a researcher, after all! I do think it is possible to do research *with* animals in ways that are, or try to be, respectful. Marc

Bekoff, for example, in studies of animals' emotions, emphasizes the value of field studies, which leave animals in their own milieu, over lab studies, which inevitably constrain animals.[33]

It is a little trickier to investigate interspecies relationships directly, of course, when the animal is a companion one whose movements will be controlled to some extent by humans. Doing empirical research in human–animal studies is undoubtedly a compromise. On one hand, research with domesticated animals can seem to bolster existing inequalities and to feed into problematic cultural constructions of what nonhuman animals are (as property, for instance). It can seem to use animals as simply commodities. In that sense, such research perhaps is always tarred with a speciesist brush. On the other hand, it is only through detailed investigations that we can begin to unravel the complex interspecies communications that can occur between us and animal others—the stuff of which human–animal bonds are forged. And better understanding might help us to find grounds for change; perhaps, in my more optimistic moments, this could mean change that benefits animals.

To me, much work in human–animal studies broadly springs from a desire to understand animal others better, drawing on a variety of intellectual traditions, and understanding is crucial to political action. Nonhuman animals throughout much human–animal studies writing—even the more theoretical—emerge as minded beings, as subjects with life stories to tell. To be sure there remain ethical questions: can we, for instance, ever be truly justified in doing research with companion animals when they cannot give informed consent (and bearing in mind that there are questions about human informed consent)? Is it always going to be a "soft" version of animal experimentation, in which we use them for our own purposes?

I would also emphasize that in studying human–animal relationships, we are investigating the complex nexuses that bind our lives and those of other species.[34] In that light, it makes sense to focus not on the collectivity of animals but on multiple forms of humanimality—a kind of hybridity. It is these intertwinings that we study. To do responsible research into human–animal relatings requires methodologies that are minimally invasive, not only of animals' bodily integrity (though certainly that!), but also of their everyday lives.[35]

In our research on horse–human relationships, we accept some degree of intervention (these are horses already domesticated and "belonging" to specific people) because we are investigating the minutiae of interspecies interactions.³⁶ We can thus focus on the workings of specific relationship between individuals and see how the horse plays a part in working together (or not). Our aim is to learn more about what might make some relationships work better than others (which has considerable implications for both human and horse), and to try to take into account the horse's perspective.

To what extent any of us succeed in taking animals' perspectives into account is debatable, and I recognize that my studies of horses may be contentious. But the point I want to emphasize here is that if we accept a need to do research, then we should be seeking methods of investigation that offer the potential to understand better the animal's point of view. It matters that we try to find ways of thinking about interspecies relating in all its complexity, and from animal perspectives. It also matters that we find ways of doing research *that are accountable* to those who are studied. This was a key argument in feminist debates about appropriate methodology, and it applies just as well to thinking about animals.

Accountability has long been emphasized by feminist scholars, keen to criticize the objectification (or complete omission) of women by researchers. Doing a study that failed to take into consideration the needs of the community under investigation (by, for example, including them in the research process) was held to be unacceptable. Including subjects was not necessarily easily negotiated but it was held up to be an appropriately feminist way of approaching research. While it is much more difficult to envisage how to negotiate research with nonhumans, accountability towards the animals whom we might study is a goal that should be part of all human–animal studies.³⁷ Even if our studies do not overtly challenge existing institutions, we can still consider how our research might impact the animals whose lives feature in the studies we write about.

To be accountable means, at a minimum, that our studies must never construct those who are studied as objects, but as subjects. It has also meant, in studies with people, thinking about the possible consequences for them of the research, as well as considering them as sentient subjects who *can engage with* the research—feeding back comments, for example, or being involved with further developments. That is not directly possible when our research involves animal subjects, and no doubt they are even less able to resist their inclusion in the study, but perhaps it is something we can think about. What role do our animal subjects play in creating and directing the research that is ostensibly "about" them? Certainly, animals can alter the progress of research in unforeseen ways, as Michael acknowledged in his account of sociological interviews interrupted by resident nonhumans.[38] How, then, do animals shape the research in which they themselves participate?

In human–animal studies we produce knowledge, but this is knowledge that can be produced jointly with those nonhuman others who are part of the subject matter of our inquiries. It is crucial that we try to foreground the part they play, though this may take some imagination on our part as researchers. Otherwise, it is knowledge produced *by* us, *about* them, thus further entrenching differences of power. Prioritizing the hybridities, the associations, the relationships, over generalized "animals" acknowledges that we humans may be privileged producers of knowledge, but we are not the only ones.

Imagining other lives is a critical part of this endeavour, not only in terms of trying to understand the experiences of different animals, but also in trying to imagine how they experience engaging with us. It is, furthermore, crucial in trying to envisage change. Stoetzler and Yuval-Davis, noting the importance of imagination in knowledge production and feminist theory, draw on Haraway's work on "situated knowledges."[39] In this, Haraway discusses what she terms partial connection and the "split and contradictory self [who] is the one who can interrogate positionings and be accountable, the one who can construct and join rational conversations and *fantastic imaginings that change history*."[40] "Imaginary horizons," insist Stoetzler and Yuval-Davis, "are affected by the positioning of our gaze. But, at the same time, it is our imagination that gives our experiences their particular meanings, their categories of reference. Whether it is 'borders,' 'home,' 'oppression,' or 'liberation,' the particular meanings we hold of these concepts are embedded in our situated imaginations."[41]

Such imaginings matter. And they are crucial to how we experience our lives with other animals or do research differently. In practice, research seems too often to be constrained by disciplinary boundaries, which severely limit the questions we might ask about living with other species and constrain the methods we might use. Too often we find that studies focus on one or the other, on how humans experience animals or vice versa, and not on the intertwining of "split and contradictory selves" that make up our partial engagements with other animals. In turn, if research imagination fails then its contribution to politics is likely to be limited; it will contribute little to the "fantastic imaginings that change history."

Envisaging subjects of research not as monolithic individuals but in terms of comings-together of selves joined partially into connection might require a leap of imagination. It certainly requires a radical leap of change in how we do research. But it might also be more consistent with the way many of us experience being with animals. We—human or not—are not bounded and solipsistic: rather we move in and out of constant engagements with others. This isn't (just) some philosophical musing but more splitting of hairs: trying to transcend separations of us and them in research is fundamentally a political question, whether the "them" refers to women or to other species of being. Imagining the multiple ways in which we and animal others conjointly construct knowledge is central here[42]—an important step in the direction of accountability.

Ultimately, of course, real accountability is unattainable, whoever the subjects of research. With humans, at least, we can adopt participative techniques, permitting some degree of collaboration with those studied. Even so, research has end points, which produce closure.[43] By this I do not mean that researchers simply see one research project as indicating need for another; rather, there is closure in the sense of one project coming to an end, under the researchers' control *and however much other participants have been involved.* Accountable research may include provision for feeding back outcomes to participants, perhaps even including their views in further projects. But it is, in the end, the researcher who makes decisions about the direction of the project, who will disseminate findings, and perhaps establish a career on the basis of the publications. It is that closure that creates a dilemma for feminist researchers, because it leaves participants out of the loop and out of the last stage of producing knowledge as a shared enterprise. And it will be much more exclusive when those who are studied are not human.

Being accountable in the political sense—part of democratic processes and shared governance—is probably not really meaningful with regard to nonhuman animals, not least because of their status as property, such that their relationship to us is determined through modes of use.[44] Use of animals frames much of what we do with them and much of the literature in human–animal studies. What does it mean to be accountable to subjects of research if they are considered someone's property? We might consider accountability as ensuring that no harms are done (though it is likely to be humans who decide what constitutes harms), and that the welfare of animals is protected, even within that framework of ownership. In principle, this might be one way in which animals' "points of view" could feed into research projects, albeit in a limited way. Accountability, in these terms, becomes at least a duty of care (though this, in turn, (re)positions animals as belonging to someone, or some institution). Nevertheless, the question of accountability to the animals we claim to care about is, I would argue, fundamental for animal studies (and politics). Given that many people involved in human–animal studies or CAS come to their inquiries from political engagement with some form of animal advocacy, the issue of whether we can be accountable to animals at the moment of studying them is central.

To take a step in this direction means ensuring that at least some of our research is relevant to animals' needs. Obviously, there are likely to be disagreements about what animals do need. "Relevance," moreover, is a loaded word, one much loved of funding agencies. I am not concerned with "relevance" to governmental policies or to economic incentives here, nor would I wish to exclude those studies that contribute broadly to our understanding of how we think about animals (some work in literature, history, and philosophy, for example). But we could think about ways to encourage researchers and activists into greater dialogue, so that those outside of academic pursuits saw research as more appropriate. One model for this might be the idea of "science shops," much publicized some decades ago, and still a worthwhile activity. The idea was that these act to liaise between community groups and researchers; the activists ask researchers how to solve a problem, and they work together on the research. This is not necessarily "science" in the narrow sense, but a model of participative research addressing the needs of specific communities. Can we conceive of research run partly by animal advocacy groups rather than universities? And, between them, can these liaisons conceive of research that allows animals greater voice?

On Partiality: Making It Personal

Throughout this chapter I have drawn on my experiences with feminist politics and tried to link it to debates about animals. There are several themes in common, but perhaps the most important is the phrase that dominated 1970s feminism: the personal is political. That, too, is a theme central to many in animal advocacy, who seek to live their lives around particular values (veganism, for example). Far from being something to be expunged from writing, personal lives with animals are a crucial part of our scholarship in CAS—something to be welcomed and celebrated in research.

Like other feminists, I think it is crucial to think about *how* we write and do research, as well as the questions asked *by* the research. It behoves us to seek ways to give voice to the voiceless, and—above all—to find ways of listening. That, to me, means thinking quite radically about relationships with animals, and about relationships between activists, animals, and scholars. Like many other feminist scholars, I would emphasize partial perspectives rather than what Haraway called the god-trick of the claim of universal knowledge.[45] Working with humanimals *is* a partial perspective; by that I mean that close engagement with nonhuman animals produces a perspective that is located in the *specific* lives of both us humans and the animals we live with, especially in the intersections of those lives and their shared meanings. But there is another sense of partiality that I want to end with, and that is that I am never *im*partial when it comes to thinking about animals and research. Years ago I was criticized by fellow scientists on the grounds that my feminism got in the way of doing "proper" research; I was too partial, too personal. These days, no doubt there are those who think that politics gets in the way of my being properly objective (read: impersonal) about animals. Good: I hope it does.

Nowadays, I am more of a researcher and scholar than I am an overt activist—though I hope these two activities nourish each other. I am saddened to see splits emerging in animal advocacy and related scholarship and have tried in this chapter to meander around some of the ways in which these splits and tensions continue to trouble my own thinking. I hope I have not become too lost in these meanderings. Ultimately, however, it is our partiality, our caring about animals, that we share across so much of the diversity of human–animal studies. I have no wish to pursue passionless research; I freely acknowledge that what makes me want to ask questions in animal studies is indeed a passion to understand animals better as well as how they relate to/with us. It is also about wanting to make the world a better place for all of us—in terms of interspecies relationships, that is another way to make the personal political. That, I hope, is a partiality we all share.

NOTES

1. Women's studies courses thrived for some time—and in some places still do. What I saw, however (at least in universities in the UK) was that there was a decline in the number of courses/teachers who had *activist* experience.
2. Best, "Rise of Critical Animal Studies."
3. I have sketched some of the ways that feminism might contribute to animal–human studies in Birke ("Intimate Familiarities?"), and how human–animal studies might influence feminist thought in Birke, "Unnamed Others."
4. See, for example, Birke, *Feminism, Animals and Science*.
5. See Birke, Arluke, and Michael, *Sacrifice*.
6. For example, Bekoff, *Minding Animals*.
7. See Birke, Bryld, and Lykke, "Animal Performances."
8. Humm, "Seven Questions," 17.
9. This was advertising a discussion at the Minding Animals conference in Utrecht, July, 2012.
10. Regarding animals as numbers see Phillips, "Proper Names"; and Birke, Arluke, and Michael, *Sacrifice*.
11. See discussion in LaFollette and Shanks, *Brute Science*.
12. Guerrini, *Experimenting with Animals*.
13. See discussion in Birke, Arluke, and Michael, *Sacrifice*.
14. Some 100 million in the US alone, for example, are believed to be used per annum, although accurate figures are difficult to obtain for the US because not all animals are included.
15. Francione, *Rain Without Thunder*.
16. Francione, "Postmodern Feminism."
17. I have to add that none of the feminists I know who identify as postmodernists would take this position.
18. Francione, "Postmodern Feminism."
19. See a discussion of human relationships to domesticated animals in Donaldson and Kymlicka, *Zoopolis*.
20. See discussion in Birke, "Unnamed Others."
21. For further analysis, see Cudworth, *Social Lives with Other Animals*.
22. Ibid.
23. Tuan, *Dominance and Affection*.
24. See Budiansky, *The Covenant of the Wild*; and Haraway, *When Species Meet*.
25. Charles and Davies, "My Family and Other Animals."
26. Writing this I was reminded of the widespread use of drugs like Ritalin to "control" the behaviour of children labelled "hyperactive," or unable to sustain attention. Again and again I have heard the argument that it is about

controlling children's behaviour to fit them into the straitjackets that we call conventional education; schools are places where kids' behaviour is highly controlled and we believe this is necessary in order to produce socially adjusted people. Controlling behaviour is just as much part of the discursive construction of "pet-keeping" as it is about child-rearing.

27. For a summary of some of this research and discussion of methodologies used in studies of animal–human relationships, see Birke and Hockenhull, "On Investigating Human–Animal Bonds."

28. Game, "Embodying the Centaur."

29. Game describes how the horse she lived with became seriously ill and was unable to move properly even after recuperation. Only when she was ridden again could the mare's muscles move properly once more, a kind of muscular memory of shared movements.

30. Thompson, "Theorising Rider–Horse Relations."

31. See also Despret, "Body We Care For."

32. Following Haraway, *When Species Meet.*

33. Bekoff, *Emotional Lives of Animals.*

34. Haraway, *When Species Meet.*

35. There are, of course, always ethical questions to be asked if research protocols intervene at all in subjects' lives—whatever the species of the subjects. With humans, ethics committees might require that researchers discuss with subjects how the research might affect them; that is more difficult with animal subjects. Ultimately, decisions about the ethics of any research that might cause interference in individual lives (and that includes some field work studies of wild animals) have recourse to arguments based on potential benefits of knowledge gained.

36. See Birke and Hockenhull, "Journeys Together"; and Birke and Hockenhull, "Investigating Human–Animal Bonds."

37. I have argued this at length elsewhere. See Birke, "Naming Names."

38. Michael, "Making Data Social."

39. Stoetzler and Yuval-Davis, "Standpoint Theory."

40. Haraway, "Situated Knowledges," 193 (my emphasis).

41. Stoetzler and Yuval-Davis, "Standpoint Theory," 327.

42. On the conjoint production of meaning between people and dogs, see Irvine, *If You Tame Me.*

43. There are some ways of making research more dialogic. In animal studies, Dawson ("Honouring Human Emotions") described her work with people who were dealing with the grief following euthanasia of a companion animal. This research, using an approach called organic inquiry, involved constant re-

engagement between subjects of research (obviously only the human, once the animal had died) and researcher, to produce shared meanings that become the research material. There is, of course, closure once the research is published, but arguably the process of the research has itself produced some degree of closure for the participants' grief.

44. Regarding animal citizenship, though, see discussion in Donaldson and Kymlicka, *Zoopolis*.
45. Haraway, "Situated Knowledges."

BIBLIOGRAPHY

Bekoff, Marc. *The Emotional Lives of Animals: A Leading Scientist Explores Animal Joy, Sorrow, and Empathy—and Why They Matter.* San Francisco: New World Library, 2007.

———. *Minding Animals: Awareness, Emotions, and Heart.* Oxford: Oxford University Press, 2002.

Best, Steven. "The Rise of Critical Animal Studies: Putting Theory into Action and Animal Liberation into Higher Education." *Journal for Critical Animal Studies* 7, no. 1 (2009): 9–52.

Birke, Lynda. *Feminism, Animals and Science.* Buckingham: Open University Press, 1994.

———. "Intimate Familiarities? Feminism and Human/Animal Studies." *Society & Animals* 10, no. 4 (2002): 429–36.

———. "Naming Names—Or, What's in It for the Animals?" *Humanimalia* 1, no. 1 (2009). http://www.depauw.edu/humanimalia/issue01/pdfs/Lynda%20Birke.pdf.

———. "Unnamed Others: How Can Thinking about 'Animals' Matter to Feminist Theorizing?" *NORA: Nordic Journal of Women's Studies* 20, no. 2 (2012): 148–57.

Birke, Lynda, Arnold Arluke, and Mike Michael. *The Sacrifice: How Scientific Experiments Transform Animals and People.* West Lafayette, IN: Purdue University Press, 2007.

Birke, Lynda, Mett Bryld, and Nina Lykke. "Animal Performances: An Exploration of Intersections Between Feminist Science Studies and Studies of Human/Animal Relationships." *Feminist Theory* 5, no. 2 (2004): 167–83.

Birke, Lynda, and Jo Hockenhull. "Journeys Together: Horses and Humans in Partnership." *Society & Animals* 23, no. 1 (2015): 81–100.

———. "On Investigating Human–Animal Bonds: Realities, Relatings, Research." In *Crossing Boundaries: Investigating Human–Animal Relationships*, edited by Lynda Birke and Jo Hockenhull, 15–36. Leiden: Brill, 2012.

Budiansky, Stephen. *The Covenant of the Wild: Why Animals Chose Domestication.* New Haven: Yale University Press, 1992.

Charles, Nickie, and Charlotte A. Davies. "My Family and Other Animals: Pets as Kin." In *Human and Other Animals: Critical Perspectives*, edited by Bob Carter and Nickie Charles, 69–92. Basingstoke: Palgrave Macmillan, 2011.

Cudworth, Erika. *Social Lives with Other Animals: Tales of Sex, Death and Love.* Basingstoke: Palgrave Macmillan, 2010.

Dawson, Susan Ella. "Honouring Human Emotions: Using Organic Inquiry for Researching Human–Companion Animal Relationships." In *Crossing Boundaries: Investigating Human–Animal Relationships*, edited by Lynda Birke and Jo Hockenhull, 113–38. Leiden: Brill, 2012.

Despret, Vinciane. "The Body We Care For: Figures of Anthropo-zoo-genesis." *Body & Society* 10, nos. 2–3 (2004): 111–34.

Donaldson, Sue, and Will Kymlicka. *Zoopolis: A Political Theory of Animal Rights.* Oxford: Oxford University Press, 2011.

Francione, Gary L. "Postmodern Feminism and Animal Welfare: Perfect Together." *Animal Rights: The Abolitionist Approach* (blog), December 5, 2007. http://www.abolitionistapproach.com/postmodern-feminism-and-animal-welfare-perfect-together/#more-13.

———. *Rain Without Thunder: The Ideology of the Animal Rights Movement.* Philadelphia: Temple University Press, 1996.

Game, Ann. "Riding: Embodying the Centaur." *Body & Society* 7, no. 4 (2001): 1–12.

Guerrini, Anita. *Experimenting with Animals and Humans: From Galen to Animal Rights.* Baltimore: Johns Hopkins University Press, 2003.

Haraway, Donna. "Situated Knowledges: The Science Question in Feminism and the Privilege of Partial Perspective." In *Simians, Cyborgs, and Women: The Reinvention of Nature*, 183–202. London: Free Association Books, 1991.

———. *When Species Meet.* Minneapolis: University of Minnesota Press, 2008.

Humm, Maggie. "Seven Questions and Some Answers." *Women's Studies Network (UK) Association Newsletter* 26 (1997): 16–7.

Irvine, Leslie. *If You Tame Me: Understanding Our Connection with Animals.* Philadelphia: Temple University Press, 2004.

LaFollette, Hugh, and Niall Shanks. *Brute Science: Dilemmas of Animal Experimentation.* London: Routledge, 1996.

Michael, Mike. "On Making Data Social: Heterogeneity in Sociological Practice." *Qualitative Research* 4, no. 1 (2004): 5–23.

Phillips, Mary T. "Proper Names and the Social Construction of Biography: The Negative Case of Laboratory Animals." *Qualitative Sociology* 17, no. 2 (2004): 119–42.

Stoetzler, Marcel, and Nira Yuval-Davis. "Standpoint Theory, Situated Knowledge and the Situated Imagination." *Feminist Theory* 3, no. 3 (2002): 315–33.

Thompson, Kirrilly. "Theorising Rider–Horse Relations: An Ethnographic Illustration of the Centaur Metaphor in the Spanish Bullfight." In *Theorizing Animals: Re-thinking Human–Animal Relations*, edited by Nik Taylor and Tania Signal, 221–54. Leiden: Brill, 2011.

Tuan, Yi-Fu. *Dominance and Affection: The Making of Pets.* London: Yale University Press, 1984.

14

Campaigning with the Enemy

Understanding Opportunity Fields and the Tactic of Corporate Incorporation

Carol L. Glasser

Many moderate animal rights organizations and campaigns increasingly seek to work with businesses and alongside corporations. From animal rights groups buying stock in companies in order to engage in shareholder meetings to campaigns working with non-vegan restaurants to develop vegetarian and vegan options, there are myriad examples of how animal rights organizations are working with corporations that participate in animal exploitation as a strategy for furthering animal rights and welfare. This is a strategy I call *corporate incorporation*.

In many of these instances organizations are seeking to work alongside corporations to achieve cultural gains, such as raising awareness of animal cruelty issues or making animal-friendly alternatives (e.g., cosmetics not tested on animals, vegan food, synthetic leathers and furs) more easily available. In other instances, there is an attempt to institutionalize "more humane" forms of animal exploitation within an industry, such as banning the use of gestation crates, or formalizing laws or other political measures to protect animals. However, by privileging the pursuit of political and cultural change, moderate animal rights organizations are neglecting, and in some cases even supporting, the economic basis of nonhuman animal (hereafter animal) exploitation.[1]

Working within corporate structures that propagate animal exploitation results in campaigns and strategies that are at best impotent, and at worse potentially harmful to the animal rights cause. Further, the failure to critique the economic bias of corporations that results in animal exploitation has led the movement down a path of institutionalization as the number of non-profit animal rights organizations proliferates.[2] This creates competition for limited resources within the social movement field and promotes professionalization and concessions over agitation and radicalism.

Economic and corporate interests are the driving forces behind both the current level of mass exploitation of animals and the repression of the animal rights movement. However, some animal rights organizations are choosing to embrace corporations that exploit animals as part of a strategy to make political and cultural shifts for animals. This emphasis on changing policies, creating laws, and shifting public opinion and individual behaviour creates a long and possibly never-ending route to animal rights. Corporate incorporation further justifies animal exploitation and prevents any possibility of achieving animal rights goals if it continues to be a prevalent strategy.

In this chapter I illustrate my points using a variety of secondary data sources and by presenting case studies of exemplar animal rights organizations and campaigns with a focus in the US. The US animal rights movement addresses a range of issues, including farm animals, companion animals, wildlife and exotic animals, animals used in research, and animals used for entertainment. Though the whole of the animal rights movement is discussed in this chapter, to keep the discussion focused I have only used case studies and examples from farm animal campaigns, including vegan and vegetarian outreach.

A Triad of Opportunity

Current theories of social movements focus in large part on the influence of the state and the political dimensions of social movement strategies, tactics, and outcomes.[3] Much of this discussion occurs within theories of the political process model and political opportunity structure (POS). From a political process perspective, social movements can be understood as being directly influenced by and reacting to the political structure of their environment: "The primary point of the political process approach was that activists do not choose goals, strategies, and tactics in a vacuum.

Rather, the political context, conceptualized fairly broadly, sets the grievances around which activists mobilize, advancing some claims and disadvantaging others."[4] Within the political process model, theories of POS focus on ways in which collective action is influenced by available political opportunities.[5] "Political opportunity structure" was formally introduced by Peter Eisinger's 1973 work on race, poverty, and riots in US cities in the 1960s.[6] This was then further developed by Charles Tilly in 1978, who used the concept of "closed" versus "open" POSs to establish a predictive model addressing how the degree of openness of a government and the political process influenced political organizing.[7]

POS comprises the stable political context (e.g., democracy, parliamentary republic, etc.) in which a social movement exists, as well as the pliable aspects of the political process in which activists hope to participate or alter. There are three key components to POS: structure, actors, and interactions.[8] A political structure can be more or less open or closed; the more open the political process, the easier it is for social movement actors to influence political outcomes through legitimate means. The key actors involved are the "protagonists," "antagonists," and "bystanders."[9] Finally, there is the context of the interaction between the actors and the political structure; the degree to which activists feel they can alter political structures and the degree to which they are willing to tailor their claims in order to have access to the political process and political elites will influence how they embrace or interpret political opportunities.

The conceptualization of POS has since been expanded to address not only formal and institutional political structures, but also the cultural dimension of the political process. Gamson and Meyer stress the importance of cultural aspects such as values, public perception, media, class consciousness, and others.[10]

Wahlström and Peterson, focusing on anti-fur campaigns in Sweden, make the conceptualization of POS more dynamic by incorporating economic factors as well.[11] They urge a reconceptualization of POS to include three separate but interrelated opportunity structures. They reframe the traditional factors associated with POS—e.g., the institutionalized political system, elite allies, and a state's ability for repression—as the *state* opportunity structure (SOS). Second, they identify the *cultural* opportunity structure (COS), as suggested by Gamson and Meyer.[12] Finally, Wahlström and Peterson add a third important aspect—the *economic* opportunity structure (EOS): "in order to achieve an understanding of the external factors

influencing contemporary social movements, one has to construct a model
of POS, including characteristics of the state and the dominant political
culture, the cultural tendencies of the action environment, and economic
actors."[13] By "economic" they are referring to the "meso- and microstruc-
tures of profit-seeking institutions" and not to the macroeconomic structure of a nation.[14] When considered together, the COS, EOS, and SOS make
up what I will call the *opportunity field*.

The concept of an opportunity field better accommodates the animal
rights movement and other new social movements: "the explanatory power
of political opportunity is limited when accounting for new types of social
movements. Political process theory assumes that social movements have
political goals and views the state or other political power as the target.
However, social movements in modern society have gradually shifted away
from the political arena, and increasingly challenge corporations, cultural
values, and other social forces."[15] Though Wahlström and Peterson's work
has not made huge waves in research framed within a political process
model, a number of scholars have recognized the importance of economic
and corporate structures for social movements. For example, Li found that
the US Computer TakeBack campaign was successful because it targeted
state, "discursive" (i.e., cultural), and economic structures.[16] Schurman
and Munro highlight that the same type of campaign and strategy can
have different outcomes if the EOS and COS differ.[17] They found the anti-
genetic-engineering movement was organized similarly in the US as it was
in Britain, but it was successful only in Britain; the economic structure of
the food supply differed between these countries, and the US public was
much more trusting of regulatory agencies but less receptive to activist
messages compared to the British public.

Wahlstrom and Peterson, Li, and Schurman and Munro all incorporated the EOS in their studies, with a focus on economic structures as *targets*
of social movement strategies. Less attention has been paid to the role of
economic structures in creating the opportunity field for social movements.
However, all structures in a social movement's opportunity field construct
the environment being reacted to and may be beneficial as strategic allies
and not just as targets. The COS, EOS, and SOS are all simultaneously generating the oppression a movement is combating at the same time that they
could all potentially engender change.

Another key element of the opportunity field is that opportunity structures influence each other: "the elements of the structure are not isolated but

interconnected, which means that an interaction in one area can *indirectly* change the structure in another."[18] It is important to take this one step further and recognize that the interaction is often very direct. For example, Wahlström and Peterson identify mass media as the most important institution of the COS. With a single headline story, the mass media can directly influence both the state and corporations.[19] One way to think of opportunity structures is as gears in a machine—they are all interconnected and simultaneously influencing each other. Like gears, some opportunity structures may be more or less powerful or integral, depending on the nature of the opportunity field.

The variable importance of the opportunity structures is another important element of Wahlström and Peterson's model. They highlight that the three structures, as well as various aspects within each structure, may differ in significance: "Depending on the goals and targets of the social movement the separate aspects of the structure differ in significance."[20]

This chapter will show that, though economic, state, and cultural structures all impact the opportunity field of the animal rights movement, they are not of equal importance. Rather, in the case of the US animal rights movement, economic and corporate interests are more powerful than the state and cultural considerations. This has not been sufficiently recognized by the animal rights movement. Animal rights campaigns often struggle to adjust laws, create policies, or change cultural attitudes while neglecting the economic underpinnings of animal exploitation. Though cultural shifts in attitude (an example of COS gains) and policies protecting animals (an example of SOS gains) may help achieve limited animal rights goals, they cannot liberate animals because they do not strike at the root of animal exploitation.

The way in which animals are culturally devalued, the lack of legal protection for animals, and the preponderance of policies that directly hurt animals are *results* of, not precursors to, economic and corporate interests. A focus on the SOS and COS is an attack on symptoms and therefore ultimately ineffective in making substantial change. With the root cause of the problem intact, politically and culturally supported speciesism and animal exploitation will continue to grow.

Successful social movements must identify the root cause of injustice and target it in their strategies. To neglect the EOS, and in particular the role of corporations in animal exploitation, is to neglect the most effective target for change. To go one step further and actually embrace corporate structures within animal rights organizing or include corporations in campaign strategies is to actively maintain animal exploitation. Even if some small gain is made, the roots of animal exploitation will be strengthened, making the overarching system of animal exploitation more difficult to defeat.

Economics of Animal Exploitation

Economic interests are the basis of the current levels of animal exploitation. Animals have become the unpaid labourers who are making the economic elite money. The process of rendering animals into commodities has created a web of industries and profit-making opportunities. There are companies that make transport trucks to take animals to slaughter, hooks and shackles to hang animals as they move down the kill line, machines to slice their flesh into various shapes, etc. Laws permit abysmal treatment of animals in most situations in which a profit can be made so people can spend very little on the feeding and care of animals, but financially benefit from their labour and bodies. The hunting and fishing industry, circuses, zoos, aquariums, animal testing facilities, research scientists, fashion designers, farmers, slaughterhouse owners, grocery stores, and animal breeders generate profit from the bodies and lives of animals.

The human–animal relationship that positions animals as commodities is not a necessary basis for human–animal interactions, but rather evolved alongside the development of current systems of trade, wealth, and stratification. Nibert finds that the oppression of animals is tied to economic interests, particularly those of capitalism.[21] Transitions from gathering-based societies to those that incorporated hunting and, later, agriculture, intensified divisions of labour between men and women, humans and other animals. Divisions of labour strengthened hierarchical structures and inequalities over time such that Western nations now operate under a patriarchal and capitalism-based system in which there are very few in power, holding most of the wealth, and within this system animals have been defined as commodities.

Economic corporate interests not only drive animal exploitation but also have a direct impact on the political process. Government officials are typically from the economic elite. In 2009, the average American's net worth was $96,000 while the average member of the House of Representatives had a net worth of $5 million and the average Senator had a net worth of

$13.4 million (US dollars throughout).[22] Government representatives in the US are so disparate from the typical US citizen that they often have economic interests that are not reflective of, and may even be harmful to, the average person. Political elites are directly influenced by corporate imperatives, leading to a political process that allows corporate concerns to dictate political processes and policies.

State officials and processes are so intimately tied to corporate interests that it has become a major concern of the state to address corporate and business requests. Furthermore, corporate interests are privileged by the established system of lobbying, in which corporations and their representatives vie for political inroads and control through campaign contributions and monetary incentives to individual politicians. In 2011, the pharmaceutical/health products industry, a primary supporter of animal testing, spent over $240 million lobbying government officials, while the agribusiness sector spent over $125 million.[23]

Through policies designed to promote corporate interests, the federal government is a major player in the corporate exploitation of animals. A stark example is provided by the system of federal subsidies to agribusiness. These subsidies artificially drive down the cost of some foods and encourage farmers to produce them in abundance. According to a 2011 article in *The Atlantic*, the nine most heavily subsidized foods in the US between 1995 and 2010 were corn, wheat, soybeans, rice, beer, milk, beef, peanut butter, and sunflower oil.[24] The cheap cost has led to the primary use of corn, wheat, and soybeans in CAFOs (concentrated animal feeding operations, one of the most egregious forms of animal farming), even though these grains are not natural food sources and can lead to painful health problems.

Subsidies also serve to drive small farms out of business (although they are more likely than corporate farms to use what some in the animal rights movement consider humane practices). In 2011, only 10 percent of US farms were receiving 75 percent of all farm subsidies.[25] This highlights the consolidation of farming and livestock operations that has led to larger facilities and greater power for a small number of corporations, power that then allows for even greater influence in the political system. The government also gives subsidies directly to the meat, egg, and dairy industries, which lowers the cost of products, thereby increasing their sales and allowing these products to remain staples of the American diet. Beef subsidies have increased 256 percent between 1995 and 2010, receiving $3.6 billion in that fifteen-year period, while milk received $4.9 billion in subsidies.[26]

These industries are also supported by the federal government on the demand side through programs that purchase large quantities of meat and dairy, often as a way to get rid of excess product created by their very own subsidies. For example, the United States Department of Agriculture's (USDA's) Special Milk Program reimburses public schools, non-profit private schools, and daycare centres for the milk they purchase. In 2011, over 5,000 schools, camps, and childcare centres used this program, which reimburses only for "pasteurized fluid types of fat free or low-fat (1%) milk."[27] Notably, by not specifying reimbursements for soy and nut milks, this program also ignores the needs of non-white children who are more likely to live in low-income neighbourhoods where schools rely on lunch assistance programs, as those not of European dissent are likely to be lactose intolerant: "95 percent of Asians, 60 percent to 80 percent of African Americans and Ashkenazi Jews, 80 percent to 100 percent of American Indians, and 50 percent to 80 percent of Hispanics. . . . Lactose intolerance is least common among people of northern European origin, who have a lactose intolerance prevalence of only about 2 percent."[28]

Corporate Catalysts of State Repression

Corporate control of the state is so powerful and pervasive in the US that it even directs state repression of social movements. When corporations that rely on animal exploitation have had their profits threatened by animal rights strategies, the state has responded with repression. The corporate underpinnings of state repression reiterate two important characteristics of the animal rights movement's opportunity field: first, that the EOS is a greater concern than the SOS, and second, that all structures in the opportunity field are interconnected.

Corporate interests have directed state repression of the US animal rights movement most directly through the passage of the Animal Enterprise Protection Act (AEPA), which was later amended and became the Animal Enterprise Terrorism Act (AETA). This bill is an exemplar of repressive legislation. It was written by representatives of the industries it benefits and legislates additional penalties for actions already considered crimes when those same actions are committed because of a specific ideology (animal rights) against a specific industry ("animal enterprise"). The industries being protected are heavily subsidized by the US government, with a peak of $25.7 billion in farm subsidies being given in 2000.[29]

Furthermore, the members of Congress who sponsored and supported AEPA/AETA were personally tied to the agricultural and/or pharmaceutical industries by campaign contributions or personal investments.[30]

The crimes, detailed as terrorist activity in the bills, focus on the economic interests of corporations, and sentencing guidelines are based on the amount of economic loss caused to the business. The concern of AEPA/AETA is clearly the protection of business interests and profit, not safety, as there are no documented cases of anyone being physically injured by animal rights activists in the US for any of the crimes prosecuted under these laws. Despite this fact, the law uses the word terrorism freely and repeatedly refers to "serious bodily injury or death."

The history of the Act makes clear that corporate economic protection, not public safety, is the reason for its creation and passage. In 1989, Representative Charles Stenholm (D-TX) introduced the Farm Animal and Research Facilities Protection Act (FARF Act) in reaction to successful, radical, direct actions by the animal rights movement. It was co-signed by 235 members of Congress. The original version of the FARF Act did not make it to the floor before the session ended, but was reintroduced in the 102nd session of Congress in 1991. The act referred specifically to the need to deter "acts of terrorism" aimed at entities that conduct business using animals, or animal enterprises.[31] In 1991 Stenholm reintroduced an amended version of the act, and it was renamed the Animal Enterprise Protection Act. It received its own section in Title 18 of the United States Code of criminal law, and was signed into law by President George H.W. Bush in 1992.

The American Legislative Exchange Council (ALEC) drafted the language that became the AEPA/AETA. ALEC holds a number of private meetings each year and drafts "model legislation" to be distributed to Congress members. It is heavily slanted toward politically conservative interests, and it is financially backed by large corporations, including ExxonMobil, Wal-Mart, and AT&T, among others. This ensures that corporate interests remain central to the legislation produced—which is evident in their model legislation.[32]

The financial ties of the politicians who support the AEPA clearly demonstrate the role played by the meat, dairy, and pharmaceutical industries.[33] Stenholm's financial interests are most explicit. Four of his top ten contributors were the American Farm Bureau, National Cattleman's Beef Association, Dairy Farmers of America, and United Egg Association—the first two of which were his first and second largest contributors. Other important sponsors of AEPA with ties to the agricultural and pharmaceutical industries included Thomas Ewing (R-IL), Herbert Bateman (R-VA), and Dave Camp (R-MI). The latter two had large investments in the meat and pharmaceutical industries, respectively, while Ewing had campaign contributors from the meat and dairy industries.[34]

One of the most important things that the AEPA did was to define the crime of "animal enterprise terrorism." Anyone who "travels in interstate or foreign commerce . . . for the purpose of causing physical disruption to the functioning of an animal enterprise; and intentionally causes physical disruption to the functioning of an animal enterprise" is engaging in animal enterprise terrorism.

Specifically, the AEPA outlines sentencing guidelines based on the amount of economic damage caused to an animal enterprise, which is defined as any "(a) commercial or academic enterprise that uses animals for food or fiber production, agriculture, research, or testing; (b) a zoo, aquarium, circus, rodeo, or lawful competitive animal event." The AEPA establishes sentencing guidelines based on economic loss and personal injury. The guidelines established purely on economic damages and political ideologies are unusual and potentially chilling of First Amendment speech.[35] Not only does this law base punishment on economic damage rather than just the act that was committed, but the guidelines establish punishments that are greater than otherwise expected for a crime such as petty vandalism. AEPA also criminalizes ideology in favour of corporate interests, since only actions motivated by animal rights ideology are prosecuted under this law.

In 2004, the Senate held a hearing, "Animal Rights: Activism vs. Criminality." This was followed in 2006 by "Oversight on Ecoterrorism specifically examining the Earth Liberation Front (ELF) and Animal Liberation Front (ALF)." These hearings led to the introduction of an amendment to the AEPA, which broadened the types of activism that could be prosecuted and created harsher penalties for violating the Act. On November 27, 2006, after a House hearing on the proposals in which only one person was called to testify in opposition to the amendment, it was signed into law under a revised name, the Animal Enterprise Terrorism Act (AETA).

The AETA broadened the scope of what was prosecutable and increased sentencing guidelines for penalties and restitution.[36] Among other notable changes under the AETA, prosecutable crimes were broadened to include "*damaging* or *interfering* with the operations of an animal enterprise" (emphasis mine). *Animal enterprise* was also redefined, and included *anyone doing business with* a company that profits from animals, anyone who works for an animal enterprise, or the relatives of animal enterprise employees.

The new sentencing guidelines included a fine and/or up to a year in prison if damages were below $10,000 and no person had reasonable *fear* of personal harm. The jail terms increased depending on economic damage, with damage over $1 million resulting in a possible twenty-year prison sentence. The AETA also provided for restitution to be paid by the defendant for any damages. Notably, under the AETA, damages include *any* loss of profit, a term left to be defined in large part by the corporations themselves; as such, damages can run artificially high, leading to high restitutions and long prison terms. The sentencing guidelines under the AETA are based on the economic interests of corporations and are extreme, particularly when considered in the context of the US penal system: "Sentencing penalties under the Act are excessively harsh and far exceed those for otherwise violent or monetary crimes under the 2005 federal sentencing guidelines that were in place just before AETA's passage. Compare 20 years for profit loss under AETA to 4.5 years for sexual assault, 3 years for manslaughter and 4 months for embezzlement or larceny."[37] Public statements made clear that federal authorities were primarily concerned with the economic impact of animal rights activism. For example, a 2006 bulletin circulated by the Department of Homeland Security emphasized the economic basis of their concern: "Attacks against corporations by animal rights extremists and eco-terrorists are costly to the targeted company and, over time, can undermine confidence in the economy."[38]

Though the impetus for this repression of the animal rights movement was driven by corporate interests (the EOS), it was enacted by legal and political sanctions awarded through formal state structures (the SOS). Furthermore, a lack of public outrage (the COS) at such a restriction of civil liberties allowed these laws to pass without objection. In the post-9/11 terrain, terrorism fear-mongering allowed corporations and the government to villainize activists. With state and corporate forces turned against activists and a lack of support from the public, the more radical strategies of the animal rights movement were largely repressed.

Repression can also be thought of as a closed opportunity structure: "political opportunity structure is also discussed within the repression literature but with the label 'political threat,' which is defined as the perceived necessity for state repression in an effort to counter challengers who (left

380 CAROL L. GLASSER

alone) could alter some form of the political-economic system."[39] The AETA closed off a portion of the opportunity field for the animal rights movement by raising the cost for confronting targets and using the tactics that most directly cut into the profits of industries that exploit animals. Indirectly, it also muted the movement by instilling a culture of fear among activists.

Importantly, repression does not function without its counterpart, facilitation: "Activists with radical goals and strategies are more likely to be subjected to repression, whereas moderate wings are more likely to receive facilitation. Thus different wings of social movements receive different strategic cues."[40] Selective facilitation and repression allow control over the pace of change a movement can achieve, and lead to movement demobilization.[41] As some strategies become more costly, others begin to seem more favourable to social movement organizations and activists, because the cost is lower. Less threatening strategies may even be encouraged by the co-operation of social movement targets with social movement organizations. Movement organizations and actors become pacified with little more than symbolic gains, such as policies that are passed but not enforced; dedicating streets, buildings, or days to social movement heroes; or using a social movement cause to promote sales (e.g., pink washing and green washing).

The trajectory of undercover investigations and "ag-gag" bills demonstrates the process through which selective repression and facilitation slows the pace of change while pacifying movement actors through symbolic gains.[42] One tactic used by the animal rights movement is undercover investigations. Activists gain access (often through employment) to a business involved in animal exploitation, such as a research facility, factory farm, circus, marine park, etc. The investigator captures evidence of animal abuse, often through wearing hidden cameras. This evidence is later reproduced in videos to be posted online to garner media attention, mobilize public support, and encourage legal action against the business. These campaigns seek to educate the public, push the state to legally protect animals, and shame corporations; they have historically been effective at getting media attention, public support, and some legal prosecutions of animal abusers.

The success of these methods was met with repression at the same time that the movement was provided a symbolic "win" and a more mundane form of activism was facilitated. In 2008, the Humane Society of the United States (HSUS) released a video of the Chino, California, Hallmark and Westland slaughterhouse in which workers forced cows who had fallen and could not get up ("downer cows") to the kill floor for slaughter. Not only were the cows being moved by abusive methods, such as pushing them with forklifts, but these downer animals were also allowed into the human food supply, which is illegal. The investigation resulted in the largest beef recall in US history and a lawsuit against the company, which subsequently went out of business.

Conversely, this investigation also spurred the onset of "ag-gag" bills in 2011. Ag-gag laws criminalize taking photographs or video in various "animal facilities," including factory farms, slaughterhouses, research facilities, and even puppy mills. Further, gaining employment with the intent to be a whistle-blower at animal facilities is deemed illegal under these proposed laws.

Since 2011, twenty US states have proposed ag-gag bills. They have been passed in five states and are currently pending in two.[43] The language in a number of these bills is identical because, like AEPA/AETA, these bills stem from ALEC.[44] Corporate interests working through ALEC drafted "model legislation" that state legislators were then encouraged to propose at the state level in order to hamper activism, specifically undercover investigations.

Simultaneous to this attempt to criminalize a legal tactic of the movement with corporate-driven legislation, the state provided the movement a "win" through largely symbolic prosecutions of slaughterhouse workers filmed in various undercover investigations. In 2010, an investigation at Conklin Dairy Farm by Mercy for Animals (MFA) resulted in the prosecution of and an eight-month prison sentence for Billy Joe Gregg Jr., a slaughterhouse worker caught on tape abusing animals. In 2012 another MFA investigation of a Butterball factory farm revealed employees kicking and stomping on turkeys; this footage led to the felony animal cruelty conviction of Brian Douglas, who was sentenced to thirty days in jail, three and a half years on probation, and a $550 fine.[45]

These prosecutions, and others like them, feign an earnest responsiveness and openness of the SOS to the animal rights agenda. Activism much more mundane than undercover investigations, such as signing online petitions to demand prosecution of the factory farm workers, was facilitated, allowing for animal rights activists and organizations to be pacified because it appeared their concerns were being taken seriously. Further, these prosecutions were merely symbolic concessions—the corporations behind the cruelty, their organizational oversight and encouragement of such behaviour, and the people who were profiting were not held accountable. A few token individuals with the least amount of power, the lowest pay, and who were acting in a way that is common in their industry, took the blame. Furthermore, the punishments for the few individuals prosecuted were remarkably light. More troubling is the way in which animal rights activists unintentionally aided in supporting a corporate narrative in which these cases of cruelty to individual animals by individual people is separated from the systemic exploitation inherent in the industry.

On the flip side, it is notable that most of the proposed ag-gag bills failed, passing in only five of the states in which they were proposed. They were not reported on favourably by the media and did not have wide public support. According to a 2011 survey, 73 percent of US adults support anti-cruelty investigations; this is more support than for any other social movement tactic, including using media to reach the public (70 percent) and filing lawsuits to protect animals (50 percent), among others.[46] It is possible that no prosecutions would have occurred if public outrage had not been stirred by the videos from these investigations and if the public did not support the tactic used. These outcomes show the intervention that the COS can have on corporate control over the state, once again highlighting the importance of the interrelated nature of all aspects of the opportunity field.

Failure of Corporate Incorporation

The US animal rights movement generally acknowledges that corporations and economic interests play a role in the exploitation of animals, which is why corporate incorporation is a strategy made use of at all. However, the role of the EOS has been misunderstood and undervalued. This misunderstanding leads to strategies in which corporations are embraced in exchange for small or symbolic gains in the pursuit of cultural and political goals.

The push for vegan options in restaurants is a clear example of this. Having more vegan options is an attempt to drive a cultural shift. The strategy aims to expose people to vegan options, remove a barrier to adopting and maintaining the diet, and make it easier for meat-eaters to reduce the amount of animal products they consume. The expectation is that if enough people choose to eat animal-free meals on a regular basis, the demand for animal products and the number of animals who are slaughtered will decrease. In terms of the opportunity field, these campaigns seek to change the EOS by way of the COS. Presumably the COS is perceived as more open than the EOS by the organizations and activists who choose this route; their hope is that through changing cultural attitudes and eventually demand, they will make corporations shift their practices. Does this strategy work?

The awareness and prevalence of veganism does continue to increase, even though the total number of vegans and vegetarians remains small. According to national polls, the number of vegetarians and vegans increased from 2 percent of the US population in 2006 to 3 percent in 2009 to 4 percent in 2012.[47] Trends regarding animal slaughter, meat demand, and per capita consumption of animal products appear promising on the surface, but further analysis suggests that cultural shifts in attitude and demand are not effective in influencing the meat, dairy, and egg industries.

The number of land animals slaughtered for food in the US has generally decreased annually. In 2011, over 102 million fewer animals were slaughtered, a 1 percent decrease from 2010.[48] Per capita consumption of meat (including fish), egg, and dairy products also declined, from 920 pounds per capita in 2008 to 873 pounds in 2009.[49] This suggests a positive trend, but a trend that must be examined more closely.

Globally, meat production has been decreasing and meat prices have been rising due to zoonotic diseases associated with CAFOs (concentrated animal feeding operations), as well as droughts in the United States, China, Russia, and the Horn of Africa.[50] Further, in the US, a high demand for ethanol has led to increasing prices and decreasing availability of corn, a staple food fed to animals on CAFOs.[51]

Economic factors, environmental factors, and an increasing population size have led to the decrease in per capita consumption of animal products;[52] whether or not an increasing number of vegans and "flexitarians" (people who reduce meat in their diets) have had an impact is still up for debate. It does not appear as if decreased consumption of meat has also translated into a decrease in demand for meat products. Demand is measured by looking at consumption relative to prices. The general consensus from economists, the US meat industry, and government agencies is that demand for most meats (pork, beef, and turkey, but not chicken) increased between 2010 and 2011.[53]

This suggests that if environmental factors change to allow for increased availability, consumers will begin to eat more meat and may return to past levels of meat consumption. To put this into the language of the opportunity field means that campaigns focused on the COS have not driven the decrease in meat production, even if they have engendered some shifts in personal behaviours and public perceptions.

Campaigns that do not decrease the profits of major corporations will not enact change, but campaigns directed at the EOS can have a quick, direct impact on animal rights goals. While the push for veganism may have opened new markets, it has not affected the current economic impetus for animal exploitation or slaughter.[54] Because corporate interests are the primary drivers of animal exploitation and the state actively works to protect these interests, any campaign that accepts the corporate interests of animal exploitation businesses by using corporate incorporation as a strategy will not make gains for animals. Campaigns that actively support corporations will ultimately fail to protect animals.

Some animal rights groups have chosen to work with fast-food restaurants to get them to purchase from factory farms with slightly better living conditions (e.g., no gestation crates for pregnant pigs) or to purchase from slaughterhouses that use different killing methods such as CAK (controlled atmospheric killing).[55] There have even been campaigns that actively promote fast-food restaurants that include vegan options on the menu. In 2008, People for the Ethical Treatment of Animals (PETA) dropped their campaign against KFC in Canada after they achieved what they called an "historic victory"—KFC adopting a "kinder killing method" (i.e., CAK) for chickens and adding a vegan option to their menu. Even though KFC's entire business model is built on the violent exploitation of animals (hence the words "fried chicken" in the company's original name), PETA celebrated and even promoted the business for these small concessions. Women wearing bikinis styled to look like lettuce leaves handed out samples of the new vegan meat alternative and a PETA employee held her wedding reception at a KFC to celebrate (and presumably bring media attention to) this shift in KFC's practices.[56]

Compassion over Killing (COK), better known in the past for radical actions such as open rescues and undercover videos, recently shifted much of their focus to getting vegan options in restaurants. Their reasoning, as stated on their website for their Restaurant Outreach Program, is as follows: "A major factor preventing numerous people from seriously exploring veganism is simply convenience. Those who've had no experience with veganism often find the thought of adopting a vegan diet very daunting. Because of this, COK greatly expanded our restaurant outreach campaign."[57] The goal is palatable on a surface level, but because it necessitates working with business interests that remain centred on animal exploitation it cannot achieve animal rights goals. In one current campaign, COK has gone so far as to actively promote a fast-food restaurant. The campaign, We Love Subway, asks people to support a vegan option at Subway. The campaign is centred on a website, run by COK—www.WeLoveSubway.com.[58] The website thanks Subway for having vegetarian options and encourages the addition of vegan meats. Since the campaign started, select Canadian franchises and three US stores have added a vegan patty; however, it is not clear this is in response to the campaign.[59]

In the earlier anecdote of PETA and KFC, there was a celebration of a fast-food restaurant after some measurable goal was attained. In this case, COK has gone further and pre-emptively promoted and celebrated a fast-food restaurant out of the hope for a "win." Notably, in both cases, the "win" falls short in great measure from the foundational goals of the animal rights movement. Killing the same number of animals who have been raised on factory farms, but killing them less painfully, is a far cry from giving animals quality of life or ceasing to kill them for food. Even in terms of the strategy of working toward animal rights through incremental changes, these campaigns fall short because of the degree to which they embrace the fast-food industry.

Since the fast-food industry is a driving force of factory farming, these gains are nothing more than symbolic; any collaboration that benefits the fast-food industry will slow the pace of change for animals. McDonald's restaurants alone accounted for 3 percent of US beef sales in 2010;[60] Subway is the largest fast-food chain in the world with 33,749 franchises as of 2010;[61] in 2011 the US fast-food industry brought in about $190 billion in revenue, an increase of $6 million from just one year prior.[62]

Any promotion of these businesses in any way that does not cut into their profit margin only serves to bolster the current system of factory farming by allowing the potential to increase profits while continuing to engage in the business of animal exploitation. Add to this the human costs tied to the fast-food industry, including the rise in obesity, heart disease, and other human health issues, cultural colonization and the rise of meat-eating globally, and the exploitation of (human) workers, and there is no pragmatic reason to work with these businesses. Unless animal rights groups organize boycotts, or at the very least demand that animal products be *replaced* (not supplemented) with cruelty-free alternatives, they are merely helping restaurants to diversify and increase profits by bringing in a new vegetarian and vegan market.

The strategy of working with corporations has also been used in attempts to secure policy and legal gains. The Farm Bill Amendment No.

2252 would have established federal regulations for the US egg industry moving forward—defining what carton labels mean, specifying space requirements for egg-laying hens, and establishing time frames within which to comply with the new regulations.[63] Even though this bill didn't pass, it serves as an exemplar case of animal rights groups and corporations working together and it highlights the types of concessions that must be made when involving animal exploitation corporations as part of a strategy to achieve political gains.

HSUS (the Humane Society of the United States) worked with the United Egg Producers (UEP), an organization established to promote and advance the US egg industry, to develop the bill. Notably, the leading sponsor on the Farm Bill Amendment was Senator Dianne Feinstein (D-CA), the same senator who actively repressed the animal rights movement by co-sponsoring the AETA.

One of the greatest achievements of the bill would have been that farms with more than 3,000 hens would be required to provide at least 124–44 square inches of living space per hen, depending on the breed. At its maximum, this requirement means that each hen is allotted an area of space equivalent to one square foot, very little considering that the wingspan of an average egg-laying hen is two and a half feet.[64] Further, farmers were being given a full fifteen years to comply with the law, essentially ensuring they wouldn't spend any extra money making transitions, as they would need to replace equipment within that time frame regardless of the legislation. Essentially, the industry would not take any loss but, by asking for only minimal welfare gains, the animal rights side made huge concessions just for a seat at the table.[65]

One argument in support of these bills is that the process of publicly pushing for these policies makes consumers aware of animal suffering, which will lead to an eventual decrease in meat consumption. However, there is little evidence to support this claim. One study found that California Proposition 2 (passed in 2008), which sought to improve farm animal welfare by eliminating the use of battery cages for egg-laying hens (among other measures), may have actually increased demand for "higher welfare" eggs while having no effect on conventional eggs.[66] Another study examining egg consumption patterns in four European countries with similar bans on battery cages found no evidence that the cultural and political discussion of these bans had any influence on consumptive patterns, as egg consumption declined in two of the countries and increased in the other two.[67]

In the previous examples, the major concerns for the animal rights movement—to save animals' lives and shift the cultural attitude toward recognizing their unique interests—are being set aside for much smaller goals. Animal rights organizations are curtailing their goals and reigning in the types of tactics they are willing to use for incorporation and access to various structures within the opportunity field.

The trade-off is particularly uneven in the partnership between HSUS and UEP (United Egg Producers). HSUS is clear that this bill is beneficial to the egg industry. The title on the web page posted by HSUS to promote the bill is: "Amendment to Improve Welfare of Egg-Laying Hens and *Provide a Stable Future for Farmers*" (emphasis mine).[68] Francione highlights that often, when legislation-based campaigns actually do succeed, the animal rights organizations promoting them explicitly state that they will benefit the animal exploitation businesses.[69]

This bill asked for less than, and would override, what HSUS had already achieved in California with Proposition 2, as well as making it impossible to challenge the federal legislation and improve conditions further by way of ballot initiatives or legislation at the state level. Further, the time periods provided to make these shifts are so long that it would be difficult to argue better welfare could not be achieved for more egg-laying hens by some other means within a fifteen-year period.

Animal rights organizations are making concessions for inclusion into the very structure that is at the foundation of the exploitation they seek to combat. Adding a vegan option may make life more tolerable for vegans, it may open up a market for vegan brands such as Tofurkey,[70] and it may even lead to more meatless meals, but it is not enough to push any significant downturn in the mass slaughter of animals for food.[71] As previously mentioned, the current downturn in meat consumption is tied more to zoonotic disease and drought than to an increase in vegan options. And even as per capita meat consumption declines, the profits of the fast-food industry continue to trend upward, likely because they sell meat-based foods so cheaply.[72]

This is not to say that any program focused on cultural or political changes will be ineffective. To the degree that these campaigns can avoid bolstering current animal exploitation industries, they do no harm, and if they are able to actually direct a cultural shift that is great enough to influence corporate profits, they can be successful. This is difficult, as was previously discussed with regard to culturally directed campaigns broadly. However, it is possible, as the Meatless Mondays campaign highlights.

The Meatless Mondays campaign promotes a cultural shift on a personal level by encouraging people to abstain from meat-eating on Mondays. Meatless Mondays is not geared around working with corporations to promote the campaign. This is a challenging tactic because it requires so many people to change their behaviour. Even so, Meatless Mondays has caught on with a critical mass of people asking for the program in their places of work or school; some businesses responsible for animal exploitation have changed to keep up with cultural shifts and fill consumer needs. The major catering company Sodexo incorporated Meatless Mondays into many of their cafeterias in 2003 and total meat purchases by customers decreased in 30 percent of the 245 cafeterias surveyed.[73]

Unlike the previously mentioned campaigns that failed by seeking corporate help in pushing cultural change, Meatless Mondays pushes corporate behaviour through cultural change. The Meatless Monday campaign highlights again the interdependent nature of cultural, state, and economic structures. In response to public (i.e., COS) support of the campaign, some catering companies, businesses, and schools (i.e., EOS) have implemented the program. The USDA (a government agency) even supported it with a post on their website in 2012, encouraging employees not to eat meat on Mondays. However, once the National Cattlemen's Beef Association put out a press release denouncing the post, the USDA immediately retracted their support and publicly stated they do not support the Meatless Monday initiative—once again confirming that corporate interests control the state and exposing the state as a less effective avenue for change.[74]

Professionalization and the Non-profit Industrial Complex

Institutionalization of a social movement refers to "the creation of a set of relationships and procedures such that the politics of an issue become routine."[75] Institutionalization is common across social movements as they move through waves or cycles of contention. Over time the pace of activism picks up and various factions of the movement work together to achieve similar goals. At the height of a wave of contention, when a movement is most active and shows the most potential for creating change, demobilization typically occurs. Some aspects of a movement are facilitated while others are repressed, movement participants leave due to exhaustion or normal life-course changes (e.g., career, children, etc.), and the moderate faction of the movement becomes institutionalized.[76] Forming working relationships with corporations, including those that exploit animals, has been a part of the institutionalizing process of the animal rights movement.

As animal rights organizations become formalized and professionalized, they become more interested in corporate incorporation, either by being included within corporate processes, utilizing the organizational structures of corporations, or working with corporations as a strategy to achieve social movement goals.

HSUS's then president, Paul G. Irwin, described the rationale in a 2003 newsletter: "We do effective work to protect animals, but if we don't promote our work and market our messages, we won't succeed in influencing people to join the effort. And corporate relationships offer a unique opportunity for The HSUS to do this. Not incidentally, such relationships also provide an important source of funding for many of our programs."[77] For HSUS, securing their position as a professional organization with financial longevity also meant tying themselves to large corporations.

Meyer describes institutionalization as a function of the US political structure, whereby dissent is routinely and predictably controlled and subdued: "Frequent elections and relatively open access to institutions allow dissident politics to be absorbed, diffusing dissent and political analysis in the process. . . . Political institutions encourage negotiation, bargaining, and compromise, absorbing dissent with minimal policy response. Paradoxically, by legitimating and institutionalizing dissent, the Madisonian political opportunity structure enhances stability and forestalls change."[78] Through a process of "co-optation," some aspects of a social movement—be they tactics, goals, ideologies, organizations, and/or leaders—become part of mainstream politics.[79] In exchange for access to some formal recognition from and inclusion in the processes of structures in the opportunity field (businesses, politics, etc.), some factions of a movement voluntarily clip their wings to accommodate the rules and routines of mainstream politics.

For access to corporate structures and decision-making, animal rights organizations are weakening their goals and accepting concessions. To the degree that they are willing to make enough concessions, corporations and the state will work with them; the number and severity of concessions required for this partnership is such that the animal rights organization's goals are watered down and may even be beneficial to corporate interests.

In addition to working within the corporate system and seeking acceptance from corporations to achieve social movement gains, the animal rights movement has embraced current economic and corporate structures by adopting formal state-sanctioned organizational configurations (501(c)(3) and 501(c)(4) status—a first step in securing many grants and receiving tax exemption, among other benefits), and running them as corporations run businesses—with social movement professionals, physical locations, and top-down organizing. This has been an integral factor in the institutionalization of the animal rights movement and along with it has come further moderation of the movement's tactics, targets, and goals.

The process of institutionalization can be seen through the trajectory of PETA from its founding in 1980 through the 2010s. PETA started as a protest organization with unabashed ties to underground radicals in the movement; as such, it was actively repressed by the state, including being targeted by a federal RICO (Racketeer Influenced and Corrupt Organizations Act) lawsuit. Over time PETA changed its tactical repertoire—embracing more conventional and institutionalized tactics, seeking corporate incorporation, and moderating its goals.[80] PETA now embraces a variety of tactics that would have been considered overly moderate for them in their early years, many of them centred on reform measures using corporate incorporation as a strategy, included attending shareholder meetings of corporations that profit from animal exploitation. As PETA explains in their *Animal Times* newsletter: "PETA's strategy for convincing companies like Smithfield Foods, Burger King, DuPont, and Monsanto to adopt new animal welfare standards involves becoming part of the very corporations that we are fighting. PETA has purchased (or recruited proxy owners of) the minimum amount of stock in top US meat processors, restaurant chains, and grocers—including ConAgra, Kroger, Wal-Mart, Wendy's, Yum! Brands (Pizza Hut, Taco Bell, and KFC), and others—which allows US to propose animal welfare improvements to shareholders at the annual meetings of these companies."[81] Not only have individual groups become institutionalized, but the movement as a whole has trended in this direction as the number of non-profit social movement organizations grows and more activists become employed by social movement organizations. Movements evolve through waves or cycles in which there are moments of intense action followed by movement decline.[82] Formalized institutional structures can be helpful for movements insofar as they serve as a sort of "placeholder" for the cause during periods of decline or abeyance, serving as "bridges between different upsurges of activism."[83] However, these formal structures are also a significant contributing factor in movement decline.

Institutionalization of the animal rights movement has come with a proliferation of formal animal rights organizations and increasing professionalization in the movement. In 1980, when PETA was formed, having a protest organization demanding rights for animals was novel as most well-known, animal-oriented organizations were geared toward service (humane societies, etc.). Since then the social movement field has grown considerably and there are more grassroots and state-sanctioned animal rights organizations. This propels the movement into complacency within the non-profit industrial complex (NPIC), a system in which organizational longevity, comradery with the state, and corporate interests take precedence over inciting dissent.

The NPIC refers to the way that political organizing and social services performed by non-profit organizations often become linked to and controlled by state and economic structures. The NPIC serves to:

- Monitor and control social justice movements;
- Divert public monies into private hands through foundations;
- Manage and control dissent in order to make the world safe for capitalism;
- Redirect activist energies into career-based modes of organizing instead of mass-based organizing capable of actually transforming society;
- Allow corporations to mask their exploitative and colonial work practices through "philanthropic" work;
- Encourage social movements to model themselves after capitalist structures rather than to challenge them.[84]

These outcomes can occur because the non-profits are beholden to the state to keep non-profit status and beholden to economic structures as they seek donations and grants. Additionally, they typically take a top-down, corporate organizing structure, creating a situation in which non-profits are working with the very structures they are seeking to change.

Increasing numbers of formalized organizations has led to a denser social movement field in which a greater number of organizations are competing for the same pool of resources, including money, volunteers, activists, and media coverage. It also leads to professionalization of activism. As Smith highlights, "[t]o radically change society, we must build mass movements that can topple systems of domination, such as capitalism. However, the NPIC encourages us to think of social justice organizing as a career; that is, you do the work if you can get paid for it."[85] Professionalization may encourage activists to think of their work for justice as something they should be paid for and it discourages activism and ideologies that are not in line with the goals of the organization signing the paycheques or the donors funding the organization.

In Staggeborg's study of professionalization in the pro-choice movement, she found that the professionalization of movement leadership and the formalization of movement organizations encouraged the use of institutionalized tactics.[86] Movement professionals are attached not only to an ideology but also to an organization; therefore, they must become more concerned with donor opinions and organizational longevity. As a professional social movement actor whose paycheque depends on organizational stability and adherence to specific state-mandated regulations, the tactical repertoire available becomes smaller at the same time that the goals sought become more moderate. Organizations need to appeal to donors and the public, and the more moderate a movement's goals and the more palatable the tactics, the more public appeal they will have.[87] Further, accepting 501(c)(3) or (4) status comes with certain prohibitions on goals and strategies. Once an organization is formalized in such a way and social movement actors are embedded in this organization, the structure of the opportunity field shifts.

As McAdam highlights in a discussion of the interaction between social movements and the POS, the "mediation between opportunity and action are people and the subjective meanings they attach to their situations."[88] In other words, opportunity structures are neither static nor objective; rather, they are *interpreted* by social movement actors. The opportunity field will be interpreted differently if an activist is a stakeholder in an organization's longevity.

Over time more organizations in the animal rights movement are becoming part of the NPIC (non-profit industrial complex); if things do not change, the grassroots ethic of collective, community-based activism in the movement will be completely co-opted and the movement will be a pawn of the state and corporations, rather than an advocate for animals.

Conclusion

Social movements are often analyzed with a political process model that views them as working within and being constrained by political structures. Theories of POSs (political opportunity structures) generally assume social movement actors and organizations will seek opportunities for inroads into the political process; when a potential opportunity is identified, the benefit of that opportunity is weighed against the concessions that must be made to achieve it. When the gains are thought to outweigh the concessions, social movement actors and organizations will develop strategies to pursue those opportunities.

POS theories are correct to a point, but they do not do enough to incorporate cultural or economic opportunities and structures. Though social movements are often thought of as political in nature, they are more than that—they are both reacting to and seeking to change various cultural aspects and economic structures as well as state/political structures. A more fruitful way to envision a social movement's constraints and potential strategies for change is by examining what I have called the opportunity field. The opportunity field encompasses COSs (cultural opportunity structures) (e.g., the media, public opinion), EOSs (economic opportunity structures) (e.g., corporations, profit margins), and SOSs (state opportunity structures, typically thought of as the POS—e.g., legislation, political elites).[89]

Not all opportunity structures are equally important. Depending on the nature of the issue a social movement seeks to address, different structures within the opportunity field will be of more or less importance, both in terms of their role in constraining the movement and their suitability as a target or an ally. In the case of the US animal rights movement, too much attention has been focused on COSs and SOSs, neglecting the fact that corporations and their economic interests drive animal exploitation and repression of the animal rights movement. US culture supports and normalizes animal exploitation in various ways (e.g., meat-eating, wearing leather and in other ways animals' skins and furs, speciesist language, advertising, etc.); however, this cultural normalization is not the cause of animal exploitation but is rather a reflection of corporate interests in continuing and expanding profits from animal exploitation. The state's perpetuation of animal exploitation is also driven by corporate interests, as is the repression of the animal rights movement.

Because economic structures are the root of animal exploitation, EOSs do the most to shape the opportunity field in which the animal rights movement is working, and also provide the quickest route to change. However, rather than challenging corporations, animal rights organizations have worked with them in efforts to create cultural change (such as increasing the number of vegan food options or swaying public opinion about animal testing) or state-oriented change (such as passing legislation to protect animals). These routes to change are not only indirect, but are often ineffective and may even be regressive. Effective campaigns would make it unprofitable to use animals as commodities, or at least *more* profitable *not* to use animals.

Economic structures, in particular corporations and their interests, are the foundation of the system that generates and propagates animal exploitation. Various forms of cultural, economic, and state/political oppressions grow and spread from there. Tackling animal exploitation that is driven by state and cultural structures is like treating the symptoms of a disease rather than its cause. If enough symptoms are suppressed through various successful campaigns, animal exploitation may appear to diminish, but at some point new symptoms of exploitation will arise or old ones will reappear. When animal rights strategies go one step further and work with corporations, they are feeding the disease, helping it to strengthen and spread.

In the case of the animal rights movement, the tactic of corporate incorporation embraces the same system that creates the exploitation the movement seeks to end. Because corporate interests are so often antithetical to animals' interests, the animal rights movement will fail to progress if it does not begin to tackle the cause of the problem and avoid incorporating corporations in strategies for animal rights.

NOTES

This chapter was written in 2013. It received the Faculty Paper of the Year award from the Institute for Critical Animal Studies.

1. I use the term "animal" when referring to nonhuman animals and "human" when referring to human animals. This is admittedly problematic language as it reproduces the fictitious human–animal binary that supports human dominance over other animals. I have made this decision for the sake of reading ease.
2. I define the animal rights movement broadly as a one that seeks to provide relief to and some sort of rights for animals, beyond basic service functions such as sheltering. I use the phrase "animal rights" to discuss the entire movement for animal welfare, rights, and liberation, including all campaigns utilized by activists and groups within this broad definition of the movement. When speaking specifically of vegetarian and vegan outreach campaigns I use the term "vegan" exclusively to make the text less cumbersome, and because all of the current major "Go Veg" outreach guides in the US only promote

veganism, regardless of whether they choose the term "vegan" or "vegetarian." The divisions within the movement are important to discuss and are worth parsing out for ideological and theoretical reasons. This has received worthy attention on movement blogs, in academic and movement literature, and in public meetings, but it is beyond the scope of this chapter.

3. See, for example, Gamson and Meyer, "Framing Political Opportunity"; Kriesi, "Political Context and Opportunity"; and Meyer, "Institutionalizing Dissent."
4. Meyer, "Protest and Political Opportunities."
5. Snow and Soule, *Primer on Social Movements*, 66–67.
6. Meyer, "Protest and Political Opportunities"; Wahlström and Peterson, "Between the State and the Market."
7. In Wahlström and Peterson, "Between the State and the Market."
8. Kriesi, "Political Context and Opportunity."
9. Ibid.
10. Gamson and Meyer, "Framing Political Opportunity."
11. Wahlström and Peterson, "Between the State and the Market."
12. Gamson and Meyer, "Framing Political Opportunity."
13. Wahlström and Peterson, "Between the State and the Market," 366.
14. Ibid., 365.
15. Li, "Opportunities in Action," 338.
16. Ibid. The Computer TakeBack campaign, started in the US and Canada in 2001, focused on getting companies that sold computers to take back old computers and manage the e-waste they generated. By 2011, all US states had either passed legislation to form e-waste recycling programs or established producer responsibility laws.
17. Schurman and Munro, "Targeting Capital."
18. Wahlström and Peterson, "Between the State and the Market," 369 (emphasis mine).
19. In the wake of the "Twitter Revolution" and in response to online social movement campaigns, some scholars now pinpoint social media as being integral in how issues are framed and in mobilizing activists (Lim, "Clicks, Cabs, and Coffee Houses") and as influencing the cultural and political landscape most starkly. Shirky ("Political Power of Social Media") elucidates this perspective: "social media's real potential lies in supporting civil society and the public sphere—which will produce change over years and decades, not weeks and months."
20. Wahlström and Peterson, "Between the State and the Market," 368.
21. Nibert, *Animal Rights/Human Rights*.
22. Jefferson, "Infographic."
23. CRP, "Alphabetical Listing of Industries."
24. 24/7 and Danello, "9 Foods."

25. The Week. "Farm Subsidies."
26. 24/7 and Danello, "9 Foods."
27. USDA, "Special Milk Program."
28. NIH, "Lactose Intolerance."
29. Cohen, Morgan, and Stanton, "Farm Subsidies."
30. Lovitz, *Muzzling a Movement.*
31. 102 Cong. Rec. 4438 (1991); see also Lovitz, *Muzzling a Movement.*
32. *Political Correction*, "American Legislative Council."
33. See Lovitz, *Muzzling a Movement*, 50–51.
34. Ibid.
35. See McCoy, "Subverting Justice," for a discussion of this point in relation to the AETA, an amended version of the AEPA.
36. See Goodman, "Shielding Corporate Interests," 848–50, for a detailed discussion of the enhancements to the AEPA under the AETA.
37. EJA, "Animal Enterprise."
38. DHS, "Preventing Attacks"; see Potter, "3 Reasons."
39. Davenport, "Repression and Mobilization," xv.
40. Koopmans, "Dynamics of Protest Waves," 645; see also Lichbach, "Deterrence or Escalation?"
41. See Tarrow, *Struggle, Politics, and Reform.*
42. Bittman, "Who Protects the Animals?"
43. Genoways, "Gagged by Big Ag." Since the writing of this chapter, more ag-gag laws have been proposed. In 2014 Idaho passed an ag-gag law that was struck down by the federal government as unconstitutional. As of September 2015, twenty-seven states have proposed ag-gag bills or quick reporting bills. They have failed or died in twenty states and passed in seven (ASPCA, "Ag Gag Bills at the State Level").
44. Potter, "'Ag Gag' Bills."
45. *PR Newswire*, "Butterball Worker Pleads Guilty."
46. HRC, *Animal Tracker.*
47. Stahler, "How Many?"; "How Often?"; VRG, "How Many Vegetarians?" These figures must be considered cautiously since these are very small proportions, making accurate measures more difficult to attain. For example, the margin of error in the 2012 survey is ±2 percent, meaning that the percentage of vegetarians and vegans, based on these survey results, could be anywhere between 2 percent (indicating no change over previous years) and 6 percent (indicating a 50 percent increase over 2009).
48. USDA, "Livestock Slaughter"; "Poultry Slaughter."
49. HRC, *Animal Tracker.*
50. Nierenberg and Reynolds, "Disease and Drought."
51. DAE, "2011 US Meat and Poultry."

52. Ibid.

53. Ibid., except see Sethu, "Meat Consumption!"

54. Key Note, *Vegetarian Foods 2012*.

55. CAK is a slaughter method in which poultry animals are killed by being placed in a container where the oxygen is removed and replaced with various gases that cause the animals to pass out and then die. Some animal rights groups promote the method as more humane because the process is believed to cause little to no pain and the birds are placed into the killing chambers while still in their transport cages, therefore they are never handled by slaughterhouse workers while still alive.

56. *Windsor Star*, "PETA Ends KFC Canada Boycott"; see PETA, "Why We Married at KFC."

57. COK, "Proud to Serve."

58. Interestingly, in another campaign aimed at getting Dunkin' Donuts to sell a vegan doughnut, they use the opposite strategy and present Dunkin' Donuts negatively, with the Dunkin' Cruelty campaign. In both campaigns, their goal is to have a vegan option and allow vegans to participate in the consumption of food at a fast-food giant.

59. According to one news report the origin of the vegan patties is disputed—in the US, COK has taken credit for the vegan options, but Subway gives credit to one of its franchise owners (*Fox News*, "Subway").

60. *Meat Trade News Daily*, "USA—McDonalds."

61. Pepitone, "Subway Beats McDonald's."

62. *Statista*, "Revenue of the Fast Food Restaurant Industry."

63. S. 3239 and H.R. 3798.

64. EFF, "Egg Laying Hens."

65. Francione ("Reflections") discusses similar campaigns in his work evaluating the utility of passing welfare-based legislation. He argues that these campaigns cannot be successful because animals, legally classified as property, will remain commodities and only be cared for 'humanely' in so far as they also remain profitable. To restate in terms of the opportunity field, this means that the SOS will shift to benefit animals only in so far as the economic considerations of corporations and businesses remain the key concern.

66. Lusk, "Effect of Proposition 2."

67. Cooney, "Battery Cage Bans."

68. HSUS website, http://www.humanesociety.org/news/press_releases/2013/04/egg-products-inspection-act-2013-042513.html.

69. Francione, "Reflections."

70. Tofurkey is a brand of vegan proteins. Many of the products have the same shape, packaging, and taste of specific meat products such as lunch meats and hotdogs.

71. I say "significant" with some reservation, as even one life saved is valuable. However, here I am referring to large, measurable changes.
72. *Statista*, "Revenue of the Fast Food Restaurant Industry."
73. Leidig, "Sodexo Meatless Mondays."
74. Harmon, "Retracting a Plug for Meatless Mondays."
75. Meyer, *Politics of Protest*, 126.
76. See Meyer, "Institutionalizing Dissent"; *Politics of Protest*; Tarrow, *Struggle, Politics, and Reform*.
77. *HSUS News* (Winter 2003), inside cover.
78. Meyer, "Institutionalizing Dissent," 163.
79. Meyer *Politics of Protest*, 130.
80. Glasser, "Moderates and Radicals."
81. PETA, "Why We Married at KFC," 19.
82. See, for example, Almeida, "Opportunity Organizations"; Koopmans, "Dynamics of Protest Waves"; "Protest in Time and Space"; Tarrow, *Struggle, Politics, and Reform*.
83. Taylor, "Social Movement Continuity," 761 (abstract); see also Staggenborg, "Social Movement Communities."
84. Smith, "Revolution Will Not Be Funded," 134.
85. Ibid., 143.
86. Staggenborg, "Social Movement Communities."
87. Downey and Rohlinger, "Linking Strategic Choice."
88. McAdam quoted in Kriesi, "Political Context and Opportunity," 77.
89. See Wahlström and Peterson, "Between the State and the Market."

BIBLIOGRAPHY

24/7 and Chris Danello. "The 9 Foods the US Government Is Paying You to Eat." *Atlantic*, July 12, 2011. http://www.theatlantic.com/business/archive/2011/07/the-9-foods-the-us-government-is-paying-you-to-eat/241782/.

Almeida, Paul D. "Opportunity Organizations and Threat-Induced Contention: Protest Waves in Authoritarian Settings." *American Journal of Sociology* 109, no. 2 (2003): 345–400.

ASPCA (American Society for the Prevention of Cruelty to Animals). "Ag Gag Bills at the State Level." Accessed October 1, 2015. https://www.aspca.org/fight-cruelty/advocacy-center/ag-gag-whistleblower-suppression-legislation/ag-gag-bills-state-level.

Bittman, Mark. "Who Protects the Animals?" *New York Times* blog, April 26, 2011. http://opinionator.blogs.nytimes.com/2011/04/26/who-protects-the-animals/.

Cohen, Sarah, Dan Morgan, and Laura Stanton. "Farm Subsidies over Time."

Washington Post, July 2, 2006. http://www.washingtonpost.com/wp-dyn/content/
graphic/2006/07/02/GR2006070200024.html.

COK (Compassion over Killing), "Proud to Serve: Reaching Out to Restaurants."
Voices of Compassion (COK online magazine), July 6, 2011. http://cok.net/blog/
2011/07/cok-restaurant-outreach/.

Cooney, Nick. "Data Suggests Battery Cage Bans Do Not Increase Egg
Consumption." Unpublished manuscript, 2011.

CRP (Center for Responsive Politics). "Alphabetical Listing of Industries." Accessed
November 20, 2012. http://www.opensecrets.org/industries/alphalist.php.

DAE (Department of Agricultural Economics). "2011 US Meat and Poultry Consump-
tion Demand." Fact sheet. University of Missouri–Columbia, Division of Applied
Social Sciences. Accessed November 21, 2012. http://web.missouri.edu/~plainr/
Papers/2011%20demand%20comments.pdf.

Davenport, Christian. "Repression and Mobilization: Insights from Political Science
and Sociology." Introduction to *Repression and Mobilization*, edited by Christian
Davenport, Hank Johnston, and Carol Mueller, vii–xli. Minneapolis: University
of Minnesota Press, 2005.

DHS (Department of Homeland Security), "Preventing Attacks by Animal Rights
Extremists and Ecoterrorists: Fundamentals of Corporate Security." *Green Is the
New Red* (blog), April 13, 2006. http://www.greenisthenewred.com/blog/
wp-content/Images/Other/DHSflyermemo1.htm.

Downey, Dennis J., and Deana A. Rohlinger. "Linking Strategic Choice with Macro-
organizational Dynamics: Strategy and Social Movement Articulation." *Research
in Social Movements, Conflicts and Change* 28 (2008): 3–38.

EFF (End Factory Farming). "Egg Laying Hens." EEF website. www.factoryfarming
.org.uk/hens.html (site discontinued).

EJA (Equal Justice Alliance). "Animal Enterprise Terrorism Act: Summary
analysis." EJA website, n.d. http://www.noaeta.org/LegalResources/
AETABriefAnalysis7.15.10.pdf (site discontinued).

Fox News. "Subway to Roll Out New Line of Vegan Sandwiches." June 14, 2012.
http://www.foxnews.com/leisure/2012/06/14/subway-rolls-out-new-line-vegan
-sandwiches/.

Francione, Gary L. "Reflections on *Animals, Property, and the Law* and *Rain Without
Thunder*." In *Animals as Persons: Essays on the Abolition of Animal Exploitation*,
67–128. New York: Columbia University Press, 2008.

Gamson, William, and David S. Meyer. "Framing Political Opportunity." In
Comparative Perspectives on Social Movements, edited by Doug McAdam, John D.
McCarthy, and Mayer Zald, 275–90. New York: Cambridge University Press, 1996.

Genoways, Ted. "Gagged by Big Ag." *Mother Jones*, July–August 2013. http://www
.motherjones.com/environment/2013/06/ag-gag-laws-mowmar-farms?page=1.

Glasser, Carol L. "Moderates and Radicals under Repression: The US Animal Rights Movement, 1990–2010." PhD diss., University of California, Irvine, 2011.

Goodman, Jared S. "Shielding Corporate Interests from Public Dissent: An Examination of the Undesirability and Unconstitutionality of Eco-Terrorism Legislation." *Journal of Law and Policy* 16, no. 2 (2008): 823–75.

Harmon, Amy. "Retracting a Plug for Meatless Mondays." *New York Times*, July 25, 2012. http://www.nytimes.com/2012/07/26/us/usda-newsletter-retracts-a -meatless-mondays-plug.html.

HRC (Humane Research Council). *Animal Tracker–Wave 4*. Report. HRC, Olympia, Washington, 2011. https://faunalytics.org/feature-article/animal-tracker-year-4/.

———. "Per Capita Consumption of Animals." *Humane Trends Study*. Accessed November 20, 2012. http://www.humanetrends.org/ht/per-capita-consumption -of-animal-products/ (site discontinued).

Jefferson, Cord. "Infographic: What Congress Would Look Like If It Really Represented America." *Good* (infographics website), April 1, 2011. http://www .good.is/posts/infographic-what-congress-would-look-like-if-it-really -represented-america/.

Key Note. *Vegetarian Foods 2012—Market Assessment*. Industry report. Key Note website. Accessed November 20, 2012. http://www.keynote.co.uk/market -intelligence/view/product/10573/vegetarian-foodspy.

Koopmans, Rudd. "The Dynamics of Protest Waves: West Germany, 1965–1989." *American Sociological Review* 58, no. 5 (1993): 637–58.

———. "Protest in Time and Space: The Evolution of Waves of Contention." In *The Blackwell Companion to Social Movements*, edited by David A. Snow, Sarah A. Soule, and Hanspeter Kriesi, 19–46. Malden, MA: Blackwell Publishing, 2007.

Kriesi, Hanspeter. "Political Context and Opportunity." In *The Blackwell Companion to Social Movements*, edited by David A. Snow, Sarah A. Soule, and Hanspeter Kreisi, 67–90. Walden, MA: Blackwell Publishing, 2007.

Leidig, Robynn. "Sodexo Meatless Mondays Survey Results." Johns Hopkins Center for a Livable Future, 2012. http://www.jhsph.edu/research/centers-and-institutes/ johns-hopkins-center-for-a-livable-future/research/clf_publications/pub_rep_ desc/sodexo.html.

Li, Junpeng. "Opportunities in Action: The Case of the US Computer TakeBack Campaign." *Contemporary Politics* 17, no. 3 (2011): 335–54. doi:10.1080/1356977 5.2011.597147.

Lichbach, Mark Irving. "Deterrence or Escalation? The Puzzle of Aggregate Studies of Repression and Dissent." *Journal of Conflict Resolution* 31, no. 2 (1987): 266–97.

Lim, Merlyna. "Clicks, Cabs, and Coffee Houses: Social Media and Oppositional Movements in Egypt, 2004–2011." *Journal of Communication* 62, no. 2 (2012): 231–48.

Lovitz, Dara. *Muzzling a Movement: The Effects of Anti-terrorism Law, Money and Politics on Animal Activism*. Brooklyn, NY: Lantern Books, 2010.

Lusk, Jayson. "The Effect of Proposition 2 on the Demand for Eggs in California." *Journal of Agricultural and Food Industrial Organization* 8, no. 1 (2010): 1–20. doi:10.2202/1542-0485.1296.

McAdam, Doug. 1982. *Political Process and the Development of Black Insurgency, 1930–1970*. Chicago: University of Chicago Press.

McCoy, Kimberly E. "Subverting Justice: An Indictment of the Animal Enterprise Terrorism Act." *Animal Law* 14 (2007): 53–70.

Meat Trade News Daily. "USA—McDonalds Account for 3% of Beef Consumption." September 25, 2010.

Meyer, David S. "Institutionalizing Dissent: The United States Structure of Political Opportunity and the End of the Nuclear Freeze Movement." *Sociological Forum* 8, no. 2 (1993): 157–79.

———. *The Politics of Protest*. New York: Oxford University Press, 2006.

———. "Protest and Political Opportunities." *Annual Review of Sociology* 30 (2004): 125–45.

Nibert, David. *Animal Rights/Human Rights: Entanglements of Oppression and Liberation*. Boulder, CO: Rowman & Littlefield, 2002.

Nierenberg, Danielle, and Laura Reynolds. "Disease and Drought Curb Meat Production." WorldWatch Institute website, October 23, 2012. http://www.worldwatch.org/disease-and-drought-curb-meat-production-and-consumption-0.

NIH (National Institutes of Health). "Lactose Intolerance: Information for Health Care Providers." Eunice Kennedy Shriver National Institute of Child Health and Human Services, January 2006. NIH Pub. no. 05-5305B. https://www.nichd.nih.gov/publications/pubs/documents/NICHD_MM_Lactose_FS_rev.pdf.

Pepitone, Jullianne. "Subway Beats McDonald's to Become Top Restaurant Chain." *CNNMoney*, March 8, 2011. http://money.cnn.com/2011/03/07/news/companies/subway_mcdonalds/index.htm.

PETA (People for the Ethical Treatment of Animals). "Why We Married at KFC." *Animal Times* (Winter 2008): 19.

Political Correction. "The American Legislative Council: A Primer on the Premier Right-Wing Corporate Lawmaking Shop." April 28, 2011. http://politicalcorrection.org/factcheck/201104280008.

Potter, Will. "3 Reasons Why Murdering an Abortion Doctor Isn't Called 'Terrorism.'" *Green is the New Red* (blog), 2009. http://www.greenisthenewred.com/blog/is-abortion-doctor-murder-terrorism/2051/.

———. "'Ag Gag' Bills and Supporters Have Close Ties to ALEC." *Green Is the New Red* (blog), April 26, 2012. http://www.greenisthenewred.com/blog/ag-gag-american-legislative-exchange-council/5947/.

PR Newswire. "Butterball Worker Pleads Guilty to Felony Cruelty to Animals Following Mercy for Animals Investigation." August 28, 2012. http://www.prnewswire.com/news-releases/butterball-worker-pleads-guilty-to-felony-cruelty-to-animals-following-mercy-for-animals-investigation-167698225.html.

Schurman, Rachel, and William Munro. "Targeting Capital: A Cultural Economy Approach to Understanding the Efficacy of Two Anti-genetic Engineering Movements." *American Journal of Sociology* 115, no. 1 (2009): 155–202.

Sethu, Harish. "Meat Consumption and Demand Both in Decline!" *Counting Animals* (blog), November 20, 2012. http://www.countinganimals.com/meat-consumption-and-demand-both-in-decline/.

Shirky, Clay. "The Political Power of Social Media." *Foreign Affairs*, January–February 2011. http://www.foreignaffairs.com/articles/67038/clay-shirky/the-political-power-of-social-media.

Smith, Andrea. "The Revolution Will Not Be Funded: The Nonprofit Industrial Complex." In *The Global Industrial Complex: Systems of Domination*, edited by Steven Best, Richard Kahn, Anthony J. Nocella, and Peter McLaren, 133–54. New York: Lexington Books, 2011.

Snow, David A., and Sarah Soule. *A Primer on Social Movements.* New York: W.W. Norton & Co., 2010.

Staggenborg, Suzanne. "Social Movement Communities and Cycles of Protest: The Emergence and Maintenance of a Local Women's Movement." *Social Problems* 45, no. 2 (1998): 180–204.

Stahler, Chris. "How Many Adults Are Vegetarian?" *Vegetarian Journal* 4 (2006). http://www.vrg.org/journal/vj2006issue4/vj2006issue4poll.htm.

———. 2012. "How Often Do Americans Eat Vegetarian Meals? And How Many US Adults Are Vegetarian?" Vegetarian Resource Group blog, May 18, 2012. http://www.vrg.org/blog/2012/05/18/how-often-do-americans-eat-vegetarian-meals-and-how-many-adults-in-the-u-s-are-vegetarian/.

Statista. "Revenue of the Fast Food Restaurant Industry in the U.S. from 2002–2016 (in Billion U.S. Dollars)." Statistics portal, 2016. http://www.statista.com/statistics/196614/revenue-of-the-us-fast-food-restaurant-industry-since-2002/.

Tarrow, Sidney. *Struggle, Politics, and Reform: Collective Action, Social Movements, and Cycles of Protest.* Western Societies Program Occasional Paper No. 21, 1989.

Taylor, Verta. "Social Movement Continuity: The Woman's Movement in Abeyance." *American Sociological Review* 54, no. 5 (1989): 761–75.

USDA (United States Department of Agriculture). "Livestock Slaughter Annual Summary." National Agricultural Statistics Service, April 23, 2012. http://usda.mannlib.cornell.edu/MannUsda/viewDocumentInfo.do?documentID=1097.

———. "Poultry Slaughter Annual Summary." National Agricultural Statistics Service, April 23, 2012. http://usda.mannlib.cornell.edu/MannUsda/viewDocumentInfo.do?documentID=1097.

————. "Special Milk Program: Program Fact Sheet." Food and Nutrition Service. Last published June 11, 2014. http://www.fns.usda.gov/cnd/milk/.

VRG (Vegetarian Resource Group). "How Many Vegetarians Are There?" *Vegetarian Journal*, May 15, 2009. http://www.vrg.org/press/2009poll.htm.

Wahlström, Mattias, and Abby Peterson. "Between the State and the Market: Expanding the Concept of 'Political Opportunity Structure.'" *Acta Sociologica* 40, no. 4 (2006): 363–77.

The Week. "Farm Subsidies: A Welfare Program for Agribusiness." *The Week*, August 2013. http://theweek.com/articles/461227/farm-subsidies-welfare-program -agribusiness.

Windsor Star. "PETA Ends KFC Canada Boycott." July 26, 2008. http://www.canada .com/windsorstar/story.html?id=d79e8d75-e2b6-430e-a2da-8bdad12c776c.

15

Nose-to-Tail Eating
A Prematurely Post-Factory-Farm Biopolitics

⊰⊱⊱⊰

Jessica Carey

"This is a celebration of cuts of meat, innards, and extremities that are more often forgotten or discarded in today's kitchen; it would seem disingenuous to the animal not to make the most of the whole beast: there is a set of delights, textural and flavorsome, which lie beyond the fillet."[1] So begins Fergus Henderson's cookbook *The Whole Beast: Nose to Tail Eating*, mass published in 2004. In the intervening five years since the 1999 publication of the cookbook's first iteration, *Nose to Tail Eating: A Kind of British Cooking*, Henderson's book and London restaurant, St. John, had already gained the respect—and in some cases, veneration—of some of the most acclaimed chefs in North America and Britain. In these words of introduction to the later edition of his seminal cookbook, Henderson manages to distill the central concerns of an increasingly influential faction in culinary culture of the global north, one that advocates a return to nose-to-tail eating and artisanal butchery.[2] Henderson's opening salvo is addressed to a mainstream food culture that seems determined to shut its eyes and mouths to all but a few cuts of meat that have been aseptically pre-selected and prepackaged for the consumer. As an alternative, he offers "a celebration" not only of other cuts of meat, but also, seemingly, of a "whole beast" that is more than the sum of its parts. Moreover, by appealing for wider recognition of the whole beast's "set of delights, textural and flavorsome," Henderson also makes legible nose to tail's promise to restore vital pleasures that are missing from our culinary and gustatory experience in the era of factory farms. In other words, despite Henderson's reputation for having somewhat humble political aims,[3] in the broader context of contemporary food politics, I argue that we can read Henderson's statement in the imperative tense: a call to see nose-to-tail eating as a form of resistance to the unprecedented dominance of an industrialized food system.

In the process, both Henderson's pithy statement and the ethos it captures articulate an ethics, of sorts, of interspecies relations. The qualifier "of sorts" is a way of signalling from the outset that once we situate nose to tail's particular interspecies ethics within the context of the broader field of contemporary animal ethics, the ethos at hand emerges as an ethical apparatus that is both more and less than it purports to be. To be more precise, in at least three key discursive areas—modern categorizations of waste, the power relations involved in interspecies care, and the biopolitical expression and experience of pleasure—nose to tail articulates what I call a prematurely post-factory-farm biopolitics. Nose to tail is biopolitical because it positions itself as a particular means of apprehending the lives of others; moreover, it does so in a way that tracks three key concerns in Foucault's description of biopolitics: the securitization of life through the articulation of norms of worthiness, the knowledge-based assessment of lives using those norm-derived lenses, and the forceful exclusion of lives that are deemed unworthy of life. Meanwhile, the ethos is "prematurely post-factory-farm" not only because the factory farm, of course, is perhaps as far as it can be from being "over," but also because nose to tail's biopolitical vision is not entirely foreign to that expressed at the factory farm—despite, perhaps, appearances.

Trash and Treasure: Tracking Waste

Nose to tail frames itself as an intervention in the contemporary problem of waste. As much is clear in Henderson's statement, which is directly concerned with parts "that are more often forgotten or discarded," but this preoccupation is evident throughout the discourse of nose to tail. For instance, for Hugh Fearnley-Whittingstall, another English celebrity chef, eating all of the edible parts of an animal is part of a broader drive for a reduction in food waste, and he advocates for nose to tail alongside his recent campaigns against discarding excess fish in contemporary fishing practices, and for the increased use of "doggy bags" in English restaurants. In both North America and Britain, the rhetoric and label of "nose to tail" often appear as an integral aspect of sustainability movements, utilized in a variety of "zero waste" efforts on the part of restaurants, food collectives, and classes in cooking and DIY butchery.

Indeed, at the current stage of capitalism the production of waste is an urgent global problem, with an undeniable ethical dimension. Zygmunt Bauman describes our will to waste as the modern problem par excellence, arising from modernity's key ontological (and ultimately, biopolitical) argument: to the extent that "[m]odernity is a condition of compulsive, and addictive, designing," we actively produce as much "waste" as we do "products," since "[w]here is design, there is waste."[4] In other words, our continual effort to order the world according to our purposes produces an ontological imaginary in which designations of "wastehood" necessarily accumulate at the exact pace of our spiralling production of "useful" commodities, both material and abstract. With this insight into the logic of waste, we now have an economic explanation for contemporary forms of waste that would otherwise seem entirely senseless. For instance, witness the spectacular scene in the 2005 Austrian documentary *We Feed the World*, in which we see truckloads of perfectly edible day-old bread being unloaded daily at a garbage dump in the Netherlands.[5] Bauman helps us understand that what feels—quite viscerally—like a prime example of gross inefficiency is also one of innumerable examples of modernity's highly tuned productive designs. We generate this copious waste in order to produce and maintain one of our most cherished cultural products: an economic apparatus premised in exponential and eternal growth. In order to produce and sustain that machine, even the bread—the supposed raison d'être for the economic structure in question—must fall by the wayside.

If one had to assess the waste problem expressed in meat-eating and only had the highly selective supermarket meat counter to go on, one could be forgiven for presuming that most of the body parts of animals, like all those loaves of bread, are simply consigned to the trash. After all, we have to strip away a whole lot of animal to get to the skinless, boneless cuts of meat we appear to covet in our culture. Yet those with intimate knowledge of industrial food production tell us that this initial presumption regarding meat's waste problem does not account for what actually happens to animal parts in the factory abattoir. Nicole Shukin notes in *Animal Capital: Rendering Life in Biopolitical Times* that recuperating and rendering non-meat animal waste has always been integral to the profit margins of industrial meat producers in North America.[6] Likewise, as Timothy Pachirat has recently illustrated in his incisive account of working at a slaughterhouse, *Every Twelve Seconds: Industrialized Slaughter and the Politics of Sight*, cattle offal—the parts our provisional supermarket lens would deem "waste"— "can generate anywhere from a tenth to a third of the income of an industrialized slaughterhouse."[7] Pachirat includes an appendix in his book that lists some of the uses to which offal is directed; my partial citation of *his* partial list for bone, for instance, includes "phosphate fertilizer, bonemeal for livestock and pet food and glue for adhesive in plywood, furniture, veneer, paperboard, match heads, sandpaper, composition cork, mother-of-pearl, gummed tape, paper boxes, and bookbinding."[8] In fact, the factory abattoir's capacity for redirecting "waste parts" is optimized to the extent that it is capable of shocking the mainstream public during rare instances in which rendering bursts into cultural consciousness: we need only recall public reaction to the "pink slime" controversy of 2012, which revealed the extensive recuperative mechanisms the food industry employs in order to make use of every last scrap of gristle and tissue—not to mention the mad-cow panic induced by the genuinely dangerous practice of including certain animal waste products in animal feed.

In short, while we seem to waste just about everything in our society, it seems that this propensity does not characterize industrial meat production: at least, not in the way that the supermarket observer—or, the casual reader of nose-to-tail practices—might assume it does.[9] If almost every part of the animal is, in fact, currently being used for something, why is nose to tail so preoccupied with the problem of waste? As a conference attendee recently asked when I presented a paper on the ethos of nose to tail, is this not a solution in search of a problem? The answer is complex: there are various kinds of waste problems, and the discursive shorthand "nose to tail" responds to a less pragmatic waste problem than the one solved by simply proving that we use every animal part for some purpose. "Some purpose," both for dedicated nose-to-tailers, and for the rest of us who either wittingly or unwittingly share some of their biopolitical logic, is not sufficient. The waste problem addressed by the particular concept of "nose to tail" has to do with the consumer's desire to retrieve animals from the industrial economy of use, and to reinsert them into a sacrificial economy of use in which the designations of value and waste lie not with the industrial ledger, but rather with the human individual in the kitchen.

In other words, the material wastage of animal parts is not so much the problem as is the perceived biopolitical wastage of "the whole beast."

Returning to Bauman's theorization of modern waste production, he observes that the spiralling logic of waste extends past material goods and services and into the biopolitical realm of the market's assessment of entire lives: "When it comes to designing the forms of human togetherness, the waste is human beings."[10] For our purposes—and paradoxically, since in a raw material sense animals are not wasted in industrial meat production— the waste is animal beings. To reread Henderson's statement, by reducing an animal to "the fillet" in the supermarket-centred realm of the spectacle, the industrial food system "disingenuously" makes the animal disappear.

Of course, over twenty years ago, Carol J. Adams posited a term for this kind of forced disappearance of the animal: the absent referent. Adams argues that "[a]nimals in name and body are made absent *as animals* for meat to exist. . . . Without animals there would be no meat eating, yet they are absent from the act of eating meat because they have been transformed into food."[11] There is no question that the unrecognizability of animal lives and deaths—their absence in the act of consuming meat—has intensified in the factory farm age. The boneless, skinless fillet spectacularly seques-ters the fact of animal life and death from our sight, to an unprecedented degree. From this perspective, we need to read differently the fact that the factory abattoir is highly efficient in rendering "waste" animal parts into non-waste: in terms of our shared conceptual apparatus concerning meat, the material efficiency of the rendering industry matters little if we never see or hear about it. Bauman might as well have the factory abattoir in mind when he notes that "[w]e dispose of leftovers in the most radical and effective way: we make them invisible by not looking and unthinkable by not thinking."[12] As far as most of us are concerned, in other words, all of those other animal parts *are* waste; we don't (knowingly) use them, and we don't think about them. Significantly, too, they are the parts that remind us most of living, breathing animals: eyes, ears, heads, entrails, tails, bones, feet. Fearnley-Whittingstall addresses this aspect of nose-to-tail eating in *The River Cottage Meat Book*: "There's no getting away from the fact that we're talking body parts here—organs and glands, no less—and that this is where meat becomes unapologetically anatomical."[13] The adverb "unapolo-getically" signals nose to tail's effort to restore the absent referent: neither the body parts themselves (thus ascribing a strange agency to the carcass) nor Fearnley-Whittingstall will apologize for reminding eaters that what they are eating was once a living animal. In fact, nose to tail's rhetorical and visual culture seems rife with overt attempts to restore the absent referent:

chef April Bloomfield's cookbook *A Girl and Her Pig*, for instance, features a front cover photo of Bloomfield standing with a pig carcass around her shoulders, and her recipe chapters are labelled "Cow," "Birds," and so on, rather than in the usual euphemistic terminology of meat. In his article on nose to tail's cultural capital, "The Modern Offal Eaters," Jeremy Strong argues that "such titillation by frankness operates as part of the hard 'truth' about animal husbandry, meat production, and food," and that nose to tail's ubiquitous visual culture of anatomical carcass diagrams "constitutes the most obvious effort to reassert that which is denied by the wiles of industry and the deliberate myopia of shoppers."[14] Yet the question remains concerning how nose to tail reckons with this hard truth: how might we interpret what happens in the wake of restoring the animal referent by seeing it and speaking about it again? For Adams, the only genuine way to restore the absent referent is to remove all metaphorical associations with the piece of meat, including the common selective tendency to reidentify meat with animal life, rather than with its prior life *and* its violent death (a tendency to which I will return below). Once all metaphor is denied, Adams argues, the "nothingness" of meat is revealed, in that "one realizes that one is not eating food but dead bodies."[15] Restoring the absent referent, in other words, brings us into contact with the unredeemable, unedifying corpse, depriving us of all possible rationales for continuing to eat meat at all.

How, then, can we interpret nose to tail's seeming recuperation of "the whole beast" from the biopolitical waste pile as a *reinvigoration* of the practice of eating meat? The answer partly emerges in a return to the question of waste: as I argued at the outset, nose to tail is not (solely) concerned with the industrial wasting of body parts that would ostensibly take place at the abattoir, but is rather more preoccupied with limiting sacrificial waste: the human individual cook's wasting of the "whole beast's" body that occurs whenever he or she does not actively use all possible parts for his or her nourishment and pleasure.

As I have observed in the course of other research on the popular rhetoric of Temple Grandin,[16] for instance, and that of Michael Pollan, the drive to restore a sacrificial value to the animal's life is a characteristic of many resistant responses to the factory farm's financial abstraction of value from animal lives. Sacrifice serves so well as a lynchpin of popular resistance to industrial agriculture not only because it provides a ready-made framework for restoring value to animal life—in a way that nevertheless seems refreshingly separate from the factory farm—but also because it legitimizes anew the status quo of killing animals for our benefit. Ultimately, it is crucial to note that while reclaiming sacrifice as a means of restoring old-fashioned trappings of value to animals may be appealing, for the animal there is likely little material difference between sacrificial and seemingly non-sacrificial killing, since ultimately as Kari Weil notes, "it is, of course, the animal alone who dies or at least perishes."[17] Consequently, we have to be careful in assessing what kind of re-endowment of animal value is possible through nose to tail: it seems clear that, like all sacrificial actions, we shouldn't kid ourselves that this ritual is really doing anything for animals.

Clearly, here I am invoking Derrida's oft-cited work on animal sacrifice, in which he argues that "[i]n our culture, carnivorous sacrifice is fundamental, dominant, regulated by the highest industrial technology . . . carnivorous sacrifice is essential to the structure of subjectivity . . . [and is] at the basis of our culture and our law."[18] As such, and given that all of our concepts of subjectivity seem to rely on notions of encountering and consuming otherness in order to both construct and immunize the self, Derrida argues that sacrifice "installs the virile figure at the determinative center of the subject."[19] In the wake of Derrida's observation, it becomes increasingly difficult to see the factory abattoir as a definitively non-sacrificial space that we might productively replace with a sacrificial practice like nose to tail. Perhaps the industrial site of animal death lacks the sense of ritual we expect of sacrifice, but it does not lack the requisite logic: animals are still valued for what service their deaths might perform for our—humanity's—benefit. In one sense, the sacrificial quality of nose to tail differs from that of industrial killing in degree, not kind: in the former practice, the sacrificial logic is simply more intense, more direct. In another sense, however, it is worth noting that nose to tail returns the sovereign power of sacrifice to the human consumer, recouping a form of sovereignty many of us long ago outsourced to the industrial apparatus: in my nose-to-tail kitchen, I decide what is waste and what is useful, and the particular uses to which I will put each part. The reinstatement of this personal power manifests most clearly in its accompanying rhetoric of renewed personal responsibility for the sacrificed animal: it is up to us not to be "disingenuous" by wasting animal parts; it is our responsibility not to let unused edible bits "decay into an unpaid cosmic debt";[20] only by open-eyed acknowledgement that our food requires a living being's death may we "pay the full karmic price of a meal."[21] Fearnley-Whittingstall is explicit: "Nobody should hog all the prime cuts. It's bad for the soul. The best relationship you can have with meat is to know it in all its parts and take an interest in every edible morsel it can offer you . . . only such a holistic approach can truly assuage the conscience of the caring carnivore."[22] Each of these claims relies on a conceptual apparatus in which we can "pay" an animal for its life with a currency comprised of our respect for the animal's value. The humanist tautology of sacrifice thus comes full circle: animal sacrifice enables not only our sense of mastery and accomplishment in the kitchen, but also our sense of ourselves as humane and respectful beings, to boot. By cooking and eating the whole animal, suggests nose to tail, no aspect of the sacrificial transaction is wasted: every body part is elevated in purpose, up from the impersonal realm of rendering bonemeal into matchstick heads, and into service in the highly selective, thoroughly humanist economy of eternal life that only sacrificial logic could dream up.

Pastoral Power: Nose to Tail and the Power of Care

Even in Henderson's brief distillation of the ethos, it is clear that nose to tail is attempting a restoration or a reclamation—but of what or whom, and to whom? In this celebratory framework that articulates itself as a lively alternative to the deadening wasteland of the factory farm, it seems we are having our animals returned to us. It is as if they strayed from us, into the oblivion of free market fundamentalism's deadly, speculative calculus of utter disposability, and have now returned to our gaze and grasp—an equally deadly place to be, but at least they will be appreciated here, in our kitchens. Not treated as an abstract number or a unit, but as a whole: a whole beast. Yet while the factory farming system and nose to tail do articulate different concepts of interspecies care, a full understanding of the distinction requires an acknowledgement of the biopolitical similarities between the two practices. Both are, indeed, biopolitical programs of interspecies governance: industrial husbandry and nose to tail share an emphasis upon marshalling power over animal populations through the human accumulation of comprehensive knowledge about animal bodies: what is normal, how to optimize desired aspects of the body, and so on. In both cases, meticulous attentiveness to the animal's body, both while it is living and after it is dead, is the key expression and performance of the caring relation. To be clear, dedicated attentiveness as a form of care is not in ethical question here as much as is the sacrificial interestedness of a given act of attentiveness. In terms of biopolitics, the starkly obvious qualitative difference in attentiveness between nose to tail and industrial systems originates solely in their vastly different biopolitical objectives, or in other words, their differing reasons for providing an interested form of care: an optimized culinary and gustatory experience on one hand, and maximized profit margins on the other.

Certainly, in order to produce the well-rounded healthy animals prized in nose-to-tail gastronomy, a biopolitical relationship that is more readily recognizable to us as "caring" is emphasized in the discourse. As opposed to the factory farm, a site infamous for the extreme manipulation of animal bodies in order to meet financial imperatives, nose to tail is supportive of a more holistic approach to animal care. Henderson, for instance, rhetorically presumes rather than prescribes in his introductory remarks in *The Whole Beast* that "[h]aving sourced happy ingredients" is a hallmark of the nose-to-tail way of doing things;[23] likewise, in celebrity chef Anthony Bourdain's introduction to the same book, he recalls Henderson appraising a roast suckling pig with the comment "[t]his was a noble animal. A happy pig."[24] Undoubtedly, the level of care required to enable even just a straight-faced claim of happiness in the animals one uses for meat is considerably higher than that offered by the factory farm.

If nose to tail's comprehensive approach to the care of an animal reminds us of an older, more traditional form of animal husbandry, then it would be useful to assess the ethos using Foucault's biopolitical descriptions of what he calls "pastoral power." Animal studies theorists have been returning to this concept recently; Nicole Shukin's "Tense Animals" and Anand Pandian's "Pastoral Power in the Postcolony: On the Biopolitics of the Criminal Animal in South India" are notable examples of such work. For our purposes here, an examination of nose to tail along the lines of pastoral power lends some insight into the biopolitical contours of the care at hand. Foucault delineates pastoral power as "a power of care. It looks after the flock, it looks after the individuals of the flock, it sees to it that the sheep do not suffer, it goes in search of those that have strayed off course, and it treats those that are injured."[25] In its ideal expression, pastoral power is other-oriented: Foucault frames the discourse as claiming that "[t]he bad shepherd only thinks of good pasture for his own profit, for fattening the flock that he will be able to sell and scatter, whereas the good shepherd thinks only of his flock and nothing else."[26] Just as the factory abattoir's impersonal mode of killing makes a "return" to sacrifice seem like an ethical alternative, factory farming's radical departure from individualized animal care makes pastoral power seem like an equally radical recuperation of interspecies respect and empathy.

Yet it is important not to get carried away by our preference for pastoral power over the factory farm's bald instrumental rationality. Pastoral power is, after all, still a powerful apparatus of biopolitical control. As Pandian asserts, it represents a form of relation quite effective in generating and enforcing disciplinary norms: in his case study of animal care in India's Cumbum Valley, Pandian finds that the logical premises of pastoral care effectively produce an imaginary that "distinguishe[s] between animals able and unable to restrain themselves,"[27] and that "emphasize[s] that everyday modulations of careful attention and stern discipline were essential to the moral subjection of these animals."[28] Moreover, as both Shukin and Pandian note, Foucault's elision of actual instances of interspecies pastoral care—in favour of its use as a metaphor that is solely useful for describing intra-human power relations—results in his overlooking of a key presumption basic to models of pastoral care. This presumption rests in a rationale of power relations that legitimizes the pastoral supremacy of the shepherd over the flock, through assertions that the flock is inherently in need of a particularly comprehensive form of care. As Pandian notes, "[r]elations between shepherds and flocks rely upon a radical difference in kind between pastors and the populations in their care. Flocks are made up of beings that would scatter, starve, suffer, die, or simply lose their way without the careful attention of someone else with better judgment."[29] Shukin echoes this observation in her rejoinder to Foucault's exclusive focus on human-to-human pastoral care: "to assume the species of the individual or population that is subject to pastoral power, is to underestimate just how contingent governmentality may be on the production and ordering of 'species' as a play of similarity and difference."[30] In other words, in tandem with the disciplinary control legitimated under pastoral care, the ideological tableau of pastoral power also works to naturalize humanity's role as a mastering species—one that possesses the unique capacity, and perhaps responsibility, to marshal a caring power over other species.

Despite potentially bucolic appearances, this "radical difference in kind" between shepherd and flock does not remain neutral or benign in the interspecies scene of pastoral care: the very logic of care that girds the scene also helps license the killing of the animals that we are looking after so carefully. First, the attributes that an apparatus of pastoral care constitutively ascribes to "the flock," which Pandian concisely sums up above—helplessness, cluelessness, and so on—only perpetuate ever more forcefully the orthodox notion of nonhuman life that presumes an animal's utter lack of future-oriented and teleological consciousness. As we have all heard before, if we deem the animal's life to be devoid of long-term interests, killing the animal does not obviate our claim that we care for the animal, as long as we kill it in a humane fashion. In fact, the sacrificial dimension of the humane, which I have already mentioned, is also central to the logic of pastoral power: to the extent that human "shepherds" alone are capable of the singularly intense mode of care required under pastoral power, not only their ability, but also their willingness to humanely consider the welfare of the animals in their charge becomes further evidence for a difference in kind between humans and animals. In this way, post-factory-farm discourses of meat-eating premised in concepts of humaneness actually reiterate the biopolitical presumption of fundamental interspecies difference, and thereby amplify the sacrificial resonance of animal killing: we are never more successfully human than when we are eating meat in what we feel is the "right way." In other words, the pastoral care we choose to extend over species lines, care that potentially includes killing, sacrificially "gives" us humaneness: a sacrificial spoil that is distinct from, if related to, our sacrificial acquisition of human accomplishment and virile mastery through animal killing. In several ways, then, the logic of pastoral power rather successfully integrates the notion of interspecies care into the justification for killing animals.

Nose to tail merely adds yet another layer to the operation of pastoral power, for it is an ethos that explicitly emphasizes our ability to continue caring for animals after they have been killed. Nose to tail's numerous assertions that we can express respect for the "whole beast" by using all of it and cooking it well constitute an argument that after death, the animal remains under our care, having merely entered a new phase of life as food. It is, perhaps, this interpretation of the animal's life that best explains a certain tendency among proponents of nose to tail: toward framing its central post-death practices—eating the whole animal and cooking it properly— as forms of care *for the animal*, not just for our own taste buds and consciences. Henderson's comment that wasting body parts is "disingenuous to the animal" supports such a reading, as do his similar remarks elsewhere: that nose to tail is "courteous to the animal,"[31] and that "[i]t's only polite to use the whole beast once you've knocked it on the head."[32] Henderson's infamous dry humour notwithstanding, this rhetoric succeeds in linking consideration for the animal as a "whole beast" with the articulation of a

post-death form of care. Likewise, when Henderson exhorts in his cookbook "On behalf of all tripe, *tripe is great* and don't hesitate to welcome
it into your gastronomic life,"[33] a curious rhetorical slippage implies not
only that tripe is alive and thus may benefit from Henderson's advocacy, but
that this advocacy forms part of an overall ethos of animal care. Another
example of this model of care emerges in Henderson's discussion of quail
meat's relative lack of cultural capital: "The quail unfortunately falls into
a kind of bird purgatory; it is not a game bird, though some describe it as
such, but is now a thoroughly farmed bird, so not glamorous enough to
warrant the 'hands on' battling the people feel justified to exert on grouse or
partridge, and is denied from joining the chicken's gang, as it is seen to be
too fiddly to eat. Then, finally, to kick the quail while it's down, people say it
has no flavor."[34] Throughout this passage, Henderson rhetorically personi-
fies both quails and chickens (whose meat forms a "gang"), describing their
"life" experiences as meat; moreover, in framing eaters' negative assessment
of the quail's flavor as "kick[ing] the quail while it's down," Henderson
frames the dead flesh as capable of experiencing insult and abuse—not as
a symbolic aftershock or residue of its killing, either, but in the form of
various denigrations of its biopolitical worthiness during the second phase
of its life, as meat. Henderson can subsequently show care to the animal
by "put[ting] forward the case for the joys of a bowl of roasted quails."[35]
Overall, however playful some of Henderson's language may be, it remains
consistent with his reliance upon a dichotomy of care in which "[y]ou can
be an unhappy carnivore, and eat pink-in-plastic, or a wise carnivore and
eat the animal with care and respect."[36]

In all of this rhetoric conjuring "meat life," multiple sacrificial discourses
of biopolitics are at play. Alongside the sacrificial benefit we appropriate
to ourselves through animal killing, nose to tail sets up a complementary
sacrificial relation in which the animal, too, ultimately benefits from its
own killing: as I have been tracing above, death enables the animal to enter
a new "afterlife" as delicious food. This narrative is a partial rewriting of
Adams's "story of meat," in which the animal disappears and the human
being becomes the sole subject of the cultural story of meat-eating.[37] In one
sense, Adams's narrative is also operational in nose to tail: as I outlined in
my description of sacrificial waste, animal death still serves us by representing, in Adams's phrase, "re-birth and assimilation into our lives."[38] Yet
the unique intervention nose to tail makes is to supplement this narrative
with one in which the animal remains a subject of the story, only now as a

symbolically animated, respect-worthy body whose experience of the after-life needs to be maximized through minimal wastage and skilful cooking. In this revised story of meat, the human eater's role is more complex: as is evident in Henderson's remarks, the pastoral framework of care desig-nates the human cook as the animal's shepherd and advocate, there to help the animal successfully navigate its afterlife as meat. The relative humility expressed in this role does not make the power relation any less genera-tive of human mastery: befitting the sacrificial discourse of the humane in which it is expressed, the humble, guiding role of the human here only *appears* to be less dominating, and as I have already suggested, the osten-sible humility of the role only works to further legitimate the human being's guardianship of the animal.

In fact, Henderson explicitly invokes the language of disciplinary con-trol over the "life" of foodstuffs, albeit in his characteristically ironic tone. Parsley in particular is subject to "discipline" through the application of light chopping: "You want to discipline the parsley with three or four chops, not whip it into submission."[39] The playful reference to the cook's engage-ment in pastoral power continues in Henderson's broader admonition: "Do not be afraid of cooking, as your ingredients will know and misbehave. Enjoy your cooking and the food will behave."[40] Again, the tongue-in-cheek tone of these statements does not invalidate my assertion that nose to tail is actively articulating a conceptual apparatus of power relations, one that emphasizes a sacrificially edifying role for the human cook and consumer consisting in taking good care of both the living and dead animal. Both the living animal and the "living" meat need our guidance, our coaxing, our careful attention, in order to reach their maximum potential of being.

To underscore this point further, I will return briefly to Strong's article on nose-to-tail eating. Strong mounts a convincing argument accounting for the movement's distaste for mechanically recovered meat (MRM), which is perhaps the factory abattoir's closest equivalent to nose to tail's effort to use all body parts as food. MRM refers to a "meat slurry" or compound product resulting from the mechanical separation of meat from bone in industrial trimmings. Along with the notorious "pink slime," or chemically treated and processed beef trimmings, MRM represents just one of the industrial meat industry's rendering methods, which I have already mentioned in the above section on waste. Strong argues that proponents of nose to tail reject MRM as a legitimate use of the "whole beast" because its relatively covert production methods subvert nose to tail's emphasis upon the consumer's cultivation of meat knowledge, which is the basis of nose to tail's cultural capital: "It is the consumer's lack of knowledge, as opposed to the insider's wisdom of the offal eater, that makes MRM bad."[41] While I think nose to tail certainly marshals cultural distinction in the manner Strong describes, I am convinced that still more is happening in the movement's dismissal of MRM: aside from the fact that it represents an industrial approach to food, which nose to tail is generally against, MRM also deprives the cook of the comprehensive, sacrificial expenditure of his or her caregiving for all parts that is enabled under nose to tail. For instance, while both MRM and nose to tail use as much of the animal for food as possible, consider the difference between MRM and Bourdain's assertion in his introduction to Henderson's cookbook that "it takes love, and time, and respect for one's ingredients to properly deal with a pig's ear or kidney."[42] The sense of accomplishment evident in Bourdain's statement stems not from simply having used all possible parts, but rather from the human subject's expansion of pastoral knowledge–power–care that becomes demonstrable in and through his or her ability to care adequately for all of an animal's body parts. For Bourdain and the nose-to-tail movement in general, using the whole animal is not a profit-motivated action, nor even based wholly in practicality or thrift, but is rather primarily experienced as an act of sacrificial interspecies care. Along these lines, Fearnley-Whittingstall asks his readers: "Are you thrifty with meat? That's not the same as stingy. Being creative with leftover meat means getting more from it. If anything, you're making it more generous to you and, in so doing, paying greater tribute to the animal that has died to provide it."[43] Again, the emphasis is not upon using all parts for the sake of using all parts, but instead, upon characterizing the meat–human relationship as a mutually rewarding exercise in pastoral care.

While Fearnley-Whittingstall has taken the extra step of raising much of his own livestock from birth, the contemporary symbolic economy of nose to tail predominantly enables those who do not farm to feel as if they are actively participating in the interspecies power relations of pastoral care. As I have outlined above, the fundamental means by which nose to tail evokes this sense of participation is through ascribing a biopolitical imperative to our interaction with the carcass: the idea that even after death, the animal needs and deserves our care. This extension of the caring relation past death is the condition of possibility for an ethos of pastoral power that has become particularly popular with urban cooks and consumers, most of whom will initiate their first contact with an animal after its death. In light of this cultural situation, I suggest that nose to tail's emphasis upon learning how to use every part of the animal serves yet another symbolic purpose: cooking and eating the "whole beast" performs a certain symbolic substitution for our "missed" care of the living animal. Fearnley-Whittingstall implies as much in his assertion that to practise what he calls "meat thrift" means not only showing "[r]espect for the animals that have died to feed you," but also "for the farmers who have (assuming you've chosen your meat well) worked tirelessly to keep those animals healthy and contented, so their meat is as good as it can be."[44] In nose to tail, in other words, the consumer enacts a symbolic sacrifice—introjection and appropriation—of the pastoral care administered before the consumer entered the scene. It is almost as if the very performance of comprehensive care involved in cooking and eating the entire animal symbolically enables us to declare that we are "all in" on the care of that particular animal—and that we always were.

The Pleasures of a Nose-to-Tail Identity

If I have been continually asserting that nose to tail bolsters the human subject in a multitude of ways, it makes sense to situate briefly some of the pleasures generated in the ethos, and their role in the formation of human identities. Our culture still primarily tends to define our pleasure in food as being primal, visceral, and since Freud, id-based; in other words, we view our pleasure in food as operating somewhat prior to politics. In popular discourse, this presumption has stubbornly outlasted the "fall" of many other naturalized discourses to the contingency of the political dimension. At the same time, it is perhaps too easy to ignore the role of pleasure in the aspects of food that *have* become a ground for politics in recent years. Nose to tail, then, is also prematurely post-factory farm with regard to the issue of pleasure: it invokes the pleasures of a strangely anachronistic ensconcing of the human within the animal world, in and through the pleasures of human exceptionalism and mastery.

Our use of highly appealing ecological models to validate our often deeply problematic actions has only increased in the current age, in which sociobiology and related fields have nearly become the official discourses of popular culture. Derrida cautions us not to slip too quickly into assuming symbiotic immersion or "continuism," arguing that "we should never be content to say, in spite of temptations, something like: the social, the political, and in them the value or exercise of sovereignty are merely disguised manifestations of animal force, or conflicts of true force, the truth of which is given to us by zoology."[45] In such explanations of politics, Derrida locates the dangerous impetus to naturalize—thus immunizing against critique—what are in fact historical (and thus deconstructable) phenomena. In other words, there is too much of a history of human chauvinism, and a record of its deeds, for it to be sufficient to declare ourselves out from under that history by assuring ourselves that what we were really doing all that time was acting like animals—as if our popular articulations of ecology and their models of competition or cooperation aren't also deeply inflected by all those things we assumed, and said, and thought about what animals were and what they were bound to do. Specifically, as we have traced above, our concepts of interspecies interaction largely remain structured by the biopolitical presumptions of pastoral power—and the claim that we may recapture a human experience "before" this biopolitical relation suggests a somewhat anachronistic contortion of the human subject. Although it is a movement of the modern kitchen, nose to tail implies that we can return to eating animals the way other animals eat other animals. Yet can we ever go home again? And when exactly to locate this relationship before exceptionalist models of human power, before even pastoral care? This time before we manipulated other lives, even if only in gathering information about them, in order to articulate more forcefully a sense of our own subjectivities and place in the world?

Yet the discourse of nose to tail often frames the pleasure of eating meat as a form of equalizing identification with other animals: a sensual immersion in animal enjoyment. Henderson's "set of delights, textural and flavorsome, which lie beyond the fillet," gestures to a pure pleasure "out there" in nature, as if waiting to be discovered. Fearnley-Whittingstall articulates a similar form of pleasure, remarking "I believe that meat, at its splendid best, helps us achieve this sense of shared contentment perhaps better than any other food";[46] and further, that we are justified in eating meat by the fact that "[w]e are not outside the natural order of things. And if we don't kill them for food, then somebody else, or something else, will."[47] Meat is thus positioned as being both universal and universally satiating. Henderson perhaps forges the pleasurable link between human and animal even more explicitly in his interview with Adam Gopnik: "So many wonders there. Spleen! Spleen is a very fine, perfectly framed organ. In fact, your spleen swells when you're in love! How can you resist an organ that does that!"[48] Here, Henderson's palpable fascination with the animal body and its capacity for pleasure lays the groundwork for a desire to eat that same body as an expression of similar pleasure. In his almost giddy transposition of human and animal, Henderson points to an ideally ecological, even vulnerable form of pleasure, operating beyond human modes of control and enabling a multitude of entanglements, shared fates, co-dependencies, and unguaranteeable benefits of interacting with others. Pleasures associated with this kind of approach to the world are the pleasures of risk and hope. Gopnik reads Henderson's intent more or less along similar lines: "In Henderson's own heart there is, one senses, a harmony between man and his food that comes from eating all of the animal there is to eat, a mysticism rooted in fatality and the fact of our being, head to toe, animals, too. We are all meat, trembling and fresh, dying and spasming, and we enter into our humanity, as we leave it, by way of our animalness."[49] Yet a significant aspect of nose to tail's pleasure that Gopnik puts his finger on here, whether consciously or unconsciously, concerns the reappearance of the sacrificial relation just when it seems to have been edged out by a commitment to open-ended connection. By asserting that we "enter into our humanity, as we leave it, by way of our animalness," Gopnik obliquely references the possibility that all of this pleasurable identification with both our animality and that of others serves a biopolitical purpose after all: if when I eat the animal I symbolically also "eat" the animal aspect of myself, am I not perhaps continually sacrificing my animality on the altar of becoming a meat-eating human? Whether the pleasures associated with feeling immersed in the ecological web always serve such a biopolitical purpose remains an open question; however, in the case of nose to tail the political dimension of this kind of pleasure seems to emerge in the appropriation of animality that is necessary to naturalize our actions in the world. The denial of difference involved in the uniquely human aspects of raising, killing, and eating other animals becomes a pleasurable, ideologically naturalized salve for our persistent ethical ambivalence regarding these practices.

However, not all of the pleasures of nose to tail have to do with ostensibly ensconcing the human within the ecological web: simultaneously, nose to tail also invokes what I call, after years of thinking about humanism and sacrifice, "old chestnut pleasures" of human separation and mastery. In other words, nose to tail celebrates a certain accomplishment of distance and immunity from other animals. Sometimes the expression of this kind of pleasure can be quite subtle in the ethos, as when Henderson comments in his note to a recipe that "[t]his may seem like a lot of hare for one weekend, but I feel it does more justice to the various bits of the animal."[50] Here, we are encouraged to experience a kind of political pleasure that is only achievable if we sacrifice some of the supposedly apolitical pleasure of eating, by eating more than our tastes desire. In other words, we accomplish a preferred biopolitical orientation to the other animal, a pleasure of caring for the flesh, by prioritizing those biopolitical achievements above (however slightly) the pleasures of visceral symbiosis articulated in "pure" enjoyment.

Ironically, at other times this sense of mastery is achieved through visual strategies that seem intended to remind us of messy identification with animal life: ever-present diagrams of animal cuts in which the cutting up of a previously living being is unremittingly explicit; Fearnley-Whittingstall's photo essay of a cow being led through the slaughtering process;[51] and the implicit shock of the real promised by the pink pig carcasses that are a recurring image in the visual culture of nose to tail, from the cover of Bloomfield's cookbook, to the cover of the spring 2012 issue of the North American foodie magazine *Lucky Peach*.[52] The latter text rather heavy-handedly emphasizes the shock of identification by presenting a photo of a pig haunch in the process of being tattooed with a human-shaped diagram of meat cuts. Yet overall, I suggest that such images function more to assert animal killing as a foregone conclusion, than to unsettle our interpretation of these practices. Ultimately, human mastery is visually confirmed rather than questioned, as these images implicitly encourage a kind of scopophilic fascination with the spectacle of dead flesh.

In other words, some of the pleasures of nose to tail appear akin to the indulgence in rubbernecking at the scene of a car wreck: there is a certain challenge built into the experience, and in proving ourselves up for the challenge, proving our willingness to see and endure, we can declare ourselves to have accomplished a sturdier humanity. To be sure, the element of virile mastery that is central to Derrida's model of sacrificial logic is in full swing in certain corners of nose to tail: as Fearnley-Whittingstall remarks, the movement's emphasis upon eating body parts that middle-class white culture tends to see as taboo or disgusting means that "offal lovers often can't resist allowing their passion to slide into a kind of competitive macho posturing, as in, 'What's the weirdest bit of an animal *you've* ever eaten?'"[53] Likewise, Bourdain notes in his introduction to *The Whole Beast* that nose to tail's adherents include "practitioners of 'extreme' eating who saw the night's fare, perhaps, as an extension of 'extreme' sports."[54]

These pleasures also hearken to ecological models of life, but only insofar as they emphasize and essentialize the predator–prey relation of competition. Representing ecology in this way is the bread and butter of a culture so deeply structured by capitalist ideologies, and again it throws into relief how we can potentially take up ecological models in an anachronistic way that masks the long violent biopolitical history of human domination, in the figure of a return to the prehuman. We only treated other animals that way because we were (and still are) winning at being predators, fighting our way to the top of the food chain, as the story goes. It is, again, a sacrificial narrative of human accomplishment, and we all know that accomplishments are pleasurable. Nose to tail is arguably more convincing in its invocation of this narrative than the factory farm has been of late, but in neither relationship is the predator role not fixed and structurally assured in a way that begs the question of whether this trope of a struggle for survival in the wild is really an apt description of what is going on in the vast majority of instances that we eat other animals. As much as there is a pleasure in imagining ourselves to be wholly and purely immersed in the ecological web of life, there is also pleasure in declaring ourselves to have mastered a clean separation from that same messy web. Nose to tail is no different from a range of other contemporary food practices in that it enables us to indulge in both kinds of pleasure simultaneously.

Yet nose to tail is unique in its intensification of both the visceral experience and the symbolic representation of these simultaneous pleasures. The idea that we get to have it all—a union with and a difference from other animals through eating—is literalized in nose to tail in that we are encouraged to develop a taste for and pleasure in every edible aspect of the animal's body that we can master with our cooking utensils and taste buds. I am reminded here of Josée Johnston and Shyon Baumann's recent sociological work on omnivorousness as a mechanism of social distinction in foodie discourse, one that sublimates the power relations involved in accomplishing privileged status by couching the discourse in terms of omnivorousness's constitutive emphasis upon inclusion. I suggest that the contradictory pleasures of nose to tail, which allow us to perform a simultaneous immersion in and separation from other animals, are indicative of this kind of omnivorous appetite for human mastery—not only over every literal part of an animal's body, but also over all the symbolic pre-post-factory farm humilities and accomplishments that, in nose to tail, may appear to be merged in a single practice.

For the health and well-being of all animals, human and "non," it is clear that we need to explore alternatives to industrialized animal farming. In claiming that nose to tail articulates a prematurely post-factory-farm biopolitics, I do not intend to collapse the differences between that ethos and the cultural logic of factory farming; on the contrary, I am attempting to unravel the terms of a binary mode of thinking that would presume resistances to the factory farm as being ethically transformative in exact proportion to the extent that the factory farm is ethically stagnant. I am convinced that identifying the structural, conceptual similarities between the two practices can only help us forge wider, clearer paths away from the factory farm in the future.

NOTES

1. Henderson, *Whole Beast*, xix.
2. The extent to which various non-Western cultural orientations to food animals predate and intersect with the current "trendy," "foodie" discourse of nose to tail examined in this chapter is, unfortunately, beyond the scope of this chapter, and remains in urgent need of further theorization.
3. Rayner, "Food Awards 2009"; Bourdain, *Medium Raw*, 143. Most profiles of Henderson emphasize his unassuming personality and approach to food. For instance, chef Tom Pemberton remarks in Rayner's article: "The thing about Fergus is that he can be quite enigmatic. . . . In all the time I worked with him he never once pontificated about British food. And he would never explain why he does something. None of what he does is to garner a reaction. It comes from a genuine love of simplicity." Similarly, Bourdain writes of Henderson that he is "painfully modest about all the adulation. His restaurant, St. John, was intended as an equally modest venture: a plain white room in a former smokehouse, where a few like-minded Englishmen could eat traditional English food and drink Claret."
4. Bauman, *Wasted Lives*, 30.
5. Wagenhofer, *We Feed the World*.
6. Shukin, *Animal Capital*, 68.
7. Pachirat, *Every Twelve Seconds*, 271.
8. Ibid., 278.
9. Of course, I am entirely leaving aside the question of excremental waste here: the "literal," biological waste of the animals at hand. It is now widely known and accepted that industrial animal farming produces unprecedented amounts of excrement that pose an urgent environmental problem: both the sheer volume and the particular nitrogen load and other chemical contents of

industrial excrement have transformed its status from that of useful fertilizer (i.e., not waste) to that of a toxic, polluting by-product. See, for instance, Pollan, *Omnivore's Dilemma*, 79. While the ethos of nose to tail is often expressed in tandem with the ethos of a return to small-scale production, the particular cultural intervention of nose to tail that I am focusing upon in this piece concerns the material reconsideration of the body parts of the food animal, rather than the holistic discourses that often accompany nose to tail, which would form part of a lengthier study of the ethos.

10. Bauman, *Wasted Lives*, 30.

11. Adams, *Sexual Politics*, 51.

12. Bauman, *Wasted Lives*, 27.

13. Fearnley-Whittingstall, *River Cottage*, 181.

14. Strong, "Modern Offal Eaters," 30.

15. Adams, *Sexual Politics*, 187.

16. Carey, "'Paradox of My Work.'"

17. Weil, "Killing Them Softly," 92.

18. Derrida, "Force of Law," 247.

19. Derrida, "'Eating Well,'" 280.

20. Philpott, "Flesh and Bone," 108.

21. Pollan, *Omnivore's Dilemma*, 9.

22. Fearnley-Whittingstall, *River Cottage*, 257.

23. Henderson, *Whole Beast*, xix.

24. Bourdain, introduction to Henderson, *Whole Beast*, xvi.

25. Foucault, *Security, Territory*, 127.

26. Ibid., 128.

27. Pandian, "Pastoral Power," 96.

28. Ibid., 97.

29. Ibid., 86.

30. Shukin, "Tense Animals," 152.

31. Reynolds, "Sexy Beast."

32. Sunyer, "At Home."

33. Henderson, *Whole Beast*, 89 (italics in original).

34. Ibid., 106.

35. Ibid.

36. Gopnik, "Two Cooks," 95.

37. Adams, *Sexual Politics*, 104–5.

38. Ibid., 105.

39. Reynolds, "Sexy Beast." See also Henderson, *Whole Beast*, 35; and Gopnik, "Two Cooks," 94.

40. Henderson, *Whole Beast*, xx.

41. Strong, "Modern Offal Eaters," 32.

42. Bourdain, introduction to Henderson, *Whole Beast*, xv.
43. Fearnley-Whittingstall, *River Cottage*, 9.
44. Ibid., 462.
45. Derrida, *Beast and the Sovereign*, 14.
46. Fearnley-Whittingstall, *River Cottage*, 8.
47. Ibid., 17.
48. Gopnik, "Two Cooks," 92.
49. Ibid., 95.
50. Henderson, *Whole Beast*, 124.
51. Fearnley-Whittingstall, *River Cottage*, 20–22.
52. *Lucky Peach* 3 (Spring 2012).
53. Fearnley-Whittingstall, *River Cottage*, 181.
54. Bourdain, introduction to Henderson, *Whole Beast*, xvi.

BIBLIOGRAPHY

Adams, Carol J. *The Sexual Politics of Meat: A Feminist-Vegetarian Critical Theory.* Tenth Anniversary Edition. New York: Continuum, 2000.

Bauman, Zygmunt. *Wasted Lives: Modernity and Its Outcasts.* Cambridge: Polity, 2004.

Bloomfield, April. *A Girl and Her Pig: Recipes and Stories.* New York: HarperCollins, 2012.

Bourdain, Anthony. Introduction to *The Whole Beast: Nose to Tail Eating*, by Fergus Henderson, xiii–xvii. New York: Ecco, 2004.

———. *Medium Raw: A Bloody Valentine to the World of Food and the People Who Cook.* New York: HarperCollins, 2010.

Carey, Jessica L.W. "'The Paradox of My Work': Making Sense of the Factory Farm with Temple Grandin." *CR: The New Centennial Review* 11, no. 2 (Fall 2011): 169–92. doi: 10.1353/ncr.2012.0005.

Derrida, Jacques. *The Beast and the Sovereign: Volume One.* Edited by Michel Lisse, Marie-Louise Mallet, and Ginette Michaud. Translated by Geoffrey Bennington. Chicago: University of Chicago Press, 2009.

———. "'Eating Well' or the Calculation of the Subject." In *Points . . .: Interviews, 1974–1994*, 255–87. Translated by Peter Connor and Avital Ronell. Edited by Elisabeth Weber. Stanford: Stanford University Press, 1995.

———. "Force of Law." In *Acts of Religion*, 230–58. Edited by Gil Anidjar. New York: Routledge, 2002.

Fearnley-Whittingstall, Hugh. *The River Cottage Meat Book.* Berkeley: Ten Speed Press, 2007.

Foucault, Michel. *Security, Territory, Population: Lectures at the Collège de France, 1977–1978*. Edited by Michel Senellart. Translated by Graham Burchell. New York: Palgrave Macmillan, 2007.

Gopnik, Adam. "Two Cooks: Taking Food to the Extremes." *New Yorker*, September 5, 2005.

Henderson, Fergus. *The Whole Beast: Nose to Tail Eating*. New York: Ecco, 2004.

Johnston, Josée, and Shyon Baumann. *Foodies: Democracy and Distinction in the Gourmet Foodscape*. New York: Routledge, 2010.

Pachirat, Timothy. *Every Twelve Seconds: Industrialized Slaughter and the Politics of Sight*. New Haven: Yale University Press, 2011.

Pandian, Anand: "Pastoral Power in the Postcolony: On the Biopolitics of the Criminal Animal in South India." In *Animals and the Human Imagination: A Companion to Animal Studies*, edited by Aaron Gross and Anne Vallely, 79–112. New York: Columbia University Press, 2012.

Philpott, Tom. "Flesh and Bone: Toward a Whole-Beast Meat-Eating Ethos." *Gastronomica: The Journal of Food and Culture* 7, no. 2 (Spring 2007): 106–9. doi:10.1525/gfc.2007.7.2.106.

Pollan, Michael. *The Omnivore's Dilemma: A Natural History of Four Meals*. New York: Penguin, 2006.

Rayner, Jay. "Food Awards 2009: You'll Have His Guts for Starters." *Guardian*, March 22, 2009. http://www.theguardian.com/lifeandstyle/2009/mar/22/fergus-henderson-st-john-restaurant.

Reynolds, Jonathan. "Sexy Beast." *New York Times*, June 20, 2004. http://www.nytimes.com/2004/06/20/magazine/20FOOD.html.

Shukin, Nicole. *Animal Capital: Rendering Life in Biopolitical Times*. Minneapolis: University of Minnesota Press, 2009.

———. "Tense Animals: On Other Species of Pastoral Power." *New Centennial Review* 11, no. 2 (2011): 143–67. doi:10.1353/ncr.2012.0003.

Strong, Jeremy. "The Modern Offal Eaters." *Gastronomica: The Journal of Food and Culture* 6, no. 2 (Spring 2006): 30–39. doi:10.1525/gfc.2006.6.2.30.

Sunyer, John. "At Home: Fergus Henderson." *Financial Times*, May 4, 2012. http://www.ft.com/cms/s/2/fe2b1594-8f82-11e1-9ab1-00144feab49a.html.

Wagenhofer, Erwin, dir. *We Feed the World*. DVD. Vienna, Austria: Allegro Film, 2005.

Weil, Kari. "Killing Them Softly: Animal Death, Linguistic Disability, and the Struggle for Ethics." *Configurations* 14 (2006): 87–96. doi:10.1353/con.0.0013.

16

The New Carnivores

John Sorenson and Atsuko Matsuoka

Producing meat entails the premature death (usually after prolonged and hideous suffering) of billions of sentient beings. Thus, activists emphasize that "meat is murder" and call for a shift in consciousness that rejects human domination of other animals through force. While Regan argues that it is morally wrong to kill animals who are subjects-of-a-life and that we should apply a principle of equal consideration to their interests,[1] Francione maintains that sentience alone qualifies an animal for moral significance and that animals should not be considered our property.[2] Questioning the ethics of a system based on speciesist violence, animal rights advocates adopt veganism to express opposition to instrumental views of animals. Noting how realities of meat production are disguised by restricted access to slaughterhouses, euphemistic descriptions and deceptive packaging, some believe that exposing these realities will lead people to think seriously about the suffering and killing of animals and to stop exploiting them.[3] While many are moved by compassion and empathy to limit exploitation, not everyone is motivated by affect. Recently, a new tendency has emerged in North America to champion meat consumption. Described as "New Carnivores" in mass media, its adherents reject vegetarianism and present themselves as heroically challenging ethical orthodoxy. This chapter examines the New Carnivores' efforts to promote meat consumption and killing, analyzing their discourse by using Cohen's strategies for denying atrocities.[4] Despite claims of being compassionate and humane, New Carnivores do not challenge exploitation but instead endorse it by offering reassurances about killing animals.

The New Carnivores

In 2009 *Newsweek* identified a "new carnivore movement" among "food-ies"—gourmets, New Age ranchers, butchers, chefs, food writers, and others with ardent or obsessive interests in food.[5] Although differences may exist within this movement (such as between those who are motivated mainly by their appetites and a search for pleasure and those who oppose factory farming and claim to care about animals' suffering), they are united in their belief that killing animals is acceptable, possibly even more so when it is done by themselves. The movement's class-based dimensions are apparent in its appeals to affluent consumers. Grocery chains like Whole Foods target such consumers with expensive meat designated "organic," "grass fed," or "local," all vaguely-defined terms.

Supposedly, the New Carnivores represent an ethical transformation in terms of the consumption of animals, a principled alternative to animal advocates who have identified the cruelties involved in modern industrial meat production. Robinson celebrates eating pasture-fed animals and "humane slaughter" in which ranchers accompany animals to abattoirs or shoot them in their fields.[6] San Francisco chef Chris Cosentino's blog, *Offal Good*, maintains that carnivores respect animals by consuming all edible parts of their bodies. Soller calls butcher Tom Myland the "herald of a new . . . meat morality . . . [the] New Carnivore movement . . . catching on at expensive restaurants [where] superb chefs . . . order . . . entire animals from local farms . . . for their overindulged patrons."[7] *New Yorker* food writer Bill Buford describes "food hysteria" driven by food writers Anthony Bourdain, Michael Pollan, and Fergus Henderson, who provided a "cult cookbook" for the movement, *The Whole Beast: Nose to Tail Eating*.[8] Magazines such as *Meatpaper* discuss "the growing cultural trend of meat consciousness," and *Gourmet* magazine reports *Meatpaper* founder and former vegetarian Sasha Wizansky's thrilled reaction to a UC Berkeley conference on butchering: "They butchered a pig in the lecture hall. . . . People were so excited."[9]

For these "foodies," concern for animals' welfare is secondary to the quest for new taste sensations and the dubious importance of being among the first who catch on to new trends. The excitement of butchering animals in public bolsters animal exploitation in general against ethical arguments made by animal advocates.[10] Killing animals and tearing apart their bodies comes to be seen not as brutality but, paradoxically, as compassion and as a radical opposition to industrial agriculture. Those who profit from and enjoy products of animal-exploitation industries have fought the animal rights movement in various ways.[11] One form of resistance to ethical challenges posed by that movement comes through creating a discourse of denial that seeks to legitimize killing of animals based on claims that smaller-scale production methods mean they are treated better before they are killed. This should be distinguished from welfarist campaigns that support abolition of animal exploitation, including killing, but believe that incremental reforms can reduce suffering. While some New Carnivores express concern for animal welfare, none object to killing animals. The contradiction in terms, obvious in any other context, is consistently overlooked in discussions about our domination of other animals.

Sexual Politics of Meat

As a signifier, "meat" is socially constructed to indicate strength, masculinity, and virility, and ecofeminists have traced analogies between exploitation of animals and oppression of women.[12] The New Carnivores, however, eagerly reassert traditional gender roles and hierarchies. In *New York* magazine's food blog, Josh Ozersky, author of *Meat Me in Manhattan* and *The Hamburger*, implicitly defines the movement's masculine identity and its embrace of killing: "The New Carnivore revels in his love of offal and game animals, exerting a macho pride in the gross-out factor connected with such dishes. (It's better still . . . to have actually stalked his meat with bow and arrow, and then butchered it himself on the kitchen table.)"[13] Rather than questioning the abandonment of ethical concerns towards others and self-aggrandizement through conformist embrace of a violent and oppressive status quo, Spartos enthusiastically describes New Carnivores "obsess[ing] over pork and butchery in a macho display of unadulterated meat-eating." The "macho display" is an expression of status: carnivores wanting respect must "name-drop cult butchers . . . [but] meat eaters looking to secure their place at the top of this town's food chain have to . . . get downright caveman—hunting down the animal and butchering it with their own hands."[14] Similarly, Ozersky advises: "If you want to be a badass carnivore, you have to be able to break animals down yourself. That's what separates the boys from the men."[15] Scott Gold presents his book, *Shameless*

Carnivore, as a "manifesto," a "call to arms" for carnivores rallying under a "blood-red banner."[16] Adopting this same aggressive, hypermasculine rhetoric to style himself as "the great and mighty warrior Beowulf",[17] Gold (nicknamed "Steakbomb") bellows resentment at being "made to feel morally lacking" by vegetarians, whose ethical arguments he shouts down by asserting that "defenceless animals taste really, really good" and "I am a carnivore and damned proud of it."[18] The New Carnivore discourse is in part a reassertion of patriarchal power expressed through domination of animals.

However, it is not only men who endorse these patriarchal power relations. Susan Bourette's *Carnivore Chic* also embraces stereotyped gender roles. As an undercover reporter at Manitoba's Maple Leaf Pork slaughterhouse, she lasts only four days; horrified by conditions for animals and workers, she leaves, determined to be vegetarian, something she has failed at twice before. Soon "lured back" by the smell of bacon, Bourette begins a quest for perfect meat, joining an Inuit whale hunt, a Texas cattle ranch and a steakhouse, a Newfoundland hunting trip, and Louisiana sausage-making classes.[19] Throughout all this, she presents herself as the Little Woman, ineffective and clumsy, hiding her meat-eating from her vegetarian boyfriend, but too queasy to eat blubber or shoot a moose. She is rescued and tutored in meat by competent males, some seemingly murderous, such as Mike the hunter who "kills bears so he doesn't have to kill people," ranchers convinced of supernatural dispensation to dominate nature, and a celebrity chef obsessed by hatred of vegetarians.[20]

Like Gold, Bourette links meat's masculine power to right-wing political views. Both praise rock guitarist and hunter Ted Nugent, with Bourette calling his arguments "compelling."[21] Nugent's widely quoted public statements included not only spiteful attacks on animal advocates but an anti-immigrant rant at Republican Texas Governor Rick Perry's 2006 inauguration, delivered while wearing a Confederate-flag shirt, symbolizing racism and slavery. At a 2007 concert Nugent, dressed in camouflage hunting gear, waved two machine guns and threatened to kill both Barack Obama and Hilary Clinton: "Obama, he's a piece of shit. I told him to suck on my machine gun. Hey Hillary . . . you might want to ride one of these into the sunset, you worthless bitch."[22] Nugent's boorishness and right-wing views are echoed by Gold and Bourette to glorify meat-eating and individualism and to express contempt for any ethical consideration of others. Amidst a steady flow of vitriol, indifference to suffering and contempt for compassion, this discourse uses meat as a symbol of power and unlimited individual freedom. Bourette refuses to limit her own pleasure in order to spare animals' lives. But her book is not simply a record of her failure to act ethically or of her inadequacies in the male-dominated world of meat. It is a political narrative, which disparages ethics and compassion as sentiments of "bead-loving hippies," dismisses liberal ideas and embraces right-wing values. In the epilogue, Bourette cooks Easter dinner for a gathering of "wolfish conservatives," striving to please Don, a right-wing speech-writer: "The prime rib is homage to his hometown of Calgary, the center of Canadian cattle country, the epicenter of the Conservative movement in Canada. And Don, who sees political context where others might not think to look, is keenly aware that our meal is almost an endorsement of the meat industry, a powerful lobby squarely in the Conservative (right-wing) corner."[23] Like Don, we, too, should see "political context where others might not think to look," such as in the New Carnivores' discourse, which espouses values essential to capitalism: individualism, selfishness, consumerism, power, and a rejection of ethical concerns about the exploitation of other animals. Below, we outline some of the discursive manoeuvres used to promote these values and to undermine animal rights. Deployed in such seemingly apolitical spaces as cookbooks, food blogs, gourmet magazines and lifestyle sections of newspapers, the rhetoric of the New Carnivores serves to maintain and justify the continued oppression and exploitation of other animals.

Style over Ethics

The New Carnivore discourse constantly works to undermine serious ethical considerations about animals' rights. Ethics are depicted as matters of fashion: vegetarianism is out of style, replaced with more aggressive and predatory values suited to neo-liberal times. Buford celebrates meat's "renaissance," cheering that "it's finally cool to be a carnivore."[24] Bourette also depicts meat consumption as "cool" and "a bitch-slap to all those reedy, high-minded herbivores ... dictating the parameters of the discussion, decreeing the rules for years. Now ... meat-eaters ... have wrested control of the food debate."[25]

Like Gold, Bourette rejects animal advocates' reasoned ethical arguments as mere "scolding." Complaining that "the sinfulness, the immorality, of meat-eating has been drummed into us for decades, ever since those first pot-smoking, bead-loving longhairs hijacked the debate and determined what the nation should have for dinner,"[26] Bourette cheers a counter-revolution, in which meat-eaters reclaim their "rights" and "replace vegetarians who "once held the countercultural high ground." In reality, there has been no "hijack[ing]," and "high-minded herbivores" have never dictated parameters, decreed rules, or deprived meat-eaters of any "rights." Vegetarians comprise only a small minority of the North American population and are ridiculed in corporate media and popular culture, as cooking magazines and "lifestyle" columnists smirk about tasteless tofu prepared by unwashed hippies, while veganism is dismissed as unthinkable and feminized in homophobic rhetoric. For example, Jacob Richler, in a "Taste" column for *Maclean's Magazine*, praises Toronto chef Marc Thuet's "showmanship" in roasting an entire bison on a spit, "a guaranteed crowd pleaser, unless you invite the guy in the pink shorts and blazer combination who asked about vegetarian options."[27] Richler's message is plain: real men eat meat while vegetarians are gay and out of touch.

The New Carnivores' constant complaint that they have been oppressed in a society dominated by vegetarians and vegans is sheer fantasy. More meat is consumed now than ever before; Bourette acknowledges that North Americans each eat an average of 260 pounds of meat per year. Nevertheless, she is much pleased to see the "high-minded . . . bitch-slap[ped]" for even raising such troublesome matters. Bourette sees moral concerns about killing as unwelcome intrusions and reduces ethics to fashion: "Now, it's the carnivores who rule cool. Meat is the new black." Gold, Bourette, and other foodies produce a narcissistic discourse of resentment and entitlement in which any consideration of the vital interests of others is dismissed as a bothersome imposition. Purchasing expensive types of meat serves as a means of social capital, distinguishing oneself as a trendy, elite consumer and demonstrating one's good taste.[28] Elite consumers purchase a sense of moral superiority by paying premium prices to make suffering seem less apparent, while marketing campaigns present the victims as happy ones. The meat industry has always employed a discourse of love and caring for animals as a strategy to conceal violent exploitation. "Humane slaughter" is just the latest version and the resulting Happy Meat is the denial of animals' suffering and death.

The "renaissance" is not simply a matter of carnivores reasserting individual "rights." Food writers serve the industry's marketing apparatus. Their associations and conferences receive direct financial support from corporations that expect favourable publicity. Food writer John Lamkin admits: "The 'no free lunch' is paying back the individuals, companies and countries

presenting you with the perks."[29] Books like *The Shameless Carnivore* reproduce information from industry groups such as the National Cattlemen's
Beef Association, never questioning their obviously self-serving claims.
Similarly, Gold's attack on PETA draws on the Center for Consumer
Freedom (CCF), a front group funded by alcohol, meat, tobacco, and restaurant industries. The CCF's strategy is to demonize activists as extremists
and "food police," harassing consumers who try to enjoy life's simple pleasures.[30] Invoking personal responsibility and consumer choice, the CCF
opposes threats to corporate profits, such as higher minimum wages for
restaurant workers, lower blood alcohol content limits for drivers, or animal welfare regulations. The meat industry and its lobbyists present vegetarianism not as an ethical practice but as the abnormal denial of pleasure
and a radical "hidden agenda" to undermine capitalism. Animal rights
fundamentally challenges animal-exploitation industries, which downplay ethical and political aspects of killing and portray vegetarianism as a
restriction on personal choice. While individual meat-eaters, not wishing
to be reminded about their role in exploiting animals, ridicule vegetarians,
the New Carnivores play an active propaganda role on behalf on animal-
exploitation industries and allow individual meat-eaters to engage in denial.

Strategies of Denial

Various social mechanisms distance people from moral concern about the
plight of others and allow them to stifle pity. Cohen describes four strategies
(denial of real harm, denying existence of a victim, condemning critics, and
denial of responsibility) used to deny atrocities against humans.[31] These
also serve to downplay atrocities against animals.[32] Some New Carnivores
do take responsibility for the death of animals but most deny realities of
suffering with images of "humane" meat and attempt to silence criticism by
attacking vegetarians. New Carnivores use welfarist concepts to reinforce
the acceptability of marketing animals and using them for food. Although
they are to be treated "humanely," animals remain only objects to be owned,
purchased, manipulated, and consumed, never subjects of their own lives
who have inherent value.

Even those who directly kill distance themselves through justifications,
selective perceptions, deliberate moral blindness, and necessary illusions.
Atrocities are typically accompanied by propaganda emphasizing group
differences. This is also true of mass production of animals for food. Killing

is justified by assertions that animals are fundamentally different from humans and undeserving of moral concern, by claims that humans have supernatural permission to use them or because they are bred for such purposes. The New Carnivores defend killing by praising "humane meat."

Denial of Real Harm

While subjecting animals to inconceivable atrocities in factory farms, meat, dairy, and egg industries claim concern for animal welfare. New Carnivores acknowledge some problems with the meat industry. Some cite environmental damage, disease or hazards to workers, but none oppose treatment of animals as property or suggest veganism as a reasonable alternative. They reject sparing animals' lives. Instead, they advocate raising animals differently, then killing them. Some promote what they call "humane slaughter," reiterating industry myths that animals can be used and killed humanely. While some killing methods may be less painful than others, humane slaughter is an oxymoron that would be obvious outside the context of dominion over animals in which almost any form of abuse is accepted as normal industry practice and Orwellian doublespeak is the lingua franca. Conditions in so-called humane slaughterhouses vary little from standard procedures. This is the first strategy noted by Cohen: denial of real harm. For example, in Britain, Animal Aid investigated a "gold standard" slaughterhouse presumed to be "one of the best."[33] Undercover film revealed extensive abuses, with animals being beaten, killed without stunning, and subjected to various cruelties. An inspector testified to the *Daily Mail* that abuses go unchecked: "If you become rigorous about enforcing the rules the slaughtermen become very aggressive. They tell you bluntly that if you're too keen, they will simply run over you with a truck or push you into a machine, but it would look like an accident."[34]

While abolitionists critique Happy Meat as a sham,[35] the tactic has increased sales, been endorsed by welfarist groups, and even convinced some vegetarians to resume eating animal products. New Carnivores use ostensible concern for welfare as a means to find tastier products; Buford, for example, praises "grass-fed beef" as "better tasting ... with "superior marbling."[36] The term "grass-fed beef" occludes animals (it is cows, not beef, who feed on grass) and emphasizing this meat's superior qualities obscures the violence required to obtain it. Similarly, Niman Ranch's website asserts that "humane and sustainable methods produce the best possible flavour" and claims to "produce the finest tasting meat in the world." Such a commodification of animals obscures the suffering of individual sentient beings, denying their existence as victims.

Tom Philpott, in *Gastronomica*, praises the "whole beast meat-eating ethos" as a revolutionary alternative to industrialized food production, "just as radical and transgressive as the complete soy-based proteins promoted by Frances Moore Lappe a generation ago."[37] Clearly, this is false: veganism rejects human dominion over animals and the New Carnivores embrace it, while promoting modified production methods.

Philpott suggests that animal exploitation is made more just through a "contract": if we raise and kill animals, "then we owe it to the animal to wring as much gustatory joy as possible out of the process."[38] Here, the contract does not even contain a clause to minimize animals' suffering; the only compensation they supposedly receive is an increase in our gustatory joy. For criminals to fully enjoy the proceeds of a robbery would hardly constitute an equitable contract in the eyes of their victim. Clearly, animals who are killed for meat have not agreed to any "contract" and the fairness of such arrangements, in which animals are deprived of their most vital interest, exists only in the minds of humans who wish to eat them, as a form of self-deception.

While repeating standard complaints about unpalatable vegetarian diets, New Carnivores use the humane myth to undermine vegetarianism. In *Food and Wine*, Christine Lennon explains "Why Vegetarians Are Eating Meat." Overjoyed that her "ethically motivated and health-conscious vegetarian [husband, and] about a dozen people in our circle . . . recently converted from vegetarianism." Lennon quotes "actress and model Mariel Hemingway" who "feel[s] more grounded" since she resumed meat-eating and notes "even chef Mollie Katzen, author of the vegetarian bible the *Moosewood Cookbook*, is experimenting with meat again."[39] Seemingly, what convinced them to abandon ethical concerns is premium-priced "sustainably raised meat," by which Lennon means flesh of cows who were allowed to graze on grass, in contrast to those fed corn, soy, and antibiotics to rapidly fatten them. Certainly, it is better to cause less pain to animals before killing them but animal rights arguments that cows should not be killed at all, regardless of how they are treated, are rejected. Lennon even calls "eating sustainable meat purchased from small farmers a new form of activism . . . striking a blow against . . . factory farming."[40] Rejecting vegetarianism, she not only ignores animals' inherent value and interests in staying alive but also misrepresents those who kill them as their friends. Recognizing that "most vegetarians" are motivated by ethical concerns about killing, Lennon acknowledges that convincing them that "eating meat can improve the welfare of the entire livestock population is a tough sell."[41]

Although it is indeed a "tough sell" to present those responsible for killing animals as their saviours, New Carnivores style themselves as friends of animals. Catherine Friend, who raises sheep for slaughter, calls herself a "compassionate carnivore." There is little that is compassionate about her: she asserts her love of meat and states forthrightly that she is uninterested in ethical debates about eating it. In the *Washington Post*, Friend explains "How to Keep Animals Happy, Save Old MacDonald's Farm, Reduce Your Hoofprint, and Still Eat Meat."[42] Her emphasis is clearly on promoting small-scale livestock operations, not on "keep[ing] animals happy." She rejects the inherent value of animals' lives, asserting that the deaths of livestock animals are not tragedies, because they are raised for this purpose.[43] Here, Friend makes the self-serving claim that the benefit she derives from violent acts justifies those actions. We might judge the worth of her arguments by comparing them to similar assertions made by owners of human slaves. Whereas Lennon prioritizes her own pleasure, Friend's key concern is the profits from her own business, but, like Lennon, Friend shifts the emphasis from sanctity of life to support for smaller-scale commercial killers such as herself. The focus is completely anthropocentric, speciesist, and self-interested.

A *BBC News* report describes vegetarians who have resumed eating meat and will pay higher prices to obtain this "from animals who've enjoyed a happy life before being slaughtered."[44] However, the report also cites observations made by Chris Lamb, of the Meat and Livestock Commission, who states that organic consumption for everyone is "unfeasible in terms of the amount of land available and the price."[45] Given the fact that so-called "humane" animal agriculture requires more land than industrial farming does, this form of production would be impossible, both environmentally and economically, on a scale large enough to satisfy the demands of all those who want to eat meat. Thus, "humane" meat can only be produced as a luxury item for affluent consumers. Nevertheless, the report notes a 14 percent increase in sales of "humane" meat over the previous year and Lamb's observation that: "organic, outdoor-produced, farm shops that make the whole thing look more acceptable, give . . . [ethical vegetarians] an easier access point back."[46] Nutritionist Marion Nestle thinks industry changes have led "even . . . committed vegetarians" to resume meat-eating and finds "a major growth opportunity, because consumers will pay more for these products."[47] In fact "committed" vegetarians are concerned about killing, not simply about modifying exploitation. More accurate is Nestle's recognition of a "growth opportunity." The *New York Times* reports: "D'Agostino, a small grocery chain in New York, said sales of meat jumped 25 percent since it added the 'certified humane' logo, though the products cost, on average, 30 to 40 percent more."[48] The key benefit of "grass-fed beef" is "more profit per animal for producers."[49]

Denying Existence of Victims

As Carol Adams maintains, meat is an "absent referent": behind meat is the animal who was killed.[50] By considering meat inanimate, humans separate themselves from the *life* of those animals, deny their individuality and subjectivity and disregard their suffering and death. We normalize their deaths, as Catherine Friend does, by claiming that the purpose of these animals is to die for us.[51] Agribusiness converts individual animals into meat, a mass term, making them simply commodities. Through concealment, euphemism, and marketing, victims are made to disappear, along with empathy or compassion. For decades, activists campaigned on assumptions that if people learned these facts, they would stop using animals for food: "if slaughterhouses had glass walls, everyone would be vegetarian."[52] However, the New Carnivores subvert this by turning killing into spectacle.

In fact, the cruelties of meat production have not stopped people from consuming it. Rather than being regrettable but unavoidable aspects of obtaining meat, cruelty, domination, and killing are the basis of meat's social value.[53] For example, veal was a prestigious product not in spite of, but because of, the extreme subjugation of animals involved in producing it, and foie gras is another obvious example; only when changing social attitudes challenged these practices did they become a liability for the industry. Meat's value depends on domination and killing; such practices confirm us as masters of the world. Although activists cite economic absurdities of clearly energy-inefficient production, this is what makes meat desirable: the more expensive to produce, the more prestigious it becomes. From this perspective, the New Carnivores' championing of "grass-fed beef" is not concern for animal welfare but another means to obtain higher status, since only elite consumers can afford it.

Rather than disguising killing, New Carnivores openly participate. Rather than being ashamed, they go out of their way to kill animals themselves, to stress personal connections with animals they transform into meat. For example, Michael Pollan buys a cow, No. 534, to follow the animal's journey from a South Dakota ranch through a Kansas feedlot and slaughterhouse and "to retrieve some steaks from the Kansas packing plant where No. 534 . . . has an appointment with the stunner."[54] Pollan does not kill the cow personally and is reassured by slaughterhouse designer Temple Grandin's notions of "humane slaughter."[55] Nevertheless, he is eager to kill animals himself. Opportunity comes at Joel Salatin's farm. Salatin, a Christian conservative, runs an "open air abattoir" where he demonstrates killing techniques and, confident in his dominionist ideology, feels no compunction about killing: "people have a soul, animals don't. . . . Animals are not created in God's image, so when they die, they just die."[56] Buoyed by such ideas, Pollan spends a morning cutting chickens' throats, which soon becomes "routine" and "no longer morally troubling."[57] Later he goes hunting and shoots a pig, which provides a "powerful upswelling of pride."[58] Afterwards, he finds photographs of himself leering over the corpse as something pornographic but soon overcomes this by looking ahead to consuming the flesh. Pollan briefly questions his involvement in killing, but he is never troubled for long. Although he acknowledges that seeing "grass-fed" animals killed might lead some to become vegetarians, Pollan hopes others will start to "feel comfortable" about killing, as he does.

Killing animals provides "authenticity." In 2008 Britain's celebrity chef Jamie Oliver electrocuted a chicken and suffocated male chicks for the program *Jamie's Fowl Dinners*, claiming he wanted to improve the welfare of birds (although obviously not those killed on camera) and to encourage shoppers to buy organic or free-range chickens (although all chickens are generally slaughtered in the same way).[59] Olivier slaughtered a lamb for *Jamie's Great Escape* and attempted to shoot a wild boar but missed. Channel 4's website describes Oliver as "close to tears" before killing the lamb, and quotes his justification for continuing: although "beautiful," the lamb is "tasty" and "a chef who has cooked 2,000 sheep should kill at least one, otherwise you're a fake."[60] Such statements normalize power relations, urging people not to feel compassion towards animals or guilt about the violence they inflict upon them but rather to embrace it as a marker of authenticity. While some viewers complained that killing the lamb was inhumane because the animal was still conscious, ideas of simply abstaining from killing and eating animals altogether were not considered.

Celebrity chef Gordon Ramsay, famous for television programs in which he abuses kitchen workers, demonstrated that he, too, was not "a fake," by killing animals on television. In 2007, Ramsay's *F-Word* program showed "two lambs being stunned with 200 volts of electricity and then being hung up and having their throats cut."[61] Ramsay raised the lambs "for three months in the garden of his London home with the intention of serving them in a shepherd's pie at his Claridge's restaurant."[62] Scott Gold authenticates himself by killing and butchering a ten-month-old calf, Ernie. Although Ernie is "cute" and "sweet," Gold finds that killing and skinning him "wasn't so bad."[63] Like Pollan, he cheers himself up with thoughts of consuming Ernie's flesh.

Reviewing chef Hugh Fearnley-Whittingstall's cookbook, Buford finds a "coherent ideology" in "unflinching" photographs of the author taking cows to slaughter.[64] The ideology is simply speciesist dominion, unchanged, but now presented as behaviour of independent-minded hipsters who refuse to follow the orthodoxy imposed by preachy vegetarians. Similarly, Buford praises chef Martin Picard's cookbook as an "unabashed celebration of meat." The *National Post* calls Picard "Canada's champion of nose-to-tail eating," noting that he is "the world's largest importer of *foie gras* using 70 kilograms a week from Quebec producers."[65] Animal advocacy group Global Action Network has exposed the cruelty involved in Quebec's foie gras industry.[66] Noting that another celebrity chef, Anthony Bourdain, identifies Picard's "genius" in giving "the whole world of fine dining the middle finger," Buford explains: "his middle-finger salute is directed not only at the world of fine dining but also at vegetarians, animal-rights defenders, anti-gun lobbyists, and anyone opposed to the killing of animals."[67] Like Gold, Bourette, and Bourdain himself, Picard offers no reasoned refutation of ethical arguments by animal advocates but merely rejects them in an aggressive show of vulgarity, as described by Buford: "The book opens with a photograph of [Picard] ... as a boxer ... in the restaurant's meat cooler ... squaring off against a dead pig before ... his bare-chested male staff, sitting in deck chairs, wearing sunglasses and swimsuits. ... It ends with Picard ... squatting in an outhouse. ... In between, ... are various photos, all ... irreverent, with animals or creatures as props: ... men wearing sea urchins like sunglasses, or pig heads arranged in a vat of boiling water so that they seem to be screaming, open-mouthed, in pain, or freshly killed birds in a mock courtship."[68] Reminiscent of the torture porn genre in cinema, Picard's "irreverent" images undermine the New Carnivores' claims to "respect" animals they kill, butcher, and consume. Instead, suffering and death become jokes, compassion is mocked, and cruelty is valorized as the hipster's postmodern detachment. Like Picard, Scott Gold deliberately aims to be crude and shocking, emphasizing the grossness of what he consumes, including blood, offal, testicles, and a penis. His quest is to eat thirty-one different animals over a month and all parts of a cow "appropriate for human consumption."[69] Gold considers no animals except humans off-limits, including endangered species such as orangutans, and says he would "gladly" eat a dog or a cat.

Surveying some of the New Carnivores' books, Buford joins them in his embrace of killing, saying that supermarkets obscure the "banal connection" between animals and meat.[70] Vegans reveal meat's "absent referent," to expose what supermarkets obscure. Buford does the same, but for opposing reasons, to defend meat-eating. He uses a rhetorical device of stating the obvious: "meat comes from an animal," but presents this as something we must accept, not challenge. While vegans make the connection to create moral shocks and awaken conscience (as well as pointing out new understandings of animal sentience, intelligence, emotions, and social relationships), Buford intends the opposite: it is, after all, a "banal connection" (though certainly not banal for the animal who is killed). Supermarkets "obscure" this truth, which Buford presents as inescapable: "the animal has to be killed." In fact, animals do not have to be killed; we choose to kill them. Meat is for tough, realistic people: "If you fear the sight of a carcass, you shouldn't be eating from it."[71] Buford allows only one possible objection, "fear," not ethical opposition to killing.

Claiming to respect animals, New Carnivores do precisely the opposite. Congratulating themselves on killing or butchering animals or eating their entire bodies, they discourage compassion and justice for animals. Indeed, they ridicule these as foolish and bothersome impositions on their own freedom. Regardless of any small improvements in their treatment while alive, they consider animals meat-in-waiting, only granted life until deemed "ready" for killing. New Carnivores reduce ethical responsibilities to suggestions that animals be treated "humanely" and embrace killing, turning it into a spectacle that lets them feel "aware" and "authentic." This authenticity is linked to the demonstration of masculinity, widely perceived as a precarious and unstable condition requiring proof and validation through public demonstrations, often involving violence.[72]

Condemning Critics

While claiming concern for animals, New Carnivores ridicule vegan ideas of reducing harm. This is another strategy for denying atrocity: condemning critics. By promoting "humane animal care," and *Righteous Porkchop*[s][73] they portray exploitation as acceptable and rather than concealing killing, they discount moral objections by denying that killing creates ethical issues. Going beyond indifference, they embrace killing as a spectacle of self-affirmation. While activists reveal the repulsive suffering and slaughter that animal-exploitation industries attempt to conceal, the New Carnivores put killing on display in order to normalize, even glorify this. While vegans work to ensure that what is normally hidden behind a meal is exposed, New Carnivores subvert this by turning killing into a spectacle. While vegetarians demand that meat-eaters accept responsibility for suffering and death, New Carnivores say they do so by openly embracing killing. They endorse human power over animals and consider exploitation acceptable. New Carnivores glorify what vegetarians reveal as shocking and cruel. By dismissing vegetarians as "bead-loving hippies" whose ethical objections are now out of fashion, they deflect those challenges. Presenting themselves as path-breakers pursuing noble quests, New Carnivores actually embrace the status quo: continued animal exploitation. A speciesist discourse of natural entitlement blocks challenges to exploitation and reaffirms human domination.

Anti-vegetarianism is a persistent theme among New Carnivores. Several bemoan their difficulties as temporary and reluctant vegetarians. Pollan briefly tries vegetarianism as an experiment but feels inconvenienced and alienated from traditions; Bourette presents it as a harrowing ordeal. Forced to become vegetarian for a week after losing a bet that he cannot go twenty-four hours without mentioning meat, Gold endures the "bland nonsense" of "slimy" tofu.[74] New Carnivores reduce ethical behaviour to matters of taste alone. Even if it were not true that vegetarian and vegan diets provide extensive variety and flavour, the New Carnivores are unwilling to consider that one should act ethically even if it is inconvenient. Unlimited individual pleasure remains their key value, even if it comes at the expense of suffering and death for others.

Those who raise ethical objections to killing animals are presented as enemies of pleasure. Philpott opposes the "gustatory joy" of eating animals to "a puritanical strain . . . among . . . vegetarians and vegans" (all unnamed).[75] Pollan claims "a deep Puritan streak pervades animal rights activists, an abiding discomfort not only with our animality, but with the animals' animality too."[76] He provides no evidence for this claim and seemingly his aim is to present animal activists as alienated urbanites disconnected from natural processes. However, the industrial exploitation of billions of individual animals is hardly natural and it is hardly "Puritan[ism]" to object to their suffering and death. It is not discomfort with "animals' animality" that motivates advocacy but, rather, recognition that we share this with them and that their lives have inherent value; vegetarians and vegans try to preserve "animals' animality" by saving other creatures' lives. Pollan's disparagement of compassion would seem jarring if the issue was child prostitution or slavery but naturalized objectification of animals allows him to completely disregard their vital interests. New Carnivores invoke "Puritanism" to dismiss compassion, ethical responsibility, and activism as abstinence and austerity, turning matters of justice into ones of aesthetics and pleasure. (Their invocation is doubly odd, given that the Puritans were notorious for their cruelty towards others, such as "witches" and Native Americans, and that their Thanksgiving festival was established in 1637 as a celebration of the massacre of hundreds of Pequot villagers.) They characterize caring, ethical behaviour as either sentimental fantasy or extremist, authoritarian impositions on "normal" people. Foodies reduce animals' lives to human choices and tastes. Thus Gold denigrates "self-righteous whining of so-called 'moral vegetarians,'" asserting: "people are free to feed themselves whatever they want."[77] He objectifies meat as merely something about which humans have different ideas, making animal victims invisible. Ignoring ethical objections about killing, Gold reduces the issue to personal choice, differences between humans in matters of taste. That animals might make a personal choice not to be killed is ignored. Rather than embracing compassion and recognizing these as matters of justice, New Carnivores attack vegetarians and reject ethical arguments.

Denial of Responsibility

Even when failing to act upon it, most people claim to be concerned about others' suffering. Generally, ethical, legal, moral, philosophical, and religious systems encourage us to be concerned about others' pain and to feel some obligation to reduce it. Strong arguments exist for extending care and consideration to animals.[78] Animal rights advocates oppose consumption of animals, regardless of claims about "humane" methods. It is misleading to label treatment of animals on "family farms" as "humane," a fantasy to think we provide happy lives to animals we kill: "free-range," "organic," "natural," and "humane" production methods involve enormous suffering for animals.[79]

The fourth strategy New Carnivores use is denial of responsibility. For example, they deny responsibility for harm by claiming that animals' suffering and death have little moral significance. Pollan expresses passing concern for "welfare," acknowledges that slaughterhouses are places of horror, agrees that good people will not want to be a part of this, and concedes that vegetarianism is a "not unreasonable" response. Nevertheless, he rejects it and champions "humane" meat, encouraging readers not to worry about cows being slaughtered because "in a bovine brain the concept of non-existence is blissfully absent."[80] Pollan's smug dismissal of the complexities of consciousness in other animals is refuted by a virtual explosion of knowledge in cognitive ethology. Concerning cows, in particular, scientists Christine Nicol and John Webster have demonstrated that these animals have a rich social life, experience intense emotions, including anxiety, fear, and pain, that they worry about the future and become excited by intellectual challenges.[81] However, even despite the fact that some fascinating advances have been made in our knowledge of the cognitive capacities of other animals (frequently at their expense), detailed in scientific journals such as *Animal Cognition*, in more accessible writing,[82] and even in corporate media,[83] their various abilities are not morally relevant in fundamental discussions about our practices of using them. It is simply speciesism to make moral judgments about the use of other animals based on anything other than sentience: if animals are sentient, we are morally obligated not to use them as resources for our own ends.[84] Thus, vegans do not base objections to meat upon animals' capacity for philosophical speculation but rather on the fact that sentient beings are killed to produce it.

New Carnivores reassure meat-eaters that they need not inconvenience themselves by acting ethically. Even those like Nicholas Kristof who believe "animal rights are now firmly on the mainstream ethical agenda" readily overlook those rights, suggesting: "For my part, I eat meat, but I would prefer that this practice not inflict gratuitous suffering."[85] Since meat is unnecessary for survival, any suffering inflicted on animals to produce it is gratuitous. In *Righteous Porkchop*, rancher Nicolette Hahn Niman critiques factory farming and praises "natural meat." Reviews on her website indicate her comforting messages for carnivores. For example, Geoff Nicholson is among those who want to "eat well and ethically" but "would rather not know" the facts of meat production or be "berated by fanatics. Fortunately for people like us there's Nicolette Hahn Niman."[86] Like other New Carnivores, Nicholson provides no refutation of reasoned abolitionist animal rights arguments but simply dismisses them as fanatical. Niman reassures Nicholson and other animal-exploiters that what they do is acceptable, even humane and revolutionary, striking blows against factory farming and improving animals' lives through methods that require no inconvenience.

Rather than engaging ethical arguments about moral duties to animals, New Carnivores simply reject them, acting as if we have no obligations to animals. They depict themselves as put-upon, oppressed by vegan orthodoxy. Bourette presents ethical considerations as bothersome impositions, complaining that "all the journalism and academic study on the meat industry took to scolding those who ate meat."[87] Scientific information on negative consequences of meat production on animals, the environment, and human health is dismissed as mere "scolding," opinions from busybodies who intrude upon personal freedom. Lennon complains: "to a die-hard meat eater, there's nothing more irritating than a smug vegetarian."[88] Holly Hughes, editor of *Best Food Writing 2006*, applauds a "backlash . . . among fed-up gourmands . . . who refuse to renounce *foie gras* and caviar just because they are produced by less-than-noble methods."[89] Buford acknowledges "no one has ever really come up with a persuasive rejoinder to the claim that a warm-blooded, pain-feeling creature's life shouldn't be taken for your supper" but rather than following through to the logical conclusion that, therefore, one should stop killing other creatures and become vegan, he praises the "cool" meat "renaissance," relieved to find "people . . . prepared to declare: Enough! I'm a meat-eater and proud of it!"[90] Clearly this is no argument at all but simply the rejection of ethical concern. Exploitation and oppression are advanced as if they were their own justification. We would hardly accept such assertions from misogynists, homophobes, or racists and they are no more convincing when the victims are other animals.

Gold disparages "militant vegetarians"[91] of the "cabbage-head set"[92] who raise ethical issues. He claims to have a "philosophy" that rises above knee-jerk reactions from a "green militia" that "we are at the top of the food chain and it doesn't matter, and that we eat meat simply because we can."[93] In fact, nothing distinguishes his views from dominionist assertions: advocating eating higher-quality meat, he provides no other justification for killing animals than his own sense of power and entitlement. Gold says his "embrace" of killing constitutes "conscious carnivorism" and differentiates him from "slob" meat-eaters. Despite the fact that "slob" eaters may not have the financial resources to purchase the more expensive meats prized by the New Carnivores, they, too, have made a "conscious decision" and reject ethical objections to killing animals. All see their own pleasure as the primary criterion and reject concern for others' suffering. Gold's only guideline is his own appetite: "defenseless animals taste really, really good."[94] He rejects ethical arguments, asserting primacy of his own pleasure over others' suffering and death:

> some practices . . . are difficult not to see as barbaric, if not downright cruel: *foie gras*, ortolan, etc. I still eat *foie gras*, though, and I love it. Sucks for the goose or duck, no doubt, but damned if it doesn't taste amazing. These are things I like to call "tragically delicious." Wrong? Maybe, but oh so tasty! But when it comes to cows or turkeys or pigs or chickens, I'll eat them, I'll enjoy them, and it'll be a chilly day in Hades when some whiney, self-rightous [*sic*] hippie dickweed makes me feel like I'm morally inferior because of that.[95]

Such statements exemplify the New Carnivores' lack of empathy for the suffering and death of other beings. Their self-centred world view presents animals only as resources, to be used for their own pleasure. They resent moral arguments as interference with their own entitlement, to be answered with furious abuse. Indeed, these foodies display determined "hostility to the very language of moral values."[96] Bourette exemplifies this, conceiving ethics as faddism. Describing a butchering class in a fashionable Toronto area, she says that previously participants would have taken vegetarian cooking classes but now embrace meat-eating as the next trend.[97] Describing herself as a "lapsed vegetarian" lacking "stick-to-it-ness" who "felt guilty," this is a minor inconvenience as she subordinates animals' deaths to her own pleasure because "meat tasted so good."[98] Bourette remains unmoved by facts and ethical arguments: "I was resolved: I was going to have my meat"[99] and "even if I was going to feel some inner conflict, I wasn't going to let it spoil my appetite."[100] Such statements are at the core of New Carnivore discourse: consideration of the ethics of killing is abandoned and self-indulgence is the sole justification for exploiting others.

Pollan appears less openly scornful of ethical arguments but uses a rhetorical technique of seeming to consider animal advocacy only to dismiss it. He acknowledges vegetarians' "moral clarity" but rather than adopting such principles he "pities" their "dreams of innocence [and] . . . denial of reality."[101] He claims to respect animals, suggesting they should have happy lives before we kill them and that we should consume their bodies entirely. However, one shows more respect for animals by not eating them at all, letting them live unmolested. Pollan briefly considers "animal rights" but only as a joke, deliberately reading Peter Singer's *Animal Liberation* in a steakhouse. Confronting Singer's propositions that animals' ability to suffer requires that they be given equal consideration and that species boundaries are not valid criteria for excluding others from such consideration, Pollan acknowledges his inability to counter them and decides to ignore them: "If I believe in equality, and equality is based on interests rather than characteristics, then either I have to take the interests of the steer I'm eating into account or concede that I am a speciesist. For the time being, I decided to plead guilty as charged. I finished my steak."[102]

Rather than changing his own consumption practices to follow ethical principles he acknowledges as irrefutable, Pollan dismisses those who do. Like other New Carnivores, he believes his own pleasure justifies any abuse.

Conclusion

The New Carnivores present themselves as constituting a different, more ethical approach to eating. Claiming to promote better treatment of animals, the New Carnivores attack animal advocacy and pursue their main objective of obtaining tastier meat and continuing their unjust carnivorous practices. The New Carnivores reject consideration for animals and turn their deaths into a joke. They believe that killing animals is justified because humans enjoy consuming their flesh. Since these are not matters of survival or nutritional necessity but trivial ones of pleasure and taste, only the cognitive dissonance characteristic of a thoroughly desensitized consciousness could consider these actions justified. Since we can prevent animals' premature deaths by becoming vegan, we cannot say those deaths are necessary or humane. These are rationalizations to make our greed for their flesh seem less selfish and cruel and to convince ourselves that killing is morally acceptable.

Through strategies of denial of real harm, denying existence of a victim, denial of responsibility, and condemning critics, the New Carnivores actually offer nothing new but merely assert their "right" to exploit animals and serve a primary function of providing exculpatory fantasies. Whether they promote neo-traditional farming methods and humane slaughter or intensive factory farming, meat-eaters share the same arrogant assumption that animals are ours to use and kill. What is most pernicious about these arguments is that they have been so widely accepted, even within the animal protection movement itself. Rather than opposing animal exploitation, groups such as PETA devote most of their campaigns to welfare reforms while the Humane Society of the United States endorses and actively promotes so-called "humane" animal products (see Chapter 14, "Campaigning with the Enemy"). The Happy Meat and "humane" myths represent a victory for agribusiness and the marginalization of abolitionist, vegan arguments.[103] Instead of accepting the spurious arguments advanced by the New Carnivores, those who are truly concerned about the protection and well-being of other animals should reject the consumption of all animal-derived products and renew their efforts to end the exploitation of our fellow creatures.

NOTES

1. Regan, *Case for Animal Rights.*
2. Francione, *Introduction to Animal Rights.*
3. Singer, *Animal Liberation*, 95.
4. Cohen, *States of Denial.*
5. Soller, "Head to Hoof."
6. Robinson, *Pasture Perfect.*
7. Soller, "Head to Hoof."
8. Buford, "Red, White, and Bleu."
9. Marx, "Vegetarian Butchers?"
10. For example, Lennon, "Why Vegetarians Are Eating Meat."
11. Sorenson, "Constructing Extremists, Rejecting Compassion."
12. Twigg, "Meanings of Meat"; Adams, *Sexual Politics.*
13. Ozersky, "'New Carnivores' Stalk Greater Fame."
14. Spartos, "Meat Wave."
15. Ozersky, "'New Carnivores' Stalk Greater Fame."
16. Gold, *Shameless Carnivore*, 3.
17. Ibid., 2.
18. Ibid., 3, 4.
19. Bourette, *Carnivore Chic*, 3.
20. Ibid., 97.
21. Ibid., 104.
22. Goodman, "Ted Nugent."
23. Bourette, *Carnivore Chic*, 196.
24. Buford, "Red, White, and Bleu."
25. Bourette, *Carnivore Chic*, xii.
26. Ibid., xiv.
27. Richler, "Men in the Pit."
28. Bourdieu, *Distinction*
29. Lamkin, "Perks."

30. Center for Media and Democracy, "Center for Consumer Freedom."
31. Cohen, *States of Denial.*
32. Cole and Morgan, "Ethical Veganism."
33. Penman, "Think Going Organic Lets You Eat."
34. Ibid.
35. Francione, "'Happy' Meat."
36. Buford, "Red, White, and Bleu."
37. Philpott, "Flesh and Bone," 108.
38. Ibid., 108.
39. Lennon, "Why Vegetarians Are Eating Meat."
40. Ibid.
41. Ibid.
42. Black, "Meat-Eating Authors."
43. Friend, *Compassionate Carnivore.*
44. Lane, "Some Sausages."
45. Ibid.
46. Ibid.
47. Quoted in Francione, "'Happy' Meat."
48. Martin, "Meat Labels."
49. Clancy, *Greener Pastures,* 3.
50. Adams, *Sexual Politics.*
51. Friend, *Compassionate Carnivore.*
52. PETA, "Slaughterhouses."
53. Fiddes, *Meat,* 44, 68.
54. Pollan, "Power Steer."
55. Pollan, *Omnivore's Dilemma,* 330.
56. Ibid., 331.
57. Ibid., 232–33.
58. Ibid., 353.
59. *Courier Mail,* "Jamie Oliver Electrocutes Chickens on TV Show."
60. Channel 4, "Jamie Sacrifices a Lamb."
61. *Daily Mail,* "Gordon Ramsay's Pet Lamb."
62. Ibid.
63. Gold, *Shameless Carnivore,* 269.
64. Buford, "Red, White, and Bleu."
65. Frenette, "Nose and Tales."
66. Global Action Network, "2nd Quebec Foie Gras."
67. Buford, "Red, White, and Bleu."
68. Ibid.
69. Gold, *Shameless Carnivore,* 16.

70. Buford, "Red, White, and Bleu."
71. Ibid.
72. Vandello et al., "Precarious Manhood."
73. Niman, "Defining Humane Animal Care"; *Righteous Porkchop*.
74. Gold, *Shameless Carnivore*, 173.
75. Philpott, "Flesh and Bone," 108.
76. Pollan, "Animal's Place."
77. Gold, "On Vegetarians."
78. Clark, *Moral Standing*; Donovan and Adams, *Feminist Care Tradition*; Francione, *Introduction to Animal Rights*; Garner, *Animal Ethics*; Nibert, *Animal Rights/Human Rights*; Regan, *Case for Animal Rights*; Rowlands, *Animals Like Us*; Singer, *Animal Liberation*.
79. Johnson, "Rare Glimpse."
80. Pollan, "Animal's Place."
81. Cited in Leake, "Moody Cows."
82. For example, Balcombe, *Pleasurable Kingdom*; Bekoff, *Wild Justice*; Bradshaw, *Elephants on the Edge*; Masson, *When Elephants Weep*; Peterson, *Moral Lives of Animals*.
83. For example, Kluger, "Minds of Animals."
84. Francione, "Only Sentience Matters."
85. Kristof, "Humanity Even for Nonhumans."
86. Nicholson, review of *Righteous Porkchop*.
87. Bourette, *Carnivore Chic*, 26.
88. Lennon, "Why Vegetarians Are Eating Meat."
89. Quoted in Myers, "Hard to Swallow."
90. Buford, "Red, White, and Bleu."
91. Gold, *Shameless Carnivore*, 1–4.
92. Ibid., 314.
93. Ibid., 14.
94. Ibid., 3.
95. Quoted in Colin, "Meat Me Halfway."
96. Myers, "Hard to Swallow."
97. Bourette, *Carnivore Chic*.
98. Ibid., 24.
99. Ibid., 26.
100. Ibid., 29.
101. Pollan, *Omnivore's Dilemma*, 362.
102. Ibid., 309.
103. Francione, "Disturbing Partnership"; LaVeck, "Let's Not Give Up."

BIBLIOGRAPHY

Adams, Carol J. *The Sexual Politics of Meat*. Tenth Anniversary Edition. New York: Continuum, 2000.

Balcombe, Jonathan. *Pleasurable Kingdom*. London: Macmillan, 2007.

Bekoff, Marc. *Wild Justice*. Chicago: University of Chicago Press, 2009.

Black, Jane. "For Meat-Eating Authors, a More Tender Approach." *Washington Post*, May 14, 2008. http://www.washingtonpost.com/wp-dyn/content/article/2008/05/13/AR2008051300581.html.

Bourdieu, Pierre. *Distinction*. New York: Routledge, 1984.

Bourette, Susan. *Carnivore Chic*. Toronto: Viking, 2008.

Bradshaw, Gay A. *Elephants on the Edge*. New Haven: Yale University Press, 2009.

Buford, Bill. "Red, White, and Bleu: What Do We Eat When We Eat Meat?" *New Yorker*, December 3, 2007. http://www.newyorker.com/arts/critics/atlarge/2007/12/03/071203crat_atlarge_buford.

Center for Media and Democracy. "Center for Consumer Freedom." *Sourcewatch*. Last modified May 7, 2015. http://www.sourcewatch.org/index.php?title=Center_for_Consumer_Freedom.

Channel 4. "Jamie Sacrifices a Lamb." *Jamie's Great Escape*, Channel 4, November 25, 2007. http://www.channel4.com/food/on-tv/jamie-oliver/jamies-great-escape/jamie-kills-lamb_p_1.html.

Clancy, Kate. *Greener Pastures: How Grass-Fed Beef and Milk Contribute to Healthy Eating*. Cambridge, MA: Union of Concerned Scientists, 2006.

Clark, Stephen R.L. *Animals and Their Moral Standing*. New York: Routledge, 1997.

Cohen, Stanley. *States of Denial*. Cambridge: Polity Press, 2001.

Cole, Matthew, and Karen Morgan. "Ethical Veganism and the Challenge of Interlocking Oppressions: How Do We Create Vegatopia?" Paper presented at the 38th IVU World Vegetarian Congress, July 27–August 2, 2008, Dresden, Germany.

Colin, Chris. "Meat Me Halfway." *Meatpaper*, March, 2007. http://www.meatpaper.com/articles/2007/0528_shameless.html.

Courier Mail (Brisbane). "Jamie Oliver Electrocutes Chickens on TV Show." January 8, 2008. http://www.couriermail.com.au/news/oliver-electrocutes-chickens/story-e6freon6-1111115279271?

Daily Mail (London). "Gordon Ramsay's Pet Lamb Slaughter 'Has Turned Viewers into Vegetarians.'" June 28, 2007. http://www.dailymail.co.uk/tvshowbiz/article-464879/Gordon-Ramsays-pet-lamb-slaughter-turned-viewers-vegetarians.html.

DeWaal, Caroline Smith. *Playing Chicken: The Human Cost of Inadequate Regulation of the Poultry Industry*. Washington, DC: Center for Science in the Public Interest, 1996.

Donovan, Josephine, and Carol J. Adams, eds. *The Feminist Care Tradition in Animal Ethics*. New York: Columbia University, 2007.

Eshel, Gidon, and Pamela Martin. "Diet, Energy, and Global Warming." *Earth Interactions* 10, no. 9 (2006): 1–17.

Fiddes, Nick. *Meat*. New York: Routledge, 1991.

Francione, Gary. "A Disturbing Partnership." *Animal Rights: The Abolitionist Approach* (blog), June 25, 2009. http://www.abolitionistapproach.com/a-disturbing-partnership/.

———. "'Happy' Meat/Animal Products: A Step in the Right Direction or 'An Easier Access Point Back' to Eating Animals?" *Animal Rights: The Abolitionist Approach* (blog), February 7, 2007. http://www.abolitionistapproach.com/?p=16.

———. *Introduction to Animal Rights*. Philadelphia: Temple University Press, 2000.

———. "Only Sentience Matters." *Animal Rights: The Abolitionist Approach* (blog), August 20, 2012. http://www.abolitionistapproach.com/only-sentience-matters/#.Vx5kIce9bdk.

Frenette, Brad. "Martin Picard: Nose and Tales." *National Post*. Last updated November 12, 2008. http://www.nationalpost.com/related/topics/story.html?id=941416.

Friend, Catherine. *The Compassionate Carnivore*. Cambridge, MA: Da Capo Press, 2009.

Garner, Robert. *Animal Ethics*. Cambridge: Polity, 2005.

Glade, Michael J. "Food, Nutrition, and the Prevention of Cancer: A Global Perspective." *Nutrition* 15, no. 6 (1999): 523–26.

Global Action Network. "2nd Quebec Foie Gras Investigation Overview." 2007. http://www.gan.ca/campaigns/2nd+quebec+foie+gras+investigation/overview.en.html?

Gold, Scott. "About Me." *The Shameless Carnivore* (Gold's blog), n.d. http://www.shamelesscarnivore.com/page_id=10/index.html.

———. "On Vegetarians (Part One)." *The Shameless Carnivore* (Gold's blog), February 7, 2006. http://www.shamelesscarnivore.com/p=12/index.html.

———. *The Shameless Carnivore*. New York: Broadway, 2008.

Goodman, Elzabeth. "Ted Nugent Threatens to Kill Barack Obama and Hillary Clinton during Vicious Onstage Rant." *Rolling Stone*, August 24, 2007. http://www.rollingstone.com/music/news/ted-nugent-threatens-to-kill-barack-obama-and-hillary-clinton-during-vicious-onstage-rant-20070824.

Johnson, Jewel. "A Rare Glimpse Inside a 'Free-Range' Egg Facility." *Prairie Progress* 8, no. 8 (2007). http://www.peacefulprairie.org/eNews/Spring07/free-rangeFarm.html.

Kluger, Jeffrey. "Inside the Minds of Animals." *Time*, August 5, 2010. http://www.time.com/time/magazine/article/0,9171,2008867,00.html.

Kristof, Nicholas. "Humanity Even for Nonhumans." *New York Times*, April 8, 2009. http://www.nytimes.com/2009/04/09/opinion/09kristof.html?_r=0.

Lamkin, John. "Perks of Being a Food, Wine & Travel Writer." International Food, Wine and Travel Writers Association blog, March 26, 2009. http://ifwtwa.org/2009/03/perks-of-being-a-food-wine-travel-writer-and-no-free-lunch.html.

Lane, Megan. "Some Sausages Are More Equal than Others." *BBC News*, February 1, 2007. http://news.bbc.co.uk/2/hi/uk_news/magazine/6295747.stm.

LaVeck, James. "Let's Not Give Up Before We Even Get Started: What the English Anti-slavery Movement Can Teach Animal Advocates about Overcoming the Politics of Pessimism." HumaneMyth.org, n.d. http://www.humanemyth.org/letsnotgiveup.htm.

Leake, Jonathan. "The Secret Life of Moody Cows." *Sunday Times* (London), February 27, 2005. http://www.thesundaytimes.co.uk/sto/news/uk_news/article100199.ece.

Lennon, Christine. "Why Vegetarians Are Eating Meat." *Food and Wine*, August 2007. http://www.foodandwine.com/articles/why-vegetarians-are-eating-meat.

Masson, Jeffrey Moussaieff. *When Elephants Weep*. New York: Delta, 1995.

Martin, Andrew. "Meat Labels Hope to Lure the Sensitive Carnivore." *New York Times*, October 24, 2006. http://www.nytimes.com/2006/10/24/business/24humane.html?_r=2&oref=slogin&pagewanted=all.

Marx, Rebecca. "Vegetarian Butchers?" *Gourmet*, April 2, 2009. http://www.gourmet.com/food/2009/04/vegetarian-butchers.html.

Myers, B.R. "Hard to Swallow: The Gourmet's Ongoing Failure to Think in Moral Terms." *Atlantic*, September 2007. http://www.theatlantic.com/doc/200709/omnivore.

Nibert, David. *Animal Rights/Human Rights*. Lanham, MD: Rowman & Littlefield, 2002.

Nicholson, Geoff. Review of *Righteous Porkchop*, by Micolette Hahn Niman. *SFGate*, March 8, 2009. http://www.sfgate.com/books/article/Righteous-Porkchop-by-Nicolette-Hahn-Niman-3168932.php.

Niman, Nicholette Hahn. "Defining Humane Animal Care." *Righteous Porkchop* website, n.d. https://www.nimanranch.com/about-us/humane-animal-care/.

———. *Righteous Porkchop*. New York: HarperCollins, 2009.

Ozersky, Josh. "The 'New Carnivores' Stalk Greater Fame." *Grub Street* (blog), April 16, 2008. http://www.grubstreet.com/2008/04/the_new_carnivores_stalk_great.html#.

Penman, Danny. "Think Going Organic Lets You Eat Meat with a Clear Conscience? This Shocking Investigation into a 'Humane' Slaughterhouse Will Make You Think Again." *Daily Mail* (London), January 12, 2010. http://www.dailymail

.co.uk/news/article-1242503/Think-going-organic-lets-eat-meat-clear-conscience
-This-shocking-investigation-humane-slaughterhouse-make-think-again.
html#ixzz1iLtLKDKj.

PETA (People for the Ethical Treatment of Animals). "If Slaughterhouses Had Glass
Walls, Everyone Would Be Vegetarian." PETA website, n.d. http://www.peta.org/
videos/glass-walls-2/.

Peterson, Dale. *The Moral Lives of Animals*. New York: Bloomsbury, 2011.

Philpott, Tom. "Flesh and Bone: Toward a Whole-Beast Meat-Eating Ethos."
Gastronomica 7, no. 2 (2007): 106–9.

Pollan, Michael. "An Animal's Place." *New York Times Magazine*, November 10, 2002.
http://www.michaelpollan.com/article.php?id=55.

———. *The Omnivore's Dilemma*. New York: Penguin, 2006.

———. "Power Steer." *New York Times Magazine*, March 31, 2002. http://michaelpollan
.com/articles-archive/power-steer/.

Regan, Tom. *The Case for Animal Rights*. Berkeley: University of California, 2004.

Richler, Jacob. "Men in the Pit against Meat on the Spit." *Maclean's* 125, nos. 25–26
(2012): 79.

Robinson, Jo. *Pasture Perfect*. Vashon, WA: Vashon Island Press, 2007.

Rowlands, Mark. *Animals Like Us*. London: Verso, 2002.

Singer, Peter. *Animal Liberation*. New York: Ecco, 2002.

Soller, Kurt. "Head to Hoof: A Butcher Helps Lead a New Carnivore Movement."
Newsweek, January 28, 2009. http://www.newsweek.com/id/182035.

Sorenson, John. "Constructing Extremists, Rejecting Compassion: Ideological
Attacks on Animal Advocacy from Right and Left." In *Critical Theory and
Animal Liberation*, edited by J. Sanbonmatsu, 219–38. Lanham, MD: Rowman
& Littlefield, 2011.

Spartos, Carla. "We've Having a Meat Wave: Macho Meat Eaters Are Entrail-
Oriented." *New York Post*, April 16, 2008. http://www.nypost.com/seven/04162008/
entertainment/food/we_re_having_a_meat_wave_106710.htm?page=0.

Twigg, Julia. "Vegetarianism and the Meanings of Meat." In *The Sociology of Food
and Eating*, edited by Anne Murcott, 18–30. Aldershot, Hants: Gower, 1983.

Vandello, Joseph A., Jennifer K. Bosson, Dov Cohen, Rochelle M. Burnaford, and
Jonathan R. Weaver. "Precarious Manhood." *Journal of Personality and Social
Psychology* 95, no. 6 (2008): 1325–39.

Walker, Polly, Pamela Rhubart-Berg, Shawn McKenzie, Kristin Kelling, and Robert
S. Lawrence. "Public Health Implications of Meat Production and Consumption."
Public Health Nutrition 8, no. 4 (2005): 348–56.

17

Rats! Being Social Requires Empathy

Leesa Fawcett

Rats seem to trouble human existence. They follow us around, hopping off boats with us in new ports and colonizing new-found lands with their presence, much as human beings have done since we started navigating the seas. Today, rats inhabit our apartment buildings, subways, sewer systems, laboratories, and our imaginations. Rats are arguably one of the most successful animals on earth if sheer numbers, adaptability, and perseverance are used as measures of success. However, along with mice and other rodents, the so-called laboratory rat is the most commonly used creature in Western experimental science. Sometimes this science, as wasteful, ugly, and bad as it may be, actually tells us something interesting and good. In a variety of recent studies on the social behaviour of rats, researchers have seen rats demonstrate empathy-driven actions, showing compassion for other rats.[1] Rats act on each other's behalf.

Although it may be difficult to understand rat "beingness," this chapter assumes enough mammalian continuity across the human/Other animal divide that we can ponder the empathic lives of certain rats and wonder what such knowledge may mean for their prospects. Rodents comprise the largest mammalian order, involving 40 percent of the world's species worldwide[2]—and those are only the ones we know about. Starting with the rats themselves, their natural history in the world and in our imaginations, then developing through ideas of sociality, particularly empathy and play, this chapter challenges the ethics of rodent experimentation. Human beings use rats carelessly in experiments for the ostensible good of other human beings. I contend that this carelessness erodes human ethics of care, empathy, and justice.

Social Rats

The natural history of rats is daunting—replete with their extraordinary, superhuman abilities. Rats belong to the mammalian order Rodentia, along with mice, squirrels, voles, and beavers; the word rodent derived from the Latin *rodere*—to gnaw, and gnaw they do with their continuously growing incisors.[3] There is evidence that rats inhabited the Earth over 50 million years ago. There is not one rat typology; instead there are over 500 species of rats worldwide, living in all environments except the polar regions. There are: blind rats that live like moles underground and "can tunnel at a rate of 1 metre every 17 minutes"; rats that build 1.5 m (5 ft) high stick nests in Australia; giant Sumatran bamboo rats with lengths over 63 cm (2 ft), weighing up to 4 kg (9 lb); and our Canadian bushy-tailed native wood rat.[4] On my way to an outhouse in Indonesia, I wandered through the kitchen and met a rat who was at least 58 cm (over 2 ft) long. We looked at one another; the rat did not scurry away or even budge. I retreated to find another route, defeated by the confident-looking gaze of a surprisingly large rat.

In Canada, we have native wood rats (*Neotoma* spp.) with bushy or hairy tails. They can be found nesting on cliffs in the mountains, in old trees, or building cactus houses in the plains. Wood rats are also called pack rats and are social animals who eat mainly nuts, seeds, and fruit. Unlike these relatively harmless vegetarian rats, the most commonly known rat species are the scaly-tailed imported Old World rats—*Rattus rattus*, the black or roof rat; and *Rattus norvegicus*, the brown or Norway rat. The roof rat is an excellent climber, often found in the top stories of buildings or running along rooftops. The larger Norway rat is more adaptable, able to withstand colder temperatures and preferring cities and farmyards. We will concern ourselves largely with the brown or Norway rat, because standardized laboratory mammals for experimentation are albino mutants of this rat.[5]

I was puzzled by the common Latin name, Norway rat, and it seems to be a mistake made early on by a British naturalist, John Berkenhout in 1769, who assumed the brown rat had arrived in England via Norwegian ships, although there isn't any record of brown rats in Norway at the time.[6]

Of course, rats could have more easily arrived on British ships returning with treasures from Asia; scientific nomenclature was deeply influenced by imperialist tendencies.

The brown rat, also known as the common or sewer rat, has grayish-brown fur and is believed to have originated from a central Asian or Chinese ancestor who lived along stream banks and migrated as rice paddies and canals spread. This may help to explain why brown rats are excellent swimmers and can dive and tread water exceptionally well, allowing them to survive in sewer and outlet systems. They are great diggers, too, preferring to tunnel into basements or under floors in a small, close-to-home range of less than 100 ft across. Brown rats are omnivores.

One of the sensational facts about brown rats is that they have a tremendous reproductive capacity, although one wonders if this isn't a co-evolutionary effect of human long-term extermination attempts and rat commensal living strategies. Brown rats, who typically live 1 to 3 years, are able to begin reproducing at 3 months of age and can have anywhere from 6 to 22 young, averaging 8 to 10, with a gestation period of 22 days.[7] Female brown rats can reproduce all year long. So by 2 years of age, 1 female (averaging a litter of 9 every month for 24 months) could have had 216 young. These possible numbers fuel the modern notions of the rat as a mass producer and mass consumer.

Rats are good pilferers of grains and foodstuff. According to the World Health Organization, rats eat over 30 million tonnes of food per year,[8] making them pretty good consumers. They take from us, and we use them. For example, rats are tethered on long leads and trained to find land mines in Tanzania[9]—a rather deadly job. Rats are good at finding things because of their problem-solving abilities and their excellent sense of smell. In fact, rats are developing even better olfactory senses, with about 2,070 smell receptor genes, and an increased capacity to deal with toxins in their liver; genetic mapping shows that rats are evolving three times faster than humans.[10]

Rats are eaten in many parts of the world, exterminated as vermin, bred as fancy pets, and ubiquitously used in experiments. The world of animal experimentation can be inconsistent, varying from respectful, difficult field research with wild animals to wasteful laboratory settings with captive animals. Nevertheless, I am pleased by the knowledge gleaned through less-intrusive experimental methods that have given us glimpses into the emotional lives of rats. Rats, like many other animals, like to play, and they learn social and physical skills while playing. Cognitive ethologist Marc

Bekoff argues that play is easy to spot: "Individuals become deeply immersed in the activity and show their delight by their acrobatic movements, gleeful vocalizations, and smiles."[11] He also believes that play is a precursor to moral behaviour as social mammals learn the rules of fair, fun play and will cease playing if the game goes awry or their playmate becomes too aggressive. In his unique and well-researched book, *Pleasurable Kingdom: Animals and the Nature of Feeling Good*, Jonathan Balcombe details video studies of rats playing, and changing their behaviour to keep the playful mood going. In one study both young and adult rats chose a box with a free rat rather than one with a rat visible but unavailable behind a plexiglas wall. They preferred the company of a rat free to play with them.[12]

Rats like to be tickled; they chirp their laughter and are empathic with each other. Rats communicate with a variety of vocalizations in ultrasonic ranges, above the hearing capacity of humans. One of their highest calls (at 50 kHz) is most plentiful when rats engage in rough-and-tumble play together,[13] when they are tickled, and when they are having sex. In a series of clever experiments exploring social affect in rats, Burgdorf and Panksepp found that rats enjoy being tickled and will seek out the hand that tickles them for more tickling.[14] Panksepp's YouTube video of rats being tickled has had over three quarters of a million viewers, so clearly some of us enjoy the rats' delight.[15]

Recently, a study investigated whether rats are capable of helping each other, based on empathic feelings. In a series of experiments, pairs of rats were housed together. To test for empathy the researchers placed a free rat in an enclosure with its companion physically trapped in a restrainer. On the first day of the test the trapped rats emitted ultrasonic alarm calls. Inevitably, at differing rates, the free rats figured out how to open the door to the restrainer and free their caged companion. To demonstrate that their acts were intentional and not accidental, the researchers showed that in other experimental conditions rats did not try to open empty restrainers or ones with toy rats inside them. They learned to open the restrainer doors when their companion was released into a separate area and there was no reward of social interaction. Even when chocolate chips were put in a second restrainer, the rats opened both restrainers and left some chocolate chips for the freed companion to eat, too.[16] Rats free each other. Rats share. Better yet, they share chocolate: something that cannot be said about all humans. To complicate the rat empathy experiments it turns out that female rats became door-openers significantly more often, and more quickly, than males. Female rats were also more active than males when faced with a trapped rat. Sex matters when you are trapped. How sexed/gendered is empathy?

Science and natural history, of course, contain their own forms of humans' socially constructed knowledge, but some types of knowledge carry more possibility and weight than others in particular times and places. A question to ponder is how deep and broad are the biological roots of empathy? Darwin was comfortable acknowledging animal emotions, such as the distress many animals experience when seeing another animal in danger.[17] Frans de Waal maintains empathy has many layers and that higher forms of empathy exist only in humans and other mammals with large brains, such as monkeys, apes, and dolphins.[18] It is one thing for apes, whales, and elephants to demonstrate empathy (given that they represent charismatic megafauna that we idolize), and quite another for shadowy rats to do so. If rats are empathic at any level, what does that mean for their ubiquitous use in intrusive experiments? What does that say about humans who use them in experiments and humans who claim benefits from those experiments? Perhaps, that we are too unimaginative, too lazy, and too stuck in our ways to devise different means of testing that do not cause such harm to so many other animals. There is ongoing refusal in science to acknowledge the emotional lives of more-than-human animals. Still, some rats, some scientists, and many activists resist, as all types of experiments continue.

Imagined and Socially Constructed Rats

In Jonathan Burt's brilliant and beautifully rendered book, *Rat*, he details the complicated boundary-crossings the rat makes in our lives: "Cultural attitudes to the rat reveal that it is a pollutant with the ability to move between bodily and symbolic boundaries with an overall trajectory that seems to make it an especially threatening phenomenon as much in the realm of language and thought as in the granary or food store."[19] Our everyday English language reveals the danger we attribute to rats and the dislike we harbour for them in phrases such as "You dirty rat!" or the notion of "ratting on someone" or trying to escape "the rat race." Rat metaphors and representations have negatively coloured and biased human rights and social justice issues. For example, Nazi propaganda, in the form of postcards and posters, regularly depicted Jewish people as rats.[20] The narrator in the Nazi film,

Der ewige Jude, opened the film by stating, "Just as the rat is the lowest of animals, the Jew is the lowest of human beings."[21] The rat was successfully deployed as a form of metaphoric warfare against peoples.

How else are rats used for human ends? In *Animal Lessons: How They Teach Us to Be Human,* feminist philosopher Kelly Oliver persuasively contends that a number of philosophers twist and "turn wild animal metaphors into domesticated beasts of burden to prove their theories about man."[22] Rats have been an active part of this circulation of power and regime of transference in Western thought. Yet, even a socially constructed rat can bite back. If we turn briefly to psychoanalysis for its unconscious processes, the appearance of Sigmund Freud's famous "Rat Man" is intriguing. The Rat Man is the name Freud gave to a patient who had a phobia about rats—a phobia that included his fear that rats would devour him or bite their way into the anus of his father (a supposed form of torture), a phobia Freud later linked to anal eroticism.[23] Simultaneously, Freud was troubled about children biting, and about children's anxiety concerning being eaten by animals. Maybe children bite as a defence, as not all biting is about being eaten—think of cornered rats who may bite to ward off capture. In the prelinguistic, embodied, and gestural world of young children they may have a unique understanding of animals. After all, in *Totem and Taboo* Freud wrote: "children have no scruples over allowing animals to rank as their full equals. Uninhibited as they are in the avowal of their bodily needs, they no doubt feel themselves more akin to animals than to their elders, who may well be a puzzle to them."[24] Freud's commentary is his way of drawing attention to the lack of sophistication in children and animals compared to cultured adults. Freud and other psychoanalysts (e.g., Lacan, Kristeva) relied in different ways on wild animals and their unpredictability to make sense of unconscious urges and desires in increasingly domesticated human beings. Gilles Deleuze and Félix Guattari rant about the psychoanalytic tendency to ignore animalness and its lived meaning: "They killed becoming-animal, in the adult as in the child. They saw nothing."[25] Deleuze and Guattari wonder if, in Freud's case of Little Hans (who had a phobia about horses), the child had actually seen a downed horse in the street being whipped (a common European occurrence then) and was deeply affected by this event. That is to say, his problems were not all Oedipal in nature—such rampant anthropocentrism, as if all meaningful encounters are only in the human-to-human domain, is tiresome. "When psychoanalysis talks about animals, animals learn to laugh," Deleuze and Guattari taunt.[26]

Rats live on despite our social constructions and exploitive uses of them. Wild rats are incredible survivors, as we like to think we are. The theme of rats symbolizing survivors is echoed in Günter Grass's novel *The Rat*, where a likeable female pet rat shows the narrator how rats survive human destructiveness and ultimately triumph over humanity.[27] Still, the adaptability of rats is perplexing, especially given extreme conditions of survival. Case in point, forty-three atomic bombs were tested in the 1940s and 1950s on the island of Runit, located in a South Pacific atoll; even with extraordinarily high levels of radioactivity to this day, making the island uninhabitable for humans for 25,000 years, rats survived and thrive on the island.[28]

In their playfully imaginative way, Deleuze and Guattari begin their chapter, "Becoming-Intense, Becoming-Animal, Becoming-Imperceptible," discussing an odd movie about a rat named Willard. Then, after a foray through the world of rat packs, assemblages, and deterritorializations, they announce that every animal is fundamentally a multiplicity.[29] Through pro-liferating connections and intensities one thing becomes something else, more than one, and flows into other possible relations—becoming a multi-plicity. To answer their question: "Or is the multiplicity that fascinates us already related to a multiplicity dwelling within us?"[30] I answer a resound-ing "Yes!" We are made up of all sorts of animal beings—from multitudes of bacteria in our bodies to the mitochondria that provide our cellular energy, as the late Lynn Margulis's theory of endosymbiosis proved.[31] Symbiotic relationships are when two different species live together and benefit from their mutual lives. Margulis cleverly showed how separate free-living organ-isms joined and evolved over time into new entities.

In concert with their notion of becoming-animal, Deleuze and Guattari urge us to "either stop writing, or write like a rat"[32] because for them the writing of a good "sorcerer" has everything to do with fully participating in the uncanny and unnatural worlds, and writing became another way to become more than human (see Chapter 6, on the sorcerer in Deleuze and Guattari). Yes. And I am doubtful many people will write rat; I am con-cerned with the material lives of rats. What would happen if more people were to empathize with rats, especially given that millions of rats have been used to stand in for human beings in excruciating experiments? It is in the uncanny world of laboratory experimentation where rats materially sub-stitute for human beings and yet in the dominant North American culture rats signify the opposite of human exceptionalism. Contradictions abound.

Sociality Through Ethology

Ethology is the study of animal behaviour—forming a long line from Niko Tinbergen to Jakob von Uexküll. In a turn away from intrusive, laboratory-based studies of animals, ethology is a field-based observational method for learning about animals in the context of their lived lives. Von Uexküll pioneered a more phenomenological and sensory perceptive approach to ethology, with his notion of "Umwelts" or lifeworlds (thus signalling the advent of later fields of sign systems from semiotics to biosemiotics and zoosemiotics). Uexküll's theory that each being has its own ways of sensing life or its specific sensory lifeworld (characterized as a surrounding soap bubble) means that rats have pretty extensive and adaptable lifeworlds.

Unlike traditional scientific ethology, Deleuze and Guattari's notion of ethology is not about defining an animal by its nomenclature (kingdom, phylum, class, order, family, genus, species, and down to subspecies) or Latin names; they are interested in the affective world of each animal. Given their relationships with the surrounding environs, what are animals capable of? Their telling analogy is to say that a workhorse is actually more like an ox (as beasts of burden) than it is like a racehorse.[33] What are the affective worlds of the brown rat?

Brown rats live and work in social units. To be social requires communication, thoughts, emotions, care, empathic responses, and a sense of what is fair and what is unfair in your collective, in order to live as convivially as possible. Jessica Pierce and Marc Bekoff argue convincingly that animals act morally, where morality is defined as "a suite of interrelated other-regarding behaviors that cultivate and regulate complex interactions within social groups."[34] Of the three moral behaviour categories they outline, rats in laboratory conditions have shown two out of the three: altruistic and co-operative behaviours, and empathic behaviours. Pierce and Bekoff believe that the third moral behaviour category—justice behaviour—is the most complex and the least widespread. Yet, as Bekoff has written elsewhere, the act of playing has elements of justice in it.[35] To be able to play with another involves understanding what is fair and unfair play. Play only continues if it is fun and fair. Rats play. So now it appears rats demonstrate aspects of all three categories of moral behaviour.

Despite my admiration for Bekoff's body of work I am not convinced justice is the most complex moral behaviour or that it is important to surgically separate altruism, empathy, and justice. Carol Gilligan's work on moral development argues that ethics of care and ethics of justice are held in tension and both are required to solve moral dilemmas and to live well with others. Of note, Gilligan is quick to point out two dangerous pathological turns in morality: (1) a justice perspective that cannot "see" the other; and (2) a care perspective that loses sight of the "self" as different from the other.[36] From the human side of the animal divide, there is a long, rich strand of ecofeminists' animal care theory that advocates for the subjectivity of animals and insists it is incumbent on us to care for other animals. For example, Josephine Donovan proposes a form of dialogical ethics as an empathic way to attend to animal lives,[37] and the late Val Plumwood promotes narrative ethics and dialogical relationships with animals in order to morally honour their differences and similarities with humans.[38] Donovan argues that animals have full relational lives and know themselves as more than commodities, so that caring humans are obliged to act on behalf of animals.[39]

Animal-Based Experimentation

Against their free will, rats serve humans as experimental commodities. The first breeding lines for the white laboratory rat (an albino form) were developed in 1906 at the Wistar Institute, in Philadelphia, to standardize animal-based experimentation.[40] White lab rats with their eerie red eyes have been the mainstay of laboratory experiments since then. But what can we learn from experiments on albino rats when it is acknowledged that albinism completely changes the chemical make-up of any animal? Albinos lack melanin, and melanin is known to bond with certain drug combinations in unusual ways. Experiments with albino rats (or mice) would tell us next to nothing about those chemical reactions,[41] besides the fact that they misrepresent most mammals who are not albino. As far as I know, rats were the first animals domesticated for scientific research; consequently, another pressing concern is the genetic variability of laboratory-bred rats. All subsequent strains of rats were developed and are in some way related to the original Wistar colony. This worries me. Even though they sell strains of hairless rats (easy to see immune responses) or Zucker rats bred for obesity research, there is not a great diversity of genetic difference. In order to compare rat responses to human responses, diversity should matter for good science.

There are more rats than people in most urban centres, like New York City, and that is just counting the rats in alleys and buildings and leaving out the rats in medical and pharmaceutical labs. The laboratory rats live secret lives that only their animal "care" technicians glimpse. Worldwide, rats and mice are the animal groups most commonly used in experiments. Rats have been hurt, tortured, and killed in experimental labs in every imaginable and many unimaginable ways. To what end? What have we really learned from the millions of experiments on rats? We have bred and domesticated rats as stand-ins for humans for human ends, whether it is for an elegant theory or a cosmetic test.

Lab rats are disposable creatures. They reproduce easily and quickly and are usually gassed and killed easily and quickly when they are no longer needed. Consumer societies destroy rodents at an extraordinary rate. In Canada, vivisection has increased with over 2.5 million animals used in 2006, compared to 1.5 million in 1997,[42] and it is quite likely that the numbers are under-reported. It is not just that rats are used ubiquitously; it is how they are used. Journalist Charlotte Montgomery reports there are categories from A to E to describe the invasiveness or severity of each experiment.

> Both A and B involve little or no pain or distress. Category C is supposed to entail minor stress or pain of short duration, such as minor surgery under anesthesia or exposure to non-lethal drugs or chemicals. Category D covers moderate to severe distress or discomfort, such as prolonged physical restraint, radiation sickness, exposure to noxious substances with no escape, or the stress of maternal deprivation. The category covers a lot of territory but stops short of death. Category E is for experiments that cause severe pain, "near, at or above the pain tolerance threshold of unanesthetized conscious animals," by CCAC [Canadian Council of Animal Care] definition. This category could include for instance, exposure to painful levels of drugs or chemicals or studies on toxic substances or diseases that last until the animal dies. Some institutions do not do Category E research.[43]

However, Sorenson tells us that in Canada the number of animals used in experiments at or above their pain threshold has tripled in the last ten years.[44] From an experimental animal's (and their advocates') standpoint, there are a number of serious issues in animal experimentation, including: validity of results, wastefulness of life, lack of imagination and development of alternative models, and the ethics of treating animals as property in general.

The thalidomide drug disaster exemplifies one of the most devastating and wrongful approaches to the validity of animal testing, the wastefulness of life, and the inexcusable repercussions to innocent victims, human beings and other animals. Thalidomide was a drug tested on rats and developed in the late 1950s by the German pharmaceutical company, Grünenthal, and sold to combat nausea during pregnancy. In fact at the time, after the rat tests, thalidomide was thought to be so safe, as CBC reported in 2007, "Canadian health regulators agreed that it could be sold without prescription: ... while as many as 12,000 babies were born with deformities linked to thalidomide."[45] The birth differences included very shortened or absent limbs, and flipper-like arms and toes attached to hips. In the Fall of 2012, Grünenthal apologized for the first time in fifty years and their apology was soundly rejected as insulting from the countries most affected: Britain, Canada, Australia, Japan, and Germany. These experiments with rats were clearly not informative in crucial, long-term ways and led to tragic outcomes.

The CCAC (Canadian Council on Animal Care) is the federal body governing the vivisection and use of animals in research. Persuasive arguments are made that the CCAC is dominated by people with vested interests in vivisection research: inspections are announced in advance; compliance is voluntary; any procedure, no matter how painful, is allowed as long as a review is conducted; reports are confidential; and there have never been sanctions imposed.[46] The layers of rationalization, legitimation, and entitlement are thick. During my graduate work, my supervisor understood my interest in animal lives and subsequently developed the first animal ethics course at that university. I vividly remember when the head of the animal care facility came to lecture, because he became so enraged when a few of us civilly asked questions. Raging, offended, blue in the face, his anger was meant to intimidate and silence us. In a CBC *Disclosure* program, John Sorenson reminds us that the head of CCAC, when interviewed in 2003, admitted that in thirty-four years CCAC had not discontinued a single experiment.[47]

In 1959, Russell and Burch proposed the three R's as a way to increase humane animal experimentation: reduction, replacement, and refinement. Since then their work has led to questions like: How many animals are actually necessary to do an experiment? Can whole animals be replaced by cell or tissue cultures? Can the experiments be refined to include computer simulations or donated human blood cells? Zoologist and feminist Anne

Innis Dagg interrogates the wastefulness of animal use in cancer research. Every year, cancer research uses millions of animals and costs billions of dollars. Dagg's citation analysis (looking at 220 animal research articles) tellingly noted the excessive number of animals used, the meagre results obtained, and their overall effect on the field (number of citations). This is a step in the right direction to actually investigate and converse about the effectiveness of using animals in research. What is our responsibility, our epistemic responsibility, as we make uncertain knowledge using rat bodies and lives?

Absent Conversations

In swirling worlds of contradictions many people have chosen rats as companion species. There are interspecies friendships between rats and humans. We do not know necessarily how the rats feel but their owners find them smart, social, affectionate, and clever problem-solvers. People talk about rats as rewarding companions and they mourn when their pet rat dies.

The silence that pervades the deaths of experimental rats is resounding. There are so few conversations about animal death. We don't know how to talk about it; we are impoverished by our inability to debate, consider, converse about this huge fact in our collective lives. Animals are killed and die all the time in laboratories and in factory farms: animals bred to "feed" us, animals bred to "heal" us. To answer Judith Butler's question: "Is the prohibition on grieving the continuation of the violence itself?" Yes. I think so. The lack of widespread public discussion is a form of culturally sanctioned denial—one of those awful secrets that erodes humanity's capacity for aliveness and compassion. Most of us collectively agree to this in a hegemonic dance of silence, but fortunately there are animal activists that resist the hegemonic holds.

Rats laugh and we cannot hear them without using ultrasonic bat detectors, and neither can we hear their cries of distress and pain in animal experiments. This is such an opportune and great loss for our empathic potential, for our very conviviality. It is also profoundly convenient for animal researchers who don't have to worry about cutting the vocal chords of rats to ignore their distress—they/we are not perceptually gifted enough to hear ultrasonic sounds. I wish I could hear rats laughing in their daily life or giggling when being tickled by whomever. My world would be so much more enriched. To so many people's astonishment the vermin giggles. What does this knowing do for our public collective conversations?

NOTES

1. Ben-Ami Bartal et al., "Empathy."
2. J. Burt, *Rat*, 10.
3. *Oxford English Dictionary*, 5th ed., 2601.
4. J. Burt, *Rat*, 28–29.
5. W.H. Burt, *Field Guide*.
6. *Wikipedia*, "Brown Rat."
7. W.H. Burt, *Field Guide*, 195.
8. Kennedy, *Living Things*, 166.
9. J. Burt, *Rat*, 101.
10. Ibid., 113.
11. Bekoff, *Emotional Lives of Animals*, 56.
12. Balcombe, *Pleasurable Kingdom*, 71–72.
13. Knutson et al., "Anticipation of Play."
14. Burgdorf and Panksepp, "Tickling."
15. Panksepp, "Rats Laugh."
16. Ben-Ami Bartal et al., "Empathy."
17. Darwin, *Expression of the Emotions*.
18. de Waal, *Age of Empathy*.
19. J. Burt, *Rat*, 12.
20. Ibid., 11; Sax, *Animals in the Third Reich*, 21.
21. Sax, *Animals in the Third Reich*, 159.
22. Oliver, *Animal Lesson*, 13.
23. Ibid., 257.
24. Quoted in ibid., 258.
25. Deleuze and Guattari, *Thousand Plateaus*, 259.
26. Ibid., 240.
27. Gunter Grass, in Sax, *Animals in the Third Reich*, 18. Sax argues that Grass's later writings use animals as alienated characters to discuss the Holocaust.
28. Kennedy, *Living Things*, 170.
29. Deleuze and Guattari, *Thousand Plateaus*, 239.
30. Ibid., 240.
31. Margulis and Dolan, *Early Life*.
32. Deleuze and Guattari, *Thousand Plateaus*, 240.
33. Ibid., 257. As much as I appreciate Deleuze and Guattari's attention to animal affects, I find their generic dismissal of people who like cats or dogs to be quite shallow.
34. Pierce and Bekoff, "Wild Justice Redux," 123.
35. Bekoff, "Play Signals."
36. Gilligan, "Reply"
37. Donovan, "Feminism and the Treatment of Animals."

38. Plumwood, *Environmental Culture.*

39. Donovan, "Feminism and the Treatment of Animals," 320.

40. J. Burt, *Rat*, 17.

41. Grandin and Johnson, *Animals in Translation*, 78–79.

42. Sorenson, *About Canada*, 137.

43. Montgomery, *Blood Relations*, 98–99.

44. Sorenson, *About Canada*, 138.

45. *CBC News*, "Thalidomid."

46. Sorenson, *About Canada*, 135.

47. Ibid., 137.

BIBLIOGRAPHY

Balcombe, J. *Pleasurable Kingdom: Animals and the Nature of Feeling Good.* New York: Macmillan, 2006.

Bekoff, M. *The Emotional Lives of Animals.* San Francisco: New World Library, 2007.

———. "Play Signals as Punctuation: The Structure of Social Play in Canids." *Behaviour* 132 (1995): 419–29.

Ben-Ami Bartal, I., J. Decety, and P. Mason. "Empathy and Pro-social Behavior in Rats." *Science* 332, no. 6061 (2011): 1427–30.

Burgdorf, Jeffrey, and Jaak Panksepp. "Tickling Induces Reward in Adolescent Rats." *Physiology & Behavior* 72, no. 1 (2001): 167–73.

Burt, J. *Rat.* London: Reaktion Books, 2006.

Burt, W.H. *A Field Guide to the Mammals of America North of Mexico.* 3rd ed. Boston: Houghton Mifflin Co., 1976.

CBC News. "Thalidomide." *In Depth Health.* Last updated November 22, 2007. http://www.cbc.ca/news2/background/health/thalidomide.html.

Darwin, C. *The Expression of the Emotions in Man and Animals.* 3rd ed. New York: Oxford University Press, 1989.

Deleuze, G., and F. Guattari. *A Thousand Plateaus.* Translated by Brian Massumi. Minneapolis: University of Minnesota Press, 2002.

de Waal, Frans. *The Age of Empathy.* New York: Random House, 2010.

Donovan, J. "Feminism and the Treatment of Animals: From Care to Dialogue." *Signs* 31, no. 2 (2006): 305–29.

Gilligan, C. "Reply by Carol Gilligan." *Signs* 11, no. 2 (1986): 324–33.

Grandin, T., and C. Johnson. *Animals in Translation.* New York: Scribner, 2005.

Kennedy, D. *Living Things We Love to Hate.* Vancouver: Whitecap Books, 1992.

Knutson, B., J. Burgdorf, and J. Panksepp. "Anticipation of Play Elicits High Frequency Vocalizations in Young Rats." *Journal of Comparative Psychology* 112, no. 1 (1998): 65.

Margulis, L., and M. Dolan. 2002. *Early Life*. Boston: Jones & Bartlett Publishers.

Montgomery, C. *Blood Relations*. Toronto: Between the Lines, 2000.

Oliver, K. *Animal Lessons*. 2nd ed. New York: Columbia University Press, 2009.

Oxford English Dictionary. 5th ed. New York: Oxford University Press, 2002.

Panksepp, J. "Rats Laugh When You Tickle Them." YouTube video. Uploaded on June 11, 2007. Accessed May 8, 2016. http://www.freesciencelectures.com.

Pierce, J., and M. Bekoff. "Wild Justice Redux: What We Know about Social Justice in Animals and Why It Matters." *Social Justice Research* 25 (2012): 122–39.

Plumwood, V. *Environmental Culture*. New York: Routledge, 2002.

Sax, B. *Animals in the Third Reich*. New York: Continuum, 2000.

Sorenson, J. *About Canada: Animal Rights*. Halifax: Fernwood, 2010.

Wikipedia. "Brown Rat." Last modified January 16, 2016. https://en.wikipedia.org/wiki/Brown_rat.

18

The Ventriloquist's Burden
Animal Advocacy and the Problem of Speaking for Others

⟫⟝⟞⟐⟝⟞⟨

Lauren Corman

To have a voice is to be human.[1]

Animal rights activists ... have long tried to put a voice to animal suffering, demonstrating through pictures, film, and sometimes animals' voices, that they don't want to be eaten, worn as clothing, experimented on, or caged for entertainment.[2]

But whether the "ventriloquist" is an academic authority speaking for the oppressed subjects or a writer putting contemporary attitudes into the mouths of historical personages, the trope of ventriloquism has come to stand for the postmodern mistrust of both mimetic and socio-political representation.[3]

This chapter addresses "the question of the animal" in relation to debates concerning what Gilles Deleuze, summarizing Michel Foucault, calls "the indignity of speaking for others"[4] and Linda Alcoff calls "the problem of speaking for others."[5] While many other movements, and affiliated fields of theory, have spent considerable time grappling with the difficulties of representing various Others, including rigorous debates about appropriation of (cultural) voice,[6] the animal movements have generally been remiss in confronting the issues that plague political representation, with some notable exceptions.[7] This seems a major oversight given that animal advocates aspire to represent groups of which they are not members.

While it is necessary to acknowledge that humans are animals, the oppression of *nonhuman* animals remains a focus of the animal movements, often even within intersectional approaches in which animal exploitation is understood as inseparable from other issues of oppression.[8] This is not to elide the problems of speaking for human animals that also occur within the animal movements. Here I focus on some of the problems regarding humans speaking on behalf of other animals.

Humans dominate other species, including those centralized in animal advocacy, such as animals within factory farms and vivisection laboratories. The large-scale industrial exploitation of nonhuman animals is conducted and supported by humans, and simultaneously, it is humans who often position themselves as animals' voices within advocacy. Such an observation seems almost too obvious to comment on: while claims to be "the voice of the voiceless," a ubiquitous aphorism within the animal movements, would likely raise the ire of other social justice activists, especially if made by those representing groups in which they do not belong, this position vis-à-vis other animals largely remains unchallenged.

The following chapter considers some of what is at stake when activists and others speak on behalf of animals (particularly when claiming to be animals' voices), how various advocates interrupt the seeming ease and at times hubris of advocates' political representation of animals, and how insights evidenced within certain pockets of activism, cognitive ethology, and posthumanism might move the conversation forward. Adding to the dialogue, I consider how certain animal advocates emphasize what I call the "dynamics of political voice," an analysis I have developed elsewhere,[9] and which names the constellation of themes typically implied through the use of the voice metaphor in its political register (in contrast to its literary/ compositional register). Even though the notion of (political) voice is overwhelmingly predicated on the assumption that it is necessarily human, as so greatly demonstrated within feminist theory and critical pedagogy (fields that centralize the voice metaphor), select animal advocates and others retain the progressive dynamics of political voice while also disentangling them from humanism. These dynamics include non-unitary subjectivity, experiential knowledge, relationality, and resistance.

Given that animal rights advocacy has largely linked representations of animals' voices to their experiences of suffering,[10] my specific engagement with the voice metaphor, and the ways in which activists suggest they speak for animals, is meant to complement a growing discursive shift in advocacy toward representations of animals' subjectivities, including but beyond victimhood.[11] Such reorientation aligns with other social justice movements and theories that challenge oppression and exploitation while they also stress agency and resistance.[12]

Before proceeding, I must specifically acknowledge Chandra Talpade Mohanty and her seminal essay, "Under Western Eyes: Feminist Scholarship and Colonial Discourses,"[13] for first inspiring my long ruminating concerns about representations of Others as pure victims, especially when such representations are figured as benevolent. To oversimplify, Mohanty analyzes Western feminist discourse, noting that "third world women" were contemporaneously constructed as a "homogenous 'powerless' group often located as implicit *victims* of particular socioeconomic systems."[14] Mohanty repeatedly points to Western feminists' constructions of women as defined by their victim status, which "freezes them"[15] as objects, constituted through victimization and thus precluded from subject status and agency. The implications are not benign but colonialist. She argues, "[w]hile radical and liberal feminist assumptions of women as a sex class might elucidate (however inadequately) the autonomy of particular women's struggles in the West, the application of the notion of women as a homogeneous category to women in the third world colonizes and appropriates the pluralities of the simultaneous location of different groups of women in social class and ethnic frameworks; in doing so it ultimately robs them of their historical and political agency."[16] We might also consider the resonance of Mohanty's theory as a springboard to encourage more self-reflection within, and critique of, the animal movements and their claims to animals' voices. As Mohanty suggests, recognition of context, pluralities, and agency is necessary; this is not to deny oppression but to resist the "colonialist move,"[17] and to attend more rigorously to the construction of groups as already constituted by victimization.

The Ventriloquist's Burden

Richard Horwitz draws a parallel between "animal liberators" and "prolifers" in *Hog Ties: What Pigs Tell Us about America*. In his chapter "Swine Rights, Liberation, and Welfare," Horwitz criticizes both groups for adopting what he calls the "ventriloquist's burden," which entails "speaking for creatures that cannot speak for themselves."[18] His primary critique, though, is really aimed at animal activists, not pro-lifers. What bothers him is the myriad assumptions animal activists make about nonhuman animals' feelings and experiences.

Horwitz, professor of American studies at Iowa University, argues that pro-lifers' conclusions about fetus personhood are based on natural rights syllogisms or observers' projections. To illustrate the type of "if-I-were-one" projection-based logic that he claims characterizes the pro-life movement, he offers the following rhetorical example: "I may not be a foetus, but I sure would not want to be sucked out [of] a hose."[19] Similarly, he maintains that animal activists enact the ventriloquist's burden through their polemics.[20] "Hogs present an additional challenge in that they plainly are different enough from people that projections of the 'if-I-were-one' sort are a radical stretch."[21]

If the problem with both animal liberators and pro-lifers is one of faulty projection, a matter of never being able to anticipate fully or interpret the experiences of others who are seemingly so different than oneself, as Horwitz suggests, then it seems to follow that no human would be able to speak accurately on behalf of either fetuses or nonhuman animals. All human claims about animals' experiences would be considered ventriloquism and, as such, damningly anthropocentric. For Horwitz, though, an unabashed hog-industry sympathizer, the question of what animals feel, and more precisely what bothers them, is available to people who "well know pigs."[22] He points to animal scientists, animal behaviourists, and farmers, or more succinctly, "people who have anything to do with them."[23] Placed at extremes, Horwitz positions animal rights activists as informed by a "bourgeois, anti-urban, and anti-industrial bias"[24] while those directly involved in farming and farm animal science are understood as the legitimate spokespeople for animals' feelings and experiences.

If we accept Horwitz's arguments, animal activists are certainly doomed in their advocacy efforts, as they are understood as too far removed from the food production chain to accurately comment on contemporary animal agribusiness and thus animal treatment within those industries. According to Horwitz, only those who are directly involved with the production and profit aspects of animal agribusiness can legitimately comment on the texture and meaning of animals' lives. Activists' concerns about animal treatment or commodification are interpreted as an affront to farmers: "Why would anyone think that getting [animals] sick, crippled [sic] and hooked on drugs saves labor and makes money? Only, I would think, if they assume that farmers are, as a rule, sadistic or stupid or both. The insult so strongly implied is awfully hard to accept, especially when it comes from some do-gooder who does not know the first thing about caring for animals as a matter of daily toil as well as self-righteous sentiment."[25] What seems puzzling is that people outside of the farm industry who care for animals "as a matter of daily toil,"[26] including animal sanctuary workers, ex-farmers, veterinarians, trainers, and animal guardians, among others, are excluded from Horwitz's analysis. Yet using his epistemological criteria, we might guess that these people, too, would be in a position to speak about animals' feelings and experiences due to their direct, daily contact with them. Still, they are subject neither to his praise nor to his condemnation: they are simply absent from his text.

Within Horwitz's occasionally vitriolic commentary exist two discrete groups: legitimate knowers (farmers and animal scientists) and ignorant activists. Therefore, for Horwitz, it is not so much that direct, daily experience is a prerequisite to know animals and thus to speak on their behalf, rather that only a very select type of experience with animals counts as legitimate grounds for advocacy. That is to say, only those within the industry are the authentic representatives of animals' experiences. Thus, the implication of Horwitz's argument is that the agricultural industry must be necessarily self-regulated, wherein only those who have a stake in production and profit are able to represent animals' experiences and feelings. While the public is generally prevented from knowing the animals they consume,[27] this same lack of daily access is counted as an automatic strike against animal activists.

Horwitz implies that it is only those who have a financial interest in farmed animals who are able to know them in any kind of meaningful way. In opposition to the "if-I-were-one" logic, Horwitz draws in part upon another equally precarious line of reasoning to support what I characterize as his "industry-knows-best" position. Namely, he points to the relationship between animal welfare and animal productivity, and thus profit: "Up until the moment the hogs leave the farm, well-being and profit are allied interests," states Horwitz.[28] His claim is based on the observation that stress in pigs diminishes feed consumption and the efficiency of the feed/marketable flesh conversion. For example, *Pork '93*'s producer's guide to hog-house flooring begins with what Horwitz considers a truism: "Pig comfort is no longer a secondary consideration. An uncomfortable pig is a stressed pig. And a stressed pig is a non-productive pig."[29]

Horwitz's claim begs the question, "What is stress?" While Horwitz argues chemical analyses still cannot clearly distinguish between "good" stress and "bad" stress in animals, he writes that "stress is readily visible in the cutting room, and packers will dock you severely for it."[30] The appearance of PSE (pale soft exudative), mushy pig flesh that results in a tasteless consumer product, is a result of "stressed-out" pigs. Before slaughter, pigs who have been abused, are hungry, feel scared, etc., will begin to accumulate lactic acid between their muscle cells. Once slaughtered, regardless of the stress experienced prior to death, the animal's body's pH level begins to drop. Slaughtering pigs in the midst of a "lactic acid storm" leads to rapid drop rates. Because acidity denatures protein, the faster the pH drops below normal levels, the more likely the flesh will show signs of PSE. Horwitz turns to PSE as a marker of animal stress to illustrate his point that animal welfare and economic interests are aligned. PSE has numerous causes, as Horwitz acknowledges, but he argues that all the causes can be adequately lumped under the term "unhappiness." The "animal that [*sic*] is challenged,"[31] the unhappy animal, is one who is high-strung, abused, or struggles to adjust to a new environment, among other difficulties. His reasoning quickly slips from the point that "hog happiness" is difficult to measure (i.e., it is difficult to discriminate between "good" versus "bad" stress on a chemical level) to a discussion of what indicates hog "unhappiness." The argument is constructed in such a way that the reader is meant to infer that an *absence* of unhappiness as Horwitz defines it (demonstrated through a lack of PSE) logically indicates hog happiness. It does not follow, however, that the absence of unhappiness signals the presence of happiness.

Further, definitions of happiness, which are based solely on some empirically measurable absence of pain or stress, neglect pleasure as a relevant factor in determining such a state. The bias of Horwitz's argument is thrown into sharp relief when the experience of pleasure is understood as indicative of happiness. "Hedonic ethology," a term coined by Jonathan Balcombe,[32] is the study of animal pleasure. This type of ethology moves beyond behavioural studies that focus on nociception,[33] or even studies of animals' *experiences* of pain. Balcombe's *Pleasurable Kingdom: Animals and the Nature of Feeling Good* offers a comprehensive survey of numerous studies and anecdotal evidence to persuasively demonstrate that many nonhuman animals experience, and are motivated by, pleasure.[34] He concludes, "[i]f animals feel, then we have a responsibility towards them. And if they feel more than just pain—if they are capable of pleasure—then that responsibility is greater than if they did not."[35] For Horwitz, advocates and consumers should be satisfied with industry definitions of animal happiness that focus on physical signs of stress and tend to ignore animals' capacities for positive experiences.

Still, Horwitz concedes, "[t]here may, for example, be a chasm between the conditions that make a hog profitable and the ones that serve its spirit, in understandable even if immeasurable ways."[36] Who might be able to make such assessments? For Horwitz, the answer is "old-timey operators"[37] who can sense that pigs are overcrowded, for example, even without confirmation from any official "herd health," "carcass quality," and profit records.[38] Concomitantly, though, calls for the return of the family farm and small-scale production methods, which might afford some animals the luxury of such attentiveness, are dismissed by Horwitz: "Wouldn't it be nice, progressives seem to say, if those people would only stay on the farm with their cute animals, content to bolster primitivist fantasies about latter-day yeomen? While we ride the Fortune 500, you can be our pet premoderns . . . [suspension points in the original] and make sure we do not hear of any pain and suffering in the process. Something must be turning horribly wrong out there, if we hear that pigs do not live like Babe."[39] The very people Horwitz claims could navigate the chasm between empirical evidence and the nourishment of animals' spirits are the same ones pressured to industrialize, which effectively divorces them from regular, direct contact with individual animals. Rather than romanticize the past and mourn the loss of the family farm (hardly a paragon of independence or virtue, according to Horwitz),[40] he rallies against activists who oppose farmers who choose to "go big" to survive, and to thrive within the current economic environment. In effect, Horwitz rescues animal scientists, industrial farmers, and "old-timey operators" from the trap of the ventriloquist's burden. To claim that animal activists commit such an offence is an attempt not only to expose the underlying pretentiousness of their advocacy, but also to increase the accusation's negative impact.

The phrase "the ventriloquist's burden" invokes Rudyard Kipling's famous 1899 poem, "The White Man's Burden: The United States and the Philippine Islands," which framed the imperialist project as one of noble obligation and justification. According to Brantlinger, "[the poem] has served as a lightning rod for both supporters and opponents of imperialism, as well as of racism and white supremacy."[41] Though varying interpretations exist, including arguments that the poem is satirical,[42] critics have largely agreed that the poem's import is both patronizing and racist. In the poem, "Kipling appealed to the American people, as he saw it—the other great half of the English-speaking race and true 'white men' as well—to share Britain's global civilising mission," writes Judd.[43] "The White Man's Burden" positioned British and American imperialists as benevolent actors who took upon themselves the burden of spreading civilization (and Christianity) or who, perhaps, even saw the uncivilized people as a kind of burden themselves. To this end, colonization is cast throughout the poem not as wanton conquest and appropriation for the colonialists' gain, but instead as the virtuous, even altruistic work of imperialists who believe themselves more enlightened than those subjected to their rule.

In Kipling's poem, American forces are urged to help those who supposedly cannot help themselves, namely, the people of the Philippine Islands. Like a parent who delivers bitter medicine to a sick and reluctant child, Americans are encouraged to bear the responsibility of civilizing the Filipino people:

> To wait, in heavy harness
> On fluttered folk and wild—
> Your new-caught sullen people,
> Half devil and half child.[44]

The condescending attitude apparent within the phrase "the white man's burden" is similarly implied through the phrase "the ventriloquist's burden," except instead of taking on the burden of "the White Man's work, the business of introducing a sane and orderly administration into the dark places of the earth,"[45] activists focus on animals as recipients of their benevolence. Read within the context of Horwitz's chapter, with its overt disdain for "PETA people,"[46] vegetarians and their ilk, those who take upon themselves the ventriloquist's burden are compared to imperialists, while Horwitz is aligned with the critics of racism and colonialism. From Horwitz's perspective, animal activists also arrogantly presume to know what is best for others, just like imperialists.

Again, as Brantlinger posits, "the white man's burden" finds echoes within contemporary discourse in relation to the invasions, or so-called "liberations," of Iraq and Afghanistan, through such neo-imperialist works as Max Boot's *The Savage Wars of Peace*, Robert Kaplan's *Imperial Grunts: The American Military on the Ground*, or Niall Ferguson's *Empire: The Rise and Demise of the British World Order*.[47] Referring to Ferguson's text,

Brantlinger contends, "[h]e doesn't quite say that America should now 'Take up the white man's burden,' as Kipling advised the US to do during the Spanish-American War: 'No one would dare,' he writes, 'use such politically incorrect language today.' Obviously he is tempted to use that language, but doesn't for fear of being accused of the racism that Kipling and British imperialists expressed. In any event, Ferguson argues that 'just like the British Empire before it, the American empire unfailingly acts in the name of liberty, even when its own self-interest is manifestly uppermost.'"[48] Likewise, it is possible that some animal activists understand themselves as animals' heroes, perhaps particularly those who identify as "animal liberationists," those who literally liberate animals through rescue, or support the goal of animal liberation, namely, "to free animals to allow them, as far as possible, to lead autonomous lives without artificial restrictions."[49]

Horwitz marshals both the shameful legacy of colonialism and critiques of its propaganda in order to admonish animal activists for adopting "the ventriloquist's burden," a slogan that signals the same corrupt underbelly as "the white man's burden." In each case, critics attempt to reveal the colonizers' and advocates' perceived altruistic heroism as self-aggrandizing delusion. Horwitz's phrase serves as an important starting point for the following work. He figures animal rights activism as sheer humanist ventriloquism, rather than as any kind of valid attempt to align with animals' interests. He points to the supposed total failure of animal rights activists to accurately represent animals. Condensed within his phrase, "the ventriloquist's burden," is a multiplicity of assumptions about who does and does not have the right to represent animals, and about the legitimate grounds for such representations.

Significantly, Horwitz suggests that there is an abuse of power implied through the act of *speaking for* someone or for a group, especially when that is done outside of direct engagements with those one claims to represent. Typically, debates about voice representation have centred on the politics of speaking for certain marginalized human groups.[50] These discussions have largely related to heated debates about how people in positions of power represent those who have been marginalized, oppressed, and colonized. The language of voice has been key to expressing these concerns.

What is interesting about Horwitz's condemnation is that he directly drives typically anthropocentric critiques about voice and representation into the realm of animal rights politics. His phrase vividly points toward central questions I think ought to be more centralized within the animal movements and critical animal studies: How have activists spoken for animals and represented their voices? What is at stake regarding animality and humanity in ethical and political voice discourses? While Horwitz's critique is overly simplistic and unfairly dismissive of animal rights, it is nonetheless useful for raising questions about activists' and scholars' engagements with the politics of representation, particularly with regard to how we claim to represent animals' voices, and indivisibly, their subjectivities.

Voice and Animal Advocacy

Voice and speech-related phraseologies operate as key tropes within the Western animal movements. Claims to be "the animals' voice" or "animals' voices," and advocates' calls to be "their voice" suggest an important way advocates and academics express their struggle to represent animals' interests and perspectives.[51] Particularly, the phrase "the voice of the voiceless" repeatedly appears in both popular and academic work about animal advocacy. For example, Erica Meir, executive director of US-based Compassion over Killing states, "From day one, it's been our mission to be a powerful voice for animals," while Paul Shapiro reflects, "I founded Compassion over Killing to take the side of the abused, to try to stand up for these animals who had no voice, and couldn't defend themselves against us, these bullies who were continually tormenting them."[52] Similarly, well-known philosopher Tom Regan, author of *The Case for Animal Rights*, describes his role as an advocate in terms of being animals' spokesperson and their voice. In the 2004 *Satya* magazine online interview with Regan entitled, "Giving Voice to Animal Rights," the influential writer states, "I obviously feel these things with great passion. My reason for being in this world is to be a spokesperson for those who cannot speak for themselves. I am absolutely certain about this. It's nothing exceptional in my case. It is true of every other animal advocate. This is why we are in the world.... As animal advocates, we have a reason to get up in the morning. A reason to rest at night. And that is to be a voice for the voiceless."[53]

It is impossible to definitively say why various advocates use such voice-saturated discourses; however, a few intersecting factors seem likely. First, the popularity of such discourses likely stems in part from the ways in which animals have been considered speechless and voiceless, "mute" and "dumb," throughout Western thought.[54] In this way, advocates are building upon certain cultural assumptions, while simultaneously challenging others, such as the disregard for animals' interests or suffering. Second, the expression "voice of the voiceless" also circulates outside of animal advocacy, and its use within the movement may partially be a testament to its more general popularity. One need look no further than Rage Against the Machine's song "Voice of the Voiceless," a homage to well-known political prisoner, writer, radio journalist, and anti-racist activist Mumia Abu Jamal, who earned the title "the voice of the voiceless."[55] The song's chorus is a repetition of the line "You'll never silence the voice of the voiceless." Third, the ways in which animals have been constructed as outside of both the political and public spheres, major sites of "voice" within Western culture, have most likely prompted activists to note animals' political "voicelessness" and, in turn, to consider themselves animals' voice or voices in these areas. Fourth, the internal rhetorical inertia of the animal movements (under the influence of the other factors) has undoubtedly helped perpetuate the discourse. For instance, a classic example of animal advocates' voice discourse is found within American poet Ella Wheeler Wilcox's popular piece "Voice of the Voiceless," from her collection *Poems of Experience*, which continues to be a commonly referenced work within the animal movements. Consider the following excerpt from Wilcox's poem, which appears on the inside cover of each *The Animals' Voice* magazine:

> I am the voice of the voiceless:
>   Through me, the dumb shall speak;
> Till the deaf world's ear be made to hear
>   The cry of the wordless weak.
>
> From street, from cage, and from kennel,
>   From jungle and stall, the wail
> Of my tortured kin proclaims the sin
>   Of the mighty against the frail.
>
> Oh, shame on the mothers of mortals
>   Who have not stooped to teach
> Of the sorrow that lies in dear, dumb eyes,
>   The sorrow that has no speech.
>
> I am my brother's keeper,
>   And I shall fight his fight;
> And speak the word for beast and bird
>   Till the world shall set things right.

Occasionally reproduced within academic writing and other printed sources, such as Diane Beers' *For the Prevention of Cruelty: The History and Legacy of Animal Rights* and Marti Kheel's "License to Kill: An Ecofeminist Critique of Hunters' Discourse," Wheeler Wilcox's "Voice of the Voiceless" now enjoys considerable currency on the Internet, through such sites as All-Creatures. org, AnimalLiberation.com, and those of the International Vegetarian Union, Brightside Farm Sanctuary, Pakistan Vegetarian Society, Jack Pine Guinea Pig Rescue, Colorado German Shepherd Rescue, and Harborough Animal Concern, among others. These sites tend to present the poem with little explanation, frequently quoting it somewhere on the main page, pre-sumably as a statement about the organization or individual's guiding values, or as a submission on the site's poetry page. Reflecting on the first four lines of the poem, Laura Perdew muses, "[m]ore than a century later, these lines are still quoted as the foundation for the mission to help animals."[56]

Additionally, many other animal advocacy organizations reference voice within their names, though it is unclear whether they are allusions to Wheeler Wilcox's famous poem. Certainly not an exhaustive list, here is a partial sample of myriad organizations that draw on voice as part of their official designation: Voiceless: A Fund for Animals (Australia), Abolitionist-Online: A Voice for Animal Rights (Australia), Animals Australia: The Voice for Animals, The Canadian Voice for Animals Foundation, Voice for Animals Humane Society (Canada), Animal Voices (Canada, Toronto), Animal Voices (Canada, Vancouver), *Animals' Voice* (official magazine of the Ontario Society for the Prevention of Cruelty to Animals), No Voice Unheard (United States), VOCAL: Voice of Compassion for Animal Life (United States), Voices for Animals (United States), Voices for Animals of Western Pennsylvania (United States), VOICE for Animals (Texas, United States), Voice for the Animals Foundation (United States), Alabama Voice for Animals (United States), DePaul Voice for the Animals (United States), SPEAK: The Voice for Animals (United Kingdom), VERO: Voice for Ethical Research at Oxford (United Kingdom), *Animal Voice* (magazine pub-lished by the Humane Education Trust in South Africa), Viva! Vegetarians International Voice for Animals (United Kingdom), and Serbian Animals Voice (Serbia).

Similarly, activist-oriented scholarship is often permeated with voice-related rhetoric. Particularly, again, the insistence that animals are voiceless and that humans are their voices weaves throughout a variety of contemporary texts dedicated to animals. For example, in *Making a Killing:*

The Political Economy of Animal Rights, author Bob Torres uses "voiceless-ness" both to name animals' experiences of suffering at human hands (i.e., voiceless suffering), and to name their ontological position as an exploited group under capitalism (i.e., as voiceless beings). For Torres, in the first instance, the key difference between exploited humans and animals relates to their experiences of suffering and exploitation: for example, he argues that "human slaves can resist, plan, revolt, and even struggle for their own freedom in some cases; nonhumans cannot meaningfully do any of these things. They are exploited and suffer voicelessly, and we rarely hear their cries."[57] While humans are exploited and suffer, they possess "voice"—as we might reasonably infer from Torres' statement—given their ability to mobilize and effect change, whereas animals cannot meaningfully do this (according to Torres), and thus they are exploited and suffer voicelessly as a consequence of their utter powerlessness to intervene in their conditions.

Torres also uses "voiceless" to name animals' position as an exploited group under capitalism. Following a summary of Barbara Noske's analysis of animal subjectivity, in which animals are perceived as "total beings" who are in relation to both physical and social environments, Torres concludes, "[h]ow we relate to animals as voiceless beings suffering under the forces of capital becomes an ethical question, much as the question of how we relate to any other group that suffers under the exploitative forces of capital."[58]

Of course, Torres is certainly not the only contemporary scholar to draw upon voice and voicelessness to construct arguments about advocacy and animals. As another example, author Diane Beers extensively relies on notions of voice and voicelessness throughout her history of animal advo-cacy in the United States. Beers ends the "Acknowledgements" of her inspired text, *For the Prevention of Cruelty*, with a dedication to her companion ani-mals: "Their spirits light every page. This book is their voice."[59] Particularly, references to animals' voicelessness sprinkle the entire text.[60] Frequently, these references appear as part of the expression "voice of the voiceless"[61] or variants of the expression, such as to "give a voice to the voiceless."[62] In Beers' writing, the "voice of the voiceless" signifies animal advocates. Implied through the aphorism, the "voice" is the activist or activists, and the "voice-less" is an animal or animals, specifically those who are abused or exploited.

As the above examples illustrate, there are common themes evidenced through animal advocates' use of voice and voicelessness. First, some advocates understand themselves as *conduits* or *translators* for animals, as Compassion over Killing, Regan, Wheeler Wilcox, and Torres' usages suggest. Wheeler Wilcox declares, "I am the voice of the voiceless: / Through me, the dumb shall speak; / Till the deaf world's ear be made to hear / The cry of the wordless weak." Torres professes, "[t]hey are exploited and suffer voicelessly, and we rarely hear their cries."[63] There is a sense that without human interveners, animals' suffering in particular remains meaningfully unintelligible/inaudible to many human beings and therefore unable to effect change on their behalf. Second, related to the first, voice is indistinguishably melted into a capacity for human speech and language. It is through human speech and language that animals' experiences of suffering are made meaningful to humans who otherwise ignore or simply fail to recognize these experiences. The conduit is then specifically human speech and language, made possible and enacted through the activists. The "hearing" discussed by authors such as Torres and Wheeler Wilcox implies being *understood* by humans, rather than simply reception of sound. Voice possession and being heard are bound concepts, and often appear in conjunction with discussions of voice. Third, voice and voicelessness are ways of describing unequal positions of power, specifically as they relate to victimhood and agency/ resistance. Voicelessness describes the experience of being a victim, while advocates' voice represents resistance to the abuse meted upon animals and the agency to effect meaningful change (or at least, meaningfully challenge those who harm animals).

We see a similar collection of voice meanings manifest in feminist debates about research and representation of the Other. In these debates, voice is unmistakeably about power as much as it is about subjectivity. Perhaps we might understand voice as the ability to define and assert one's subjectivity, or the power to have one's subjectivity recognized by those who refuse it. According to some, it is simply not enough to speak one's experience because the speaking itself does not guarantee truly being heard. Language and speech also become metaphors for agency and resistance. As such, only those privileged enough to actually be heard can effect change, because they are able to speak a language that is heard. For example, in her essay, "We Are Different, but Can We Talk?" Saraswati Raju confronts the difficulty of speaking on behalf of others, particularly as suggested by postmodernist feminist discourses that challenge universalizing theories and meta-narratives. Specifically, Raju considers the problem of first world women speaking on behalf of so-called third world women, herself identifying as the latter. Cautious of treating either category as monolithic (she qualifies both groups as composed of women who are disparately oppressed), she argues,

> The point that speaking for others is often value-laden and amounts to
> epistemological violence and that speaking for those who are less privil-
> eged may be a way to get out of guilt are well-taken. But then what? . . .
> Ideally, the researched should speak for themselves, but what if they
> cannot? Not because they do not have knowledge, but because they are
> not equipped with the language that can be heard and responded to by
> those who make the decisions. Do the privileged remain silent even if
> their speaking, however tinted and biased their voices might be (assum-
> ing that they would be), makes a difference?[64]

I find Raju's imperative quite compelling. I am especially struck by her
assertion that sometimes the researched cannot speak for themselves: "Not
because they do not have knowledge, but because they are not equipped
with the language that can be heard and responded to by those who make
the decisions."[65] This sentiment well summarizes the briar patch of ethical and political questions about representation that permeate the animal movements, which are indivisibly also shot through with questions of
power. Perhaps the question is not, "Do they have a voice?" but instead, "Are
their voices heard?" Or, more precisely, "Are their voices heard by those in
power?" In absence of an affirmative answer, they *are* largely voiceless
in that respect. In absence of reception and response by those in power to
"make the decisions" that help animals, their subjectivity is not recognized,
but that is much different than the assumption that it does not exist.

Voice functions paradoxically because it both attempts to highlight
subjectivity at the same moment that it inadvertently erases it (through the
proclamation that animals are voiceless and advocates alone are their voices).
Indeed, it is the animals' expressions of suffering that have inspired advocates to "be their voice." Recall Wheeler Wilcox's poetic lament, "From street,
from cage, and from kennel, / From jungle and stall, the wail / Of my tortured
kin proclaims the sin / Of the mighty against the frail." Wheeler Wilcox *did*
hear their voices. The animal advocates discussed below explicitly grapple
with the complexity of voice and the potential dangers it encompasses.

Interruption

Some animal advocates offer a more complicated rendering of animals'
"voicelessness," at times directly disrupting its seemingly perfunctory and
rote reproduction. For example, animal advocate and scientist Marc Bekoff
offers at times a paradoxical and contradictory understanding of animals as
both voiceless and voiced: "We must continue to be the voices for voiceless

animals and add to their 'vociferous voices of suffering' as philosopher Graham Harvey puts it. Numerous animals are really crying for help and they are not truly 'voiceless.'"[66]

Similarly, pattrice jones more directly critiques animal activists' use of voice in her presentation at the Grassroots Animal Rights Conference in 2005.[67] She questions the language that superficially appears benevolent but perhaps, in a deeper sense, points to both a latent arrogance and paternalism that ought to be challenged. As one of few documented instances of an activist critiquing other activists' use of voice, jones is worth quoting at length:

> We must take responsibility for ending human exploitation of the earth and other animals, just as men must actively support women in the struggle against sexism and white people must work hard to divest ourselves of the illegitimate power and privilege that come with being white. Of course, feminists would never tolerate men trying to run the movement against sexism. And, could you imagine what would have happened if, when I was doing anti-racist work, I had run around saying "I am the voice of the Black man"!?
>
> There are no such natural checks on self-importance in the animal liberation movement. We have people running around claiming to be "the voice of the voiceless" as if animals don't have voices of their own. That heroic attitude makes it easy to assume that you know what's best for the animals without stopping to wonder what they might say if you asked them and were able to understand their answers.[68]

Bekoff's and jones' challenge to activists' seemingly uncritical use of voice as a signifier of (a lack of) political power and agency prompts questions not only about the strategic use of language, but also perhaps more importantly, highlights animals' subjectivities and provides a reconfiguration of "the animal" within the movement and larger public. Both authors position animals as active agents rather than passive victims. Bekoff's claim that "[w]e must continue to be the voices for voiceless animals" is held in tension with his proceeding statement that "[n]umerous animals are really crying for help and they are not truly 'voiceless.'"[69] How do we reconcile these positions?

Bekoff seems to be wrestling with different understandings of voice. Embodied and metaphorical voice (in this case, political voice) rest against each other like layered sheets of coloured vellum. Where does one hue begin and the other end? Or, to use an auditory metaphor, the metaphorical and the material are two notes harmonizing. They resonate together, almost indistinguishably. When he writes that "we must continue to be the voices for voiceless animals," Bekoff acknowledges the lack of animals' political voice, but the material or embodied voice of animals seems to bleed into his first interpretation (i.e., "We must continue to be the voices for voiceless animals"). From Bekoff's standpoint, animals do indeed have voices (i.e., "Numerous animals are really crying for help") such that, seemingly, he recognizes how their embodied voices haunt the phrase "the voice of the voiceless."

Birke and Parisi also gesture toward a distinction between political voice and embodied voice regarding animals when, in "Animals, Becoming," they write, "Nonhumans may not have a political voice in Western culture; but they have political interests and can form alliances. We must pay more heed to the deep interconnections between many kinds of politics."[70] Here, voice is qualified. It is not that animals do not have voices, but that they do not have political voices, or to use their phrasing, "a political voice," perhaps implying a collective and singular voice. Differentiating between political voice and embodied or material voice seems useful because it offers an approach for thinking through activists' claims to be animals' voices, or calls to be animals' voices.

However, such neat bifurcation between political voice and embodied voice is potentially problematic. First, the assumption that animals do not have political voices (or a political voice) forecloses the possibility that they do participate or influence political realms. Additionally, the denial of animals' political voices perhaps also forecloses an appreciation of the dynamics of political voice that animals do possess and enact. Specifically, is the denial of animals' political voices tantamount to a denial of their subjectivity, experiential knowledge, capacity for relationships/dialogue, and ability to actively resist those dynamics of voice often employed in reference to humans' social justice struggles?[71] Second, it also implies that their embodied voices and potential political voices do not overlap or blur together.

Scholars and advocates such as Marc Bekoff point to a discursive tension between an appreciation of animals' embodied voices and the possibility of political voice or voices. It is unclear if Bekoff is referring to either a metaphorical (i.e., political) or an embodied voice when he states, "Numerous animals are really crying for help and they are not truly 'voiceless.'"[72] The phrase "cry for help," in reference to humans, is not always associated with a physical cry (such as when self-damaging behaviours are termed a "cry for help"), although it certainly can be. Yet Bekoff, a cognitive ethologist, is very much interested in the emotional and cognitive experiences for animals. Given the disciplinary context from which he writes, it is quite likely that he wants us to attend to the physical cries (and other vocalizations or voices) of animals, so that we may ask questions about the motivations and meanings involved in such expressions. For him, the physical cry and metaphorical cry merge. A "cry for help" can literally be a cry for help.

Still, legitimate questions might be posed about whether the presence of an embodied voice (or a particular kind of embodied voice) is necessary for one to be acknowledged as having a political voice. Is it correct to say that when an animal cries that he or she is asking for assistance or reaching out in some way? Does one (human or nonhuman) ever cry just for the sake of expression rather than the elicitation of response? I think there is a real danger in suggesting that embodied voice, when defined as the audible production of sound, is understood as the prerequisite for political voice. If this is the case, all sorts of speciesist oversights will certainly be committed in the name of animal advocacy. What about animals who never "cry" or "cry out"? What about injured animals who stay silent to avoid predators? What about animals who seemingly do not produce sound, or sounds that we can hear and recognize as voice? For example, humans cannot hear certain whale sounds either because they are too high or too low.[73]

Further still, as some have claimed, silence can also be a voice. For example, consider H-Dirksen L. Bauman and Jennifer Drake's essay "Silence Is Not Without Voice." The essay describes a course taught by Bauman and Drake entitled Narratives of Struggle, which was part of the Binghamton enrichment program. The course showed how "the Deaf are a 'real' cultural community,"[74] such that Deaf identity was taught as an integral aspect of multicultural curriculum development. Within Narratives of Struggle, Deafness is positioned as culture in contrast to deafness as disability (the authors distinguish between Deafness and deafness, where the latter refers to the repressive education models based on medical views of deafness and the former refers to bilingual/bicultural education): "For the Deaf, recontextualizing Deaf identity in a cultural framework alongside Latinos, African-Americans, Chinese-Americans, gays and lesbians, and other cultural/racial/ethnic groups represents significant advancement toward the recognition that the Deaf community is a linguistic minority in the United States. In addition, hearing students introduced to the relevant historical, political, and social issues surrounding Deaf culture are encouraged to expand and to challenge their existing notions of multiculturalism, disability, and language."[75] It seems significant that the essay, which focuses on the importance of including Deaf culture within multicultural education, uses the trope of voice in its title. The voice trope seems to offer a way of acknowledging "Deaf persons as cultural subjects,"[76] although the title is not explicitly explained in the essay. Cultural subjectivity gestures toward voiced subjectivity, and vice versa. Notably, class discussion of Deaf culture first occurred during the Resisting Silences/Finding Voices week. A paper by Youlla, a student in the class, is summarized by the authors, who write, "Youlla continued to connect the inability to 'hear' with the inability to listen and to empathize in order to argue that the dominant culture is 'disabled' by its inability to listen to the 'voices' of different communities."[77] The conventional meanings associated with language, (multi)cultural identity, voice, and silence are intentionally troubled within the course, Narratives of Struggle. Those who are silent, or are understood as silent, are not without voice, in the sense that they are expressive and cultural beings.

Voiceless?

Karen Davis's polemical essay, "Thinking Like a Chicken: Farm Animals and the Feminine Connection," disputes the epistemological assumptions of Western science, and deep ecology in particular, and conceives of voice as neither strictly metaphorical nor exclusively embodied. Her questions challenge not only what experiences count within these frameworks, but also in correlation, whose voice counts. Her aim is both to reveal the epistemological assumptions of certain modes of ecological thinking, and simultaneously to represent those experiences (and beings) that are elided, specifically those of chickens and other farm animals. Against the powerful voice of the scientific expert is—within her understanding—the ignored voice of the chicken.

Although her critique also extends to science and environmental ethics more generally, Davis takes specific aim at J. Baird Callicott's influential essay, "Animal Liberation: A Triangular Affair," which extensively draws on Aldo Leopold's famous "Land Ethic." Leopold's ethic prioritizes the biotic community, wherein species have greater moral value than individuals, and wild animals have greater moral status than domesticated animals. An individual "nonhuman natural entity" is valued to the extent that it contributes to the "integrity, beauty, and stability" of the community.[78]

Callicott applies Leopold's moral framework, which strongly delineates between things that are "unnatural, tame, and confined" and things that are "natural, wild, and free," to discount arguments for animal liberation.[79] Callicott claims that farm animals have been "bred to docility, tractability, stupidity, and dependency," and similarly, like tables or chairs, they are "creations of man."[80] Consequently, animal liberation is understood to be as preposterous as efforts to free furniture. Against Callicott's sweeping generalizations, Davis introduces Viva, a hen who recently escaped slaughter. She discovered the partially deformed and filthy animal within a chicken shed. In the months before her death, Viva lived at Davis's house.

The appearance of Viva's story in Davis's text also signals the appearance of voice. Davis's description of voice, in relation to the hen and elsewhere throughout the piece, suggests a clear challenge to Callicott's reification of farm animals. In the following passage, Viva's voice exemplifies her expressivity and responsiveness, which in terms of Davis's argument, helps shift the portrayal of farm animals from objects to active subjects:

> One of the most touching things about her was her voice. She would always talk to me with her frail "peep" which never got any louder and seemed to come from somewhere in the center of her body which pulsed her tail at precisely the same time. Also, rarely, she gave a little trill. Often after one of her ordeals, in which her legs would get caught in her wings, causing her terrible confusion and distress, I would sit talking to her, stroking her beautiful back and her feet that were so soft between the toes and on the bottoms, and she would carry on the dialogue with me, her tail feathers twitching in a kind of unison with each of her utterances.[81]

Davis' positioning of Viva as a being who talks and who participates in dialogue seems particularly significant. Consider hooks' (1989) supposition that dialogue is "necessarily a liberatory expression"[82] because it indicates a recognized voice as opposed to a soliloquized voice. If we apply hooks' interpretation of dialogue to the above account, which seems reasonable given Davis's argument, Viva is shown not to engage in "the mere making of sounds," as Aristotle would contend, but to be a subject in responsive relation to another subject. "Only as subjects can we speak," contends hooks.[83] As Gilligan maintains, "speaking depends on listening and being heard; it is an intensely relational act."[84] For hooks, Gilligan, and Davis, voice is about being subjects in relation; Davis goes further than either Gilligan or hooks through her representation of animals as voiced subjects.

Returning to the oral and aural again, Davis moves from descriptions of dialogue to a musical metaphor, again emphasizing Viva's voice, and that of other farmed animals. Notably, in the following excerpt, Davis does not suggest that chickens are voiceless, only that their voices become obscured within the cacophony of certain environmental discourses: "I think to myself, listening to the trumpet blasts and iron oratory of environmentalism, how could the soft voice of Viva ever hope to be heard here? In this world, the small tones of life are drowned out by the regal harmonies of the mountain and their ersatz echoes in the groves of academe."[85] As hooks emphasizes and Davis implies, the possession of voice alone is not sufficient for liberation; the struggle for voice is to be heard.

The importance of voice is further made clear through Davis's essay within an essay, "Clucking Like a Mountain." Davis's employment of voice, though directed toward deep ecology and environmental ethics generally, offers a specific response to Leopold's wish that we "think like a mountain" and identify with the ecosphere. Particularly disturbing for Davis is the recognition that Leopold's plea for eco-holistic thinking, which she agrees with in sentiment, has provided a rationale for some environmentalists to exclude farmed animals from moral consideration. Davis further laments that Leopold likely would have denied domesticated animals such as chickens a voice at the Council of All Beings, a popular exercise inspired by his work.[86] In response, keeping with the exercise form in which "beings are invited to tell how life has changed for them under the present conditions that humans have created in the world," Davis writes from the perspective of an imaginary factory farmed chicken.[87] Her testimony is divided into two paragraphs: one detailing her current conditions experienced as a battery hen, and in contrast, another describing how she would have lived "[i]n nature or even a farm yard."[88] The paragraphs' juxtaposition emphasizes the abject conditions experienced by most "layer" hens. I provide an abridged excerpt of the speech below:

Megaphone please.

I am a battery hen. I live in a cage so small I cannot stretch my wings. I am forced to stand all night and day on a sloping wire mesh floor that painfully cuts into my feet. The cage walls tear my feathers, forming blood blisters that never heal. The air is so full of ammonia that my lungs hurt and my eyes burn and I think I am going blind. . . .

My mind is alert and my body is sensitive and I should have been richly feathered. . . . Free, I would have ranged my ancestral jungles and fields with my mates, devouring plants, earth-worms, and insects from sunrise to dusk. I would have exercised my body and expressed my nature, and I would have given and received, pleasure as a whole being. I am only a year old, but I am already a "spent hen." Humans, I wish I were dead, and soon I will be dead. Look for pieces of my wounded flesh wherever chicken pies and soups are sold.[89]

In one of the more poetic sections of "Thinking like a Chicken," Davis again returns to the auditory, comparing environmentalists' disregard for individuals to the dismissal of individual notes in a song. Yet, none who love music negate individual notes; like William Blake who inspired his readers to see the universe in a single grain of sand, Davis urges, "We must learn with equal justice and perception to hear the music of the spheres in the cluck of a chicken, starting with the hen who, historian Page Smith says, 'is rich in comfortable sounds, chirps and chirrs, and, when she is a young pullet, a kind of sweet singing that is full of contentment when she is clustered together with her sisters and brothers in an undifferentiated huddle of peace and well-being waiting for darkness to envelop them.' If I think like a mountain, will I be able to hear this hen singing?"[90] Davis further pairs voice with individuality in the Epilogue. First, in response to Callicott's argument for a single ethic, which appeared in his later conciliatory piece, "Animal Liberation and Environmental Ethics: Back Together Again," she writes, "I believe that we need a single ethic in which we are a voice not only for life but for lives—for all the soft and innocent lives who are at our mercy."[91]

Davis expresses her discontent at the rejection letter authored by the *Environmental Ethics*' editor, regarding her submission "Clucking Like a Mountain." In the letter, the editor turns to the work of professor of Christian theology John Cobb to argue that the "right to life" principle applies more to certain animals than others; namely, the principle applies less to animals such as chickens and veal calves and more to gorillas and dolphins. From Cobb's perspective, whereas the potential experiences of gorillas and other animals presumed within their class are particularly distinctive, the lives of animals such as chickens are not. Additionally, neither these animals nor others are greatly concerned with their deaths. According to Davis, the editor's arguments precisely enact the type of positions she critiques; subsequently, she concludes that the letter "seeks to shout down the voice of the individual animal and author and to delegitimate me as a speaker who knows chickens in deference to the 'experts' with whom the world order and divine mind just happen to agree that animals humans like to eat (such as chickens, veal calves, and tuna) and animals who like to eat humans (such as sharks) have less valuable personal and interpersonal experiences and a lesser part in the universe. How do the experts know? They decided."[92] Davis' jab at "expert knowledge," characterized in what she later calls the "voice of the expert,"[93] relates to her earlier critiques of deep ecology, specifically the great extent that it adheres to the prevailing scientific world view. According to Davis, this "domineering construct of our era" eschews personal experience as legitimate grounds for knowledge.[94] For example, her years running a chicken sanctuary and her many personal relationships with chickens were dismissed by the article's reviewers. As one of the "Clucking Like a Mountain" referees (whom Davis speculates is a poultry scientist) chastised, "too much first person singular" and "sixteen billion chickens cannot tell me the psychic price of scientific enlightenment."[95] Davis queries, "[w]here is the voice of the voiceless in the scientific literature, including the literature of environmental ethics?"[96]

In other words, Davis' argument maintains that science is not the sole purveyor of truth. Following Adams and Procter-Smith's claim that "the voice of the voiceless offers a truth that the voice of the expert can never offer,"[97] she posits that the language of science is unable to represent the "truths of subjugated knowledge."[98] Instead, she calls for the realization of a different voice: "This voice requires a different language from the language of experts, a verbal and lyrical equivalent of the subjective and intersubjective experiences linking humans to one another and, through an epistemology rooted in our evolutionary history, to other animals and the earth."[99] In conclusion, Davis contrasts "the expert's" voice with Viva's voice, and Viva comes to represent an ambassador for all farmed animals. In this sense, she is both acknowledged as an individual and as a species representative.

Davis directly enters the sticky terrain of representation of the (animal) Other throughout her essay: she gestures toward Viva's own voice as a way of unseating not only Callicott's and other environmentalists' claims about farm animals, but also unseating the assumption that her (human) voice alone can represent Viva's subjectivity. I appreciate the self-consciousness of her attempt. Davis's "voice" claim to her own experiential knowledge, resistance to hegemonic discourses, and emphasis on dialogue reverberates with voice in its contemporary political register. She goes beyond such descriptions, though, by disrupting the humanism of political voice through her attempt to include Viva's embodied voice. We can understand that gesture also as an effort to acknowledge her political voice, and in relation, her subjectivity. It is this latter voice that is so often lacking within social justice and even animal advocacy texts, such as Torres' *Making a Killing*. My argument is not to undercut the significance of the texts and their myriad contributions. Crucially, we hear of animals' suffering within advocates' work, and in this sense, we do undoubtedly achieve some insight into and description of their subjectivity. However, Davis deepens these kinds of efforts by providing a more extensive "voice" of nonhuman animals within her writing, including not only a representation of their abject suffering but also their capacity for dialogue, complex emotionality and sociality, including the reciprocal giving and receiving of pleasure.

Of course, Davis's approach does not immunize her from accusations of adopting the "ventriloquist's burden."[100] Yet, Davis grounds her efforts to speak on Viva's behalf within experiential knowledge generated in relationship with her and other chickens. Recall Davis's question, "Where is the voice of the voiceless in the scientific literature, including the literature of environmental ethics?"[101] While she employs the phrase "voice of the voiceless" with regard to animals, she does not simply substitute herself as their representative without trying to bring their "voices" centrally into her discourse. In this sense, she acknowledges that animals are "voiceless" only in some contexts, but not all, and their construction as "voiceless" is not inevitable.

Generally, for animal advocates, voice is linked to an ethical imperative to act on behalf of those who are suffering. Advocates, aware of animals' suffering and also animals' inability to end this suffering, are motivated to speak out about this otherwise unheard (and, synonymously, unacknowledged) pain. Advocates' descriptions of animals as "voiceless" are ways in which they attempt to name not only animals' suffering, but also the general human ignorance and/or dismissal of such suffering. As much as they position themselves and their work as animals' voices (in the sense that advocates enable public recognition [i.e., *hearing*] of animals' suffering), they likewise necessarily position animals as being unheard, which signals their condition of suffering as one of profound victimhood. Animals are understood as unable to *politically* express their suffering and meaningfully intervene to stop it: they are seen as helpless. In this sense, voice is wedded to political agency and resistance; animals' suffering prompts an ethical response from advocates who are motivated to politically act on their behalf. How discourses of voice (and voicelessness) function in such instances is clearly articulated, as previously mentioned, by Birke and Parisi who state that animals do not have a political voice in Western culture.[102] In part, voicelessness names political impotence; voice names the capacity to affect political change. (The change being demanded often relates to the alleviation and end to animal suffering and use.)

At the same time, some advocates' critiques of voice relate to a concern about the erasure of animal subjectivity that is (potentially) implied through phrases such as "voice of the voiceless." Such concern makes particular sense when considered within a broader cultural context of voice: a major dynamic of political voice is subjectivity.[103] In its political register, voice typically signals the presence and assertion of subjectivity. In certain activists' constructions there is a tension in the recognition that animals are often unable to affect change in their lives (especially, with regard to escaping or alleviating their suffering),[104] while there is also a discomfort in the presumption that they lack subjectivity and agency. When activists such as Bekoff and Jones attempt to disrupt discourses of voice in the animal movements, they articulate a form of coalitional politics that suggests a shift away from a construction of animals as passive victims to a foregrounding of animals as subjects, and in relation, as agents who can also resist. Birke and Parisi's claim that animals can build alliances suggests a similar orientation Davis's variously repeated highlighting of Viva's voice (and those of other farmed animals) offers a view of animal activists more as partners than as (entirely) saviours.

Nonetheless, Bekoff pragmatically realizes that advocates are ethically required to be the "voice of the voiceless," being that animals are voiceless in a major sense because they are not "heard" (i.e., do not have their suffering recognized) by the majority of people. Political voice is frequently figured as relational and dialogical; its presence is made possible only in the context of reception. Consequently, based on the advocates' rhetoric presented throughout this essay, we can conclude that in a significant way, animals *are* voiceless in the sense that their suffering is not heard by humans. However, we can also say that they *are not* voiceless in the sense that they are seen by advocates as subjects who have desires, perspectives, and interests (regardless of human recognition of this fact).

While most animal advocates are quick to point to animals' interests in not suffering, others (such as Davis and Bekoff) go further, and simultaneously offer fuller descriptions of their subjectivities, as evidenced in their more nuanced constructions of voice. Their claims about animal voices (and, necessarily, their subjectivities) confront the humanist assumption that subjectivity is strictly a human phenomenon. In other words, what is so striking about Bekoff's, jones's, Davis's, and Birke and Parisi's discourse is their explicit challenge to the humanism that typically undergirds the political register of voice. These authors do not presume that voice is necessarily human. Indeed, they actively and overtly work against that supposition. Despite their understanding of animal suffering, and the lack of political will directed to that issue, they are unwilling to simply argue that animals are voiceless and that advocates ought to be their voices. They are unsatisfied with conventional constructions (by both animal advocates and others, ostensibly) that suggest voice is only human. As such, they also offer interpretations of animal subjectivity that are often only afforded to (certain) human beings. They share an ethical and political lineage with earlier advocates such as Montaigne who explicitly refused to frame animals as voiceless.[105]

Animal Subjectivities in Advocacy

Collectively, those interested in changing large-scale exploitative relationships with nonhuman animals are primarily interested in wresting animals from their categorization as objects. In many ways, the problem, which is consistently described and resisted, is that animals are understood and treated as things, resources, (live)stock, capital, property, etc. Consequently, we are at a vital crux. How do we move forward from this point? Cary Wolfe is asking us to seriously reconsider adopting a notion of subjectivity that contains within it the anthropocentric and speciesist trappings of humanism. For example, as Wolfe notes, the push for animal rights is fraught given that the Western construction of rights is predicated on the exclusion and differentiation of human from nonhuman animals.[106] The achievement of rights has been the achievement of (necessarily) *human* rights. Those included within the Western sphere of rights-holders are permitted to be there due to their human species membership. The wish for various marginalized others to be included in this sphere is the desire to be recognized as fully human and thus rights-holding subjects. Indeed, the boundaries that define rights (i.e., who is entitled to them) are based on the exclusion of nonhuman animals. We can clearly hear Audre Lorde's claim that "the master's tools will never dismantle the master's house"[107] in Wolfe's critique.[108]

In *What Is Posthumanism?*, Wolfe elucidates the potential of disability and animal studies to expose the limitations of the liberal humanist model:

> I am not suggesting that working to liberalize the interpretation by the courts of the Americans with Disabilities Act is a waste of time, or that lobbying to upgrade animal cruelty prosecutions from misdemeanour to felony status is a bad thing. What I am suggesting is that these pragmatic pursuits are forced to work within the purview of a liberal humanism in philosophy, politics, and the law that is bound by a historically and ideologically specific set of coordinates that, because of that very boundedness, allow one to achieve certain pragmatic gains in the short run, but at the price of a radical foreshortening of a more ambitious and more profound ethical project: a new and more inclusive form of ethical pluralism that it is our charge, now, to frame. That project would think the ethical force of disability and nonhuman subjectivity as something other than merely an expansion of the liberal humanist ethnos to ever new populations, as merely the next room added onto the (increasingly opulent and globalizing) house of what Richard Rorty has called "the rich North Atlantic bourgeois democracies."[109]

Wolfe is advocating for a pointed critique of humanism within the animal and disability movements, which also prompts questions about the validity of the liberal humanist subject more generally. The point should not be the shift of nonhuman animals from object to subject when the framing of both is firmly entrenched within a liberal humanist paradigm. A very narrow conceptualization of subjectivity still plagues initiatives such as the Great Ape Project, which advocates for a recognition of nonhuman ape personhood, largely through discourses of what legal scholar Taimie Bryant calls the "similarity argument" (i.e., those who are most like us are seen as most deserving of rights). She writes, "[i]f humans are defined in some significant measure by a particular characteristic (such as tool making ability, self-awareness, or the capacity to suffer), questions of justice arise when animals are sufficiently similar to humans as to the characteristic and justice is defined as requiring like entities be treated alike."[110] As Bryant contends, the similarity argument has been a key strategy of the animal rights movements; it is precisely this argument that drove the Western civil rights movement, the feminist movement, and the disability rights movement. She acknowledges that this orientation is an important first step for these movements, but that ultimately, asking potential rights-holders to possess similar characteristics of existing rights-holders is a limiting gesture that flattens, rather than celebrating, respecting, and actually benefiting from difference and diversity. Wolfe's desire for a "new and more inclusive form of ethical pluralism" shares a similar starting point with Bryant,[111] one that values diversity and questions the conventional measuring sticks used to deem one a worthy recipient of justice, and necessarily the very meaning of "justice" (legally defined as treating like entities alike).[112]

While Wolfe's arguments regarding subjectivity and justice are astute, particularly as they help describe an orientation and set of (what I also believe are) useful "coordinates" under the banner of "posthumanism," others not working within this particular language are nonetheless very much engaged in the kind of intervention that he proposes. On the one hand, Wolfe turns to philosophers such as Derrida as crucial interlocutors for posthumanism. For example, he takes guidance from Derrida's eloquent assertion (one that I think largely summarizes much of Wolfe's argument): "there is not one opposition between man and non-man; there are, between different organizational structures of the living being, many fractures, heterogeneities."[113] On the other, I turn toward Smuts' research on embodied communication with nonhuman animals,[114] and other similar projects, which are also directly and centrally involved in the appreciation of nonhuman subjectivities that very much run counter to a liberal humanist one.

Smuts' article, "Between Species: Science and Subjectivity," for example, describes a version of subjectivity that is constituted in relation (as opposed to atomized individuality) and that recognizes elements of subjectivity outside of typical linguistic modes so highly valued within Western philosophical traditions. I recognize that Wolfe is primarily engaged in conversations with philosophy, literature, and cultural studies, but I find a perplexing absence in his exclusion of Smuts' research, particularly as he is provisionally responding to the question, "What is posthumanism?" Haraway is very much part of his discursive landscape, perhaps because she, too, is dialoguing with philosophers such as Derrida. Yet, it is people like Smuts who so strongly influence Haraway in texts such as *When Species Meet*, and Haraway's descriptions of "companion species" are very much inspired by (and modelled on) the kinds of relationships forged within Smuts' grounded research with dogs and other nonhuman animals. Haraway's understanding of companion species is primarily based on relationality, and it points to ethical responsibilities that are borne out of relations between human and nonhuman species, and within each.

Haraway's theory is rightfully acknowledged by Wolfe as part of an emerging posthumanist literature. However, I want to petition for Bryant,[115] Balcombe,[116] Bekoff,[117] Noske,[118] Smuts,[119] Davis,[120] and Birke and Parisi,[121] among others, to also be recognized as part of this posthumanist turn. Not only does it help balance what seems dangerously like an old-boys' club of posthumanist scholars (Haraway excepted, of course) counted within Wolfe's *What Is Posthumanism?*, but because these authors have long been involved in describing (and engaging in) human and nonhuman subjectivities quite contra to the liberal humanist subject constructed in the West, one which is relentlessly predicated on the disavowal of "the animal."[122]

More than just a rallying cry for inclusivity, though, my point here is that we ought to pay close attention to these alternative versions of subjectivity because, I believe, they can be enormously helpful to the animal rights and liberation movements. They can help foster a deeper and more radical animal politics. This assertion returns me to voice. Given that voice is a powerful metaphor within Western social and environmental movements, including the animal movements, part of what I find exciting about the voice metaphor is its dedication to and articulation of a kind of subjectivity also grounded in relationality. Further, the relationality implied through the voice metaphor is intimately tied to a project that recognizes and values difference. As Gregory Alexander contends, part of the role of the voice metaphor is to highlight difference.[123] Bekoff and Smuts, to name two groundbreaking academics, are working with precisely such differences—heterogeneities—that both intensely acknowledge individuality and recognize the subject as never divorced from or defined outside of sociality.[124] Smuts, for example, writes extensively about "intersubjectivity" among and between species.[125] For aforementioned animal-focused authors, the social sphere is not understood as strictly the province of humanity, as is incorrectly assumed by many social scientists and others.[126]

Aspects of the voice metaphor in its political register that indicate non-unitary subjectivity, experience, relationality, and resistance in other, human-focused social justice struggles are clearly evidenced in Balcombe's, Bekoff's, Davis's, and Smuts's descriptions of nonhuman animals' lives and human–nonhuman animal relations, but in ways that do not simply swap old characteristics for new ones demanded of nonhuman animals in order not to be objectified. They are also vigorously trying to unsettle the anthropocentrism and speciesism inherent in Western humanism. This is vital work.

NOTES

1. Gilligan, *In a Different Voice*, xvi.
2. DeMello, *Speaking for Animals*, 8.
3. C.B. Davis, "Reading the Ventriloquist's Lips," 133.
4. Deleuze, *Intellectuals and Power*, 209. In a conversation between Deleuze and Foucault, originally published in 1972 in *L'Arc*, Deleuze reflects on Foucault's efforts to establish the conditions where, through the Information Group for Prisoners, prisoners could speak for themselves: "In my opinion," states Deleuze, "you were the first—in your books and in the practical sphere—to teach us something absolutely fundamental: the indignity of speaking for others. We ridiculed representation and said it was finished, but we failed to draw the consequences of this 'theoretical' conversion—to appreciate the theoretical fact that only those directly concerned can speak in a practical way on their own behalf" (ibid.).
5. Alcoff, "Problem of Speaking for Others," 6.
6. E.g., Kohl and Farthing, "Navigating Narrative."
7. E.g., DeMello, *Speaking for Animals*; Munro, "Strategies."
8. E.g., Nocella et al., *Defining Critical Animal Studies*.
9. See Corman, "The Ventriloquist's Burden?"
10. DeMello, *Speaking for Animals*.
11. E.g., Balcombe, "Animal Pleasure"; Bekoff and Pierce, *Wild Justice*; Best, "Revolutionary Implications"; Bryant, "Similarity or Difference"; Colling et al., "Until All Are Free"; Donaldson and Kymlicka, *Zoopolis*; Hribal, "Animals Are Part"; *Animal Planet*.
12. E.g., Denov, *Girls in Fighting Forces*; Hill, *500 Years*; Lindroth, "Paradoxes of Power"; Manchanda, *Women, War and Peace*; Mohanty, "Under Western Eyes"; Law, *Resistance behind Bars*.
13. Mohanty, "Under Western Eyes."
14. Ibid., 57 (emphasis in original).
15. Ibid., 58.
16. Ibid., 72.
17. Ibid., 71.
18. Horwitz, *Hog Ties*, 45.
19. Ibid.
20. The similarity Horwitz finds between pro-life and animal rights activists' "if-I-were-one" projections suggests little recognition of the different contexts in which animals and fetuses reside, and the implications of these contexts: namely, animals exist independently, and fetuses are dependently located within independently existing bodies. As Francione notes, fetus-protection laws could only be enforced through an egregious invasion of women's

personal privacy, via a direct state intervention and manipulation of women's bodies. However, in the case of animal protection laws, an animal may be taken away without any intrusion into the personal privacy of another. Francione argues, "[w]hen a vivisector seeks to exploit a nonhuman in a biomedical experiment, the situation is much more analogous to one of child abuse, not abortion" ("Abortion and Animal Rights," 150).

21. Horwitz, *Hog Ties*, 45.
22. Ibid., 46.
23. Ibid., 49.
24. Ibid., 43.
25. Ibid., 42.
26. Ibid.
27. Arguably, most North Americans do not clamour for the opportunity to meet the individual animals they eat.
28. Horwitz, *Hog Ties*, 47.
29. As cited in ibid. Fox problematizes the term "productivity," as used by many animal scientists. Despite what the rhetoric implies, "productivity" is not simply an individual's "conversion efficiency in relation to its rate of growth or egg or milk yield per day per unit of food consumed" (*Inhumane Society*, 33). Instead, "productivity" of a pen or cage of animals is determined in conjunction with costs related to labour, equipment, and feed. Fox also argues that often efforts used to reduce animals' physical expression of stress do not address the psychological distress (*Inhumane Society*, 32).
30. Horwitz, *Hog Ties*, 47.
31. Ibid. I use *sic* here to interrupt the speciesist assumption that the appropriate pronoun for animals is one that defines them as objects (signalled by "that"), while the appropriate pronoun for human beings is one that defines them as subjects (signalled by "who" or "whom"). My contention is that animals are also "who" and "whom." While some grammar sources indicate that "that" can also be an acceptable pronoun for human beings, "who" and "whom" are used exclusively in reference to people.
32. *Pleasurable Kingdom*.
33. Nociception does not imply the experience of something adverse, only that an animal's nervous system is stimulated in a way as to prompt a reflex to avoid the stimulus.
34. Balcombe emphasizes that evolution and experience are compatible not only for humans, but also for animals. To exclude one from the other is to create a false dichotomy, one too often made by the scientific community. Concentrating on pleasure, Balcombe describes multiple studies that show the many ways animals seek out and experience pleasure, including through food, sex, play, and others. Keeping in mind the individual differences among animals, Balcombe points to

the continuity between humans and other animals: experience and evolution are wedded. He states, "[t]he physical pleasures of life—like the pain—are current, even though they have evolutionary significance. It is these experiences, not the evolutionary forces underlying them, that put wind in the sails of a raccoon's existence. And a mouse's. And a pigeon's" (*Pleasurable Kingdom*, 8).

35. Ibid., 209.

36. Horwitz, *Hog Ties*, 48.

37. Ibid.

38. Ibid., 48–49.

39. Ibid., 43.

40. See Horwitz, "Meet the Big Guys," in *Hog Ties*, 66–76.

41. Brantlinger, "Kipling's 'White Man's Burden,'" 172.

42. E.g., Snodgrass, "Poetry of the 1890s."

43. Judd, "Diamonds Are Forever?," 42.

44. Kipling, "White Man's Burden."

45. Kipling as cited in Brantlinger, "Kipling's 'White Man's Burden,'" 178.

46. Horwitz, *Hog Ties*, 47.

47. "Kipling's 'White Man's Burden.'"

48. Brantlinger, "Kipling's 'White Man's Burden,'" 186.

49. Bernstein, "Legitimizing Liberation," 98. According to Best, animal welfare colludes with animal-exploiting industries through their joint acceptance of the property status of animals. Animal rights and animal liberation are more closely aligned to each other than to animal welfare. Best argues that animal rights provides the philosophical foundation for the ALF (Animal Liberation Front), and therefore, in his view, animal liberation in general. For Best, the crucial distinguishing feature between rights and liberation is the use of direct action by the latter. "While those who adopt the animal welfare position seek merely to reduce animal suffering," explains Best,

> supporters of animal rights aim to abolish it, demanding not bigger cages and "humane treatment," but rather empty cages and total liberation. Animal welfare philosophy accepts the property status of animals, but animal rights philosophy insists that animals are subjects of their own life and no one's to own. Whereas animal welfare philosophy reinforces the moral gulf between human and nonhuman animals and allows any use of animals so long as it furthers some alleged human interest, animal rights theory puts human and nonhuman animals on an equal moral plane and rejects all exploitative uses of animals, whether human beings benefit or not. Clearly, animal rights is the guiding moral philosophy of the ALF, but whereas animal rights often is a legal fight without direct action, animal liberation is an immediate confrontation with exploiters. ("Behind the Mask," 26–27)

50. E.g., Collins, *Black Feminist Thought*; Keeshig-Tobias, "Stop Stealing Native Stories"; Lugones and Spelman, "Have We Got a Theory"; Rowell, "Politics of Cultural Appropriation."

51. The term "advocate" finds its etymological roots within voice. As a noun, *advocate* is contemporarily defined as "[o]ne called in, or liable to be called upon, to defend or speak for" (*OED Online*, accessed 2008). From Middle English via Old French *advocat*, "advocate" ultimately stems from the Latin *advocātus*, which means one summoned or "called to" another, especially one called in to aid one's cause in a court of justice (*OED Online*, accessed 2008). *Advocātus* is the past participle of *advocāre*, which combines *ad* "to" and *vocāre* "to call" (*Oxford Concise Dictionary*, 1995, 9th ed.). "Advocate" remains the Roman law courts' technical title for a person who pleads someone's cause in a court of justice. Notably, *advocate* finds a shared etymological root with voice through *vocāre*. Voice defined as a "sound made by the human mouth," stems from Old French *voiz*, from the Latin *vōcem* (nominative *vox*) "voice, sound, utterance, cry, call, speech, sentence, language, word," related to *vocāre* (*Online Etymological Dictionary*, 2001–16, s.v. "voice," http://www.etymonline .com, accessed 2008). A shared relationship between "advocate" and "voice" is explicitly shown through the contemporary definition of "advocate" as a transitive verb: "To plead or raise one's voice in favour of; to defend or recommend publicly" (*OED Online*, accessed 2008).

52. CoK, "20 Years of Compassion!"

53. Regan, "Giving Voice to Animal Rights."

54. Consider, for example, some early connections made by animal advocates regarding speech and voice. Diane Beers argues that the birth of the organized animal advocacy movement in the United States began in April 1866, with the inauguration of the ASPCA (American Society for the Prevention of Cruelty to Animals) in New York. Henry Bergh declared at the end of the first meeting, "[t]he blood-red hand of cruelty shall no longer torture dumb beasts with impunity" (*Prevention of Cruelty*, 3). Founded in 1869, the oldest animal welfare society in Canada, the Canadian Society for the Prevention of Cruelty to Animals (CSPCA)—now known as Montreal's SPCA—has claimed for over a hundred years to have fought for "those who cannot speak for themselves" (Johnston, *For Those Who Cannot Speak*, 1). Similarly, like other organizations, the Denver Dumb Friends League invokes speech through its name. Choosing to retain the outmoded nomenclature, "dumb," the organization states, "When our organization was founded in 1910, it was named after a London, England, animal welfare group called 'Our Dumb Friends League.' In those days, the term *dumb* was widely used to refer to animals because they lacked the power of human speech. Today, the Dumb Friends League, headquartered in Denver, is the largest community-based animal welfare organization in the Rocky

Mountain region—providing a strong, compassionate and steadfast voice for those who cannot speak for themselves" (Dumb Friends League, "About Us").

55. Finley, "Lyrics of Rage."
56. Perdew, *Animal Rights Movement*, 20.
57. Torres, *Making a Killing*, 39.
58. Ibid.
59. Beers, *Prevention of Cruelty*, xii.
60. Ibid., 7, 11, 30, 40, 56, 58, 59, 60, 134, 155, 196, 198.
61. E.g., pp. 7, 30.
62. E.g., pp. 134, 196.
63. Torres, *Making a Killing*, 39.
64. Raju, "We Are Different," 174.
65. Ibid.
66. Bekoff, "Animal Emotions," 38.
67. The conference was held in Manhattan, New York City, in the spring of 2005.
68. jones, "Power of Grassroots Movements."
69. Bekoff, "Animal Emotions," 38.
70. Birke and Parisi, "Animals, Becoming," 71. This statement follows their discussion of feminism, animals, and science, which is informed by Deleuze and Guattari's notion of "becoming." Through their piece, Birke and Parisi offer critiques of feminism, animal rights, and biology. They look to "becoming" as a move toward respecting heterogeneous difference, challenging the extensionist tradition of animal rights (where boundaries themselves are not challenged), and calling for a "nondeterminist science" (ibid.).
71. See Corman, "Ventriloquist's Burden?"
72. Bekoff, "Animal Emotions," 38.
73. Rothenberg, *Thousand Mile Song*.
74. Bauman and Drake, "Silence Is Not Without Voice," 310.
75. Ibid., 311.
76. Ibid., 310.
77. Ibid.
78. Leopold, in K. Davis, "Thinking Like a Chicken," 193.
79. K. Davis, "Thinking Like a Chicken," 193.
80. Callicott, in K. Davis, "Thinking Like a Chicken," 194.
81. K. Davis, "Thinking Like a Chicken," 194–95.
82. hooks, *Talking Back*, 24.
83. Ibid., 12.
84. Gilligan, *In a Different Voice*, xvi.
85. K. Davis, "Thinking Like a Chicken," 198.
86. The Council of All Beings is a ritual designed by John Seed, Joanna Macy, Pat Fleming, and Arne Naess to encourage humanity's reconnection with a larger "ecological self" (Seed et al., *Thinking Like a Mountain*, 20).

87. Seed et al., *Thinking Like a Mountain*, in K. Davis, "Thinking Like a Chicken," 200. Typically, the Council is a spoken and collective exercise, conducted in a group of people.
88. K. Davis, "Thinking Like a Chicken," 200.
89. Ibid. (italics in original).
90. Ibid., 203.
91. Ibid., 206. However, Davis does not concede Callicott's point that farmed animals' ontology is tied to the roles humans have ascribed to them, nor does she support Callicott's position regarding the conscience-soothing belief of an unspoken evolutionary "social contract" between humans and domesticated animals. In effect, suggests Davis, Callicott's application of social contract theory legitimates unequal social relations between humans and animals, and ignores hierarchies of power.
92. K. Davis, "Thinking Like a Chicken," 208.
93. Ibid., 209.
94. Ibid., 208.
95. Ibid.
96. Ibid.
97. Adams and Procter-Smith, "Taking Life or 'Taking on Life'?: Table Talk and Animals."
98. Adams and Procter-Smith, in K. Davis, "Thinking Like a Chicken," 208.
99. K. Davis, "Thinking Like a Chicken," 208.
100. Horwitz, *Hog Ties*, 45.
101. K. Davis, "Thinking Like a Chicken," 208.
102. "Animals, Becoming."
103. Corman, "Ventriloquist's Burden?"
104. E.g., Bekoff, *Strolling with Our Kin*; K. Davis, "Thinking Like a Chicken"; jones, "Power of Grassroots Movements."
105. Montaigne, *Apology for Raymond Sebond*.
106. *Zoontologies*.
107. Lorde, *Sister Outsider*, 110.
108. *Zoontologies*.
109. Wolfe, *What Is Posthumanism?*, 136–37.
110. Bryant, "Similarity or Difference," 207.
111. Wolfe, *What Is Posthumanism?*, 137.
112. Bryant, "Similarity or Difference."
113. As cited in Wolfe, *What Is Posthumanism?*, 139.
114. Smuts, "Between Species."
115. "Similarity or Difference."
116. *Pleasurable Kingdom*.
117. "Animal Emotions" and *Emotional Lives of Animals*.
118. *Beyond Boundaries*.

119. "Encounters with Animal Minds" and "Between Species."
120. "Thinking Like a Chicken."
121. "Animals, Becoming."
122. Oliver, *Animal Lessons.*
123. "Talking about Difference."
124. Bekoff, "Animal Emotions" and *Emotional Lives of Animals*; Smuts, "Encounters with Animal Minds" and "Between Species."
125. "Encounters with Animal Minds"
126. Noske, *Beyond Boundaries.*

BIBLIOGRAPHY

Adams, Carol J., and Marjorie Procter-Smith. "Taking Life or 'Taking on Life'?: Table Talk and Animals." In C. J. Adams (Ed.), Ecofeminism and the Sacred, 295–310. New York: Continuum, 1993.

Alcoff, Linda. "The Problem of Speaking for Others." *Cultural Critique* 20 (1991): 5–32.

Alexander, Gregory. "Talking about Difference: Meanings and Metaphors of Individuality." *Cardoza Law Review* 11 (1989): 1355–75.

Balcombe, Jonathan. "Animal Pleasure and Its Moral Significance." *Applied Animal Behaviour Science* 118, nos. 3–4 (2009): 208–16.

——. *Pleasurable Kingdom: Animals and the Nature of Feeling Good.* New York: Palgrave Macmillan, 2007.

Bauman, H-Dirksen L., and Jennifer Drake. "Silence Is Not Without Voice: Including Deaf Culture within Multicultural Curricula." In *The Disability Studies Reader*, edited by Lennard J. Davis, 307–14. New York: Routledge, 1997.

Beers, Diane. *For the Prevention of Cruelty: The History and Legacy of Animal Rights Activism in the United States.* Athens, OH: Swallow Press, 2006.

Bekoff, Marc. "Animal Emotions and Animal Sentience and Why They Matter: Blending 'Science Sense' with Common Sense, Compassion and Heart." In *Animals, Ethics, and Trade: The Challenge of Animal Sentience*, edited by Jacky Turner and Joyce D'Silva, 27–40. New York: Routledge, 2006.

——. *The Emotional Lives of Animals: A Leading Scientist Explores Animal Joy, Sorrow, and Empathy—and Why They Matter.* Novato, CA: New World Library, 2007.

——. *Strolling with Our Kin: Speaking for and Respecting Voiceless Animals.* Jenkintown, PA: American Anti-vivisection Society, 2000.

Bekoff, Marc, and Jessica Pierce. *Wild Justice: The Moral Lives of Animals.* Chicago: University of Chicago Press, 2009.

Bergh, Henry. *Prevention of Cruelty.* Athens, OH: Swallow Press, 2006.

Bernstein, Mark. "Legitimizing Liberation." In *Terrorists or Freedom Fighters? Reflections on the Liberation of Animals*, edited by Steven Best and Anthony Nocella II, 93–105. Herndon, VA: Lantern Books, 2004.

Best, Steven. "Behind the Mask: Uncovering the Animal Liberation Front." Introduction to *Terrorists or Freedom Fighters? Reflections on the Liberation of Animals*, edited by Steven Best and Anthony Nocella II, 9–63. Herndon, VA: Lantern Books, 2004.

———. "Revolutionary Implications of Animal Standpoint Theory." *State of Nature: Online Journal of Radical Ideas* (Summer 2012). http://www.stateofnature.org/?p=4904.

Birke, Lynda, and Luciana Parisi. "Animals, Becoming." In *Animal Others: On Ethics, Ontology, and Animal Life*, edited by H. Peter Steeves, 55–73. Albany, NY: SUNY Press, 1999.

Boot, Max. *The Savage Wars of Peace: Small Wars and the Rise of American Power*. New York: Basic Books, 2002.

Brantlinger, Patrick. "Kipling's 'The White Man's Burden' and Its Afterlives." *English Literature in Transition, 1880–1920* 50, no. 2 (2007): 172–91. doi: 10.1353/elt.2007.0017.

Bryant, Taimie. "Similarity or Difference as a Basis for Justice: Must Animals Be Like Humans to Be Legally Protected from Humans?" *Law and Contemporary Problems* 70 (Winter 2007): 207–54.

Callicott, J. Baird. "Animal Liberation: A Triangular Affair." *Environmental Ethics* 2 (1980): 311–28.

COK (Compassion over Killing). "20 Years of Compassion!" Video. *YouTube*, December 13, 2015. https://www.youtube.com/watch?v=mgdd3cBdv7Q.

Colling, Sarat, Sean Parson, and Alessandro Arrigoni. "Until All Are Free: Total Liberation Through Revolutionary Decolonization, Groundless Solidarity, and a Revolutionary Framework." In *Defining Critical Animal Studies: An Intersectional Social Justice Approach for Liberation*, edited by Anthony Nocella II, John Sorenson, Kim Socha, and Atsuko Matsuoka, 51–73. New York: Peter Lang, 2014.

Collins, Patricia Hill. *Black Feminist Thought: Knowledge, Consciousness, and the Politics of Empowerment*. London: HarperCollins, 1990.

Corman, Lauren. "The Ventriloquist's Burden? Animals, Voice, and Politics." PhD diss., York University, 2012.

Davis, Charles B. "Reading the Ventriloquist's Lips: The Performance Genre behind the Metaphor." *TDR* 42, no. 4 (1998): 133–56.

Davis, Karen. "Thinking Like a Chicken: Farm Animals and the Feminine Connection." In *Animals and Women: Feminist Theoretical Exploration*, edited by Carol J. Adams and Josephine Donovan, 192–212. Durham, NC: Duke University Press, 1995.

Deleuze, Gilles. *Intellectuals and Power: A Conversation Between Michel Foucault and Gilles Deleuze*. In *Language, Counter-Memory, Practice: Selected Essays and Interviews*, 205–17. Edited by Donald F. Bouchard. Ithaca, NY: Cornell University Press, 1977.

DeMello, Marg, ed. *Speaking for Animals: Animal Autobiographical Writing*. New York: Routledge, 2013.

Denov, Myriam. *Girls in Fighting Forces: Moving beyond Victimhood*. Report prepared for the Government of Canada. Ottawa: Canadian International Development Agency, 2007.

Donaldson, Sue, and Will Kymlicka. *Zoopolis: A Political Theory of Animal Rights*. New York: Oxford University Press, 2011.

Dumb Friends League. "About Us," n.d. http://www.ddfl.org/about-us/our-story/.

Ferguson, Niall. *Empire: The Rise and Demise of the British World Order and the Lessons for Global Power*. New York: Basic Books, 2003.

Finley, Laura L. "The Lyrics of Rage Against the Machine: A Study in Radical Criminology." *Journal of Criminal Justice and Popular Culture* 9, no. 3 (2002): 150–66.

Fox, Michael W. *Inhumane Society: The American Way of Exploiting Animals*. New York: St. Martin's Press, 1990.

Francione, Gary L. "Abortion and Animal Rights: Are They Comparable Issues?" In *Animals and Women: Feminist Theoretical Explorations*, edited by Carol J. Adams and Josephine Donovan, 149–60. Durham, NC: Duke University Press, 1995.

Gilligan, Carol. *In a Different Voice: Psychological Theory and Women's Development*. Cambridge, MA: Harvard University Press, 1993. First published 1982.

Haraway, Donna. *When Species Meet*. Minneapolis: University of Minnesota Press, 2008.

Hill, Gord. *500 Years of Indigenous Resistance Comic Book*. Vancouver: Arsenal Pulp Press, 2010.

hooks, bell. *Talking Back: Thinking Feminist, Thinking Black*. Cambridge, MA: South End Press, 1989.

Horwitz, Richard P. *Hog Ties: What Pigs Tell Us about America*. Minneapolis: University of Minnesota Press, 2002.

Hribal, Jason. "'Animals Are Part of the Working Class': A Challenge to Labor History." *Labor History* 44, no. 4 (2003): 435–53. doi:10.1080/0023656032000170069.

———. *Fear of the Animal Planet: The Hidden History of Animal Resistance*. Oakland, CA: AK Press, 2011.

Johnston, Beatrice. *For Those Who Cannot Speak: A History of the Canadian Society for the Prevention of Cruelty to Animals, 1869–1969*. Laval, QC: Dev-Sco, 1970.

jones, pattrice. "The Power of Grassroots Movements." Paper presented at the Grassroots Animal Rights Conference, April 2005, New York. http://www.bravebirds.org/GARC1.html.

Judd, Denis. "Diamonds Are Forever? Kipling's Imperialism." *History Today* 47, no. 6 (1997). http://www.historytoday.com/denis-judd/diamonds-are-forever-kiplings -imperialism.

Kaplan, Robert D. *Imperial Grunts: The American Military on the Ground.* New York: Random House, 2005.

Keeshig-Tobias, Lenore. "Stop Stealing Native Stories." *Toronto Globe and Mail,* January 26, 1990.

Kheel, Marti. "License to Kill: An Ecofeminist Critique of Hunters' Discourse." In *Animals and Women: Feminist Theoretical Exploration,* edited by Carol J. Adams and Josephine Donovan, 85–125. Durham, NC: Duke University Press, 1995.

Kipling, Rudyard. "The White Man's Burden." *Literature Network,* n.d. http://www .online-literature.com/keats/922/. First published 1899.

Kohl, Benjamin, and Linda C. Farthing. "Navigating Narrative: The Antinomies of 'Mediated' Testimonies." *Journal of Latin American and Caribbean Anthropology* 18, no. 1 (2013): 90–107.

Law, Victoria. *Resistance behind Bars: The Struggles of Incarcerated Women.* 2nd ed. Oakland, CA: PM Press, 2009.

Lindroth, Marjo. "Paradoxes of Power: Indigenous Peoples in the Permanent Forum." *Cooperation and Conflict* 46, no. 4 (2011): 543–62.

Lorde, Audre. *Sister Outsider: Essays and Speeches.* Trumansburg, NY: Crossing Press, 1996.

Lugones, Maria C., and Elizabeth V. Spelman. "Have We Got a Theory for You! Feminist Theory, Cultural Imperialism and the Demand for 'The Woman's Voice.'" *Women's Studies International Forum* 6, no. 6 (1983): 573–81.

Manchanda, Rita. *Women, War and Peace in South Asia.* Thousand Oaks, CA: Sage, 2001.

Mohanty, Chandra. "Under Western Eyes: Feminist Scholarship and Colonial Discourses." *Feminist Review* 30 (Autumn 1988): 61–88.

Montaigne, Michel de. *Apology for Raymond Sebond.* Translated by Roger Ariew and Marjorie Grene. Indianapolis, IN: Hackett, 2003. First published 1580.

Munro, Lyle. "Strategies, Action Repertoires and DIY Activism in the Animal Rights Movement." *Social Movement Studies: Journal of Social, Cultural and Political Protest* 4, no. 1 (2005): 75–94.

Nocella, Anthony, II, John Sorenson, Kim Socha, and Atsuko Matsuoka, eds. *Defining Critical Animal Studies: An Intersectional Social Justice Approach for Liberation.* New York: Peter Lang, 2014.

Noske, Barbara. *Beyond Boundaries: Humans and Animals.* Montreal: Black Rose Books, 1997.

Oliver, Kelly. *Animal Lessons: How They Teach Us to Be Human.* New York: Columbia University Press, 2009.

Perdew, Laura. *Animal Rights Movement.* Minneapolis: ABDO, 2014.

Raju, Saraswati. "We Are Different, but Can We Talk?" *Gender, Place and Culture: A Journal of Feminist Geography* 9, no. 2 (2002): 173–77.

Regan, Tom. "Giving Voice to Animal Rights." Tom Regan's website. Accessed 30 May. http://tomregan.info/giving-voice-to-animal-rights/.

Rothenberg, David. *Thousand Mile Song: Whale Music in a Sea of Sound.* New York: Basic Books, 2008.

Rowell, John. "The Politics of Cultural Appropriation." *Journal of Value Inquiry* 29, no. 1 (1995): 137–42. doi: 10.1007/BF01079071.

Seed, John, Joanna Macy, Pat Fleming, and Arne Naess. *Thinking Like a Mountain: Towards a Council of All Beings.* Philadelphia: New Society, 1988.

Smuts, Barbara. "Between Species: Science and Subjectivity." *Configurations* 14, nos. 1–2 (2006): 115–26.

———. "Encounters with Animal Minds." *Journal of Consciousness Studies* 8, nos. 5–7 (2001): 293–309.

Snodgrass, Chris. "The Poetry of the 1890s." In *A Companion to Victorian Poetry*, edited by Richard Cronin, Alison Chapman, and Antony H. Harrison, 321–41. Oxford: Blackwell, 2002.

Torres, Bob. *Making a Killing: The Political Economy of Animal Rights.* Oakland, CA: AK Press, 2007.

Wheeler Wilcox, Ella. *Poems of Experience.* London: Gay and Hancock, 1915.

Wolfe, Cary. *What Is Posthumanism?* Minneapolis: University of Minnesota Press, 2010.

———, ed. *Zoontologies: The Question of the Animal.* Minneapolis: University of Minnesota Press, 2003.

About the Contributors

LYNDA BIRKE's life has been hugely enriched by whole herds of nonhuman animals, who know far more than she does about human–animal relatings. In another life, she is a Visiting Professor in biological sciences at the University of Chester. Her research is mainly interdisciplinary and mainly in human–animal studies (HAS). Her most recent research has been on horses, giving her ample excuses to be with them. She has published widely in both feminist studies and HAS.

GARRETT M. BROAD is an Assistant Professor in the Department of Communication and Media Studies at Fordham University. His research investigates how globalization, storytelling, and communication technology shape contemporary communities and networked movements for social and environmental justice. His work on animal subjects has been published in *Environmental Communication, Gastronomica: The Journal of Critical Food Studies*, and the *International Journal of Communication*. He is also the author of *More Than Just Food: Food Justice and Community Change* (University of California Press, 2016).

JESSICA CAREY is a Professor of Literary and Cultural Studies at Sheridan College in Ontario, Canada. Her research focuses on the biopolitics of food movements and human–animal relationships, and in her current work she is exploring appeals to nostalgia in food advertising and cookbooks. She has published articles on a wide range of topics, including Temple Grandin's animal-oriented rhetoric, representations of interspecies responsibility in the novel *Wild Dogs* by Canadian author Helen Humphreys, and biopolitical uses of care rhetoric in animal cloning discourse.

JODEY CASTRICANO is Associate Professor in the Faculty of Creative and Critical Studies at the University of British Columbia, Okanagan, where she teaches in the English and Cultural Studies programs. She is a Research Fellow with the Oxford Centre for Animal Ethics and was a member of an International Working Group with the Oxford Centre for Animal Ethics and the British Union for the Abolition of Vivisection (BUAV), which has recently released *Normalizing the Unthinkable: The Ethics of Using Animals in Research* (http://www.oxfordanimalethics.com/wpcms/wp-content/uploads/ Normalising-the-Unthinkable-Report.pdf). In literary studies her specializations are in nineteenth-century literature (gothic) as well as in cultural and critical theory. In the case of the latter, her primary area of expertise and ethical concern is in posthumanist philosophy and critical animal studies with extended work in ecocriticsm, ecofeminism, and ecotheory. She has presented and published essays in ecocriticsm and critical animal studies and was the editor of *Animal Subjects: An Ethical Reader in a Posthuman World* (Wilfrid Laurier University Press, 2008). She is co-editor with Rasmus Simonsen of *Critical Perspectives on Veganism* (Palgrave Macmillan, 2016) and the author of *Cryptomimesis: The Gothic and Jacques Derrida's Ghost Writing*. Forthcoming is *The Gothic and Psychoanalysis* (U of Wales Press).

LAUREN CORMAN is an Associate Professor of Sociology at Brock University. She teaches in the areas of Critical Animal Studies and contemporary social theory. Her intersectional research draws on feminist, anti-racist, posthumanist, post/anti-colonial, and environmental approaches to the "question of the animal." Her scholarship investigates ideas related to agency, resistance, and (interspecies) subjectivity. As such, her interdisciplinary work bridges the social and natural sciences through cognitive ethology, which explores nonhuman animal cultures and societies. Broadly, Dr. Corman is interested in coalition-building across social, environmental, and animal movements, and links her work to larger anti-capitalist struggles. She maintains her longstanding commitments to critical pedagogy, and also publishes in this area. She hosted and produced the animal advocacy radio show *Animal Voices* for about a decade. She is currently collaborating with filmmaker Karol Orzechowski (*Maximum Tolerated Dose*) on a documentary about nonhuman animals and intersectionality.

J. KERI CRONIN is Chair and Associate Professor of the Visual Arts Department at Brock University. She is also a Faculty Affiliate in Brock's Social Justice and Equity Studies graduate program and a member of the Faculty Steering Committee for the Social Justice Research Institute at Brock. She is the author of *Manufacturing National Park Nature: Photography, Ecology, and the Wilderness Industry of Jasper* (UBC Press, 2011) and the co-editor (with Kirsty Robertson) of *Imagining Resistance: Visual Culture and Activism in Canada* (Wilfrid Laurier University Press, 2011). Her current research explores the ways in which late-nineteenth- and early-twentieth-century animal advocacy groups used visual culture in their campaigns. In the summer of 2012 she curated an exhibition called *Be Kind: The Visual History of Humane Education* for the National Museum of Animals & Society (NMAS), and is currently serving as the Chair of the Advisory Council for NMAS. As part of her commitment to knowledge mobilization beyond traditional academic audiences, she writes a monthly column called Picturing Animals for the online magazine *Our Hen House.*

MANEESHA DECKHA is Professor and Lansdowne Chair at the University of Victoria Faculty of Law. Her writings on species, race, gender, and culture, which the Social Sciences and Humanities Research Council has generously supported, have appeared in law reviews as well as the *American Quarterly*, *Ethics & the Environment*, and *Hypatia*. She is the recipient of the US Humane Society's Animal and Society New Course Award and has held the Fulbright Visiting Chair in Law and Society at New York University in relation to her animal law scholarship. She is currently completing a book project on feminism, postcolonialism, and animal law.

LEESA FAWCETT lives beside the Nottawasaga River, along the spine of the Niagara Escarpment in Hockley Valley, with a varied assortment of rescued, wild, companion, and feral Beings. She initiated the study of human–animal relations at York University. She teaches courses in animal studies, environmental philosophy and advocacy, environmental education, children's studies, and natural history. Current research projects include a multi-year study of human–wildlife encounters in the Greater Toronto area, and an arts-based experiential education project with Nishnaabe-Aski Nation youth. Leesa is Associate Dean (Teaching and Learning), and

Coordinator of the Graduate Diploma in Environmental and Sustainability Education, in the Faculty of Environmental Studies at York University.

CAROL L. GLASSER is an Assistant Professor of Sociology at Minnesota State University, Mankato. Her research examines social movements, critical animal studies, and gender inequality. When she is not research-ing or writing, she is committed to helping create a more egalitarian world through teaching, volunteering her research skills to grassroots and non-profit organizations, engaging in activism toward freeing nonhuman ani-mals from their position of oppression, and working as an ally to other movements advocating for social justice.

LORI GRUEN is the William Griffin Professor of Philosophy at Wesleyan University. She is also a professor of Feminist, Gender, and Sexuality Studies and coordinator of Wesleyan Animal Studies. She is the author and editor of nine books, including *Ethics and Animals: An Introduction* (Cambridge, 2011), *Reflecting on Nature: Readings in Environmental Philosophy and Ethics* (Oxford, 2012), *Ethics of Captivity* (Oxford, 2014), and *Entangled Empathy* (Lantern, 2015). Her work in practical ethics focuses on issues that impact those often overlooked in traditional ethical investigations, e.g. women, people of colour, non-human animals. She is a Fellow of the Hastings Center for Bioethics, a Faculty Fellow at Tufts' Cummings School of Veterinary Medicine's Center for Animals and Public Policy, and was the first chair of the Faculty Advisory Committee of the Center for Prison Education at Wesleyan. Gruen has documented the history of The First 100 chimpan-zees in research in the US (http://first100chimps.wesleyan.edu) and has an evolving website that documents the journey to sanctuary of the remaining chimpanzees in research labs, The Last 1000 (http://last1000chimps.com).

PETER HOBBS is a PhD candidate in the Faculty of Environmental Studies at York University. The title of his dissertation is "Chemical Intimacies—Toxic Publics," in which he tracks different multi-species ecologies and political assemblages that have emerged as a result of the proliferation of industrial toxins. The goal of his work is to reveal the politics and chemistry behind the various ways in which we make toxins and how toxins in turn remake us. Along with his interest in chemicals and material semiotics of dogs, his recent publications include a queer-ecologies tour of Toronto (co-authored with Cate Sandilands), and an artist book that documents a series of site-specific séances he performed with the artist-shaman AA Bronson. Peter in nutshell: dogs, chemicals, queers, and ghosts.

RHYS MAHANNAH, holder of a BA (hons.) in English from the University British Columbia, is currently a masters student at the University of Victoria, British Columbia. Following a life-changing undergraduate animal studies class with Dr. Jodey Castricano, Rhys has since focused his scholarly lens upon literary theory, including and especially posthumanist and critical animal studies.

ATSUKO MATSUOKA is a Professor in the School of Social Work, York University. Her research has addressed the importance of understanding of intersectionality of oppression among immigrants and refugees and ethnic older adults, and issues related to animals. She has co-authored a book on the Eritrean diaspora, entitled *Ghosts and Shadows: Constructions of Identity and Community in an African Diaspora*, and a Japanese book, *Critical Social Work and Analysing Practice Through Deconstruction: Experiential Learning*. She integrates anti-speciesism into social work education. She has written on animal exploitation and co-edited the book, *Defining Critical Animal Studies: An Intersectional Social Justice Approach*.

ANTHONY J. NOCELLA II, Ph.D., an intersectional scholar-activist, is an Assistant Professor in Sociology and Criminology, Gender and Women's Studies, Environmental Studies, and Peace and Conflict Studies at Fort Lewis College. Nocella has published more than fifty scholarly articles or book chapters; co-founded eco-ability, disability pedagogy, academic repression, and critical animal studies; co-founded, and is director of, the Institute for Critical Animal Studies; National Coordinator of Save the Kids; is the editor of the *Peace Studies Journal*; and has published more than twenty-six books, including *Terrorists or Freedom Fighters? Reflections on the Liberation of Animals* (Lantern Books, 2004), *Call to Compassion: Religious Perspectives on Animal Advocacy* (Lantern Books, 2011), *Igniting a Revolution: Voices in Defense of the Earth* (AK Press, 2006), *Love and Liberation: An Animal Liberation Front Story* (Piraeus Books, 2012), and *Earth, Animal, and Disability Liberation: The Rise of the Eco-ability Movement* (Peter Lang, 2012). His website is http://www.anthonynocella.org.

KELLY OLIVER is W. Alton Jones Professor of Philosophy at Vanderbilt University. She is the author of over one hundred articles, thirteen books, and ten edited volumes. Her books include *Hunting Girls: Sexual Violence from The Hunger Games to Campus Rape* (Columbia University Press, forthcoming), *Earth and World: Philosophy after the Apollo Missions* (Columbia UP, 2015), *Technologies of Life and Death: From Cloning to Capital Punishment* (Fordham, 2013); *Knock Me Up, Knock Me Down: Images of Pregnancy in Hollywood Film* (Columbia, 2012); *Animal Lessons: How They Teach Us to Be Human* (2009), *Women as Weapons of War: Iraq, Sex and the Media* (2007), *The Colonization of Psychic Space: A Psychoanalytic Theory of Oppression* (2004), *Noir Anxiety: Race, Sex, and Maternity in Film Noir* (2002), and *Witnessing: Beyond Recognition* (Minnesota, 2001). She has published in *The New York Times* and has been interviewed on ABC television news, various radio programs, and the Canadian Broadcasting Corporation. Her work has been translated into seven languages. Recently she published two novels in the Cowgirl Philosopher Mystery Series.

ROD PREECE is Professor Emeritus at Wilfrid Laurier University. He has written twenty-one books, either authored or edited, several book chapters, and numerous articles in learned journals on German and comparative politics, political philosophy and animals ethics, including *Animals and Nature: Cultural Myths, Cultural Realities*; *Brute Souls, Happy Beasts, and Evolution: The Historical Status of Animals*; and *Animal Sensibility and Inclusive Justice in the Age of Bernard Shaw* (all UBC Press).

MARGARET ROBINSON is a vegan scholar and a member of the Lennox Island First Nation. Margaret grew up in *Eski'kewaq*, Nova Scotia, and holds a PhD from the University of Toronto. She is an Assistant Professor in the Department of Sociology & Social Anthropology at Dalhousie University in Halifax, where she teaches in the Indigenous Studies program. She lives with her partner of twenty years and their four cats.

JOSHUA RUSSELL is an Assistant Professor at Canisius College in the Department of Animal Behavior, Ecology, and Conservation and the Anthrozoology master's program. His phenomenological research investigates children's lived relationships with the more-than-human world as well as the various educational programs and materials that mitigate and influence those relationships. His chapter was written with the support of a generous research fellowship granted by the Animals & Society Institute in partnership with Wesleyan University. Joshua lives in southern Ontario with his partner Sean and their rescue dog, Penny.

JOHN SORENSON is a professor in the Department of Sociology at Brock University in Canada, where he teaches critical animal studies. His books include *Critical Animal Studies: Thinking the Unthinkable* (Canadian Scholars' Press); *Defining Critical Animal Studies: An Intersectional Social Justice Approach* (edited with Atsuko Matsuoka, Anthony Nocella II, and Kimberley Socha; Peter Lang Publishers) *Animal Rights* (Fernwood); *Ape* (Reaktion); *Culture of Prejudice* (with Judith Blackwell and Murray Smith; Broadview/University of Toronto Press); *Ghosts and Shadows* (with Atsuko Matsuoka; University of Toronto); *Disaster and Development in the Horn of Africa* (Macmillan); *African Refugees* (with Howard Adelman; York Lanes Press); and *Imaging Ethiopia* (Rutgers).

Index

Books in the Environmental Humanities Series
Published by Wilfrid Laurier University Press

Animal Subjects: An Ethical Reader in a Posthuman World
Jodey Castricano, editor / 2008 / 324 pp. / ISBN 978-0-88920-512-3

Open Wide a Wilderness: Canadian Nature Poems
Nancy Holmes, editor / 2009 / 534 pp. / ISBN 978-1-55458-033-0

Technonatures: Environments, Technologies, Spaces, and Places in the Twenty-first Century
Damian F. White and Chris Wilbert, editors / 2009 / 282 pp. /
ISBN 978-1-55458-150-4

Writing in Dust: Reading the Prairie Environmentally
Jenny Kerber / 2010 / 276 pp. / ISBN 978-1-55458-218-1 (hardcover),
ISBN 978-1-55458-306-5 (paper)

Ecologies of Affect: Placing Nostalgia, Desire, and Hope
Tonya K. Davidson, Ondine Park, and Rob Shields, editors / 2011 /
360 pp. / illus. / ISBN 978-1-55458-258-7

Ornithologies of Desire: Ecocritical Essays, Avian Poetics, and Don McKay
Travis V. Mason / 2013 / 306 pp. / ISBN 978-1-55458-630-1

Ecologies of the Moving Image: Cinema, Affect, Nature
Adrian J. Ivakhiv / 2013 / 432 pp. / ISBN 978-1-55458-905-0

Avatar and Nature Spirituality
Bron Taylor, editor / 2013 / 378 pp. / ISBN 978-1-55458-843-5

Moving Environments: Affect, Emotion, Ecology, and Film
Alexa Weik von Mossner, editor / 2014 / 296 pp. / ISBN 978-1-77112-002-9

Found in Alberta: Environmental Themes for the Anthropocene
Robert Boschman and Mario Trono, editors / 2014 / ISBN 978-1-55458-959-3

Sustaining the West: Cultural Responses to Western Environments, Past and Present
Liza Piper and Lisa Szabo-Jones, editors / 2015 / 380 pp. /
ISBN 978-1-55458-923-4

Animal Subjects 2.0
Jodey Castricano and Lauren Corman, editors / 2016 / 542 pp. /
ISBN 978-1-77112-210-8

www.ingramcontent.com/pod-product-compliance
Lightning Source LLC
Chambersburg PA
CBHW060017030426
42334CB00019B/2077